GEORGE CALDERON

GEORGE CALDERON

Edwardian Genius

PATRICK MILES

Sam&Sam
Cambridge

First published in 2018
by Sam&Sam,
29 Highfield Avenue
Cambridge CB4 2AJ

Typeset in Dante MT by James Miles

British Library Cataloguing-in-Publication Data
A catalogue record for this book is available from the British Library

ISBN 9781999967604

Printed and bound in Great Britain by Clays Ltd, Elcograf S.p.A.

2 4 6 8 10 9 7 5 3 1

To the Memory

of

Lady Petra Lambe

(1905-1990)

née Corbet

CONTENTS

ILLUSTRATIONS

Cover: George Calderon, c. 1912, by Frederick Hollyer

Who 'Is' and Who 'Was'?

George Calderon brought the plays of Anton Chekhov to the British theatre. He was the first person to direct Chekhov in Britain (1909) and the first to publish English translations of Chekhov's plays (1912). His versions of *The Seagull* and *The Cherry Orchard*, together with his published views on the originality of Chekhov's plays, did more than anything in the twentieth century to embed Chekhov in our classical repertoire and national consciousness; Chekhov became, in Irving Wardle's words, 'Britain's second favourite, and most loved, dramatic author'. It is the mission of this book, however, to show that there is far more to George Calderon than his Chekhovian legacy.

Lieutenant Calderon was an avant-garde writer killed leading his platoon into action at Gallipoli on 4 June 1915. His fate may call to mind that of Rupert Brooke, Wilfred Owen, or Isaac Rosenberg. But the similarity ends there. These were young men still when they died in the Great War, whereas Calderon was in his forty-seventh year. His creative achievement lay in the pre-War period and is Edwardian in the best sense. These poets' reputations lay in the post-War future. They have outgrown Calderon's reputation and, to a large extent, that of his friends the poets Laurence Binyon and Henry Newbolt. To discover Calderon, we have to penetrate beyond what has been called the 'long shadow' of the First World War – a shadow that still lies upon us. We have to discover the *Edwardian* world. For despite his famous Spanish name, Calderon was an Edwardian Englishman through and through.

The Edwardians have had a bad press almost since the end of the War, which they have been accused of causing, or not preventing, or at least murderously mismanaging. There has been a popular interest in the love life of Edward VII and his courtiers, say, or the Edwardian elite's conspicuous consumption of wealth, and even the life of the Edwardian working class. But the life of the Edwardian professional class is relatively unknown to the nation. Since the 1960s we have tended to think of its military, imperial and familial male representatives as starched, tight-lipped, probably sadistic 'bastards'. Even Julian Fellowes's *Downton Abbey*, whose protagonists' mindset was certainly formed under 'King Teddy', did little to improve the Edwardians' image. When it comes down to it, we don't like them and we prefer not to think about them.

This is strange, because as Roy Hattersley has written the Edwardian period was 'a watershed in British history [...] the time when a modern nation was born', and in many ways we resemble the Edwardians ourselves. We share their obsession with sport, style, international travel and new technology. If the Edwardians believed passionately in versatility (now deplored as their 'dilettantism'), we have invented multi-tasking and the portfolio career. If they had an excess of disposable income, which they believed should be spent on pleasure and luxury, we have our ever-growing inequality of wealth and our culture of self-gratification. Perhaps we too are more interested in appearances – 'spin' – than in truth? Perhaps our preference for political correctness over political initiative mirrors the determined hesitancy of Edwardian Liberal governments?

I first encountered George Calderon in 1978 when I was asked by the National Theatre in London to appraise all published and unpublished English versions of *The Seagull* for a possible production. I was astonished by the economy and theatricality of Calderon's translation; and even more by the insights of his essay on Chekhov's plays. Yet we agreed at the National Theatre that his version was too 'quirky', its language too 'Edwardian', for us to use. Even in his photographs Calderon looked utterly Edwardian, or what I took then to be Edwardian: pallid, clinically shaven and groomed, with snow-white starched collar and the same menacing intensity as, for instance, Lord Curzon or Henry Newbolt. I did not like the look of Calderon. I suspected, from the socialistic perspective of the 1970s, that he was another 'Edwardian bastard'.

Three years later, I was commissioned by the Russian Academy of Sciences to write a history of Chekhov's plays on the British stage and had to take a closer look at Calderon. From the only published memoir of him, Percy Lubbock's *George Calderon: A Sketch from Memory* (1921), I learned that he was living in St Petersburg at the very time *The Seagull* was premiered there, returned to England in 1897, got a job at the British

Museum, married, wrote articles about Russian literature, published two comic novels, made an anthropological study of Tahiti, became a star reviewer on *The Times Literary Supplement* (*TLS*), was active in a number of political causes, wrote a dozen plays, worked with the Ballets Russes, insisted on becoming a combatant at the age of forty-five, and disappeared at Gallipoli. I was flabbergasted by what I read. *How* had Calderon come to live in Russia for three years, as I had myself in the twentieth century? What had he done there? Whom did he marry? Why did he go to Tahiti? How did he become interested in Chekhov's plays? What were his politics? Above all, how could one man combine so many talents and achieve so much by his mid-forties, only to throw it all away on a military adventure bungled by the Edwardian officer class – an adventure that he was not obliged to join? I decided I must look at Calderon's extant archive, but there was none. His wife had disappeared from London without trace after his death was confirmed in 1919. There were no children and, apparently, no papers.

I shall recount in my Acknowledgements how an extremely lucky break led me to George and Katharine Calderon's papers in a Scottish attic. As I sat there in the bracing cold, reading letters, documents, memoirs, diaries, and contemplating 700 photographs and watercolours, my preconceptions fell away: George Calderon was clearly a highly original man, a risk-taker, even a maverick, but kind, penetratingly intelligent, explosively witty, dynamic, courageous; he had a passionate affair with Katharine before they married, they were in some ways a very modern couple, and I found Katharine ('Kittie') every bit as impressive as him. I immediately felt the lack of a full-length biography of Calderon. As a theatre person, ex-Russianist, and something of a risk-taker myself, I sensed I was the person to get on and write it. The book you are reading is the result.

George Calderon was a very sociable man. But contemporaries did not find him easy to know or understand. As I researched his biography, I began to feel the same. What *had* he done in Russia? He never talked about it and the evidence at first seemed minimal. When he courted Kittie, his friend Archie Ripley's widow, he addressed his letters to her in different hands and pretended he was in places that he wasn't. He loved mystification and dressed so differently at different times that his life appeared one long disguise. The closer I thought I was getting to George Calderon, the more he resembled a black hole. For at least half of its existence this book was entitled *Black Pot: The Mysterious Life of George Calderon*, playing on the meaning of his Spanish name

But computers have revolutionised biographical research. Calderon letters are rare, Calderon manuscripts even rarer, but as more archival institutions worldwide put their catalogues online it became possible to track such documents down, even buy some that were advertised in obscure places, then marry all this material to the core Calderon Papers from the Scottish attic. The *TLS* had cracked the authorship of its unsigned Edwardian reviews, put the attributions and texts online, and this enabled me to read all of Calderon's fifty-four contributions as the work of a single writer – probably the first time it had been done. Other online newspapers, databases and sites throughout the world made it possible to follow George's sea voyages, locate reviews of all his plays, reconstruct his activities in the suffrage debate and strikes, and plot his brief military career. All of this would have taken a decade to do 'manually', if it had been possible at all. Information technology and my subsequent sojourns in libraries and archives began to make the narrative of Calderon's life clearer. Above all, the nature and meaning of that life emerged as I discovered who his family, wife, friends and colleagues were and as I learned more about the times in which he lived. The journey of this book, therefore, has been towards understanding the Edwardians better as people, revising our image of them, and proposing a concept that previously, perhaps, would have been regarded as a contradiction in terms – 'Edwardian genius'.

Nevertheless, one cannot deny that George Calderon is little known... I have lost count of the times I have been asked whilst writing this book, 'Who is George Calderon?' Others have spluttered at me, 'But nobody's ever heard of him!', as though I must be mad to choose such a subject for a biography.

I should like to address this question from a slightly different angle. I was once sitting next to a lady (whom I did not previously know) at a dinner, and the conversation went like this:

SHE: Who is this man you are writing about?
ME: He is Edwardian.
SHE: *Is* Edwardian? Surely you mean he *was* Edwardian?
ME: Well no, he's Edwardian.
SHE: No no, you can't say that. He *was* Edwardian!

Even this lady asked who 'is' this man, not who 'was' he, but to say he 'is' Edwardian was a step too far for her, as she knew nothing about him. He could exist for her, if at all, only in the historical past, whereas for me, his biographer, he and the Edwardians were already a 'second presence'. Conversely, those who ask 'Who *is* George Calderon?' are seeking an existence for him in the information-bearing pattern of the present, so to speak, and implying that he has none. Yet there have always been figures from the past who took generations to acquire a present, for example Emily Dickinson, Franz Kafka, or Wilfred Owen. For such people to acquire a present, it first has to be established, through biography, who they *were*.

That is what this book sets out to do for George Calderon. But because it is necessarily also a biography of Calderon's wife and their 'set', it could not be told in the chronological straight line of a so-called traditional biography. Different kinds of Time ripple through its story, from the intimate 'real time' of love letters, or Calderon's time past on Tahiti as he himself recalled it, to the Victorian and Edwardian *aeons*, or the futurity that Kittie increasingly lived by after George left for Gallipoli. Moreover, if any self seems to me discontinuous, Calderon's does, and this encouraged me to depart from the strictly chronological sequence.

Biography should be an experimental genre. As Ruth Scurr, biographer of John Aubrey, has admirably expressed it, the fundamental problem of biography is 'always the same: how to find a narrative form that fits the life (or lives) in question'. My first biography (*Brief Lives: Anton Chekhov*, 2008) was preset at a hundred pages, but this was the perfect length for embodying in minuscule chronological chapters the personal view of Chekhov's life and works that had grown in me over the previous forty years. As I researched my biography of Calderon, I realised I could not prescribe its length, but I had no doubt about its narrative form. It opens

with Kittie Hamilton's marriage to Archie Ripley and goes straight into
Calderon's affair with her after Ripley's death, and her own relationship
with Nina Corbet. It then flashes back to Calderon's time in Russia, and
beyond that to his birth, education, and decision to go to Russia, before
returning to the 'present' of his marriage in 1900 and his literary career up
to 1906. This stretch of linear narrative then has to be suspended for seven
years, because in that period he was seriously pursuing so many activities
at once that they demand to be shown in concurrent 'thematic' chapters.
After August 1914, however, a single narrative reasserts itself, and in fact
can be followed almost day for day on my internet 'blography'
calderonia.org for the last ten months of Calderon's life. The concluding
two chapters follow Kittie's life after George's disappearance at Gallipoli,
as her life is intimately connected to his *after*life and, indeed, rounds the
whole book.

It is not in fact true to say that nobody knows who Calderon is.
Derwent May has even spoken of Calderon's 'rediscovery' in recent years.
But the way in which he is known is itself part of his story. A large number
of people know George Calderon well in their specialised spheres. Theatre
historians know him for his role in the New Drama and for introducing
Chekhov to the British stage; experts on Edwardian fiction are familiar
with his proto-modernist satire *Dwala*; Russianists know his essay on
Chekhov's plays; aficionados of the *TLS* know him as a brilliant early
reviewer; Tahiti specialists will have read his classic posthumous book
about the island; ballet historians will certainly have come across his
seminal article on the Ballets Russes. These are separate spheres that have
little cause to talk to each other. Calderon, however, comprised all of
them. The fact that in his lifetime people encountered him only in their
own sphere meant that he was never seen in his entirety, even by Percy
Lubbock, who knew Calderon personally but was unsympathetic to many
of his interests. It also has to be said that Calderon himself probably saw
his life in separate compartments. Thus he is a figure who has never been
presented in the round, in all his vital Edwardian diversity – a failing that
this book aims to rectify.

Since this is a story rather than an academic biography, I have
dispensed with footnotes. However, every fact presented has its material

source. Letters quoted are held by the collections named in my Acknowledgements. Books and authors quoted are to be found in the Bibliography. The original spelling and punctuation of letters is usually retained, including underlining and the characteristic Edwardian use of dashes; very occasionally, small changes have been made to clarify meaning. Everything in square brackets is my own. In chapter 4, all dates are according to the western, Gregorian calendar ('New Style', N.S.) unless otherwise stated ('Old Style', O.S.). Russian names are transliterated using the Library of Congress system except where there are long-accepted English versions, e.g. Tchaikovsky, Novikoff, Fokine. In quoted texts, transliterations are kept as they are in the original. The formal diminutive of Katharine was 'Kittie', so I use that in my own text, but correspondents also wrote 'Kitty' when they knew her well and were thinking of it more as the affectionate form of 'kitten'. 'Victorian' usually refers to the Queen's reign (1837-1901), whilst 'Edwardian' is used in a wider sense of approximately 1897-1916.

I have deliberately used some long quotations from Calderon's own works and letters, since most readers will not be acquainted with his writing and style. It seemed important to allow George Calderon wherever possible to tell us himself who he was.

Cambridge, December 2017

1

The End of 'A Veritable Child of Earlham'

A *haze* of tweed...no other word for it. The dots on the soft, floppy shooting jacket, waistcoat and bags are so tiny that they might be simply the grain of the photograph. Is it a plain 'hounds-tooth', or just a fine check? Does it look less substantial than the shooting rig of the other six men in the photograph because the man wearing it has stood back and is slightly out of focus, or because it is more worn, possibly a hand-me-down, or even because it is of *superior* quality?

Here is a photographic portrait of the same man, in a two-inch-high oval frame crowned with a silver garland. In his left lapel is a fresh flower. Is it an orchid? An iris? A daffodil? What might each tell us about him? And the chipped, carmine enamel border round the bevelled glass: is that 'ribbed', or 'milled', or as they said *'guilloché'*, and is the intended effect what was called 'sunburst'? What did these details say about the owner of the portrait? Did she have the support at the back made specially like an A, because the name of the man was 'Archie'?

This is the past. It is not so much a different country as a different language (although the language is still 'English'). Why did lovers, spouses, friends call each other 'Peter' in their letters? What precisely, in the 1890s, did 'coodling' someone involve? What really did 'I want you' mean then? What were the feelings of a speaker in the 1900s when he or she chose the words 'charming', or 'fitness', or 'staunch'? What medication was a 'Cockle'? What were 'Swipes'?

You could never learn all the language of a past – its language of words, codes, objects, clothes – and in that sense the past can never be known or understood. 'But of course,' you exclaim, 'that's what makes it the past!' Yet when these dead people are still so recognisably human, or British, or 'like us', the urge and even yearning to understand 'their' past is difficult to suspend or brush aside.

Despite the fact that the seven men in the first photo (see Fig. 1) have
'the same' bodies and faces as ourselves, can we even read their body
language accurately? Three of the younger men (who are brothers) have
burnt-out pipes in the corners of their mouths, as though they are
'sporting' them, and the one in the middle of the front row seems to be
'posing' with his hands in his pockets and his deerstalker on his knee. But
in 1886, when this photograph was taken after a day's shooting at
Earlham, just outside Norwich, were these the affectations *we* feel them to
be? Were they expressions of the insecurity of youth as we know it
ourselves, or were they just social conventions?

Be all that as it may, Archie, the young man in the atomised tweed,
does seem to have stepped back and apart, and to stand more stiffly. He
stares intently, even anxiously at the camera. He is slighter by far than the
others, his hands are white and small, and there is a startling void in the
sleeve around his left wrist. Although only nineteen, there might be
particular reasons for this more 'delicate' appearance.

He was born Archibald Edmund Ripley on the last day of 1866, when
his mother, *née* Laura Pearse, was forty-two. He was the last of her ten
children, of whom six died before they reached forty-five. From an early
age he suffered from what was described as 'lung trouble' and 'asthma',
but was probably TB. In the Admissions Register of Trinity College,
Oxford, he wrote that he had been educated at Norwich Grammar School
and 'privately'. It was his ill-health that delayed his entry to Oxford until
he was nearly twenty-one. He was admitted in October 1887 at the same
time and to the same college as George Calderon, who was then only
eighteen.

But Ripley was nothing if not plucky. He was almost desperately active
and ambitious, as the darkly focussed gaze on many of his photos perhaps
conveys. He was highly sociable, a conversationalist par excellence, and
according to a note written by his widow in 1945, 'beloved both by
undergraduates and dons', becoming President of the Oxford Union 'after
a walkover election'. Precluded from energetically physical sports, he took
up golf, which was becoming a national craze, and won a Blue.
Nevertheless, his final degree, awarded in the summer of 1891, was an
aegrotat (in Natural Sciences). When he and Calderon embarked on a
Norfolk golfing holiday in May 1892, it was interrupted by Ripley's ill-
health.

Fig. 1 Earlham, 1886. Back row, extreme right: Archie Ripley

Archie was also a passionate traveller. Possibly as early as 1882 he visited North Africa and brought home the photographs and two live eagles to prove it. In 1888 he was in Norway, Sweden, St Petersburg and Moscow, and seems to have made a return journey via Switzerland. Whilst in Paris the following year, he obtained special permission to take his own photographs of the Venus de Milo in the Louvre.

We do not know when Archie Ripley and Katharine Hamilton met, but they were certainly corresponding in the spring of 1894, when she was accompanying her friends Sir Walter and Lady Caroline ('Nina') Corbet on a European tour. From Amalfi on 20 April she wrote 'I am so sorry – so sorry that you have been ill again – I was afraid of it', but added next day: 'Surely it is not much wonder – for it always seems to me you burn the candle at both ends and in the middle as well.' Ripley appears to have been engaged at one time to the London beauty Nesta LLoyd, a cousin of Sir Walter's. But that summer, possibly at a ball in Oxford, Ripley and Katharine had what he referred to as 'that beautiful experience', about whose significance they were 'one as we always shall be in mind as in everything else'.

In the nine surviving letters from Archie to Kittie whilst she was holidaying with the Corbets in the Scottish Highlands throughout September 1894, he is perhaps exaggeratedly frank about himself and his situation. He drinks 'to excess' at the Savile and other clubs and is a heavy smoker. He goes off to play golf rather than turning up for work at the firm of solicitors where he is training. During an interview with a barrister who might give him 'devilling', he discovers that 'I am strongly antipathetic to him and this is a very rare experience with me and men'. Indeed, another of his problems was that although he constantly 'wanted' (i.e. 'missed' or 'longed for') Katharine, he was so used to male company that he had doubts about being married to her. A friend named Common came to visit him occasionally at 211 Piccadilly, but 'although he is my Nina I suppose, […] I shouldn't think he was nice to kiss which your Nina must be I know'. Another friend, when he stayed the night, was 'so nice and warm'.

During this month apart, Ripley had a typical bout of his illness. His 'ulcerated' throat was so sore that he had to send for opium, then for a doctor to 'cauterise' it. This condition and his 'rather bad diarrhoea' left him bedridden, able to eat only Brand's Essence of Beef, and 'not really up to writing a decent letter'. Yet he was beguiled by the TB-sufferer's delusion that this was his 'last fight with opposing Nature and that when I have won this one, which may be tomorrow or any day my happy and healthy years [...] are to begin, spent with my Kit'.

Archie Ripley was gnawed by anxiety that he was not yet physically strong enough to marry, that he could not afford accommodation of the quality to which he aspired, and that he would not earn enough to support children. At the end of September 1894, therefore, he decided to ask for leave from his current job at Brodrick and Partners, Great Trinity Lane, London, and go home to Norfolk to 'try and get strong' in the hope of marrying in February. Even this proved not enough. In December he embarked on a four-month restorative cruise via Colombo to Sydney, thence to China and Japan, and home via Vancouver. His passion for Kittie never dimmed on the voyage, his health was at least stabilised, and they were married at Chelsea on 30 April 1895. Eventually they took up residence at 17 Golden Square, Soho, together with Kittie's mother, Mary Hamilton, who was by then seventy. Perhaps this was the solution to not being able to afford, on their own, to rent more than an apartment. Before long, however, Kittie also became her mother's main carer.

The intensely English context of Archie Ripley's life was that he was a 'son of Earlham', the Norfolk hall that formed the subject of Augustus Hare's two-volume *The Gurneys of Earlham* (1895) and Percy Lubbock's classic *Earlham*, which has rarely been out of print since it appeared in 1922. This sprawling red-brick house dating from 1642, and its large park, three miles from the centre of Norwich, are forever associated with the Quaker Gurneys who lived there from 1786 to 1847. In 1841 Ripley's mother married John Gurney, an Anglican minister, and together they moved into the house in 1854, opening a long new chapter in Earlham's history. Her husband died in 1856, she stayed on with her children, and in 1859 she married the Revd William Nottidge Ripley, by whom she had five more children. The whole of Archie Ripley's childhood, then, was centred on Earlham.

The name evokes a particularly potent idyll. On the one hand, Earlham had been the home of Friend John Gurney, a highly respected banker, then of his Quaker son Joseph John, who was raised mainly by his own sister, Elizabeth Fry. Gurney's Bank in Norwich was a byword for honesty, reliability and investment nous. In the words of R.H. Mottram, it was 'part of that solid axle of ability and integrity' around which Victorian England 'turned'. John Gurney toured Britain and Western Europe with his sister calling for prison reform and the abolition of capital punishment. He was also a campaigner against slavery: there was a stretch of garden path at Earlham called 'Wilberforce's Walk' because Gurney had conferred there with the great reformer. Earlham, then, was permeated with an atmosphere of moral clarity and philanthropy. On the other hand, it was also an aesthetic idyll, with its great lawn, mature trees, brilliant flower beds, its south front festooned with vines and roses (Katharine Ripley's painting of this side was used as the frontispiece to *Earlham*), and indoors the Chinese jars and faded velvets so lovingly described by Percy Lubbock. Archie Ripley possessed two massive albums of photographs of Earlham's interiors and park taken, possibly by himself, at the very time that Lubbock recalls (1886-88). Moreover, the infinitely kind and mild William Nottidge Ripley and his wife perpetuated the Gurney tradition of good works in the Norwich community. Lubbock's book is rounded by memories of his step-grandfather taking morning prayers in the front hall of Earlham and Sunday evensong in his diminutive church nearby. On both occasions all the family and servants attended. Earlham comes across as a model Victorian Christian household.

Yet Percy Lubbock freely admits that this idyll is 'romance', 'poetry'. In his case it is the product of a *recherche du temps perdu*, namely the summer holidays he spent at Earlham before the First World War. It is a creation of his own ornamental, somewhat orotund style. In reality Earlham was neither the Gurneys' nor the Ripleys' ancestral hall, because both rented it. Everything was enabled by great banking wealth. Even Percy Lubbock questions Laura Ripley's role as Lady Bountiful and suggests that Earlham 'discountenanced' art and the creative imagination. But Archie's brother Philip, in his 'Annotations' to *Earlham* privately printed in 1929, makes even more exalted claims for the place: it was a 'blessed house' from which the 'Eternal Gospel emanated', a hearth of 'unostentatious benevolent thoroughly English domesticity'. Earlham, of course, is hazy too, a 'dissolving view'.

Another ingredient of Victorian Earlham, however, was 'mirth'. Archie's father had a gentle, ironic turn, Laura Ripley a silvery laugh. Their sons were always ribbing them and each other. Conversation flowed freely at Earlham's hospitable board and Archie was, in Lubbock's words, the 'most shameless' of the brothers in his 'ribaldry' and 'effrontery'.

Presumably it was partly this that Lubbock was referring to when he wrote to Kittie that her and Archie's home, 17 Golden Square, had become 'a veritable child of Earlham'. Fellow-members of the Savile Club, friends from Archie's life and travels, young and old, irrespective of social station, gathered at 17 Golden Square for evenings of conviviality, smoking, and above all conversation. The subject-matter was limitless, it seems, but often revolved around politics, the future of mankind, 'free and enlightened youth', and Archie's sense of community with the world. His own fluency and buoyancy cast a spell and he was a master at unlocking conversation in others. He soon had his own 'circle', as Percy Lubbock put it (in his late teens Lubbock was part of it).

Again, though, we are conscious that the past is a different language. 'Mirth' is not a word used very much today. At Earlham it signified 'horseplay', 'effrontery', 'ribaldry'. It was neither subtle nor particularly kind. A brother of Archie's, in his twenties, was quite capable of shooting his leg out suddenly in the porch at Earlham to send his five-year-old niece Violet Lubbock flying. Some of Archie Ripley's own recorded mirth most resembles mockery; even the word 'jeering' is used of him presiding over an evening at Golden Square. Perhaps this explains why, according to Kittie's 1945 note, he was 'virulently detested by a few' at Oxford. We should remember that the sons of the simply ecclesiastical Revd and Mrs Ripley were still 'young gentlemen', and some of them doubtless behaved like Hooray Henries. Archie Ripley's own ebullience, however, was perhaps born more of frustration, even bitterness, at his own physical debilitation.

When he and Kittie married they were both twenty-eight, which then was relatively old for a woman. But as the youngest Hamilton daughter she had lived with her mother ever since her father died in 1884. Moving with her mother from St Andrews to London, she was absorbed in attending her, in training as an artist under Briton Rivière and at the A.S. Cope and J.W. Nicol School of Painting, mixing with students at the Slade, and accompanying her many girl friends in their social whirl. Yet she was clearly not deterred by the prospect of nursing two adults in the marital home. She was probably attracted by Archie's clean-cut, boyish handsomeness, his high spirits, and his cultured interests. His large, gleaming eyes held great pathos. On the backs of a series of photo portraits of him Kittie commented lovingly on how accurately they captured the features of the original. And if Archie masked his disabilities with energy, mockery and a love of pleasure, she was every bit as feisty.

Kittie's father, the Anglo-Irish philanthropist and religious writer John Hamilton, was sixty-seven when she was born to his second wife, then forty-two. It could not have been easy for the teenage Kittie, living in reduced circumstances in a rented apartment at St Andrews for the last three years of her father's life. But it was still a household of culture, intellectual curiosity, and vigorous debate. As well as painting, she wrote wittily, unpredictably, fluently. Both the Ripleys and Mary Hamilton must have been delighted at this union of two eminent Protestant families.

After his marriage, Archie Ripley picked up the pieces of his career as a barrister. Increasingly, however, it was interrupted by respiratory problems, and at some point in 1897 his health deteriorated significantly.

One afternoon early in 1898 Kittie Ripley returned to 17 Golden Square from walking Jones, their young Aberdeen terrier, removed her hat in the columned, black and white marbled hall, and heard a new visitor speaking to her husband in the high studio or music room beyond. The man, of medium height for today, looked like a foreigner. In Laurence Binyon's words, 'he wore cropped hair *à la brosse*, a pointed beard, prodigious moustaches'. This was George Calderon, recently returned from Russia.

Katharine Ripley had never met him before and according to Lubbock she was viewed 'critically' and 'not without some mistrust at first'. Calderon came to visit Archie Ripley more and more often. Kittie could not know – very few did – that when he had been living at home in Burlington House after graduating, he would sit for hours with another contemporary, the portrait painter Charles Furse, cheering him up during his bouts of consumption, and that he read regularly to patients in the Ophthalmic Ward at St Thomas's. Clearly, Ripley and he had much to talk about. According to Calderon later, Archie was 'the only friend with whom I could tell and be told everything'.

On Thursday 20 October 1898 Calderon went to fetch a doctor for him. 'He had pneumonia', he wrote to his mother Clara Calderon, 'and with his asthma and weak condition it soon got too much for his lungs.' Archie died on the Sunday afternoon, 23 October. In death he looked calm, almost contented. He had, after all, packed a great deal into his short life. Kittie carried his deathbed photograph with her in a small green wallet for years after – possibly her whole life.

The next morning, Calderon received a short note on paper headed '17, Golden Square. W.': 'Dear Mr Calderon, I know Kittie wants to see you this morning – Come if you can – She does not know that I am asking you – I am Kittie's friend Nina Corbet.' We know from Kittie's memoir of George Calderon that he did come, and 'talked and talked and talked' with her about Archie.

Meanwhile, she was deluged with condolences, mainly from men, written immediately on receiving the news. 'Archie was the <u>one</u> person', wrote the nineteen-year-old Percy Lubbock, 'whom I felt as a friend older and wiser than myself, and at the same time <u>exactly</u> on equal terms with myself.' The man in whose chambers Archie had read for the Bar, E. Forbes Lankester, told her:

You know better than anyone the peculiar way in which Archie gained the affection of everyone who knew him well. […] Dear Mrs Ripley it is simple truth to say that he was loved by other men as few are, and that in return he gave a constancy and warmth of feeling which few men can give.

His brother E. Ray Lankester, an eminent zoologist and another member of the Savile Club, wrote Kittie perhaps the most emotional letter of all, concluding: 'This will be your comfort – that you did everything to make him happy and that he knew it and loved you truly, and was very happy.' 'He was a <u>real</u> person and a <u>real friend</u>', wrote Arthur Royle from

'Sutherlandshire': 'I shall never forget those evenings in Golden Square – they were unlike any others elsewhere.' The composer Charles Villiers Stanford, with whom the Corbets and the Ripleys mixed socially, felt it was 'at any rate a little consolation to know that so lovable a man was so very deep down in the affections of his friends, and that they won't forget his sympathetic and kindly and sweet personality as long as they remember anything'.

Archie Ripley's body was brought to Earlham on Tuesday 25 October 1898 and the first part of the funeral was conducted in the Hall next day. The coffin was then carried by his friends and Earlham's servants across to the little church of St Mary's evoked so powerfully by Lubbock in the closing pages of *Earlham*. Here it was buried in the family plot. Neither part of the service was conducted by Canon Ripley, who had married Archie and Kittie but was by now seventy-four. The following day Mary Hamilton registered the death at Westminster. Very soon after, Nina Corbet accompanied Kittie back to Golden Square. She wrote to Laura Ripley that Kittie was 'very very tired bodily' and that she was going to stay with Kittie almost another week. Nina's six-year-old son, Jim Corbet, wrote from Acton Reynald in a letter headed 'Jim's love to Auntie Kittie': 'Isn't it nice to think that Cousin Archie is in heaven.'

Whatever Percy Lubbock might write to Kittie six months later about 17 Golden Square itself being 'a veritable child of Earlham', without Archie Ripley, its master of ceremonies, Earlham in London was over.

But within ten weeks, in January 1899, Katharine Ripley was again at Earlham, this time for the austere but impressive funeral of Laura Ripley herself. The local newspaper wrote: 'It was touching to see so many of the very poor present, who had come out from Norwich to see the last of a lady whose kind heart and open hand were ever ready for their help.' A few months later, William Nottidge Ripley left the Hall and settled closer to the city of Norwich.

For many, this was the end of Earlham itself.

2

EASTCOTE MAN

In October 1898 George Calderon was living at Southill Farm in Eastcote. Although only a dozen miles from the centre of London as the crow flies, this was indisputably 'the country'. It was a Middlesex village of about 600 people, with three grand houses – Eastcote House, Haydon Hall and High Grove, of which only the last has survived – and a cluster of small farms, cottages and 'lodges'. One of the latter was Haydon Lodge, an arresting mock-Elizabethan pile designed by the architects George and Peto in 1881 and still standing on the corner of Southill Lane and the High Road through Eastcote to Ruislip. Almost opposite it was a pub, The Case Is Altered, and further up Southill Lane from that was Southill Farm.

'There is a placidity about living in the country which makes one quite contented', Calderon wrote to his mother on 22 June 1898, a week after moving in. Probably the real attraction of Eastcote for him was its proximity to Pinner, which was a 'dormitory suburb' that had had its own station on the London Underground's Metropolitan Line since 1885. In about fifteen minutes Calderon could cycle from Southill Farm half a mile up the High Road towards Cuckoo Hill, then across the fields to the main road into Pinner from the south, turn off it down a footpath along the edge of West House (now Pinner Memorial Park), and ride under the railway bridge up to Pinner station. From there it was only twenty-five minutes to Baker Street.

For a twenty-nine-year-old earning his living from translation and his own writing, the rent must also have been advantageous. Two furnished rooms, utilities, breakfast and evening meal cost him seven shillings and sixpence a week (around £600 a month today). 'The butcher is good and the cooking also. Dairy products are at hand. At night it is cold', he told his mother. At least some of the time, it seems, he sub-let one room to a contemporary from Trinity College, Arthur B. Lowry, who was starting a career in London as a civil servant. Two medical students were also living in the house.

It was a Queen Anne farmhouse with seven bedrooms, offices and other rooms, two W.C.'s, a stable, coach house, flower garden, and 'hard and soft water'. The person who managed it all was the forty-something widow Rose Tobutt, who farmed twenty-five adjoining acres presumably with the help of her grown-up sons. She, her fourteen-year-old daughter and three sons were domiciled in the farmhouse with no live-in servants. A photograph (Fig. 2) captioned 'George Calderon on Return from Russia 1898' shows him in his beard and a homburg playing croquet possibly on the back lawn of Southill Farm.

Fig. 2 George Calderon, 1898

To say that George Calderon 'lived' at Eastcote, however, is an exaggeration. There is no evidence that he involved himself in the community. Despite being a sportsman and looking out onto one of Eastcote's cricket grounds, he did not play there. He preferred to play golf two miles away at Northwood, or further up the Metropolitan Line at Amersham, where he stayed with friends. Nor does he appear to have introduced himself to the wife of the tenant of Haydon Hall, Mrs Harry Bennett-Edwards, who was the local author (she wrote romantic novels), certainly his social equal, and frequently to be seen about the village.

Basically what Calderon did in Eastcote was write. He would go up to London to research and read in the British Museum, then bring his notes and copying back to work on them at Southill Farm. In the autumn of 1898 he was writing at least three long pieces: an article on 'old Tolstoy, who has a 70th birthday soon', another on Nicholas II's initiatives for a Peace Conference, and '100-odd pages to Edmund Gosse, a sketch of a history of Russian literature, only a sketch for his eye, poor man, to tempt him to order a book'. He may have been writing already for *Literature*, but reviews there were anonymous and the candidates for his authorship look doubtful. He was certainly working freelance for 'Flowerdew's technical translation office', for whom, according to their testimonial, he performed 'important and difficult translations', presumably mainly from Russian. And he was writing stories.

In October 1898 *The Cornhill Magazine* printed 'Richard K. Whittington', signed 'George L. Calderon'. The eponymous hero of this story is American, like the heroine of Calderon's first story published by the *Cornhill* (1897) and protagonists of the two novels he would write in the next five years. Evidently he was already bemused by the otherness of the 'Yankee' world and confident in his handling of its language. He even placed accents on some English words in 'Richard K. Whittington' to indicate where they were stressed in American. Where had he acquired this command of 'Yankee' vocabulary, pronunciation and colloquial style? We do not know; although there is just a hint that he had an American girl friend in his last year at Oxford. If so, were her whole family 'over' perhaps, as in his novel *Downy V. Green* (1902), and Calderon frequented their home?

'Richard K. Whittington' is set in Liverpool Docks and ironically modulates the idea that, as its hero puts it, 'it's a most curious thing how history repeats itself'. The American Dick Whittington has heard the bells telling him 'turn again, three times Pres'dent of the United States of Amurrka!' and believes his cat will bring him to the White House. In fact his cat brings him one disaster after another. Following a voyage to the Fiji

Islands, for instance, Whittington is presented with a bill for damages caused by his cat, including fifty cents for 'cork toes':

That derned puss got foolin' around and killed some half-a-dozen of the sacred white rats they kept there. The king had some notion of impaling my friend the Captain, but by a judicious offer of warming-pans and thermometers, which they fortunately had in cargo, the Captain got away with nothing worse than the loss of his thumbs and big toes.

Deprived of his capital, a legacy, and his fiancée, still Richard K. Whittington believes in his cat and his destiny. 'A stoopid lot, them Yankees,' murmurs an old docker who has heard the tale; 'they never knows when they're ill off.'

Whilst lodging at Eastcote, Calderon paid many visits for days at a time to old friends from school, university and St Petersburg as far afield as Oxford, Newcastle upon Tyne, and the Norfolk Broads. He also occasionally stayed with his widowed mother in Kilburn. It would be very difficult, then, to predict when he would actually be at Southill Farm. This led at least one of his friends to doubt whether that was his permanent address. Calderon was adamant that it was. Yet something mysterious remains about his residence in Eastcote: he lived there and he did not... It meant he could 'be' in two places at once, namely Eastcote in people's minds and somewhere else in reality. This was to prove very useful in his growing relationship with Archie Ripley's widow.

She was an utterly believing Christian and a regular churchgoer. She did not need reassurance or comfort where Archie's life beyond the grave or his essential goodness were concerned. She had scores of girl friends in London thanks to her social contacts and her time as an art student. But, excepting the Ripleys and Gurneys (who lived far from London), she seemed to have no men amongst her immediate acquaintance who had known Archie really well and whom she could trust simply to talk about him. And, of course, male company was what she missed most.

Quite apart from his 'social charm' and 'truly Spanish courtesy', as his friends described it, George Calderon could empathise with her the most because in the year since he returned to England he had himself drawn closer than ever to her husband. Through the rest of 1898, on Calderon's visits to 17 Golden Square and in letters, he and Katharine shared all they remembered and loved about Archie Ripley.

The first such letter of Calderon's that has survived was written at Eastcote on Wednesday 14 December 1898. It plunges straight in:

I have by me a book of Lamb's Poems and a few Essays, edited by Ainger, Macmillan 1888, blue marbled sides, red leather back and corners, containing the inscription G.L.C. 2nd Dec. 1889. A.E.R. That was when I was 21, at the beginning of our 3rd year at Oxford. Michael Furse [older brother of Charles] had just come up. Michael took me to help at a penny reading that term where I fell in love. Archie steered me through it, very badly I think [...]. I remember one summer evening, very late, only I and Archie still awake; I was – not the worse – but the more open and garrulous for some kind of liquor. We walked in big strides round and round in the moonlight, our heads together, round the front quad, while I told Archie all about it; and we chuckled and drifted off, I suppose into other matters, and laughed at things together. Cannan our Dean complained that we had kept him awake all night, when he saw me at Logic next day. (She, by the bye, is also 'another's' as I heard with pleasure three months ago, and forgot to tell Archie.)

Then its mood changes. Calderon was 'in the 4th day of illness; all over me'. He had been 'sitting very lean and drowsy toasting my toes all day, without the heart so much as to read'. Writing to her, however, had 'awoken my dormant appetite' and he started to eat some stewed apples that Mrs Tobutt had sent up to him. Suddenly 'the door opened and in came two black figures, a little and a big, Mother and Evy [Evelyn Calderon, his younger sister] from home on a visit, hearing I was ill'. His recovery, perhaps, had been delayed by drinking 'the red stuff the doctor gave me in a bottle', which 'may have been lotion'. After they left, he sat down at the piano and 'proclaimed health and vigour fortissimo through the village'.

And now my muddled mind has come round to what I had been meaning to say any time these 4 days. If my last letter was brutal it was not delightfully brutal, but stupidly and clumsily. Sense is sometimes rightly brutal to weakwitted sensibility; I know no other case of delightful brutality. Granting me sense for the sake of argument, have you ever displayed anything resembling the other thing? Of course not; you go straight on like a big barge, not disturbed by little winds and currents. When you say you can throw light on my life, you are right, because you have knowledge and will; rather – you would be right if I had any life – you will if I have. 'So can anyone' is nonsense if it puts you on a footing with 'anyone'.

We do not know in what sense his 'last letter' was 'brutal', or what she meant by being able to 'throw light' on his life as 'can anyone'. Had he already said to her, as she put it twenty-two years later in her memoir, 'You know I won't always talk of Archie – I know myself and I won't and you mustn't mind', and stressed that she must live in 'the present'? Would she be 'throwing light' on his life because she was such a persuasive Christian, or simply because she was 'maturer' than him (she was nearly two years older)?

He concluded the letter: 'Shall I be in the way if I come and dine with you on Saturday and stay over into Sunday? Yours G.'

We do not have any of Katharine's letters to Calderon from this time. Probably they were burnt on her instructions after her death, together with most of Ripley's letters. However, Calderon's next letter, written on 19 December, after the weekend, starts: 'Your last letter gave me the impression […] that for some occult reason you didn't want me to come and sleep at your house; and that for another occult reason you hadn't the frankness to say so.' He suggests she has tried to compensate by 'heaping kind enquiries and material benefits upon me' (she had sent him a portmanteau by rail); he objects to 'being treated as an impersonal object of philanthropy'. In the two letters he received from her next day he found she made apologies 'for something, I haven't the vaguest notion what – something about "strange growths" (my hair?)', and expressed 'wishes', i.e. perhaps regrets. 'Don't waste wishes: you *are* all over prickles', he replied. 'They tickle me wonderfully.' Nevertheless, she had made a 'discovery' about him that had given her a 'disagreeable sensation'. Was this the discovery that, whilst the 'best of friends', he had seen 'far enough down into you to find a kindred spirit at the bottom'? Or the fact that he was not 'occult' and did not subscribe to Christian morality?

On New Year's Eve Calderon wrote 'Dear Kitty' (the more intimate spelling) a long letter from Eastcote. Evidently he had recently visited her again at Golden Square: 'It was very sweet of you to have Archie's photo for me all ready in its frame; it stands, frame and face, as a natural whole on my mantelpiece.' The last day of 1898 was Archie Ripley's thirty-second birthday and she was facing the new year without him. Calderon addressed the subject perhaps 'brutally':

There is no sorrow in this anniversary – nor in any anniversary. You would 10,000 times rather have had the meaning in your life and lost the word for it, than never have had the meaning at all. I rejoice with you. But anniversaries are nothing – mere conventions: tomorrow is nothing; the New Year without Archie or with him is only a new number at the top of the newspaper. Yet you will feel perhaps differently; believe that your friends, dear friend, are alert to feel your feeling and help you if you need it.

This was all a single paragraph near the end of the letter. The rest, closely written, was devoted to clarifying his, George's, relationship with her.

He began: 'Why should you scold at me and call me names – as you did – for telling you that your immaterial gifts were greater and preferable?'

I often thought that, desiring to benefit me, you nevertheless preferred to benefit me in the cheaper coin of material goods, counting the immaterial too precious for me, reserving them for more deserving cases, and yet unable to keep them from me entirely from the very nature of things […]. Must I really explain in what these immaterial benefits consist? […] What you have done – you have given me a new friend, opened my eyes wider on an old one, drawn me from vegetable inertia into activity and sympathy, taught me how even I might be a buffer between a dear soul and her pain (a little; better than nothing), taught me a little to distinguish the upper and the under in my own self, done your best to give me a spiritual world like that in which you and millions of good people live – a thousand other things which were new to me.

It is almost as though Katharine has been attempting to convert him to the beliefs by which she and 'millions of good people' live, but he is encouraging her to continue… Moreover, she is so determined to see the 'credit side' of his character that he believes even if he were 'put in

Holloway for stealing milk cans' she would 'preserve' him from 'letting go altogether in self-contempt' by writing or coming to see him 'through the bars'. 'Moral bars', though, do 'divide' them 'even out of Holloway'. Yet the thought that she will always put out a 'friendly hand' through the bars is 'a consoling reflection for blue-devil days' and suddenly he talks of 'alliance':

allied with you I am allied with a bold honest mind, a clear warm mind exercised in things above and beyond my experience (I respect that mind, Kitty, wherever it doesn't touch on political economy); [...] I believe that you will use it for seeing my faults and mistakes, and that you will know that it will be a pleasure to me and not an offence to have them pointed out; [...].

In fact, my good ally, I haven't enough half sheets to tell all the immaterial benefits that you can and have conferred, and I beg that you won't tear any hairs at all out of your head, for I think your heart is in your head, and they serve to keep it warm.

Obviously, the combination of self-abasement, moral challenge and disarming 'frankness' on Calderon's part could be interpreted as skilful psychological manipulation. But there was undoubted truth in his concluding paragraph:

If you groan under the burden of my friendship, blame yourself for it; you drew me in (for which I thank you); and when I was half ready to withdraw discreetly – not yet knowing you – you detained me (for which I thank you much more).

Yours G.

Had she made herself too vulnerable in her grief? Had he even identified an opportunity to further his career by marrying a well-off widow? Or was he irresistibly attracted to her? The relationship was direly complicated by the circumstances in which it came about, but perhaps this letter was as near as he could come to a declaration of love, without once mentioning the word or the emotion.

The next day, Sunday 1 January 1899, Laura Ripley died. George Calderon collected Jones, the Aberdeen terrier, from Golden Square and looked after him at Southill Farm whilst Kittie attended the funeral. Mrs

Hamilton was ministered to by Ada, the parlour maid, and at least one other servant. By Saturday 7 January Calderon was getting concerned:

What is the use of friends if you don't keep in touch with them when you are going through difficult times? Are you doing all that you hoped? Is it not true that Mr Ripley finds more natural help in you, poor detached thing, than in his married sons?

You went away looking so strong and hopeful, and resolute – for you thought much more than you said.

On 9 January he received a letter from her that persuaded him she had been 'getting along much more smoothly than I expected'; indeed he seems disconcerted by the sense that she was having 'pleasure' at Earlham. Perhaps he feared that she was drifting from him under the spell of Earlham and her past. Immediately, he sought to narrow the divide that he had referred to in his letter on New Year's Eve: 'I expressed myself badly; the moral bars that divide us was meant to mean "that <u>would</u> divide" us if I stole moral milk cans; that I hope won't divide us. Don't be hurt.' In her letter she appears to have enclosed some money for looking after Jones ('it <u>is</u> a lot').

During the following week he was due to attend a ball at 'the Furses' in London – presumably the home of C.W. Furse, Archdeacon of Westminster. She had invited Calderon to stay that night at Golden Square and he hoped she would be back by then. Instead, she sent him her front door key and stayed on and on at Earlham.

In his long letters, Calderon could not resist delivering some 'prickles' of his own and he created a human persona for Jones. 'Being the Sabbath', he wrote on Monday 9 January, 'I and a friend did 42 holes of golf round the fields, and Jones came as caddy.' Jones was 'covered with mud and tenderly affectionate. This comes of two biscuits a day. Poor half-starved little man, he is beginning to fill out again [now that he had received more dog-biscuits through the post]. He's a little Barnado 5 shilling boy, that's what he is'. Calderon also began to share with her what he was writing. A story featuring 'Nadezhda' (the Russian woman's name meaning 'Hope') had come 'marching home again hurrah from a publisher's' – and has never been seen since. Another, which he had just written, he sent her so that she could tell him 'what you think is the worst nonsense in it, that must be cut out'. His accompanying comments tell us much about his literary values at the time:

Consider length, proportion, justice, relevance to the main idea (such as it is); try to discover the main idea (if there be any, beyond the fact): uncertainty in that on the part of the author spoils even the flimsiest story. Note which passages came most tediously in the reading. (My directions are already disproportionate to the thing they direct.)

The story (which has not survived) may have been provisionally called 'Jetsam'. Evidently 'Dear Kit' came back to him with some criticisms:

Of course you are quite right about the thing. [...] It is a joke and too long. I don't a bit agree with your canon, that the slighter a thing is the beautifuller it should be written. I don't know what beautiful writing means, except that it is a very offensive thing used by affected essay-writers. But I do know stories which have hardly any outward incident in them and yet are charming in detail: but that is because the sentences constructing them contain worthy facts, observations of small events, or clarifications, or opinions.

However, her 'opinion' so agreed with his own, namely that he had not 'worked out the joke right (and 3 times too long)', that he was sure 'we are both right'. Yet he remained 'convinced' that the idea or 'point' of the story was sound. He returned to the subject in another letter the same day (18 January 1899) and we gather from this something of the story's plot:

The idea (begin with that) of the besiegers outside watching the procession coming: a long line of heroic women with husbands, taking it very solemnly, and then the good Haus-frau, such as you see working in a tub in London back gardens as you pass in the train; with all her gear about her, thinking only of the institution, the family and its wants; and as naturally as she scolds her children when they interfere with the current of everyday things, so naturally throwing away the unnecessary husband. I insist on squeezing a story out of it some time. Then, quite generally, a woman with 12 children, her future assured [...]; her husband has served all his uses; there is no more romance, no more economic service, nor anything to be got out of him. He has converted her into the institution it was her object to become, a family instead of a woman. Why not eat him as the she-spider does? Or kick him out as the bees? It is an everyday story: but the husband is usually tolerated in a small smoking-room at the back instead of being dropped in a ditch.

If only I could put that, obvious as it is, into a 3 page story, I'm sure it wouldn't be a bad story. It isn't worth more than 3 guineas; so don't let's waste £5 worth of consideration on it – discussion rather – as much consideration it may have as it needs.

In view of Calderon's stance in the debate about women's suffrage ten years later, the 'idea' of this story is interesting. His belief that the 'idea' or 'point' of a story is first conceived, then 'embodied' in the work, rather than discovered or explored in its writing, is also significant. 'Charming' sounds warning bells, and there is certainly no evidence here that he had understood *Chekhov's* achievement as a story-maker, even though he had probably read some of his prose. Finally, Calderon clearly felt the need for 'feedback' – dialogue – about his writing, but when he got it he appeared vulnerable and even unstable:

Your general remarks upon the necessity of excellence are apposite, I have never been so slothful or easily contented as during the last many months, 7 or 8, during which I have had more need of industry and exactingness than ever. Pray keep me up to the mark. But not, mind you, by moral expositions of the evils of sloth etc or I shall hate you. It cannot be done by words or even hints (nothing is so easily detected as a hint, or so much destroys friendly confidence) or looks (which are hints badly expressed). It can only be <u>infused</u>. Infuse. Thankyou for so long a letter: it makes up for 2 consecutive postcards. At least, it mitigates them.

G.

In the meantime, Calderon had attended the ball at the Furses' and returned Kittie's key. He had come to London 'dull and dispirited, resolving to return early to bed', but 'I felt as if I were revisiting the scenes of my youth; as I was indeed; for I revived impressions of first acquaintance with the Furse interior'. 'She' (not a Furse) was there, but 'she affected me, neither to plus nor to minus'. He conversed with his 'chief ex-rival' on 'friendly and playful terms' and felt like saying to him:

'Bless you my boy, go in and win.' Although 'she' did not 'throw a glamour over all that surrounded her', the glamour 'was there, from the brightness of each circumstance (relations chiefly) and she revolving drew the light into herself and became the nucleus. She is no longer the nucleus, but the surroundings are as bright as ever'. There was a 'pervading something in her family, an essence, penetrating keen and refined, in all of them', which she had 'localised or typified' for him and he had once made a declaration to her 'in a hansom-cab'; but 'I have my head above it all now'... So he went on over seven small letter-pages.

He had got back to Golden Square 'at about 4'. The ever loquacious and inquisitive Mrs Hamilton pumped him for 'ball-room gossip' over breakfast, 'but I could tell her nothing, except that all the young ladies were equally charming and the music excellent'. Together, they calculated from Kittie's 'demand for chemises' that she would be away another week.

A few days later he was still uncertain when he would be bringing Jones back and staying over at 17. She had invited him for Friday 20 January, 'but if we are not to come on Friday you will of course let us know'. By the end of Wednesday he had decided that he and Jones would be coming on the Saturday. 'But it is possible that my chief-golfer will come on Saturday and stay with me into Sunday: in which case I would come up with him on Sunday for dinner (supper?) and stay till Monday.' There is no indication in his letters of when she was returning to London at all, but he was encouraged by something she had written in her last letter: 'What a tempter you are, baiting with egotism: you have much to say[,] you say; but I may be comforted for lots of it is about me.'

On the Saturday, 21 January 1899, *Literature* published an unsigned review which we know was by Calderon because he told his mother so in a letter. It is a review of Constance Garnett's translation of Ostrovskii's classic play *The Storm* and is exceedingly interesting for two reasons. First, it puts between Calderon and Garnett – two of Victorian/Edwardian England's pre-eminent translators of Russian literature – the clear blue water that was to separate them for the rest of Calderon's life. He begins by acknowledging that Constance Garnett 'surpasses the last generation of translators from the Russian' because she is more accurate. Unfortunately, he continues, it is peculiarly difficult to translate Russian plays because 'Russian is probably the best dramatic language yet discovered. From six words you may tell a man's birth, education, habits, character, and point of view'. Garnett is not adequate to this quality of dialogue:

> The even current of slang in the translation, while obliterating all the superficial distinctions of character, necessarily fails to represent the nervous vernacular of the original: the vulgarness of the original is the robust vulgarness of surviving antiquity; Mrs Garnett's is a debilitated vulgarness of the new growth. The old-fashioned commonness of the terrible mother's diction in the play is greatly misrepresented by such a rendering as 'My, what a stuck-up thing she is! Here she is in a huff directly!' It is, no doubt, his 'untranslateability' that has prevented Ostrovsky from becoming known abroad.

This was Constance Garnett's first attempt at translating a Russian play and it was a disastrous choice because her social background, perhaps, had not equipped her with demotic English (she excelled at Turgenev's literary prose and even the dialogue of his upper-class heroes). Moreover, she was probably well aware that she did not have an 'ear' for theatrical dialogue. Calderon, then, in this review had immediately put his finger on two of her weaknesses as a translator, which are now widely recognised.

But as far as we know, this review is the first time that Calderon had expressed in print any of his views about Russian literature. They are original. 'Ever since the Song of Sorrow sprang up and blossomed in the wilderness of Russian medieval literature,' he claims, 'the keynote of Russian invention has been the triumph of Sorrow.' The capitals probably refer to the genre of 'laments' in Early Russian Literature, traceable as far back as 'The Lay of Prince Igor's Campaign'. He continues:

Man and God are banded together to fight against an overmastering αναγκη [Necessity]. Sometimes it is the power of winter, of famine, of government; in Ostrovsky it is the inevitable evil of human relations. 'The Storm' is a picture of fate, as embodied in the reactions of character. […] It is not tragedy as we know it in the tradition of the classical school; it is the sadness of life itself, reduced to dramatic dimensions. It bears the same relation to tragedy as the modern pathetic does to the old-fashioned sentimental, for the vigour of it springs from the admixture of the commonplace.

One is tempted to suggest that Classics had given to Constance Black, as she was known as an undergraduate at Cambridge, a flying start in translating Turgenev's, Tolstoi's or Dostoevskii's syntax, and to Calderon a perspective for Russian literature. But Calderon also identified the element of the 'grotesque', and absurd, in that literature:

The woman [in *The Storm*] who terrifies Katerina into confession by her talk of hell-fire is no hell-mouthed Cassandra, but a little mad old lady, followed by two tall footmen in cocked hats. A touch like this adds a poignancy far beyond the reach of academic tragedy.

Here Calderon's own vision of the play was far beyond the reach of most Russian appreciations of it.

He returned Jones to 17 Golden Square on Sunday 22 January. That night he and Katharine Ripley sat up late and had 'a great talk together'. Judging from the letter that Calderon wrote from Eastcote on the Tuesday, much of their talk revolved around a visit she had had earlier that weekend from Michael Furse and others – possibly Oxford friends of Archie's.

Michael Furse (1870-1955) was the member of the Furse family Calderon was closest to. 'Mike' had overlapped with him at Trinity, Oxford. He was well over six foot tall, strongly built, a rower, but with a gentleness that one of his biographers has even described as 'femininity'. He had histrionic talents and these brought him into contact with Calderon in Trinity's drama club. Furse was strongly influenced by his High Church father and his father's friend Charles Gore. In his first year at Oxford he joined the Christian Social Union recently launched by Gore and others. Participation in Trinity College Mission at Stratford in the East End helped form Furse's inimitable brand of 'muscular' Christianity and social engagement. He was ordained in 1897 and by 1899 was Fellow, Chaplain and Sub-Dean of Trinity. We shall have occasion to refer to his charisma as a bishop later. Suffice it to say that by 1899, in addition to fundamental differences, Calderon had taken against 'Michaelism' – Furse's personal mixture of Anglo-Catholicism, 'straight talking', and robust activism. Even so, after the ball at the Furses' he had written to Kittie: 'I renounce all disloyalty of decaying affection for Michael and Michaelism; for he and his charmed me thoroughly.'

It is not easy to work out what Furse said to Kittie that became the object of such heated discussion between her and Calderon. This is partly because the only documentary evidence we have of it is the letter Calderon wrote on Tuesday 24 January 1899 to Jones the dog! Kittie, it seems, had written a letter the day before in the persona of Jones, thanking 'Uncle George' for looking after him whilst 'Mum' was at Earlham. Calderon's reply, therefore, was prefaced:

For Master John Jones. Not to be opened by anyone else on any account. Would Mrs Ripley be kind enough to give it to him? Mr Calderon did not like to address it to him directly for fear the parlour-maid should think it was a joke.

By 'address' here Calderon meant the front of the envelope. Ada the parlour-maid generally took delivery of mail sent to Golden Square and, indeed, posted most of the outgoing letters. As we shall see, this was a not insignificant factor in Kittie's and George's communications.

Calderon wrote that he wasn't sure that he and Kittie did not 'misunderstand one another a little', but 'it may have been myself who misunderstood' Furse's 'humour':

Anyway, I'll tell you what I thought. Your Mum told me what Michael said about himself, and she seemed to think it strange for him to say it to a woman, especially to a woman who might have expected 'pastoral help'. What the bearing may have been in Mike's mind I don't know – personal, I thought, as between him and her, unless 9/10 general, merely for matter of conversation; I thought she took it as personal, between the two (by the bye – how one's mind does stray – 'ramify' as Mum says – I like being called Uncle […]).

One surmises from this and later in the letter ('As to your remarks about parasites, my dear Johan, of course you know more about that than I do') that in Kittie's conversation with Michael Furse the question of her vulnerability had arisen. Had she perhaps admitted that she still needed commiseration, comforting and cherishing, but was wary and afraid of being taken advantage of? Did Furse perhaps counter that anyone in the position of comforter could become fond of her, that there wasn't anything necessarily 'wrong' about that, and added with 'humour' (as

Calderon put it) that if he, Michael Furse, were giving her 'pastoral help'
he might experience tender feelings towards her himself? If so, her
'looking a little angry', as Jones reported to Calderon, was possibly
because she thought Furse was making a pass at her himself.

Almost certainly, she was severely stressed by the thought of breaking
two taboos. The first was that of becoming romantically, let alone
physically, involved with another man so soon after her husband's death.
But was she also entering the 'forbidden zone' of a love relationship with
someone whose 'professional' role was as a counsellor? Did she feel angry
at the thought that Calderon was abusing her trust and that Furse seemed
capable of it too? Was she confused and angry with *herself* for
'encouraging' these men and other 'parasites'?

At Golden Square on the night of Sunday 22nd January, Calderon
continued to Jones on 24th, 'it seemed to me strange that she should not
see that Mike's proposition about pastoral help would have an application
to other people as well'.

So, in the most brutal fashion, I cross-examined her; as for my voice, I think it was
much the same as usual, rather soda-watery perhaps; but hers was a little wooden
note that came out at the back of her head; we were shouting at one another over
a brick wall with glass bottles on the top. You see I thought that she regarded me
something in the light of a sofa-cushion that can be leant on and talked to without
its expecting to be referred to the same genus as the visitors. So I was really
protesting, superfluously (?) for my humanity.

In fact, he now suspected that Furse's 'proposition' was intended to refer
to him, George, and 'that may have been almost the whole point'. Clearly,
as in his New Year's Eve letter, he was determined to persuade her that
although a friend and comforter, he had a right to 'unprofessional' human
emotions for her. He pressed this home:

I should like to have a gossip with you, Jones my boy, about the High Church
question and other matters. I shall be at 17 on Wednesday, unless Mum puts me
off. I shall be sitting up pretty late, as I can't sleep early in London; so you can just
run down to the studio when they have all gone bye-bye; I hope nobody will
interrupt us. [...] I quite agree with what you say, Johan my lad, about Michael:
he ought to give the pastoral help if it falls within the scope of his business, or the

natural line of his progress; and take the consequences as they come. It would be absurd to consider the consequences, unless there was something disastrous, dishonourable or impossible among them. If I were a parson, Jones, I should dismiss all consideration of the consequences from my mind; neither think of them, nor talk of them except in a superficial, outside, episodic, anecdotal, conversational way: because, putting aside all bible notions and S.P.C.K.ness, the best rule of life is to live by and in the present [...] and if there is nothing wrong in the present, but on the contrary, everything, or a good deal, that is of the best, (even though there be a lot of poppies among the corn) then be sure that the harvest will be all right.

According to Calderon, then, what was happening to them, 'in the present', was authentic, 'of the best', the product of neither an exploitation of trust on his part nor enticement and consent on hers. Nevertheless, he ended his letter to Jones: 'Tell Mum to telegraph before breakfast if I am not to stay at 17.' He was coming up to London early next day, 25 January, to work at the British Museum.

If he did stay at Golden Square on the night of Wednesday 25 January, he must have stayed the following night too as we know from another letter that he had breakfast there on the Friday morning. But what happened next is impossible to verify. On Saturday he wrote to his mother from Notting Hill Gate, where he had stayed overnight at the family home of Hugh Bradby, his golfing partner and contemporary at Rugby. Prior to that, he told his mother, he had been 'away in the country, at home, without budging'... Now he was on his way to Oxford – 'to stay with Michael Furse'! There was, understandably, no mention of his visits to Golden Square, but on 8 February he was due to attend a literary dinner given by Reginald Smith, editor of the *Cornhill Magazine*, and he had already decided to 'put up with [i.e. *chez*] Mrs Ripley, as being handy', rather than stay with his mother in Kilburn. By the evening of Monday 30 January, however, he was back at Golden Square. Had he made a flying visit to Furse from the Saturday afternoon to the Monday? If so, what was the purpose?

That Monday night in the 'studio' at 17 Golden Square Calderon and Katharine Ripley made love, in the Victorian/Edwardian sense, for the first time. The sixteen-page letter he wrote her from Eastcote the next day seethes with excitement, themes, and tenderness. 'My darling wife', it begins astonishingly,

I find nothing on arriving to reconcile me to my return: only an MS returned from the *Fortnightly*, my Peace Rescript article, once a book, the fruit of 2-3 months hard and enthusiastic work. I turn back in face of that little squall straight into the harbour; I lay my head on your broad white bosom, under the protecting head, within the protecting arms, screened from the outer world, globed about by Kitty from what I took for infinity and finding infinity truly within, in that endless inner world created a day ago by you and me for you and me, and holding everything else within it. Kisses for the dear face and eyes and for the hands, on the back and on the palms. You are [...] a perfume and the warmth of a summer sun – and I suppose I am a little blustering and intoxicated to write such stuff.

There follows a description of reading over lunch Emerson's account of his interview with Wordsworth – 'young America looking at old England, digesting advice with an inward smile' – then Calderon drops another bombshell: he has shaved off his 'moustache and imperial'. Evidently she had suggested he shed the beard, but

If little George is to have no beard he cares for none of the preliminaries to it; he will uncase his individuality, and the sooner the better, lest his mouth look sore and constrained at the 'literary dinner'. A broader and better area moreover for drinking Kitty's soul from the surface of her flesh; what vulgar people call 'kissing'.

Implying, perhaps, that he had been in Oxford that weekend and obtained Michael Furse's blessing (so to speak), he continued:

I feel all the happier in knowing that well qualified people regard you as 'ripping' – Michael, for instance; [...] Cis [Cecil Lubbock, nephew to Kittie by marriage, married to Edith Furse, Michael Furse's sister]; everybody in short. You are just grand, and if these things went by competitive examination, whose should I be? If I didn't know [...] the utter steadfastness of the woman with no phases, I should say – You are as free as air to cast me off when you please. You have been rushed; you have been taken in an attack at dawn, when but just awakening out of sleep.

[…] I have still a hundred things to say. Some will be better said in your private ear, murmured in your forgiving lap.

Then he was back to literary matters: he would send her his article on Nicholas II's 'Peace Encyclical' of December, to read and send on to the *Edinburgh Review* or the *New Century Review*, and 'Michael is going to introduce me to the Editor of the *Quarterly* for the article on Tolstoi. I think you had better read it lest there be anything we should be sorry for afterwards in it'. The latter, as well as implying that she had become his regular 'reader', probably means that he was apprehensive about expressing in print religious and literary views that might offend her family and 'circle'.

Next he asked whether there was 'an etiquette by which I must stop sponging on you now'; yet a page later he was asking her if she could give him 'some money' to help him out, concluding 'it is only too plain that I am a designing villain'. Thence he flitted to the difference between them in age and experience:

Dear grandmother, you are younger these days than…you were; that expression in your veiled eyes, tender and half ironical in look, is the expression of your girlhood, the days of the miniature [see Fig. 3] and the hanging locks; the tiny smile, the little look of bliss – these are spring buds coming out again with the new year of love. There are rich individual tones in your voice (I heard it as you went to the bath this morning) all girlish and graceful, that strike on an inward ear in the heart. […] Yours is an everlasting youth, for it is not grey locks that make old age, but grey thoughts and grey opinions. Your love will be always a girl's love, though tempered by the wisdom and selflessness of a woman. You are a school-girl, granny; come and sit on old Uncle George's knee.

But how were they now to pursue their love affair by post? Wouldn't the blue-green envelopes 'coming often' 'with the postmark Pinner' arouse suspicion? 'Does Ada look?' He thought Ada already had 'an inkling', which is why, presumably, he had written this letter on black-bordered paper: observing Kittie reading it over breakfast, Ada would assume Calderon was still writing to her mistress in his capacity as a bereavement counsellor… But will Kittie post her own letters now? For his part, he will mystify:

I will vary envelopes and pens and postmarks, so far as I can without making it worse. Do not be afraid of deceitfulness. It would be a holy joy were our right deceiving others' wrong. Right deceiving right should be neither a pleasure nor a pain; it is a necessary here. I know no limit to it, but the limit of detection.

Will tomorrow's first post bring me my first love-letter? With my name in the dear square firm handwriting.

A thousand kisses all over you, my dearest. […] God bless you, darling wife; Fate bless you; your own goodness is an everlasting blessing to you, and I stand in the shadow of your wings. Pray to your God to make me pure. […] Your God sent me to meet you in the valley of the shadow of death; I went unknowing into the arms of a white angel, and the valley as we walk down it is a valley full of flowers. When I am weak it is a pleasure and happiness that will make me cry.

Goodbye, wife. G.

Had he proposed to her the previous night? Had she accepted? Or was it all wishful thinking? Or was he calling her 'wife' simply to reassure her of his intentions?

As with most of Calderon's letters, the expression of this one is vigorous, fluent, replete with direct emotion – the work, one might say, of a born writer. But the mood swings in it are considerable. The sixteen-page one that he wrote her the following morning, 1 February 1899, is unmistakably depressed. 'Am I the city of desolation, dear Kit?' he begins. 'I feel empty and deserted while the inhabitants are away.' Even the letter he had received from her that morning felt like the equivalent to

peeping in at the gate. I and you were sitting in armchairs, apart, fearing the parlour maid. Send me another, dear love, with a pressure of hands in it, with the tenderness of your chin and cheek laid upon my hair, with a blessing of me as I lean in your lap.

He will not address what she has said in her letter, other than to ask her to 'write for <u>me</u> this time, rather than for yourself'. He even goes back to her 'Jones' letter and the issue of Michael Furse and 'pastoral help'. His quotation from it reveals she had written that he sometimes 'frightened' her 'into smithereens'. Quite possibly this was the effect that his next proposal had on her:

If only we had some little bower near to Golden Square where we could meet fearless and in our own right, some dainty, tiny, fresh, clean bower, a temple of love and a school of life, where I could sit at the prophetess's feet, fondling them and learning. A little lodging, each with a key – it seems too Parisian; a little heaven where you would not be ashamed to enter. […]

Dear dark love, there is time and space for souls as well as bodies, in spite of the addle-headed philosophers; souls are more limited by these conditions [of physical separation] than bodies. Your body is more with me here than in the studio, for it is not so clothed with spirit. Therefore my love for you is better when I am with you than when I am away. Partly this is wrong in me and I must correct it; but partly it is to be remedied by being with you.

Then suddenly, on page eleven, it emerges what was the trouble with her letter:

Archie laughs with me at the humour and irony of this morning's post: my first love-letter half spent in telling me how my love was in bed with another man. (Did you know that I could be so coarse and blunt?) Do not think there is any jealousy or reproach or sense of pain in this. I was bound to know it (you felt) and writing was the only way of picking up the crumbs of truth dropped in the telling. Two more crumbs – Did you know of Archie's London life before you were engaged? Did you know it before that night at Oxford?

He understands that she wants him to 'have the whole story clear' and he protests: 'Darling Kit, there is no atom of antagonism between us even in the confessional.' Evidently she had referred to aspects of her marriage to Archie as 'rocks' in her 'side' and on the path of her relationship with George. In a very characteristic flash, Calderon places them in a completely different, fundamental context: 'The supreme difficulty of one human being taking another into itself so transcends your tiny rocks that they are not worth the mentioning, were they as big as St Paul's.' The letter ends, though, where it began: he had 'happiness at 17, not here. Write me a letter as good as a kiss; it will have to be long to come up to that greatness. G.'. The envelope was addressed in a slightly disguised script and black-bordered.

Fig. 3 Katharine Hamilton, 1885

Calderon wanted 'love' letters from Kittie, letters as passionate as his own. This was far too dangerous for a woman of her class so recently bereaved; and perhaps she still distrusted her own emotions for him. Instead, she decided they must share their pasts frankly with each other before she could be sure of them moving towards a full love affair and marriage. Later that day (1 February) Calderon received from her a note – 'only half a sheet!' – which made him 'happy again'. She seems to have confirmed to him that she would marry him, but only after the statutory three years. That evening he replied: '3 x 365 is fortunately beyond my arithmetic, or I should cry. One piece of good news, 1900 is not a leap year.' 'It is because you are my wife and not my sweetheart only that I am impatient […] I know that you are my wife because sweethearts never know one another as you and I do.' Intriguingly, he also refers to her writing 'to tell me all about Sir John'. Was this Sir John Conroy, described by Kittie on the back of a photograph of him as 'Archie Ripley's tutor at Oxford and a much loved friend'? What 'all' was there to tell? But Calderon finished the letter: 'Dear love. Thank you for your darling little note; it is so sweet. It is a kiss. Dear love. Tell me everything.'

Kittie's response to the creation of a love nest ('eyrie' in Calderon's word) seems to have been equally cautious. In a letter next day, 2 February 1899, he claimed:

I have a very short memory. All your features and the details of your form were so vivid 4 or 3 days ago. But now I cannot picture any part of you. Only sometimes when I think of the profile at the writing table with the great ball of black hair behind the head, my gracious black swan swims back into my memory.

Next morning, 3 February, before dashing off to catch the 10.41 from Pinner, he announced: 'Today I shall hover about Golden Square seeking the eyrie. It is urgent, pressing. We cannot continue apart.' He had received a 'dear fat letter' from her, presumably telling him more about the past. He could not 'munch' it now and 'say what I think over each thing', all he could answer was: 'I respect and love your love and your capacity for love, your genius for love, the more I know it; it is a rich intoxicating fluid, and now that I have drunk it all other wine is too thin for me.'

That lunchtime he wrote to her in pencil 'from a Vegetable Chop-House in St Martin's Lane' to say that he had looked at five lets in the vicinity of Golden Square and was about to set off 'on the prowl' for others. Two hours later, writing from an ABC cafeteria also in pencil, he announced that he had found a suitable room for an 'enormous price' at 21 Great Titchfield Street, closer to Baker Street, and joked that it was 'handy for my high church sister's church, All Saints Margaret Street'. He would come up next day on the 9.12 from Pinner and 'be installed by 10.10 a.m. From that time till 11.45 a.m. I shall wait for you'. Both of these letters were posted that afternoon in a white envelope addressed in a disguised hand.

At 10.15 the next morning, Saturday 4 February, he was 'settled at the table' at 21 Great Titchfield Street 'with my writing-case and the article on old Tolstoy', writing to her 'in case you should not come, dear Kit'. As he waited, he tried to console himself and her about their situation:

Don't you see the beauty of our three years [...]? So much depends upon me – virginal wedlock, not waiting but contented – with the hopes and cares that belong to it, the hidden pleasures and school-child freaks...far more beautiful than the everyday man and wife; a sunny picture to which we shall always look back with romantic regret.

In terms of Calderon's ambitions as a writer, however, most revealing is what came next:

Your money – put that on one side, out of your mind [...]; no need to consider what is already in the larder; are you enough identified with me to put yourself into my place? To help me all you know in seeing to a line what I do best, and helping me to do it? You are more than half a 'literary woman'. You appreciate a certain disdainfulness, even when it is discredited by insolvency – a certain pride or conscience which makes it impossible to write interviews with Little Tich or Herbert Campbell [music hall stars], for the *Windsor Magazine*. I think no-one could better feel my feelings and be my helper in the mere matter of work; and that is surely something between man and wife, isn't it? .... Why don't you come? [...] Why don't you write or telegraph? Can't you?

In addition to love and sensual attraction, then, he was looking for a partner who would value what he was trying to do in his writing; would in a deep sense *work with him* in his literary career.

But 'doubts' and 'tears', as we know from his letter from Eastcote next day, had prevented her from coming to Great Titchfield Street. So he pressed her to come the following day, Monday 6 February: 'At 10 I shall be sitting in the eyrie, (don't forget the address) cosying by the fire waiting for my love to come to me.' He offered a literary analogy for their relationship, which ingeniously developed his theme that anyone in their situation should live 'by and in the present':

Your poor sad letter, my dear one! When a poet writes an epic he designs and sees the whole plan; then he goes to each part and creates it anew from its own centre; the part is still a part of the whole, but it has a life of its own, and the plan of the whole is forgotten in the making of the part. So with your epic of love. You are busied now on the making of a new part; you do no wrong in throwing yourself all into the part; it is designed beforehand as a part of the whole; but it is not designed in detail; the plan[,] the 'point of view'[,] says 'love George', no more. Love him, dear love, and even while you forget the plan of the whole, you are not departing from it.

Even so, before dashing off to play golf with Hugh Bradby (it was Sunday again) he wondered whether he 'understood' her 'troubles', her 'feelings'. 'Cannot kisses mend them at ten o'clock?'

Given that a later letter of Calderon's reveals that the landlords of the Great Titchfield Street 'eyrie' accepted his and Kittie's 'relation' and 'received' them, it is possible that she did go there on 6 February. But if so, she had some unwelcome news for him: she was shortly leaving again for Earlham. She may even have arrived there next day, leaving him to stay at 17 Golden Square on his own for the 'literary dinner' on Wednesday 8 February and return to Eastcote with Jones on Thursday.

There is no indication why Kittie did this. Had she been invited by Canon Ripley for a family gathering, perhaps marking his departure from Earlham? Was she simply drawn back there by all her memories? Was she finding her relationship with Calderon *impossible* and needed to get away from London?

The six letters that he wrote to her at Earlham over the next four days – beginning on black-bordered paper and totalling fifty sides – provide some clues. Writing in the early evening of Friday 10 February 1899, he apologises for his previous 'cruel' letter (now lost), as he realises 'you have much more to fear and to bear than I have'. 'Poor pretty darling, poor dear Kitty, my love – I should have written to cheer and to help you. But it is best to see me as I am – not an admirable character; very weak; ready to take, having nothing to give.' Something, it seems, happened before she left London that makes him imagine her whispering to herself 'Archie would not have ['done' is crossed out] been so'. He reproaches himself for robbing her of 'that poetry of love which you might duly expect of me',

for being 'defiled with desire'. When she first arrived at Earlham, she
wrote him 'such beautiful things [...], picturing and seeing Archie walking
about the house'. Did she now, as he put it, 'think of ' both Archie and
George? 'Do not confuse and weigh; think that each human being is
worthy only by what is individual in him, and the individualities of men
are not commensurable.' In fact he was sure she had 'long since found
means (if ever you had to seek them) to reconcile the double love'.

Evidently he had spoken, or written to her, of an 'expurgated week in
[an] undiscovered village' – 'a monstrous thing for a man to say under the
circumstances; but I suppose I am a monster'. He did not 'withdraw'
anything he had said about that. He merely admitted he was 'tempting'
her, and 'shall love you the better if you refuse'.

The nature of the problem is intimated by his repeated imagining of
their physical contact. After the above, he continues:

Poor, dear dear Kit, forget my shortcomings: let all this pass in a long kiss. And
when the kiss is over, leave your hand in mine.

Dear blessed darling; let us lean back side by side, with our heads together
against the back of the chair, your arms about me, mine about you.

Writing the following morning, Saturday 11 February, he says that he is
'less moody, more myself', because he has spent twelve hours in bed and
she herself is 'partly to blame':

Once you seemed to be there with your face just in front of mine, smiling in upon
me. I have been able clearly to recall all your prettiness, the angle of your chin,
the corners of your mouth, the atmosphere of love about you. I desire you.

Not surprisingly, their trysts in the 'studio' after Mrs Hamilton and the
servants had gone to bed were putting them under great stress – moral for
her and physical for him.

Whilst Calderon waited for her next letter, however, he shared news,
views, asides and humour with her, all in his inimitable fluent style. On
the Friday, for instance, he had been at the British Museum 'still at Servian
translations'. This is a surprise, as it implies that as well as Russian he

knew Serbo-Croat. Perhaps he had had to teach himself the language at short notice: he was labouring at these 'translations' chiefly to produce 'an effect upon Traill [the editor of *Literature*] – the sort of man who decides useful opinions upon who knows about what'. This, Calderon admits, is 'a bad sort of motive', but he cannot help it: 'I am undermined in all my actions by the desire to please an audience. It is the worst of vices, of the gentler sort.' He tells Kittie this in case she has not 'discovered' it already; and in terms of 'knowing' Calderon it is certainly an interesting confession.

On the Friday, he had drunk 'five whiskies, two at supper, the rest irrelevantly'. This had only been possible because he had money in his pocket from her: 'I should not have dared it in my customary poverty.' Writing to her next day, he was 'smoking a cigarette; I oughtn't to be'. All of this is because 'I throw myself too much for support upon you; I feel as if I had no more any need of self-government', and he misses her so much. If only she were with him at that moment, 'we could ramble out into that sunshine; stroll over to Ruislip Church, bribe the clergyman…'.

Meanwhile, he had 'indited a long letter to the *Daily News* on "Plethoric London"', which he was pretty sure they would publish 'because it is so sensible'; but this only led him to another disarming confession:

Dear heart, I am awfully afraid of becoming a bore. I have the makings of a bore in me. Will you tell me at once, do you think, when you find that I bore you? How are you most likely to be taken with the feeling? Will it be when I talk of my work? Of my friends? Of my mental experiences? Or when I grow enthusiastic over something you are not interested in?

Beneath it all was the need to hear from her again. 'I think you will have to write more than once from Earlham.' He was assuming she would return to London on Tuesday 14th February and he feared there would be 'no Eyrie on the Wednesday. Perhaps. Will you come? Shall you be glad to see me? […] Were you at all jealous when I wrote to you how I had enjoyed the Furses' dance?'.

At about half past eleven on the Saturday morning, having finished his first letter of the day to Kittie, Calderon left on his bike for Northwood, about two miles away, where he was to give 'golfballs to the pro to be remade' and could post both letters to her, thus obtaining a different postmark from usual. That afternoon he played golf with Bradby, presumably at the Northwood Links. His game was 'not worth a hang today; but we have done our thirty holes and come in tired. So we are fairly satisfied'. Having had no letter from her during the day, in his letter that evening he described at length some instances of what was to remain a favourite activity of his all his life: encountering and conversing with ordinary men and women of the 'lower classes'. The first was a road-mender, the second a 'china hawker', the third the Scottish golf professional, who was drunk, and the fourth the latter's landlady, a policeman's wife, who together with Calderon tried to persuade the professional 'at least three times to go to bed'.

Taking this as his starting point, Calderon fantasized wittily but somewhat dangerously. Supposing 'my Scotchman' accused him of *stealing* the sovereigns he kept offering Calderon for his 'twelve bad golfballs', what would Calderon's defence be?

I am a man without visible means of support: if I am asked for my accounts, to show where my money comes from, what shall I say? I shall tell the police that I cannot bring your name into the court but they must make private enquiries of you and they will find it is all right. I am in love with you, I shall say, and we are going to be married; then up jumps Col. Monsell (the head of our district). 'In love with Mrs R.? Not a bit,' he will say; 'he's in love with my daughter.' Penal servitude for life; and you will be allowed to come once a month for ten minutes, to an Eyrie with bars and a fat warder looking on. Just think if we were separated by bars. Supposing I were Dreyfus. Would you wait for long? 7.30 and dinner is coming in. One kiss for an appetizer, my love. Dear heart.

In early 1899 Dreyfus was still in solitary confinement on Devil's Island. The 'joke' behind 'Col. Monsell' was that he was not only a Chief Constable in the Metropolitan Police, but the father of Geraldine Monsell, the twenty-three-year-old 'she' at the Furses' ball and a cousin of Michael Furse.

But there was a delay with dinner, which was presumably brought to Calderon's room(s). He had borrowed the Tobutts' family bible 'to look

up Peace' (whilst working on his article about the encyclical?) and Bradby
now read out a gloss from it explaining that woman had not been created
from the head of man, or his feet, 'but out of his side to be equal with him;
under his arm to be protected by him; near his heart to be beloved by
him'. This impelled Calderon to continue his letter:

It is extraordinary how sensible clergymen and people who write notes in bibles
are. I am sure I shall offend you in your religion some day; for I feel an active
enmity to so many of the circumstances of it; I can't stand professionalism; these
wretched Bishops seem to be on a par with the French Chamber over the Dreyfus
case. But I shall not really offend you; there is nothing over which we should
disagree in it all, except the divinity of Jesus, which I do regard as against reason
and very badly evidenced; besides, not meaning anything. Even over that we
could never fall out. Could we really fall out over anything?

Although the following day was a Sunday, there was still an early morning
postal delivery. Calderon spent 'all the intervals of waking in the night [...]
waiting for daylight and the promised letter', but all the postman brought
him was 'a booklist from Mudie's' (the Circulating Library).
    That evening Calderon resumed his writing to her:

Very sleepy, dear Kit. Jones and I have been sitting dozing side by side in front of
the fire this hour; for we have been out all day in sun and wind and rain, playing
golf. I feel quite a new man tho' tired; cold wind and driving rain on bare head
and neck, air whistling under one's shirt, have refreshed me. I have been reading
your letters of this past fortnight; my unnatural wife has sent me no new one to
read. [...] Very sweet – much that is in your letters – one of them is full of
warmth and light from page to page – one in which you say that you love my
name – I never cared for it till now; I always thought it rather ridiculous; but it is
an honest name, for it [George] means a tiller of the earth; though I never do any
digging except when I am playing golf.

As a dramatic diagram illustrated, Jones had excelled himself whilst out
with Calderon and Bradby by running around in circles 'almost mewing
with excitement' after a rabbit that had shot off in a straight line. Another
drawing in the letter showed a small spider that had 'come dangling down'
out of Calderon's hair as he was writing. This he interpreted as a good

omen for a letter next day, because 'araignée de soir, grand espoir'.
Consequently, he would go to bed early 'so as to bring post-time nearer'
and he would get as much sleep as he could 'till Wednesday to bring our
first kiss nearer, our first words, our first looks, and the first touching of
our hands nearer'.

On Monday morning, 13 February, Calderon received her letter; and
exploded. He was in 'such a nasty peevish cantankerous mood that I
cannot answer your letter worthily'. She appears to have become
overwhelmed at Earlham with shame and guilt at their relationship, and
by the conviction that others, including servants, looked upon her as
'impure', that George himself took her to be 'impure', that she really was
'impure'. He remonstrated:

If I wanted to know whether a tablecloth was clean, I should look at the
tablecloth instead of enquiring of the housemaid what and when had been spilt
on it. Do I not know that you are utterly pure? I see you as you are, the fruit of
your behaviour, and utterly pure. All that is of a piece with your marriage: you
have had a passion for one man; if it has had anything in it that seemed strange to
you, it was all towards him; it is all one thing. Had you and he lived together till
seventy you would have felt no self-reproach. What difference does his death
make? You would have felt nothing of it but for me; do not alter your feelings for
me; and as for myself I feel that it has nothing to do with me.

It is unlikely that we shall ever know what it was that now, after becoming
intimate with Calderon, seemed 'strange' to Kittie about her marriage to
Ripley, whom she had loved to the extent that Calderon calls it a 'passion'.
It is quite conceivable, however, that Calderon's love for her was more
erotic than Archie's, that she had assumed Archie's was 'pure' and
'normal', and Calderon had awoken in her a physical ('impure') response
that for her was quite different from what she had experienced in her
marriage. As we have seen, Archie Ripley may even have been uncertain
of his own sexual orientation. It is likely, moreover, that Calderon was
more impetuous, less self-controlled than she was accustomed to because,
like a lot of young men of his background who rejected prostitution, he
actually had no experience of 'love-making'. When he referred in his letter
of 31 January to receiving his 'first love-letter', perhaps he meant 'ever'?

He referred to her in a letter the next day as a 'prophetess' of 'love and life', at whose feet he would sit 'learning', so perhaps he had been emboldened in his advances ('designs', she called them) by the very fact that she was older, more experienced, and could 'teach' him?

Equally, especially whilst at Earlham, she must have 'felt' Archie's body still; longed for it; not have been able to turn from it, or rather its remembrance, to another, real one. This, it seems, is what produced Calderon's most explicit outburst in his letter of 13 February:

More…I want to hear nothing of your passion for another <u>body</u>; I know of it; but why should you keep it before my eyes?

I told you I was peevish. But consider my case. I love a beautiful pure woman; and an irrelevant showman keeps leaping irrepressibly up in front of the picture insisting that she is neither beautiful nor pure and introducing me to things which it is against my instinct to hear more than once; just once, to put away, with my own judgement on them; not a case for argument, but a free judgment and no more said. Let us pay off the showman for he is a liar and he spoils the picture.

It is unfortunate – though perhaps even intended – that the 'showman' is first read as a kind of spirit-form of Archie, when its more settled meaning, surely, is as a metaphor for the whole concept of physical purity (in Kittie's case probably of religious origin).

At this point, Calderon 'capitulates', in the sense that he is prepared to forgive her anything, agree to anything, and place her on the pedestal, or throne, that he has known all along she deserves. But he immediately qualifies it with arguments that foreshadow his position on women's suffrage a decade later:

Here is your crown and sceptre. But do not think I give them you because you ask for them. It is that against which I rebel in Woman (with a big W). She demands. You demand. I care nothing for unbased demands; her only claim to any royalty is the free admission of it by man. That is where you and I disagree. There is no throne at all for wives, as wives. There is one for Kitty, as Kitty: not in the least on account of her sex, only on account of her individuality. […] Men are equal and women too: that is to say, they are to be weighed without any irrelevant allowances, such as for birth, sex etc. And the height of absurdity is to expect reverence for a defect – such as that of being a woman – it draws no reverence; but only the gentleness of compassion. This is a radical disagreement between us.

Revealingly, however, Calderon is adamant that differences in ideas, beliefs, 'need not lead to a breach', as they 'never go near the bottom of things', i.e. what lovers really have in common. 'Being' precedes for him 'ideological' agreement or disagreement.

'Carping a little more – pure carping', he quotes a sentence from her letter: 'Instinct, Reason, Love – all say the same thing – No.' He counters that Reason is wrong, 'perhaps', in telling her that if their relationship moves further down the path he has taken it then he might '"make what is now hard impossible"', since 'there is no question of the hard and the impossible; it is a question of unhappiness and passive functions of health'. Repression of intimate acts, he seems to be saying, is simply unhealthy. Further:

I do not understand what Love answers when it 'insists on its own strength and integrity'. But what of instinct? Unless Instinct has contradictions in itself, I would rather it had been on my side. Or should I not? I do not understand the instincts of a pure woman: but does it mean that my body is less loved?

Calderon had indeed 'revealed myself so much to you in these last few days', but now all the firewalls came down:

I am almost jealous of Mike. You affect him as you affected me. While away you do not affect me so now; at any rate not today. I think Mike must have been thinking only of himself when he was 'humorous' to you about pastoral help. Would you rather I stepped aside?

I am piling nasty things on nasty things: but you told me to do so. [...]

Even when you write me caresses in your letters, I do not really believe that you love me; I shall not believe that till I see you again. [...]

Perhaps so discontented a man as I am ought not to marry: do you think I ought? Your going away is much more disturbing to my work than your being in London. [...]

Dear love, love me and forgive me.

This was despatched to Earlham from central London at 12.15 p.m. that day, Monday 13 February 1899. He must have wondered whether, as in January, she would now stay on longer at Earlham than she had said.

Only three hours later he was sitting in an ABC cafeteria writing her an elated letter. His mood had changed completely since the morning. He had had lunch, presumably by arrangement, with 'Mammy Ham' at Golden Square, and

She and I were utterly agreed upon the grandeur of your nature; after lunch I went into the studio, inhaled your atmosphere, murmured caresses (you will find them there when you reach home) [...] – dear dear Kit, you are so much too great and splendid for me, there is such an Old Testament grandeur in you – you cannot but be mistaken [in her self-deprecation] – you are a million, million times too good for this poor crawling creature.

Dear dear Kit, I led Mammy Ham on at lunch for the pure delight of paradoxes; I could not help talking of you. She thinks you will never marry. Women marry twice, but they never love deeply twice. You have loved so well, that you cannot love much again; and without loving much (we were both agreed) you could never marry again. Dear darling woman. Do you know your own value?

He had gone to look at another potential 'eyrie', but 'the housekeeper felt assured (with red and white patches on her face) that no lady would think of visiting a man at his chambers'. 'Do you mind my telling you this, dear love?' he asked – because it contained an imputation of 'impurity'. The fact was, he concluded, the lower the class of the area 'the more savagely correct is the deportment', and he had decided to take the Great Titchfield Street 'eyrie' for another month precisely because the Simmintons, who ran it, 'understand our relation'.

Mrs Hamilton had confirmed to him that her daughter was returning next day (Tuesday), so he begged Kittie to come to him at the Eyrie on Wednesday morning, before he 'officially' returned Jones to Golden Square that lunchtime:

Dear dear dear darling, I long for you, not basely, not spiritually, but with the whole of my being, – undistinguishedly. [...]

Whatever you say, whatever you write, I shall be at the Eyrie on Wednesday morning at 10 o'clock, hungry for the sight and for the touch of you. I know you are merciful and kind, and if you do not come to me soon I shall be miserable, but only with a temporary passing misery, for I shall know that you would come if you could. Dear dear love; write to me there [...] if you cannot come. [...] Jones will be there; let that be an inducement.

Calderon did not post this letter immediately but took it with him to Kilburn, where he was 'staying the night with my people'.

There, at nine o'clock in the evening, he resumed the letter and related to Kittie some interesting literary news. In Bloomsbury earlier that day he had visited E.V. Lucas, the prolific writer whose cricket classic *Willow and Leather* had come out the year before. Calderon included a drawing of Mrs Lucas, whom he described as 'a large weird incisive clinging creature with French hair and deep luminous snake-charming eyes close up under the eyebrows. She sits still as if she were a camera photographing you'. Mention of E.V. Lucas, who edited Grant Richards's increasingly popular series 'The Dumpy Books for Children', prompted 'Marge', Calderon's elder sister, to attack Richards's 'reader' of a collection of fairy stories by her friend 'Bertha Harrison of Burlington House' (later a leading anti-suffragist). Both the author and Marge 'guess at the sex' of the reader 'from the extravagance of the abuse' and suspect the reader of 'rivalry and gross intemperate vindictiveness'. What they don't know is that the reader was Kittie!

Calderon also alludes to his long letter published in the *Daily News* that day, 13 February 1899. It was printed as a 'tail-piece' to one of the extended articles that appeared day after day about overcrowding in London and is a good example of Calderon's ability to have a rigorous view about anything. He begins by stating what seems to be the obvious: 'In the village where I live there are far fewer houses than in London, but we are not in the least overcrowded.' The 'chief characteristic of London as a place', however, is 'the large number of people which it houses'. Hence 'the more houses you put together in one place the less living-room will there be for the people that will come there'. This sounds like the kind of paradox beloved of Calderon since his student days. Any modern town-planner would agree with him, though, that to ease overcrowding you have to decentralise. The 'most immediate cure of the evil', he suggested, was 'to spread the knowledge of what a beastly place London is for a working man to live in – even if the knowledge has to be spread by extension courses'.

Calderon's mother thought his letter 'wise and good, so you may be sure that it is so, for one's mother would hardly be prejudiced'. But he was most concerned to know whether Kittie approved of his putting his name on it 'in full'. 'I thought if it was sensible and people thought so, that there was no reason to leave the credit of it unoccupied.' Pushing his byline even in this simple way was part of his strategy for leaving journalism behind: all his previous publications in newspapers and journals were unsigned, except his stories.

'I shall sleep in your arms tonight love', he closed the letter metaphorically, and sealed it in an envelope. Next morning he opened it again and added two more sides, because he had had an experience that he must tell her about. He knew that it was in her arms he lay, because 'there are no others that could enfold me so tenderly, there is no other bosom where I could lie so tranquilly, no other body that could send such a genial warmth into mine'. More even than that:

I had a gleam of the feeling that you call prayer. It seemed to put me for an instant into such close communion with you that I am sure you must have been praying and thinking of me at the moment. It was just after twelve last night. If I know what God is then it was love coming from him and going to him. Though that is speaking in your language, not mine. And again at 7.30 this morning I felt so loved, that you must have been thinking of me.

He had practised a new piano piece, by Grieg, which he wanted her to hear because he felt that when he played 'really special pieces' he was 'talking through music right into your heart'. He now re-sealed the envelope, addressed it in a heavily disguised hand, and posted it on his way to the British Museum so that she would receive it when she returned home that day, which was St Valentine's.

Whether they met at Great Titchfield Street on Wednesday morning we do not know, but a great clarification took place in the studio that night. Judging from Calderon's letter written at Eastcote on the morning of 13 February, Kittie had implied to him that she had 'reconciled all feelings' at Earlham. Calderon presumably succeeded in convincing her now that there was nothing 'impure' about their relationship. We have no letters written by him between 15th and 23rd February, but it is quite clear from the four that have survived from the end of the month that their love had moved onto a different plane.

Calderon now addressed her as 'Titten', 'Titteny', or 'Tittenish', adaptations of 'kitten' ('kitty') that most likely play on her distinctive laugh but in any case sound intimate. 'Dear love,' he writes to her on 24 February in a heavily disguised envelope postmarked Uxbridge, 'I am so glad we have been through these trying things, over these hillocks, because the ground slopes down the other side', and next day: 'It is fine weather with us love; the cyclonic disturbance has passed clean away.' He has not had 'any blue devils' and feels 'perfectly good and cheerful and permanent and vigorous' at the thought of 'you loving me with all your immense warm power'. He is even 'a little set against the Eyrie (at present)', because:

It presents you just in that detached way which makes it easier for me to take a wrong and selfish view of the thing. I hadn't sufficiently realised – not exactly the duty which is appended to love, but the necessity of standing up on one's own individual legs, not just climbing into the bosom and squawking like a peevish baby for want of something to be discontented about.

The child of her friend Kathleen Skipwith (a sister of Nesta LLoyd) has died and he offers Kittie his support, because he knows that her unique gift for comforting will be greatly called upon:

You will have an effort of comforting, Titten; – it is an effort probably, though you may not think it so – and if you can draw any strength out of me to help you with all efforts of doing and enduring, draw, draw, draw.

Indeed, in the set of studio portraits of Kittie with Jones taken at about this time (see Fig. 4), though 'lovely' and 'gracious' in Calderon's words, she looks drained; her hair is greying; and one realises with a shock, from the colour of her bag, of the bow at the back of her hair, her choker and the ribbon in her dress, that she is wearing mourning. The 'best' of these photographs Calderon had framed and kept at Eastcote.

Fig. 4 Katharine Ripley, 1899

Four months after Archie Ripley's death, then, despite 'moods', 'peevishness', 'monstrous demands' on Calderon's part and shame, guilt and downright fear on Katharine Ripley's, their love had achieved an acceptance of who they were and how they would conduct themselves before they could get married. For the first time in his letters Calderon uses the symbol of a circle with a dot in the middle, meaning in context 'your arms about me' or 'my arms about you'. 'With you I enjoy a perfect liberty, because there is nothing I have not told you', he wrote to her on 24 February, and the following day: 'In the half-sight of waking I see your face in the fold of the bedclothes smiling in on me, brush my lips over the cotton work, love and am loved.'

Nevertheless, as Calderon admitted in his letter of 24 February, his capacity for 'fermenting difficulties out of nothing' was formidable. Not far into this letter he announced: 'I have challenged Mrs Dowdall to go to see the murderers at Mme Tussauds with me on Monday; she accepts cheerfully.' 'Mrs Dowdall' was the twenty-three-year-old Hon. Mary Borthwick, married to one of Calderon's closest friends from Rugby and Oxford, the barrister Harold Chaloner Dowdall. She was svelte, auburn-haired, vivacious and unconventional. She and her husband were settled in Liverpool but visiting London. Two years later she became the invaluable confidante of Augustus John's wife Ida, by whom she was known as 'the Rani' (i.e. maharani).

Challenging Mary Dowdall 'to see the murderers' is a Calderon joke, since she was pregnant with her second child and might fear a miscarriage. Calderon continued:

I daresay we shan't go there, but somewhere. [...] Does it stir any *arrière pensée* in you my determined way of seeing Mrs D? Ought I not to like to see any other nice women now? I think, on the contrary[,] that my pleasure in them is rather enhanced by being in love with you: it gives a definiteness to one's relation. I wish I had left out this paragraph. [...] Of course I don't mean anything about j-l-sy; but about whether I seem to be trying to prove something – I haven't a notion what.

He simply could not 'leave well alone'. He closed his letter of 25 February, immediately after 'the cyclonic disturbance has passed clean away', by fretting: 'What if Nina Corbet dissuades you from loving me?'

3

WHITE RAVEN AND BLACK RAVEN

Nina Corbet was born Caroline Douglas Stewart on 6 June 1867 at Brantford, Ontario. She could trace her ancestry to Robert II, the first Stewart king of Scotland, and beyond. As her daughter expressed it to me in an interview in 1986, the circumstances of Nina's childhood were 'very romantic'. Her father, James Affleck Stewart, a captain in the 11th Hussars, had been sent on a mission to Canada, where he fell in love with and married the 'very lovely' Eliza Vale. Three weeks before Nina was born he died in Canada at the age of twenty-eight. After a few years, his widow brought their daughter to the Stewart family home, St Fort House outside St Andrews, to acquaint her with her native land. However, Eliza was given the cold shoulder by the Stewarts and forced to live with Nina at the other end of the country – in 'The Nest', Torquay. Thereafter she was known as 'Mrs Stewart of Torquay'.

Kittie's mother's family, the Simsons, had lived at Pitcorthie House, eight miles from St Andrews, and been friends with the Stewarts for generations. Kittie's own childhood was spent mainly on her father's estate in Donegal. Possibly, then, she and Nina first met when they were young girls visiting their respective grandparents in Fife. By 1881 Kittie was actually living in St Andrews with her parents and Nina had moved to the area, too. This was because the Stewarts were facing a dynastic crisis: Nina's only uncle had died childless, leaving Nina her grandparents' only heir.

By their late teens, Kittie and Nina were inseparable friends. They loved dancing and went to balls together. When they were staying in the same house, they usually shared a room and sometimes a bed. They called each other by turns 'Dina' and 'T'Other'. 'Dina' perhaps derived from the popular music hall song 'Villikins and his Dinah'. In letters they addressed each other as 'Darling', 'My own', or the mysterious 'Peter'. Although not tall, Nina looked the classic 'statuesque' beauty of the time (see Fig. 5), and was always having to watch her weight. Kittie was shorter, had a minute waist, and was always being asked if she was eating enough. Both were extremely lively and enjoyed gossip and intrigue, but Nina was the more flirtatious. As a girl one Christmas Eve she had put her 'drawers' on inside out when she got up, was dared by her maid to wear them like that all day, 'and I <u>did</u>'. In social relationships she sought a frisson of risk, whereas Kittie seemed always restrained by the moral values that she had assimilated as a child from close contact with her father. Nina greatly relied on Kittie for advice and support in adversity.

Fig. 5 Caroline ('Nina') Corbet, c. 1890

In 1888, just after her twenty-first birthday, Nina Stewart married
Walter Orlando Corbet, heir to a baronetcy in Shropshire derived from
the knight Hugo le Corbet (Crow or Raven) who had come to Britain with
William the Conqueror. It is thought to have been a marriage of
convenience. Walter was eleven years older than Nina and in letters is
referred to by her and by Kittie as 'poor boy', 'dear old Walter', 'poor old
dear'. But at thirty-two he was still a dashing, physically fit Captain of the
Coldstream Guards who had fought in the critical battle of Tel-el-Kebir in
Egypt six years earlier. Kittie's grandmother, Mary Simson, read his palm
in November 1888 and plausibly identified 'extraordinary energy, and
power of activity in all muscular performances [...] great tenacity of
purpose and extreme conventionality'. Others said that he did not have an
enemy in the world. In Kittie's words he was 'a typical Englishman of his
kind – nice to look at and nice right through'.

Nina and Kittie's relationship grew even closer after Nina's marriage.
She needed a unique confidante to relieve the strains and expectations of
being an aristocrat's wife and bearing his children. As she wrote later, 'any
great change of life such as Marriage is like a Pack of Cards being
thoroughly shuffled. It only remains then to sit down, and play the game
of Patience!'.

Three months after her wedding she presented Kittie with a red
leather-bound, gilt-edged book stamped in gold 'Kittie', on the flyleaf of
which she had written a quotation from Bacon: 'But one thing is
admirable, which is, that this communicating of a man's self to his friend
works two contrary effects; for it redoubleth joys, and cutteth griefs in
halves.' On the first seven pages of this 'Friendship Book' Nina also wrote
out extracts from Rider Haggard, Elizabeth Barrett Browning,
Wordsworth, Erskine and others. Their themes were not so much
friendship as love, fidelity, and the connection between human and divine
love. 'What is the true way of loving one's friends?' reads the entry from
Fénelon. 'It is, to love them in God, and God in them; to love what he has
made them, and to bear for love of Him with what he has not made
them.' Later in the book, Kittie wrote out 'from Nina' Elizabeth Barrett
Browning's sonnet beginning 'How do I love thee? Let me count the

ways | I love thee to the depth and breadth and height | My soul can reach'.

After their marriage, Nina and Walter Corbet lived at St Fort. Corbet resigned his commission in 1889 with the rank of Captain and became a 2nd Lieutenant in the 1st Fifeshire Light Horse (Volunteers), as well as Master of Fife Fox Hounds. But the couple also spent much time staying at one country house or another in England owned or rented by members of the Corbet family. This entailed as many as four balls a week, sometimes lasting till three in the morning, at which on Nina's own admission she flirted, 'chaffed men's heads off', and made 'great pals' and 'conquests'. From Acton Reynald, the Corbet family home, she wrote to Kittie at about this time:

My darling do write me often. It <u>does</u> help me so. Your Sunday's letter did me <u>real</u> good, you are a clever gurl [*sic*] to write so A1-ly. Oh, if I could – if I could – not write but act but I fear my influence is <u>not</u> roselike. [...] Pray for me Quincki an you love me. In hot haste very tired out shooting all day your ever own and loving thro' everything and for always Nina.

The Corbets' first son, Vincent, was born in 1890. Later, following an acute illness or a miscarriage, Nina sent to Kittie from yet another country house a tightly folded note in faint pencil that read:

All through my pain I've been buoying myself up with the hope that you were happy – <u>really</u>. Is it so? I couldn't write before and I'm not allowed to now so I just say I love you and I want you. This may be superfluous write to me soon – Tomorrow. I fear you will not like, [*sic*] I am <u>so</u> thin – you would laugh if you saw me – I've never been so in my life.

Both young women were occasionally on the verge of tearful breakdown, but could not show it in the social milieu within which they moved. Kittie had unhappy fallings in love and declarations of love made to her, which were perhaps complicated by her belief – a leitmotif of quotations in the 'Friendship Book' – that love should involve self-sacrifice and pain. She needed Nina Corbet's support too, which if they had not

been separated, Nina implied, would have been more physical: 'Neenee
does coodle you up, and up and up – all round and over and under you –
you're just tired my darling – but I can't bear to think of Keetee crying and
lifting up her voice with no slip-body to comfort her!'

In 1891 Walter Corbet inherited the baronetcy and Nina became Lady
Corbet. The Corbets' heraldic symbol was a raven, with the motto 'Deus
pascit corvos' ('God feeds the ravens'). It may have been around this time
that Kittie and Nina took the names 'White Raven' and 'Black Raven'
respectively. Probably not too much should be read into this, as Kittie was
simply very pale-skinned and also known as 'Swan'. But there is no doubt
that the sobriquets were also intended to suggest that Kittie was good and
Nina bad. Nina regularly reproached and denigrated herself in her letters.
Kittie's 'good' influence, she wrote, 'comes from the real real you – and
the real real me is horrid, loathsome, and so cannot fail to exhale loathly
vapours'. She also experienced unaccountable bouts of anaesthesia, when
she could not feel what she knew she ought to. In 1891, when the Corbets
were in Japan on a world cruise, they received news that their friend Sir
Richard Sutton, married to Walter's sister Constance, had died suddenly at
the age of thirty-seven. Nina wrote to Kittie:

I feel numbed. I can't think. When Walter dashed into my room yesterday and
gave me the telegram, I of course thought in my selfishness it was Vincent. [...]
Poor poor Constance. I have written to her, but [...] such a letter [...] hard and
unfeeling. I can't cry. Walter has cried a lot [...] I don't know what I'm made of. I
can think of nothing else – it stains through everything [...] It seems too
appallingly selfish to think of myself even – but it has brought home my own
misdeeds more clearly I think than anything could. If it had been Walter [a line
blacked out] I can't write any more I am too miserable.

What 'misdeeds' was she referring to? Most likely, what she thought of as
acts of 'emotional infidelity' towards her husband, her flirtations and
'involvements' as she called them. She had unfailing affection and respect
for Walter, she even loved him, but she had never fallen in love with him.
Her consequent emotional openness to other men never became sexual,
but it was in utter contrast to her fidelity to 'White Raven'. All the

evidence of her letters and entries in the 'Friendship Book' points to her being 'in love' at this time with Kittie.

After Nina, the woman closest to Kittie was, in fact, Constance Sutton. Like them, in 1891 she was twenty-four. She was a believer seriously interested in contemporary theology. In the 'Friendship Book' Kittie wrote out several pages from Constance's copy of *Letters from a Mystic of the Present Day* by her father's cousin the 'post-Tractarian' Revd Rowland William Corbet. But the death of her husband severely shook her faith. She could feel nothing 'beyond' the 'aching void' that her husband's death had left behind. 'I can't realise often that he is happier where he is – is he Kittie? – and feel that he must be as lonely as I am.' 'Faith – hope – belief are so easy in the abstract […] just when they become a necessity they seem to slip out of one's grasp.' From Japan Nina wrote to Kittie: 'I know what a comfort you can be to Connie – I should have been of no use – you know just what to say and do, and what not to say and do.' Kittie did this throughout 1891 and 1892 in letters to Constance that were primarily religious and sought to restore her faith in the 'love of God' and the 'Life Beyond'. On 29 December 1891 Constance wrote to her: 'I don't think you know – or ever <u>will</u> know perhaps – the help that your <u>living faith</u> has been to me […] and is <u>now</u> – for one requires faith in the Unseen more not less as the time goes on I find, so help me still, dearest friend, won't you?'

All three women were much exercised by what they referred to as 'Self'. Nina and Constance speak of it as almost by definition bad. One of the worst words in their vocabulary is 'selfishness', which they regularly accuse themselves of. Consequently they always seem in pursuit of 'self-control'. In some highly revealing pages entitled 'Thoughts and Musings' that Nina Corbet wrote in 1893/94 we read:

Every day do something that you <u>dislike</u>. […] To have one's mind and body under control is the most difficult thing in human life – but every time you violate self by forcing it to do that which it dislikes and which you <u>know</u> to be right, you strengthen your character all round, not only the particular weakness you are combatting.

So far so conventional, one might think, for Victorians and oppressed Victorian women especially. However, Kittie Hamilton as a young woman comes across not as negatively obsessed with 'Self' – her own self – but as positively preoccupied with other people's selves. This differentiated her fundamentally from Nina and Constance, and it was of course one source of their lifelong friendship with her.

Nina directly addressed why she thought women were 'given to be deceitful'. 'Society (with a big S)' had imposed 'customs' and 'certain rules of daily life' on women which rendered 'certain hypocrisies' and 'little polite lies' inevitable. For a start, a woman 'can never show her feelings or her preference for a particular man, unless he comes forward first'. If a man is rebuffed, 'all he has to do is go away and enjoy himself – big game shooting – soldiering – yachting', whilst a woman must 'stay at home with the eyes of her family and friends always on her. She must laugh and smile as before, while her heart is breaking'. Nina felt 'very strongly', therefore, that it was 'not entirely women's fault' that they were 'not honourable as a rule'. 'They are taught from earliest youth to hide their feelings and this is the result!' 'In some ways', she concluded, 'men are infinitely more large minded than women – but I think their sense of honour is greater towards each other, than towards women.'

Both Nina Corbet and Constance Sutton involved themselves in Kittie's career. Kittie made a life-changing decision in the early nineties that she was not going to be just a lady of leisure and good works, but become a painter. There was artistic talent on both the Hamilton and Simson sides of her family, she had had drawing lessons as a child, and she now threw herself into sketching and painting, whether at St Fort or Constance's rented home of Combermere Abbey in Shropshire. Both Nina and Constance were alarmed by the spectacle of a woman 'working' so hard. They also supported her when she was depressed about her paintings being rejected for exhibition. Things seem to have come to a head in December 1892 when Mary Hamilton gave her son John Pakenham Hamilton a thousand pounds but was hesitating over continuing to fund Kittie's course and studio fees at the A.S. Cope and J.W. Nicol School of Painting. Kittie was encouraged to continue by the established painter

Briton Rivière and Nina stepped in to pay some of Kittie's studio fees from the generous allowance she received from her husband.

Walter Corbet himself thoroughly approved of his wife's relationship with Kittie Hamilton. He found Kittie's vivacity delightful, addressed her as 'darling', and when the couple were in London he invited her to accompany them on excursions. She was the perfect chaperone for Nina on the European tour that the Corbets made in April and May 1894, on which he referred to them as his 'girls'.

A wacky illustrated journal of the tour kept by Nina and entitled *The Log of the Two Girls and the Boy with the Sailor Hat* meshes closely with seventeen letters written home by Kittie to her mother – the longest series of Kittie's letters known to have survived. On the voyage to Naples and in Italy itself the Corbets were travelling with a predominantly male, upper-class company and it seems that accommodation and some activities were divided by gender. In Florence the 'girls' bumped into a fellow art-student of Kittie's from London, the American Louise E. Bagg, and together they visited an artist's studio where, Nina recorded, there were 'some very clever pictures, notably one of Kittie with no garments'. Meanwhile Kittie wrote enthusiastic, newsy and playful letters to 'Mammie Muffles', 'Hammie-Mammie', 'Mammie Ham', 'the Mother of La Katrinella', 'Mammery Hammery' and 'You Dear Old Lady', in which a constant theme was whether her mother was being 'good', looking after herself, and even dressing appropriately. One has the impression that Mrs Hamilton was a 'liability'. In her last letter home, from Antwerp on 24 May, Kittie asked her to have a 'big Tub' of 'hot hot water' ready for her, but 'Mammie dear do <u>not</u> ask any sole male or female [round] – more especially male! I'll be really angry if you do – and you know what that means!!!'.

From all of Kittie's relationship with Archie Ripley, only one letter appears to have survived from her to him. It was written at Amalfi on 20 and 21 April 1894 and some of it has already been quoted. At twelve pages in length, however, it covered many subjects. It is literary yet authentically conversational, immediate yet very clearly expressed, and as others have pointed out her handwriting is quite 'masculine'. In the absence of any of her religious letters to Constance Sutton, let us quote what may be a kindred passage of 'encouragement' to Ripley:

[In your last letter] I thought you were sad or depressed not about any particular thing […] but in a sort of general way – and that Life which might mean so much meant so little – and that shadow deepened deepened – and the sun went down-down – . And that that partly was why you wished others – and me amongst them – to live in the sunshine and absorb it. […]

But the Sun is for us all – all – and it is more wicked to turn from it than to fly from the shadow – for the sunlight is the gift of God – the shadow is the shadow of Sorrow and Sin – yes – cast from we know not where – but anyway not from God... Sometimes for oneself one is I think too apt to turn from the Sun, no matter how one may appreciate – and long for it for others – to feel that for us it is not. Do not think I am in any way talking this at you […] but in a purely general way do you not think this is so?

Elsewhere in the letter Kittie has referred to following her teacher Briton Rivière 'blindly as to my work in so far as what is bad and good for me in the execution', but in everything else having to live in her 'own way' and 'at certain pressure or I'd die'. 'I know myself – and the only way I can do any good at anything […] is at what people who think they know more about it than I do myself call "at fever point".'

Ripley's attitude to Nina Corbet, and particularly to her physical closeness with Kittie, shifted as his engagement progressed. On 30 August 1894, three months after Kittie had returned with the Corbets from Europe and five weeks after becoming engaged, he saw Kittie off at King's Cross for a 'driving holiday' with Nina and Walter based at Gobernuisgach in Sutherland. In the ten minutes that he was waiting for a bus outside the station afterwards, he wrote that evening, 'I was accosted (you know the technical term) three times. Figure to yourself the contrast, me just leaving you'. He finished the letter: 'Hug-gz, and kiss Nina for me. Hugg her on the mouth. I like you better than Nina but not much.' At 10.00 p.m. next day he wrote to Kittie: 'I fancy you now in bed with Nina in a Z[izz?]. I like to think you are with her. […] I wish you were in my arms, I wish I were in Nina's place, you know what I wish.' In a later letter before Kittie returned, he considered the idea of reducing their rent as newlyweds by 'sacrificing the guest room', which would not mean 'not having Nina for I

could sleep in the drawing room or go out and she with you on those
delightful occasions'. But he immediately qualified it: 'I have no hesitation
in telling you plainly darling that I shan't like sleeping away from you a bit
when we have once begun it in fact I don't now but for Nina of course.'
He had begun this letter by telling her that his fellow clubman Common
was staying with him for a night but he did not believe Common was 'so
near to me as he was[.] I doubt whether we shall ever be so near again.
[...] I don't think he is changing, it is I and the egoism of the family (you
and I) is growing on me'.

Only one letter from Kittie to Nina appears to have survived. Judging
from the reference to Dreyfus, it was written in the second half of October
1894 whilst Ripley was convalescing at Earlham (Dreyfus was *charged* on
15 October, but not 'condemned' until after Archie had left on his world
cruise). It is worth quoting at length, because it surely catches the spirit of
Kittie and Nina's relationship on the wing:

> Peter – what are you? Where are you? How are you?
> I'm beginning to get anxious I own.
> I would necessarily. Only so many things public and private have occurred and
> no sound of you since Sunday. – Dreyfus condemned, I back in London – and
> now this morning you doubtless see in the paper, Nina smashed up on her bicycle
> – and no-sound – no letter – no wire –
> Oh dear – if you are ill –
> I don't expect I'll go to Emmetts [the Lubbocks' home in Kent] at all – Mother
> was so shaken at hearing of Nina's accident that she said she'd rather I didn't
> leave here till I return to A.R. [...] whenever they want me –
> Poor poor Nina – her nose fractured and a great big bit of bone had to be cut
> out Δ – and very much skinned and contused all down one side – and Gladys'
> [LLoyd's] head badly cut – she also in bed. All this happened the afternoon of the
> day I left – I only heard this morn. of course. Her Mother was there and Gwen
> [LLoyd] – so I bide my time till there is need of me –
> For Heavens sake make some sign – either in person or by letter. <u>K.</u> [circle
> with dot in the middle and emphasis-line below]

The whole incident with the bicycle is a fantasy, but the desperation of the
last paragraph and the force of the symbol meaning 'I hug you very
tightly' are manifestly not.

On Kittie's side, her marriage certificate was signed by her mother and Walter Corbet. It is surely an indication of how much a part of the Corbet ménage she had become, that she was presented with an eight-inch high silver goblet inscribed 'To Miss Hamilton on her marriage from Mr Curr and Cottars [tenant workmen] on St Fort Estate April 30th 1895'.

Six months later, Nina visited Kittie and Archie at Earlham, taking with her one of her dogs, probably a Pekinese. On 2 November she wrote from London: 'Dina – I'll do your Com. [?] I hope you'll approve – I'm coming by the 2. something. [...] Oh! I want you 1000 times more than you want me. [...] I am so brainless I shall go noggity all the time I am at Earlham!'

In her letter to Laura Ripley of 29 October 1898, following Archie's funeral, Nina wrote: 'you must let me say now from my heart I thank you for allowing me to be with Kittie – and with all of you, during the last few days. No one knows what Kittie has been and is to me, and to be of any smallest use to her – or anyone connected with her – is my greatest comfort.'

4

Who Had He Been?

Why and exactly when George Calderon returned from Russia in 1897, we cannot say. Possibly it was because his father was seriously ill: Calderon senior's death certificate suggests that he was diagnosed with 'pelvic cancer' in the spring of 1897, although he did not die until April 1898. Possibly the fact that George was still wearing his bearded Russian identity throughout 1898 indicates that originally he was not intending to stay long in England before returning to St Petersburg or Moscow to further his plan (so Percy Lubbock tells us) of securing a university post in Russia.

Whichever, uncertainty on this point is nothing compared with the question of what Calderon *did* in Russia in 1896 and 1897. His subsequent spoken and written fluency in Russian, his intimate knowledge of contemporary Russian life, his scholarly command of Russian history, folklore and literature, were to become his principal professional qualification; the one for which, amongst so many other interests, he was probably best known and on which he could most rely for an income. Yet what did he do in Russia in those years, where did he go and whom did he meet, that imparted to him this specialist knowledge? Given the formative influence, as some of his friends saw it, of his Russian experience on his whole life, these questions comprise the single biggest mystery in Calderon's biography.

There are several, rather final reasons why we know so little about what Calderon did in Russia after 1895. First, no letters from him in Russia appear to have survived other than seven written to his parents between October and December of that year, although he certainly wrote to them and some ex-university friends after that. Then we know that he contributed pieces from Russia to the *Pall Mall Gazette* and *Standard*, but these were always unsigned and can be identified for sure only when he refers to them in his letters. Percy Lubbock stated that Calderon's despatches describing the coronation of Nicholas II in Moscow in May 1896 would be found 'somewhere in the files of the *Standard*', but neither these files nor those of the *Pall Mall Gazette* now exist to identify Calderon's authorship. Finally, although Calderon had to register with the police wherever he went in Russia, and have dealings with officialdom (for example, he had to take an examination in St Petersburg qualifying him to teach in 'Gymnasia and Progymnasia'), these documents reveal nothing of his friendships and writing activities. In fact he probably went to some lengths to conceal his most interesting excursions and acquaintances from official eyes. No letters have survived to him from Russians in this period.

The long, illustrated letters that Calderon wrote to his parents in his first three months in Russia hint tantalizingly, however, at the breadth of his activities. He obtained his passport in London on 20 September 1895, probably left Tilbury between 6 and 8 October, and at six in the morning of 12 October 'we anchored at Cronstadt in a beautiful big harbour bristling with fortresses'. That day, from the Hôtel de France, he wrote to his mother his first fresh impressions, which are a mixture of humorous delight and anthropological precision. The city 'swarmed' with cabbies:

All along the side of every road they stand or move along in lines, and most of them offer to drive you. They are all dressed alike, – and look like a blue set of Yeomen of the Guard [sketches of back view and front view]. The skirt is within a foot of the ground and shoots stiffly out: the hat is about 4 inches high. At the latter end are topboots. They drive with a rein in each hand, wide apart. The archway forming the background of the left hand illustration is the dougá, or yoke over the horse, to which the ends of the shaft are attached. All vehicles seem to have this; and apparently the poorer the conveyance the richer the decoration of the douga.

Coming from London, Calderon found St Petersburg 'most beautiful':

Full of bright colour, free of advertisement; all the streets I have seen are clean. You frequently come upon gardens, bridges, canals, the river. The bright Prussian blue of the cabmen (izvoshtshiki) gives a variegated look to the roadway. The shopmen seem to write up the names of their goods for information rather than advertisement: they paint old pictures of them outside – more, I think, for the beauty of the street than from any naughty boastfulness. The milk shop has pictures of cows at a well, cows being milked; good nursery pictures of cheese and butter and what not. At every corner is a fine man with a big sword.

This was a Russian policeman, who kept a directory of people's addresses from which Calderon was able to locate the British Consul, John Michell, and the Whishaw and Hubbard families. He had letters of introduction to all of these people, who were first-rate contacts for him. The Whishaws and Hubbards had lived and done business in Russia for generations. James Whishaw – 'charming man [...] does every possible thing that can be good for one' – was the Vice-Consul and together with a member of the Wylie family (also long-established in Russia) was able to advise Calderon on acquiring private pupils.

Eight days later he was writing to his mother from 79 Nevsky Prospect, the main avenue of the city, where however his room, number six, looked onto Pushkin Street. He had called on, or dined with, about twenty people, who all thought it would be 'easy' for him to set up as a tutor; so he had decided to place an advertisement in the largest daily newspaper, *Novoe vremia*,

stating that I am Mag. Artium Univ. Oxford; ready to teach English and Latin; for this necessary to get leave from Head of Police showing Diploma. Yesterday sent in thumping letter, 12 inch words on foolscap, to Head of Police enclosing letter from Presdt of Trinity. Have not yet been arrested for bad grammar.
Beer and tobacco are cheap. Love to all.

Within a fortnight, Calderon had two 'pups' (pupils), to whom he presumably taught English, and another had different requirements, as he explained to his mother:

A young lady who wishes to go up to Oxford and read philosophy (Russians are nuts on philosophy[,] the bookshops are full of translations of Buckle's Hist. of Civilisation in England, Mill, Darwin, Herbert Spencer, Comte etc also all the political socialist philosophers). She proposes, I hope, to run through the dead languages under my tuition. She has been in England learning English; so the channel of instruction affords no difficulties. Draw a deep breath and make up yr mind to a large parcel, rolled up in brown paper and a dusting-sheet or whatever fancy may suggest.

This was to contain '1. My whacking big Greek Lexicon, Liddell & Scott [...] weight say 10 lbs' and '2. My whacking ditto Latin Dictionary, Lewis & Short [...] weight say 7 lbs'. His 'defence' was that it would have been

the height of rashness to bring great heavy books out here on the off chance of getting lessons in Gk and Latin to give when I had all sorts of other notions of how I would catch the rollicking rouble: I would have needed another box, cumbered my lodgings, trammelled my movements and perhaps have delayed the ship. As it is be comforted by the reflection that I shall have no merry time going down to the sea-canal and the custom-house to meet my goods (such I am told is the process of receiving parcels): and above all the Censor will have a bad time looking the books through to see that there is nothing seditious in them.

The letter concludes with a vital observation about Russian dress: 'Please don't send me my grey tails: a tail is the badge of servitude. I mean to go in for pea-jacks [plausible translation of *pidzhaki*] as they call roundabouts [short jackets] here.' Who the young *émancipée* was, and whether Calderon's relationship with her remained formal, we know as little as we do of another 'female pup', who was 'plump, not uncomely', and lived with her sister in a 'jolly log-house' on one of the islands – which by the middle of December he was able to walk to across the frozen Neva.

Meanwhile, he had started writing. Interestingly, the *Times* veteran Russian correspondent George Dobson called on *him* (Calderon appears to have acquired a letter of introduction from the newspaper's foreign editor, Donald Mackenzie Wallace). Dobson, who was forty and dressed 'like a clergyman', was 'not discouraging as to possibilities of writing for papers', but convinced Calderon that in his present situation he could have 'no opportunity of gleaning any new news'. 'After all', George wrote to his mother on 6 November, 'what can the average foreigner in Gower Street know of the immediate political past, present and future of England? far more the foreigner down the Nevsky, acquainted with one Russian.' But he could write from his own, immediate experience of the Russia about him, and by the end of November he had sent off four articles to the *Pall Mall Gazette*, all of which, to his surprise, were published.

'A Russian Tavern' came out on 10 December 1895. It describes a visit to the 'Dmitrii Donskoi' traktir (pub) on Liteinyi Prospekt, a major street off Nevsky. 'It is not very respectable to dine at such a place', Calderon began, but 'from an economic point of view, one must – as the Russian proverb has it – stretch one's legs according to one's coat.' After removing your hat, the first thing you must do upon entering a traktir 'if you are Orthodox, is to bow to the eikon in the far corner, and cross yourself several times'; 'for the heathen', however, the priority is to make for the zakuski on offer at the 'well-furnished bar' in the first room. The zakuski are the '"fore-bits", or preliminary snack':

Plates of unknown dainties lie piled one upon another, and the fancy is bewildered with seductions. Caviare – on toast, of course, – there is, and slices of generous sausage. For myself, I choose without hesitation a portion of raw herring dressed with oil and minced onion. Having selected your snack, you must prelude it by tossing off a glass of neat vodka: this is absolutely *de rigueur*; no sipping, but a 'volley' [*zalpom*], as the Russians call it. The vodka in the traktirs is a pure colourless spirit obtained from corn, resembling whisky rather than any other Western liquor; but vodka, generally, is spirit of whatsoever origin and flavouring.

From here he graduated to the main eating and entertainment room, which resounded to an 'electric organ, with a great show of shining pipes and trumpets'. The observations he made here are accompanied by generalisations which, considering how little time he had been in Russia, are impressive. The room had 'many windows, richly looped with bright curtains, paper of flowered blue and gold, furniture of green and red, and much brass work'. In his second letter to his mother he had been struck by 'pink walls, blue walls, yellow walls; red roofs and green roofs; […] old peasant women in gorgeous cottons, with a leaning to vermilion', so he had already been sensitive to the different 'palette' of Russian life. But to comment, as he did parenthetically in this article, that 'the Russians have a talent for the collocation of vivid colours', is a perception of a different order: in the twentieth century semioticians were to dilate precisely upon the *collocation* ('*sopostavlenie*') of particular tints in Russian life and art. Calderon was also affected by the directness of Russian music, although his use of 'deep contented' here suggests he retained an ironical distance:

The organ booms out one of the old old peasant songs of the Russians, with its sad deliberate elaborations, accompanied by rapid forked flashes in the treble, full of that deep contented melancholy which inspires so great a part of the music and literature of Russia. You lean back and sigh and listen. The music does not wait for approval; it has an instant chemical effect on you.

On a more mundane level, he generalised that 'rich and poor, everybody in St Petersburg is engaged off and on all day in drinking tea' and 'no-one shouts to call attention in Russia, it is vulgar and rowdy; even the errand-boy on the top of the tram-car only gives a low hiss to make his friend at the corner look up', and this, he claims, is how you should summon a waiter. Discussing the women he can see in the *traktir*, he notes that the 'frequent smile' of one 'shows a shining row of strong teeth', and he speculates that this is because 'the acid rye-bread of the country has a chastening effect on the teeth'. Another woman has 'a face like an angel and a body like a piano-organ'. Already he has concluded that Russian women are 'sometimes pretty from in front' but 'seldom in profile'. In general, 'the Russian woman has not a willowy form – it is rather perhaps oaky; but her movements are accurate and impressive; even when she wipes her nose on her sleeve she does it with a certain dignity…'.

The theme of feminine corpulence was reprised at the beginning of Calderon's next article in the *Pall Mall Gazette*, 'I seek Lodgings in St Petersburg' (19 December 1895). Like many foreigners in Russia, he was finding it difficult to achieve things with the alacrity he was used to. 'How many obstacles there are to getting about!' Before he can get out of the building, for instance, he is detained by 'my landlord's "relative" in the hall – a limp man in a grey uniform, who frequently visits our flat, leans against doorposts, wears his cigarette with a droop, pants in arm-chairs, scratches his beard,' and questions him in rudimentary French. (Quite possibly the man was an informer.) Emerging into the courtyard, Calderon is in time to see two peasants rush the archway with a horse-drawn car containing 'a vast load of hay' – it 'sticks in the arch like a cork in a bottle' and he has to clamber over a wheel to reach the street. Here, 'the Russian women are all so broad that it is impossible to pass them without running up and down doorsteps or out into the road'. Progress is further impeded by the fact that 'astonished yokels' visiting the city always walk hand-in-hand, the husband carrying 'a club, like the giant in the pantomime, the thick end of which bristles with spiky roots'.

Much of this article was in fact concerned with the life of the large Polish community in St Petersburg. One of the lodgings Calderon visited was run by a Polish lady married to a Russian. She said:

I must dine with the family; it will be an advantage to me, for I can improve my Russian ('Lussian', she called it). Her husband, she said, was a great chatterbox, and loved to sit over his beer of an evening and discuss 'questions'. Charming! I thought. Conversation with this Old King Cole will be full of local colour. I left her, promising to return in an hour to view the husband.

Calderon spent the hour in a 'Polish tavern', where he ordered 'shnail-klops and huckleberry kvass'. It was 'a most disastrous dinner': 'Shnail-klops is stock-meat which has served its time in the soup, thinly disguised under a coating of brown boot-polish and cochineal. The Poles are not suppressed half enough; shnail-klops should entail Siberia.'

When he returned to the lodging:

The door was opened by a dishevelled cockroach four feet high. This was Old King Cole! Klops or no klops, I could never dine with this! I must get out of it discreetly. They brought me to a table where there was an urn under full pressure. I said I must have till the morning to think of it. They halved the price. I said I was by nature irresolute. The beetle rose behind the table, smote it with his fist, and said I must decide now or never. I said I would rather decide never.

That evening he received through the post a long poem eulogising England. The accompanying anonymous letter was addressed in English 'To the Right Honourable Sir G.F. Calderon' and explained that the work was written 'in Poland language'. Calderon ended his article: 'It cannot be

from the landlady; it must be from the eating-house keeper, to make up
for the shnail-klops.'

As Calderon explained in a letter to his father dated 27 December 1895,
it was difficult for him to find single subjects 'that will run to 1400 words'
as the *Pall Mall Gazette* required. This is why his next piece, published on
21 December, was split into 'I Engage Lodgings in St Petersburg' and 'In
Search of a Father'.

In the first, it transpires that he is now lodging in a very traditional
Russian family (he does not say where). Over his bed are three icons, with
a blue fairy lamp in front of each. 'On Saturday evening they humbly
asked permission to light up the lamps to honour the eve of the weekly
festival.' Interestingly, he remarks that as a consequence he 'spent the
evening in some fear of English visitors'. Meanwhile, the '*dvornik*, or
courtyard concierge', had come to tell him that the police were not
'satisfied' with his registration at this address:

They must know my calling, my patronymic, and my religion. My calling, I said,
was of a somewhat complex character: he suggested that 'agent' would probably
cover everything. As for patronymic, I declared that I had none to give; but he
insisted and I am new-christened 'Algernonovitch', Barney Algernonovitch.

Fortunately, the primary meaning of 'agent' in Russian at that time was
not 'spy', but if the St Petersburg police compared his registered Christian
name and patronymic with the details of his British passport, they must
have wondered.

The second half of the feature turned on a classic 'longevity' canard of
the type that young foreign correspondents are still known to pursue in
Russia today. Someone (who?) had told Calderon that there was a man
called Ivan Fedorovich Kuz'min living in St Petersburg who was 138 years
old. Calderon 'sought him in the hospitals in vain', so inquired at the city's
'Address Office', which enabled him to interpolate a sketch of minor
officialdom:

Here the visitor is, among other things, informed in the English tongue that
'Smooking is forbidden'. Written inquiries are tossed in at a pigeon-hole; they

come out in course of time at a half-door further along, where an official rolls out the names in the midst of an eager crowd... 'Anton Astafyevitch Nogayef, province of Tula, district of Yefremof, village of Clean Ponds, peasant! Vassily Dmitrevich Sapozhnikof! Avdotya Polikarpovna Korovinskaya! Nadezhda Constantinovna... What surname?' ... 'Mokraya' (Wet) pipes a feeble voice – whereat everybody laughs, and after a pause a town wit says: 'Aha!... Not Dry?'

Armed with an address, Calderon 'found the rambling house, but for the life of me could not find lodging 117 where Kouzmin lived'. A boy painting a wall in the yard and two bearded students up at a window directed him but he could not light on the correct back door – an experience familiar to foreigners visiting friends in nineteenth-century blocks in St Petersburg today. Eventually, 'by dint of many matches', he penetrated to the door of Kuz'min's flat and knocked:

A smiling artisan of some twenty-five years appeared and shook hands with me. I said, 'Kouzmin?' He bowed. I asked if Ivan Fedorovitch would receive me. He said that Vanka was having his head washed... 'Vanka?' I cried... 'Head washed!' 'Every Monday...his mother,' he explained. This was coming it rather strong. 'And you?' I asked. 'Fedor Kouzmin,' he replied, crossing his hands on his breast. 'Then Ivan Fedorovitch is...?' 'My son,' he said with a blush.

Calderon could not have produced a finer climax if it had been a short story. In fact was it fiction? He ended with a plausible journalistic sentence – 'I am sorry I could not find the patriarch: I wanted to go round and have a romp with the old boy, and ask him how he does it' – but there are enough touches of irony in his account of the Methuselah's life at the beginning of the piece to make one suspect that it is as creative as the biography of, say, Lieutenant Kije. Moreover, the name of the 'patriarch' contains elements of one of the most enigmatic figures in Russian hagiography, Fedor Kuz'mich, the longevous Siberian monk thought by some to be Alexander I in disguise. In this contribution to the *Pall Mall Gazette* Calderon had touched on some themes of Russian folk mythology potent to this day.

His last contribution in this batch, 'On and Off in Petersburg', which was not published until 7 January 1896, resembles a short story even more.

Calderon was an excellent sportsman and, as he described in his letter to his mother of 14 December 1895, he was much taken by 'the skating-ground, Yousoupof Garden, along my street', where 'the skating is mostly done at night 8-11'. Here, he tells us in 'On and Off in Petersburg', he made the acquaintance of an aristocratic student, one Petr Petrovich Golovenko, who is practically an ice-dancer:

We would meet and chat in the main cloak and skate room, or over a glass of coffee in the refreshment-room – conversation on the ice was too fugitive for me; he was always round the other side of an island by the time I got to the verb.

Golovenko is enamoured of a lady named Mariia Andreevna, whom Calderon describes as 'a grave damsel of medium height, who exhibits that happy mixture of *embonpoint* and dignity which is characteristic of Russian girls. She has, as Golovenko himself described her, "real Russian eyes, long, black, tip-tilted, and serious like a dog's"'. She sits by the rink and is 'fascinated' by Golovenko's 'graceful and varied turns at improbable angles'. Rejoining Calderon indoors, he 'clapped me a terrible clap on the thigh, and said "It's on!"', meaning 'Mary, his own dear iceberg, had promised to meet him at the ice-hills the next day'.

The 'ice-hills' were artificial structures on Krestovsky Island, three miles north of central St Petersburg, and Calderon's extended description of them, of how they function for tobogganists, and their social attractions, are fascinating for admirers of Chekhov's famous short story 'The Little Joke', which is partly set in such a place. Golovenko, who has invited Calderon along, is naturally 'a real master of the art' of gymnastic tobogganing, but Calderon seems more professionally interested in Mariia Andreevna: 'She looked very charming in a fur-tippet with tails all over it, a suggestion of pansy-velvet and black lace somewhere, and a bonnet which, for want of technical information, I can only describe as a "dream".' She agrees to 'go down' with Golovenko, which involves her sitting on one 'velvet toboggan' and Golovenko kneeling on another behind, holding hers. Unfortunately:

Whether it was that Golovenko had not taken a good grip of the lady's sledge, or whether she wriggled at the preliminary terror of the descent, I cannot say: all I know is that by the time they had reached the bottom of the slope the toboggan had parted company, and while Pyotr Petrovich sprawled through the snow partition on to the return run, Marya Andreyevna plunged head foremost into the bank of snow on the other side.

Everyone at the top laughs, but Calderon hopes that 'her position' prevented her from hearing them. She 'put aside all further offers of help from Golovenko and walked back alone to the steps' with a Russian girl's characteristic dignity.

But she was swathed in snow; I fear that she was wet (the sun was shining very strongly on that bank of snow). I thought I detected a tremor which meant some down the back; and the bonnet! – alas! the 'dream' had had a rude awakening.

As Calderon and he sledge back to the city, Golovenko is 'very taciturn'. 'At parting, all he said was: "It's off, my boy, it's off!".'

According to the Julian ('Russian', 'O.S.') calendar, by which of course Calderon was 'living' in St Petersburg, this tale was published twelve days earlier, on 26 December 1895, the day after Russian Christmas Day. But the British community had celebrated Christmas on 13 December O.S., because back in Britain (according to the Gregorian, 'western' calendar, 'N.S.') that was the 25th of December... This dichotomy focussed Calderon's mind on what in a deeper sense he was 'doing' in Russia – what his priorities there were.

He wrote to his mother on 2 December O.S.: 'My Xmas won't be spent in an English house for my host is Russified: has a Russian wife and Russian children and has Swedish cousins within reach. I have every hope that it will be as Russian as possible.' Having written that, he seems to realise that he may have given the impression that he is 'going native'. He hastily adds: 'I and the English colony are not neglecting one another. I dine with the Alf. Whishaws on Tuesday[,] other English on Wed.' In fact, he spent 'English Christmas evening' (i.e. 13 December O.S.) at another Petersburg English family's, the Wildings, together with seven Whishaws and 'two young Wylies'. They had 'turkey and plum pudding with methylated spirits', crackers and paper hats, and played charades. The same evening he was invited by Mrs James Whishaw to celebrate the 'Russian Xmas' with her family, but had to decline presumably because the invitation he had already accepted from his 'Russified host' was actually for Russian Christmas on 25 December O.S. (6 January N.S.). At least this demonstrates that the Vice-Consul welcomed the opportunity for a double Christmas celebration. But if, as Calderon writes, his 'Russified host' was an 'Americo-Suedo-Spanio-Anglo-Franco-Russian' paper manufacturer, did he actually experience a full traditional Russian Christmas at all, with fasting on Christmas Eve until the first star appeared, peasant boys walking around in the snow carrying a star on a stick and being given treats, a house festooned with decorations, a tree hung with gold- and silver-covered walnuts, and all the special dishes that went with the prolonged entertainments on Christmas Day?

The correspondence suggests that Calderon did not particularly *want* to spend Christmas with the English community, he wanted to find out what *Russians* did on this religious holiday. Yet it was not proving easy for him to meet 'real' Russians – to get on the 'inside' of Russian family life.

Some help here must have been provided through an English naval engineer, Archibald Campbell Ross, who befriended him. Ross was a year older than Calderon and had been in St Petersburg three years already, working for a Newcastle company that was advising the Tsar's navy on building battleships. He spoke fluent Russian. On 1 November 1895 he wrote to his brother: 'Called on Calderon and had talk with him. He is distinctly nice and amusing, says really witty things at times. Knows a lot of Russian, tho' he speaks very little, he says.' Ross was deeply in love with an eighteen-year-old Russian girl, Mariia ('Manya') Guseva, and introduced her to Calderon. She responded to his outgoing personality, his determination to speak more Russian, and his curiosity about Russian life. She was very lively and direct, one might say 'quintessentially Russian'. She undoubtedly helped him improve his spoken language, and she probably introduced him to her own extended St Petersburg family. Manya and Ross were married in the spring of 1896. They remained friends with Calderon all his life.

As Anthony Cross, an authority on the St Petersburg British, puts it, by the 1890s the British Colony was 'no longer as monolithic as it had once appeared'. It was 'blurred' at the edges, but 'even here a certain stubborn adherence to British traditional ways and customs was observed'. Most of the middle-class British in St Petersburg did not socialise with Russians, they simply did business with them. Calderon was therefore wary of becoming ensconced amongst them. But he could hardly elaborate on this to his parents, as they had gone to great lengths to set up such contacts ('introductions') for him. Calderon's *entrée* to the Whishaw clan, for instance, was almost certainly thanks to his father being a close associate of the painter William Frederick Yeames, creator of 'And When Did You Last See Your Father?'. Yeames was born in Taganrog on the Azov Sea, his uncle was British Consul General at Odessa, and the Yeames family were closely intertwined with the Whishaws.

From the six letters that have survived to his mother from Russia in 1895, one also has the impression that Calderon knew she worried about him. After all, as far as we know, he had never lived abroad before. He stresses to her that 'the kuchmister's', where he often eats, is clean and 'frequented by the most respected people only; not a low haunt of peasants and labouring-men'. Although she had read in the English press that St Petersburg was flooded, he 'heard no guns' and assures her 'the flooded part is some three miles from here'. He asks her not to send out the payments that are accumulating for him in London from Flowerdew's translation agency and the *Pall Mall Gazette*, but to 'tell Father I have no need of money with many thanks'. She has asked him how he spends his day, so he begins an hour-by-hour account of 3 December:

Got up, say at 8. No bath. (I bathe *à la russe* : that is to say I go once a week to a place about 300 yards from here where a most luxurious steam bath is to be had for 20 copecks. There will be say 20 people bathing at the same time.

He continues the parenthesis for another eleven lines, culminating gleefully in:

Then you take a great bunch of greens, birch with all the leaves on, sweet smelling, and gently beat yourself all over. This opens the pores. Give the pores a chance; then shower bath, cold slosh, divan, towel, great coat and go home. Very jolly.)

However, on re-reading the letter he realises that the idea of a cold shower immediately after a 'hotter and hotter' steam bath might alarm his mother, so he adds underneath in smaller writing: 'No danger to health: even children of 6 go there.' This description Calderon worked up into a 1400-word piece, 'A Russian Bath', which was published in the *Pall Mall Gazette* of 7 April 1896 and reprinted in the *Leeds Mercury* of 30 April.

The only letter we have from Russia to his father (27 December 1895) is less structured and possibly less self-censored. 'You must not suppose that my pupils fill my time – they only fill my pockets. I have whole days vacant', he writes; although 'these are profitably spent in tootling about, reading, polishing my tongue (the Russian one), reading the papers [...] and often sending home translations of them.' He knows that his father loves games, so he describes those played at the Wildings', a session at 'the skating ground' that evening, and a game of Russian billiards 'with Dr Scheckauer':

Table as in England. Three big reds planted on spots down the middle of the table[,] 2 whites; the game is pure potting. The Russian calls a pocket a 'loser' [*luza*]; whether borrowed from the English I don't know; they also say '*khoróshi shot*' for 'good shot'.

In fact *luza* comes from the French *blouse* for a billiard-pocket, but Calderon's experience of playing billiards in Russian proved invaluable about fifteen years later when he came to Gaev's lines in *The Cherry Orchard*, could translate them accurately, and usefully point out to actors that Gaev 'always plays a declaration game of billiards, no flukes allowed'.

The five 'sketches', as he called them, that have been named so far as written by Calderon and published in the *Pall Mall Gazette* 1895/96 were, like most contributions to that newspaper, unsigned. They can be attributed beyond reasonable doubt either because they are named in Calderon's extant letters to his parents, or because general references to them there match textual evidence. (A sixth, 'Feenya and Fyodka', is named in his letter to his father, but appears not to have been published.)

Unfortunately, the fact that we have no letters of Calderon's from Russia during the whole of the rest of his stay means that we can only suggest on circumstantial and stylistic grounds what else by him was published in the *Pall Mall Gazette* in 1896 and 1897. Strictly speaking, we cannot be sure that *anything* by him was published there other than these five sketches. The rigorist view, indeed, would be that 'we do not know' whether he continued writing there – it is a 'mystery'.

Nevertheless, a prime candidate for attribution to Calderon must be the feature published in the *Pall Mall Gazette* of 20 February 1896 as 'Some Diversions of Petersburg'. It concerned three distinct locations, which would tally with Calderon's complaint to his father that it was difficult to find one continuous subject that would 'run to 1400 words'. The first section was headed 'The Circus' and began: 'Often in the days of childhood my soul yearned for just such a circus – a circus without horses. Give me clowns, I used to cry.' The second was 'The Krestovsky Winter Garden', a kind of night club on the same island as the ice hills. It focusses on the gypsy women, 'Little Russian' (Ukrainian) women, and 'Cossack girls' who perform there, and ends: 'Four o'clock? Well, it really is time to be getting home to bed.' These two pieces read as reportage, but the third piece, 'The Custom House', is much more of a story and strikes me as a small masterpiece:

If a parcel is sent from abroad to a man in England he finds it one fine morning on the breakfast-table. Not so in Petersburg. A few days ago I received a notice that 'a package' awaited me at the Custom House, a journey of many versts. Entering, I found a room cut in two by a counter surmounted by a screen of wire with pigeon-holes.

On the far side were some twenty officials in and out of uniform, chatting, smoking, drinking tea, and consulting in groups over entries in the books; on the near side was a handful of mere men in various attitudes of exasperation and despair. A proud and beautiful lady received my paper through a pigeon-hole. After a deal of travelling here and there it was brought and laid on a desk by another pigeon-hole, labelled 'Delivery of packages'. The stool by this desk had, alas! long been tenantless. Round this stool centred all the hopes and fears of the assembled public. Some of them gazed towards it haggard and silent; others paced up and down before it like caged lions. At two o'clock a polyglot Swiss gentleman spoke up for himself and his fellow-sufferers. He put his head through the wirework and hailed an idle man in gold epaulettes who was smoking a cigarette on the corner of a table. 'Please send someone here!' he cried. 'Send? Send whom?' 'Why, the man who ought to be here.' 'Ought to be there!' More haggard silence, more caged chafing. Then in a soft and silvery voice our Swiss enquired if there was not a billiard-room in the establishment where he might pass the time. No answer.

At three o'clock an under official came up with a troubled look, took a paper and walked twice disconsolately round the official compartment with it; then came back, put it down again, and went aimlessly off somewhere else with the same look of distress upon his face. An elderly peasant rose from a bench behind me, seized the man who takes care of the great-coats earnestly by two buttons, and asked whether his parcel was ready yet. '*S'chas!* – in a moment!' was the conventional reply. The elderly peasant crept back, and sat softly sobbing in his corner.

At four o'clock the Swiss gentleman, after some outbursts of maniacal hilarity and sarcasm witheringly polite, swept out of the place, vowing that he would leave his parcels to rot in the Custom House rather than come back – a species of revenge which the officials will no doubt appreciate. At last they brought me a number of papers to sign, demanded money under various headings – customs, censor, outdoor porterage, indoor porterage, lighterage, demurrage, insurance, bottomry, &c., – and then gave me my package. It proved to be a small pamphlet (privately printed) by my dear old tutor, on the 'Ontological Value of Consciousness'. I have lent it to a friend out here who goes in for that sort of thing, and am sending my tutor a box of caviare and some cucumbers in return.

For a man of reflexive disposition there are few pleasanter ways of passing a couple of hours than at the Petersburg Custom House.

This could have been based on Calderon's experience of fetching the 'whacking big' Greek and Latin dictionaries he had asked his mother to send him on 6 November, or of receiving the fine edition of *Reynard the Fox* illustrated by his brother Frank which his parents sent him for Christmas. The confident pacing of the narrative, the verbal absurdity ('demurrage, insurance, bottomry'), suppressed anger and supreme irony of the last sentence, definitely suggest the pen of George Calderon.

But he did not merely submit sketches to the *Pall Mall Gazette*. As he wrote to his father, he patronised a 'circulating Russian library with a reading room attached' in which he read 'the papers', and he 'often' sent home 'translations of them to H.W. Wilson who concocts them in to articles and plies the editors with them; with what success I don't know'.

Nor do we. Herbert Wrigley Wilson was another Trinity, Oxford, man, although two years senior to Calderon, and his speciality was the navies of the European powers. As Calderon wrote to his mother on 3 December, Wilson was 'just bringing out a book on Ironclads in Action'. Wilson would 'construct articles' from the translations Calderon sent him, 'get them into papers & share the swag'. It seems, therefore, that Calderon was combing the Russian press for information about the Tsarist navy, perhaps picking up nuggets from Archibald Ross as well, and passing them to Wilson – activities that even then may have been regarded as intelligence-gathering. Did he send this information home through the open post? Quite possibly, in those days, but there is a suggestion in a letter to his mother of 17 March 1899 that he sent back politically sensitive material *pri okazii* as the Russians call it, i.e. with a traveller: he had directed to his mother a 'long' article from Russia about Finland ('you see it is being suppressed by the Tsar') and this they had codenamed 'Finnikins'.

Wilson, however, was an all-round journalist (he went on to become assistant editor of the *Daily Mail* from 1898 to 1940) and may have placed in British newspapers a range of Calderon's translations from the Russian press; on 14 December 1895 Calderon wrote to his mother that Wilson had 'most heroically been using his good offices on my behalf'. It is conceivable that the abstracts from *Novosti* [*sic*] 'Reconciliation of Russia and Bulgaria. Opinion in St Petersburg. (From a Special Correspondent)', *Pall Mall Gazette* 17 February 1896, and 'A Russian View of Disarmament', *Pall Mall Gazette* 6 March 1896, were contributed by Calderon. As we learn from his letter to his mother of 3 December 1895, he also 'looked up in a magazine' articles on 'something dull from which to plagiarise and send results to *Standard* or what not'. Perhaps, then, the small semi-statistical items about the Russian economy, cholera in Russia, or the Russian Fleet, that appeared in the *Standard* at the end of 1895 and in the first four months of 1896 as 'Through Reuter's Agency', were also culled from the Russian press by him.

The more important question is, what did Calderon do and what of his was published whilst he was in Moscow for the coronation of Nicholas II in May and June 1896?

We have only Percy Lubbock's word for it that Calderon was a coronation correspondent for the *Standard* in Moscow, and his peculiar choice of words ('somewhere in the files of the *Standard* [...] are his impressions of the ill-omened coronation of Nicholas II') suggests that Calderon's despatches were not published! Since the 'files' of the *Standard* for 1896 seem not to exist, we cannot compare the original (signed) despatches with the copious edited reportage about the coronation actually printed in the *Standard* at the time. Was Calderon in Moscow, then, at all, let alone as the *Standard*'s correspondent?

Fig. 6 George Calderon, St Petersburg, 1895

Here we are helped by some pictorial evidence. We have two portraits of Calderon, face-on and in profile, taken by Denier on Nevsky Prospect 'for passport', as Kittie wrote on the back, i.e. probably for the police registration of his residence in St Petersburg in 1895. On these he has cropped hair, a goatee beard, and 'prodigious moustaches' as Binyon described him (see Fig. 6). He is wearing a formal bow-tie and looks like a Russian intellectual or writer. Then there is another, 'taken', Kittie informs us, 'by police', at the studio of Oskar Meier on Trubnaia Square, central Moscow. In this he is wearing the same suit but has short hair with a parting, a shaven chin, a neatly trimmed moustache, a florid butterfly, and looks the very image of a western correspondent (see Fig. 7). This, then, confirms that he was in Moscow at some time – long enough to need to register once more with the police – and suggests that he really was a newspaperman whilst he was there.

Оскаръ Мейеръ МОСКВА
ТРУБНАЯ ПЛОЩАДЬ ДОМЪ ГУЧКОВ

Fig. 7 George Calderon, Moscow, 1896

If we look at the coverage of the coronation in both the *Pall Mall Gazette* and the *Standard* (two of Victorian Britain's most popular newspapers), we find that the former is divided between pieces 'From Our Own Correspondent', 'From Our Special Correspondent', and pieces with no byline at all, whilst the latter is divided between 'From Our Special Correspondent' and 'Through Reuter's Agency'. The *Pall Mall Gazette*'s 'Own Correspondent' in Moscow cannot be Calderon because this writer has just arrived from Berlin, his transliteration of Russian is Germanic, and his style too flat. Writing on 8 May 1896 for the *Standard* of 14 May about the preparations for the coronation, its 'Special Correspondent' says that he has just arrived from St Petersburg. The *Pall Mall Gazette*'s 'Special Correspondent', in a piece published on 6 May 1896, writes that he too has just arrived from St Petersburg. His articles (as opposed to those of 'Our Own Correspondent') bear stylistic resemblances to those of Calderon's in the *Pall Mall Gazette* earlier. By and large, until tragedy struck on 30 May, the *Standard*'s 'Special Correspondent's' reportage is factual, respectful, and neutral, as befits despatches probably based on the press releases supplied by the Press Bureau to the foreign press corps of which he was part. However, there are again some stylistic features in these pieces that remind one of Calderon's 'sketches' for the *Pall Mall Gazette*.

From all this we could form the hypothesis that Calderon travelled from St Petersburg to Moscow in the first week of May 1896 at the convenience of 'the special bureau established for ensuring the comfortable transit to Moscow of all persons officially connected with the Coronation ceremonies' (*Standard*, 14 May 1896) as Special Correspondent for both the *Standard* and the *Pall Mall Gazette*, and that he wrote in different genres for each, although the former was by far the bigger and more lucrative job. This, in turn, suggests a wider hypothesis. Nicholas II had succeeded to the throne eighteen months earlier. It had been known there was going to be a coronation for almost a year before Calderon left England. Notices periodically appeared in British newspapers that set it for the spring of 1896. Possibly, therefore, Calderon had, as Lubbock put it, a 'commission for occasional correspondence' with the *Pall Mall Gazette*, but signed an actual agreement with the *Standard* long before he set out for Russia, to cover the coronation for them, which his knowledge of

Russian would have eminently qualified him in their eyes to do. It might have been this secure job, set to last from the beginning of May to 7 June, that persuaded him he could take the financial risk of going to Russia in the first place.

As befitted an empire of 125 million people with two capitals and a ruling dynasty confidently looking towards its tercentenary, the coronation events from the arrival of distinguished visitors in Moscow to the re-entry of Nicholas and Alexandra to St Petersburg covered nearly two months. Naturally, representatives of all European monarchies and governments attended. But it should be remembered that the overwhelming majority of the Tsar's subjects were still peasants. This led the 'Special Correspondent' to comment in the *Pall Mall Gazette* of 6 May:

Undoubtedly one of the most interesting, if not the most interesting, feature of the coronation festivities will be the People's Fête, which will take place on Saturday, May 18 (O.S.). [...] It is characteristic of the Russian system of government, and significant of its attitude to the common people, that the 'Fête Populaire', as it is termed in the official programme, is the only fixture in a course or round of festivities which will embrace a period of three weeks that can be said to partake of a popular character.

In a piece published two days later entitled 'Some First Impressions of Moscow. The "Masses" and the "Classes"', a *Pall Mall Gazette* correspondent developed the theme surprisingly frankly:

A greater contrast could not be offered than that presented by the appearance of the 'masses' and that of the 'classes' in Russia. The former are, generally speaking, robust-looking and seemingly well-nourished. The latter, and especially the men, look more like semi-galvanized corpses than living beings. I attribute this striking contrast entirely to the Russian manner of living, which, so far as the 'classes' are concerned, is unhealthy in the extreme. Joined to exceedingly high living, late hours, and all sorts of enchanting but enervating dissipations, the Russian system of easy existence absolutely refuses to admit of the necessity of bodily exercise. It is no exaggeration to say that the well-to-do Russian never, to use a homely but expressive phrase, walks a yard. His person, moreover, is nearly always loaded and encumbered with furs, even in summer-time; and as he heats his house and restaurants to a positively preposterous extent, the bad effects on his health of the combination of these evils may be easily imagined if less readily described.

The 'common people', however, 'lead a comparatively healthy existence' because they are in the fresh air more, are perforce more abstemious, and their staple food is the 'nutritious and easily-digested black bread of the country', which is 'an excellent means of preserving their health under the very severe social and sanitary conditions under which they live, and of building up, as it were, "muscle and bone"'. Even the rank and file of the Russian army are a finer 'body of men' than their officers, and the writer concludes: 'I maintain that this surprising difference and contrast is entirely due to the Russian system of high-living.'

Although this piece has no byline at all, and seems far more hastily written than Calderon's 'lucubrations', as he called them, in St Petersburg for the *Pall Mall Gazette*, stylistic touches such as 'semi-galvanized corpses', 'enchanting but enervating dissipations', and 'never walks a yard', suggest his authorship.

On 12 May 1896 the *Pall Mall Gazette* published 'Russian Life and Character. The Streets of Moscow'. This was 'From Our Special Correspondent' and even more critical of aspects of Russian life, from the potholes in the streets to the drunks, the police, and the autocracy itself:

It is amazing that with so many particular sources of well-doing at its command, the Russian system of government should produce so dismal a result. What is the use of an autocracy if it fails in those very respects out of which it expects, or expects others, to justify its existence? [...] Everyone that comes to Russia complains of ineffectiveness of the system.

The writer's harshest words, however, are reserved for Russian priests, than whom it would be 'impossible' to find 'a more untidy, unkempt, and uncouth-looking body of men'.

They wear beards and moustaches, long hair and long coats. Their goloshes are generally worn down at the heel, and the skirts of their garments are covered with mud. They look for all the world as if they never combed or washed their hair, brushed their clothes, or interviewed their tailors [...]. The mental qualifications of the Russian priest are as bare and unprofitable as their externals are unprepossessing. They are illiterate in the highest degree, and anyone who condescends to address them on topics unconnected with their narrow sphere will be rewarded with an ignorant stare or a no less expressively ignorant silence for his pains. Their sole qualification consists in repeating the prayers of their Church, which also appears to be their sole occupation.

The unsubtle tone of this piece argues against it being by Calderon, but he was anti-clerical before he even went to Russia, and possibly the pressure of his job in Moscow and the stresses of Russian life provoked this outburst from him. Certainly the next Moscow feature published in the *Pall Mall Gazette*, 'Russian Life and Character. The Music-Halls. (From Our Own Correspondent)', 14 May 1896, seems linguistically far too thin and unironic to be his.

Meanwhile, the 'Special Correspondent' of the *Standard* was filing daily reports, mainly about the 'Arrivals in Moscow' and the precarious state of the weather. On 20 May the newspaper also published a two-column description by him of the Kremlin, sent four days earlier. Its limpidity and precision qualify it to be by Calderon, rather than a translation by the Press Bureau. On 22 May the Special Correspondent reported on the 'State Entry into Moscow. Imposing Ceremony' in a very formal style and with long lists of dignitaries; presumably he witnessed only a fraction of it and most of the despatch derived from a press release. The next day his communication was headlined 'The Coronation of the Czar. Reception of Ambassadors', three days later 'Moving the Regalia', and this was followed by a Reuters report of the banquet given on the evening of 24th by the Russian press 'in honour of the representatives of foreign journals now in Moscow', at which the press baron Aleksei Suvorin, a close friend of Chekhov's, proposed a toast. Presumably the *Standard*'s Special Correspondent was there.

On Tuesday 26 May (14 May O.S.) Nicholas was finally crowned in the Kremlin's Uspenskii Sobor. The *Standard*'s account, over eight columns, was headlined: 'Brilliant spectacle. The ceremony in the Cathedral. Imperial manifesto. Amnesty and remission of taxation. (From our special correspondent.) Moscow, Tuesday evening.' One assumes the 'Special Correspondent' was present in the Cathedral, as he uses the phrase 'fresh from witnessing the splendid scene', but his account of the ceremony is so procedural that it could have been taken from an official script of what was 'going' to happen. There are no really alive, personal touches, so perhaps the 'Special Correspondent' was *not* present. Alternatively, according to Suvorin's diary the service lasted nearly five hours, so perhaps this left correspondents with no time or energy for originality. The *Standard*'s Special Correspondent managed more verve, however, in reporting the 'Banquet and Illuminations' next day, the 'Imperial Levée' the day after that, and especially the *grande toilette* of the English ladies at the State Ball on 29 May. It must have been a great relief to him that the most demanding part of his commission was over and he could now describe some quite sincere rejoicing.

Then everything departed from the script. In the early hours of 30 May (18 May O.S.) about half a million peasants and workers gathered on a huge common called Khodynka Field to the north-west of the city, in readiness for the distribution of a gift from the Tsar (a coronation mug, some food and a brochure), which was advertised to start at 10.00 a.m. It had been organised to take place from 150 booths at the edges of the Field. However, none of the organisers had seen fit to prepare the access to the booths, which included a deep cutting about fifty yards across with pits in it and two poorly covered wells. For some reason, at around five o'clock in the morning the crowd began to move towards the booths. It could no longer be controlled by the police present, so the people manning the booths began to distribute the 'gifts'. In the surge through the cutting, many people lost their footing and were trampled to death, or fell down the holes and wells, and hundreds more were crushed in the funnels created around the booths. Throughout the day, about 1300 corpses were removed from Khodynka Field and carted through the streets of Moscow, often followed by mourning *narod* ('common people').

Next day, the *Standard*'s Special Correspondent telegraphed an account that appeared on 1 June under the headline 'Terrible Disaster in Moscow. Panic at the Fêtes. Two Thousand Lives Lost. The Czar and the Victims'. He evidently had not gone to Khodynka himself, but he was not entirely reliant on official accounts either; he could make some personal observations:

People are highly exasperated against the Chief of Police for not having taken proper precautions and his life was yesterday considered to be in danger. [...] This sad event has taken all the interest out of the other items of the Coronation festivities, which will be gone through mechanically, the general feeling being one of painful oppression.

Later that day he filed a second story, having visited the 'People's Cemetery' as he called it, Vagan'kovskoe, where 'the victims are laid out in rows upon the ground, which is guarded by military with fixed bayonets'.

An enormous crowd has all day been passing in one gate and out at another, seeking for missing friends [...]. Quite a hundred thousand were gathered in the cemetery. The bodies are placed in rough shells [light coffins]. A Moscow manufacturer has given a hundred pieces of calico, and a number of women are hard at work sewing shrouds for the victims. Comparatively few have been identified, but some have been carried away for private burial, whilst others have been buried by relations.

A plot of ground has been reserved as a common grave for the larger number, who will be buried tomorrow morning. The grave is now being dug by Army workers, who are forming a deep trench more than a hundred yards long.

On 2 June the *Pall Mall Gazette* ran a piece entitled 'A Moscow correspondent telegraphs', which it said was also from the *Standard*'s special correspondent. It pointedly stated that the 'festivities' were continuing and 'not a flag' had been lowered or 'a shutter closed'. The same day, the *Standard* had: 'The Moscow Disaster. Three Thousand Victims. Message from the Queen. (From our special correspondent).' He was now explicitly critical:

Almost universally, the disaster is attributed to the total want of precautions, usually so conspicuous in Russia when they are wanted least, and to the lack of foresight, and even of elementary common sense, shown in the arrangements for the distribution of the gifts. [...] The exasperation of the people is intense.

That evening (2 June) he drove out again to the cemetery. The corpses were 'in most cases, laid three deep, and one trench has been left open to receive the further victims that are expected'. He dwelt on the 'fatal well' that had contained twenty-eight bodies.

If the *Standard*'s special correspondent for the 'Khodynka Tragedy' was George Calderon, one can only speculate on the psychological impact it had on him. This was the worst 'stampede' disaster to date in recorded history. He was twenty-seven, from a secure, fun-loving Victorian family, and as far as we know he had had little experience of death. He first visited the cemetery on the same day as Suvorin, and we know from the latter's diary that the stench was overpowering, the victims' clothing was shredded, their bodies mangled or bloated, their faces so pulped as to be unrecognisable. This, perhaps, is why the 'Special Correspondent' kept repeating in his despatches that 'a very large number of the victims are still unidentified'. Not once, as far as our sources can tell us, did Calderon refer in subsequent life to having witnessed the enormity of 'Khodynka'. Of course, that may have been because he was not the 'Special Correspondent' at all. Equally, though, it could be because the experience was so traumatic that he could not bring himself to speak of it. He may have tried to leave the memory 'behind' him in Russia.

There was another dimension to the tragedy, however, which the special correspondent(s) of the two newspapers displayed exceptional insight into. Let us recall that on 6 May in the *Pall Mall Gazette* he had drawn attention to the fact that the 'People's Fête' of 30 May was the only event planned for the 'common people' and this was 'significant' of the Tsarist government's attitude to them. A week later in the same newspaper he wrote that it was 'amazing' that a system with such a complete monopoly of power 'should produce so dismal a result'. These were precisely the realisations that the Khodynka Tragedy jolted Russian society towards. The truly pitiful fact was that half a million of the *narod* had converged on Khodynka to receive the 'Tsar's gift' because *they had nothing*. The autocracy ran everything, so the autocracy was responsible for the disaster; it was callous towards its own people and unfit for purpose. Even such a supporter of the regime as Suvorin began in his many diary entries about Khodynka to think in that direction. On at least two occasions, incidentally, the Special Correspondent had stood within yards of Suvorin in the coronation events, but it is highly unlikely that they met. Chekhov, who had no illusions about the autocracy anyway, was detained at Melikhovo until 11 June, when he joined Suvorin in Moscow and on 13 June they visited the cemetery together. No coffins or bodies were visible, but in Suvorin's words 'there was still an odour above the graves'.

By then, having described 'An Imperial Pilgrimage' to Zagorsk, 'Dinner at the British Embassy', and a 'Grand Military Review', the *Standard*'s special correspondent appears to have left Moscow. Whether he went straight back to St Petersburg or took the opportunity to travel in the Moscow region, possibly paying a call on Tolstoi at Yasnaya Polyana as many correspondents did, we cannot confidently say. Someone, at any rate, was able to report in the *Pall Mall Gazette* of 6 July 1896 on the 'quiet little affair' of the Tsar and Tsaritsa's 'entry into St Petersburg', and the content and style suggest Calderon:

In spite of the ghastly accident that darkened the coronation, he has begun as auspiciously as most Tsars. He has done nothing in particular, but he has done it very well. And the presumption is that he will maintain that respectable, if not sensational form. Russia does not want a Parliament, a free press and the rest of it. Not quite so much Siberia, not quite so much persecution of dissident creeds would be improvements which would not take much bringing about. Otherwise, the strength of the Tsar is to sit still and let Russia go unreflectingly on. That kind of role suits it, though other countries would be driven to a revolution in less than a fortnight. But Russia is Russia, and constitutionalism cannot be manufactured out of a peasantry. The Tsar might as well try to make a ball dress out of bark cloth.

Not many liberal Englishmen suspected, or could stomach, the blunt truth that few Russians *wanted* democracy. Behind the resigned humour of this extract, one senses its author's exasperation with such a country. If one adds to this his exasperation with its officialdom, its priesthood, its self-indulgence and the government's contempt for its own people, one wonders whether he could endure life in Russia much longer.

Between July 1896 and May 1897 there are only two pieces in the *Pall Mall Gazette* that can reasonably be ascribed to Calderon. Although the first, which appeared on 25 July 1896, is entitled 'The Nijni-Novgorod Fair', it does not suggest that he himself attended the fair, which was one

of the biggest trade events in the world and lasted several months. He had
come by a 'little tractlet' issued by the Finnish Steamer Navigation Society
about Nizhnii and the two capitals. It was a good example of a classic
Russian phenomenon – translation into English by someone whose native
language was not English – and Calderon spent half of his article relishing
its nonsense:

'Nischny Novgorod', says this little brochure, 'is the most important of Russia is
situated on pictures que bells, from where, the Oka is flowing in the Wolga.' [...]
(I should mention in passing that commentators understand 'pictures que bells' to
be another way of expressing 'picturesque hills') [...] 'Well werthy of notice',
further remarks the little tract, 'is Peter the Great's house, where the great
Reformer lived and worket, here still stand his boot, and armchair.'

The focus on linguistic hilarity is a good indication that the piece is by
Calderon. But its second half strikes out into completely new territory:

In pleasant contrast to the hopeless tedium of everything civil, political, or
commercial in Russia, things military are for the most part bright and interesting.
The *Scout*, the little military weekly, contains more good reading than all the rest
of the *Novostis*, *Novoye Vremyas*, and various *Vedomostis* put together.

That week's issue described an exercise carried out by a special scouting
detachment of the First Battalion of the Ivangorod Fortress, in Poland.
The main part of the exercise consisted in hastily constructing 'with reeds,
logs, planks and barrels [...] little rafts, upon which they loaded their
clothes and equipment', then swimming 'a distance of about a quarter of a
mile' across the Vistula 'pushing their rafts before them'. The regimental
dog was 'trained seriously with a view of being of service in time of war',
in particular to sit a few yards in front of a sentry and wake him up by
growling whenever it heard a sound. 'Any sheep-dog,' the piece
concluded, 'could be trained to perform this duty, and would be an
invaluable assistant to the obtuse paleface in conflict with the wily savage.'

As well as testifying to the range of Calderon's reading in the Russian
circulating library to which he belonged, this and the short factual
abstracts on Russian military matters that appeared in the *Pall Mall
Gazette* over the next year could indicate that he had made new friends in

St Petersburg amongst army men, perhaps through Manya Ross's brothers.

But if after returning from Moscow he did not write regularly again for the *Pall Mall Gazette* or *Standard*, he must have done something else to earn money. In a c.v. produced in 1899, he stated that he held a 'certificate granted by the Awarding Committee of St Petersburg Education District [...] qualifying to teach in Gymnasia and Progymnasia', i.e. secondary schools. In the second half of 1896, then, perhaps he exchanged his unpredictable income as a private tutor for a regular income as a part-time schoolmaster? This might be verifiable from the records of the 1896-97 census of the Russian Empire, instigated by the very Petr Semenov (Tian-Shanskii) whom Calderon had had an introduction to from Edward Delmar Morgan, member of the Hakluyt Society, in 1895. But we do not know at which St Petersburg address to look.

One thing seems certain, and that is that Calderon did not see the first production of *The Seagull*, at the Aleksandrinskii Theatre in St Petersburg between 29 October and 17 November 1896. Judging from a list of his library made in 1922, whilst in Russia he bought Chekhov's early collections of stories *Motley Tales*, *In the Twilight*, and *Stories*, as well as the volumes *The Duel* and *Ward No. 6*, but nowhere (it seems) did he mention having seen the Petersburg *Seagull* or heard about its disastrous reception – and there were plenty of contexts in which he surely would have, if he had been in the city. This is in marked contrast to Constance Garnett, who visited St Petersburg in 1894, probably heard about the 1896 premiere from her friends the Vengerovs, and within a month of the last performance wrote to Chekhov requesting a copy and permission to translate it.

It is possible that in the last year of his stay in Russia Calderon contributed non-fiction and fiction to a number of other publications. For example, in his 1899 c.v. he says that he has written for the *Journal of Education*. Perhaps, then, he wrote the piece on Russian education that appeared there on 1 February 1897. It is very factual and statistical, acknowledging in part an American source, but the initial generalisation followed by a list that becomes a *reductio ad absurdum* is, as we have seen, characteristic of Calderon's style:

Very Russian are the conditions of admission to the Universities. In St Petersburg [...] students are only admitted, except in special circumstances, who have completed the gymnasium course – the St Petersburg educational circuit; and each student must send in with his request for his admission his gymnasial certificate, the dates of his birth, baptism, and confirmation, a passport permitting him to quit the commune where he is a resident, the certificate indicating accomplishment of military duties, three photographs of himself, and a certificate of good moral character.

Similarly, we know that Calderon submitted fiction to *Temple Bar*, 'A London Magazine for Town and Country Readers', so perhaps he was the author of the unsigned 'A Russian "New Woman"', From the Russian of Loukinov' that appeared there in the second half of 1896? 'Loukinov' is a writer unknown to Russian literary historians (although 'Luk'ianov' – L.A. Polonskii – was a contemporary writer). I would venture that the story's English is too good to be a nineteenth-century translation, its construction and punchline-ending are Calderonesque, its detailed, sensual portrayal of the heroine and her clothes is comparable with that of 'On and Off in Petersburg', yet perhaps it is *too* polished for Calderon. Fred Whishaw, a London-based cousin of James Whishaw, placed several of his stories of Russian life in *Temple Bar*, but 'A Russian "New Woman"' seems to be too sophisticated to be by him. Yet again, in the absence of external evidence, we have to suspend judgement on whether an excellent piece of Russia-related writing is the work of George Calderon. Regrettably, however, we can say with some certainty that the first-ever English translations of short stories by Chekhov, which appeared in the May 1897 issue of *Temple Bar*, were not by him as their transliteration system is German and their language far too stiff.

If, from about the middle of 1896 until he left Russia in 1897, Calderon had a regular small income from teaching in a state school, it would have freed him to concentrate on a project which we know had become close to his heart. In a letter of 1896 to his father, the original of which has been lost, he wrote that he had sent to a British publisher a 'sketch for a book' whose working title seems to have been *Demon Feasts*. Its subject, he explained, was

An inference of the first beginnings of religion in the Indo-European race, way back some 6000 years, by a comparison of customs, languages etc. The method and the inferences are new; but I find that the gist of my conclusions is supported by the results of other people's inquiries. The book requires some knowledge of Greek, Latin, Slavonic languages, a smattering of Sanskrit, and the ability to read French, etc. [...] so there is no waste of education. I class this book among Slavonic Studies, inasmuch as the Slavonic side of it is as important as all the rest put together, and constitutes the main value of the work. I have discovered some very astonishing Bulgarian folk-lore.

What had got him interested in this? Had he met Russian folklorists and early anthropologists who were working in this field already? Was it with them that in 1896 he envisaged working 'on the staff of a Russian university', as Percy Lubbock puts it? He had possibly read Andrew Lang's *Myths, Ritual and Religion* (1887), and probably Frazer's *The Golden Bough*, which had created a sensation when it appeared in 1890. But in any case he would not have been in Russia long before he heard of folklore 'demons' such as the *kikimora* (a kind of Banshee) or the *domovoi* (house spirit), and pagan rituals that were still practised among the peasants. The book sounds as compendious as Frazer's, and had already led Calderon to acquiring a reading knowledge of Bulgarian. As we shall see, it became a lifetime project.

Although unsigned, 'Scene in a Russian cemetery. Grave and gay. (From an occasional correspondent)', which appeared in the *Pall Mall Gazette* of 11 May 1897, is therefore likely to have been by him. It describes, and lightly analyses, a classic occasion on which pagan and Christian rituals are mixed in Russian public life. This is *radonitsa/radunitsa*, traditionally observed on the Tuesday after Low Sunday. Families visit their relatives' Christian graves with painted eggs and other food specially prepared for the Easter just passed, consume some of it sitting on a graveside bench or at a table, and actually leave some on the graves. To quote the last two paragraphs:

In its fullest form, preserved in fragments in the provinces, the celebration consists of two well-defined parts, the mournful and the merry. In Little Russia [Ukraine] the rite begins with weeping and a rhythmical chant in honour of the dead; after this Easter eggs are trundled over the tombs from sloping boards. In Baltic Russia, where this sport is also practised, the eggs are afterwards given to the poor. Next follows the meal, and last of all in the ancient celebration come dancing and music: for this purpose in many places the mourners repair to some neighbouring tavern; but in the good old days the graveyard was attended by professional clowns who took the lead in the merry-making.

The following is a song appropriated to the occasion of this feast and endowed with a full share of that mystic inconsequence which seems to endear their popular ditties to the Russians:

> The son-in-law brewed beer for his mother-in-law:
> He brewed his beer against Carnival.
> He invited his mother-in-law for Radonitsa,
> But she came on the Eve of Christmas Day.

The mention of a mother-in-law and her characteristic perversity in preferring to come when not invited might tempt one to believe the quatrain humorous; but it may have served as a hymn in Pagan days, in as much as beer is, in fact, brewed and drunk ceremonially in honour of the dead at the three festivals named.

There are details here that Russianists today might query, but Calderon's researches for *Demon Feasts* had taken him into a subject that would be richly developed by twentieth-century cultural anthropologists and thinkers such as Bakhtin.

This is the last article published whilst Calderon was in Russia that may be plausibly attributed to him. On 22 June 1897 Archibald Ross wrote to his wife in Russian from the shipyards of Nikolaev on the Black Sea: 'There is an English banquet here this evening, to celebrate the Jubilee [Queen Victoria's Diamond] and I really don't want to go to it. Did Calderon and [Basil?] Cameron come to see you on Sunday, with Sasha and Sergei [her brothers]?' This is the last documentary allusion we have to Calderon being in Russia, and of course he might already have left and therefore not have visited her on Sunday 20 June 1897, the day of the Jubilee. At any rate, when Calderon did leave she presented him with a photograph of herself in a feather boa taken in November 1895 (Fig. 8), on which she wrote in Russian: 'With fond memories and as a token of sincere friendship, from Manya Ross.'

Fig. 8 Manya Ross, St Petersburg, 1895

What did Calderon bring back with him from Russia? In the first place a
Russian library, along with items of embroidered linen (presumably for his
mother), and an icon. His knowledge of Russian, Manya said, was

'thorough' and he wrote it 'so well it would be difficult to detect the style was not that of an educated Russian'. He had had to manage his accommodation, meals, travel and other expenses extremely carefully – lessons that proved useful when he transferred to Eastcote – and if we accept that he was the *Standard*'s Moscow correspondent, then he learned in Russia how to write and file stories to a deadline. But above all, he had been so light on his feet in Russia, so curious about every aspect of Russian life, and so determined to 'Russify' himself in order to see that life from the inside, that I believe he returned to England with a broader and deeper understanding of the country than most of his British contemporaries who had been there.

The great period of Anglophone experience of Russia and speculation about its nature and future was still to come, in the form of, say, Carl Joubert's *Russia As It Really Is* (1904), Maurice Baring's *The Russian People* (1911), and Stephen Graham's *Undiscovered Russia* (1912). But there was a magisterial work in this genre published before 1895 which Calderon could hardly not have read: Donald Mackenzie Wallace's two-volume *Russia* (1877). This was the fruit of travelling all over the Russian Empire between 1870 and 1875. It was an instant success, went through several editions, and was translated into many languages. Mackenzie Wallace was actually present with the *Standard*'s Special Correspondent in the Cathedral when Nicholas II was crowned, and met Suvorin afterwards, who wrote in his diary that he (Suvorin) had 'said a few nice things to him'. But by then Mackenzie Wallace had become something of a conservative Russophile and establishment figure.

His thick volumes had covered every conceivable surface feature of imperial Russia from the railways to the history of the 'Noblesse', nationalities, Church and State, the serfs, and the Judiciary. However, as he acknowledged in his Preface, he was 'assisted' in his 'efforts to reach the best living sources of information' by 'Madame de Novikoff', a Tsarist apologist and agent living in London. His book has wonderful breadth, is not at all without immediate experience of Russian life, but on aggregate it gives the kind of 'arms-length' view that in the Soviet period was associated with British ambassadors making raids on 'Russian life' from their embassies. Calderon's experience of Russia was close to the ground;

he was absorbing, and trying to convey in his writing, what it *felt* like to be living amongst ordinary Russians. In particular, although Mackenzie Wallace and the Hon. Maurice Baring had a sense of humour, they were not comic writers, as Calderon was. Calderon had a sense of the ridiculous, nonsensical and absurd that enabled him to see far deeper into the nature of Russia. Although disparate, his various pieces for the *Pall Mall Gazette* demonstrate this. He not only relished the grotesquery of certain Russian types (e.g. the 'dishevelled cockroach'), but could convey the extreme frustration and angst of living in a despotic, anti-rational system. Calderon even appreciated the 'mystic inconsequence' of Russian *pribautki* – nonsense verse – such as the quatrain quoted in his article about 'Radonitsa'. His perception, then, was closer to Lewis Carroll (whose *Through the Looking-Glass* he was reading in December 1895), or Chekhov (who once said, 'What an absurd, cack-handed country our Russia is', and himself as a young man wrote nonsense verse), than to Mackenzie Wallace. At the same time, living in Russia without diplomatic privileges, and experiencing the 'Khodynka', gave Calderon a comprehensive *critical* view of the Russian state. As Percy Lubbock put it, Russia was not a country for which Calderon had 'any predilection'.

Yet again, though, we must remind ourselves how incomplete and speculative the above account is. We do not know where else Calderon went, outside Petersburg and Moscow; we do not even know the names of his Russian friends other than Manya's family, the Gusevs; above all, we cannot be sure that articles published in the *Pall Mall Gazette* and *Standard* that could be by him really are by him. We assume he left Russia in the summer of 1897, but it could have been at any time up to Christmas.

*   *   *   *

By contrast, the facts of Calderon's life up to his departure for Russia are comparatively well documented and can be briefly told.

He was born George Leslie Calderon at 9 Marlborough Place, St John's Wood, London, on the morning of 2 December 1868. His father was Philip Hermogenes Calderon and his mother Clara Marianne, *née* Storey.

That day, P.H. Calderon wrote to his mother-in-law offering a pen sketch of a bawling infant, with the comment: 'He is very dark, and has long hair, and promises to be like his father.' 'His father' had been born in Poitiers of a French mother and Spanish father. Technically, their full Spanish name was Calderón de la Mancha, but they were collaterally related to the great seventeenth-century playwright Pedro Calderón de la Barca. When still a child, P.H. Calderon was brought to England, where his father became Professor of Spanish at King's College, London, and a minister of the Reformed Church of Spain. 'I have lived here ever since,' P.H. Calderon wrote in a family history of 1884, 'married an Englishwoman and my children are English born and bred. Indeed, I feel so entirely an Englishman myself that it requires a mental effort to realize the fact that not one drop of English blood runs in my veins.' He became naturalized in 1873.

Clara Calderon, three years younger than her husband, was the sister of the painter George Adolphus Storey. He lived nearby, or possibly even in the same house, for this was St John's Wood and in the 1860s the young painters Calderon, Storey, Henry Stacey Marks, William Frederick Yeames, David Wilkie Wynfield and others were known as the 'St John's Wood Clique'. They took family holidays together (in 1867 P.H. Calderon rented Hever Castle for this purpose) and loved games, practical jokes, fancy dress and entertaining one another. P.H. Calderon was highly sociable and counted Dickens and Trollope amongst his friends. According to Storey, his wit was 'un peu malin'. His nickname was 'the Fiend', as he was given to dressing up as Mephistopheles. At parties he specialised in histrionic singing.

The St John's Wood Clique were not bohemians and there has never been the slightest suggestion of impropriety in P.H. Calderon's life. He was a highly skilled painter of portraits and historical scenes, a very hard worker who achieved considerable financial success and in 1887 was appointed Keeper of the Royal Academy. Thus after a succession of addresses in St John's Wood and Kent the family moved into Burlington House. As Keeper, P.H. Calderon was in charge of the 'schools' at the Academy and threw himself into teaching. In this capacity, as his obituary in *The Times* put it, 'Calderon was a great success, his kindliness of heart and geniality making him a general favourite'.

Nevertheless, P.H. Calderon owed much of his upward mobility in the art world to being a master of self-presentation and giving Victorians glimpses of what they wanted. He cultivated the image of a tall, hirsute, immaculately dressed grandee. He specialised in painting beautiful young women in ways that appealed to Victorian sentiment and captured what was termed 'the charm in womanhood'. It has been said that British painters of this period wanted to paint female nudity as their French counterparts did – and as British art-goers wanted to see – but they could do so only if there was a pretext, for instance historical. From this point of view, P.H. Calderon's 'The Renunciation of St Elizabeth of Hungary' is a masterpiece. It shows the twenty-something saint kneeling completely naked in profile at an altar, with a rapacious-looking monk in close attendance. Exhibited at the Royal Academy summer exhibition of 1891, the painting created a national uproar. Catholics found it grossly offensive for suggesting that the 'immodesty' of the depicted saint was accepted Catholic ritual, when the original Latin sources for the incident do not say that she literally stripped herself bare. Others were outraged at a woman being shown nude in the presence of men. Controversy raged for weeks in the press and even Parliament, but Calderon kept his counsel. To the modern spectator the painting seems unmistakably voyeuristic and 'tacky'. Entirely benevolent though P.H. Calderon was, one is bound to wonder what effect his self-dramatisation and tendency to vulgarise had on his children's own values.

Clara Calderon, however, was thoroughly conversant with the painterly personality, utterly supportive of her husband's professional activities, and a classic Victorian superwoman. She had eight children between 1861 and 1873, of whom George was the sixth and her fifth son. Two others, Frank (born 1865) and Fred (born 1873), also became painters. In 2012 their father's painting 'Captain of the Eleven', showing a boy cricketer with a very straight bat, sold for £289,250 – 'a new world record for this artist', the auctioneers Bonhams declared. It was used in Pear's Soap's Christmas Annual for 1898, then widely reproduced throughout the twentieth century. Bonhams described it as 'the perfect image to represent the Victorian view of children as models of truth and honesty'. Since it was painted in 1882, it cannot depict George himself; but it does bear resemblances to him and his siblings. P.H. Calderon himself was too busy to appear on family photographs or attend his children's school speech days, but Clara's engagement with her children seems to have been complete and extremely loving. The Calderons remained a very close family.

Whilst living at 16 Grove End Road in the 1870s George Calderon attended St John's Wood School. Four letters from him to his mother have survived from this time. They demonstrate an early proficiency at long hand. Aged eight, he wrote to her at Boulogne, with no spelling mistakes: 'Nurse wishes me to tell you that the cistern is quite finished. The workmen have almost finished the studio-steps. Amelia does water the flowers in the drawing-room, the flowers out of doors do not want watering as it rains so very much.' At the age of eleven George won a copy of Samuel Smiles's *A Boy's Voyage Round the World* as the school's form prize for Latin.

A good grounding in Latin was, of course, a prerequisite for a place at a public school. In the Entrance Examination for Rugby George's performance was rated 'very satisfactory' by the Headmaster, Thomas William Jex-Blake, and he started there as a Scholar in September 1883. Unfortunately, although he is thought to have written to his mother from Rugby every week, only letters from his last six months at the school appear to have survived. However, fairly complete school reports exist from 1885 to 1887 and they are revealing. Calderon was extremely lucky to escape the headship of the fearsome John Percival, who arrived in May 1887 and had no time for 'originality' in a boy. Jex-Blake, in the words of the Rugby historian Hope Simpson, had 'an abiding interest in art and a firm belief in its educational value'. Calderon boarded at School House, which was run by Jex-Blake himself, and it is noticeable from reports that in his first years Calderon worked better for him than for other teachers. In July 1885 Jex-Blake summed him up as an 'unstable, quick-witted, unreflecting pleasant soul'; six months later he was a 'very good lad in every way: bright and pleasant also'; by April 1886 Jex-Blake was writing that Calderon's work for him was 'excellent', he had 'real literary power' and was 'good in character; though with a flippancy that had better, and probably will, disappear'. A repeated theme of reports, however, was that Calderon was 'much too often late for morning Chapel', where he occasionally played the organ.

At Rugby Calderon was nicknamed 'Stew', short for 'Stewpot', as in Spanish his name does indeed mean 'a large cooking pot'. He was an active runner, 'footballer' (i.e. rugby-player), and slow-bowler. As far as we can tell, George was the first of Clara's children to be educated away from London and home; she therefore worried incessantly about him. In March 1887 he casually mentioned that 'the nose-rash' was going round the school. 'How I wish I had never mentioned the disease to you!' he wrote soon after. 'I am of course perfectly safe on account of the little balls of poisoned sugar that you make me swallow'... His strongest subjects were Classics, French, and Mathematics. A contemporary wrote of his 'independence of mind', his 'abundant vitality' and 'friendliness and humour', but added that 'George either did not do [his work] at all or slaved at it'.

In 1886 and 1887 Calderon did slave at it. From having stood halfway down a class of thirty-two the year before, in December 1886 he was elected to a Classical Exhibition at Trinity College, Oxford. In January 1887 he announced to Clara that he was giving up the vice-presidency of the Debating Society, writing for the *Leaflet*, singing in the choir and performing in a House Concert. 'That's pruning. Now all my sap can run up the bifurcated stem, exercise of mind and exercise of body.' In the Christmas holidays he had already been reading for the Queen's Gold Medal for an Historical Essay, which was to be on 'the influence of Mahomet upon Europe for good and evil'. This was the most coveted of all the school prizes and with encouragement from his father he won it – regrettably, however, the essay itself has been lost. Calderon's reading aloud of his essay was the first item on the programme for the school's Speech Day on 25 June 1887 and later in it he played Pistol in scenes from *Henry V*.

By then he still did not know the outcome of all his cramming for Rugby's own awards to future undergraduates. But it had clearly taken a toll. In a superb letter to his mother of 24 July 1887 he described how he had been clandestinely burning the midnight oil when he fancied he was being visited by the 'much-dreaded "Middle Passage Ghost"', which turned out to be a prowling 'Jerry' (servant) who reported him to the new Head, Percival. Following that, he smashed out a window pane whilst ridding himself of a 'fat moth' ('I have a mortal terror of moths'). Three days later he was able to telegram his parents: 'Equal third for Major Exhibition, first for Mathematics [i.e. a Minor Exhibition], Total sixty pound' (per year at Oxford). The printed table of the Sixth Form's combined term-marks and examination marks for Summer Term 1887 makes, however, interesting reading: Calderon's examination marks were consistently high and placed him fourth in the 'Upper Bench', but in his term work he did not hit 50% for Composition, Divinity, History or Grammar and was the only person to score 0/15 for 'Repetition'.

He went up to Trinity College, Oxford, with his friend from Rugby Harold Dowdall in October 1887 and, as we know, Ripley, Binyon, Lowry and Furse were some of his contemporaries there. Like all Oxford colleges, Trinity was extremely sociable. I am indebted to its historian, Clare Hopkins, for her personal communication that under President Henry G. Woods the college 'settled comfortably mid-table. Trinity had no great tutors – but there were some decent ones. The college didn't dominate at sport – but it held its own. It wasn't spectacularly rich or grand – but it managed nicely'. The thirty-seven letters from George to his parents that have survived from 1887-90 suggest that he combined an active sporting, social and debating life with frenetic swotting, bouts of economy, and persistent maternal fretting about his health and safety. After an inauspicious start with rowing ('I had been on the river for 2 minutes and in the river for 5'), he concentrated on rugby, later taking up golf. His initial outlay at Trinity included buying a piano and moving it into his room. As at Rugby, organised religion played a significant part in college life: 'Morning chapel is a dreadful concern at 8 a.m., it consists of "Morning Prayer" including the 2 lessons. We managed it in 16 minutes this morning.' As an exhibitioner, he took his turn to read the lessons.

Inviting friends to breakfast or to evening 'smoking parties' was an established undergraduate custom. On 7 November 1888 Calderon wrote to his mother asking her to send him 500 cigarettes. 'I do not smoke them myself', he told her, but 'they are the most elementary instrument of Oxford hospitality' and he 'found' that 675 had been 'consumed' in his rooms since January. His father, who was paying the bills, complained a month later that 'pleasure preponderates in my scheme of occupation'. According to George, however, he and Dowdall (who lived next door) 'breakfast and lunch together and urge one another on in the path of virtue and economy. We live on porridge and bread and butter'. As a spoof of Trinity's 'Claret Club', they had founded the 'Swipes Club' – 'swipes' being the poorest quality beer. It would, George assured his father, be

a club that should substitute frugality for profuseness and intellectual joys for corporeal pleasures.

[…]

It shall be held after hall once a week. Beer shall be the only refreshment provided, and pipes the only smokes allowed. I wished to enforce 'Churchwardens' [long clay pipes].

The members shall sit in plain chairs at a round table.

So much for the body. Now for the luxuries:

We will enjoy the works only of the gigantic minds of the world: whether the communion with them be by books, music, or art.

We will decide in conclave what minds are desirable as gigantic; we shall probably elect such as Confucius, Shakspere, Bhudda [sic], Browning, Mahomet, Wagner, Phidias, and Aristotle.

We shall enjoy them by having them read by members that have studied them, and can offer an explanation of the meaning; by having them exhibited (if works of art) by those that possess or borrow them, and can indicate their meaning; by having them performed (if music) by those that know them.

The impression of hedonism that he had possibly been giving was, he wrote to his mother, 'a delusion arising from the fact that I enlarge upon my pleasures, that you may taste them and I may ruminate them'. We know from a contemporary that the 'Swipes Club' did exist.

The college was all-male, but undergraduates were surprisingly able to socialise with women of their own class. These might come to Oxford, chaperoned, to meet their male friends in college and go out with them during the day. In a letter dated 9 December 1888, Calderon told his mother that Dowdall and an Oxford 'damozel ycleped Violet Hunt' were 'on terms of intimate acquaintance; and from day to day she brings new chaperones to his tea-parties', whom George evidently met. Miss Hunt was none other than the future novelist and mistress of H.G. Wells, Somerset Maugham and Ford Maddox Ford, to whom Oscar Wilde had allegedly proposed in 1879, when she was seventeen! As we have heard, whilst assisting Michael Furse at a 'penny reading' – possibly a town event – George fell in love with someone he met and the infatuation lasted until the following summer. This is not to mention the Commem. Balls held after summer examinations. Writing to his mother on 17 June 1890, he seems to suggest that his 'best girl', whom he would be meeting at Trinity's 'dance', was a 'fair American'.

Another annual Oxford event was the 'reading party', when a group of undergraduates under the supervision of a college Fellow would go off to a wild part of the country for a combination of heavy reading for examinations and healthy outdoor exercise. Calderon proposed joining one of these at Easter 1889, to swot for 'Greats' (the second part of his four-year course). Unfortunately, he described it to his mother as 'mountain-climbing at the Lakes', rather than 'hill-walking'. She panicked and persuaded his father to oppose it. George had to defend the activity at length, describing the Dean as 'an experienced Alpine climber' and the 'mountains' as 'only toy mountains: Primrose Alps. To climb them is like bull-fighting with sheep, or prize-fighting with gloves'. He persuaded his parents to let him go, but a fortnight later was writing to Clara: 'My dear mother, I do not think you need to be nervous about the punts at Oxford. The river is never very broad, even when flooded, as it was on Saturday when the St John's man was drowned'...

Calderon does not seem to have developed any exclusive relationships at Trinity; rather, he knew everybody and, as Binyon put it, was 'universally liked and admired'. From 1888 he was active in the college debating society, specialising in proposing amusing amendments to the motion which were usually rejected. For example, on 13 May 1888 he moved to amend 'That this House desires to express its approval of the duty on bottled wines, and the taxes on pleasure-horses, vans and wheels' to 'whilst approving the tax on pleasure-horses strongly disapproves of the duty on bottled wines and the tax on vans and wheels' (defeated).

Surprisingly, on 28 October 1888 George moved 'That too much attention is paid to Athletics in this University' – and lost 4:21. The motions were extremely varied, but usually serious and topical; one imagines that they were vigorously debated. He voted in favour of Higher Education for women and liberalising the marriage laws. In 1889, with Ripley, Dowdall, Furse, Binyon and Lowry, he joined the Gryphon Club, whose membership included Fellows and was limited to twenty. They debated and read papers 'on any subject', the Rules emphasised. According to the *Oxford Magazine*, on 17 November 1890 George 'read a particularly interesting and amusing paper on "Women"'. The year after, he became the club's President.

At the same time, he was drawn to the theatre. In November 1888 he performed in an evening of recitations with Henry Irving Junior – 'a perfect and absolute travesty of his father' – and acted under him in Oxford University Dramatic Society's 1890 production of Browning's *Strafford*. But in Binyon's words he 'did not take up acting seriously, but played in the college burlesques'. As Michael Furse explains in his autobiography, these were spoofs of O.U.D.S. productions 'for home consumption' in Trinity. Judging from the few photographs of them that have survived, they were improvisatory, 'camp', and very funny. Furse himself acted in them and described Calderon as their 'leading spirit'. George was also in much demand as a piano accompanist. At a Trinity College 'Smoking Concert' on 29 November 1890 he sang in the catch 'My Celia's Charms' and recited F. Anstey's poem 'Burglar Bill'.

Where academic work was concerned, he continued his pattern at Rugby of following periods of play with stretches of ferocious exam-swotting that undermined his health; but this was a common student syndrome. Revising for 'Mods' (part one of the B.A.) in January 1889, he wrote to his mother that he was 'doing a regular 9 hours per diem', had 'given up football: [it] saves nervous energy', had bought a 'new duplex lamp', and wore an eye shade. Ten days later he informed her he had resumed rugby-playing and reduced his swotting to eight hours a day because he had reached the point where he was quoting Quintilian in his sleep. Clara was so anxious that she sent him 'meat lozenges'.

Calderon took a Second Class in his Finals in the summer of 1891. Having won awards at both Rugby and Trinity, he was doubtless disappointed. Laurence Binyon wrote of George as a student that 'there seemed to be a freakish vein in his mind. Paradox attracted him' and perhaps this 'prejudiced his work' in the B.A. examinations. Binyon even described him as 'something of an enigma': 'All were agreed about his gifts, but no-one was confident of the direction in which they would carry him.' We must remember, however, that Calderon's Oxford degree was in 'Literae Humaniores' – i.e. Latin and Greek languages, history and philosophy – and his strongest subject at Rugby had been Mathematics! The only boy who had come near George's final mark for maths at Rugby was Dowdall, and he had gone on to read Natural Sciences at Trinity (like Ripley). If we seek an explanation of why George did not do the same, it probably lies in Headmaster Jex-Blake's perceptive estimation that he was 'sound but not advanced' in mathematics, i.e. was not a career mathematician.

But by far the most intriguing of Binyon's memories of Calderon at Oxford is the following:

One day in George's last term, when his mother and sisters were in Oxford, he asked me to join in rowing them to Kennington [i.e. Rose] Island. His friend H.C. Dowdall completed the party. Lying on the grass under the trees, we fell to discussing life after Oxford; and George surprised me by announcing in his most completely decided manner that as soon as he went down he was going to study Russian. Why Russian? It seemed so unrelated to anything he had done hitherto. Nothing seemed to have influenced him except the abstract consideration that Russian was little studied in England; it was a subject with a future, and promised an interesting field of work.

Binyon may well have been taken aback, but George's decision was probably not an 'abstract' one at all: more likely, he was influenced by the very concrete opportunities that Russia and a knowledge of Russian seemed to offer Englishmen at this time. The Russian economy was booming and foreign players warmly welcomed. As it happened, at Rugby Calderon had been friends with Alfred Bertram Whishaw, whose family had been successful business people in Russia for generations, and at

Trinity he met Victor Francke, who was related to the paper-mill owner 'along the Moscow line' from St Petersburg with whom George spent Russian Christmas 1895. The early 1890s saw a sharp increase in articles about Russian literature, features about Russia such as Fred Whishaw's, translations of Russian authors, and interest in Russian music. There was every sign of 'Russia' being a growth industry. It is a great shame that not one letter of Calderon's to his parents in 1891 seems to have survived, as he must have discussed his Russian plan with his mother, who plainly knew about it before he graduated, and supported it. To his father he seems to have said merely that he wanted to pursue a 'supplementary profession', namely writing, before 'going to the Bar'.

From the autumn of 1891 Calderon was based at Burlington House and began reading for the Bar in the chambers of William English Harrison at 2 Paper Buildings, Temple. How, in addition to reading for the Bar, did he learn Russian?

Since he had been taught Latin, Greek and French from grammars, and was conversant with the *structure* of Western languages, in the first place he probably taught himself Russian from works such as Ivan Nestor-Schnurmann's 1884 *The Russian Manual* or W.R. Morfill's classic *A Grammar of the Russian Language* (1889). Morfill was Oxford's first Reader in Russian and it would be tempting to think that George had read his inaugural *Essay on the Importance of the Study of the Slavonic Languages* published by O.U.P. in 1890. Possibly, even, he pursued a correspondence course in Russian run by Nestor-Schnurman, who had some kind of connection with Rugby. But he needed live Russian conversation practice too, and we know from his third extant letter to his parents from Russia that this was provided by 'a Russian lady'. A Russian police official characteristically asked him whether it was 'Mme Novikoff', but it was not. A prime candidate for this person's identity is the mysterious 'Mrs Shapter', who features in several of his 1895 letters, clearly lived in England, but gave him numerous introductions in St Petersburg. Perhaps she was a Russian married to a Briton of that name.

Calderon threw himself into his barrister training with gusto. 'He was I thought very ambitious and keen to begin in Court', wrote English Harrison later. 'He never shirked any necessary labour and assisted with enlightened common sense and humour the solution of the different problems with which we had to deal.' Presumably he occasionally met Archie Ripley, who was reading in chambers at the same time, but apart from letters describing their golfing holiday in 1892 there is no evidence that they had any other contact between 1891 and 1895. George became a member of the Inner Temple and was called to the Bar in 1894.

Meanwhile, since he was living at home the only letters that we have to his parents in this period were written when either he or they were away on breaks. In April 1893 he went on a walking holiday in Northumberland with a group that included Godfrey Bradby, an assistant master at Rugby; in September 1894 he was on holiday at Midhurst, Sussex, with his sisters Margie and Evy; Christmas 1894 he spent with the Teale family at Leeds; in May 1895 he was staying at Amersham, probably with the family of his friend Evan Hodgson. These sojourns had two significant things in common: in each place the holidaymakers mixed with the local clergy and put on entertainments for their hosts. One such was a melodrama George 'concocted' with Michael Teale. In Northumberland, he and Bradby wrote the first of at least two plays they collaborated on. All of these dramatic works are now lost.

By 1895 Calderon was impatient. He wrote much, but there is no evidence that any of it was published. He frequented the British Museum, where he presumably read Russian books or researched pieces that he wrote. Perhaps this is what English Harrison was referring to when he recalled: 'The time of waiting for Briefs is always a weary one, and he became interested in other subjects which drew him from the practice of the Law.' For George, however, it was much more dramatic. He felt he had reached a turning point in both his legal career and his writing. His parents were on holiday at Broadstairs. Having first told his mother that he was 'going to write to Father in a few minutes and [...] my letter will contain debatable matter', he penned one on the same day, 28 August 1895, that is so pivotal that it must be quoted at length:

My dear Father,

I have been conscious for some time that a crisis has arrived in my worldly affairs: that it is against nature that I should any longer be drawing my subsistence from a family treasure-chest which is none too large. I therefore resolved some time ago that I positively must be supporting myself by the end of this autumn. You know that I delayed going right to the Bar for a little time in order to furnish myself with training for a supplementary profession. I have not had any success with the supp. prof. Plays, articles, stories – all have been haunted with a fatal home-sickness which has brought them back to the cupboards and drawers of Burlington House. I have also looked round for pupils, but they have not come.

In fact I have done pretty well everything that I could to keep myself going until the Bar should begin to pay – without interfering with Bar-prospects. But this Bar very much limits the sphere of choice. There are so very few other professions that can be carried on without sacrificing the Bar. In fact, this keeping up the Law is generally no more than a fiction. All the interest is transferred to the other subject and one gives up the Bar at last instead of giving it up at first. [...]

There are fine sort of Self-Help stories of great lawyers who stuck to it starving in Temple garrets and at last became famous. But these are old-fashioned stories. A man two generations ago thought he was starving at the law if he only got a brief a fortnight. He could not have conceived of an era when there should be about 50 barristers to one brief; the present proportion.

If the law were a very noble end, if one were set upon being a Q.C.M.P., if present circumstances did not imperatively forbid further waiting, if one were gifted specially for success in the Courts, if one were interested in the Law – then it would perhaps be worthwhile submitting to all sorts of things, in order to achieve final success. But if one is not ambitious of much money, and if one feels that all one's interest and most of one's capabilities lie in other directions – then it is at any rate certainly not worthwhile letting the Law be a bullet [i.e. cannonball] on one's ankle to keep one growing old in inglorious dependence at home while the rest of the family have been earning their living for years.

I have no reason to suppose that I shall do much at the bar [sic]; the Law is like a business – it does not pay unless a great deal of capital is put into it; I cannot wait any longer for the 'living wage'.

The commonplace consolation that everybody has to wait, especially at the Bar; that Charles Russell etc that Lord Eldon etc – is no consolation at all. If they waited in dependence on those who really had not the money to support them there was nothing admirable in their patience in the least.

It comes therefore to this, that I have tried to reconcile the Bar with the necessity of self-maintenance, and I have failed.

It remained therefore to find a means of maintenance without the Bar. This, of course, is not a difficult matter. I have turned things over in my mind and arrived at a solution which is not merely satisfactory, but which positively warms me with its attractiveness.

But having got so far perhaps I have got far enough for this morning. It is ages since I put so much inside one envelope.

[...]
Your loving son
George.

'Positively' is perhaps a little over-worked in this letter, and in the circumstances George's statement that finding a 'means of maintenance' is 'of course, [...] not a difficult matter' takes one's breath away. But the boldest stroke of all was not to tell his father what the 'solution' was!

Calderon went down to Broadstairs to explain his plan. On 9 September he wrote to his mother that he had 'offered tomorrow as a day for newspaper editors to see me if they like'. Five weeks later he was in St Petersburg.

★   ★   ★   ★

The above, then, is some of what George Calderon had been – in a sense 'was' – when he returned from Russia in the second half of 1897.

He took up residence again in Burlington House. The only siblings also living there were probably his two sisters. Doubtless his presence was a comfort and help to his mother as P.H. Calderon's condition worsened. George had free board and lodging (we presume) right in the centre of London. But what was he going to do to earn his own money?

The fact that he retained his exotic appearance possibly indicates that he was hoping to 'sell' himself as a 'Russian hand', an expert on all things Russian, and a knowledgeable writer about Russia. However, he was not the last Russian correspondent of a British newspaper to return home to find that, however well-known his despatches were to the public, it was incomparably more difficult to make a living from his Russian expertise in this country than it had been in Russia. There is no evidence that Calderon picked up the threads again at the *Pall Mall Gazette*. How could he, as he would only be able to write from his past experience of Russia and the newspaper demanded hot news. Ever since the editorship of W.T. Stead (1883-89), who was hopelessly entangled with the Tsarist agent Olga Novikoff, leader-writing about Russia had been a highly sensitive occupation at the *Pall Mall Gazette*, one that George Calderon was far too young to be entrusted with.

Many hoped, and probably expected, that he would write a book about 'Russia' fresh from his experiences of it. Yet this too was problematical. The most popular recent book about Russia was again by W.T. Stead. His *Truth About Russia* (1888) was almost entirely concerned with grand politics and the question of war or peace with Russia. These and such issues as despotism, democracy, and the persecution of the Jews in Russia, were what most interested people about the country. Although Calderon certainly had his own political views about Russia, this is not the kind of book he could have written, or wanted to. If he had collected his articles for the *Pall Mall Gazette* and stitched them verbally together, they would have conveyed a strong 'existential' sense of Russia: what it was like to live amongst such differentness, daily unfreedom, absurdity, bureaucratic torment, and brutality. But this was not the kind of perception of Russia that Victorian readers wanted, and the fragmentary, rather than panoptic approach, would have been years ahead of its time.

Similarly, one might have expected that Calderon would immediately get down to translating Russian literary classics and make his reputation that way. But Tolstoi's novels were already well provided for, and whilst Calderon was in Russia Heinemann had brought out in Constance Garnett's translation seven of Turgenev's greatest works. The Garnetts – Constance with her translation ability, her husband Edward and father-in-law Richard with all their reviewing and publishing contacts – had cornered the market. Moreover, just as (whether they realised it or not) Mackenzie Wallace and Stead were associated with the far Right, the Garnetts through their ex-terrorist friend Stepniak and others were associated with the far Left. This again would deter Calderon from entering the English world of Russian literary translation. Dostoevskii was ripe for translation, but perhaps George did not find him congenial, and he would have had to create the demand for him almost from scratch (Garnett herself did not start translating Dostoevskii's novels until fifteen years later). We know that Calderon came back from Russia with copies of many of Chekhov's works in Russian, but the simple fact may be that he sensed no demand for them and therefore was not going to attempt them. Perhaps, to paraphrase Henry Vaughan, he was also apprehensive that 'those who want the genius of original writing, fall to translation'.

The first signed story by Calderon to be published after his return was 'Laughing Aspen', which appeared in the December 1897 issue of the *Cornhill Magazine*. It is set in America. The eponymous heroine is an American Indian who has had a 'European education' at an 'excellent boarding-school in Brighton'. She is forced by her father Wampum Mittens to return prematurely to her Reservation, but elopes with a brave, Maple Sugar, who has no 'European education'. She decides that the only way they can make a living is by marketing her husband as an authentic American 'Noble Savage' who writes deep poetry. The first volume is in fact written by a 'professional literary man' (Walt Whitman?) who has spent 'thirty years trying to get a publisher for his "Wild Grasses" – about the forest and the prairie and that sort of thing'. He is 'bought [...] book and all' for thirty dollars a month and 'does the rhymes' in the second book. Maple Sugar is a huge social, literary and commercial success until the real poet drunkenly spills the beans. Although epistolary and simple in construction, the story is full of pace, verbal invention, and grotesquerie. It touches on three subjects that were to fascinate Calderon for the rest of his life: the modern noble savage, American civilisation (commercialism), and the minutiae of women's fashion.

His next story to be published, 'Lipa Sidorovna' in *Temple Bar* for February 1898, is completely Russian in inspiration and not comic. A very religious old lodging-house keeper in St Petersburg has erected a 'wooden house with glass doors' over the tomb of her only son, who was murdered in Moscow many years before. On Sundays and 'all the major saints' days' she spends hours at the tomb. At 'Radonitsa' she has a meal at the table inside the wooden house and 'scatters the table afterwards with bread-crumbs and chips of shell from Easter eggs, by way of provender for the departed'. She has 'long talks with Sasha', 'dreams often of her boy', and is even visited by him in the night and told that 'he had a white house of his own where they would be dwelling together'. The life of the lodging house, the characters of the other lodgers than the narrator, and Lipa's religiosity, are realised in convincing detail in the first half of the story. In the shorter second half, the real Sasha turns up, on the run from Siberia. He explains that all those years ago he murdered a friend for his money and convinced the police that the victim was Sasha and he a passport-less escaped convict. Now he wants pity and money from his mother; but she refuses and turns him over to the police. 'She clung relentlessly to her little hoard', the narrator comments. 'She was struggling between the demands of the innocent long-cherished Sasha, who needed a [new] roof to his tomb, and the sordid unacknowledged reality, who wanted the means to live.'

The themes of this story – religious mania, dream/reality schizophrenia, the *neudachnik* (male failure) – were very Russian and very rich. For some reason the story was not signed, but we know that it was by Calderon because in 1922 Kittie revealed that George's most popular one-act play, *The Little Stone House*, was based on his story published 'some years ago' in *Temple Bar*.

'Tarakanof's Idyll', published in the *Cornhill Magazine* of March 1898 with the byline 'George L. Calderon', is biographically intriguing and superficially resembles an early Chekhov humorous short story. Tarakanof (which means roughly 'Bugford') is a middle-aged academic anthropologist, author of *Materials for a History of Modern Superstition*, who is a guest at the country home of the Zamarashkins ('Dragglesworths'). The Zamarashkins' eldest daughter Vera is a student of Tarakanof's and he decides he will be doing her the greatest favour in the world by marrying her. Repeatedly rebuffed, he proceeds (purely for experimental purposes, of course) to cast a love-spell that he has collected from a local *znakharka* (wise woman), but is thwarted by the young people with hilarious consequences. Tarakanof departs ignominiously, but is comforted at the close by the news that his paper on 'The Psychology of Superstition' has been awarded 'the Bezobrazof ['Direface'] Silver Medal by the Kazan Academy'.

In 1898 Calderon himself was undoubtedly continuing his research on Slavonic folklore in the British Museum. We know that he had also resumed translation work (presumably 'technical') for the Flowerdew agency in London. He is said to have begun writing on Russian subjects in *Literature*.

On 30 April P.H. Calderon died at Burlington House aged sixty-four. His death certificate states that George was 'present at the death'. By his very short will made twenty years earlier, Calderon senior gave 'all my real and personal estate whatsoever and wheresoever unto my dearly loved wife Clara Marianne Calderon for her own use absolutely' and appointed her his sole executor. In terms of average earnings, he left the equivalent of £2,740,000 today. Very soon both Clara and George were looking for new accommodation. By the middle of June George had moved into Southill Farm and was recommending to his mother a house he had found at Rickmansworth, but in the autumn she actually moved into one of the more salubrious parts of Kilburn. Whether her daughters Margie (aged thirty-four) and Evy (aged twenty-seven) lived with her is unknown, but her brother was still alive and she had plenty of friends.

There is no evidence that George Calderon knew before leaving for Russia that Archie Ripley had got married, or where he, Kittie, and Mrs Hamilton were living. Given that Golden Square is less than a quarter of a mile from Burlington House, perhaps Calderon simply bumped into Archie in central London sometime in late 1897. That Kittie did not meet George until 1898 is indicated by the fact that she always remembered his return from Russia as being in that year.

5

THE GREAT ENTERPRISE

When Calderon asked in his letter to Kittie written at Eastcote on the evening of Saturday 25 February 1899 'What if Nina Corbet dissuades you from loving me?', he added: 'You are not much swayed by opinion.' But there is no evidence that Nina tried to sway her. Later in life she told George that he had 'always' had 'a very warm corner in my heart'. In any case, the intimacy that he and Kittie shared at 21 Great Titchfield Street in the third week of February completely bonded their relationship. It is clear from his letters that Kittie was his mentor here. In the same letter of 25 February he wrote: 'I love my own body now, flirt with the pillow and sheets, feel so comfy in bed, your arms about me.' The last statement was in his imagination only, but it was partly through their imaginations that they both found a way to survive their 'virginal wedlock' – the very long 'engagement' which, it seems, was never officially announced. In a letter written earlier that day, which he knows she will receive on Sunday morning, he asks her to imagine whilst she is at church that 'there is a warm crude thing on her left looking out for a prayer and a lesson' from her; apparently a lesson in touch. Letters become for him love toys. The one that he times to arrive on 27 February is a part of himself: 'How delightful to come in out of the raw morning here into the fragrant warmth of your bed, and nestle into your warm bosom and sweet lips. Smile on me and the smile will carry to Eastcote.' 'Darling, darling love. Take my letter right into bed if you are still there. Happy happy letter.' When he returns from London, having visited her at 17 Golden Square that afternoon, he imagines that it is 'my careful dear wife' who had 'ordered me a fire when I got back', which 'bathed' the room in 'cheerful glow' (actually, he had 'passed on the order' himself to Mrs Tobutt). He half-fantasizes: 'It is delightful to be looked after personally in this way; to have a value of one's own; at home I was only one of many; so all this is quite new to me.' He 'sees' her sitting in the armchair before him. When he has no visitors, he puts her portrait up in his room so that she is 'there'.

It is clear that by the end of February 1899 their 'working relationship' had been sealed, too. He was giving her his manuscript articles to read, possibly also his stories, inviting her reactions, and practically treating her as his literary agent. This was of absolutely crucial importance to him, as he felt so insecure about his vocation:

Dear Titten, what am I good for? I have a mind of sorts: what office has it in the world? Too practical to be academic, too academic to be practical – I suppose if one goes steadily along any road one hits the intended main-road at last. Dearest, dearest – I am very glad not to be alone.

These lines, from the letter that Calderon wrote her on the morning of 25 February, express better than any the 'problem', 'dichotomy', or even 'conflict', that Percy Lubbock and others thought they identified in Calderon's literary legacy and personality. 'Too practical to be academic, too academic to be practical' is so relevant to 'Who was Calderon?' that we shall return to it. The important point at the moment is the depth of Calderon's relief that Kittie was at his side in his pursuit of an 'office' in the world.

This letter accompanied a copy of Edward Carpenter's book *Towards Democracy*, which Calderon had borrowed from one of his sisters and was asking Kittie to post back to Mudie's Circulating Library from 'Miss Calderon', and the manuscript of 'that silly dull essay on Servian translations', which he wanted her to read and then forward to the editor of *Literature*.

The fate of this 'essay' (not 'review') is typical of the metamorphoses and peregrinations behind Calderon's non-fiction publications in the late 1890s and early 1900s. He took months to research and write them. We have no idea what these 'Servian translations' (of Serbian literature?) were, but he had obviously already been working on the project a while at the British Museum when he mentioned it to Kittie in his letter of 10 February. Was he in fact translating pieces of Serbian literature himself, to illustrate his own essay? No review of books on Serbian literature appeared in *Literature* at the time. Nine months later an article entitled

'Foreign Letter. Serbian Literature' was published there. It is certainly well-informed, but appears to have been authored by someone who has 'seen a Montenegrin column on the march', which as far as we know Calderon had not. It is also purely historical and the style too colourless to be by him. Was the essay that he originally sent to *Literature* via Kittie cannibalised by Traill to produce this published piece?

Similarly, we know from George's letter of 14 August 1898 to his mother that he had been 'working away' in the British Museum on an article about Tolstoi for the writer's seventieth birthday, 9 September; but the date passed without one appearing in *Literature*. Possibly this was because they had already published a leading article on Tolstoi on 30 July in conjunction with a long review by M.H. Spielmann of an English translation of *What Is Art?*. Possibly, if Calderon was a Russian consultant to Traill, he had an input into the leading article, but there are few stylistic hints of this. As we know from his letter to Kittie of 4 February 1899, he was still writing 'the article on old Tolstoy' then, having contemplated submitting it to the *Quarterly Review*. Possibly it grew into two articles: the long signed piece on Tolstoi's novels published in *Literature* in 1901, and the more famous one, on Tolstoi's religion, published in the same year in England, America and Russia. George's thinking about Tolstoi therefore took possibly three years to gestate and see the light of day.

A more extreme example is Calderon's article on the writer Korolenko. By the merest chance, a letter has survived in New Zealand from Calderon to the editor of the *Nineteenth Century* asking for the manuscript back 'if you have no use for it'. The letter is dated 7 January 1898, so presumably that article was written in 1897. No further references to it appear in Calderon's correspondence before the piece 'Korolenko' was published in the *Monthly Review* of September 1901. Had the same article been going the rounds of the reviews for four years, or had it been rewritten in the meantime – and if so, in what ways?

That editors used the facts and translated material contained in George's submissions to produce, with his collaboration, unsigned pieces that were more in line with the needs of the moment and the periodical's house style, is suggested by what may have been the eventual fate of his article about Finland. We recall that he had written a 'long' article codenamed 'Finnikins' on this subject whilst he was in Russia. In a letter to his mother in March 1899 he implied he was updating it and sending it off. The only piece on Finland ('The Downfall of Finland: An Object-Lesson in Russian Aggression') in the core literary periodicals of this time appeared in the July 1899 number of *Blackwood's Edinburgh Magazine*. Stylistically the text does not resemble Calderon in the least, but it contains long translated quotations that might well have come from him. He probably also continued to act as Russian consultant and translator to H.W. Wilson, whose articles on naval matters were regularly published. Similarly, although we have identified only one article in the *Journal of Education* as being possibly by Calderon, the editor gave him a testimonial that suggested a sustained working relationship.

The longest-running of all George's non-fictional writings, however, concerned Nicholas II's initiatives for world peace. In August 1898 the Tsar had issued his 'Rescript' calling for an international conference to stop the arms race and address 'the longings for a general appeasement' which 'in the last twenty years' had become 'especially pronounced in the consciences of civilized nations'. That autumn Calderon wrote his 'Peace Rescript article', described by him as 'once a book'. It was returned to him by the *Nineteenth Century* probably in December 1898 and then by the *Fortnightly Review* at the end of January, 1899. In the meantime, Nicholas II had put forth what is known as the Russian 'Circular' or 'Encyclical', raising the stakes and presenting topics for discussion at the proposed conference. George's letter to Kittie of 31 January suggests that he wrote an article on that too, which he was sending her to read and submit to the *Edinburgh Review* or *New Century Review*. Neither article seems to have been published as such. In the summer of 1899 the conference actually met and signed the first Hague Convention.

All this was extremely high politics and inevitably, at Olga Novikoff's instigation, W.T. Stead was involved. He interviewed the Tsar in November 1898 and attended the conference the following summer. What George Calderon really thought about it all, we do not know, as the only periodical publication that his articles may have fed into – 'A Note on the Peace Conference' in the *Quarterly Review* of October 1899 – is too impersonal to judge. But he evidently kept his file on the subject open, because he was able in December 1900 to deliver a paper to the Anglo-Russian Literary Society entitled 'Russian Ideals of Peace'. Even on the eve of leaving for Flanders in 1914, his thinking about the War was influenced by his knowledge of Tsarist ideology and Tsarist international intentions.

By the beginning of March 1899 Calderon felt so secure in his relationship with Kittie that he was able to tell her without anguish that there could be 'no pretence of the British Museum on Wednesday to Saturday [1-4 March] this week (inclusive) for the *Daily News* advertises it shut those days'; therefore he could not drop in at Golden Square on that pretext, nor could he go up to London as if to the British Museum but actually to meet her at Great Titchfield Street, and therefore they could not see each other. Instead, 'heavily laden with your golfbag over my shoulder and my luggage in my hand [sketch]', on 2 March he cycled much of the way to the Hodgsons at Amersham to play golf for two days. He even enclosed for her to read 'a letter I have had from little Mrs Dowdall', one that simply showed how at ease Mary was with one of 'the Bear's' (her husband's) best friends. He concluded his letter to Kittie that evening:

Are you well? Are you happy? Will you miss me tonight? You will sleep the sounder for my being away. I should have much to say to you were we together, sleepy as I am; rather, I expect I should fall to sleep in your restful arms. G. Kisses for neck and hands and lips; sleepy ones, childish.

He would see her 'the day after tomorrow', i.e. probably the evening of Saturday 4 March. On 3 March, still at Amersham, he wrote: 'Do not forget me during this long absence (long for me). I have bidden Mrs Tobutt keep a pat of butter for your birthday', which was Sunday 5th. He signed off: 'Best of blessings. G. alias Peter', and in front of 'Peter' he drew a cat. Perhaps this suggests that in both Kittie's correspondence with Nina and George's with Kittie, 'Peter' was chosen because it was a traditional name for a tom popularised recently by Louis Wain's cat drawings, and it complemented 'Kitty'. This is the last letter we have from George to Kittie until 1903.

In the April issue of the *Cornhill Magazine*, however, a story appeared that as well as private jokes between them contained a paean that must have made Kittie very happy. The story was called 'The Academy of Humour'. For the only time in the *Cornhill*, Calderon's authorship was credited at the beginning immediately under the title. This might be because the editor, Reginald Smith, was keen to promote Calderon as one of the strongest new humorous writers in his stable and the story addressed two key interests of his young readers: wooing a wife, and being 'amusing' in society.

As with 'Laughing Aspen' and 'Tarakanof's Idyll', the story is told in letters, and as with the latter its hero is an academic bore. Bilbury J. Jones, writing to his uncle from 'Woodham Daintry, Essex', explains that he has not 'abandoned my long cherished ambition of at last securing the Chair of Metaphysics at one of our Universities; not for one moment!'. But he has realised that in order to defeat his rivals for the hand of the girl he has fallen in love with, he must become 'humorous'. 'I had been so long preoccuppied with serious things that I had lost the art of being amusing.' He has therefore signed up for a ten-week course at 'Professor Larrion's Geleological College, or Academy of Humour. Geleological – the word, as I need hardly point out to you, comes from the Greek γελοίος – is the science of the laughable or ridiculous'.

Jones met the love of his life whilst staying with his uncle's friend Admiral Timminer:

As soon as I set my eyes on Miss Kitty Timminer [...] Chairs of Metaphysics had no longer any charms for me, if Miss Kitty could not share them with me. [...] If anyone had described her to me beforehand I should have said at once that she was the last person in the world with whom I need have feared I should fall in love. I never met anyone *less interested* in serious things in the whole of my life. You know her, of course; you must have seen her when you have visited the Timminers at Chelmsford; so I need hardly describe the many particular beauties whose synthesis is so utterly bewitching. I really cannot write about her; whatever adjective I find is so hopelessly inadequate and tawdry. I cannot understand how *anyone* who has seen her, even for a moment, can *ever* think of marrying anyone else.

Professor Larrion is 'a man of powerful intellect', but 'his face wears such an air of imperturbable gravity that it is often hard to know whether he is being funny or not'. He gives po-faced lectures on the History, Philosophy and Art of Humour, his students learn by heart lists of anecdotes and puns, inflict incessant practical jokes on each other, and take walks in threes with a hired professional bore 'in the middle of each trio'. 'The country people fly with every sign of terror when they see us approaching, for somehow or other the absurd rumour has got about that Mr Larrion's Academy is a private lunatic asylum.'

To Jones's dismay, his chief rival, the already 'witty' Captain Bunching of the Essex Light Infantry, also signs up for the Academy, with the aim of learning to '*bombard* Miss Kitty with jokes', and invites her and her father to the end of term ball, where all the students will flaunt their gelastic skills to the top of their bent. Bunching ruins his chances, however, by inviting Admiral Timminer to carve a 'tremendous [inflatable india-rubber] turkey', which explodes. 'The Admiral was very indignant, as was Kitty.' Subsequently, another student stains the front of Kitty's dress with black ink from a trick scent bottle, and the irrepressible Bunching causes her to tear it by inviting her to sit on an ottoman with a false top. Kitty runs up to Jones and leads him into another room with the words 'You, at least, will not be funny, Mr Jones' – which indeed he had been too nervous to be all evening. She gives the whole 'ghastly entertainment' a piece of her mind:

She said that the perpetual stupid jokes, idiotic riddles, and facetious answers that she had had to listen to perfectly sickened her, and she hoped she would never meet a funny man again. I comforted her as best I could; the conversation became more and more intimate, and suddenly I found that I had proposed and been accepted.

But the story actually ends with an excellent further twist. The Admiral consents to the marriage and invites Jones to spend Christmas with them. Over Christmas dinner, Jones involuntarily perpetrates a heinous pun on 'port' and 'starboard':

There was no effort; it simply dropped out. A long pause followed. We all seemed to be gasping for breath. Imagine my utter astonishment when Kitty suddenly jumped up, pale and trembling, from her place at the table, and said, in a low, firm voice:

'Bilbury, if you ever make a joke again I shall break off our engagement.'

I did not seek to fathom her motives. I was ready to make even this sacrifice *for her sake*. I promised her I would never make another. And I never will!

The foreground action and language of this story are genuinely hilarious. The parody of academic discourse, and the pervading sense that nothing can be duller than analysing humour, give it a darker, shifting perspective as well.

But if George and Kittie were confident of their own secret engagement, there were still two major obstacles to their marriage, and these were linked.

In his first letter of 25 February 1899, Calderon asked: 'What news of Mummy Hum? Has she let off any bombs?' As Kittie expressed it later, her mother was 'a very delightfully original, humorous and generous-hearted person – but she made no effort ever to veil her feelings'; and made none now. For her daughter to meet regularly and correspond with a man only four months after her husband's death was simply improper. 'This would have been the same', Kittie wrote, 'whoever the man might have been.' The servants Ada and Lena would, everyone assumed, have been equally shocked and might have left. George was therefore going to even greater lengths to conceal from them and Mrs Hamilton who it was writing to Kittie. 'Send me envelopes which you get from other people', he wrote in the same letter. 'I want a whole packet of specimens to copy addresses from.'

Equally, however, Mrs Hamilton was right if she objected that George would not be able to support her daughter financially, or even perhaps himself. It must have been a mystery to her how he earned a living. Almost certainly his mother had paid him a legacy from his father's estate in 1898, with which he set himself up at Eastcote and financed a not uncomfortable lifestyle. This was surely running out. When Mary Dowdall invited George to stay with her and 'the Bear' in March 1899, she acknowledged that he would have to 'sell your hat or something' to afford the ticket.

One can see that Calderon could just about cobble together a living from technical translation, bits of work as a journalist, stories that paid three guineas a time (£300 today using the RPI), and occasional donations from Kittie, but it was undeniably precarious. His main research in the British Museum, for the comparative book on folklore, brought no income at all. It might, indeed, look as though he was back in the situation he had languished in before he left for Russia in 1895: submitting all kinds of writing (including the short history of Russian literature) to a wide range of publications, with only slightly better results.

At this point, it seems as though Calderon felt he had to improve his income if he was going to seem 'worthy' of Kittie, and sustain it when they were married. He therefore began to look for a permanent job.

In mid-May 1899 he stayed with the Dowdalls in Liverpool, then went on to Newcastle upon Tyne to visit Manya and Archibald Ross. On 24 May he wrote to his mother from the Rosses' home at 4 Collingwood Terrace:

I write with a purpose. I want you, if you can, to look up in *The Times* what you saw there about a lectureship in Russian at Oxford; for if it is open to all comers I mean to put in for it. But I want every possible detail; who elects; who gave; to what institution; for what purpose; everything. If possible I shall at once send in a scheme of lectures.

Ever supportive, Clara had clearly alerted George to this job first. However, the announcement in *The Times* of 10 May actually read:

UNIVERSITY INTELLIGENCE

Sir David L. Salomons, of Gonville & Caius College [Cambridge], having offered to provide a stipend of £50 a year for five years for a University lecturer in Russian, the General Board of Studies are of the opinion that the offer be gratefully accepted, and they further recommend that they be authorized to appoint a lecturer at the stipend named for five years, the lecturer to be in connexion with the Board for Medieval and Modern Languages.

Thus innocuously began a notorious Cambridge University 'affair' that dragged on for over a year and has been variously described as a 'storm in a teacup' and an 'Oresteia' with consequences reaching almost into the twenty-first century.

It was characteristic of Calderon that he should at once set about devising 'a scheme of lectures', presumably on Russian language, literature, history and folklore, to accompany his application. However, if he did make inquiries into 'for what purpose' the lectureship was being set up, he would have discovered that Cambridge dons were confused about it. For the previous three years Ivan Nestor-Schnurmann had travelled to Cambridge for two days a week to train Foreign Office Interpreters in Russian, Bulgarian and Czech. He was a first-rate language teacher. This arrangement had come to an end, but the Medieval and Modern Languages Board believed it would be a good thing 'for teaching of Russian to be provided', and the new lectureship was advertised as being in *Russian*, not Russian Studies. Schnurmann, then, could confidently expect to continue his excellent work.

Fifty pounds a year was not such a negligible sum. In terms of the RPI it might be worth only £4500 today, but in terms of average earnings it might be equivalent to £17,500. The successful candidate would probably have to lecture only two days a week in two out of three terms. If he 'resided', which was what the members of the General Board wanted, he could become a member of a Cambridge college, possibly a College lecturer, and accrete extra income in a number of ways. There was a feeling among some dons, therefore, that Salomons's offer warranted appointing not just a language teacher but a 'scholar'. Given the by then established interest in things Russian, a range of highly qualified 'Russianists' might apply. Kropotkin even wrote to the Vice Chancellor warning him against 'Mme Novikoff's friends'!

Calderon submitted his application. He did not enclose a 'scheme of lectures', but one of his referees, Reginald Smith the publisher, forwarded with his testimonial the manuscript of George's 'Sketch of Russian literature', which was described as 'readable, and indicating intimate knowledge'. None of his seven testimonials has survived verbatim, but they were succinctly summarised by someone for members of the General Board of Studies who were selecting the best candidate. Calderon's first referee, his last Rugby headmaster John Percival, who was now Bishop of Hereford, testified that he had 'unusual gifts as an interesting teacher' and 'high character as an English gentleman'. Charles Cannan, George's tutor at Trinity, wrote of him as 'a man of exceptional acuteness and vivacity who must without doubt be a brilliant teacher'. Traill referred to the 'high literary merit' of his contributions to *Literature*, and his 'faculty of lucid and critical exposition'. The comments of the other three referees – the editor of the *Journal of Education*, Messrs Flowerdew, and Manya Ross – have already been referred to.

Meanwhile, Calderon heard that the Library of the British Museum was intending to appoint an Assistant in Printed Books with special responsibility for Russian and other Slavonic-language works. Researching regularly at the British Museum, he may have heard about this post on their grapevine, or he may have been tipped off by Laurence Binyon, who had been working there since 1893. Whether with George's knowledge or not, in mid-June 1899 Kittie wrote to E. Ray Lankester, now Director of the British Museum (Natural History), about the post. Lankaster replied that he did not know 'what will be the nature of the vacancy and who will be the possible candidates', but he would 'do all that I can for your and Archie's friend'. The chairman of the Trustees of the British Museum was the Speaker of the House of Commons, whom Lankaster would 'tell' about George, and the Speaker would 'give some regard to my opinion'. Lankaster also wanted to 'talk with Calderon' and 'see you [Kittie]', for which purpose he invited himself to lunch.

The library post would involve passing Civil Service examinations in Russian and French and possessing a good working knowledge of Serbian, Bulgarian, Polish and 'Bohemian' (Czech). Calderon probably already had a working knowledge of Serbian and Bulgarian, so he applied and set about learning the others immediately. On 29 August 1899 he wrote from Southill Farm to his mother in France:

I am working vigorously (but I hear nothing about the British Museum); having broken the back of Polish I am hard at work at Bohemian. I get my books cheap straight from Prague: I expect my Bohemian postcards cause them some wonderment and amusement. Each language seems harder than the one before it; but each is a new and fertile region of exploration.

He sat the Civil Service examinations and scored high marks in Russian and French. Edward Cazalet, who examined him in Russian, thought that Calderon's 'extensive knowledge of Russian lore was scarcely approached by any former candidate at the Examinations'.

In late autumn 1899, the members of the General Board at Cambridge turned to the task of appointing their first University lecturer in Russian. George must by then have informed them of his application to the British Museum, as the summary of his submission to Cambridge noted that he was 'a candidate for appointment' in London. He 'thinks that duties would not clash', but 'apparently would not reside'. The latter, of course, was in the dons' eyes crucial. Schnurmann would not 'reside', nor would the third candidate, Captain Henry Havelock (who had a reference from Morfill in Oxford). The fourth candidate, Ellis Minns, would 'reside', as he was already a Fellow of Pembroke College. He also had a Double First in Classics from Cambridge, had 'studied Russian at the École des Langues Orientales in Paris', lived in Russia for a year, 'studied at [the] University of Moscow', and had five professors of that university as his referees. In addition to being able to 'teach Russian and Church Slavonic, especially in its relation to the classical languages', Minns was evidently an up-and-coming Cambridge scholar. The members of the General Board chose him.

But, it will be remembered, the lecturer was to be 'in connexion with the Board for Medieval and Modern Languages', i.e. the latter had a say in the appointment. 'Unprecedentedly', as the minutes of the Council of the Senate recorded, this Board rejected the General Board's nomination of Minns. Their stated reason was that Minns did not have the necessary experience for the post – which, of course, Schnurmann did. The real reason may have been that they did not think that they needed a 'scholar' in the post, but a language instructor who could teach to their own standards of scholastic exactitude. Schnurmann, moreover, was supported by the vocal Fellow of King's College Oscar Browning, to whom he had taught Russian. Strictly speaking, we have no evidence that Calderon was even seriously considered.

The way that the Council decided to resolve this situation was by rescinding the original Ordinance for the lectureship, announcing a new one (which was to be called the 'Salomons Lectureship in Russian'), and nominating the lecturer themselves (for which purpose they appointed their own committee of three). This scheme went ahead in January 1900. Whether George Calderon had by then been offered a post at the British

Museum, or had simply read the writing on the wall of the Cambridge lectureship, we do not know; but around this time he withdrew his candidacy. In March 1900 he took up his appointment at the British Museum.

According to Laurence Binyon, in 1891 Calderon said he was taking up Russian because it was 'a subject with a future'. We ought, then, to evaluate whether this prediction came true – for Calderon personally or for the subject nationally. In terms of the latter it is worth noting what happened next in Cambridge.

For the second round of the contest the three remaining original candidates were joined by three more. One of these was Alexander Porter Goudy, who was a graduate of two Scottish universities, knew ten languages, had taught Russian at University College Liverpool for three years, and offered to reside. As a language teacher he was academically better qualified than Schnurmann. Both the latter and Minns were therefore passed over by the Council's selectors in favour of Goudy. But the Council's 'Grace' appointing Goudy was promptly rejected by the Senate! The Cambridge air thickened with flyers: a Fellow of Pembroke College regretted that 'if Mr Goudy is elected, the best candidate [i.e. Minns] will be excluded, probably for life, from doing recognised service to the University as a student and teacher of Russian', another don believed that '*in paribus ceteris*' it was 'an accepted principle' to favour Cambridge candidates, and several eminent Cambridge figures came out in support of Minns. It was beginning to look as though Goudy was being rejected because he was not a 'Cambridge man'. This stiffened the Council's resolve, they renominated him to the post, and on 24 May 1900 swung his appointment by 149 votes to 105.

Goudy remained Cambridge's Russian and then Slavonic Lecturer until 1936. Like his counterpart at Oxford, William Morfill, he was essentially a grammarian. His only book publication appears to have been an accented Russian edition of Tolstoi's *Sebastopol Stories* (1916). He was undoubtedly an effective Slavonic languages teacher, but could not possibly be described as a scholar of international stature or a man to put the study of Russian culture on the map in England. After his retirement, the Cambridge Department of Russian/Slavonic Studies remained essentially a high-quality language teaching academy for another fifty years. Even in the 1970s, the professor believed that it was 'not a research department' and that the proper place for the study of Russian literature was the University's Faculty of English (*sic*).

With the benefit of hindsight, we can say that Ellis Minns and George Calderon were the best professors of Slavonic Studies that Cambridge never had. Minns rose to occupy the Disney Chair of Archaeology at the university, continued to speak beautiful Russian and be passionately interested in Russian culture for the rest of his life, and in Anthony Cross's words retained 'the friendship and esteem of leading Russian scholars, particularly archaeologists, art historians and historians of antiquity'. By the outbreak of World War I something similar could have been said of Calderon. But Calderon would also have brought to Cambridge Russian a vitality, openness, breadth of knowledge and power of critical thinking that might have transformed a 'language department' into a centre of excellence for the study of Russia and Russian culture. As it was, like most British 'Russian' departments over the next ninety years, the Cambridge one produced instruction in Russian literature, history and thought that was saturated with historicism and very low on critical thinking.

Curiously enough, Calderon's very next publication after the Cambridge fiasco addressed part of this problem. On 31 March 1900 *Literature* published his review of K. Waliszewski's history of Russian literature that had come out in English and French. 'As a popular historian of the literature', Calderon conceded, Waliszewski had 'hardly been surpassed even in Russia.' However, this was 'apart from all questions of criticism'; for Waliszewski was not a *literary critic*. 'He is deficient in what is beautiful in mere literature; he is not much interested in it; he has read authors' unpublished letters, but he has not read the books they wrote with any degree of attention.' Indeed, Waliszewski had misread fundamental details in Turgenev's novels. 'M. Waliszewski knows all about the Turgenev controversies, what Katkov said, and what Turgenev wrote to Mr Ralston, but he does not know Turgenev's novels.' Moreover Waliszewski had no grasp of the wider spiritual and cultural contexts of Russian literature: referring to Dostoevskii and Korolenko, Calderon claimed that 'the kindly Russian sympathy for sinners' was a 'sealed book' to Waliszewski.

What Calderon was warning against here was mistaking an historical narrative about Russian literature for a literary-critical one about the mainly synchronic apprehension of specific texts of Russian literature. It was a distinction that very few in British Russian Studies seemed alert to, or even able to comprehend, for decades to come.

To conclude this episode in Calderon's life, we have to remember that what Sir David Salomons was offering in 1899 was not a chair in Slavonic Studies but a lectureship in the Russian language. Both Minns and Calderon would surely soon have chafed at the limitations of the post. It is impossible to imagine George not becoming bored with academic life pretty quickly, and the fact that he would not 'reside' strongly suggests that he himself saw his future as lying in the metropolis. He never applied for an academic post in Russian Studies again. Where the future of Russian as a 'subject' in England is concerned, the most we can say is that the jury is still out on it.

In the spring of 1900, then, Calderon was making his usual daily journey on the Metropolitan from Pinner, but probably on an earlier train and certainly without proceeding to Great Titchfield Street, as he was on his way to paid work at the British Museum Library.

If he had not known it already, he would soon have discovered the 'context' at the Library that he was walking into. Richard Garnett, father-in-law to Constance, had just retired from the top position, Keeper of Printed Books, which he had held since 1890. Garnett had considerably improved the Library's Russian and Slavonic collection after the anarcho-communist Petr Kropotkin, resident in Britain, pointed out its lacunae in 1888. Kropotkin was still an active donor to the Russian section. But Garnett's daughter Olive, and Constance Garnett, had also been close friends of Sergei Stepniak-Kravchinskii (killed in an accident in London in December 1895), who with others founded the Russian Free Press, and since 1892 this émigré revolutionary organisation had been supplying the Library with publications banned in Russia itself.

From Calderon's point of view, it was probably a good thing that Garnett had already retired and been succeeded as Keeper by G.K.

Fortescue, who did not have a special interest in Slavonic books. It meant that Calderon did not have to perpetuate the Garnetts' personal relations with the Russian revolutionary community. On the other hand, he was specifically replacing the department's senior Slavonic specialist, the Pole John T. Naaké, who had been on the staff since 1860 and in the words of the Library's official historian 'became insane in 1899 and retired'. As well as assisting readers, Naaké's duties had been to select and catalogue Slavonic material together with his colleague Robert Nisbet Bain. When Calderon started in the post his tasks were described as 'cataloguing of Slavonic books', 'correcting errors in the titles of Slavonic books in the catalogue', and 'suggesting purchases of Slavonic desiderata', but we know from other sources that he liaised with readers and answered enquiries. He was probably not involved in the selection of new books from bibliographies and catalogues produced in the countries concerned, as this was the responsibility of Bain at the time, who was a grade higher than Calderon. Nevertheless, he had the opportunity to suggest works that might also be of interest to him in his own research. All recommendations were eventually submitted to Fortescue, who would revise them and send orders to agents such as Asher & Co., who had an office in St Petersburg. The cataloguing, which involved meticulous application of the British Museum's transliteration systems, may well have appealed to George's exact mind. Manuscript catalogue entries had to be as perfect as possible, because printed copies would be prepared from them for general use.

Sometime that summer, Calderon moved closer to his work. With his university friend Arthur Lowry he took up residence at 1 Great College Street, close to Westminster Abbey. Although the rent must have been higher than at Eastcote, he was saving on travel and was now just over a mile from Golden Square.

Perhaps it is an indication of how energy-consuming he found his new job that he appears to have published only one other item that year: 'The Lieutenant's Heroine' in the November issue of the *Cornhill Magazine*. This is a story set in the contemporary Caucasus but with overtones of Lermontov's *A Hero of Our Time* and Pushkin's stories of the officer class. The narrator is an English painter visiting the region, the hero a lieutenant in the occupying Russian army. At the start of the story the lieutenant keeps consulting the future in the cards, which repeatedly tell him he is to fall in love with an 'heroic' woman and that this is imminent. He complains to the narrator:

'I had always hoped that I shouldn't marry a heroine: I can't stand your masculine women.' He sighed with Slavonic resignation, and added, '*Róku ne minovát*', which is Russian for *Kismet*.

I pitied him from the bottom of my heart, and was glad that the cards had no such power over destiny in England as they have in Russia.

The last sentence is, as it were, the 'thesis' of the story, much as at the beginning of 'Richard K. Whittington' it is that there is no such thing as bad luck.

Arriving at the isolated Russian house that the soldiers and painter are to defend against a band of Chechens, the lieutenant meets the owner's daughter Varvara Petrovna, 'a tall, handsome young woman, with a high aquiline nose and a commanding presence', whom he immediately assumes is his 'destiny'. She is a chip off her father the Colonel's old block and joins the soldiers in blazing away at the Chechens 'as if it were the most natural thing in the world'. Her cousin Sonia is 'a little slender figure' with the 'less heroic charms' of a 'soft and pretty voice'. She jumps on a chair when a mouse appears, bursts into tears when the cat pounces on it, and faints when a bullet grazes her hand. Nevertheless, when a corporal is shot and lies gasping for water, it is Sonia who kisses, caresses and comforts him and risks her life to go outside to the spring with a bucket in her hand. When the Chechens see her, they stop firing and their young chief fills the bucket for her and escorts her back to the house. 'I congratulate you, sir, upon the valour of the women of your garrison,' he tells the lieutenant, 'but Chechens do not fight with women', so all of the tribesmen ride away. A year later at a dance in Tiflis the narrator meets the lieutenant again, who tells him that he is married and the cards 'were true prophets'. 'I congratulate you, my dear fellow,' the narrator automatically responds, 'Varvara Petrovna seemed to me a woman whom any man might be proud to...' But the lieutenant cuts him short: actually he married Sonia!

The English narrator's thesis that there is no such thing as foreknowledge thus seems disproven (the lieutenant did marry a 'heroine'), then proven (he did not marry the 'heroine' Varvara Petrovna), then finally disproven (Sonia *was* a heroine).

At the moment, searches of literary periodicals appearing in Calderon's lifetime indicate that this was the last story he ever wrote, or that was published. All six stories we have looked at are genuinely witty and written with a fine touch. In 'The Lieutenant's Heroine', for instance, Calderon modulates the association of white with Sonia to suggest now peace, now cowardice, now beauty. The details in his stories are always very concrete ('I was in my terra-cotta silkette with the squash-coloured streamers' ('Laughing Aspen')). Usually his fictional prose is light, uncluttered, and fast-moving. His strongest point is his command of direct speech. It is hardly fortuitous, therefore, that three of the stories are purely epistolary. Yet they only present one side of the correspondence; the total effect is rather monologic and artificial. Above all, as we know from George's 1899 letters to Kittie, each story was first conceived as an ingenious 'idea', which in practice means a plot with a reversal in it, a surprise ending, and a punchline. The success of a Calderon story depends on how well this plot is conducted and the ending brought off. 'Idea' in the sense of thematic suggestiveness, or psychological richness, is, with the exception of 'Lipa Sidorovna', absent. The stories are phenomena of technical control, and sometimes it slips from showing into telling. Perhaps, then, the reason that Calderon stopped writing stories in 1900 was that he tired of having to perform the same 'trick' each time of conceiving a story, conducting it, and 'finishing' it (nearly all the endings are very closed).

On the other hand, the stories were written to be entertaining and are entertaining. We should surely not disparage entertainment, lightness, playfulness and sheer humour. Although comprising only fifty pages of print, an attractive first book of stories could have been made from them that would have sold, as they perfectly exemplify the contemporary popular taste in short narrative fiction. The fact that Calderon did not do this suggests that he did not see himself as a developing short-story writer. We are left with the impression that he had 'done' short stories now and was moving on. Indeed it is possible that the publisher of the *Cornhill*, Reginald Smith of Smith, Elder and Co., had already persuaded him to attempt a longer humorous work.

Presumably Calderon's main writing project in 1900 was his Slavonic *Golden Bough*. Although he was no longer visiting the British Museum principally to do his own research, he must have had plenty of opportunities to look things up and to stay abreast of Slavonic publications in his 'field'. Several of his predecessors had also had research ambitions: for instance, in 1874 whilst on the staff Naaké had published his *Slavonic Fairy Tales*, and Bain was translating a collection of Tolstoi's stories. Possibly Calderon even returned to the Library in the evenings. As usual, we do not know that, or, of course, what stage his research had reached – in particular, whether he had yet taken the fateful decision to move it into other, non-Slavonic languages.

Without doubt, as 1900 wore on the overwhelming focus of his life became his approaching marriage. Not only would it mean that he and Kittie could at last love and live openly together, it would be the beginning for them both of a great artistic enterprise. In 1899 he had asked her 'are you enough identified with me to put yourself into my place? to help me all you know in seeing to a line what I do best?' and now she was. She read and constructively criticised everything he wrote; she acted as his agent in sending off his submissions; she had excellent contacts with publishers already and was raring to network on George's behalf, as her initiative to E. Ray Lankester showed. Elegant, feisty, humorous, from a famous family and perfectly at ease in society, she would be a natural literary hostess. The enterprise was to launch Calderon as a writer and it could be the perfect partnership. At the same time, she continued to paint in the studio at Golden Square and as a weekend painter himself George would be able to join her there. Thanks to his parents, his contacts in London's art world were considerable and could be of help to her. By the autumn of 1900 Kittie and he must have been excited at the prospect of their new *working* life together.

Their engagement (which ostensibly dated from January 1899) was not announced in the press, and perhaps was never discussed with Mrs Hamilton. At some point in the autumn, however, they must have broken to her that they intended marrying by the end of the year. This was only just over two years since Archie Ripley's death, but socially acceptable as it was in the third calendar year. From what we know of Mrs Hamilton's and George's relations after the wedding, it is possible that she now found him congenial as a man and acceptable as husband to her daughter because of his career prospects. It is not ascertainable whether she attended the wedding, which took place only ten minutes walking distance from Golden Square, but clearly she acquiesced in it.

Most of Kittie and George's friends, however, were taken completely by surprise when they were informed of its imminence. Around the end of October Kittie wrote to tell Catherine Lubbock, Archie Ripley's half-sister, and on 2 November her twenty-one-year-old son Percy wrote somewhat complexly from King's College, Cambridge:

I can't easily tell you the real joy that mother's news is – you are too good a friend to us for it to be possible not to accept your happiness as ours – and the feeling that yours is Archie's too makes all perfect. I don't say this without meaning it – it is a very real thing; and I don't only congratulate you (that too), but I am glad myself, and it is delightful that you should stay at Golden Square, a place that now means so much to us.

I think you could hardly doubt what the feeling of all of us would be – and I expect Mother told you that we had looked forward to just this. I should like to be at your wedding – may I?

Writing to George in Russian, Manya Ross was more direct:

Don't tell me you are getting married, too?! How unlike you it is, – that you are in love, I can believe, – but that you are getting married and so soon – it's simply incredible. I approve of your choice, but am sorry to lose you as a dear, good friend and an interesting person to talk to. I know that both of you will be happy, because you are both suited to each other, I felt that immediately I saw your darling Kittie. She really is wonderful, and her old mother too. I send you my parental blessing. I am sorry that we shan't be at your wedding, much as we would like to be, it's your own fault, you should have told us earlier. Your devoted and ever-loving Manya.

It seems that George and Kittie had given their friends at most a fortnight's notice. Judging from an undated letter from Nina Corbet, Kittie sent her the letters of congratulation she received, which led Nina to say 'indeed you are lucky to have such dear brothers-in-law' and describe 'Mike' Furse's letter as 'very good and expresses what one feels so well'.

The main actors at the wedding on Saturday 10 November were presumably apprized of it well in advance. Nina Corbet appears to have given Kittie the pattern for her wedding dress and recommended to her wearing Paris stays, as her own were 'himmlische [...] never mean to wear any others – and my tummy is nil'. She also wanted to 'give George something he would like and use'. Whereas Sir Walter Corbet, Mrs Hamilton, Laura Ripley and two others had witnessed Kittie's first marriage, Sir Walter was probably away now at the Boer War, so Nina took his place, and the only other witness was Arthur Lowry. If Mrs Hamilton was there, why was she not a witness? And if Clara Calderon attended, could not she too have signed the register? Or one of George's brothers? This may indicate that the wedding really was hurried and there was even some uncertainty on the Calderon side. There could hardly, however, have been any criticism of the choice of venue or officiant: Wren's church of St James's in Piccadilly, and 'Michael B. Furse, Fellow and Sub Dean of Trinity College Oxford'. The marriage was announced in *The Times* on Monday 12 November 1900.

6

RUSSIANIST, CARTOONIST, NOVELIST

In terms of publishing, the years 1901 to 1905 were the most productive period of Calderon's life. The 'great enterprise' began with a bang when within three weeks of returning from his and Kittie's honeymoon in Paris he delivered a paper entitled 'Russian Ideals of Peace' to the Anglo-Russian Literary Society (ARLS). This was on 4 December 1900, two days after his thirty-second birthday.

Calderon had only just joined ARLS. It must have seemed a promising way of raising his profile as a Russian scholar. One wonders, however, how congenial he found its membership. Tolstoi was officially member number six, but a glance at the nearly 500 other members' names in the society's *Proceedings* for 1900 reveals that the Russian contingent were mostly from the establishment class of Tsarist society and the British predominantly conservative, too. The Garnetts and their Russian friends were conspicuous by their absence. The Tsar, Tsarina, and Grand Duchess Mariia Aleksandrovna (married to Queen Victoria's son Alfred) were the society's patrons. This itself was a sensitive issue for the Russian authorities and the Russian embassy doubtless reported back to them about the society's 'loyalty' (after 1905 the imperial couple withdrew their patronage). Further, there was a sizeable component of British military men, since one of the society's objects was to provide a centre where officers who had become British interpreters could read Russian newspapers and listen to topical lectures. Meetings were held at the Imperial Institute, South Kensington, and the *Proceedings* printed by the Army and Navy Cooperative Society. The president was businessman and Russia-enthusiast Edward A. Cazalet, who has been described by Dorothy Galton as 'a rather cantankerous, self-opinionated and pompous autocrat'.

Before such an audience, how was Calderon going to take a critical look at Nicholas II's Peace Rescript, the Peace Encyclical, and the Hague Conference that followed? If, as his despatches from Russia seem to suggest, he vigorously rejected the autocracy and believed Russia needed 'a Parliament, a free press, and the rest of it', how could he interact with people who generally believed the opposite? Only eight weeks earlier Aylmer Maude, the English Tolstoyan, had had a very cool reception when he lectured on Tolstoi's beliefs – and declined to join the society. Would George be compromised by what he had described to Kittie as his habitual 'desire to please an audience'?

One could be forgiven for thinking that he had decided to bore his audience into submission. He told them that his 'purpose' was to

trace in this paper, as well as I can, the development in Russia of the idea that Universal Peace should be one of the main objects of a Christian's life. My paper will fall into two parts: the first will deal with the education of the nation to that idea by the Gospel of Peace as the duty of the individual; the second will deal with the progress of the ideal in national politics, and I shall endeavour to show in each part the influences which led up to the final result.

Accordingly, he began with Christ's message of the Kingdom of God ('in secular language the Millenium') and traced its influence on Russian dissenters from the earliest Bogomils, Strigolniks, Judaisers and Molokane, to the Moravian Brothers, the Mennonites, and the 'native species of Quakerism' the Dukhobors. Although efficiently presented, all this was purely factual and narrative, as was the excursion that followed about Henry of Navarre's scheme for Perpetual Peace and the influence of that, the Quakers, and Mme Krüdener on Alexander I's contribution 'to the ideal of Universal Peace'. Calderon was probably quite a fast speaker, but he had now been talking for nearly thirty minutes and it is difficult to believe that many of his audience could have taken in so much information or understood where it was 'going'. It dawns upon one that he probably *had* written 'a book' on this subject, as he told Kittie back in January 1899, and was simply recycling a chunk of it.

However, he had now reached Alexander I's 1815 draft of the Holy Alliance and suddenly presented his own evaluation of it. The Holy

Alliance, he said, 'was a daring scheme, aiming at nothing less than the introduction of the Christian virtues into the sphere of public life'; but

I may say that the effect of the Holy Alliance was almost wholly disastrous. A kind of Federal system ensued in the form of periodical conferences of the Foreign Ministers of the chief powers, and these conferences soon resolved themselves into meetings of conspirators plotting against the liberal aspirations of one another's subjects. [...]

    Canning conferred a benefit on mankind when he broke up this Federation of Reactionaries. But Alexander never could understand why people found fault with it. His intentions, as he explained to Grellet [the British Quaker] at a later date, were of the best.

Calderon was saying, then, that the end result of Alexander I's 'Ideals of Peace' was to entrench the status quo in Europe and insulate Russia from liberal contagion. The idea that these political aims were combined with an unawareness of them on the 'peacemaker's' part, was an interesting paradoxical model for explaining the peace initiatives of the more recent tsars.

    But Calderon could hardly apply it to Nicholas II before this audience. It would have involved elaborating on the liberal aspirations, particularly democracy, that the tsar was intent on thwarting. Instead, George chose to explain the peace policies of Alexander III and his son in terms of Slavophilism and Hegel's philosophy of history. 'It is an essential part of the Slavophil doctrine', he told his audience, 'that Russia is destined to bring in the final reign of Universal Peace.' The Russians saw this as the destiny that Hegel's Weltgeist had prepared for them; theirs would be the last and best 'National Civilisation' that would achieve 'the final "synthesis" of universal history'. The 'final reign of Universal Peace', moreover, would be the 'aeon of Orthodox Christianity – of forbearance and consent'. All that Russia had to do was 'be faithful to her Orthodoxy, gently wrest the hegemony of Europe from German hands, and then – the synthesis'. According to Calderon, Alexander III acquired this belief from the Slavophile friends of his youth and Nicholas II was continuing his father's strategy with his Peace Encyclical.

In the penultimate fifteen minutes of his lecture Calderon had displayed a detailed knowledge of the history of Slavophilism and confidently presented an Hegelian hypothesis for the motivation of the last two emperors' peace offensives. Unfortunately, this hypothesis was purely abstract. Contemporary Russians were, as he had written his mother from St Petersburg, 'nuts on philosophy', but there is no evidence that the tsars and their advisors were. Even the regime's chief ideologue, Konstantin Pobedonostsev, kept the Slavophiles at arm's length. The notion that anything was going to 'gently wrest the hegemony of Europe from German hands' would have been laughable to these men. They were certainly Russian nationalists (not Slavophiles), but there is no evidence that they had imperial designs on western Europe.

It is disappointing that, for reasons we can only imagine, Calderon did not examine the *realpolitik* behind Nicholas II's Encyclical, analyse the documents themselves, or evaluate what the First Hague Conference achieved. Historians have indeed compared the last tsar's peace initiatives to Alexander I's and the general view is that Nicholas II probably was motivated by a sincere Christian desire for an end to war. However, it is very clear from the 'Rescript' of 24 August 1898 (which Calderon confuses with the 'Encyclical' of 11 January 1899) that a vital part of the Tsarist government's motivation was economic. The official translation of paragraphs four to seven reads:

The financial charges following an upward march [in arms production] strike at the public prosperity at its very source.

The intellectual and physical strength of the nations, labour and capital, are for the major part diverted from their natural application, and unproductively consumed. [...]

National culture, economic progress, and the production of wealth are either paralyzed or checked in their development. [...]

The economic crises, due in great part to the system of armaments à l'outrance, and the continual danger which lies in this massing of war material, are transforming the armed peace of our days into a crushing burden, which the peoples have more and more difficulty in bearing.

Nicholas II wanted peace with the Great Powers because he knew military defeat was a powerful engine of change in Russian society – change that he

did not want. But the Rescript surely implies that he and his advisors
feared economic collapse for the same reason. Structurally, then, his
motivation was similar to that of Alexander I's: he believed in 'Universal
Peace' *and* he wanted to save his autocracy from 'disaster'.

Naturally, one could say that Nicholas's desire for international peace,
his aspirations for 'public prosperity' and 'economic progress', and the
declarations of the Hague Convention of 1899, were entirely laudable.
Only seven months before Calderon's lecture, however, Tolstoi had
excoriated the Hague Conference thus (in Maude's translation):

It was particularly becoming that the Russian rather than any other government
should be the *enfant terrible* of the Hague Conference. No-one at home being
allowed to reply to all its evidently mendacious manifestos and rescripts, the
Russian Government is so spoilt that – having without the least scruple ruined its
own people with armaments, strangled Poland, plundered Turkestan and China,
and being especially engaged in suffocating Finland – it proposed disarmament to
the governments in full assurance that it would be trusted!

In Tolstoi's words, the Tsarist regime's proposal was 'indecent [...]
coming at the very time when it was preparing an increase of its own
army'. Here was some of the critical thinking that seemed absent from
Calderon's exposition. George had even said that Slavophilism 'in its
purified and mitigated form' seemed to him 'the doctrine which lies at the
root of all that is enlightened and wise in Russia's policy of today' – a view
which Olga Novikoff must have had great pleasure in reporting to her
political masters.

Nevertheless, at the very end of his lecture Calderon was able to land a
personal punch:

We of the *gniloi zapad* [Rotten West] [...] may well doubt whether the idea
embodied by the Russian nation – to speak in Hegelian terms – is the final
synthesis in the Weltgeist's development, whether in fact Russia is capable of
teaching us the ways of the Millenium. I believe that it is Russia's view of her own
mission, but I do not think it will be universally accepted in England. [...] It is
hard to believe that the secret of mankind's perfection has been entrusted to the
Russians of our own day; for the conflict between the individual and the
community in Russia is as keen as ever. Russia must be strong to fulfil her
national mission of peace; and the needs of her strength still exact the military

service of Molokans, Duchobortsy, and all who preach the individual gospel of peace.

In his concluding words he even attacked Tsarist racism. A nation that aspired, in Dostoevskii's word, to be 'pan-human' could 'hardly be a nation which guards the purity of its blood so jealously'. Somewhat mysteriously, he felt it must 'rather be a nation which combines the racial elements and the ideas of every continent – some nation perhaps which is only now in process of formation'.

Judging from the published record, none of these strictures was responded to from the floor. Cazalet opened by thanking Calderon for his 'admirable paper' and declared ex cathedra that 'the common Russian people were eminently peace-loving'. The Secretary, Alexander Kinloch, seconded those thanks and referred to an article that had just appeared in the *Fortnightly Review* entitled 'A Plea for Peace – An Anglo-Russian Alliance'. The general drift of Kinloch's and Manya Ross's contributions, as printed in the *Proceedings* at least, was that everyone should work 'zealously to remove misapprehensions and to further peace and good-will between the two great peoples'; which happened to be one of the stated aims of this Society for Anglo-Tsarist Friendship... However, 'Mr Havelock' (the Captain Henry Havelock who had applied for the Cambridge job) took a different line:

Doubtless the Tsar, personally, was sincere in his desire for peace, but with such a large military class and civil service, was it likely that his desire should be shared by many of his people? [...] The idea put forward by Mrs Ross as to Russia stemming the hordes of barbarians was highly creditable, but at present her stemming seemed to consist in going with the stream [!].

Havelock thanked Calderon for what he actually called 'the most instructive and pleasantly-delivered paper they had listened to'.

George's debut on the Anglo-Russian lecturing circuit had been a success. They had probably been won over by his charm and actorial skills. He had realised his 'desire to please an audience' without, presumably, being 'undermined' by that desire too much. It may appear strange that he had devoted so much time to the numerous pacifist dissenter sects in

Russian history, given that the leaders of 'national politics' were Orthodox, but this did add a unique, Russian perspective to the modern peace movement and probably explains why his original article/book had been called 'The *Evolution* [my italics] of the Peace Encyclical'. Quite possibly this narrative was new, interesting and instructive to his audience. His critique of Alexander I's Holy Alliance invited comparisons with Nicholas II's peace offensive, but Calderon avoided making them. Instead he floated his Slavophile-Hegelian interpretation, which must have been congenial to many present. Yet here too, briefly, he had managed to inject criticisms.

One imagines that Christmas 1900 at 17 Golden Square was a happy one.

The new year began with an increased workload for Calderon at the British Museum. He and others were asked to assist Bain in dealing with the Slavonic items in a Subject Index covering the years 1881 to 1900. In the second week of January he received a letter from Kropotkin accompanying 'a few socialist pamphlets for the Library' and took it home with him. Home, which was not a large house, was always full of people, activity, and animals. In addition to four female servants, a sick nurse came and went for Mrs Hamilton, there were constant visitors, and the Calderons had acquired another Aberdeen terrier, the puppy Joan, to go with Jones. According to Kittie, George left work 'latish afternoon', which gave him some time to pursue literary networking in central London, then after dinner he would work on his own projects. Mrs Hamilton did not approve of the 'hard close studying George was doing in Folklore and Anthropology' at this time – she favoured writing that had 'bubble and buzz' – and referred to *Demon Feasts* as 'that old stodge'.

It was at about this time that a series of amateur photographs was taken of George at 17 Golden Square by Violet Lubbock, Percy's nineteen-year-old sister. They show that he had a long and prominent nose, dark hair parted in the middle, and the strong eyebrows of his Calderon forebears (see Fig. 9). He is wearing a full-length artist's smock and in two of them a strange flat cap. Presumably Violet was spending the weekend with them, it was Sunday afternoon, and Calderon had just emerged from the Studio to have these snaps taken. What, then, could he have been painting?

Fig. 9 George Calderon, 1901

Calderon's fortes as an artist were line drawings and watercolours. None of the latter seem to have survived from this period, but there is a thick sketch book half-full of cartoons by him that seems to have been started early in 1901. They are mostly on literary, historical and painterly subjects and somewhat in the manner of Max Beerbohm, whom Calderon probably knew at Oxford and whose exhibitions we know he visited. The first dozen pages include parodies of the painters C.H. Shannon, William

Rothenstein, W. Strang, and Augustus John, whose work Calderon must
have viewed at the Carfax Gallery in St James's, Piccadilly. (As Mrs Ripley,
Kittie had sat for her portrait by Augustus John in 1897.) The cartoon on
page twelve is of Edward VII 'Trying on the Coronation Robes', so it must
have been drawn after the death of Queen Victoria on 22 January 1901.
But the first cartoon in the book, and one of the best, was of Tolstoi (Fig.
10), which strongly suggests it was drawn at Golden Square in 1901, as this
was the year in which Calderon's research on Tolstoi begun in 1898 came
to spectacular fruition in publications.

Fig. 10 'Count Leo Tolstoy', by George Calderon

On 7 March 1901 Tolstoi was excommunicated from the Russian
Orthodox Church. Konstantin Pobedonostsev, the state's custodian of the
established church, had been wanting to do this for years and with the

assistance of senior clerics had at last succeeded. Tolstoi himself, however, had left the Church years before and was completely unruffled by Pobedonostsev's highly publicised action. Yet Tolstoi's 'followers' and many other Russians protested loudly against it. This was the context into which George hurled his signed article 'The Wrong Tolstoi', published in the May 1901 issue of the *Monthly Review*.

He began with a flight of the irony and *reductio ad absurdum* that enlivened the piece throughout:

The Holy Synod has excommunicated the Count, who has been busy these many years in excommunicating the Holy Synod. The Synod's long delay in issuing this *accusé de réception* of Tolstoi's thunderbolts can only be explained by supposing that the watchfulness of the Censor has hitherto prevented their librarian from securing a copy of Tolstoi's religious works, or that Mr Pobedonostsev has not been at leisure to read them.

Given that Tolstoi and his followers reject basic articles of the Church's faith (e.g. the divinity of Christ), 'together with all its ritual and ceremonies', one might think that they would bear the 'blow' of excommunication 'with equanimity' –

that the disciples would not be indignant with the Church for denying to their leader the consolations which he had spent so many years denouncing as frauds and impositions. But, on the contrary, they are inviting the civilised world to join them in bitter outcry against this latest instance of priestly tyranny.

What, Calderon asks, can be the source of this inconsistency?

The explanation he proposes tells us much about his own values of education and critical thinking. 'The spread of earnestness among the half-educated classes', he writes, has brought about 'a new public, full of noble but untutored aspirations, which wants the Millenium in cash down', i.e. simple 'drastic' solutions. Because such people are not educated enough to understand why the professionals do not have dogmatic answers to all life's problems, they turn to 'the prophets':

When a prophet comes preaching that doctors know nothing of medicine, nor philosophers of metaphysics, that priests and politicians practise their crafts only for their own personal advantage, they receive him with enthusiasm – it is what they more than half suspected themselves – and they become Christian Scientists, Theosophists, Tolstoyites, and the like. [...] They assume that because the men who have the gifts and the knowledge necessary for dealing with those difficult subjects have failed, therefore success must surely fall to those who are hampered with none of their gifts and none of their knowledge; at once they yield their allegiance to the destructive critics whose revelations seem to have invested them with authority in all these matters by right of conquest.

Interestingly, despite the fact that Russians were already well known for their propensity for sectarianism and cults of personality, Calderon is clearly not limiting his arguments to Russians. He would seem to be associating 'half-bakedness' and lack of rigorous thinking with the growth of 'mass education' through the media at the end of the nineteenth century generally.

   'It seems a hard saying', he continues, 'that this is the public in which Tolstoi has found his following, for Tolstoi is endowed with genius and piety – two attributes which are not necessary in appealing to that multitude.' But it is the case, and for an obvious reason:

There was no other public open to his teaching. He taught that doctors, lawyers, clergymen, statesmen, scientists, and philosophers were all blockheads or humbugs; that the world must give up its civilisation, knowledge, arts, crafts, creeds, food-stuffs, liquors, laws, armies, navies, and social order. This was too much for the educated men of the world: if for no other reason than that they were all doctors, lawyers, clergymen, soldiers, sailors, statesmen, scientists, landowners, licensed victuallers, or the like.

Calderon's favourite device of the 'bathetic list' works to good comic effect here, but he hastens to add that there is a 'graver reason' why Tolstoi's 'gospel' has not been espoused by the 'well-informed', and that is that it is riddled with inconsistencies. 'Inconsistency, though the mark of an honest man, is out of place in philosophy.' But the 'enthusiasts' – the 'half-educated' – have no problem with it:

The faculty of believing contrary things at the same time, of believing that which they cannot understand, or that which they know to be false, is the most characteristic feature of that large and growing class. Yet their opinion is by no means to be neglected; for they are the makers of reputations; they are the light-kindling stuff which sets the solider world on fire.

This directly leads Calderon to explain the title of his essay. The 'mass audience', as we might call it today, has made a *celebrity* of 'the wrong Tolstoi' and left the 'right Tolstoi' out in the cold. And by these two Tolstois he does not mean what we might assume:

I am not speaking of Tolstoi the novelist, who has a separate reputation of his own, founded on the opinion of judicious men; I am speaking of the two Tolstois of later years: the right Tolstoi, who leads his kindly, weak, lovable life at Yasnaya Polyana, and the wrong Tolstoi, who writes the books and pamphlets decrying all the best that mankind has achieved.

This 'duality' enables Calderon fundamentally to deconstruct Tolstoi the 'prophet' whilst preserving every affection for Tolstoi the man.

The wrong Tolstoi 'writes pamphlets to show that a man should have no truck with property, wives or children', while the right Tolstoi 'lives with his family on a comfortable property in the Province of Tula' – and Calderon quotes from the paper given by Aylmer Maude ('one of his apologists') at a meeting of ARLS on 2 October 1900, to illustrate the very difficulties Tolstoi had in acting consistently with his published views. Pressing his point with destructive irony, Calderon continues:

That little difficulty of not being able to 'do good' without harm, of creating anger and bitterness in the hearts of those nearest to him, is one that is very likely to crop up when a man – especially a married man – tries to practise a scheme of life which involves poverty and celibacy. In fact, that difficulty always does crop up; and there is a touch of personal feeling in the indignation of the Tolstoyites when the reproach of inconsistency is brought against their master: for though Tolstoi has thousands of disciples in every part of the world, I think I may safely say that not one of them has ever practised the Tolstoi scheme of life for twenty-four hours together, any more than their teacher. And this feature is all the more curious and interesting in a religion of the militant sort, which declares all other religions mere 'frauds', invented to justify the criminal lives of their adherents.

In fact, the only community of 'true Tolstoyites' are the inhabitants of the Nicobar Islands, who 'enjoy the only conditions in which Tolstoy's political economy can be realised' (although their 'rum and tobacco and the black top-hats have no place in Tolstoyism'); and the only land in Europe where Tolstoi's agrarian utopia is possible is 'that strip of South Russia which goes by the name of the Black Soil, and there only in favourable years'. 'If the world were to go mad one day and accept Tolstoyism as a working theory of government', much of its European population would have to be resettled on 'the Black Soil, the Nicobar Islands, and one or two other favoured spots, on freehold estates of about nine square yards each'.

So far Calderon had been teasing out arguments from the topical fact of Tolstoi's March excommunication, although some of them had probably been maturing in his mind since 1898. Now he turns to a different critique, which we know he must have been engaged with in the summer of that year, as in the letter to his mother of 14 August he recommends Tolstoi's *What I Believe* to 'the Dean' (Michael Furse?) as 'light theology' and describes Tolstoi's Bible scholarship as 'weak'.

The wrong Tolstoi, Calderon continues in 1901, has in effect exploited the 'authority of Jesus Christ for the philosophy which he teaches', as 'he could not have gained all these disciples without the name of the Gospel'. It is 'only fair', then, to examine 'whether his biblical basis is sound'. Calderon looks at six examples of Tolstoi's exegesis in his book *Harmony of the Gospels*, and finds them woefully flawed. In Tolstoi's retranslation of John 1.1 he is 'quite reckless of genders', he censors a verse in Matthew 19 because it contradicts his, Tolstoi's, own views on 'the promise of a future life', he mistranslates a verb in Mark 10.30 for similar reasons, and produces a 'ludicrous note' on another Greek word. Considering the depth of Calderon's education in classical Greek at Rugby and Oxford, one is inclined to believe him in these matters rather than Tolstoi, who 'taught himself Greek at the age of forty-one'.

But now Calderon returned to his main point – the dissonance between the wrong Tolstoi and the right – and went for the jugular:

The system once made, good or bad, it behoved Tolstoi to live by it, if he believed in it. He had declared governments, law and property bad, and it was his duty to eschew the advantages of them. Incidentally he had rejected also tobacco, alcohol and meat. But life was hard with him. His brother-in-law says that, so far from being happy when he had evolved this scheme for the only possible happiness, he became depressed in his spirits. His wife and children had no idea of giving up the property at Yasnaya Polyana and working in the fields for their daily bread. Then, again, he was troubled by visitors. [...] Romantic ladies came – a sort he could not abide – and wanted to 'learn life'; practical ladies came and threatened to blow out their brains if they could not have a thousand roubles on the spot. The wrong Tolstoi says that if people ask for money it is not charitable, but only polite to give it to them; he also says that if people steal things it is because they need them, and therefore have a right to them; but history relates that when these ladies came the right Tolstoi lost his temper and the Countess sent them away.

Tolstoi refused to appear as a witness in a law case, because he rejected the state and would not swear an oath; but he bought himself out of appearing by paying the fine for non-appearance before the court even met. His efforts to give up smoking, as described by the Tolstois' German governess, were 'pitiful' and hilarious. Of an afternoon, she wrote, Tolstoi 'wanders about [...] with a hatchet in the woods'. Calderon comments: 'There is something charmingly ingenuous in the picture she gives of Tolstoi, the amateur Tolstoyite, coming back from the fields with a conscious smile of achievement and the smell of manure about him.' In spite of his Puritanism, he also has a bicycle for exercise 'and even joins the young people in the despised and immoral game of lawn-tennis'.

Clearly, Calderon has no problem with the 'good Tolstoi', the 'real Tolstoi, the kindly old man of Yasnaya Polyana': 'Altogether it is a delightfully human picture, that of Tolstoi, the Squire of Yasnaya Polyana, living in the great house with his Countess, in his sheepskin-overcoat, playing at being a Tolstoyite.' But the 'wrong Tolstoi [...] seems altogether to have missed the charm of the right Tolstoi's whimsicality and weakness, which have in them something of the appeal of a child's helplessness'.

Worst of all, in *The Kingdom of God Is within You* Tolstoi has devised the 'curious theorem', or hypothesis, of the 'Parallelogram of Moral Forces', which has been seized on by his disciples but in reality is only a sophistical let-out from the charge of 'inconsistency' (hypocrisy). If one of the moral forces in our lives is our 'animal' nature and the other 'divine perfection' as taught by Christ, then according to Tolstoi our lives will actually move along the 'resultant' of the two forces and that is the most we can expect. Yet this is an hypothesis that can excuse any 'inconsistency', since the 'animal force' could be extremely large and the Christian force nearly non-existent, yet the 'resultant' would still be acceptable. Further:

The doctrine seems hard to apply to public life. What resultant will the Parallelogram give us in the matter of fighting? Shall we forswear war and settle our quarrels with pitchforks? Or what compromise will the Parallelogram make between the abolition of law-courts and our depraved inclination for justice? Is Lynch-law the resultant?

Finally, Calderon tells us, it is the Parallelogram that explains the 'apparent contradiction' between Tolstoi's condemning women to 'perpetual virginity' in the epilogue to 'The Kreutzer Sonata' (since 'the Christian cannot look upon carnal connection otherwise than as a sin') and his belief expressed in *What Then Must We Do?* that to women is given 'the law of childbearing'. 'Tolstoi means us, of course, to trust to the Parallelogram of Forces for the continuation of the species'!

There can be little doubt that Calderon was right to focus on the cognitive dissonance in Tolstoi's 'system'. As Kierkegaard had written fifty years earlier: 'Most systematisers [...] do not live in their own enormous systematic buildings. But spiritually that is a decisive objection. Spiritually speaking a man's thought must be the building in which he lives.' George had also demonstrated that as an hypothesis the 'Parallelogram of Moral Forces' was fallacious because it could always be proved but never disproved. Like Flat-Earthism or some conspiracy theory, it could be adjusted indefinitely to accommodate belief and practice. No wonder, he implied, it was so popular with Tolstoi's disciples. Although Calderon had not been able in this article to 'set forth the whole bulk of the contradictions which [the disciples] have swallowed', his readers might now be more able to appreciate 'the mental condition of those who, at one and the same time, declare the doctrines of the Church an impious fraud, and complain of the cruelty of the Holy Synod in dissociating Tolstoi from any participation in them'.

Nevertheless, Calderon was determined to leave his readers on a positive note by returning to the 'good Tolstoi', the kindly real Tolstoi whom people genuinely loved as a man of conscience in a society with no moral leadership. Tolstoi, he concluded,

is not a Tolstoyite: he is an amiable character who has somehow strayed out into real life from the pages of *Tristram Shandy* or [Bulwer-Lytton's] *The Caxtons*. And perhaps we who are also not Tolstoyites may consistently be sorry that the Church of his native country – which, no doubt, he loves in his heart of hearts – should have declared war on him. For, separated from his 'system' – and the separation is easy – he is not more unorthodox than thousands in and out of his own country who live and die at peace with their Established Churches, to the comfort of their friends and relatives.

This is, however, a complex denouement. Comparing Tolstoi to an 'amiable character' from a comic novel seems gratuitous. Who are the 'we' who may 'consistently' regret his excommunication – members of the Church of our own 'native country'? Surely there is *considerable* doubt that Tolstoi 'in his heart of hearts' loved the Russian Orthodox Church? Or is it his 'native country' that he so loves, for syntactically it is impossible to distinguish? The inclusivity – 'thousands in and out of his own country' – is particularly interesting, as it may describe Calderon's own 'Tolstoyan' position as an agnostic surrounded by Victorian Anglicans.

This essay has a claim to be the best-informed and most rigorously argued piece of writing about Tolstoi as a 'thinker' before George Orwell's 'Lear, Tolstoy and the Fool' of 1947. And it sparkles with irony, comic timing, verbal economy and a sense of the ridiculous. It is a masterpiece of Calderon's polemical writing.

The metropolitan literati noticed it. On 4 May 1901 the anonymous diarist of the *Academy*'s column 'The Literary Week' summarised the essay and reproduced a long passage from it. Interestingly, he twice used the term 'trenchant' of Calderon's critique, and described the 'account of Tolstoi's experience of his own system' as 'slightly malicious'. This seems to prefigure the problem Calderon had in his later interventions in public issues: his superior knowledge and rigorous thinking were interpreted as personal animosity. Whether because his article was syndicated, or George himself had submitted it to them, it was reprinted in the following month's issue of the American review *Living Age*. But its most sensational reappearance was on 25 May 1901 in Moscow.

One of the indefatigable Olga Novikoff's occupations was sifting the British press for references to Russia (this is how she had talent-spotted W.T. Stead when he was still working on the *Northern Echo*). It was most probably she, then, who alerted Pobedonostsev to George's article. She had known the necrotic Procurator-in-Chief of the Holy Synod for a long time and had direct access to him through members of her family at court. Pobedonostsev understood well the power of the Russian and foreign press, and was an arch-manipulator of both. Tolstoi's excommunication had badly misfired in Russia. Since Calderon's essay was critical of Tolstoi 'the thinker', Pobedonostsev seized on it as a way of defending the Holy Synod's action; and the fact that it was written by a foreigner and appeared in what Pobedonostsev described in a preface as 'the well-known London journal *Monthly Review*' would give it more credibility than if he had written it himself.

A Russian source has claimed that Pobedonostsev translated the article personally. This seems unlikely, as when W.T. Stead met Pobedonostsev, and even stayed with him, they communicated in German. There is no doubt, however, that the translation was made very soon after publication, that it was rushed into print by the Holy Synod's press, and that it was unscrupulously twisted by Pobedonostsev for his own purposes.

He introduced the text thus: 'In the cause of truth and common sense we consider it useful to acquaint Russian readers and writers with [this] article about Tolstoi [...]. Its author, Mr Calderon, has entitled it "The Wrong Tolstoi" ["*Lzhe-Tolstoi* "].' The Russian title, however, is a 'spun' translation that means rather 'The False Tolstoi'. '*Lzhe-*' is a prefix attached to proper names in the sense of 'Pretender', and an accurate translation into Russian would have been '*Ne tot Tolstoi* '. This shift in sense set the tone for the rest of Pobedonostsev's editing. Naturally he had deleted the mention of himself in the first paragraph of the original – and with it almost all of George's irony throughout the essay. Tolstoi's rejection of 'other things by which the Church stands' became 'all that the Church is founded upon'. Calderon's disquisition on the 'earnestness' of the 'half-educated classes' was grossly simplified and the emphasis placed on Tolstoi's pretension to being a 'prophet'. The phrase 'Tolstoi is endowed with genius and piety' was removed. The long quotation about and discussion of the Nicobarese was simplified ('None of them does any work') and a sentence, 'This is Tolstoi's ideal realised', was written in. Half of George's discussion of Tolstoi's political economy was cut, the long quotation from Tolstoi's *The Kingdom of God Is within You* was not given in Tolstoi's original, and a short rhetorical paragraph replaces the whole of Calderon's humane concluding one. Pobedonostsev had transformed the essay into a pamphlet redolent in its crudity and dogmatism of Soviet propaganda.

The question arises, did Olga Novikoff ask Calderon if he would agree to his essay being published in Russia? Perhaps the positive views expressed by him at the ARLS lecture about contemporary Slavophilism imply that he was sympathetic to her beliefs and even knew her? This seems unlikely. She moved in much higher social circles than him – this of course was part of her cachet – and there is no documentary evidence of their meeting at this time. (In November 1904 he and Kittie bumped into her at a restaurant, she 'threw her hands about in ecstasy over her lunch, praised K's profile and wanted to know where I had picked her up', George wrote to his mother.) Russia had no copyright treaty with Britain, so Novikoff did not need to ask anyone's permission to republish the piece. In any case Calderon could hardly have approved of the distorted version in which it came out in Russia. Probably he was deeply embarrassed by it and felt he had been shamelessly compromised. The Russian publication is never mentioned in his extant correspondence.

The *Monthly Review* had been coming out since October 1900. It was edited by Henry Newbolt, the barrister turned professional writer who had shot to fame in 1897 aged thirty-five with his volume *Admirals All and Other Verses*. He seems to have first met Calderon when both were researching at the British Museum in 1898. *Habitués* of the Reading Room gathered for meals at the Vienna Café in New Oxford Street. As Newbolt recalled forty years later, among the 'happy little crowd' there George was 'by nature happier than the rest of us'. They became lifelong friends.

It was probably the success of 'The Wrong Tolstoi' that led to the potentially career-furthering invitation from *Literature* to write a six-page signed article entitled 'Tolstoy's Novels' for an issue devoted to Tolstoi. Before then, however, the household at 17 Golden Square had undergone a complete upheaval – one which may well have affected the quality of the piece Calderon produced.

In the winter and spring of 1901 Mrs Hamilton was very ill. Quite apart from her chronic rheumatoid arthritis, she probably caught bronchitis or a chest infection. Kittie wrote of this time in her memoirs: 'I remember going into her room one evening. "Oh dear," she said rather fretfully, "I hoped you were George." This meant that he both amused her and raised her more comfortably in bed than anyone else.' But Calderon too was ill at this time. He put this and his mother-in-law's sickness down to the fact that they were living at the centre of the Smoke. He therefore set about finding somewhere else. In Kittie's words, 'on a soaking Saturday afternoon' he went out to Hampstead and in the appropriately named Vale of Health found 'the adorable little old house we lived in for so many years – Heathland Lodge'.

Even by Edwardian standards 'little' seems a misnomer. Forming an L-shape over a hundred feet long, it had an imposing stuccoed gable, three smaller gables, a belvedere, a conservatory, a creeper-covered concrete extension that was probably the kitchen, huge leaded windows, expanses of red hanging tiles, and at least twelve tall chimneys and stench pipes. It had been built in the 1860s but made over by the Arts and Crafts architect George Birch in the 1890s. The Vale of Health, it seems, was just becoming popular with the professional classes, so Heathland Lodge was not cheap: the freehold cost £3500, which would be well over a million today using average earnings. Mrs Hamilton provided £2500 of this as a mortgage and the rest probably came from the will trust of Archie Ripley managed by his brother William, a solicitor in Norwich.

It is easy to see why the Calderons were so pleased with this house. It faced southwestwards and the 'range' that they lived in was filled with light. In front of these quarters was a large sunny garden. Yet the house was secluded, being at the extreme edge of the Vale and not inviting on the side by which it was approached. It also had direct access to the Heath, which was ideal for walking their dogs. Living and working in Heathland Lodge you were in an enclave within an enclave.

They finally moved in around November 1901. On 30 August George wrote to his mother from the British Museum: 'We are *still* not finished yet at Hampstead: we still have painters and carpenters all about us. But we begin to see the end', implying that much had to be done to get Heathland Lodge how they wanted it. 'Kittie works hard too, putting a lot of mind into the decoration of the house and garden. She is swallowing Robinson on the Flower Garden in great gulps.' The latter was William Robinson's encyclopaedic masterwork *The English Flower Garden and Home Grounds*, which he had given her that month inscribed 'Kittie from Peter'. This was probably the first garden Kittie had created; although she had undoubtedly learned a lot about the subject from Frederic Lubbock, the creator of the gardens at Emmetts (now a National Trust property), who had employed Robinson himself.

'Tolstoy's Novels' came out on 31 August 1901. As a piece of writing it is the opposite of 'The Wrong Tolstoi'. It is eclectic and does not present a closely reasoned argument. There are strange errors. *War and Peace* is termed for part of the article *Peace and War* and Bezukhov unaccountably referred to as Bezuchi. The first work Calderon discusses is 'The Cossacks', which Tolstoi subtitled 'long short story' – a distinction George might have profitably analysed. Given that the article displays a good knowledge of Tolstoi's biography and the secondary literature, he must have known that Tolstoi himself insisted that *War and Peace* was not a novel, either; but this is not addressed. In fact there is little in the article specifically about the novelistic elements of the works referred to. Some of its flaws may be the result of very poor editing: Traill had died in 1900 and no-one's name appeared as editor on the masthead of *Literature* ever again. Perhaps George had had to cobble this article together in haste from his previous writing on Tolstoi, and in the process of moving home.

However, if the article has a proposition about Tolstoi's novels it is this, stated in its opening paragraph:

As the world is an unsatisfactory affair from almost every point of view, the great novelists have all agreed in being discontented with the greater part of it; and the thing in common between them all is satire – discontentment barbed with wit. Tolstoy has been more dissatisfied and therefore more satirical than any.

Tolstoi, we are told, is 'a satirist' and the 'chief value' of his novels lies 'in the presentation of the world at large, […] in the satirizing of thousands in the person of typical instances'. Yet the sense in which Tolstoi 'satirises' is not considered. Clearly his novels are not 'satires' in the sense that every element in them is organised to ridicule aspects of the world outside them. Yet if Calderon meant 'satirise' in the loose modern sense of a *tone*, one of criticism merged with derision, this too hardly applies to Tolstoi. Tolstoi's technique is rather to undermine, devalue and degrade his victims in such careful 'realistic' ways as to deceive us about what he is doing. Calderon does allude to Tolstoi 'reading his dismal doctrines' into his characters and 'filling them with his own arrogant and repellent creed, that all other men and women are swayed only by the will of the flesh', but his view of Tolstoi as fundamentally a 'satirist' remains superficial.

It is also disappointing that Calderon presents Tolstoi's male heroes according to a simplistic typology drawn from Russian journalism ('superfluous men'), interprets works biographically ('Nechliudov […] is no other than Tolstoy himself'), and forces on them conventional wisdoms about Russian social history. It may be true that one of the aims of *War and Peace* is 'to picture the beginning of the new national life, to show how it rose bright and fresh […] while the mincing shadows of the old French life vanished into disrepute', but that is not its novelistic heart and it seems strangely inadequate to describe it as 'mere narrative without *arrière pensée*'. Projecting onto *Anna Karenina* the 'disillusionment which followed on the Liberation of the Serfs' and viewing it essentially as 'satire of society at large' is even less adequate. Calderon does not begin to analyse the tragedy of Anna (or Vronskii, or Karenin). He does not show any awareness of the complexity with which the moral issues are actually laid bare in the novel, despite Tolstoi's own epigraph and demonization of Anna. Calderon appears to accept it as a straightforward *roman adultère*. He does not even broach the extraordinary grasp of social life and the emotional understanding of men, women, children and even animals that Tolstoi displays and inducts us into as readers. There is no appreciation here of the existential intensity and ambivalence that we value today at the heart of Tolstoi's novels. Almost the highest accolade Calderon bestows is the quintessentially Edwardian 'charming' (four times).

Nevertheless, he does have some perceptive, and witty, things to say. Referring to *War and Peace*, he writes:

Tolstoy is, above all things, a good hater. He wants to lower Napoleon, his chosen enemy, in the eyes of the world. The ascription of his successes and failures to Fate is a splendid humiliation; there is such a crushing moderation about it.

And George goes on to show how inconsistently Tolstoi applied the hand of Fate to the French and Russian armies, and how close Napoleon's own recorded view of a good general was to the qualities Tolstoi ascribes to Kutuzov. He also draws an original and thought-provoking analogy:

Tolstoy is one of the few artists who is able to paint a whole family on a single canvas, with all their nice differences of character, so that not a figure could be taken from the composition without marring the whole. In this faculty he most resembles Jane Austen.

Calderon rounds off his article on 'Tolstoy's Novels' by discussing the short 'peasant stories, half realism, half fable', in which genre 'Tolstoy stands almost alone'. These demand 'unusual powers', since they are in competition with 'the folk-stories handed down from mouth to mouth – [...] the work of generations of narrators, cutting and polishing old tales, which survived through the centuries only by a process of the severest natural selection'. In his concluding sentence he describes one such tale, 'The Three Old Men', as 'one of the most classically perfect works of art ever produced in any medium'. This suggests that Calderon felt more at home with works of this length than *War and Peace* and *Anna Karenina*, whose 'design' he found lacking in 'a balance of proportion'.

One could not conclude from this article that Calderon was a literary critic. It contains *aperçus* but no sustained literary apprehension. Despite being one of the first overviews of Tolstoi's fiction up to *Resurrection* (which appeared in English in 1900), it has been forgotten, which 'The

Wrong 'Tolstoi' has not. Calderon never wrote a signed article for *Literature* again.

However, the following month, September 1901, the *Monthly Review* published an exemplary article by him on Vladimir Korolenko. Yet again, his departure point is Tolstoi:

> In Russia as in England, the great novelists have passed away. Tolstoi remains as a monument of the past: but Tolstoi has put fiction from him, with all the other vanities of this wicked world. Still, in this new generation there are some notable men, and perhaps most notable of all is Korolenko. He has not the great novelists' gift of even skill over large canvases, but some of his small canvases come very near perfection.

It is intriguing that Calderon has chosen Korolenko as the 'most notable' of the 'new generation', considering that Chekhov is incomparably more original, by 1901 had been at the height of his powers for several years, and Calderon owned copies of Chekhov's major works. But Korolenko, who was seven years older than Chekhov, was certainly a major prose-writer of the previous generation and had influenced Chekhov himself.

Having given a perceptive potted biography of Korolenko, Calderon plunges straight into one of Korolenko's most famous short stories, 'Makar's Dream', which he aptly describes as 'a prose epic of destiny, containing the essence of all that [Korolenko] had thought, seen and felt while he lived among the half-breeds of the Yakut district'. He very skilfully retells the story, varying the narrative with comments of his own and translations of two long passages, and concludes:

> Over whatever depths of pathos or poetry Korolenko carries his readers, from time to time he plumbs the waters with some line of humour that serves to show them just how far below lies the hard ground of their everyday mood. Grand and touching as is the scene of Makár pleading before the throne of justice, the reader has always before him the […] log-hut, the big scales, the angel-servants listening open-mouthed in the doorway, the old priest twitching Makar's coat […]. Its realism, its Yakút anthropomorphism, contrasting with the sublimity of the subject, give it a humour that drives the pity of it right home.

Next Calderon compares a number of passages from 'Makar's Dream' in its anonymous 1892 English translation with 'What Korolenko Says'. This is an unrivalled way of engaging with the actual style of a writer, since translation itself should involve a very close reading of the original. Unfortunately, the conclusion is that, 'unconstrained by any bonds of reverence or taste', Korolenko's English translators 'hew' his carefully constructed stories into 'shapeless masses', 'paraphrase his language as they go', and 'debase the style to the standard of fifth-rate English fiction'. Calderon's analysis is a sobering reminder of the crass awfulness of many English 'translations' of the time (even, for example, of *Anna Karenina*). The editing and self-gratificatory ad-libbing that they practised are astounding. Calderon was undoubtedly right as well to lambast their 'ignorance of common words and common objects' and their sheer amateurism:

It would be tedious to enumerate the occasions on which the translators call birches 'beeches', sedge-warblers 'sparrows', etc. Yet one would have thought that if they were not better at guessing, they might at least have looked the things up in a dictionary.

What George omits to mention is that the passages he labels 'What Korolenko Says' are translations by himself. They are accurate, very sensitively phrased, and because they incline to literalness they always evoke the sensation of reading a writer in an 'other' language. They certainly suggest that if Calderon had taken to translating the Russian classics he would have been greater than Constance Garnett. The fact that he singles out a French translation of Korolenko because it is 'literal, correct, and complete', suggests that the latter were his own translation values too.

From here he proceeds to describe Korolenko's 'methods' as a writer, including his use of 'raw material' stored in notebooks (it would be interesting to learn how he knew about this). He examines other key works of Korolenko's, makes short critical observations, for example 'a Russian critic has remarked a certain quality of description which Korolenko shares with Dickens. There is more restraint in the Russian writer', and illustrates them with his own translations. Finally, he attempts to explain why Korolenko has 'to some extent disappointed the hopes which he raised by his work in the eighties'. He is essentially a Slavophile and 'a *naródnik* or student of "the people"'. He has 'given too much time to observation and not enough to creation. He has internationalised his pity for "the people"' and become a human rights institution. It is difficult to disagree with Calderon's conclusion. He had written a model of how to introduce readers to a writer whom they cannot read in the original.

Calderon's final contribution to the *Monthly Review* in 1901 was possibly his most brilliant. 'Dobrynia: A Russian bŭilina' was published in December. A *bylina*, as we would write it today, is a long narrative poem of the kind that arose 'in the neighbourhood of Kiev some thousand years ago', as George put it in his introduction, and is sung. One of Newbolt's ambitions for his review was, in his own words, 'a desire to bring about a change in the estimate of Poetry then held by the reading public'. To achieve this, he was more interested in publishing long works than short. In his memoirs *My World As in My Time* (1932) he makes it clear that he was so proud of printing Calderon's 'Dobrynia' as of other long poems by Binyon, Bridges, and Yeats.

As a common noun '*dobrynia*' means 'a kind, straightforward, simple-hearted man', but it also became the Christian name of one of the most popular heroes of the *bylina*'s, Dobrynia Nikitich. Calderon explains that there are 'many variants' of the Dobrynia poems and he has 'compounded' his translation from them. This in itself moves his translation towards original creation, although he still insists it is 'literal'. Calderon had come across the *bylina*'s in the course of his Russian folklore research, which was now in its sixth year, and he presumably knew them very well. He gave a brief account of how they were collected and written down in modern times, then added this paragraph:

For the interpretation of the poem here given, readers may follow Vsevolod Müller, who believes it to be no more than a corruption of a certain Turkish tale; or Orest Müller, who regards it as a sun-myth. For Dobrynia is a dragon-slayer like many sun-gods, and in this poem the speculative may find a solar allegory in his rapid flight over the earth at evening, like the rays of the sunset; and they may find a likeness to Apollo in his skill upon the cittern.

Evidently, by 'interpretation' Calderon did not mean 'literary' but 'ethnographical'. These lines probably give an accurate insight into the *magnum opus* he was labouring on. Whereas we might have expected him to discuss the astonishing verbal beauty of these *bylina*'s, or the counter-suggestible complexity of Dobrynia's personality, or the sheer grace with which the female characters are presented, he appears to be offering the poem as an object of anthropological speculation. Footnotes later 'interpret' events in 'Dobrynia' such as the gift of an arrow from a woman to a man and the 'crowning' of bride and groom.

But if the contextualisation and apparatus of Calderon's translation are academic, the poem he has produced on the page is not. We cannot compare it with a single original, so we cannot verify that the translation is 'literal'. He claims more for it, however, than that: 'My object has been to preserve the spirit as well as the body of the original, by imitating as far as possible the manner of the telling, according to the different genius of our language.' This may seem contradictory. The 'spirit' of the *bylina* is only perceptible through its 'body', i.e. the characteristics of its verse, and Calderon departs from the most fundamental one: the original is iambic and anapaestic, with no set number of stresses to the line, but he opts for a strict trochaic tetrameter. Yet the polysyllabic 'body' of the Russian language is lithe enough not to slow the pace of each line in the original, and Calderon is right to feel that this pace can only be retained in English with a shorter, less polysyllabic line. Moreover, although *bylina*'s rarely use exact rhyme, preferring assonance, repetition, morphological similarity and parallelisms, Calderon reproduces these effects faithfully with English equivalents:

> From the midst came young Dobrynia,
> Came Nikita's son Dobrynia.
> Deeply, deeply had he drunken
> Of the Rhenish and methaglin:
> Yet he stood and never tottered,
> Yet he spake and never stuttered.

In addition, he reproduces the pauses for breath in the *bylina*'s, the indented refrains of lines, and even internal rhymes. Consequently the 'translation' reads fast, but has a vocal architecture like the originals. It is also effortlessly archaic in its diction:

> Sadly, sadly wept his mother,
> Timoféyevna Mamélfa,
> For her darling son, Dobrynia,
> Till her face was wan with weeping,
> And her eyes were dim with greeting.

In short, although the 'translation' starts out from a precise, even academic knowledge of the source language, it is completely oriented to its 'target language': it is a brisk, absorbing, exhilarating read in English. As Newbolt appreciated, Calderon had produced an English poem in its own right.

The only problem was, Calderon's contemporaries automatically associated the trochaic tetrameter of his version with Longfellow. As someone (judging from the handwriting, it may have been Ellis Minns) wrote on a Cambridge University Library copy of the published text:

> There is too much Hiawatha
> In the art of this translator,
> Making simple Russian ballads
> Sound like modern Yankee metres,
> Yankee metres by Longfellow
> (Coming out in many volumes...)

Yet this was much more of a problem for contemporaries than it is for us. Imitations, parodies and cantata settings of *Hiawatha* were then ubiquitous. Like Longfellow himself, Calderon knew that the Finnish epic *Kalevala* was composed in a form of trochaic tetrameter and judged it appropriate for translating *bylina*'s, which are emphatically not ballads. It is a pity that he did not imitate the *Kalevala* more: the monotonous feminine ending of every line of his translation is certainly contrary to the 'genius of our language' and not a feature of the *bylina*'s either. However, he avoided the plodding trochaic rhythm that contemporaries associated with *Hiawatha* by rarely having lines containing four full stresses, and especially by 'scudding' the first foot. As in the originals, the line he produced in his translation is actually what Russians call *gibkii*, i.e. flexible and attuned to a voice. It is essentially dramatic and suited to public declamation, which was again appropriate to a *bylina*.

This was Calderon's *annus mirabilis* as an independent Russianist. No-one in Britain published such a variety of original, deeply researched work in this field in 1901. However, we have to remember that at least two of these publications had been drafted four years earlier. What was he writing in 1901 that was *new*? On 30 August he wrote to his mother that he was 'working away pretty hard, besides my routine Museum work; but I am not writing anything'. Presumably the 'pretty hard work' was his continuing research for *Demon Feasts*, but what stage that was at remains an enigma.

The situation changed dramatically in the new year. On 26 March 1902 Cecil Rhodes died. Within ten days the British press was publishing rumours about the contents of his will. It was leaked that Rhodes had endowed a system of generous scholarships for students from the British Empire, the USA, and Germany, to pursue courses of up to three years at Oxford University. Media speculation was so febrile that the indefatigable W.T. Stead edited the will for publication and brought it out in June 'with elucidatory notes to which are added some chapters describing the political and religious ideas of the testator'. This confirmed that the Rhodes Scholarships were being set up.

It must have been at this time, then, that Calderon took to Reginald Smith of Smith, Elder and Co. the idea for *The Adventures of Downy V. Green, Rhodes Scholar at Oxford* – and Smith recognised a winner. Americans were topical, the Rhodes Scholarships were topical, even Oxford was topical because a public debate was raging over whether Greek should be dropped as a condition for admission. Above all, the book to which George's title alluded, Cuthbert Bede's *The Adventures of Mr Verdant Green, an Oxford Freshman* (first published in three parts 1853-57) was a perennial favourite with the reading public and would give Smith's advertising a following wind. George was an 'Oxford man' and could be relied upon to know his subject. Finally, and quite exceptionally,

Calderon offered to illustrate his book himself, just as 'Bede' (Edward Bradley) had done. Perhaps he showed Smith his 'cartoon book' to prove he could do it. Smith signed him up, but obviously the book had to be written as quickly as possible if it was to take full advantage of its topicality. It appeared in the second week of November 1902.

Astutely, the book opens by parodying the first page of the original and establishing Downy Verdant Green's ancestry. His paternal grandfather was the hero of Bede's book, who became a high court judge, Calderon tells us, because he had 'that indefinable quality so essential in a judge [...] a certain freshness, and ignorance of matters of common knowledge'. His son Tony discovered 'a secret for the preparation of soap from petroleum' and emigrated to America to make his fortune from it. There he married Miss Angelica Downy, 'a penniless New England beauty', and it is Downy V. Green's maternal grandfather who reads about Cecil Rhodes's will and proposes his grandson apply for one of the scholarships to Oxford.

Here it is worth noting an ambiguity in the name Downy. One might assume it is just a plausible surname taken, say, from the photographers W. and D. Downey who were responsible for celebrity portraits including that of Rhodes in the front of Stead's publication. Without the 'e' it could imply that this Verdant is so green he is still covered in down. But it could also play on a contemporary slang meaning – 'knowing', 'canny'. This Calderonian paradox is, in fact, central to the book. Old Man Downy has made a meticulous analysis of the qualifications needed by a Rhodes Scholar and concludes that they amount to 'thirty per cent for knowin' Lattun an' Greek, an' the other seventy for bein' tall'. Downy V. Green *is* tall, and has 'a natural imperturbability of countenance – which the Americans catch from the Red Indians – [that] made him look wiser than he really was'. His grandfather withdraws Downy's name from the contest when the local press starts digging out the dirt on candidates' family history; then when 'none of the candidates but Downy had a shred of character left' he pops back in to take the Scholarship. Similarly, Downy's grandfather, who is to accompany him to Oxford, cannily insists that they learn Bede's original by heart, because it 'contains a keerful study of the ways an' manners of the young Britisher at Oxford, and invaluable disquisitions on the institootions of the place'.

Once in Oxford, however, the Downies discover they are sometimes too 'knowing' by half. Old Downy is convinced that the British, and Oxford dons in particular, are 'not men of business', but he discovers the Master of his grandson's college obsessed not with Greek particles, as in Cuthbert Bede's day, but with share prices and property. He tries to 'bargain' with him over his grandson's rent, but fails, and even has to sign a bond for £200 that the College has instituted for Rhodes Scholars 'for our own protection'. At this point he decides to 'vamose the beef-run' back to the States, with the parting advice: 'Recollect you come of the conquerin' race. Recollect we've taught these Britishers most everything they know.'

That evening in hall, Downy discovers that Oxford undergraduates no longer dress in 'a shaggy jacket with saucer-buttons, and trousers of three-inch check' as Bede had depicted and Downy copied; 'the prevailing fashion in Oxford was one of almost ostentatious simplicity'. He also learns that it is absolutely not done now to shout for your scout to bring you a drink. Downy is 'sconced' for this, i.e. punished by being brought 'a quart pot full of beer'. But he turns the tables on his companions by draining it in one, which means that *they* are all sconced. This is a pattern that recurs throughout the book. Downy is not just green, but capable. At a breakfast given by the President of the College Rowing Club (modelled on Calderon's Trinity contemporary Hugh Legge) Downy is the only student present who knows who Cardinal Newman was. Downy's natural vigour and candour make short work of 'smugs', whom he defines as 'low-spirited prigs' and who include a temperance Christian, wine bores, and poetasters.

Although these early chapters are pungent and obviously based on Calderon's own experiences at Oxford (his illustration of the college breakfast features caricatures of several contemporaries and himself), the most important relationship in the book is between Downy and a family of other Americans. Chadbank Cheney is another Rhodes Scholar, but he has been able to bring the rest of his family with him to Oxford because the scholarship is so generous. In chapter eighteen he invites Downy to 'a little tea-romp up [at] my wigwam', to meet 'the whole caboodle'. A Dr Robinson has also been invited, who is 'one of the leading champions of the cause of Greek'. Discussion over tea turns to what Cecil Rhodes

expected his international scholarships to achieve. Robinson has no
doubts: 'Oxford is the representative of a – a very high form of culture;
and Mr Rhodes evidently wished the world to participate, so far as they
were capable, in that culture.' But Mrs Cheney vehemently disagrees:

> 'Then you think you're goin' to civalise the world?'
> 'That is surely the only way of looking at it?' [Robinson replies]
> 'No sir! You've gotten hold of the wrong end of the toastin' fork this time. [...]
> The object of Cecil J. Rhodes' Will is to civalise Oxford by the infiltration of the
> Ameracan element. Turnin' out pore imitations of the trash that some coloured
> folk down South scribbled on sheepskin two thousand years ago [she means
> Homer] is not Civalisation. Civalisation is Life: livin' better, doin' better, thinkin'
> better. And that's what I do not find in Oxford. No, sir; Oxford will need some
> tittavatin' before you can make it the hub of the Universe. [...] If you want to see
> Civalisation, go to Ameraca. Look at our Cahnstitootion, look at our Trade! Look
> at our overhead railways, steam-heat, and hydrahlic ullavators in the poorest
> quarters! [...]
> 'But surely, my dear madam, you don't mean to say that this is the ideal of
> civilisation to which we are to aspire?'
> 'No, sir, I do not. It is the bed-rock on which you have to plant the scaffoldin'.'
> 'But all the things you speak of represent only the material.'
> 'An' ef you can't manage the Material, what business have you to be foolin'
> with the Ideel?'

Over the next four pages Mrs Cheney expounds her own philosophy of
education, derived from Dr MacGuffin of Goober Valley's *Outline of
Mindology* ('Mindahlagy, she pronounced it'). As a result, Downy
conceives a great admiration for her – 'a re-markable woman'. He is never
far from her family for the rest of the novel and she introduces him to its
only love-interest, the parasol beauty Miss Ada Shelmerdine.

   Perhaps the turn to the security and practicality of the Cheney family
mirrors Calderon's own adoption of an American family at Oxford, his
own education at 'fair American hands', as he described them. Might the
photo (by W. & D. Downey) of a middle-aged American-looking lady
amongst Calderon's Oxford papers be of a matriarch who adopted him,
and might the 'typical American girl' described as Miss Cheney be her
daughter?

In his discursive review of the novel, Newbolt concentrated precisely on the positive impact of the Americans on Oxford. He pointed out that in George's 'ingenious frontispiece' an academically attired Britannia 'sits at the receipt of nations' with the motto '*Qui docet discit*' ('He who teaches learns') above her head. At Oxford, Downy decides to 'give Greek another chance'. 'We too, at this rate, shall soon be giving Greek another chance', Newbolt continued. 'Under the wholesome stimulus of American contradiction – if it is to contradict that they are coming – we shall experience a revival of faith, we shall realise that man does not rise by ullavators alone' and the 'first and best of the things [Oxford] will be taught will probably be a keener love of learning and especially of classical learning.' Calderon's illustrations were compared to Kipling's and both authors accused of 'raising the standard of authorship to a height beyond the reach of ordinary genius' because they drew as well as they wrote.

Other reviews were lavish in their praise of the book's humour and George's knowledge of American. 'Primarily intended to amuse, and really amusing', wrote the *Athenaeum*. A long piece in *The Times Literary Supplement* described it as 'full of overflowing spirits and laughter'. 'It is one of the best bits of fooling we have read for a long time, and is written by one who knows Oxford perfectly, and has a command of American slang which Mark Twain himself might envy', the *Daily Telegraph* told its readers, even claiming that it 'deserves as wide a vogue as its predecessor "Verdant"'.

The book was a hit. Within less than a month Reginald Smith was writing to Calderon to tell him that a second impression was imminent and returning 'the drawings', which had 'fulfilled their mission admirably well'. Mary Cholmondeley, author of the 1899 bestseller *Red Pottage*, had just published *Moth and Rust*, which was also well received, and wrote to George: 'How nice for you and me to think we have written the two books of the season!!!!!!!! Cockadoodle-*doo*!!!' She invited him to come 'straight on here from the Museum' next day, to 'dine with us quite informally in morning dress'. Kittie had probably known the Cholmondeleys for some time through Nina: like the Corbets, they were an old Shropshire family.

Much of *Downy V. Green*'s success was undoubtedly due to what the *TLS* reviewer called 'a perfect carnival of American slang'. Phonetical spellings and colourful expressions abound and the Edwardians evidently found them screamingly funny. The *New York Times*, however, commented that 'the writer is by no means a master of the American dialect. His "Mr Downey [*sic*] Green" talks after the manner of "Sam Slick" – a manner which never had any resemblance to anything American'. Calderon would not necessarily have disagreed. What he had actually done was take the knowledge of American that he himself had acquired from American friends and combine it with phrases from a book of American slang (he collected such books) to create an artistic language that no American ever spoke but which was as hilariously grotesque as, say, Brobdingnagian.

Unfortunately, the topic of American Rhodes Scholars was a fleeting one and slang quickly ages. The book went into at least three impressions, but its popularity was short-lived, even amongst Trinity College alumni who thought they possessed the 'key' to its characters. It is possible, however, that *Downy V. Green* is the ultimate source of the successful film *A Yank at Oxford* (1938) and its remake *Oxford Blues* (1984). Today the book on which its 'idea' depends, Cuthbert Bede's *Verdant Green*, is itself not widely known. Amongst Oxonians, however, the latter is something of a cult text, and it seems that this continues to benefit George's sequel. Although there has not been a completely new edition of *Downy V. Green* since 1902, four different print-on-demand versions are currently on offer on the Net and several copies of the original in the States.

But Bede's and Calderon's books could not be more different. In many ways they are characteristically Victorian and Edwardian respectively. At about 135,000 words, Bede's had to be printed in a small font to fit into 350 pages, whereas at a mere 40,000 words Smith decided to print Calderon's in large type with wide line-spacing and generous margins, and it covered 184 pages. Bede's illustrations were scratchy, full of hachure and realistic detail. George's are smooth and continuous in line, with minimum detail and maximum white space. Whereas Bede revelled in prolixity, Calderon was limpid. Bede took an almost Dickensian delight in detailing the food, drink and tobacco that his heroes consumed; although these feature in *Downy*, they leave no taste or smell. Whereas Mr Verdant Green took a healthy interest in milliners and barmaids, and nearly a third of Bede's book is devoted to his courtship of the pert young Miss Patty Honeywood, whom he marries whilst still a student, Downy falls at the very end of Calderon's book for a thirty-five-year-old 'dizzy blonde' and 'bachelor-girl' who says only two words and whose face George has not shown us in his illustration (only her minute stippled waist).

In fact, it is the feeling of emptiness, coldness and sterility about *Downy V. Green* that puts some modern readers off. There can be no doubt that Calderon intended to produce this feeling, however, and that it is characteristic of a certain style of Edwardian humour. It is the void beneath the surface that one associates with Juvenal, but also, say, with Swift's treatment of the Houyhnhnms, or with Evelyn Waugh (whose own illustrations have similarities with George's). At the Oxford of *Downy V. Green*, the literary club The Upas Union is named after a tree that kills everything around it, meetings of the philosophical Swipes Club break up as soon as the earthenware pot containing the beer is turned upside down empty, and the 'selectest club', the Kaloikagathoi ('Beautiful and Good People') is so vacuous that Downy refuses their invitation to join it. As if to stress an essential sterility about the tease Ada Shelmerdine, Mrs Cheney tells Downy that she 'ain't the sort men marry, let alone boys'; she is not only a 'bachelor-girl', but a 'college-widow'.

The unsettling 'black holes' in *Downy V. Green* are satiric negation, whereas Bede always remained the sympathetic Victorian humorist. Yet Calderon's book is not 'a satire' either, as it is not always satirical. The laugh is by no means always on the American hero, because he also learns from his life in Oxford. Perhaps then, as the frontispiece suggests, *Downy* is about education, particularly in an age when, as Newbolt put it, the Americans were 'coming'. It is a kind of satiric Bildungs-novella.

By the end of 1902, it seems, Calderon was pretty tired. Although Heathland Lodge was commensurate with Mrs Hamilton's expectations – and she was obviously paying many of the running costs – it was beyond her daughter's and George's means. Kittie therefore wrote in November 1902 to Constance Sutton for advice about selling her pearls. Constance,

Nina's sister-in-law, had been married to one of the richest men in England and four years after his death she married Hubert Astley, who was also from a wealthy family. As well as Dick Sutton (now aged eleven), she had borne Philip Astley in 1896 and Ruth Astley in 1900, who was another of Kittie's godchildren. In a fifteen-page reply from Italy, Constance therefore proposed 'lending' Kittie £500-800 'on the security of your pearls' which she felt her daughter Ruth might wear in 'another 15 years'. This sum, Constance wrote, was 'lying idle in the Bank – and bringing me no interest – so that I shall not in any way be the loser'. In fact it was enormous: over a quarter of a million pounds today in terms of average earnings. 'I am afraid,' she wrote, '"George" will consider this the most abjectly unbusinesslike and womanish letter he has ever had to digest!' She had ordered a copy of *Downy V. Green*, incidentally, and enclosed the *Daily Telegraph*'s review. It is not known whether the Calderons went ahead with 'pawning' Kittie's pearls in this way.

Christmas 1902 was probably when they began the 'institution', as Kittie called it, of inviting George's brother Frank's family round for the day from Hampstead. This included his children Philip (aged nine) and Joan (aged six). They arrived at ten in the morning and in Kittie's words 'by 4.30 a charade of real quality had to be produced and performed before a large audience of all our friends who had children and some who had not'. Philip Calderon, 'a particularly good actor', and Joan were 'capital collaborators'. Whilst George was dressing in the morning, he would 'evolve a plot', and by the time they arrived 'it would be sketched out on half a sheet of paper'. In the morning and afternoon this would be worked up into a whole play complete with 'topical verses written of course on the spur of the moment by George and sung to some easily picked up and remembered tune'. Calderon played the 'central character holding all the strings and leading the others into saying exactly the right thing', and Kittie supplied the costumes, illustrated the programme, and was stage manager. It was a 'really remarkable performance' and sometimes repeated at Frank Calderon's later. Evidently, although the Calderons had no children of their own Heathland Lodge was the hearth of a truly family Christmas. After Christmas, George and Kittie may have visited the Lubbocks at Emmetts, or other friends in the country.

Despite these relaxations, in the new year Calderon took an irrevocable decision: he was going to give up his job at the British Museum. On 7 February 1903 the Keeper of Printed Books, G.K. Fortescue, reported to the Principle Librarian that George 'desired' to 'retire' on 28th. The word 'retire' is perhaps intended to convey that he was not so much breaking off his employment as completing three years.

Kittie's memoirs, however, tell a different story. Since moving into Heathland Lodge, Calderon's routine had become to get up 'very early' and walk the dog, then 'bath, dress, breakfast' and leave for the Museum, return late in the afternoon, possibly 'play a quick game of crazy croquet', then 'rush off to work till Dinner', after which he would work a third shift in his study until Kittie made herself so 'disagreeable and disturbative' that he had to give up around eleven. 'As it was', she wrote, 'he had not the physique to stand it.' They both 'hoped giving up official work at the B.M. would make all the difference'.

At the same time, when George had spoken in 1891 of Russian being 'a subject with a future' he had surely not envisaged that after investing ten years of his life in it he would be a 'Second Class Assistant', as the *London Gazette* put it, in a library. It was a far cry from his once-ambition to teach and research in a Russian, or British, university. He must have felt that the British Museum post had served its purpose well, but was a dead end for him.

Yet presumably there was also a positive factor in his decision, namely that he *wanted* to concentrate on creative writing and finishing the anthropological work that could make his name. How he and Kittie could afford for him to give up salaried employment is another matter. Kittie earned something as an occasional publisher's reader and editor, particularly of children's books, and George could have taken up technical translation again and provided journalistic services on Russian matters, but there is no evidence that he did. He probably made a useful sum out of *Downy V. Green* – this was the 'golden age' still for authors and publishers – but obviously that would not last long. Perhaps, then, Kittie did sell her pearls, or pawn them to Constance?

There is no doubt that Calderon had been valued at the British Museum. Fortescue wrote fondly of him to Kittie in 1906 and regretted that he was not able to accompany George on a restorative cruise. Calderon's colleague Robert Nisbet Bain, who was fourteen years older than him, presented him with copies of his translations *Tales from Tolstoi* (1901) and *Tales from Gorky* (1902). Calderon was highly qualified in his field, humorous of course, and ineffably courteous. He also made friendships with eminent Slavists visiting the British Museum. One of these was Paul Boyer (1864-1949), holder since 1891 of the first chair in Russian at the École des Langues Orientales in Paris and the man who had taught Minns his Russian. Boyer wrote to George in Russian from Yasnaya Polyana on 10 September 1902, reporting that Tolstoi was 'well and in very good spirits and working like a young man'. A letter in French from Boyer dated 15 November 1902 suggests that they knew each other well enough to have discussed intimate issues.

Boyer had asked Calderon 'an indiscreet question: one of those that we are sometimes rather embarrassed to ask men of your nation'. It seems to have been about English social and sexual *mores*. In his reply, which has not survived but which Boyer called 'a veritable act of moral consultancy' exposing 'the state of mind of today's Englishmen', George had written that in both areas of intercourse Englishmen display 'modesty' but have a 'secret "tother thing"'. One wonders what exactly he was referring to. Boyer proposes that this is not 'hypocrisy', but 'a natural reserve'. In view of George's own comments about French stage plays later, it is interesting that Boyer believes the 'translations of French vaudevilles acted on the London stage [...] are an embarrassment to everyone' as the English find their titillations 'either boring or disagreeable'. Calderon and Boyer exchanged publications, Boyer visited the Calderons when he was in London, and as we shall see George had a substantive discussion with him about the *magnum opus* when he was in Paris in 1905.

Kittie's phrase about 'giving up official work at the B.M.' suggests that after the end of February 1903 Calderon carried on working there in an 'unofficial' capacity, i.e. as a reader and presumably on the *magnum opus*. But in March he embarked on two other literary projects.

The first was published in the April 1903 number of the *Monthly Review* under the title 'The Obstinacy of the Romanovs'. Although short, it is crucial for understanding Calderon's political stance on Russia. He does not seem to have ventured into print on the subject again until 1914.

On 11 March Nicholas II proclaimed what is known in Russia as the 'Manifesto of 26 February 1903'. This aspired to foster religious tolerance, improve the 'material position' of Orthodox clergy, financially help peasants to break away from their communes – although 'the fundamental principle of property in common is to be held inviolable' – and spoke very vaguely of 'reform [...] by local representatives in provincial government and district administration'. According to the *Daily News* of 13 March 1903, in Russia itself the manifesto was 'held to proclaim the advent of a new era of self-government [...]. It is considered to be the most significant Act of State since the Imperial manifesto on the emancipation of the serfs'. Even a modern Russian historian believes 'its traditionally grandiloquent style cloaked an unambiguous hint from Nicholas that his aspiration was to create a popular legislature, a State Duma' (Kulikov, 2012). Whatever the truth of this, Calderon's point was that British newspapers were interpreting the manifesto as proof that

the Tsar's belated country is going to mend its ways and make a beginning of conforming to the Western system of social life known as 'Civilisation'. Nicholas II is pictured as yielding at last to the humanising influence of the 'Anglo-German Tsaritsa', shaking off the baleful spell of that 'grim fanatic', M. Pobedonostseff, dealing a death-blow to the Orthodox Church [...].

This is the Western form of compliment. Not one word, however, of the manifesto itself seems to justify the belief that Nicholas is going to Westernise his country. Quite the contrary.

Calderon had no difficulty in showing that 'in each separate article of his manifesto Nicholas makes clear his rejection of Western methods', for instance of parliamentarianism. The manifesto was in his view 'a counterpart in home politics to what the Peace Conference was in foreign politics; both are expressions of the Slavophil scheme of national life'.

Yet this was not the nub of George's article, either. He now urged his readers to accept that Russia was 'different', that it had a political culture of its own:

It is natural enough to thank heaven that we are Britishers; but it is wholesome at times to try and realise that there are other civilisations in the world, and that in their poor way, and for the poor folk that are born into them, they have a *raison d'être*. It is unjust to picture the Tsar as a benighted Oriental potentate, scion of a house of tyrants, waking at last from Asiatic sloth, as he listens to his German Sheherazade telling him what is being done in the Western world. The Romanoffs have seen and rejected our civilisation since Romanoffs were. They have borrowed our mechanical arts, but never our social order.

He even claimed, with justification, that 'English opinion of Russia' was 'educated chiefly by exiled revolutionaries, yet it might be surmised that many Russians actually approve of the system under which they live'. We in Britain might live under a form of democracy, but if 'we never tire of abusing the faults of our civilisation', from the 'evils of our political system' to slums and the 'licence of the press', what was so superior about it? Our Parliamentary system was not even representative, since 'in each constituency there is a large minority, the unsuccessful party, which has no representative in Parliament at all'. This notion is 'abhorrent to the Russian creed of justice'. The Tsar, according to Calderon, 'sits for minority as well as majority, and for the Country as well'; consequently 'theoretically there is much to be said for the autocratic system'.

This was superbly provocative, but purely declarative. It foreclosed discourse. It led nowhere. The problem is one very familiar to modern culturologists. To understand a country we must 'go into it' as deeply as possible, we must study every aspect of how its people feel and think. But if that is all we do, it risks becoming merely a descriptive academic pursuit and we ourselves risk becoming merely 'acculturated'. As Mikhail Bakhtin pleaded, we must 'come out of' the foreign culture again, back into our own, in order to view the other culture critically, to have something new to say about it, from our own point of view; indeed for any discussion ('dialogue') about it to be possible.

It was admirable that Calderon should be stressing the 'differentness', the 'autonomy' of Russian political culture, but what from his cultural point of view *was* the 'much' that was to be said for autocracy? What reservations lay behind that word 'theoretically'? He seems to have found the Russian system disastrous when he was living there. What of the many

Russians who *wanted* western-style democracy? Were they wrong? If the British 'never tired' of criticising aspects of their own political life and society, was that not precisely what democracy was for? Calderon's determination to pursue acculturation in this article led him to what some might regard as a characteristically paradoxical extreme: he claimed that 'serfdom was an Anglo-Saxon institution imposed upon Russia by a usurper, and abolished a few years before the Anglo-Saxons gave up keeping slaves', but he never told his readers who this 'usurper' was or when serfdom was abolished in England.

The article ended extremely lamely:

This is less a plea for admiration of the system than an endeavour to explain how it may justify itself to its upholders: partly it is a protest against a habit of gauging every foreign civilisation by an inapplicable British scale of 'progress'.

Calderon had lost his way in this piece because he could posit no value for 'coming out of' cultures again in order to respond to them critically from one's own angle. Nor had he considered the question of 'universal' values, political or otherwise. Finally, his apparent acceptance of the Russian, supposedly Slavophile system, left him vulnerable to misrepresentation by its propagandists. In later parlance, he looked like a 'fellow-traveller'. He risked being used by Olga Novikoff and her ilk in the political sphere as he had been by Pobedonostsev in the religious.

Calderon's other project in the spring of 1903 was his novel *Dwala*. Since its hero is a 'missing link' between apes and *Homo sapiens*, it may have been conceived in 1902 after he read and annotated the copy of *The Origin of Species* given him by Kittie for his thirty-third birthday, and then read *The Voyage of the Beagle*. He also annotated the sections of the Tertiary and Human periods in his copy of Geikie's *Text-Book of Geology*, which, he recorded inside, had been given to him by 'Canon Ripley 1902'. On 29 August 1903 he wrote to his mother that he had finished 'two thirds' of *Dwala*. In a letter to Kittie in October he wrote that he had heard 'nothing from Smith Elder', so presumably it had been submitted to them some time earlier, perhaps before he left for Paris at the very end of September.

He went to Paris to accompany Kittie's nieces May and Kittie Hamilton to a 'charming house in a St John's Woody suburb', where they were to improve their French. He himself had business, perhaps of a Slavonic nature, in the Bibliothèque Nationale. He introduced himself there 'as a colleague', but it availed him nothing: he was passed to a 'decrepit imbecile of 45 in the "administration" who gave me futile advice', and ended by telling this person that 'if *he* came over to the British Museum he would not have such things said to him'. He was also reading 'a dismal life of the Comte de Chambord written by an imbecile Royalist, with a view to my play'. Presumably the latter was historical, but nothing more is known of it. On the evening of 2 October he went to see Puccini's *La Vie Bohème*, which seemed to him 'as imbecile a travesty of the book as it is possible to construct'. Evidently, the madhouses of Paris had been opened specially for his visit.

The following day he was invited to the Boyers, where he at last met 'the mysterious wife', Russian and five years younger than Paul Boyer. Calderon was soon in his element and had a 'delightful evening':

We sat at a table and drank tea à la russe, and smoked cigarettes, and talked incessantly, also à la russe, altogether – about endless subjects leading nowhere, never ending – socialism, royalism, riches, poverty, democracy, functions (social etc) of women, etc. etc. till eleven o'clock.

Boyer's habit of frank discourse seems to have been perpetuated, as he asked 'whether there were any children arrived or on the way: my coming alone seemed to portend accouchement, I think'. Calderon does not say what his answer was. He accepted an invitation, however, to dine with them '*tout à fait sans cérémonie*' two days later, even though this meant selling his ticket for a performance of Beaumarchais's *Le Barbier de Séville*, 'which I should have adored to see'. In a gentle dig, he wrote to Kittie that on 4 October, it 'being Sunday, I went twice to the theatre', where he saw Sophocles's *Oedipus Rex* and 'a mad farce in four acts with ugly women and charming men'. The farce involved a male sharing a bedroom with the heroine disguised as a soldier, and much business with a 'pedestal', which seems to have been a portable chamber-pot cupboard. 'Things vulgar which shock us in England', George wrote Kittie, 'are really very amusing – why exclude them? […] laughing, I realised how there is entirely no reason for being ashamed of being amused.' On the other hand, along with the Louvre and Notre Dame, the list of places he had 'not been to' included 'Moulin Rouge, Folies Bergères […] Variétés'.

By 5 October he was beginning to find his time in Paris 'what one might call tedious'. Evidently he did not have to take May and Kittie Hamilton back with him, so he soon set off for Emmetts, the Lubbocks' home in Kent, where his own Kittie was already staying.

This was the second break the Calderons had taken in six weeks. The first had been four days in Norwich at the end of August and its circumstances are revealing. Working long shifts at his desk, Calderon had decided, in Kittie's words, that 'hard manual labour would do him good'. Every afternoon, therefore, he worked with the gardener at Heathland Lodge to 'level a sloping lawn so as to make an almost full-sized croquet-ground'. 'He used to work like a navvy […] wheeling barrows of earth – they made the lawn level but it was far too heavy work and only helped on that approaching collapse.' 'I got that exhausted', he wrote to his mother on 29 August, 'that we had to go and have a change.' Doubtless, whilst in Norwich they had visited Canon Ripley, who lived with his son William, Kittie's solicitor. They had seen Archie's father twice, then, within a year. Probably they also visited Earlham and Archie's grave, and possibly this is when Calderon painted a watercolour of Earlham's south front matching one by Archie from the 1890s.

They had not been back from Emmetts ten days, when the Corbets' heir, Vincent, died at Eton of appendicitis aged thirteen. He had been a page-boy at Kittie's wedding in 1895. She went to join Nina at Acton Reynald and was present at the interment in Moreton Corbet churchyard on 22 October 1903. George did not go, but wrote a letter of comfort to her the day before:

My dear Kee, You will get this just about the time of poor little Vincent's funeral. That over they will be able to settle down to a dull progression of getting used to it; a feeling of finality. The great thing to go on is certainties. One thing certain is that a sweet and definite little personality has existed, and is so much to the good; whatever is lost in the future, the past is not lost and is all pure gain – the loss of the future is a miscalculation of the unknowable. The past remains, unspoilt by any of the chances of maturer life. Any comfort that can be found more than that verges into uncertainties. Clerical comforts will not stand abrupt strains: it must be with survivors as it is with people dying; they suddenly doubt the clerical comfort – so a parson has told me, so far as concerns dying people – though certainly he put it in the form of a sudden onslaught of the Devil. Every man and woman must have onslaughts of Agnosticism when brought closely face to face with the hard fact.

This letter follows the pattern of many of Calderon's personal responses to boundary situations: it opens with 'full-on' statements that could even seem offensive ('dull progression of getting used to it'), but grows increasingly engaged and moving. The first section echoes the rationalism and agnosticism that we saw in his letters from Eastcote. It was bound to irritate Kittie, and after the last sentence she actually wrote on the letter: 'Yes, but the Love of God asserts itself to the inner consciousness at such times – not our faith – but the power of God and his love. K.' Possibly she wrote this response long after, when she was re-reading his letters, and Calderon never saw it. However, he continued:

Give Nina my very best love and sympathy. Vincent presents himself to me most vividly in his bedroom, just in bed, me visiting him – I think by invitation; perhaps not. Eagerly playing the host, entertaining me, keenly watching me, hoping he could please: showing me his Waverley novels – pointing the way to them rather, from his bed – asking me how I liked the wallpaper, which he had chosen; sorry when I went; blinking in a quick way when the words were trying to pour out.

Through its combination of tentativeness and eidetic recall, this description enacted what Calderon had written in the previous passage, namely that 'the past is not lost': his own words had brought Vincent 'alive' again for his reader.

Whatever he was working on in the autumn of 1903, we may be sure that Calderon's social life was busy. Not only did he and Kittie regularly entertain their relations living in or visiting London, as well as passing Russianists such as Boyer and the literary historian Semen Vengerov, by now they had made many friends in Hampstead itself. Chief amongst these were William and Alice Rothenstein, who lived at 26 Church Row.

Here the Rothensteins gave suppers for a group of artists and writers that included Augustus John, Max Beerbohm, Joseph Conrad, H.G. Wells, W.B. Yeats, James Pryde, and W.H. Hudson. Calderon probably met most of these through Will Rothenstein, although there is documentary evidence only of Rothenstein and Beerbohm attending what the former called 'the Calderons' enchanting parties at the Vale of Health'. These parties might include 'pot cricket' and croquet on the lawn of Heathland Lodge, and were generous with food and wine.

Both Rothenstein and George were early risers. They often met for walks on Hampstead Heath. As Rothenstein recalled:

Above all else Calderon loved discussion, deeming the spoken word greater than the written one. With his friends, and, since I was so near a neighbour, with me perhaps most of all, he daily practised dialectics. [...] He and I went for long walks over the Heath, discussing art, ethics, literature, politics, religion, folk-lore – there was nothing about which Calderon could not theorise brilliantly. [...] Tolstoy's pamphlets still troubled me; Calderon, who admired Tolstoy's novels – no-one without knowledge of Russian could appreciate the force and splendour of Tolstoy's prose, he would say – didn't approve [of] his later writings. He foresaw the disintegrating menace of revolutionary tendencies everywhere at work. A settled authority was needed, we agreed, that we might be free to do our work; work suffers when men become too political.

According to Rothenstein, 'Calderon sometimes annoyed people who didn't understand his character, by waving, so to say, a red flag in their eyes; he annoyed Conrad.'

Possibly Conrad was intrigued to meet George as a collateral descendant of the European dramatist whom he read and admired: in 1896 he had used Pedro Calderón's line from *La vida es sueña*, 'Man's worst crime is that he has been born', as the epigraph to *The Outcast of the Islands*. But given Conrad's family hatred of the Tsarist regime and the fact that he understood Russian radicalism far better than Calderon did, he may have regarded George as a naïve apologist of a 'Slavophile' autocracy, although this does not seem to have led to a rift between them. In Rothenstein's words, Calderon also failed to arouse any response in A.E. Housman. I remember how Calderon, after meeting Housman at our house, remarked, as I accompanied him downstairs: 'Well, William, so far from believing that man wrote *The* [*sic*] *Shropshire Lad*, I shouldn't even have thought him capable of reading it!'

It is generally believed that Rothenstein became one of George's closest friends; possibly the closest after the death of Archie Ripley. Rothenstein was also extremely fond of Kittie, to whom on her birthday in 1904 he presented the original of his portrait of the Liberal politician John Morley – conceivably one of her heroes as he supported Irish Home Rule.

But how close were Rothenstein and Calderon really? As Michael Holroyd finely analyses in his biography of Augustus John, Will 'sacrificed himself' for a vast range of people because he felt he 'lacked the mysterious spirit of charm' and the gratitude he earned from them was 'a substitute for the love he felt he could never attract'. The effect that this apparent self-ingratiation had on some of Will's 'friends', for instance Augustus John, was downright anti-Semitic. But with their cosmopolitan backgrounds, both Conrad and Calderon knew and understood Jews, and there is no evidence that their lifelong affection for Rothenstein was anything but sincere. As we shall see, Rothenstein stood by George and Kittie closely during the biggest crisis in George's life.

Heathland Lodge also fed and encouraged a number of young people, particularly Percy Lubbock. He had miscalculated in his plans to apply for a fellowship at Cambridge and been obliged to take the Civil Service examinations, which he passed. On 26 December 1903, from the midst of a family Christmas at Foxwold Chase in Kent, he wrote to George and Kittie:

I don't know if my dolorous piece of news has reached you – but anyhow it is this – the brutes have given me a place in the Education Office and I start there next Saturday. I can't view this calmly. But you are two of the very few people who will send me sympathy and not congratulations. [...] I can't really in my heart of hearts feel convinced I am right in doing what it implies – and that is giving up indefinitely my one ambition, which is to be one day (a good long way ahead) an artistic writer.

The idea of sitting at an office desk 'looking over applications for new fireplaces in village schools' was 'BEASTLY in a way that you will understand, though so dreadfully few people do'. He needed their advice and moral support, so 'Shall I come to lunch Thursday?'. Obviously, this was a subject that the Calderons understood well. Possibly they also sent him to see their friend Mary Cholmondeley, as a fortnight later he was writing to tell them that 'a conversation of about two hours with Miss Cholmondeley' had 'beautifully helped me to make up my mind' to leave the Civil Service 'next Jan. 1, 1905 at latest'.

We know from an hilarious red-ink letter written by the twelve-year-old Dick Sutton to 'Auntie Kittie' on 30 December 1903 that around this time 'Mr Kalderon' had been ill. Whether this was a specific illness or some side-effect of overwork, is not known. By March 1904, however, he was certainly suffering from exhaustion, as that month he took what seems to have been the first of his lifelong series of recuperative sea-voyages.

Why was he exhausted? A plausible hypothesis is that since completing *Dwala* he had thrown himself into one intensive language course after another. *Demon Feasts* seems to have been particularly etymological in approach. He therefore needed to delve into one Indo-European language after another. In Percy Lubbock's words, he tackled each 'with a zeal that was as methodical as it was devouring'. He 'surrounded himself with grammars and dictionaries, filled a notebook with a new vocabulary, and rehearsed it on a system mathematically calculated to lodge it in the memory within the shortest possible time'. He took a copy of *Chambers's Etymological Dictionary of the English Language* (568 pages), had it rebound in three volumes with a blank page between each pair of printed ones, then went through every entry in it supplying synonyms in numerous languages on the facing pages. He was constantly learning lists of words, starting with his morning shave. Anyone who has undergone an intensive language course knows that six weeks of this is about as much as you can take. Calderon was inflicting it upon himself for month upon month. In this way he covered at least Flemish, Italian, Spanish (of which he had known little before), German and some Sanskrit, to add to his existing knowledge of French, Latin, Greek, and five Slavonic languages.

Perhaps it was necessary to undertake this grinding mental labour. But when could he say he had 'learnt' that particular language and dialect? This part of his project risked becoming self-perpetuating. In all his occupations before resigning from the British Museum, he had had his work structured by others' deadlines and timetables. He had had no experience of being, as it were, full-time self-employed. Perhaps, therefore, he now failed to structure his working-time himself. It is tempting to feel that occasionally he was expanding his work as an 'independent scholar' to fill the time available. The combination of Parkinson's Law and his innate tendency to go at things 'like a bull at a gate' might drive him to exhaustion, if not worse. The only remedy was to take the work away from Calderon, or Calderon away from the work. Kittie and he decided on the latter and bought tickets for him on the *S.S. Shropshire* from Liverpool to Marseilles on 31 March 1903, and on the *S.S. Warwickshire* from Marseilles around 11 April. The need to go must have been urgent, as he surely knew that *Dwala* would come out whilst he was away.

On the train journey to Liverpool there was a bonus: he shared a compartment with the 'Rani'. 'Very pleasant and composing', he wrote Kittie from the ship, 'with Mrs D's eyes opposite – talking of death and duty and writing and the uses of squires and artists; I filled her with piety, such as I had.' Dowdall himself was 'thin and harried; touched with an insanity of worldly push'. Calderon spent forty-five minutes at their house, during which Mary seemed to him 'like [W.H.] Hudson's humming-bird at rest; rather dull and dark and different'. Before the ship left he continued to Kittie: 'The people aboard look quite possible; not a greater proportion of semi-idiots than usual.' And this is all we know of his experiences or itinerary on the cruise. The *Warwickshire* was returning to Tilbury, and from Portland on 15 April he posted Kittie a letter and some notebooks: 'You'll find my diary in these books – not very amusing, not very delicate and decent – not a thing for young people like Mrs Ham to be let see.' Like all the other notebooks he kept on his travels, it has been lost. Ominously, he signed the letter 'Your Peeky Wee [Man]', a formula he used sheepishly about himself when he felt the worse for wear.

Arriving back at Heathland Lodge, Calderon found three reviews of *Dwala* awaiting him. The first, which had appeared in the *TLS* a week before, was the worst and potentially the most influential. The book exhibited 'in parts a fine dashing reckless cleverness', and was even 'brilliant […] in an odd, baulking sort of way', but it was 'a book of brilliant beginnings which sputter out'. 'Lady Wyse the social "monster", Hartopp the tyrant-beggar, Prosser the burglar-valet' were all undeveloped, the reviewer (A.B. Walkley) complained: 'Evidently Mr Calderon has a fresh invention in fantastic caricatures; but when they are once invented he has no further use for them.' In a letter to Kittie probably written whilst George was still away, Percy Lubbock suggested that this view had 'some justice'. (We shall return to it.) But the reviewer's overwhelming thrust – one might say obsession – was that *Dwala* was an attempt to 'improve on a classic', viz. Thomas Love Peacock's *Melincourt*, which features an unspeaking orang-utan elected to Parliament. Calderon had 'forgotten', as Peacock did not, that Dwala was 'an ape', and made him into an 'interesting Oriental' who becomes 'a Saviour of Society', turning the book into 'a wild hodgepodge of social and political satire which does not arride us'.

This is completely misguided. There is no evidence that George had ever read *Melincourt*, and Dwala is explicitly not an ape but the Missing Link who has to evolve fast into 'an Englishman, a Londoner'. As Lubbock put it to Kittie, 'the [reviewer] *is* an ass'. We should also note in passing that 'hodgepodge' is one of the original classical meanings of the word 'satire'.

The other two reviews, which appeared on 16 April 1904, were in journals. The *Spectator* dismissed any resemblance to *Melincourt*, or to H.G. Wells and G.K. Chesterton. In *Dwala*, it wrote, Calderon had 'plunged […] into the deeper and more dangerous waters of tragic-comedy' and his 'meaning' was 'to illustrate the slenderness of the barrier that divides the primitive man from the most elaborate product of civilisation'. Nevertheless:

when it is impossible for the reader to tell whether he is meant to laugh or cry, he ends by doing neither. Mr Calderon's method is too sketchy to be impressive, his satire too anarchical to be convincing. One rises from the perusal of *Dwala* bewildered and dismayed by the misdirected expenditure of so much talent on the working out of a fantastic plot on lines which nothing short of genius could render engrossing.

The *Athenaeum*, however, paid tribute to the subtlety with which George conducted Dwala's metamorphosis from Missing Link to 'Man', even concluding that 'one of the marks of the soundness of the workmanship is the fact that, to the very end, a sort of grotesque pathos attaches to the figure of Dwala. It is a daring, original, and very clever piece of work'.

There is little doubt that with *Dwala* Calderon intended to make the leap from comedy to full-blown satire. It would tally with his increasingly intellectual ambitions as a writer and observer of the British body politic. Even in 1901 he was becoming over-concerned with Tolstoi as a 'satirist'. There is evidence that around the time of writing *Dwala* he re-read *Gulliver's Travels* and Horace. If *Dwala* was conceived as satire, then, how successful is it as satire?

The main criticism levelled at *Dwala* was that it was jumbled, 'unfinished', and even 'anarchical'. A brief summary of its narrative will bear that out. It opens with a long chapter set in Borneo in which we are introduced to the hominin that his American captor has been educating as a man. We watch the hominin returning to the jungle when he learns that he is to be taken by a menagerie to London in his old cage as the Missing Link. This is a highly accomplished piece of writing in the realistic novel style, complete with crackling Yankee dialogue. The second chapter is less than four pages long and presents an encounter between the hominin and 'the Panther' in a symbolistic, almost expressionist style. After this the creature wanders into the village of the local tribe, who are seeking a saviour from the European gold-diggers currently invading their forest. This gives Calderon scope for some admirable anthropological burlesque. However, dramatic dialogue almost disappears at this point and the narrative turns from showing to telling: 'The old king was promptly clubbed on the head [...] Politically speaking, the result of all these events was that the war party had captured the machine.' The hominin is proclaimed the new king, given the name 'Dwala' ('Him-of-Two-Names'), but taken prisoner when the British army is called in to 'pacify' the natives. These events are narrated in such generic language as to resemble fable.

But with the arrival of the Liberal 'pro-Boer' M.P. Mr Wyndham Cato, who has conceived the mission of persuading the Foreign Office to set 'Prince Dwala' up in London in a style befitting his royal status, dialogue returns in plenty and the narrative style plunges for long stretches into that of the comic social novel. There is a proliferation of characters from the social elite with bizarre names: Lord Griffinhoofe, Pendred Lillico, Baron Blumenstrauss, Warbeck Wemyss, Captain Howland-Bowser, Sir Peter Parchmin, Mr Disturnal... The text teems with contemporary and even personal references: the 'Eastern Question', an 'Aerated Bread' shop, Sherlock Holmes, 'R[othenstein], the artist', a charwoman called 'Mrs 'Amilton, who washes the steps, pore thing, of a Saturday'... Even so there are sudden switches from novelistic realisation to bald narration and commentary; very short chapters are suddenly interpolated; other chapters present 'non-events' as in *Downy V. Green*. Above all, three lower-class characters are introduced – a kleptomaniac, a conman, and an orphan – who it seems the novel could easily dispense with, yet they remain to the end. Dwala becomes Prime Minister, with his 'Aegeria' Lady Wyse he pulls the country out of its collapse following the 'Great Crisis' and 'Famine', but unbeknown to him he is already infected with the disease of modern metropolitan man: tuberculosis. When his memoirs are stolen and sold to the press, the secret of his origins and the fact that he has a tail is out. In a menagerie van he is hustled onto a steamer bound for Borneo, but dies before he can get there. These events are narrated at breakneck speed, almost perfunctorily, but at the very end a long, slow passage intervenes describing Dwala's burial at sea, and the novel ends with a limpid, abstract paragraph for all the world like a 'moral'.

One can understand the bewilderment of many readers at the apparently chaotic switches in style, plot and tone in *Dwala*; its 'messiness' and 'inconclusiveness'. Yet this is the very essence of one form of satire – the *lanx satura*, or 'medley', that Juvenal even termed 'farrago'. One of the most common adjectives used of this kind of satire is 'Protean'. The satirist has constantly to do the unexpected, even at the risk of appearing anarchical, otherwise the 'dullness' of his victims will overwhelm us all. The 'satiric plot', Alvin B. Kernan has written, is characterised by 'disjunctiveness'. It 'violates narrative lines', in Michael Seidel's words, and 'satiric action is a kind of bad seed'. 'An extraordinary number of great satires are fragmentary, unfinished', Northrop Frye pointed out. Who remembers the ending of *Gulliver's Travels* or is satisfied by the ending of *1984*? Similarly, one of the hallmarks of satire is that character is deliberately not 'developed'.

In terms of these features *Dwala* is brilliantly satiric. However, a satire must attack something, manifestly attack it, and it is not easy in the case of *Dwala* to see what that is. The exposure of the 'socialist' conman Hartopp and the high society do-gooder Lady Lillico is extended and complete, and the portrayal of politicians, civil servants and society types is always amusing, but there is no sense of what essentially is being objected to beneath the surface. In a true satire one would expect to have been compelled to this sense by the author's all-pervasive irony and skills of indirection. Instead, we are *told* rather explicitly at key moments what the 'problem' is. Dwala's objection to the lounge lizard Pendred Lilico is that 'he has no eye' and Calderon explains the meaning of this over two pages using philosophical terms. In fact the phrase is a devastating judgement on most of the humans Dwala encounters in London society (basically it means '[lacking] a consciousness of individual independence'), but we have not been brought to perceive this ourselves. We are told that the Great Crisis and Famine that bring England to its knees do not arise from

any cynicism in the ruling classes, but from our system of government itself. The evil begins in the polling booth, where men are elected, not to sit for England, but to sit for a party or for local wants. The interest of the nation is the only interest unrepresented in the House of Commons.

But we have not been persuaded of this ourselves by the play of irony and satiric wit, we merely have the author's word for it. In fact, for a satire there is a disconcerting *lack* of irony and indirection in *Dwala*. There is also a lack of self-irony, which permits Calderon to commit sentences such as: 'The stately innocence of Nature grew lovelier in a sudden trouble of virginal consciousness.'

However, with an eponymous hero who is originally an example of *Pithecanthropus erectus*, there is a strong overarching sense of allegory about *Dwala*; and successful allegory has often been at the root of great satire. The 'two names' that 'Dwala' signifies appear to be not so much 'ape' and 'man' as 'animal' and 'human'. How, then, do these two natures interact with the other forces in the novel?

The *Spectator*'s reviewer missed the allegory when he concluded that *Dwala* illustrated 'the slenderness of the barrier that divides the primitive man from the most elaborate product of civilisation'. London civilisation, with the exception of Lady Wyse, is shown as entirely lacking in atavistic vigour. Its politicians are etiolated, vacillating, and third-rate. Dwala takes intensive deportment lessons and throws himself into 'the distractions and pursuits of the best society', but the 'animal' part of his psyche has not been superseded. With the instinct of the animal he can assess immediately whether a person has 'eye', as he has himself. We are told that as he rose through Edwardian society 'Man' thrust names and attributes on him, but these were merely a mask for the 'real naked Nature-given personality' that he possesses and to which 'Man's eyes [are] blind'. This seems to be the *political* import of the allegory. We do not know precisely what Dwala's 'Great Policy', 'New Charter', 'new Civilisation' and 'New Humanity' as Prime Minister were, but we are told they amounted to a 'revolution' and that this flowed from his 'hectic strength and clearness', an heroic animal vitality that unites the electorate round it. In Lady Wyse's word, the last thing their policies will be is 'dull'.

By the end of *Dwala* its target has become the fissiparousness of contemporary British politics. Undoubtedly this reflects upper-class impatience with the splits in the Liberal Party over the Boer War and the Empire, and in the Conservative government over Free Trade (which is alluded to). But in the last fifty pages of the novel Calderon seems to attribute these failings to 'Democracy' itself. The concluding paragraph reads:

There is no remedy for the errors of Democracy; there is no elasticity of energy to fulfil purposes conceived on a larger scale than its every-day thought. Other systems may be purged by the rising waves of national life; but Democracy is exhaustive.

The somewhat Bergsonian terminology seems to suggest that British politics needed an injection of Dwala-like 'vitalism'; and in fact contemporaries felt that it was time for 'new blood' to bring both parties into the twentieth century. But the lines quoted earlier about 'men' being 'elected, not to sit for England, but to sit for a party or for local wants' directly connect with Calderon's challenging words in his 1903 article about the Romanovs: 'It is the fundamental idea of autocracy that the Emperor sits for minority as well as majority, and for the Country as well, a constituent not represented in our Parliament.' Was he, then, advocating a form of 'autocracy' to cure Britain's ills – a 'one-nation' dictatorship perhaps?

If so, it is disappointing that he never considered the extension of suffrage instead. In 1904 only about thirty per cent of the adult population could vote in parliamentary elections, and they were men. *Dwala* itself satirises the elitism of national politics at the time, but there is no suggestion that broadening the franchise would improve the situation; inject new 'vitalism' into it. Nor does Calderon consider Proportional Representation. Nevertheless, it should be noted that Dwala is *elected* Prime Minister, and after his zoological exposure he resigns in favour of a Government that will presumably call a General Election. Thus although Calderon attempted in *Dwala* to think outside the 'box' of Democracy, he never abandoned its fundamentals.

Dwala is not a coherent satire, but it is satire. Its mishmash of genres eminently qualifies it as modern satire. The cinematic jerkiness of its text may even qualify it to be called 'modernist' satire. Of all twentieth century satire it most resembles Aldous Huxley. There is a similarity in the formation of characters' names and in the science fiction (or fantasy) that sources both authors' narratives. Huxley's *After Many a Summer* is similarly predicated on a single 'scientific' fantasy, and as in *Dwala* its denouement is celebrated as 'a joke'. Given that Aldous Huxley's father was a reader and editor for Smith, Elder and Co., and Kittie had dealings with him, it is even possible that Aldous read *Dwala* as a young man. *Dwala* has an honourable place in the cult worlds of 'Prehistoric' and 'Lost Race' fiction. The parallels between *Dwala* and Kafka's report by a 'civilised' ape to an Academy (1917) are intriguing, and the 1979 film *Being*

There, starring Peter Sellers as Chauncey Gardiner, reproduces the paradigm of Dwala's rise to supreme power.

But *Dwala* is now an extremely rare book. In recent years it has even disappeared from online catalogues of print-on-demand specialist publishers. Yet the more one reads it, the more provocative and enjoyable it becomes. One should relish the element of sheer play in its rapidly changing focus, style, and tone. For Calderon himself did not take it too seriously: in his letter to his mother of 29 August 1903 he described it as a 'penny novelette'!

The book was dedicated to Kittie, who must have found the portrait of the London *beau monde* entertaining, and she did her best to promote it amongst her friends and literary contacts. Percy Lubbock gave a copy to his college contemporary E.M. Forster, who may be the source for the remark quoted in Percy's letter: 'It is a book that makes the ordinary "intelligent criticisms" more wretchedly beside the point than usual.' Percy hoped it would sell well, 'yet I somehow feel that for it to be a success would stultify it really'. Although palaeontological expeditions to find the 'Missing Link' featured in the newspapers of the time, *Dwala* did not have the up-to-the-minute topicality that had launched *Downy*; and few people understood its political message – what Lubbock went so far as to call 'the extraordinary hard concentration of thought' in it.

Realising that the reviews so far had done *Dwala* few favours, Calderon sent a copy to Joseph Conrad, who occasionally wrote literary criticism and was an admirer of Anatole France. But on 2 May 1904 Conrad replied from Pent Farm that he was 'groaning under a grievous burden of arrears of work; and I want to read your prose with a free mind. Therefore I have not yet opened the book'. No review by him appeared.

At a party thrown by Kittie at Heathland Lodge, Rothenstein praised *Dwala*, Max Beerbohm 'expressed agreement, and she, delighted, plied him with questions, wishing to know which parts of the book he most admired'. But Rothenstein adds that 'Max' had not in fact *read* the novel… One senses, even, that the Calderons' friends were embarrassed by it. Perhaps they had not expected him to produce social satire so near their bone. On 7 May, however, the *New York Times* described *Dwala* as 'an elaborate satire', credited Calderon with having 'devised a new theme for a story', claimed that the book had made 'a decided sensation' in London, and predicted 'a large sale'. In June the *San Francisco Call* told its readers that *Dwala* was as 'diverting' as *Downy V. Green* had been.

Dwala went into a second edition in 1904, but unlike *Downy V. Green* it did not make a third. Possibly Calderon was disappointed. In its review of *Downy* the *Daily Mail* had said 'he has it in him to become a humorist of the first order'; but he had higher pretensions. After a satire on the whole of English society, where could he go? He never published another novel.

In the summer of 1904 he threw himself back into his anthropological project. It was possibly at this time that Lubbock spent a day with him, recalling that

The morning was given to a correspondence with a professional 'thought-reader', whom he had fallen in with somewhere and whose imperfect system of remembering everything about everyone he had taken to improve; the rest of the day being devoted to a minute tabulation of the different dialects in the poetry of the Walloons.

This seems to suggest a loss of perspective on the research subject itself, as well as on the amount of reading, concentration and memorising that it needed.

On 11 July Calderon wrote to his mother mentioning three visits to Heathland Lodge by a doctor. This was probably Albert Tebb. He was Mrs Hamilton's doctor, but it is just as likely that these visits were to attend to George himself. Tebb had a practice in Hampstead, treated the working class at the Hampstead Provident Dispensary, specialised in TB, but was also a master at treating the neurasthenic breakdowns of artistic people, including Conrad and Hueffer. In the middle of September 1904 Tebb and his three-year-old son Christopher joined Calderon on holiday in northern France, and it is clear from George's letters then that he was suffering from nervous problems.

Kittie and he appear to have gone over to Cap Gris Nez in the first week of September accompanied by Archie Ripley's one-time employer W.H. Gray. They stayed at the Hôtel de la Sirène in an idyllic spot on the sands and a professional photograph was taken of them in front of the long ridge of rocks still visible in the bay today (Fig. 11). Around 8 September Kittie returned to London with Gray, leaving George at the Grand Hôtel at Wimereux. From here next day he wrote describing a performance of Delibes's opera *Lakmé*, which was partly based on Julien Viaud's Tahitian novel *Le mariage de Loti*. Considering George's own encounter with Tahiti two years later, it is interesting that he could not 'sit out' the performance. He wrote Kittie vignettes of the other English guests at the hotel, drew caricatures of them, and claimed preposterously:

I just saw Mrs Ham (I am sure it was her) going hand in hand with a sailor in a sou'wester into the water and being jumped up and down by him among the breakers. I didn't like to call out to her, as it was the first time I saw her in these clothes.

Calderon's daily letters to Kittie from here are the longest series to have survived from him anywhere on holiday. They are packed with fluently expressed news, observations about the people around him, opinions, and scenic descriptions. They fully justify the comment in her memoirs that he wrote 'never a dry word' to her.

On 10 September Calderon was back at 'La Sirène', and the Tebbs arrived there that evening. 'Tebbie' had evidently paid a visit to Heathland Lodge before leaving, as he informed George that 'Mrs Ham [...] thinks you [Kittie] and me very silly to risk our lives by coming and staying in a "house built on the sands"'.

On 11 September 'R.L. Napoleon Stevenson' left the hotel. 'He told me he was going; his time was up', George wrote Kittie, 'but M.Lormier [the proprietor] rolls his eyes and says "Je l'ai mis à la porte!".' Dramatic M.Lormier!' Unfortunately the cook went to see 'Stevenson' off, stayed to 'go on a spree' with him, and M. Lormier had to dive down to the kitchen at the last moment and 'improvise a dinner for us all'. (The real Stevenson had died in 1894.)

Calderon and Christopher built 'a castellated fortress' and 'sand boats', whilst Tebb 'peered about in his distracted spectacled London way among the rocks; catching shrimps by ones and twos, with his trousers tucked up, in the pools'. Otherwise, Calderon's main occupation seems to have been reading French novels. Through the 1890s and 1900s he bought paperback

Fig. 11 W.H. Gray, Kittie and George Calderon, 1904

editions of Balzac, Daudet, Viaud ('Loti'), Maupassant and others, and had them bound in an identical style. One that he read at Cap Gris Nez was Flaubert's *Salammbô*. He wrote Kittie a frank critique of its language, but was impressed by its visual images and generally 'glad' to be reading it. In a letter to him, Kittie criticised the women in Bernard Shaw's *Plays Unpleasant* (1898) for being monsters. He responded:

It doesn't matter to me whether his women in his plays are 1st rate or 2nd rate. [...] He is writing of Ibsenists and the like. He is not representing well behaved or ill behaved women, but elements of character. [...] A playwright's personages, it seems to me, are not individuals or even types, but characteristics embodied; and if a single characteristic embodied makes a personage who is unpleasant to a well-educated mind, it's the fault of the characteristic. By representing only 'nice' women etc one would get no forrader; they are not plastic; they could not be moulded about a moral idea. I hope to make some monsters before I have done.

This is interesting for his view of 'a playwright's personages' at the time, but also for indicating that he was still intent on writing plays though none he had written so far had been staged or has survived.

One way in which Calderon had hoped to relax at Cap Gris Nez was by sketching and painting. Kittie had painted some rather heavy water colours of the bay whilst she was with him, and he bought himself materials in Wimereux after she left. But by 15 September neither Calderon nor Tebb had 'made any sketches' and there seemed to be a 'social' problem about Calderon painting in public: 'I have enquired of the Patron, what effect my blouse would produce; the answer is doubtful; I have hardly the courage to wear it.' At some point, however, he managed to complete a fine watercolour looking inland through the dunes. Telegraph posts and wires span the entire middle distance, but are very lightly touched in. The washes of sky and dune are far more delicately laid than Kittie's, and the overall effect is intriguingly abstract and contemplative.

In his letter to Kittie on 17 September Calderon compared the Patron's need to 'quiet his stormy nerves' by drinking cups of limeflower tea, with his own relaxed condition: 'For my nerves, the place is enough; [...] the silent sunshine on the hills, titillated by the purring waves and the rare

sounds of the fishermen and the seawall builders.' But on 21 September he
was writing to her in an unstable hand:

Undermined by a 3 day habit of waking before daybreak my nervous system went
pop at midday yesterday – but only a little pop. Bromide and bedroom and
chauffe-pieds ensued, absolute indolence on the terrace, sleeping draught at night.
Odd, isn't it? in such a healthy place.

His plan was to leave for Boulogne that day and cross the Channel the
next:

Everything here is on my nerves now; the noise of the sea and the look of the
rocks. That is why I want to travel, to change the scene utterly. Tebb accuses the
monstrous East wind, and my supposed habit of secreting uric acid until it
reaches a bursting point and I go pop. Tebbie doesn't look at all well himself; and
I think we suffer a great deal from the loneliness of the place, which is all the
more intensely felt where Nature is laid on with a big brush; seas, like mountains,
prey upon the solitary mind.

He had been about to take a glass of bromide, but 'am taking you instead',
and after writing two pages to her already felt 'so much better'. He longed
to meet her at Emmetts, but 'honour compels me, if I am well, to see
Tebbie through'. The reference to uric acid suggests that Tebb thought
Calderon suffered from gout (like Conrad); and there is some evidence
that Calderon thought so too. Next day, 22 September, when enumerating
to Kittie what he wanted her to bring for him to Emmetts, he included 'a
box of cigarettes' but also 'a few aloines for old sake's sake' – aloines being
laxatives.

By the time the party was ensconced in the Grand Hôtel du Commerce
at Boulogne on 23 September, Calderon declared he was 'the only robust
one', but could not 'sit down to a comfortable walk, or take a good read'
as he had to be in attendance to a 'sickly' Tebb and recovering
Christopher. 'I wish we were coming home', he complained to Kittie, 'but
there seems no motion to it on Tebb's part. […] I shall sob in bed tonight,
to think I might be at nice Emmetts, instead of grousing about here with
nothing to do, and nobody to play with me.' It seems unlikely that they
left early enough for Calderon to join Kittie at the Lubbocks', but that did

give him time to paint the view from his bedroom window at a second hotel, the Grand Hôtel du Nord in Rue de Boston. It is precise, full of rectangular shadows, and verging on surreal.

The indications are that Calderon returned to London refreshed and relaxed. He remained on excellent terms with his mother-in-law, with whom he played cards. 'I have an improved variety of Picquet for Mrs Ham', he wrote Kittie on 19 September, 'but I shall not tell it you in case you should steal my patent.' From Cap Gris Nez he had written to Paul Boyer and Manya Ross, possibly advising the former on a Russian matter and to the latter about giving another paper to ARLS. Probably he settled down to his anthropological research again, and to planning his paper, which would be published.

1905 began with important developments in the Calderons' extended family. On 5 January Percy Lubbock wrote to Kittie to tell her that his sister Violet was engaged to 'Evey' – Charles Evelyn Pym, whose family home 'Foxwold Chase' was at Brasted, a couple of miles from Emmetts. Violet was twenty-three and Pym, a professional soldier, twenty-five. 'Tell Mrs Ham', wrote Percy, 'one of the first things said was "When can we go and see Mrs Ham?" and Violet will come soon.' Despite their age difference of fifteen years, Kittie's relationship with Violet was to become one of the most mutually supportive after Nina Corbet, and 'Foxwold' almost a second home for the Calderons.

In early February Nina herself wrote to Kittie from Acton Reynald:

Beloved Dina,
    Walter and I want you to be a godmother to our wee one. Her name isn't settled – but that's a detail.
    She is rather beloved – when she doesn't scream – which she does frequently. [...] Very <u>dark</u> blue eyes [...] a <u>hideous</u> nose and a lovely mouth, an exceptionally lovely mouth. No hair much – but what there is a <u>bright</u> corn colour – with a <u>distinct</u> red tinge, when the sun catches it. [...] She knows her own mind in the most killing manner. Oh! I do so pine to show her to Vincent. He would have so loved her. I miss him more now than I have almost ever done – and at times feel it more than I can bear. But probably it is becos I am weak physically. I can't say this to anyone – so praps that's why I feel it a relief to write it. Bless you darling Dina. A 1000 lovings from yr T'other.

The child had been born on 27 January 1905 and was christened Lesbia Rachel. She was called 'Lesbia' because she had 'a beaming eye' as in Thomas Moore's poem, which the Corbets knew from their friend Charles Villiers Stanford's 1895 arrangement of Moore's 'Irish Melodies'. She was to become so close to her godmother Kittie that at times she regarded her almost as her mother. The 'Lesbia' in Moore's poem alludes to Catullus's mistress of that name.

At the beginning of April 1905 George visited Paris and Versailles with G.F. Bradby, the Rugby master five years his senior. Clearly it was another convalescent holiday, as he refers to himself in a letter to Kittie as 'pore little Peeky'. Bradby was researching his book *The Great Days of Versailles*, which came out the following year. On 11 April 1905 George wrote to 'My pretty Catharine' from Versailles after a detailed tour of the first floor of the palace with Bradby, who was 'terribly well informed on the historical associations'. There is no mention of the French historical play that Calderon had been researching in Paris in 1903. Instead, he introduced Bradby to the *spécialité de la maison* (duckling) at the Tour d'Argent restaurant, conversed with eloquent waiters ('even if they do not *invent* ideas, they own them, these Frenchmen'), and watched French farces, with which he was again delighted.

On the evening of 9 April Calderon called on Paul Boyer. He was slightly annoyed, it seems, that Boyer 'examined' him 'at length' about his 'projected book', raising 'no fewer objections' than Calderon had when he read the proofs of Boyer's *Manuel pour l'étude de la langue russe* the previous year. But one cannot help feeling that an external view of George's protracted research was exactly what it needed. To Kittie he criticised Boyer for having

the obedient professorial mind, which is ready to believe all manner of questions closed which are as open as hungry oysters. He believes anthropology an uncertain vague field of knowledge which must be brought into no alliance with such a perfected scheme as comparative philology.

This seems unfair about Boyer (whose *Manuel*, incidentally, remained in print for the next sixty-two years). The fact that Boyer objected to anthropology being 'brought into alliance' with comparative philology does not mean that he thought anthropology itself was 'an uncertain vague field of knowledge'. He may have felt that anthropology *based* on comparative philology – which there is evidence George's projected book was – would be 'uncertain' because it was not so much empirical as subjective; in other words was not anthropology. Revealingly, perhaps, George 'hadn't any wish to discuss it with him'. They argued about it into the night, however, 'with great candour on both sides'.

The two long letters that have survived from this trip are especially tender towards Kittie and affectionate towards 'Mrs H.', Violet, and 'Master J[ones]'. Although Kittie's daily letters have not survived, it appears from George's of 11 April that she had been reproaching herself over some religious matter. He retorted:

As for you and your religious practices, Madam, to be dissatisfied with yourself is irreligious; for you are not idle or 'careless', but very energetic in yr static way, and you follow the dictates of your own personality, which is far better than accepting habits of childhood like yr friends. Besides, as if it mattered what you do; you are only affected by what you are, and if you change yourself I shall regard it as a breach of our marriage-contract.

He was more concerned that he had received from her 'no directions about yr stays'. Evidently Kittie had taken Nina's advice of five years before and liked her underwear to come from Paris. George was about to visit the shop, run by a Mme Gaches-Sarraute: 'Any injunction about the busks?'

He returned to Hampstead on 17 April and only two days later the whole family left for an unknown destination. By then Calderon's paper for ARLS must have been in a fairly final state, as it was delivered at the Imperial Institute on 2 May 1905.

The title 'Beauties of Russian Literature' may suggest an informal, impressionistic discourse of the kind that was appreciated at the time as 'literary criticism'. Nothing could be further from the truth. George had applied all his art to seeming conversational, tentative, even dilettante, but actually the paper presented some profound ideas about Russian literature that were the result of a decade's meditation and are hardly to be found in the writings of his Russianist contemporaries.

He began with 'a confession which will at once prove my incompetence for the post of critic which has been thrust upon me'. For him, he claimed,

the bulk of the literature of every country is a desert and a waste; it makes no appeal to my imagination; it affords me no pleasure, and if I read it it is in moments of vanity, when I am bitten by the madness of being well-informed.

This was the usual 'in-your-face' Calderon opening; he had already warned his audience that he believed 'my duty is not so much to inform you as to provoke you'. He implied that he was not interested in a country's 'literature' as such, i.e. as some historical entity, and therefore did not actually 'know' Russian literature; but the examples on which his paper is based prove otherwise. He himself explained that by 'desert and waste' in a country's literature he meant

the literature which despises common life, the literature which represents life, not as it is, but as it pleased the gentry of genteel periods to fancy it; the literature of heroic passions, high courtly language, and courtly sentiments which cannot bear the friction of common life. In other words, the classical period of every nation's literature.

My barbarous creed is this: that which is not original in literature is not good: that when a writer imitates an old form, it is his new matter which is good, his improvements and additions, not his fidelity to his model.

According to Calderon, 'the imitative period, the genteel and lifeless period of Russian literature, was very long'. It was 'hardly therefore till the literature of the nineteenth century' that his 'search for beauties' could begin. Yet he promptly proceeded to discuss such beauties in the *oral* literature that preceded classicism.

After quoting in Russian the first seven lines of 'The Lament of Boris Godunov's Daughter', which was written down in the seventeenth century by an Englishman in Russia, and after reading his own translation of all of it, Calderon said: 'This seems to me excellent, because the poet realises the essential likeness of all human beings. In a poem of the gentry the woman would speak like a princess; in this poem [...] the princess speaks like a woman.' He then discussed the 'commonplace in England' that Russian literature is 'pre-eminently sad'. Drawing no doubt on his own experience, he remarked that 'Life in big countries, with big governments and big disasters, is always a melancholy business'. However, 'for that very reason, it seems to me, the people who live in these big sad countries deliberately cultivate the art of gaiety' and this was nowhere clearer than in the 'ballads' (oral poetry). With three famous examples he sought to show that 'the feats and adventures of the old Russian heroes are told [...] with a sly exaggeration and relish of surprise which is endlessly refreshing'. His listeners must have been entertained by his reading of the 'sonorous' originals, and by the quality of his translations. 'Simplicity', he concluded, was 'perhaps the greatest merit of these poems', but it was not to be confused with 'baldness': it was 'the simplicity which comes from a rigid exclusion of all thoughts but the largest and most apposite'.

Calderon now executed a transition from the 'old' oral literature to modern Russian literature that is both clever and likely to appeal to English readers today. Pushkin, he said, came closest to the 'spirit' of the ballads in the poems that he wrote 'under the inspiration of his old nurse, even where he does not endeavour to imitate the metre of the folk-song'. Then George cited 'Natasha's dance':

Somewhere in Tolstoy's *War and Peace* Nikolai Rostov goes to a country house where his sister, Natasza, at the sound of music, steps out into the middle of the floor and prepares to dance, with a sort of sly gay smiling and a roguish swaying of the shoulders. For the moment her brother feels awkward and ashamed, as if she were doing something unseemly; then it suddenly comes over him that what she is doing is the most harmonious thing in the world and wholly Russian. It does not need much sympathy in a foreigner to understand that.

'Natasha's dance', Calderon explained, is prefigured in the lines of Pushkin's 'Tale of the Dead Princess and the Seven Heroes' describing the wicked stepmother before her magic mirror – lines 'which seem to me extremely beautiful; and like Natasza's outburst, beautiful through being wholly Russian'. After reading Pushkin's lines in Russian, he commented:

Here in the first place is an admirable picture, in that it conveys more than it actually describes. One sees all the movements of the creature's neck and the pitch of her feet on the carpet, as in some painting by Sargent. But what makes it so marvellous is the liquid ease with which it is described, an ease which the writer could hardly have found, so far as I know, in any language, ancient or modern, except Russian.

He then considered some morphological, grammatical, and phonetic features of Russian that particularly suit it to lyric utterance, and 'the greatest master' of that in his mind was Lermontov.

Following his own abridged translation of a classic passage in Gogol's *Dead Souls*, and an excellent commentary on its beauty, Calderon turned to Turgenev and Tolstoi. He agreed with de Vogüé's description of them as 'apostles of social pity', but only in the sense of 'pity for those whose destiny is worse than their own'. George put his finger on the problem that was to bedevil English expositions of the Russian novel for the rest of the century:

One must guard against misinterpreting the word 'social', and confounding this 'social pity' with the concern of our own novelists about social problems. I think the reason why Russian novels have become international property more than the novels of other nations, is that they deal more with man as man, and less with man as the occupant of a certain social position, than other novels. If the distinctions of our numerous English social classes were suddenly abolished a very large mass of our novels would become unintelligible – the key would have been lost.

Although in *Fathers and Sons* 'there is certainly a sharp social contrast between Bazarov [...] and Pavel Petrovitch', the 'whole interest and pathos of the book lies in the contrast of the two generations with their different ideas; and the gulf is just as wide between Bazarov and his parents as it is between Bazarov and Pavel Petrovitch'. The novel was therefore not social in the sense of the 'social school of novels, which we favour so much in England', it was concerned with visceral issues of human biology and communication.

Similarly, George continued, Russian novels lacked 'the religious element as it is understood by British novelists'. The latter 'make the interest of their books depend on the minor contrasts of different shades of creed' (low church, high church, Trinitarian, Unitarian are mentioned!), but carry their 'analysis' no further. Yet 'if we understand religion in the [...] sense of our relation to the rest of the created world and the conduct to be based on the sense of that relation, then I should say that the Russian novels are eminently religious'. He then discussed a 'religious story' which 'seems to me to be very beautiful' – his favourite 'Three Old Men' by Tolstoi.

In the last five minutes of his talk Calderon touched on Chekhov. He saw him in the context of a short story form which 'I think was invented by the French and has been very indifferently cultivated in England'. In this 'some dramatic moment or incident sums up the whole interest of a man's life, or the relations of different sorts of people one to another'. Rather surprisingly, Calderon describes Chekhov, who had died the previous year, as 'an uncertain artist in many ways, uncertain as to his own convictions, uncertain in his selection of subjects, uncertain in his judgment of his own work', and one who produced 'many failures'. This sounds more like the conventional wisdom of Chekhov's 'sociological' Russian critics than a view based on George's own evaluation, and there must be a suspicion that he had not actually read Chekhov's longer, greatest and latest stories. Nevertheless, his choice of the early short work 'Verochka' was discriminating, and his treatment of its qualities apt.

When introducing Calderon as 'lecturer', Cazalet had said that 'besides his excellent knowledge of the Russian language and literature' he was, 'as we all know', a 'popular and ingenious author in other fields'. The audience could not have been disappointed. George had maintained a light touch throughout and certainly provoked the discussion that he said was his object. But he had also addressed issues about Russian literature that had hardly been broached in English before: the aesthetic *realia* of its best verse, its focus on the existential rather than the social, its intense pursuit of human rather than ecclesiastical values.

After this, Calderon presumably returned to his research. But the summer of 1905 became increasingly digressive and disrupted for him.

In June he took a thick ruled exercise book and numbered three hundred pages of it according to a complicated system that he explained on the inside cover. The book was intended to be the first in a series examining chapter by chapter 'the canonical books of the Christians, in chronological order; so far as one can easily arrive at it'. He began with Thessalonians I. The project seems to have been a fundamental attempt to consider the evidence for Christianity. He clearly had access to Cheyne and Black's *Encyclopaedia Biblica* of 1899, and had read biblical scholars such as F.C. Baur, because he refers to them. He may well have been reading in the original Greek, although he generally quotes from the Authorised King James Version. His resultant commentary is a fluent mixture of factual notes, personal responses, paraphrase and translation. It does read as if written down after reading each verse. He is particularly concerned with whether St Paul believed Jesus was 'a son of God before he was [the man] Jesus', with St Paul as 'a Christian by conviction, not study', and with 'folklore cases' of the doctrine of Christ's redeeming blood. Some of this commentary is written in the personal shorthand that Calderon was developing at this time, and to which he left keys. Nevertheless, he abandoned the project after fifteen pages.

For at least the past year, in fact, Calderon had been studying Taoism. In a letter provisionally dated 7 July 1904 he thanked Rothenstein for 'finding me *Taoist Texts*', the punctuation of which implies that he was already familiar with fundamental texts like the *Tao Te Ching*. For her birthday on 5 March 1905, he gave Kittie what is now a classic Edwardian version of the latter published that year, *Wisdom of the East: the Sayings of Lao-Tsŭ* translated by Lionel Giles. Given George's scepticism about Christian theology, one can see that a philosophy without a personal God, focussed on existence, spontaneity, compassion and personal conduct, might well attract him. The central role of paradox would also have appealed to him. However, the very fact that the Taoist is exhorted by Laozi to 'follow diligently the Way in your own heart, but make no display of it to the world' means that if George had embraced Taoism he would hardly have told anyone – and indeed, there are no discursive references to it in his writings. Nevertheless, there are a number of small facts that suggest his interest in the Taoist view of life continued to at least 1912, and we shall note these in passing.

The marriage of Violet Lubbock and 'Evey' Pym took place on a grand scale in London on 7 June 1905 and the Calderons were present. Shortly afterwards Evey's twenty-three-year-old half-sister Carol Pym became engaged to Violet's thirty-four-year-old brother Guy Lubbock. Carol was beautiful, humorous, an accomplished artist, and very close to both Calderons. In July George wrote to congratulate her. He began in his usual challenging way ('Guy is […] such a respectable, eminent, ingratiating thing to have at your side'), but was soon rhapsodising:

I used to hate anyone getting married (that was partly because I wanted to marry everyone myself); I like it now, especially if they marry Guy. So often they marry some pale moustachioed pushing fellow in pince-nez and a tie tied too tight, who looks over my shoulder and treats my conversation as an irrelevant parenthesis. But Guy! I don't remember two people marrying more considerately, more conveniently to my feelings, choosing an object so equidistant from the apple of my eye. Do it quickly.

There is a terrible irony in these last words, for on 1 August Carol Pym died at Foxwold of meningitis. The impact on George and Kittie must be imagined. Mrs Hamilton believed she had been responsible for the match.

It is a plausible hypothesis that about this time Calderon became absorbed in devising a 'universal language'. According to Percy Lubbock, George had examined Volapük, the 'international language' created by Johann Schleyer in 1880, and its successor Esperanto, and found them wanting. His own attempt would be 'really rational and logical'. Presumably his intensive courses in the Indo-European languages and his drive to find linguistic resemblances as part of his research had tempted him down the path of 'conlanging', as it is called today (i.e. constructing languages). But 'conlanging' is notoriously time-consuming and according to Lubbock Calderon expended 'enormous toil' on it.

Not that the Calderons lacked holidays in the summer of 1905. They probably stayed with the Lubbocks at Emmetts, they appear to have stayed with the Stuart-Menteths at Rownham's Mount, near Southampton, and they certainly visited Netherhampton House in Wiltshire, as photographs have survived from their stay and Kittie painted a lush watercolour of the garden. These visits would last about a week each. On holiday Calderon would sometimes spend the morning working, but according to Kittie 'on his holidays George completely enjoyed himself' talking, playing games, accompanying people at the piano, taking long walks. Perhaps at times, though, he found the atmosphere slightly claustrophobic. At Netherhampton in 1905 Cecil Lubbock and his young family were also present, and Cecil was married to Michael Furse's sister Edith. Another brother of Edith's, the sculptor Henry Furse, was the principal tenant of the house and Newbolt's wife Margaret was drifting into an affair with him. George particularly enjoyed talking to 'old Mrs Coltman', presumably the mother of Ella Coltman, Margaret's lover and Newbolt's mistress. Henry Furse, incidentally, had sculpted the figure of Mercury placed on top of Vincent Corbet's tomb. It may have been a relief for George, Kittie and 'Mr Jones' to move to Hale Farm in Sussex on 26 August to stay with the newlyweds Violet and Evey.

But unlike the year before, Calderon's health did not improve through the autumn. It seems that he always tended to turn to drawing and painting for therapy. At about this time he produced a series of excellent crayons of Jones. One Sunday afternoon in December he and John Fothergill (Rothenstein's friend and a future celebrity restaurateur) sketched each other and a mysterious guest called Mrs Lapp on the backs of Heathland Lodge writing paper. On 27 December Kittie and George visited Foxwold as the guest of Evey's stepmother and in the company of an old friend of the Pyms, the comic novelist and *Punch* contributor Anstey Guthrie. The day after, Nina's son Jim wrote to Kittie from Acton Reynald expressing the hope that 'Uncle George's' health was better.

There is hardly any documentary evidence of what happened next. Extrapolating back from April 1906, however, it is clear that in the new year Calderon's mental and physical condition deteriorated steadily. It seems that he was still obsessed with the universal language, and this may have been when, in Percy Lubbock's words, after a Saturday morning's hard work on it he went for a walk on Hampstead Heath and blacked out 'while he sat on a bench with five Polish Jews, who were keeping the Sabbath there; they escorted him home, all talking Polish together'. After this, according to Lubbock, 'the universal language was fortunately heard no more'.

What, in present-day terms, was wrong with Calderon?

Obviously he was 'over-studying', overworking mentally on his 'folklore' book and on the 'universal language', but what was *driving* him to do this? What were the psychological roots of these obsessions? In so far as both projects involved the elaboration of enormous abstract systems, they could be said to lie potentially in the autistic spectrum. Yet Kittie's memoirs and the testimonies of George's friends speak of him as a very sociable man, supremely sensitive to his surroundings and other people; a man of quick feeling and empathy. Was the trouble, then, that his whole Victorian education had been in competitive 'extreme male' environments, he aspired to eminence in those terms, yet he was thus forcing himself relentlessly against his own grain? If true, this might explain his particular nervous exhaustion: he had rare intellectual abilities, but he could not 'win' in these quasi-Aspergic projects, as they were contrary to his deeper nature.

Fig. 12 George Calderon, c. 1902

Whether Calderon also suffered from physical ailments, such as gout, we do not know, but photographs of him between 1901 and early 1906 show startling changes. The photograph probably taken after moving to Hampstead (Fig. 12) shows a young, athletic-looking postgraduate (it was Kittie's favourite). The Calderon in photographs taken at Cap Gris Nez in 1904 is bronzed and still robust-looking. The man sitting next to a smiling Kittie in the garden of Rownham's Mount in 1905 (Fig. 13) wears a stiff wing collar and three-piece suit, and looks like an academic dragged from his study. Studio photographs taken of him in the same suit in late 1905 or early 1906 display cavernous eyes, brows that appear hormonally out of control, and possibly a skin complaint. Kittie had one of these blown up and mounted, because it shows George radiantly laughing (Fig. 14); but he is holding the end of a cigarette between black-stained fingers and thumb. At this point, presumably, he was a chain-smoker.

Fig. 13 George and Kittie Calderon, 1905

Fig. 14 George Calderon, 1905 / 1906

Had Calderon simply 'lost his way'? This, surely, is too negative an
interpretation. In the previous five years he had published a sensational
essay on Tolstoi that had gone round the world, fine articles on other
aspects of Russian literature, a bestselling comic novel illustrated by
himself, an entirely different novel based on a profound science fiction of

his own, and delivered lectures which no contemporary British professor of Russian, it seems, could rival. It is an extremely impressive body of work, which contains hardly any element of repetition. After each achievement, as with his short stories, Calderon moved on to something new. Today even his 'universal language' – of which not a word has survived – might be regarded as 'cutting-edge art' and worthy of inclusion in one of the courses of 'conlang studies' offered by American and European universities. It would seem more accurate, then, to view the years 1901-05 as a single cycle (hence the length of this chapter) in Calderon's intellectual and creative life, a cycle that was completed as it began with a paper to ARLS. He did not believe in repeating himself, so where was he to go now? He did not publish, or as far as we know complete, anything in the first quarter of 1906. His condition developed into what Percy Lubbock actually called 'a very serious illness'.

Kittie's solution was for him to go on a long voyage. He would be leaving her to care for her mother, and this was one reason why she could not accompany him. But she was entirely positive about him going. As well as travel being 'the thing, the only thing, to set him up', she believed '*Adventure* was essential for George – and a man can't have completeness of adventure if he has got a woman with him'. Perhaps in February, then, they began to discuss where he might go. Rather than a circumnavigation like the one Archie Ripley had made, it seems they were attracted by advertisements that had appeared in the newspapers for voyages to 'New Zealand, Tasmania, Australia, calling at Cape Town' run by Shaw, Savill, and Albion Co. Ltd using their 'magnificent Royal Mail Steamers from London [...] every Four Weeks'. Calderon, however, thought of a project that would take him beyond New Zealand into the Pacific. A letter to him from Joseph Conrad dated 25 March 1906 reveals that George had consulted the former merchant seaman about 'sailing' to various archipelagoes. Conrad advised him to take steamships to Tonga, or Fiji, or Tahiti, 'and if you wish to explore a particular archipelago you may find means to do so from the principal port of each group. I imagine you will get as much *sailing* in that way as you'll care for'. At some point, we do not know when, Calderon chose Tahiti.

Judging from William Rothenstein's letter to Kittie of 5 April 1906, George was got onto his ship in a delicate state. He was seen off by a 'bearded brother' (presumably Frank), a 'nice and cheery' nephew (presumably Philip), and Rothenstein himself. The latter wrote:

It was very hard for me to leave him […] I wish I could have stayed with him, and kept him company. I love him very much, and I pray he may come back as strong and robust as he was of old.

Evidently Kittie was not there. Rothenstein's letter is addressed to her 'c/o Lady Corbet' at Acton Reynald.

7

'C'EST UN TYPE': RECOVERY IN PARADISE

With Calderon's visit to Tahiti, this biography enters another of the 'tourbillions of Time' (Robert Graves, 'On Portents') to which it is subject. This is because hardly any documentary evidence about the visit exists outside Calderon's own book about Tahiti, which was assembled and published by Kittie six years after his death. As she records in her Preface to *Tahiti*, George himself did not start to write it until 'the winter of 1913-1914', i.e. seven years after he had the experience. He stimulated his memory with the diaries, sketches and letters that he regularly sent home to her. Apart from four watercolours, none of this material has survived. The present chapter, then, is mainly dependent for its biographical facts on a (partly fictive) narrative that appeared fifteen years after George visited Tahiti. It recounts the 'events' from *Tahiti*; the book will be discussed as a book in chapter fifteen.

Calderon left Tilbury on board Shaw, Savill and Albion's 6237-ton *Waiwera* on 4 April 1906. We do not know what all of its ports of call were, but possibly from Plymouth he posted the only letter to Kittie from his trip of which a fragment has survived:

To plunge out again into the fresh-smelling sea, to new faces and new talk, it is a pleasant thing! And at the end a slim black figure and a little dog perched on the white cliff of England. Au revoir, my little best.

The *Waiwera* then called at Tenerife and Cape Town, where George painted two watercolours from offshore. He was growing back his old 'Russian' beard. The ship next stopped at Hobart, and arrived at Wellington on 27 May. In a letter to his mother from Auckland dated 12 June he explains that he spent ten days in Wellington, where the 'letters of introduction' that he brought with him were 'very useful': he was 'put up' for three clubs there, was writing now from 'the chief club' in Auckland, and the Bishop had given him 'a good introduction' to the British consul on Tahiti. He was 'strong and healthy and in this lovely New Zealand climate feel lively even in adverse circumstances; the little accidents of a bad night or the like do not have any considerable effect on me'. He was due to leave Auckland for the Society Islands at four o'clock that afternoon on 'a nice picturesque old-fashioned fruit-smelling trading ship'. This was the *Hauroto* (renamed the *Rangatira* in George's book).

Leaning over the rail that evening talking to another passenger, Calderon discovered that the person was a Russian professor who, in Kittie's words, enjoyed working nowhere so much as in the British Museum Reading Room, where the only person he had got on with was 'one George Calderon'. He had not recognised 'the man with the pointed beard and moustaches to whom he was talking nor had George recognised him'. He was Aleksandr Aleksandrovich Vasil'ev, a professor of Byzantine History at the University of Iur'ev (now Tartu in Estonia), and a great traveller. He was a year older than George, had a 'bull head' and 'Mongolian' eyes, in George's words, and a large straggly moustache. He too was heading for Tahiti, but only for a month.

The *Hauroto* called at Rarotonga in the Cook Islands, probably elsewhere, and came into Papeete harbour at night on 22 June:

A crowd was assembled to meet it – white men and brown men in ducks [coarse cotton] and linen, and numberless brown women in night-gowns and Gainsborough hats. The chattering natives on the wharf lighted matches and held them up to find their friends aboard, and the native deck passengers stooped laughing over the ship's side and blew them out.

Calderon and Vasil'ev booked themselves into what in *Tahiti* is identified as 'Pandora's Hotel'. It seems to have been the staff here who transmogrified 'George' and 'Aleksandr' into 'Tihoti' and 'Aritana', the names by which they were now known. Calderon rapidly grasped the layout and functioning of the hotel, noting particularly the input of 'the multitudinous swarm of *fetii*, or native friends and relatives', i.e. the extended family. 'There is gaiety and movement at the hotel', he wrote, 'and everybody wants to have a hand in it.'

At the Casino, he discovered that the entertainment 'consisted in fact of a cinematograph, displaying scenes of European life'. He and Vasil'ev were ushered by 'Monsieur Percier of the Governor's Chancellerie' into the kitchen, where 'about twenty young Frenchmen and native women were drinking bottled beer'. George was particularly struck by the dancing of Tupuna, a 'thin girl with black hair and a sorrowful smile, dressed in a white gown, with a garland of flowers on her head':

The dancer stood with naked feet immovably planted on the dirty boards, and all her attention seemed fixed on the movements of her haunches, which described circles and ellipses in various planes. The movement of the haunches was ugly, but there was beauty in the sleepy face, in the languorous smile, in the downcast eyes, in the gestures of the high narrow shoulders and the slender arms; she slapped her palms together as she threw out her hands alternately.

Later that evening Percier (probably not his real name) took them to a garden with 'sweet-smelling bushes' where more 'Bayadères' and 'Nautch dancers', as Calderon calls them, performed over a bottle of rum. 'Slender Tupuna' was again present, and later he described her 'exquisite taste in dress', her life story, her hands and her whole personality. This was based on visiting her 'more than once' where she lived with 'the ugly Marotea'. The girls made a living as hostesses. George told her 'what a charming person I thought her. *Mais...il y a une belle fille en Angleterre, à laquelle j'ai promis de faire le tour du monde sans embrasser personne*'. '*Embrasser*' here and subsequently is undoubtedly an Edwardian euphemism. But Tupuna was not offended: '*Ah, c'est beau ça!*' she said, '*Je te ferai un chapeau pour ça!*', and made him one with a lining 'embroidered in silk with blue forget-me-nots'.

Both Calderon and Vasil'ev were pianists. George sketched 'Aritana' as he played light music and sang in French, Russian and Italian to Europeans on the hotel's garden verandah after dinner. A native girl stole in and kissed Vasil'ev on the neck, and a 'giant' Tahitian 'peeped round the window-post' to watch Vasil'ev's 'muscular fingers tripping nimbly up the treble'; this was 'too much' for the Tahitian and he 'suddenly doubled up with laughter and drew swiftly back into the darkness'.

Calderon was intent on discovering what 'real' Tahitian music was like. When Tupuna had danced in the Casino, she had been accompanied merely by 'two monotonous bars of music on an accordion'. In the garden the girls had sung songs deliberately '*à la Canaque*', i.e. (Calderon concluded) in the pseudo-Polynesian style beloved of Europeans. Even what was known at the time as 'the Tahitian National Anthem', a 'slow, dreary song called *E Mauruuru a Vaú* of which [Tahitophiles] never tire', was sung to a tune 'taken from the French Baptist hymn-book' in a harmonisation that had 'no semblance of Tahitian music' in it.

One evening the fat little waitress at the hotel, Maná, took them to a house on the shore outside Papeete 'to hear some native singing'. As they entered:

The room was dimly lighted by two oil-lamps, standing on the floor. Behind the lamps sat a semicircle of a dozen girls and women, and in the shadow behind the women half-a-dozen men, who rolled their bodies about and sang 'Umph! Umph! Umph!'. The song ended in a long note and a general 'Umph!' all round.

This seemed more authentic. But when George asked Maná what the song was about, she replied: '*C'est une chose qui s'est passée en Galilée. C'est la naissance de Jésus-Christ*'. Another song commenced with a child throwing back its head and uttering 'a sharp sequence of words on one shrill, cracked note':

The rest followed rapidly after, and the chorus brayed its way to the close with a sustained, rushing volume of sound that hummed and crackled in the roof, calling to mind newspaper boys, coster girls, crickets, pigs and policemen's rattles.

After a song of welcome had been sung to 'Tihoti and Aritana', Calderon proposed sending out for 'a bottle or two of wine to regale the company', but Maná 'laughed uneasily and told us we had said a *chose affreuse*'. This was because all the songs had been *himénés*, Christian songs written by native poets, and the occasion was in fact a religious meeting. When, shortly after, they stayed the night at a chief's house, it was again *himénés* that were sung for their entertainment, although the tunes were

apparently native ones. Calderon's quest for 'real' Tahitian songs and
music continued.

Whilst Calderon was still in Papeete, he and Vasil'ev also visited the
Roman Catholic mission school, the French Protestant school, the
Mormon mission, and the colony of ex-Pitcairn Islanders (descended from
some of the mutineers of the *Bounty*), who were Seventh Day Adventists.
Established western religions and sectarianism were everywhere in Tahiti.
Given Calderon's own agnosticism, this was a feature of life there that
interested him greatly. It became a major theme of his eventual book.

Vasil'ev now took a house in Papeete, for which he needed a
housekeeper. Maná recommended her sister, who was about eighteen and
called Tahiri-i-te-rai ('Fan the sky'). Calderon made an extensive study of
this girl's character. She was outwardly shy and demure, but had her own
agenda. After the Russian had explained her duties to her, she 'said that
she must have a broom and some other implements, and sent him out to
buy them'. She asked him how to use them, and 'she watched Aritana's
demonstrations with great apparent interest. Then she went home and
resumed her normal life'. She occasionally turned up 'to see how Aritana
was getting on', or would suddenly appear with a dish of bread-fruit
'smoking hot from her mother's ground-oven half-a-mile away', but it was
soon understood that she did this 'in the capacity, not of a servant, but of a
friend' – in fact simply as one of the *fetii* at the hotel who had crowded
round laughing when Vasil'ev 'interviewed' her for the job on the '*fetii*-
verandah'. 'All the work I saw her do for Maná', Calderon wrote, 'was to
throw a banana skin over into the road, then lean moodily against a post
and ejaculate: "*Que je déteste le travail!*".'

Tahiri 'rarely tells the truth, because it is dull'. Calderon and Vasil'ev
admired the autobiographical novel *Rarahu*, or *Le Mariage de Loti*, by
Julien Viaud ('Pierre Loti'), and asked her to show them 'Loti's Pool', the
'sylvan paradise which we remembered in *Le Mariage de Loti*, with its
long grass, its rocky basin, its scented shade beneath the mimosas', where
Loti had met his heroine coming down to bathe. Tahiri took them straight
there. But what they saw was:

a narrow and rather muddy pool between two brown, sloping banks; even the waterfall had disappeared. A few yards away a sort of stone kiosk and a wooden trap-door in a patch of weeds, fenced round with a [*sic*] barbed wire, marked the head of the Papeete waterwork system.

Tahiri sat in a tree listening to them reminiscing about the scene in the novel. 'How it has changed!' they exclaimed. 'Yes, everything has changed since the flood,' she told them, meaning the tsunami earlier that year. When Calderon asked her what the native name for the pool was, she replied, '*Cochon tacheté*' (spotted hog). In fact, as she very well knew, 'Loti's Pool' was about a mile further up the Fautaua river. It and the waterfall exist to this day. Calderon and Vasil'ev visited it later and contemporary photographs of people bathing in it survive in George's archive.

Whether by nature or by assimilation of the European image of Tahiti, from time to time Tahiri could speak only of '*amour*'. When, in a discussion about beauty, Calderon praised 'the saying of Lao Tsze that "the sage delights in that which is insipid"', Tahiri protested strongly. 'Every evening at dusk', Calderon claimed, he found her standing by the entrance to the hotel garden with 'a little white scented flower for me, wrapped for shelter from the rude world in a sheath of coiled green leaf'. It smelt 'like a jasmine, fresh and virginal' and he discovered later that it was 'the *tiare maohi*, or native single gardenia, the flower *par éminence* of the island'. However, when he asked Tahiri what it was called, she said, '*C'est la fleur du coeur.*'

She says it sentimentally, in that shy murmur which she keeps for her more audacious jokes. She knows quite well that it has no such name: she has made it up on the spur of the moment. She is laughing at me, at herself, at lovers' trysts on summer nights. Another time the flower is a little faded, and she murmurs as she gives it to me: '*Fleur fanée, coeur aimé.*'

Tahiri did not reveal to Calderon that she would be 'married *pour tout de bon* when a certain schooner comes home', but he discovered it anyway. She was to become a key player in the poetry of his book.

A local character whom he was keen to meet was an American university man known as Barefoot Bill, *Taáta huruhuru* (Hairy Man), or *L'Homme Nature*. He lived 'alone on a mountain at the back of Papeete, the only mountain-dweller on the island', and according to Calderon his name was Dumford, but this could be fictionalized (Frederick O'Brien (1921) suggests his real name was Ernest Darling). To reach him involved climbing through a forest of orange trees, giant ferns, bread fruits, and 'solid polygons of [spider] webs six feet high and four feet thick'. Calderon did not manage it at his first attempt. Arriving 'on another day' at the top of the mountain, he found 'a tiny brown hut with fire-blackened earth all about it' and beheld 'a tall, lean man, as naked as Isaiah, hacking a hole in the ground'.

He had a handsome, civilised American face, with clean-cut nose and eyes, short, soft, tangled beard, hair falling in locks of dusty yellow on his shoulders, and the general aspect of an Ober-Ammergau Christ. His tanned skin threw the little fine flaxen hairs of his body into relief. He said: 'I am glad to see you, brother', and led me to his [hut].

Dumford had arrived in Tahiti calling himself 'Professor' and hoping to create 'a sort of social revival among the Tahitians'. 'You've got to go right back to Nature, brother,' he told George, 'and live according to her rules. What you need is pure air, hard work and a diet of non-acid fruits.' He gave George a copy of his Ten Commandments, which were 'spelt according to a phonetic system of his own'; one was 'Thou shalt not eet meet', another 'Vizit troppikle cuntriz'. He invited Calderon to come and live with him when he, George, was 'ready', whereupon he would teach him how to obey Nature and they would 'sing up here together like the morning stars, and shout for joy like the sons of God'.

There is an undeniably homoerotic element to Calderon's encounters with Nature Man. He made his second visit to him at night. 'Clothed like Robinson Crusoe', Dumford led George to his hut, 'laid me a bed of sacking on the floor, put out the lights, climbed into a hammock and talked and talked.'

In the night he got up and lit a candle. He said that he was hungry. I offered some biscuits that I had brought in my bundle.

– Your cookies can't satisfy the hunger that I'm suffering, brother.

It was not bodily hunger that afflicted him, but some sort of aspiration after the ideal.

Dumford was given to 'throwing a pirouette in the air' and leaping naked into a large pool below his drinking hole (which he called 'the Fountain of Youth'). George worked with him for an hour or two on his 'plantation' and on his third visit was joined by 'another Nature Man', called Betts, who was likewise a vegetarian but wore 'trousers for decency'.

One cannot escape the impression that despite the voyage, the climate, and the relaxed ambience, Calderon was still nervously challenged. Why had he set out the first time to meet Dumford at four in the morning? On that occasion he had had to turn back. On the second occasion, when he had struggled up the mountain *in the dark*, he had lost his way, lain down, and 'cried aloud for the Nature Man with faint hope of response'. Dumford himself diagnosed George's case 'very flatteringly as one of "mental over-stimulation due to excess of educational facilities"'.

After about a fortnight in Papeete, during which he had 'scraped a quite insufficient acquaintance with the native language', Calderon set out on foot along the road that leads down the eastern coast of Tahiti to Taravao on the isthmus with the Taiarapu Peninsula, or *Tahiti iti* (Little Tahiti).

He had an introduction to a man called Temaeva at the village of Vaapuru, which would appear to have been not far beyond Papenoo, a town eleven miles out of Papeete. But he made slow progress because he was dazzled by the landscape and 'hundred different sorts of trees and bushes of which I did not know the names'. He stopped every so often to make notes, and when he was hot he would experience the 'rich delight' of going up a hollow into the hills round which the path ran, 'undressing and going down into a tiny rill among the flowering grasses and bathing there beneath a little cascade to the sound of the murmuring water and of a turtle dove cooing in the trees overhead'.

By the evening of the first day he had probably covered only half a dozen miles. He rounded a point, 'creeping by between sea and cliff', and found himself in a sheltered bay, where a *pater familias* named Moitua put him up for the night. With the whole household listening, Moitua interrogated George about the British royal family, especially 'Peretue' (the Prince of Wales, i.e. Edward VII) and 'Arafata' (Prince Albert). What had become of the latter, Moitua asked.

'He has been dead these fifty years.'
'Dead these fifty years? Well, in that case, *Aita ra'au*, there is no tree.'
Long and earnestly I pondered over this saying, pacing up and down in the darkness among the palms, till I saw that he meant not tree, but herb, in the sense of medicine. I had come on my first Polynesian joke.

Calderon was much taken here by a girl called Marae, who sang for him later, and the 'beautiful build' of a man present from 'one of the islands noted as the most barbarous and still addicted to cannibalism'. He made fine drawings of them both.

The next morning he hitched a lift on the mail-cart to Papenoo. Here he was looking for the French teacher, Lantérès, whom he had been directed to for advice and knowledge of Tahitian life. Lantérès decided Calderon needed a horse, and went to look for one. Meanwhile, George drew his native wife, who gave him a language lesson and invited him to stay. In the bamboo house he saw a Tahitian inscription in European letters and speculated: 'the fact that Tahitians carve European letters from right to left [...] suggests that they had a script of their own, now lost.'

Lantérès had first worked in the French administration on Tahiti, but could not stand it. 'He loved liberty.' He now lived a completely Tahitian life, with an extended family, gathering wild food, breeding pigs, and presumably teaching some French for the Catholic mission. Whilst George ate lunch with them, a piglet ran about the floor wolfing the babies' food; during his siesta he could see 'scores of mice entering gravely in parallel lines all along the floor, like Association football players lined out'. That evening he had a 'gorgeous feed':

As we sit hornets keep falling from the roof. A girl wanders in from another house and brings me a sweet-smelling garland of *tiare maohi*. [...] Lantérès and I lie in *pareus* (waist-cloths) and garlands in the sun on the plateau, looking through the tops of coco-trees on to the blue sea.

What they talked about will be discussed in chapter fifteen. George hired a horse here for a week.

At last he reached Vaapuru, where he discovered that his host Temaeva lived in a European house with at least three generations of his relatives. Before the assembled family, Calderon's letter of introduction written in Tahitian was read out by Temaeva, his wife, and even George himself. Like Moitua's, this was a religious household. When the guest had been 'put to bed' he heard family prayers being murmured in the rest of the house. They were in fact Calvinists. On Sunday 'everybody put on all the black clothes they could find, as if it were Christ's funeral instead of His resurrection that they were celebrating'. In church, Temaeva sat 'with his arm round my waist and an affectionate smile on his face'.

But Calderon had brought with him something that cut across all their cultural and religious preoccupations. Alone one afternoon with an invalid relation, he lent him a copy of *Ali Baba and the Forty Thieves* in Tahitian and French that he had found 'on a dusty shelf at Papeete'. Another relative took it from the invalid and went onto a verandah where he read it aloud to himself. That evening Temaeva's father read it. As George lay in bed that night he thought he could hear family prayers again, but they went on much longer and sounded unfamiliar. He got up, and found 'all the members of the household assembled in another room, the invalid sitting up, much better, with a smile on his face, while Temaeva read *Ali Baba* aloud'. After the church service, a large part of the congregation came back to Temaeva's to hear the deacon read the story to them, and a few hours later he 'read it through once more by general request'.

Although George was fond of Temaeva, and the household sang Tahitian songs to him, one senses that he was not at ease in such a 'European' family. This was not what he was looking for. In one respect, though, they were thoroughly Tahitian. Calderon's letter of introduction had said he was 'rich and will recompense you for what you spend on him'. 'Deceived' by this, Calderon says, he left money behind him on a table. Temaeva's wife in particular was deeply offended.

Unexpectedly, and presumably by horse, Calderon now returned to Papeete. His purpose was to say goodbye to Vasil'ev, who was leaving on the next ship. It may now have been 9 July. The capital was 'already astir with preparations for the annual festival of the Quatorze Juillet', but George regarded this as the sole (and colonial) survivor of the great communal festivities of Tahiti's pre-Christian past and did not want to see it. Nevertheless, he and Vasil'ev went to hear the 'Papeete chorus' rehearsing, among whom were many of the 'Bayadères'. Their conductor was a fierce little old man with a whip 'like a white fishing rod'. Tahiri-i-te-rai came up to George afterwards, 'very bold; she had been with officers of the *Zélée*; she blew cigarette smoke in my face and went away'. Perhaps on 11 July, he set out again on the road to Taravao.

This time he must have made faster progress to Papenoo, where he returned the horse and continued on foot, presumably beyond Vaapuru. At a place Calderon calls Vaanui, which could be present-day Faauanu six miles beyond Papenoo, he was offered lunch by an old woman whose husband was 'a chief'. After visiting a ninety-year-old Dutch naval deserter who lived on his own and was nicknamed 'the Spider', he encountered a group of natives returning from the mountains, carrying yams, plantains, and green bamboo canes. One of them, with 'a broad, good-natured face, [...] nose and lips flattened like a negro's, [and] splendid limbs', was called Amaru. George walked along the road with him:

We soon came into a sheltered cove at the foot of a little valley, where the road was carpeted with mossy grass in the shade of chestnut-trees. On a green knoll on the inland side was a little native house with bamboo walls and pandanus-thatched roof; thickets of hibiscus, purao, banyan and guava surrounded it, and before the door rose a group of three or four coco-palms, holding up their drooping crests with a sinuous grace of strong, slender women.

Two children ran down the knoll to meet Amaru and he addressed to George in French the traditional Tahitian welcome 'come and eat'. This was 'so open-hearted an invitation that I readily accepted it'.

Basically this was a family of four living in a modest house from the fruits of their own labours. Calderon got on very well with Amaru and his wife Vava, who were presumably in their early thirties, and he loved playing with the children, the girl Arii-Roo and the boy Te-Hei. He found it so congenial that he stayed in the first instance for over a week.

From Amaru he learned the reality of Tahitian kinship patterns. The woman who had given him his first meal at Vaanui was Amaru's 'mother'; in fact his adoptive father's wife. Another woman they visited was also Amaru's 'mother'; this time his foster-mother. His biological mother lived on the west coast. Arii-Roo and Te-Hei were not his and Vava's biological children; like 'most of the children in the island' they were adopted. This was because it was customary, Amaru explained to George, 'when a child is born for some great friend or near relation to come to the father and the mother and say: "I will call this child 'N' or 'M'", and by the mere naming the child becomes theirs'. When George asked whether the biological parents sometimes refuse, he was told: 'A stranger one might refuse, but a brother, a sister, or a near *fetii*, how could one refuse?'

In Calderon's subsequent book this leads into a profound discussion of the European belief that the Tahitians were not emotionally attached to their children, and an extended hypothesis (their 'aristocratic principle') for the infanticide supposedly practised by them in the pre-Christian era.

This family too were religious, but instead of going to church on the Sunday that George was with them, they took him up the valley to 'an open, grassy place among orange and banana trees', where *utes* were to be performed and fermented orange juice drunk. *Utes* were 'secular songs', 'love songs', which Lantérès had told George were 'obscene, according to European ideas'. This is hardly visible from the examples George took down and translated, but his description of this '*ute* festival' certainly suggests that the *performance* of them could be erotic. He compared the occasion to a scene from Rabelais. Children were not allowed to hear *utes*, so Arii-Roo and Te-Hei had been left at home. After a while, George returned to the house to 'eat oranges and play hide-and-seek' with the children. Their parents were so late that eventually he went to look for them. He found them on the seashore, 'singing and dancing with unabated energy' in the moonlight, and both 'exhaled a strong fragrance of orange'. Evidently he had been able to give the couple some 'quality time' together. He does not mention whether they had ever had children 'of their own'.

Living with this family gave Calderon rich material on Tahitian music, poetry, magic, manners, language, superstitions, jokes, play, and

occupations. Food was scarce and the couple worked hard. Amaru also
had to feed his 'fathers and mothers' and made regular expeditions into the
mountains to gather food for humans and pigs. Vava spent her day fishing,
cooking, fetching fresh water and sea water, tending her vanilla crop,
catching wild chickens, or producing bamboo strips for Papeete market.
Calderon, meanwhile, passed

idle, lotus-eating days with the children, sprawling on the ground of the grassy
knoll, looking out to the open sea, stringing my glass beads [which he had
brought with him] on threads of *purao* bark for Arii-Roo, strolling along the shore
or into the woods with naked feet.

It was superb therapy. His brain was very active, he never ceased to be
inquisitive, to ask questions and ponder, to keep his diary and to sketch,
but no-one made him do anything. The landscape, the sea, the way of life,
he found completely restful, yet he was accepted in a stable, vibrant
family, as he had always needed to be. When after a week he mentioned
leaving, Amaru 'sat down on a box and cried; [...] his wife cried with her
shirt to her eyes, and the children looked at me with round, sad eyes'.
Eventually they parted, 'with kisses and flowing tears'. If Calderon did not
come and stay with them soon, Amaru told him, 'I shall seek you out and
bring you here'.

The path beyond Vaanui was washed by innumerable streams. In order
to keep his trousers dry, George took them off and donned the native
pareu. He also stripped to the waist. The surface of the path was a hard
compound of rock and broken coral that reduced his shoes to 'lumps and
balls under my heels'. On arrival at Taravao he went straight to the French
fortress to post a letter for someone he had met on the way. The fat
gendarme in charge, known as the Brigadier of Taravao, told him he was
wearing 'the costume of a savage', would not accept his letter, and bawled
at him: '*Je! ne! vous! per! mets! pas! de vous présenter devant mon bureau
dans cette tenue-là!*' George went into a thicket to put his trousers back
on, 'sat down by the roadside to meditate', and it was at this moment, he
claimed later, that he conceived the idea of writing his book, 'respectfully
dedicated to the French administration of Tahiti'.

But things only got worse. At Taravao Calderon had, as he put it, 'come again into the full stream of the civilisation of *papaas* [foreigners] and unredeemed Chinamen' – 'unredeemed' because they had a monopoly of shops and business all over the island, were brazenly exploitative, and impervious to civilising influences around them. 'Everyone' on the isthmus was 'rude'. Perhaps its very narrowness generated tension. When Calderon asked the shopkeeper he had just bought food from which of the two roads outside his door was to Tautira on Tahiti iti, he was told 'I do not know'. Nor could the shopkeeper sell him shoes or tell him where the next shop was (it was actually a hundred yards away). Failing to buy shoes, he tried to hire a horse, but with no more success. In the end, Calderon was offered accommodation by a Protestant deacon. This, however, led to him being cut dead by all his previous Roman Catholic acquaintances as they passed through.

Calderon had been offered the hospitality of Amaru's *fetii* at Tautira, halfway along the northern coast of the Taiarapu Peninsula. As today, at Taravao you could either continue on the road westwards around *Tahiti nui* (Great Tahiti), or take the road onto *Tahiti iti* as far as Tautira. Calderon did neither. He seems to have collected some legends here, and he worked 'hard at the language', but on his own admission he grew 'despondent', even 'irresolute'. He impulsively decided to get a horse and retrace his steps fourteen miles to Mahaena, because he had heard that this was 'the place of pre-historic simplicity'. However, absolutely no-one at Mahaena would put him up for the night. He told one inhabitant it was 'an accursed village full of savages', and rode back to Taravao. Sitting on the deacon's verandah next day, 'again the sense of depression close[d] over me, of desolation and of the fear of death alone on the seashore, away from England'. He seemed stuck in the cul-de-sac of Taravao.

He was rescued by Amaru, who came looking for him on a horse and whisked him back to Vaanui. Although they arrived when everyone else was asleep, 'Madame Amaru' ironed 'sheets and pillow-cases, smiling all the time', and George was put to bed. 'In the morning she gave me a beautiful hat she had made for me in my absence.'

After recuperating, Calderon set out again for the Taiarapu Peninsula on foot. As he approached Taravao the natives looked 'disdainful' and 'pass[ed] without salutation'. He reminded himself that in olden times *Tahiti iti* had been regarded as lawless, savage, and with 'no reputation for friendliness'. This time at Taravao he fell in with three Catholic priests who were having a picnic. He had a 'heated discussion' with them about everything from Dumford to Darwin, ending by telling them that 'if they had lived in the time of Christ they would have crucified Him'. His vehemence perhaps indicates how stressed Calderon was still; although they 'parted as good friends as ever'.

At Pihaa on the peninsula Calderon met the retired gendarme Piétry, of whom everyone had spoken well. George was due to stay with Amaru's *fetii* Taua, a little further on at Pueu, but Piétry assured him the accommodation was too poor for a white man, he would be 'tormented to death' by fleas and mosquitos, and should lodge with him. Calderon politely refused. Taua turned out to be an industrious matriarch of sixty who ran 'a well-ordered household' and on reading Amaru's letter invited George to stay. The family worked in the copra trade and were not poor, but they did not seem very friendly and they gave him his meals with them on the ground. Then it transpired that the reason they lived in 'a hut which is only a roof on four posts, open at all sides' was that their old house and furniture had been washed away by the tsunami...

One of Calderon's purposes in coming to *Tahiti iti* was to find the house that R.L. Stevenson had lived in for two months in 1888 and talk to people who had known him. Taua knew of him as 'Teritera' and said his house had been destroyed by the flood. Twice in *Tahiti* George tells us that he was 'too footsore' to pursue this inquiry further. He spent two evenings with Piétry, who gave him all the local news and gossip, and one afternoon went with Taua's son-in-law to drink fermented orange juice and listen to *ute*-singing. It was a group of 'beautiful people assembled in a hut behind the chief's house; richly favoured, full-juiced men and women; garlanded with a profusion of wild flowers, and very friendly'. Taua now began to cherish him more. He transcribed a song from her. One of her daughters, Uupa, made 'very soft eyes' at him and Taua had 'the air of offering her to me as a companion'.

Calderon was particularly taken by the women of *Tahiti iti*. They were of beautiful form and face, with immense masses of coarse hair bound up behind their heads; they offer no salutation; they turn their eyes neither to the right nor to the left, but steadfastly go on their way, with the majestic tread of Greek goddesses.

The men too were 'of richer temperament and greater stature' than on *Tahiti nui*, 'with whiter teeth, coarser hair, blacker and more vivid eyes; with brighter smile and tranquiller gravity'. Altogether, he felt the 'Taiarapuans of today' had retained 'the fresh-blooded vigour of the age of gold'. But still they were not 'near and familiar to me like Amaru, Temaeva and the rest'.

Perhaps on 3 August, Calderon reached his final destination, the village of Tautira twelve miles from Taravao. It had 'a brilliant indigo bay [...] sand-rimmed and fringed with distant dim blue coco-palms'. As today, the coastal road ended here because the strand gave way to cliffs and rugged terrain all the way round to the south coast. Calderon set off back to Taravao without exploring that unspoilt coast, which is home today to the 'heaviest wave in the world' at Teahupoo. Instead, at Taravao he turned left and made for Papara, fifteen miles along the south coast of *Tahiti nui*, in order to visit the site of a bloody battle of 1768 in which the king of Taiarapu had won independence from the northern 'mainland'. Unfortunately, as he walked out onto the historic promontory he heard a voice singing the 'spurious national anthem of Tahiti' and saw natives 'joining in it with complacent grins'. 'No bitterer historical irony could be invented than that', so he walked away 'hastily' and set off back to Vaanui, where in three days time he was due to start with Amaru on 'a ride round the island'.

Calderon's reasons for going to Tahiti were to do with his health and his interest in anthropology, but it is clear that whilst he was there he became increasingly preoccupied with what it meant to live 'close to Nature', and whether this was possible for a European in the twentieth century. Dumford was a figure debated all over the island. Previously at Vaanui Calderon had met a young Frenchman named Vaillant, who had given up an office job in Sydney to live what he called a life of 'Paradise' and 'independence' here. In fact he was a complete sponger. He had billeted himself for three years on Piriri, Amaru's adoptive father the old

chief, used all the latter's *fetii* as if they were his own, and was now going
to set up his house next door. Vaillant too became a term in Calderon's
'return to Nature' calculus. When George got back to Vaanui this time,
Amaru gave a 'pigling feast' in his honour, to which Piriri and his wife
were invited but not Vaillant. A very interesting conversation ensued
about Piriri's belief that 'in the old days' most Tahitians lived in the
mountains – in 1906 they still contained 'everything that man needs for
life' – and Piriri demonstrated how to make fire with two pieces of wood
even in the rain.

Next morning, with ferny wreaths on their heads made by the women,
George and Amaru set off on horseback. The circumference of *Tahiti nui*
is approximately seventy miles. They rode straight to Taravao, where
Amaru had to pay the gendarme a fine for letting his pig stray on the road,
and overnighted at a European dentist's. The next morning they passed
through Mataiea, about eight miles along the south coast, where Rupert
Brooke was to stay in 1914. One stretch of road beyond that was according
to Amaru 'a terrible place for *tupapaus* at night' – these being ghosts or
spirits. Amaru described them to Calderon and how to get rid of them.
That afternoon they must have passed through Papara. The next sizeable
commune was Punaauia, where Gauguin had lived in the 1890s. Calderon
had already visited it with Amaru during his first stay by riding round the
north coast, but the settlements in the next fourteen or so miles between
Papara and Punaauia would have been entirely new to him. It is strange,
then, that he does not mention them. On the contrary, he and Amaru rode
on through the night and through Punaauia, arriving at Faaa at one in the
morning. They had therefore covered thirty-five miles in a day. For
George the real spice of this trip, it seems, was not the sightseeing but his
conversations with Amaru.

From Faaa they went in early next morning to Papeete, where each
had his own business. They must have set off again that day, because 'that
evening as we rode along the road we met Dumford on his bicycle'; but
where they spent the night is unclear. The caption to the 'legend of the
stars in the Tail of the Scorpion' in *Tahiti* implies that Calderon heard it
from Temaeva at 9.00 p.m. on 10 August 1906. Since Temaeva lived at

Vaapuru, beyond Papenoo, they probably regained Vaanui later that night.

Within a day or two George left Vaanui for the last time, intending to see Amaru and his family again in Papeete.

As he walked into the capital, he passed two Frenchmen from the administration. One, whom he did not know, asked the other: 'Who is that?' 'Don't you know?' said the second, who was Monsieur Percier. '*C'est Monsieur Calderon*.' The first riposted:

'*Tiens! Impossible!* Ah, see to what such imprudence leads. Two months ago that man came here rich, full of money; he threw it right and left, squandering it on liquor and harlots. Now see to what he has reduced himself by his extravagance. He is obliged to go about like a beggar.'

Percier protested that it was not like that at all, and George still had 'money'. 'Then what explanation is possible?' asked the other. '*Voyez-vous*,' replied Percier, '*c'est un type*.'

George booked into 'Pandora's Hotel' again and prepared to leave the island. He visited Tupuna and the other 'Bayadères' and found that Tahiri-i-te-rai was suffering from a bout of consumption. 'I tell Tahiri that she is a naughty girl to be ill. She says: "I don't want to be ill; *c'est le Bon Dieu qui m'a fait* [sic] *malade*".' He gave Maná English lessons and sat at the feet of Madame Drollet, who knew 'as much of the ancient language and traditions of the island as few natives'. She gave him Tahitian poems and told him legends. Amaru and his family now arrived, with a young coconut for him to drink at once, a sack of oranges, and 'three or four hats to take with me'. Calderon went to the cinematograph, arriving during an interval, when girls 'burst out of the inner room, hung about with roses and other flowers'. One 'appropriated me, danced me round, led me to a seat and decorated me with all the flowers she was wearing herself. It was pandemonium and I soon fled'.

On 17 August Amaru and his wife came to do his packing for him, whilst Tahiri and Maná sat on the bed looking on. His ship, the *Hauroto* again, left later that day and as he looked over the side he could see Amaru, his wife and the children 'standing in a row on the wharf weeping'.

We do not know when he reached Auckland, but on 8 September he was writing his mother a brief postcard from which it is clear that he had picked up his mail there and was just about to board a ship for Wellington. 'In six or seven weeks I shall be back in England; a bearded and a wiser man.'

We know that on 12 or 13 September 1906 he left Wellington on Shaw, Savill and Albion's 5563-ton *Karamea*. It appears to have begun a new service sailing *eastwards* from Wellington via Cape Horn and Rio de Janeiro to 'West Coast ports of the U.K. and London'. When George had used the phrase '*faire le tour du monde*' to Tupuna, then, it looks as though he meant it literally.

8

PERFORMING FOR THE *TLS*

All of the letters, diaries and sketchbooks that Calderon sent home to Kittie from his travels in 1906 probably reached her. It was not so easy for her, however, as she had to know exactly which ports he was going to be at when, and time her letters to be waiting for him when the ship docked. Thus he may not have known until the *Karamea* reached Tenerife on 22 October that Kittie's mother had died on 30 August.

Mrs Hamilton possibly accompanied Kittie to stay with the Corbets at Acton Reynald when George left for New Zealand in April, but she must have become increasingly bedridden thereafter. Dr Tebb described her as 'confined to her room with Rheumatoid arthritis etc' and suffering from attacks of 'pneumonia, bronchitis, phlebitis etc etc'. 'During the whole time', Tebb says in the testimonial that he wrote for Kittie in 1914, 'the daughter took an active daily share (with the regular nurses) in the nursing, lifting etc.' At some point Mary Hamilton moved to a nursing home at 18 Crossfield Road in Hampstead, where she died. Tebb certified the causes as 'Acute Bronchitis (capillary) 6 days Heart failure'.

At the beginning of September, then, not only had Kittie not seen her husband for five months, but she had lost her mother, with whom she had lived for most of her unmarried and married life. She was drained by the experience of the last few months. George finally appeared on 30 October and their reunion must have been tearful.

It is possible that for reasons connected with Mrs Hamilton's probate, or other reasons, Kittie vacated Heathland Lodge in October. Certainly, by November the house was profitably let to the family of Hermann Sielcken, the 'Coffee King', and George and Kittie were living at 33 Buckingham Mansions, about a mile away. They moved back into Heathland Lodge on 13 April 1907, but had evidently decided to sell it. A grand farewell garden party was held there on 8 June. However, when the house was put up to auction on 25 June, it did not sell. After a month visiting Emmetts in Kent, Evey and Violet's home in Sussex, and the Newbolts at Netherhampton, they returned to 33 Buckingham Mansions, having found another tenant for Heathland Lodge. They seem to have finally moved back into Heathland Lodge at the end of 1907, staying for the next five years but probably taking occasional lodgers.

In a memoir from the 1940s, Kittie wrote that George's 'sea-voyage' brought him 'new vigour'. But George's diary for 1907 – the only one of his known to exist – tells a more complex story. His visit to Tahiti was definitely followed by a new cycle of creativity, but this had very uncertain beginnings.

Although George kept what he described as 'diaries' on his various cruises, these were perhaps more like journals, since there is no evidence that he normally kept a diary and the idea seems difficult to reconcile with his passion for living life 'forward'. Several things suggest that the point of the pocket diary which he kept in 1907 was in fact to help him organise a new literary career and focus his mind on it from day to day. Thus after three months of almost entirely social entries, on 8 April he notes in Russian: 'Began to draw up programme of projects.' By the end of May he is 'at work on *Chenda*' (the first title of his play *The Fountain*). Memoranda through the summer record his work on a 'Tahitian article' and *Chenda*. The latter is 'finished' on 20 July, 'typewritten' by 24 July, and being revised at the beginning of August. But the work took its toll. Against four days in July he put large ink and crayon crosses, which seem to indicate bouts of depression. After seeing a doctor in Farnham, George took to his bed for five days 'with gout' and his writing became shaky.

On 6 August 1907 the Calderons left for three weeks holiday at Acton Reynald; except that from 20th to 26th George made a 'solo tramp', as Kittie described it, from Shrewsbury to Leamington Spa. He probably slept rough. It must have felt like a throwback to his time on Tahiti. Judging from the picture postcards that he sent Kittie from each town, he was happy and relaxed.

By the end of the first week of September, when the Calderons were staying at Alresford in Hampshire, George was 'reading the history of the Reformation' in search of a subject for a history play. On 13 September he was 'designing *Cromwell*, a play of the Reformation', but he had an accident that put his arm in a sling and he was treated by two doctors at Stoke Mandeville. Nevertheless, he continued 'designing *Cromwell* and collecting material', on 5 October he 'began to compose it', and he worked away at it all that month as well as 'looking over *Chenda* for revision'. Then he went down with a bad cold and, diary notwithstanding, lost his way.

He admitted on 8 November that he was 'shillyshallying between different books to write'. A week later, he was still 'shillyshallying' but '(apparently) settling down to write the book on Tahiti'. He was 'afraid of *Cromwell* and uneasy about *Chenda*'. On 7 December he 'laid the outline of *Tahiti* and began to write'. His memoranda directed him throughout December to continue with *Tahiti*, but by the end of the month he seems to have abandoned it, and even the projected article.

Altogether, Calderon published nothing in 1906 or the first half of 1907. On the evidence of his pocket diary, his health was still not strong enough for sustained literary work.

It was probably Percy Lubbock who found for him the perfect way of easing himself back into print. The magazine *Literature*, to which George had contributed possibly half a dozen reviews between 1897 and 1902, was sold by *The Times* at the beginning of 1902 and incorporated with the *Academy*. Immediately afterwards, *The Times* launched its own *Literary Supplement*. By 1907, under its shrewd and far-sighted second editor Bruce Richmond, it had taken off. Percy had started contributing in 1904 at the age of twenty-five and was highly thought of. Virginia Woolf was another star among the paper's young guard of 'brilliant, questioning and sceptical minds' as Derwent May, historian of the *Times Literary Supplement*, has described them, and Calderon became part of this group.

Evidently it was as a Slavist, folklorist and ethnologist that he was first taken on, since four out of the five reviews he contributed in 1907 are on these subjects. They display a fine knowledge of recent Balkan history, folklore medicine, and Maori legends. Already in the fifth review, however, published on 6 September 1907, he is branching out. Its subject was a book by G.F. Abbott entitled *Israel in Europe*. This was 'a synopsis of the history of the Jews in Europe' and George found it 'interesting in subject, comprehensive in material, and lucid in expression'. But he voiced a fundamental personal disagreement:

To our mind the whole book seems to disprove the thesis which the author sets out, perhaps as an afterthought, in his introduction – that the sufferings of the Jews in Europe have arisen from their obstinacy in holding themselves aloof from their Christian neighbours. On the contrary, it is the active part which they have played in the affairs of the Christian continent which has been at once their service and their disservice, their claim to our gratitude and the motive of our envy. [...] It is the essence of every grievance against them only that by their superior talents they have reaped so abundantly in every country the rewards offered for certain forms of work.

The book also moved him to express a personal literary belief: 'Mr Abbott has many qualities good for the business of writing, but he lacks the chief quality, certainty of opinion; a defect in daily conversation, but the very life of letters.'

In 1908 the number of reviews by him shot up to thirty-one. He began on 6 February with a piece over two thousand words long that examined with vivacious erudition three books: one on Muslim, Christian and Jewish folklore of the Holy Land, one entitled *Jamaican Song and Story*, and one on Russian and Bulgarian folklore stories. This review may well throw light on some problematic aspects of Calderon's own work in this field.

'Nations may be judged by what they have made of their primitive fictions', he opened. The peoples of the Middle East, and the Indians, had

excelled all the other nations of the earth in the sublimity of their treatment of this material. The raw stuff, being converted by them to the uses of wisdom, has thereby gained immeasurably in literary value. Some of it, encrusted into the fabric of religion, has spread from these centres all over the world; what remains unsanctified is the subject-matter of folklore.

Not surprisingly, then, the transmission, or as George calls it 'diffusion', of folklore narratives becomes the personal focus of his review. 'That tales should spread from the Holy Land to Europe is not remarkable; there is a continual coming and going of Christian and Moslem pilgrims in the Russian and Turkish Empires.' The concrete similarities between the Bulgarian/Russian folktales that he quotes and certain Jewish and Palestinian ones in the first book under review appear to corroborate an hypothesis of transmission in these cases. But suddenly – and the abruptness could indicate faulty editing – there is a break in his argument: 'The belief that pearls are made from raindrops is almost universal; Columbus recorded it as Mexican; Pliny says dewdrops. No doubt some things have gone conversely by the Hadjis' road from Europe into Asia.'

The idea that components of folklore are 'universal' implies polygenesis rather than diffusion (obviously Calderon is not suggesting that the image of pearl-raindrops was transmitted from Europe or Asia to Mexico before Columbus). The brilliant series of comparisons of folklore stories from Jamaica, Australia, China, and Sanskrit that George entertains and impresses us with next are *analogues*, not examples of 'diffusion', and the latter argument has disappeared entirely. He conceives no empirical term, for instance 'morphology' or 'structure', between 'universal' (polygenesis) and 'diffusion' (transmission). This gets him into deep water when he comes to discuss the Jamaican story 'Mancrow'. He believes it is

curiously interesting as a study in transmission, because one can lay one's finger on its original with tolerable certainty and see the transformation which it has undergone in adoption. The 'little yawzy fellah' who goes out with his 'six bow and arrow' from Kingston to shoot Mancrow is almost certainly the Russian Ilya of Murom, the bird-slayer, whose heroic career was prefaced by thirty years in a 'yawzy' condition, while he sat on the stove. When he wanted to go and fight the Robber Nightingale (Solovéi in Russian), who sat in the trees like Mancrow and 'darkened' the country about him, he was set back by his elders with just this, 'Tche, boy, you better go sleep a fireside than you go to the wood to go dead.' [...] What clinches the identity is the name Solidáy, which is Solovéi transferred from the fowl to the man.

In what sense 'is' the 'little yawzy fellah' (i.e. Solidáy) Il'ia of Murom? Calderon qualifies the statement with 'almost certainly', but he seems so eager to believe in this tautology that he attributes a line from the Jamaican story to the Russian. And most people's initial reaction to the fact that the human hero of 'Mancrow' is called Solidáy would surely be that it tends to *dis*prove any identity, not 'clinch' it. Yet he is so far persuaded of it himself that he presses 'transmission' into its service: 'It is certainly curious to find a Russian story so far astray; but runaway sailors have, no doubt, had more to do with the transmission of ideas in every age than has been generally taken into account.' In fact all of this is assertion and speculation.

Interestingly, in Calderon's next long review of a folklore work, published on 7 May 1908, he appears to reject the linguistic approach that he himself may have practised: 'The extravagance of the Max Müller school, who looked for the explanation of every myth in the corruption of language [...] became too absurd to be tolerated.' In its stead, he writes, came 'the sect of Traditionalists, who obstinately refuse to admit any other explanation of folk-tales and folk-customs than that of "survival" from a more primitive state of being'. The book under review, George Gomme's *Folklore as an Historical Science*, was an extreme case of this approach. Calderon relentlessly deconstructed Gomme's claims for folk 'tradition' and the 'historical value' of fairytales, then took the argument in an entirely fresh direction. Gomme, he wrote, was intolerant of the 'psychical point of view' in anthropology, under which heading he included 'visions, hallucinations, and trance conditions, natural and induced', in other words 'clairvoyance' and shamanism. This was modern indeed. The whole review demonstrated not only George's analytical powers and command of the subject, but the openness of his mind to new approaches.

However, the most unexpected development in his reviewing for the *TLS* in 1908 was that he was invited to review novels and ended by reviewing more of them (fifteen) than anything else. This possibly came about because he was given a new book by G.K. Chesterton to review on the assumption that it was non-fiction, but in fact it was the novel *The Man Who Was Thursday*. Calderon produced a masterly critique in only 211 words, published on 5 March. Chesterton's 'ordinary function', he claimed, was 'to entertain us with slow-moving, long-drawn epigrams; something at once ponderous and roguish'. This book, 'as an entertainment', was only 'half a success; it is full of witty turns, but they are like the flashes of blue light in a tube railway, irrelevant expenditures of motor energy. As literature, it is a hopeless *confusion de genres'*. George's reviewing of novels, the vast majority of which were ephemeral, began the week after.

Richmond must have been delighted by Calderon's light touch. George was thoroughly conversant with the classic English novelists, we know from his surviving library that he had worked his way through modern French fiction, and he knew the Russian novelists well. His critical standards were very high. But he also understood that 'the practised reader devours a volume a day' and was not as demanding as himself. Consequently his reviews of novels, although almost all negative, rarely demolish and are usually gentle, understated, even complimentary.

Many of these novels enabled George to exercise his taste for the absurd. Reviewing on 12 March 1908 a novel 'with an unfortunate name, *The Virgin Widow'*, he found

It is an altogether curious and uncomfortable world which these people inhabit. They live in solitary cottages by unfrequented roads, and have absolutely no occupation to while away the time, though the poet smokes a little when things are darkest.

Similarly, from a review published on 29 October 1908:

The people of Trescas, the Cornish village in which Mr Morley Roberts lays the scene of *David Bran* [...] are not quite like the people of other villages. Their speech is full of dark sayings about wisdom and destiny and the heart of man; they pass their lives in a state of wonder at each other and at the ways of heaven. They are cast in heroic mould; the women all have strong hearts and strong hands; the men are giants; and as for David himself, seven at a blow would be nothing to him.

The eponymous hero of Algernon Blackwood's 'metapsychic and occult' novel *John Silence* (19 November 1908) is an imitation of Sherlock Holmes, but his pursuits are

not after delightful criminals, but after tedious bogeys, women who turn into cats, men who turn into wolves, and Egyptian 'fire elementals' living with asbestos rabbits in a wood. To delight in the mystical symbols of prehistoric times is a sure sign of mental degeneration; and the enlightened will be warned of the sort of thing they have to expect in this volume by the svastika stamped on its cover.

Very occasionally, as in this review of Maurice Hewlett's *The Spanish Jade* (14 May 1908), Calderon turns his irony on the novelist himself:

It is the work of a practised craftsman, skilful and ingenious in execution; but, like the work of so many practised craftsmen, it expresses so little that the skill and ingenuity rather tantalize than satisfy. If he had a tale to tell, one feels, how well he would tell it; how exquisitely he would moralize if he had any moral to impart. His language is fastidious and nice; he is witty, he is tortuous; he is like a clown at the circus straining his muscles to lift a lump of wood painted to look like a cannon-ball, or a man dancing a ballet to draw a cork.

Examples of the straight-faced *reductio ad absurdum* in George's reviews could be multiplied. He is far more of a humorist in this genre than a satirist.

His reviews of two 'quality' works of fiction, on the other hand, give interesting insights into his own beliefs at this time. Writing on 10 September 1908 about Somerville and Ross's *Further Experiences of an Irish R.M.* he remarked:

It is to be understood in no disparaging sense, when we say that the chief gift of the authors [...] is the amateur quality of their work. The Zeitgeist rebels a little against professionalism in art. [...] We rejoice at the coming of an amateur with all his artistic innocence and the smack of real life, from which he emerges, on him.

Amateurism in this sense later became one of Calderon's tenets. But his review of H.G. Wells's *The War in the Air* (5 November 1908) suggests beliefs about war far removed from those he held six years later. Did Wells think, asked George, that 'one international conflict would really provoke the whole world to war', or was this 'only a way of giving grandeur to his tale'? Like many Edwardians who had never known a European war, in 1908 Calderon seemed to think the vital question was that of pacifism, or at least whether Britain should acquire 'armaments'. Wells, however, posited that 'the appearance of being unarmed does not contribute to keeping the peace, but, in fact, provokes the attack' and that modern war would be total. In George's view, this 'moral' from *The War in the Air* 'will not bear looking into'.

After novels, the largest group of reviews that he wrote for the *TLS* (eleven) concerned Russia, Russian literature, and Tolstoi. This contained its fair share of aristocrats' memoirs and journalistic writing about Russia ('in great vogue at the present time'), although even here Calderon could find positive things to say. For example, reviewing on 11 June 1908 Brayley Hodgetts's *The Court of Russia in the Nineteenth Century* he admitted 'the emergence of one clear and original thought (almost on the last page of the book)', namely that 'Absolutism and Nationalism are incompatible, and that Alexander III, by accepting Slavophily [Slavophilism] as an official creed, signed the death warrant of the autocracy'. The point was 'ingeniously argued' and it was 'an interesting notion to think of Pobednostseff as the destroyer of the autocracy'! In a review of A. Brückner's *Literary History of Russia* (11 November 1909) he was scathing about Minns's verse translations of Russian poetry, but praised Havelock's sensitive rendering of the book from German.

The most important 'Russian' books that George reviewed were by Aylmer Maude and Maurice Baring. Both were non-academic Russianists; 'amateurs' in the sense of which George approved. Readers might feel, however, that his treatments of their work were less than fair.

Reviewing on 11 March 1909 the first volume of Maude's monumental *The Life of Tolstoy*, Calderon conceded that 'no other Englishman can claim the same advantages as biographer – knowledge of Russia and the Russian language, intimacy with Tolstoy's works, and acquaintance with the man himself'. But Tolstoi was himself 'one of the most perfect autobiographers' and 'his own criticism of himself is so searching that he leaves those that come after him no scope'. As a 'personal friend' of Tolstoi, Calderon claims, Maude is too close to get a handle on him and settles for a 'morbid conscientiousness about chronology' and amassing the facts to which he has unique access:

It is right and natural for Tolstoy himself to tell us about his bull-dog and his estate and the siege of Sebastopol; but what we want from his biographer is a history of his mental development; we do not want to know the circumstances through which he passed except in so far as they bear on that.

These strictures are, of course, a salutary warning to biographers everywhere, but one cannot wholly agree with them since intellectual biography is only part of the 'story'. In his review of the second part of Maude's biography, published in the *TLS* on 6 October 1910, Calderon even hardened his criticism to saying that Maude had 'serious faults as a biographer. He is enormously prolix, he tells us things that we do not want to know, and omits those that we do'. In his first review he had strongly suggested that as a writer in English Maude was a dilettante: 'He knows Tolstoy and Russia well enough, but he does not know us and our words and our ideas.' In other words, again, he was too acculturated to Russia. Nevertheless, Calderon recognised that in his second volume Aylmer Maude

lays his finger on the radical weakness of Tolstoy's manner of thought when he speaks of his 'ethical arrogance', his readiness 'to condemn the achievements of those whose work has been remote from his own experience, and to impute base motives to men and movements he knows almost nothing of'.

Altogether, indeed, George characterised the second volume as 'an acute criticism' and Maude himself as 'a man of a rare sort, himself an idealist, a seeker, an experimenter, of keen intelligence, devoted to public good'.

Calderon's critique of Maurice Baring's books may appear less judicious. Reviewing his *Russian Essays and Stories* on 22 April 1909, George admits immediately that 'what interests us is the author's method rather than his matter; and his volume affords an opportunity for appraising the theory and practice of that particular school of realism of which he here appears as a disciple'. He claims that in his essays on Russian life and his stories drawn from it Baring thinks that realism consists in selecting 'almost at random what he will tell us'. Baring regards 'the search for causes as a kind of insincerity', whereas 'what we want [...] is truthful records of typical people, real or unreal, seen through the medium of a general notion of Russian life derived from combined observation and reasoning'. Moreover,

The depth of his error as to realism may be seen in what he says about Russian plays. He believes it to be a peculiarity of Russian dramatists that they aim at depicting real life, and suggests it as a novel experiment for the Western stage that we should imitate them. 'I believe,' he says, 'that plays written about real life, in which the characters live and behave as they do in reality, would be not only interesting but successful in any country.' As if the making of such plays were not the perpetual aim of dramatists! But a dramatist would be putting chaos and not real life on the stage if he presented imitations of unselected people doing unselected things at unselected moments.

This hit home with Baring and in his next book, Landmarks in Russian Literature, he tried to refute it. Unfortunately, to do so he brought in Chekhov, asserting that 'the difference between Tchekov and most English and French dramatists [...] is that the moments which Tchekov selects appear at first sight to be trivial'. In his copy of the book Calderon wrote beside this: 'The reverse of true', and proceeded to attack it in his review of 24 March 1910:

The *differentia* of Tchekhof is that the extraordinary moments which set the pistols going are never the result of sudden causes, but are always brought about by the cumulative tragedy of daily life; not ordinary daily life in the sense of everyone's daily life, but the life of men tragically situated, like Ivanov and Uncle Vanya. But that is a very different thing from choosing trivial moments.

To obsess about this theme in Baring's books was certainly subjective, and Calderon seems guilty of wilful distortion in his review of The Russian People (2 November 1911) when he presents Baring's discussion of the 'paradoxes' of 'the Russian character' as contradictions in Baring's own writing. Nevertheless, he did pay tribute to Baring's knowledge of the Russian language and people, and even declared that he had 'the chief part of the outfit of a critic; he has enthusiasm and the power of communicating it' (24 March 2010).

George's fundamental, if not explicit, criticism of Maude and Baring was that they had immersed themselves in Russian culture but not come out of it again sufficiently to say something innovative about it; in other words, that there was little critical thinking in their books. Indeed he implies that neither of them knows *European* culture well enough to have anything comparative and critical to say. Certainly Baring seems to have assimilated some of the waffle on 'realism' churned out by contemporary Russian academic literary historians and *engagé* journalists. Calderon also bemoaned the authors' errors of translation, transliteration, stress and fact. Correspondence about these followed on the pages of the *TLS* and largely vindicated him. If Maude and Baring were in the best sense 'amateur' Russianists, Calderon comes across here as the professional.

In 1908 and 1910 Calderon wrote on Chesterton's non-fiction at some length. His review of *Orthodoxy* and *All Things Considered* (1 October 1908) developed his earlier take on Chesterton as a great entertainer ('His writing has all the qualities of the best journalism, and, chiefly, it conveys the sense of mental energy without the appearance of effort'), but also grappled with Chesterton's religious conservatism and irrationalism. 'What he wants', George protested, 'is the old dogmas; the more the merrier, and the older the better.'

His motives in philosophy are in fact not rational, but wholly aesthetic. [...] He does not understand the fine romantic incalculability of true reason (which is always being deflected from its straight course by the *data* which it discovers); it presents itself to him in the image of a big Reading Gaol, spreading its whitewashed corridors in vistas of infinite gloom. He refuses to believe in the first postulate of science, the uniformity of Nature; it is too dull to believe in. He prefers perpetual miracle.

Reviewing *What's Wrong with the World?* (30 June 1910), Calderon claimed that 'Mr Chesterton writes about himself and says it is mankind. The reason why he can never be a convincing critic [...] is that he [...] does not perceive the virtues, the "identity" or "tao" of the thing that he attacks'. But the worst thing in the book was his mockery of 'gentility'. Chesterton believed that gentility was 'a kind of rather offensive paste smudged over boys at public schools'; he did not see that it 'goes to the roots of things, permeates the being and is a philosophy of life for all classes'.

If public schools teach the manners of the Polynesian or the 'gentle parfit knight' to the sons of grocers Mr Chesterton should not sneer, but rejoice. Cleanliness is praised by the gentry, not because it is a private luxury, but because it is a public benefit; 'playing the game' is not helping one's side to win but being generous to adversaries; what Mr Chesterton calls insincerity and indifference to truth is really compromise, not infidelity to principle, but the submission of private opinion to the needs of public action; again, a deep social virtue, not a private and superficial vice.

If Newbolt's most famous poem is being alluded to here, George's interpretation of 'playing the game' is surely wrong. But as we shall see, when he wrote in this review of a man subjecting his 'own personality' to the 'convenience of the community' he was expressing one of his deepest beliefs.

Two final groups of reviews are on subjects that may seem surprising: tramps (or in the case of A.C. Benson a rambler), and psychical research.

On 14 May 1908 Calderon reviewed W.H. Davies's *The Autobiography of a Super-Tramp* together with *Never Say Die* by a Russian Grand Duke. At Eastcote he had chatted with unemployed workmen, on Hampstead Heath he conversed with tramps, and he himself enjoyed rambling with minimal possessions. He found Davies's book sympathetic and G.B.S.'s preface to it 'delightful'. But what he sought to understand was the dissatisfaction of both the tramp and the Grand Duke. He concluded:

The really essential difference between tramps and Princes is that, while the destinies fight against the tramp, the sorrows of Princes are almost wholly of human manufacture. [...] The Prince, having what the vagrant needs, does not feel grateful for it or desire more of it; his demands on life go over into the sphere of the romantic, with which Mr Davies (whose world seems to contain no women but landladies) is wholly unconcerned. The Prince does not realise the benefit of what he has, but only the privation of what he lacks.

As George saw it (in a review of 2 June 1910), H.G. Wells tried to jump on the Davies/Shaw bandwagon by sponsoring the autobiography of George Meek, a down-and-out maker of bath chairs. Compared with Davies, however, Meek was 'artificial, a product of free libraries and cheap reprints; he goes about with his eyes shut and sees, not the world, but what his newspaper tells him is the world'. Meek had 'a grievance', but 'the question is, Is Society really responsible for all this? Is it our fault?'. Calderon thought not. The bath-chairman was under the illusion that 'all his life he has been somehow "exploited" by a "predatory" class; but if you come to think of it there is really nothing exploitable in Mr Meek. He has been receiving more than giving all his life'. In 1985, at the height of Thatcherism, the *TLS* reprinted this review in its column 'Seventy-Five Years On'.

Calderon's approach to the books he reviewed about 'spiritualism' was open-minded but cautious. He did not spare fraudulent mediums and Mme Blavatsky. On the other hand, as an anthropologist he believed the study of 'psychical phenomena' was 'of incalculable value for the proper understanding of the history of human thought' (review of 27 August 1908). He was therefore prepared to consider the findings of the Society for Psychical Research (SPR), whose 'standard of evidence required' was 'about five times stricter than that required to hang a man for murder' (review of 8 September 1910). The difficulty about the hypothesis that spirits communicated through mediums was 'the unmistakable colour which the communication gets through the medium' (review of 9 July 1908). Similarly, these 'ghosts' make 'all manner of mistakes of fact which the dead could not make' – even the 'spirits' of deceased members of the SPR could not read the 'sealed test letters' that they themselves left behind for this purpose (review of 8 September 1910). Although George put forward a 'provisional theory' of his own, involving ambience and the deceased's belongings, which 'avoids some of the objections to the telepathic and *outre-tombe* explanations', he was forced on 9 July 1908 to admit:

We are not very much nearer to a definitive theory of the phenomena than we were before; we are perhaps on the threshold of a new world of thought, peering across it, as it were, but we are still very far from stepping over it.

Nevertheless, his knowledge of and thinking about this subject were to have an impact on one of his plays, and possibly on Kittie after his disappearance at Gallipoli.

The immediacy and wit of Calderon's contributions undoubtedly owe something to the *TLS*'s 'house style' at this time. The first person singular was replaced by a collective 'we', irony was the order of the day, and reviewers' candour was protected by anonymity. Even so, as Derwent May has written, George's reviews are outstanding for their 'dashing intelligence' and 'often sparkled on the pages of the *Lit Supp* as brightly as Virginia Woolf's'.

A number of personal beliefs emerge clearly from them. He was no anti-Semite. He defended the right of 'the smaller and remoter nations of Europe', such as Serbia and Bulgaria, to self-determination. He was appalled at the destruction of the '*joie de vivre*' of the 'brown races' by 'sombre forms of Christianity'. Russian genocide in the Caucasus was an 'unpardonable crime'. He empathised with 'the excitement of getting a job' and 'the misery of not getting one'. He felt it was impossible to know where political actions, e.g. pogroms, originated in Russia, because 'the country is too big; the government is too loosely organized'. Nothing was 'true' about Russia 'except paradoxes'. For all the absurdity of his 'system', Tolstoi had 'roused thousands from their apathy towards the shocking state of society' and made Christianity 'a living thing for many who had taken no interest in it before'. Writers, as opposed to journalists, should not practise 'a sort of random impartiality, a readiness to hold two opposite opinions at the same time'. 'Good performance in all the arts' requires 'firmness of purpose [...] firmness in carrying out the general plan of [a] work, firmness in facing the facts which bear on it.' He supported those 'poorer townsfolk of this country' who were struggling to better themselves by working hard and acquiring 'the love of good manners and the domestic virtues'. Egotism was a bad thing, 'gentility' in the service of the community a good thing.

The high point of Calderon's involvement with the *TLS* was the year 1908, when he contributed thirty-one reviews, of which fifteen were of novels. The invaluable TLS Historical Archive tells us that the thirty-one reviews totalled 30,192 words. Contributors were paid £3 per column, which was roughly 1250 words. Using the Retail Price Index, this suggests that in 1908 he earned from his reviewing the equivalent today of about

£6200, or four times that if we use Average Earnings. It must have been an extremely welcome addition to the family finances.

However, by the end of 1908 he had evidently had enough of reviewing novels. He tackled only one more, and that was in 1910. Given that most of the personal beliefs just summarised featured more than once in 1908, perhaps he also felt that he had said all he had to say and was in danger of repeating himself. In 1909 he contributed eight reviews, specialising in Russia and Tolstoi. The following year he reviewed only seven books, but most of them were major publications. He reviewed only single works in 1911 and 1912.

There is hardly a superfluous word in Calderon's reviews for the *TLS* and as usual with him they read zestfully. They must have cost him a great effort of compression and polishing; but the evidence is that he enjoyed the experience immensely. Working on the *TLS* was so successful as therapy that he had become almost 'prolific' again. However, he clearly did not feel a long-term commitment to the paper. He had placed all his intelligence, up-to-the-minute knowledge, and writing skill at its service, but in 1910 he moved on.

9

THE TROUBLE WITH SUFFRAGISM

If 1908 was remarkable for George's productivity as a reviewer, it was even more remarkable for a totally new development in his life: he became a political activist.

The Women's Social and Political Union (WSPU), whose members were known as 'suffragettes', was founded in 1903 to hasten the enfranchisement of women by militant methods. The much older and more popular National Union of Women's Suffrage Societies (NUWSS) sought to bring pressure to bear on Parliament by peaceful methods and should be referred to as 'suffragists'. Although the suffragettes had been heckling Cabinet ministers, chaining themselves to public monuments and assaulting policemen for some years, after Asquith became Prime Minister in April 1908 their campaign moved to a new level of mass lobbying, window smashing, and hunger strikes. Not only was women's suffrage the great domestic issue of the day, Hampstead was a hot-spot of debate about it as so many intellectuals lived there.

Calderon contributed to public meetings in Hampstead about the female franchise, and 'hearing that a Hampstead lady intended to publish a pamphlet in favour of Woman Suffrage, with the Priory Press [Hampstead printers]', he 'undertook to publish another in answer to it'. According to him,

when the time came, the lady, still mindful of the privileges of her sex, changed her mind, and proposed on the contrary that I should set up the ninepins and she should knock them down; a proposal to which I was obliged to consent.

Thus (he would have us believe) was born his 9000-word pamphlet *Woman in Relation to the State: A Consideration of the Arguments*

Advanced for the Extension of the Parliamentary Suffrage to Women, published in the summer of 1908.

Nothing, probably, has put people off George Calderon more than his opposition to votes for women. Yet as well as considering his arguments, we must view them in their full historical context – which has been painstakingly reconstructed over the last thirty-five years by 'revisionists' such as Brian Harrison, Martin Pugh, and Julia Bush. It should be remembered that women did have the franchise in local government. Successive opinion polls had established that the majority of them did not want the parliamentary vote. Several of George's arguments are identical to those presented by the Women's National Anti-Suffrage League (WNASL) in its manifesto. The thrust of his case, therefore, would not have seemed strange to contemporary readers. It was the way in which he elaborated it, and his tone, that were peculiar.

Characteristically, he had researched the literature in several languages and even listed it in a bibliography. 'The arguments of Mill, Condorcet, Bebel,' he concluded, 'tend only to assert what I, for one, joyfully admit: that in mental and moral capacity Woman is at least the equal of Man.' This was a restatement of what he had written to Kittie on 13 February 1899: 'Men are equal and women too.' In the opinion of a reviewer in the *New Age*, it 'gives his whole case away'. 'After that, why clink the cannikin?' 'But', Calderon swept on, 'that is no argument for giving [Woman] the suffrage.'

To us this may seem incomprehensible, since if men and women are 'mentally and morally' equal subjects of a single state, they must qualify for equal political rights. In George's view, however, this would be false logic. He did not even consider the inference, because like most people who opposed female suffrage he was overwhelmingly concerned with the *difference* between men and women.

He starts from the belief that 'Man' created 'the State'. In a passage of potted anthropology, he recounts how, whilst 'Man' went out to hunt and make war, 'Woman specialised more narrowly and developed the home; grew lovely, and softened the manners of men'. 'Both sexes desired justice, and sought to establish it by different methods.' 'Woman invented persuasion; but the most immediately effective method was Man's own, of

Force', and with it 'Man [...] established justice-by-compulsion and called it the State'. The 'great Woman's Grievance Myth' of the time is that 'Man has somehow "collared" the State for his advantage over downtrodden Woman'. But having created the State, 'Man did not "exclude" Woman; she never had any part in it'. Woman is 'an important member of the Community, but has no part whatever in the State, except to enjoy the benefits which it secures her'. One of these is protection (by males). Christabel Pankhurst claimed that 'with the progress of civilisation spiritual force replaces physical force as the controlling element in human affairs', but 'with what spiritual force shall we repel invaders?' asked George, invoking the spectre of 'German regiments dropping from the clouds in Zeppelin airships'.

Moving swiftly on from the premise that women have no Nature-given role in the management of the State, he focussed on what he called 'the essence of the grievance', namely 'that woman's voice is not heard in the councils of the world'. He refuted this with spirited rhetoric:

Now in what conceivable sense is this so? They write books, have journals of their own, swarm on the staff of the public newspapers (men have no papers of their own); we hear them speak on every platform, and hear them gladly when they are not merely ejaculating or ringing dinner-bells. If ever a Royal or Parliamentary Commission sits on a question affecting both men and women, it is an open scandal what partiality the members of it show towards a woman witness. Competent women are heard willingly in every department. The historic names which the women suffragists hurl at us so defiantly from their procession-banners, are all memorials of men's readiness to listen. In what wild realm of imagination, one wonders, can these ladies have lived who complain that woman's opinion goes for nothing in this man-ridden world?

Woman has powers at her disposal for moulding the destinies of the people, far transcending our pitiful politics; and these are social opinion and sexual selection. [...] Everywhere deprived of political power, everywhere Woman governs Man; and we rejoice in our servitude. Who made the goddesses and worshipped them? Man.

Calderon then argued, with many concrete examples, that women had as much freedom in British society as men; that in law 'woman really holds a position of enormous advantage' because her husband is in many cases held responsible for her actions; and in matters of property married women were excessively protected by the male State, even being able to 'repudiate their debts and evade bankruptcy'.

Next he attacked the suffragists for believing that their acquisition of the vote would 'mend' a whole series of 'grievances' concerning 'things which lie altogether outside the law'. Primogeniture and paternal custody of children were 'prehistoric customs' that were 'not the work of Parliament at all' and in practice had already been adjusted in women's favour. Admitting women to university degrees was not a matter for Parliament, although 'personally, I think it a pity that the Universities, College of Surgeons, etc, do not admit women to these degrees', because 'it is a matter of public convenience to have all useful talents measured by the same standards'. Suffragists obsessed about the lack of wage equality, but this was not the result of male discrimination, it was caused by the 'competition of women for whom the wage is a supplement and not a livelihood'. Being herself a political economist, not even Millicent Fawcett (president of the NUWSS) thought that 'legislation is one of the possible means of raising wages'.

But his real target was the suffragettes. He claimed they were so counter-suggestible that they opposed 'legislation proposed for the protection of their own sex against degrading occupations' and extending the maternity leave of women employed in factories. 'If some doctor discovered a drug capable of giving us all perfect health, it is certain that Miss Pankhurst and Miss Gore Booth would lead processions of hospital nurses to Hyde Park to protest against the use of it.' The violent methods of the suffragettes were 'frankly anti-social'. They claim that interrupting meetings and attacking the police are 'the only way', but when they get their wish and are imprisoned they re-invent themselves as victims:

I must confess that the glamour of their heroism is a little dimmed for me when they keep writing to the papers explaining to an indifferent public what a hardship it really is to be in Holloway [...]. There was never any need to explain this sort of thing about being burnt at the stake or thrown to the lions. Nor is it made any better by those who agitate and petition Mr Gladstone [Home Secretary] to make it more comfortable for the martyrs in their jail; as who should plead for not quite such big lions or not quite such a hot fire.

The 'genius' of the WSPU founders had been to replace the 'tedious old meetings' of the NUWSS with 'a jolly uproar with young folk at Caxton Hall [...] such spouting and shouting and banner-waving and general freedom from "deportment"; with expeditions and amusements together, bun-shop cocoa-sprees, keen arguments and long cosy talks, arms twining round waists'. 'With the advent of Miss Pankhurst the spirit of Dionysos descended on the movement.'

It is clear by the middle of George's pamphlet that what he believes the suffragettes want is 'political power' and what he most fears is 'Feminism'. Both mean to him the same thing: female hegemony. In its historical context, this was a common and understandable fear. No-one knew how enfranchised women would vote; successful suffragism could lead to a Woman's Party; and the female population was over a million greater than the male. The 'leaders of the woman suffrage party' had stirred up 'a bitterness and jealousy against our sex'. They had lost their 'self-control'. The suffragettes claimed that when they had got what they wanted they would 'behave like reasonable people'; but given their penchant for violence perhaps they would behave like Maenads?

The core of George's argument is the classic one of contemporary female and male anti-suffragists that the 'spheres' of women's and men's activities are 'separate'. His presentation of it, however, is extreme and dogmatic. 'Antis' like Mrs Humphry (Mary) Ward and Lady Margaret Jersey were less concerned with the *apartness* of the spheres than their pragmatic *difference*: women were best at philanthropic activity in the community, at nurturing, at helping the disadvantaged. Since they had the vote in local government, on school boards and in health authorities, there was enormous scope for their vital work. It had a future and could complement men's work. But by locating gender difference in prehistory, George made it quasi-absolute and deprived it of a future. A franchise was merely 'a particular licence [...] from the sovereign power', not a right. And the 'position of women in relation to the State is fixed once and for all by their physical constitution': because their 'muscular force amounts perhaps to about 35 per cent of the whole adult muscular force of the country', they are incapable of enforcing anything and therefore unqualified for the 'licence'. 'While the State lasts, it is men's.'

Throughout the pamphlet there are flashes of chivalric charm which may well be genuine. 'In thought' the whole thing is 'dedicated' to 'dear Madam', who has a 'vague but noble political faith which is all your own', and

if you [...] descend from the splendour of the general to the mean detail of the particular, if you hold me out a programme in place of an ideal, and label yourself mere Liberal, Tory, Socialist or what not, then your pedestal is no longer a pedestal but a platform, and your political influence over me no more than that of Mr Balfour or Mr Asquith.

But there were hardly any 'particulars' about the real work of hundreds of thousands of real women in the real 'Community' without which, in fact, the 'State' in the wider sense would have collapsed. There is no sense in George's pamphlet of complementarity or what the future of women might be. It is almost entirely negative, even sterile.

The apparent intransigence is reinforced by his tone, which is set by a Latin epigraph adapted from Juvenal and meaning 'indignation makes the book'. Irony, sarcasm and satiric exaggeration abound. 'Women have practised medicine ever since the world began, but so inefficiently, that in all these centuries their collective medical wisdom has never risen above a few health-destroying herbal superstitions.' 'The legend that woman is neglected and unheard has spread (for the communicability of such hallucinations see Esquirol, *Des Maladies Mentales*).' One could understand George's 'indignation' at single-issue fanatics, but here it seems to engulf suffragettes, suffragists, and women in general. Nevertheless, as the passage quoted above about lions illustrates, he had not lost his gift for the ridiculous. His portrayal of the 'Lambs of the Men's League for Women's Suffrage, the society formed by some of our sex for transferring our political power to the other' is hilarious.

In fact George's pamphlet may have been too amusing to have an impact. The WSPU's *Votes for Women* did not comment on it. William Rothenstein appreciated it and in August 1908 George wrote to him:

It is charming to be praised by a person of understanding, when so many people of no understanding see no merit in one's performance. The two or three reviews which I have had all agree that I have no serious views on woman suffrage, and wrote a pamphlet for a joke. One of them tells its readers that I am a suffragist and wrote against woman suffrage out of good nature, because someone else who was to have done it failed at the last moment.

He then gives an interesting account of how he and Kittie spend their time (he was writing from a country house in Hampshire):

I look forward to the Autumn and the beginning of a new London year, with its street and café life, its hopes and delusions, and the meetings of the learned and unlearned societies which I frequent. Meanwhile we wander for another few weeks; on Friday to the Lubbocks in Kent for the second time, then Kittie to Shropshire, and myself, to wind up the gaieties of the summer, with a Congress on Religions at Oxford.

The latter was the Third International Congress for the History of Religions, held between 15 and 18 September 1908. Although George did not give a paper himself, he was a discussant at the sections on 'Religions of the Lower Culture' and 'Comparative Religion and Sociology'. After a sensation-seeking German paper entitled 'The Ethnology of Galilee; or, Was Jesus a Jew by race?', according to the *Manchester Guardian* George stated that 'there was no Aryan race, and Jesus was undoubtedly a Jew by religion and nationality'.

But the autumn of 1908 turned out very differently for the Calderons from his prediction. Whilst they were away, prominent male anti-suffragists led by the imperialist Lords Cromer and Curzon and the Liberal M.P. John Massie had moved towards organising men opponents into a parallel body to WNASL. It is not clear how Calderon came to be in this network, but there was a strong Oxford component to the anti-suffrage movement of both sexes. He evidently volunteered to organise the calling of a Men's Committee for Opposing Woman Suffrage and to make Heathland Lodge its temporary address. As many eminent supporters as possible had to be found. Arrangements for the first meeting had to be clandestine in order to minimize suffragette disruption. When George did not have time to write a letter personally, Kittie acted as his secretary. The fluidity of the new organisation can be judged by the fact that she first headed a letter of 15 November to William Rothenstein 'C.O.W.S.', realised what it spelt out, and changed it to 'C.O.F.S.', the Committee for Opposing Female Suffrage, which it briefly became. The letter appealed on George's behalf for 'the names of any men that you think likely to be in sympathy with this movement which it would be desirable to invite' and George added his own postscript: 'Soldiers, sailors, millionaires, bishops, writers, lawyers, doctors, socialists etc are wanted.' Hundreds of such correspondences had to be conducted and it was possibly at this time that they had the five secretaries working in the house whom Kittie mentions in her memoir. It is also possible that the Calderons paid for these themselves, as a later letter signed by George and preserved in the London Women's Library makes it clear that there was as yet no fixed subscription and 'the Committee will of course need money for its work'.

It met at Westminster on 3 December 1908 with John Massie in the chair. Lord Cromer moved that the time had now arrived when it was 'incumbent on those who believe that the extension of the franchise to women would be contrary to the best interests of the country and the Empire to give effect to their convictions by united action'. This was carried, the meeting resolved itself into a 'general committee for opposing female suffrage', and an executive committee was unanimously appointed. Messages of support were read from Curzon and Austen Chamberlain. The next day *The Times* published a list of 140 men who had 'already joined the committee'. They included a Duke, six earls, a score of members of the House of Lords, more M.P.'s, Charles Villiers Stanford, Rudyard Kipling, and Henry Newbolt. George is named last, as the 'hon. secretary'.

All through December he, Kittie and others laboured to recruit new members for the second meeting. Obviously, most of the personages named by *The Times* were too grand to be involved in this donkey-work. An interesting sidelight on the Calderons' own commitment to it is provided by Kittie's comment that they often used to think how Mrs Hamilton would have 'loved to be *in it*', i.e. all the activity at Heathland Lodge, 'so much more than we did really!' Another question is to what extent Kittie agreed with George's anti-suffragism. She almost certainly opposed women's suffrage herself, as she believed passionately in female public service and most of her friends were from the class that was 'anti'.

But she may well have objected to George's perceived misogyny in the matter. His references in his pamphlet to the legal privileges of 'my wife' suggested that he was a hard-done-by husband, which he clearly was not. Possibly the extreme aspects of his argument and expression led to one of the 'very rare' 'tornadoes' she refers to in her memoir. She felt that he sometimes 'prevented people seeing the truth of what he was upholding by being too violent'. Nevertheless she worked with him for the anti-suffrage cause.

At its second meeting, on 19 January 1909, the Committee was formally renamed the Men's League for Opposing Woman Suffrage (MLOWS), with Cromer as President. George remained Honorary Secretary, the League still operated from Heathland Lodge, and George was one of its most active members. On 26 January he attended what *The Times* described as 'a demonstration in support of woman suffrage' held in the Queen's Hall 'under the auspices of the Men's League for Women's Suffrage'. Sir John Cockburn moved the motion 'That the exclusion of women from the Parliamentary franchise is both unjust to women and detrimental to the best interests of the State'. Whenever Asquith, Herbert Gladstone or Mary Ward were mentioned, the audience hissed. The resolution was carried 'with only a few dissentients', amongst whom was undoubtedly George, and they too were 'hissed as they held up their hands'.

A much fiercer encounter took place at the Queen's Gate Hall on 19 February 1909. Fliers announced a public debate on the motion 'That in the Opinion of this Meeting the Parliamentary Franchise should be extended to duly-qualified Women', proposed by Helen Ogston of WSPU and opposed by George representing MLOWS. Ogston already had a high profile. At a meeting of the Women's Liberal Federation addressed by Lloyd George at the Albert Hall on 5 December 1908 she had been 'first heckler'. When stewards tried to eject her she drew a dog-whip and flicked it at them, an event recorded on the front page of the *Illustrated London News*.

Since Ogston was twenty-six, tall and elegant, this is probably the debate witnessed and described by Percy Lubbock: 'The lady began it; her fluent, attractive appeal was listened to in a charmed silence, broken occasionally by a few happy sighings and purrings; she was a beautiful figure of a Diana, earnest and brave and free.' George, by contrast, seemed a 'Mephistopheles': 'With his arguments and his sarcasms, his crude interrogations, his facts and his dates, the atmosphere was chilled and the shining spaces contracted.' Instead of trying to win his audience over, he had decided to perpetuate the tone of his pamphlet. But the satirist is a man people fear. First the audience hissed, then it produced 'a running fire of indignant interruption', finally 'a squall of exasperated dissent'. The hall was packed with suffragists/-ettes and it was probably a foregone conclusion that George would lose heavily, but he made no attempt to turn his considerable charm on them, or to attack the Achilles' heel of the motion – the words 'duly qualified'. Why did suffragists/-ettes want a female franchise limited by economic and marital status, rather than a universal one?

Calderon's next contribution was connected with this issue. A private member's bill brought in by Geoffrey Howard proposed adult suffrage for men and women subject to a three-month residential qualification. It was due to have its second reading on 20 March 1909. The day before, a long letter appeared in *The Times* signed by Lady Jersey and three others for WNASL, and Lord Cromer and three others for MLOWS, including George. It called on 'those members of the House of Commons who may have yielded, at one time or another, good-naturedly and somewhat light-heartedly, to the pressure put upon them, to lay aside all mere personal considerations and take their stand now against this revolutionary Bill', and appealed to the 'Press and the public' to support them. If passed the Bill would 'increase the electorate from seven and a half millions to at least twenty millions, and the majority of electors in the United Kingdom would be women'. This, of course, was these Antis' main objection, and they promptly repeated their classic arguments against the female franchise. They also stressed that even Millicent Fawcett and the Pankhursts rejected the Bill. Moreover, an anti-democratic note in general can be heard in the letter: there is no doubt that for Edwardians like Cromer 'democracy' was a pejorative word approximating to 'government by the ignorant'.

As this letter implied, M.P.'s had become steadily converted to the suffragists' cause. Howard's Bill passed its second reading by thirty-five votes and was going to a Committee of the Whole House. To keep up the pressure, WNASL presented to the House of Commons a petition containing 243,000 signatures and organised a large meeting at the Queen's Hall on 26 March. The platform was packed with peers, peers' wives, M.P.'s and other eminent persons, including Lady Lubbock and George. Mary Ward was repeatedly cheered as she described the 'practical work' that WNASL had achieved in the eight months of its existence. Intriguingly, however, the rest of the evening was devoted to speeches by Lord Cromer and Austen Chamberlain. In fact Howard's Bill had no chance of becoming law, as the Conservatives had an impregnable majority in the House of Lords.

By now the MLOWS office had moved from Heathland Lodge to Bridge Street in Westminster, but George remained Honorary Secretary. On 13 April 1909 *The Times* published a long letter from him in that capacity, dissecting the common claims of suffrage supporters that having the vote would raise women's wages. He mocked the idea that market forces would 'magically' respond to the 'raised status' of enfranchised women by increasing their pay. He asked: 'If women workers are to be enriched, out of whose pockets is the money to come? Is it out of the employers', or out of men workers' in the same trades?' The suffragists appealed to the fact that women's wages had already risen in countries where they had been given the vote, but

When this statement is looked into it invariably turns out that the women whose wages have been increased are simply and solely Government *employées*, to whom their Governments, either corruptly or on the basis of a false Socialistic creed, have given, at the expense of the taxpayers, salaries above the market value of their work – schoolmistresses and post-office *employées* as a rule.

The interesting word here is 'corruptly'. It may mean 'in defiance of market realities', 'to buy them out', or it may mean 'in the name of equality'. Certainly, of course, equal rights have not led to equal pay for women, so George may have had a point about invidious market forces.

In the first six months of MLOWS's existence Calderon must have been one of its most energetic members. Generally it did 'very little work, much less than that of the women', Cromer wrote to Curzon later. By July 1909 the Women's League had held meetings all over the country, opened a hundred branches, and acquired more members than the WSPU. As Brian Harrison has written, the Men's League was 'more a collection of major public figures than a nation-wide movement'. These figures' professional lives were centred on Parliament. George Calderon was not a public figure in that sense, he could find more time than they to be active in the anti-suffrage cause, and he obviously relished it. In the absence of branches of the Men's League he spoke at branches of the Women's League, for instance at Windsor Town Hall on 3 March 1909, at the Hampstead Conservatoire on 11 March, and at Hove on 29 April.

There is no documentary evidence of Calderon's involvement in MLOWS between May 1909 and July 1910. Possibly he even relinquished the honorary secretaryship. There were no major political developments on the suffrage front in early summer 1909; presumably he and Kittie were at country houses through the summer itself; in the autumn they were in Glasgow for productions of George's play *The Fountain* and his translation of *The Seagull*; for most of December they were living in St Andrews; and they spent Christmas with the Corbets at Acton Reynald. Generally, then, he must have followed events such as the mounting suffragette vandalism, the first forced feeding of hunger-strikers, and suffragettes' physical attacks on politicians, from afar. In 1910 he was again based in London, the parliamentary struggle over suffragism took a new turn, and in the summer he became more actively involved than ever.

A Conciliation Bill to enfranchise a million women was put forward by an All-Party Committee and passed its second reading on 7 July 1910 by 299 votes to 189. Under pressure from his Cabinet, Asquith had agreed to give the Bill parliamentary time. It might therefore become law. The prospect galvanized both suffragists and anti-suffragists. As *The Times* remarked, 'it seems that the battle of women's suffrage is only just beginning in earnest'.

The MLOWS 'proconsuls' Cromer and Curzon disdained open-air democracy and the senior leaders of WNASL preferred private meetings.

According to WNASL's *Anti-Suffrage Review*, however, in July 1910 an 'Anti-Suffrage Outdoor Campaign' was begun, when 'two members of the Men's League hired a cart and held a meeting on Hampstead Heath'. Most likely these were George Calderon and his friend Alfred Maconachie. It appears that younger bloods from both Leagues now formed a sub-committee to promote a 'forward' policy of open-air meetings in London, particularly at places favoured by their opponents, and this was called 'the Trafalgar Square movement'. Prominent on the sub-committee were George for MLOWS and his exact contemporary the linguist and archaeologist Gertrude Bell for WNASL.

Calderon and Maconachie appear to have been responsible for organising and publicising the large anti-suffrage demonstration held in Trafalgar Square on the afternoon of Saturday 16 July 1910, whilst Bell's task was to arrange for WNASL members to attend in force and even speak. The handbill for the event, which can be seen in the Museum of London and is headed VOTES FOR WOMEN. *NEVER!*, names the instigator as 'Anti-Suffrage Campaign' (at the MLOWS address) and talks only of 'Several Platforms. Several Speakers'. There seems little doubt, however, that the demonstration was intended to be a joint MLOWS/WNASL venture – Bell had sent George £150 (£13,000 at today's prices) 'to cover the expenses of the meeting', and her father was donating another £50.

On the morning of the demonstration an 'atrocious article', as Kittie described it, appeared in *The Times*. Most of it was devoted to enunciating the 'six reasons why Lord Cromer objects to granting the suffrage to women' as contained in 'a special leaflet which Lord Cromer has drawn up for the occasion'. It then gave a long list of men from whom 'messages of sympathy with the object of the meeting' would be read out in Trafalgar Square, but who were possibly too exalted to attend. The final paragraph read: 'The meeting is organised by the Men's League for Opposing Woman Suffrage; it is not a demonstration by the Women's National Anti-Suffrage League and women are not expected largely to attend.'

When Bell and Calderon read this, they must have felt that the ground had been cut from under their feet. The whole object, of course, had been to demonstrate the solidarity between 'forward' male and female Antis in their common cause. Now the members of WNASL present would probably be outnumbered by female suffragists. Even Mary Ward would not be attending or speaking. Rather suggestively, however, when her message of support had been published in *The Times* with Curzon's two days before, unlike him she had not said she was *unable* to be present. It looks as though at the last moment the Executive of MLOWS had persuaded WNASL to pull out, or the Executive of WNASL had taken fright, and the 'Great Popular Meeting', as it was billed, would be an all-male affair. The 'atrocious article' was immediately followed by an account of a 'drawing-room meeting' the day before convened by the East Marylebone branch of WNASL and chaired by...Lady Cromer.

The somewhat bemused account of the demonstration that appeared in *The Times* on Monday 18 July 1910 remarked that the 'literature' available was 'irreconcilably divided into two streams', one of which was 'very much larger than the other'. The reason was simple: 'Shortly before the speaking began one or two hawkers distributed leaflets on behalf of the promoters of the demonstration, but they were anticipated by an hour by "suffragettes", who showered their leaflets and their badges on friend and foe alike.' About 2000 people were present, but were 'fairly evenly divided into men and women' and most of the hecklers at the five platforms addressed by M.P.'s and others were women. The reporter claimed that 'the promoters were well satisfied with the result', but the resolution put from each platform – 'That this meeting protests against woman suffrage in any shape or form, and calls upon the Government to give no further facilities for any Bill enfranchising women without previous reference to the judgment of the electorate' – was carried by only 'a small majority'.

George immediately wrote to Bell asking her if she knew who had put the 'message' in *The Times* deterring WNASL members from attending. She replied in a letter of Monday 18 July that she did not, nor did anyone in 'the office of the Women's League'. On the contrary, 'when I read it I thought of course that it was of your drafting as I know no other source for any announcements that have appeared in the newspapers'. Obviously, Calderon and Bell had been overruled by the highest councils of MLOWS and WNASL. However, Bell's letter suggests that she and George had themselves acted unilaterally: 'My very strong feeling is [...] that we ought not to have embarked as a sub-committee upon a step which would compromise the reputation of the Leagues without their approval.' Deeply embarrassed, she had to ask for her father's cheque back. She took the blame for 'having been unable to help you in the way you should have been helped'. 'Fortunately,' she wrote, 'thanks to your strenuous endeavours, the meeting was not a disaster; it was only a little absurd.'

There is no documentary evidence that George was associated with either League after this date. Perhaps he did not agree with plans to merge the two, as his name does not appear on a list of supporters of the proposal published in the *Anti-Suffrage Review*. Amalgamation happened on 6 December 1910, when they became the National League for Opposing Woman Suffrage (NLOWS). Cromer told Curzon that dissolving MLOWS's Committee was 'rather a troublesome business' and eventually he had had to 'squash out the Men's League'. Did George fall victim, then, to this purge?

It seems unlikely. NLOWS would need a full-time organising secretary and office secretary, and Cromer and Curzon had raised the funds to pay for them. Obviously Calderon did not have time to do the first of these jobs, even if Cromer had wanted him to. In the first week of September 1910 George took himself off with Walter Crum, the Coptic scholar, to the World Fair in Brussels. By 28 September a Mr Scott had been appointed Organising Agent of NLOWS. In November, incidentally, the Conciliation Bill was dropped, because another general election had to be called. In the ensuing protest, 200 suffragettes were assaulted by the police.

Percy Lubbock's assumption was that Calderon dropped the anti-suffrage movement suddenly, as (Lubbock thought) he did other campaigns: 'He knew precisely the moment when he had made his peculiar contribution to a cause and could not usefully give more. At that point [...] he would be gone, like the Red Queen.' But this is manifestly not so. Calderon continued to write biting letters to the press about suffragism over the next three years, and above all in 1911 he published a fourteen-page pamphlet with the Priory Press entitled *The Organisation of Buying: A Policy for Women*.

This is far less conservative than his anti-suffrage pamphlet. In the febrile atmosphere of 1910 following the 'People's Budget', there was widespread fear of rising food prices and resentment that consumers were becoming political footballs. George proposed forming a National Consumers' League which would not only regulate fair trading, vet quality and 'encourage sound workmanship', but 'put an end to under-payment, to over-work and non-employment', secure a realistic minimum wage, produce a kind of *Which?* of good employers, abolish sweat-shop production, award a 'registered label to be affixed to goods produced under satisfactory conditions', and monitor 'workshop sanitation, wages, pensions, overtime, holidays'! Obviously this shares certain ideals with the Cooperative movement and the Labour Party. In calling for fair trade and a National Consumer Council George was well ahead of his time. But his most radical proposal was that all this should be run by women. Women consumed 'a good deal more than half' of the 'marketable wealth of the country'; 'in the act of buying, each woman has daily in her grasp the control of all the mysteries that go to the making and distributing of what she buys'; and women excelled at 'voluntary or local' organisation. A women's consumer protection league should be set up 'at once' and George ended the pamphlet by giving the address of a Miss E.H. Tipple, who had 'kindly undertaken the first steps' to organising it.

It has not been possible to discover what became of this initiative. One has the impression, however, that it was grounded in a much humbler appreciation of the scale and seriousness of women's civic work in Edwardian Britain than he had evinced in *Woman in Relation to the State*. According to George in his 1911 pamphlet, woman's 'communal activity' was directed to a nation's 'health and comfort, as rearing, teaching, tending', but also, intriguingly, to 'equalising the distribution of wealth'.

What did Calderon's activism on behalf of anti-suffragism achieve? How, a hundred years later, should we make sense of his views on the subject?

In March 1912 Lord Curzon succeeded to the presidency of NLOWS and, as Brian Harrison has observed, 'Curzon's movement [...] was, up to August 1914, on the winning side'. In George's lifetime anti-suffragism did not fail. Surely his own efforts contributed significantly to the fact. After women over thirty received the vote in 1918, however, Kittie wondered whether 'that great energy that he poured forth' for the cause had been wasted. Some of his friends regarded all of his activism as 'Quixotic'. But as the 1920s wore on Kittie became 'more certain' than ever that his efforts had not been in vain, for

energy of that absolute great true-hearted sort – the child of deep straight thinking – breeds energy in others of the same type – it may only be in flickers by comparison – but it is by the spreading abroad of that sort of energy in the souls of men that at last regeneration will come.

It could, indeed, be claimed that enfranchisement was a victory for conservative women. As Mark Bostridge has written, 'The overwhelming weight of contemporary opinion leads to the conclusion that suffragette violence by 1914 wasn't working.' On the outbreak of war, Emmeline Pankhurst called a halt to all militancy and suffragettes threw themselves into voluntary work beside suffragists. WNASL members like Lady Jersey, Mary Ward, Violet Markham, or Gertrude Bell – feminists in their own right – had, of course, always identified this as women's special sphere of activity, and they provided outstanding public service now. There seems little doubt that these developments between 1914 and 1918 complexly assisted the achievement of women's suffrage. George too, in his pamphlets and a long letter published in *The Times* on 23 May 1913, had argued strongly for women to 'get themselves a life'.

Given that George Calderon was a rationalist and a qualified barrister, it is not surprising that he derived his anti-suffragism legalistically from the 'masculine functions' of the State. His basic arguments do not differ substantially from those of the chief theoretician of male anti-suffragism, the Vinerian Professor of English Law at Oxford Albert Dicey. They are put far more dogmatically than Dicey's, however, and one finds oneself wondering what lay behind George's vehemence.

Among the male Antis there was, of course, a faction who simply did not like women. Calderon cannot conceivably be classed with them. We know from various letters that both before and after he met Kittie he was strongly attracted to many women, and they found him unthreatening, chivalrous, entertaining, even magnetic. He always worked well with women. In *Woman in Relation to the State* he wrote: 'We men, with few exceptions, are all Mormons at heart. We have made the great sacrifice of monogamy, and much must be forgiven us.' The inclusive 'we' suggests he knew only too well that this described himself. He was particularly susceptible to women in their early twenties, and flirted with them. Yet there is absolutely no evidence that he ever broke his own marriage vows; the idea is unthinkable, given his lifelong belief in straight-thinking and plain-dealing. More than that, he could not *live* without Kittie. As she wrote later:

He seemed acutely conscious all the time that one was there – and to need one to be there – with the result that I hardly ever went away even for a day when he was at home. He at once seemed to feel left and lost. He absolutely needed one. Of course I did not want to go away. I only say this to show how closely natural human life held him though seemingly so up to the eyes in ideas, work, and play.

Woman seems to have been for him the ultimate human 'other'. Conceivably, his reaction to suffragists and suffragettes was so bitter because they deeply threatened the identity of this 'other' in his mind and heart. In particular, perhaps, he found suffragettes frighteningly masculinized, or as Lord Cromer put it 'unsexed'. Some of them he called 'Viragettes'. As he saw it, the Pankursts' fanaticism had unleashed on society a wave of Bacchae-like frenzy.

In her important study *Women against the Vote: Female Anti-Suffragism in Britain*, Julia Bush has written that 'from a longer-term perspective' the women Antis' 'sturdy defence of gender difference' was 'far from irrelevant to later generations'. Indeed, there is a debate to be had about gender difference and it is being had. I suggest that Calderon's activity on behalf of anti-suffragism was at root about his emotional perception of women's identity. In any 'broader project to restore neglected conservative dimensions to British women's history', as Bush expresses it, Calderon's views on gender difference deserve to be consulted.

10

George Calderon the Dramatist

> This general ignorance is the oddest feature of
> modern life. I knew a case of a temperance
> mission entirely supported by brewery shares.

> James Wren, *The Fountain*

Although readers of the *TLS* doubtless appreciated the brilliance of
Calderon's reviews, few could know that he was the author of them.
Reviewing hardly contributed, then, to raising his national profile.
Similarly, his anti-suffrage work was concentrated in the metropolis. It was
actually his career as a playwright that most brought him to the nation's
attention, and he pursued it at the very same time as his journalism and
political activism. If this sounds amazing, it was; but the relatively rich
documentation of George's theatrical career suggests that he planned it
extremely carefully and with Kittie's help was able to promote it with
maximum efficiency.

It will be recalled that he had collaborated on various dramatic texts
before he went to Russia and in 1903 was even writing a play drawn from
French history. Some of these scripts were only for amateur performance,
but it is quite possible that he submitted others to professional theatres. If
so, they stood zero chance of being accepted, as George was not an actor
or an insider of the commercial theatre in other ways, nor was his literary
prestige outside the theatre compelling enough. No more is heard of this
kind of play-writing after 1903. What, then, had changed to enable his
theatre career to take off five years later?

His letter of 14 September 1904 to Kittie from Cap Gris Nez suggests
that he was already familiar with Shaw's *Plays Pleasant and Unpleasant*
and with Ibsen. According to a letter from Dr Tebb to Ford Madox Ford

dated 26 July1935 and published by Martin Buck in 1998, after George returned from Tahiti he set about reading 'the whole of Labiche's plays'. Eugène Labiche had been dead for twenty years, but his vaudevilles and well-made 'imbroglio' farces such as *Un chapeau de paille d'Italie* were still internationally successful. Calderon admired Labiche as a comedic craftsman and he and Kittie were particularly fond of *La Cagnotte*. It is possible that this is also when George translated Musset's play *On ne badine pas avec l'amour*. His version was entitled *Perdican and Camilla* and published posthumously. The fact that he divided up Musset's chorus, transposed some lines, and added lengthy psychological stage directions, suggests that he was using it as an exercise in honing his own stagecraft. Whether because he wanted to, or felt that he had to if the play was to pass the censor, he sanitised Musset's amatory and anticlerical language. Even so the translation was not performed in George's lifetime, which is hardly surprising as the original itself was not staged in full until 1923.

Later, Laurence Binyon wrote that he was 'amazed at the thoroughness with which [George] prepared himself for his dramatic work. He was not satisfied till he knew everything about the theory and philosophy of drama, as well as every practical detail of the theatre'. Amongst the more recent dramatists George studied were the French writers of 'thesis plays' and the British exponents of the 'Theatre of Ideas', i.e. the 'New Drama' as it was called.

Whereas Edwardian commercial theatre – the plays of Pinero, say, Sutro, H.A. Jones, or J.M. Barrie – probably held little attraction for George, one can see that plays about 'ideas' would interest him intensely. Shaw's plays had been very slow to be staged, but the Vedrenne-Barker seasons at the Royal Court between 1904 and 1907 suddenly created an audience for them and brought other practitioners of the Theatre of Ideas to the fore, such as St John Hankin, John Galsworthy, and Granville Barker himself. Here was a superb opportunity for George. He seized it.

The way into the alternative theatre was through the Incorporated Stage Society, which was founded in 1899 and by 1907 had about 1200 members. Shaw and Barker were prominent in it, Frederick Whelen was its President, and Hankin was on its Council of Management. Will and Alice Rothenstein were members and Calderon seems to have joined in

1907. He finished *Chenda*, his first version of *The Fountain*, on 20 July 1907 and offered it to Barker – 'ineffectually', as he recorded in his diary. On 30 July the Rothensteins came to supper and he read it to them. 'Calderon was himself an actor born,' Will wrote in his memoirs, 'and to hear him read a play was a delight.' Next day George offered the play to H.B. Irving, but again to no avail. Evidently he now decided that the Stage Society was his only hope. Over the next ten months he changed the play a great deal, for instance introducing the small but significant part of a 'South Sea Islander', and he seems to have read it to the Rothensteins again in June 1908. He particularly valued Alice's opinion and the couple probably had influence in the Stage Society. With a new title, *Charity*, the play was submitted to the Society, accepted, and performances scheduled for 28 and 29 March 1909. By then it was called *The Fountain*, 'a comedy in three acts'.

The reason there would be only two performances – a Sunday evening and Monday matinee – was that these were the only consecutive days that a major theatre would be available (in this case the Aldwych), as well as actors otherwise engaged in the commercial theatre. Since the performances were open only to members, they qualified as private and were immune from the censor. But it would be a mistake to think that Stage Society productions were insignificant. Edwardian Britain was in the grip of, in Joseph Donohue's words, 'a contagious enthusiasm for things theatrical that had never been higher and would perhaps never again rise so high', and Stage Society premieres aroused great interest. Thus the Society's cuttings book alone contains thirty national reviews of George's play published over the next ten days.

Stage Society productions also attracted some first-rate performers, who were eager to be seen in them. In a long letter to Alice Rothenstein Calderon named the best-known of them in the cast and expressed his delight that the play would be directed by the experienced Norman Page: 'I couldn't have wished for a better […]. He understands it all much better than I do, and has just the light touch that it wants.'

Before the first night, the Calderons moved up to stay with the Lubbocks at 26 Cadogan Gardens. They shared a box with them in the theatre, which was full. The audience included relations and friends going

back many years. Although the curtain-raiser, *Unemployed* by Margaret
Mack, was slated by the critics, it did at least prepare the audience for the
subject of George's play, as according to *The Times* it showed 'how a
tramp [...] died of starvation at the feet of two idle middle-class persons
just as they were talking flippantly about the problem of unemployment'.
Then *The Fountain* commenced. As several reviews put it next day, the
play was 'well received' throughout and according to the *Daily Telegraph*
'there were loud cries for the author at its close'.

Almost all the reviewers found the play 'entertaining', 'amusing',
'witty', 'never dull', and above all 'clever' (a term then of the highest
praise). 'After a season of much indifferent or wrong-headed work, the
Stage Society springs upon us a most enjoyable surprise' wrote the *Star*,
and the *Winning Post* even called it 'one of the brightest and wittiest plays
that have recently been seen on the London stage'. The *Daily News* found
it 'packed full with good things', the *Sunday Times* reviewer wrote that
'not for a long time' had he 'laughed so much at a conceit which is tragic
in its undertones, but exceptionally comic on the surface'. Several
compared *The Fountain* with Shaw to the latter's disadvantage. The
Outlook found George's language superior: 'Such dialogue as Mr
Calderon's is more than rare. There is nothing quite like it. He approaches
Mr Shaw's standard of brilliancy without any of his difficulty or freakish
unconvincingness.' 'We have here', the *Sunday Times* continued, 'a
humorist who has many of the gifts of G.B. Shaw without playing the
wire-puller to his puppets.' The *World* ventured:

Mr Calderon seems to be the playwright we have been looking for [for] so long.
He has an exuberant humour, an observant eye, a neat trick of drawing character,
and a pretty talent for rapid cut-and-thrust dialogue: all these in addition to his
ideas. He does not pull a long face and pound his views into us with the heavy
earnestness of a social science lecturer. He is a laughing philosopher.

The play was assumed, of course, to be George's 'maiden effort'. As such,
reviewers found it 'a very promising creation' (*Daily Mail*), 'undeniably
brilliant' (*Manchester Despatch*), even 'magnificent' (*Court Journal*).

On the face of it, Calderon had been incredibly fortunate with his
actors. '*The Fountain* was exceedingly well acted', announced the

Standard, and 'members of the cast could hardly have been improved upon' – indeed not a hard word seems to have been printed anywhere about the 'playing', which was repeatedly described as 'capital'. Mary Jerrold, the future film actress, was well cast as the heroine, Chenda Wren: 'Sparkling, like a sunbeam, instinct with life, humour and animation, Miss Jerrold never lost hold of her audience for a moment, and not one word too much of her did they have' (*Winning Post*). For several reviewers the character actress Nancy Price's performance as an East End virago, Dinah Kippin, was a 'triumph'. Frederick Lloyd was warmly praised as the 'Oxonian socialist' James (Jimbo) Wren. But the fact is that George had written a supremely actor-friendly play. No-one's part was heavy or too light. All were individually realised and their speech was direct, colloquial, vigorously paced, and above all crafted to elicit audience rapport. This is perhaps why Mary Jerrold, for example, was able to act 'with such freedom' (*Sunday Times*).

Nevertheless, two fundamental criticisms of the play were made in review after review. The first was that it was 'Shavian' in inspiration: its subject was too reminiscent of *Widowers' Houses* and James Wren's logorrhoea too similar to that of John Tanner in *Man and Superman*. The other criticism was 'technical': the play was too long, its 'construction' was faulty, it had too many 'interludes', was 'chaotic', and the dénouement 'altogether too obvious' (*Daily Chronicle*).

Unfortunately, the first criticism was voiced most vehemently by the doyen of London critics, A.B. Walkley, who had a thousand words on the subject in *The Times* of 30 March 1909. He began by accusing Calderon of tendentiousness:

It is probable that our latter-day missionaries of the West [End] to the East [End] are not all fools or windbags; and, in ignoring this probability, the author of *The Fountain*, whilst he has written an amusing comedy, has written it at the cost of scrupulous fairness and veracity. […] We should have liked to see just one sensible philanthropist among Mr Calderon's crowd, for the simple reason that it might then have been a credible as well as an amusing crowd.

Walkley jumped to the conclusion that George's 'nearest approximation to a sensible person, as he conceives that person', is the 'Fabian Socialist'

Wren, who has 'no belief in "charity" at all' because it is 'society' that
needs fixing. The 'Shavian school', according to Walkley, was 'the school,
in short, of the Jimbo Wrens'. There were 'several Jimbos among the
purveyors to the Stage Society' and Walkley plainly assumed George was
one of them:

It is a school of people who have plenty of ideas about social problems and who
can juggle with those ideas to the accompaniment of a good deal of what, we
fear, must be called 'patter', but who either do not know or do not care [enough]
about the broad and simple facts of human life and character to make a
substantial play out of them.

He was patronising about the play ('it is only amusing now and then') and
about the playwright ('they are amusing in their way, the play-writing
Jimbos'). The *Pall Mall Gazette* carried an even more 'horrid' review, as
George put it.

These attacks were so wrong-headed that George felt justified in
replying to them in print. In his Preface to the published text of *The
Fountain* (1911) he denied that Wren was 'an exponent of orthodox
socialism' and that he himself was 'a disciple of Bernard Shaw':

Wren is a member of the Fabians, it is true; he goes off to one of their meetings at
the end of Act I; but, like many other members of that Society, he is not a socialist
at all; he only thinks he is a socialist.

   As for myself, I am very grateful for some of the things implied when the word
'Shavian' is applied to my comedy; but *distinguamus*. Mr Shaw has no exclusive
copyright in talkative heroes. [...] My inspiration was certainly not derived from
Widowers' Houses. The plot of *The Fountain* was developed by a severely logical
process from a philosophical basis.

The philosophical basis in question could well have been Taoism, as
Wren's paradoxical belief in 'doing nothing' in order to 'achieve wonders'
because 'Progress is Nature's affair', strongly suggests the doctrine of *wu
wei*, 'action through inaction'. This 'basis', George continued, was 'as
Anti-Shavian as can be' and had led to his 'tremendous discovery' that 'all
the Evil that matters is produced, not by evil intention, as is generally
supposed, but by good intention working through the complicated

channels of our social system' (not 'economic' system). In fine, 'all the people who together cause the miseries of Boodle Court are good' – positively Liberal, in fact, in their intentions.

How naïve and old-fashioned after this seems *Widowers' Houses*, with its slum-landlord grinding the faces of the poor! Bernard Shaw, like Lloyd George and all those nurtured in the socialism of the early eighties, still believes in the fantastic old Wicked Rich myth. Wren's jaunty epigram 'Villains are a literary invention which the Elizabethan drama inherited from the demonology of the Middle Ages' [...] expresses a truth which has certainly never entered the Shavian head. Mr Shaw's villainous landlord does not correspond to anything in real life, but is derived straight from the Iagos and Don Johns of the Tudor stage.

This in its turn over-simplifies Shaw, but George's 'discovery' explains why at least one reviewer felt that 'the chief virtue of *The Fountain* is its rich, warm, genial humour, which, while not blinded to the folly or even the wickedness of man, perceives the good in the worst of us, and makes the best of it' (*Star*).

The idea that poverty is not caused by the existence of wealth, and the sustained impression conveyed by *The Fountain* that 'benefits' sap independence and personal initiative, clearly align it with conservative thinking. Moreover, Wren's 'Fabian' approach is presented as sheer verbal fantasy. It is quite surprising, then, given the left-leaning membership of the Stage Society and Shaw's role in it, that the play was accepted for performance at all! Possibly George's friendship with Hankin had helped. Possibly the Council were simply bowled over by the play's energy.

The plot of *The Fountain* is as follows. Chenda Wren (22) has left her husband Jimbo (32) because he has spent three months since their wedding talking about 'revolutionising the world', without *doing* anything. She has decided to tackle 'one of the plague spots of East London' by ploughing her income from a Trust Estate into a mission run by its local vicar, her cousin Tom Oliver, who is trustee of the estate. She gives, 'lends', and exchanges money for objects pledged by the large cast of Boodle Court, without getting any back. Wren arrives and lectures everyone on how 'charity' is merely the rich taking money from the poor and recycling some of it to them. A rumbustious rent-collector with a wooden leg

pursues the tenants onstage and off and lets it be known that the landlord
of Boodle Court is raising the rent. Chenda's next project is to create a
'Settlement, Old Age Pension House and Sanatorium' by taking a lease on
Glengarry House opposite. For this she needs more money. Oliver agrees
to arrange it through the Trust. Chenda signs the lease on Glengarry
House 'Resolving on a breach of covenant', as the stage direction tells us;
namely a covenant that it is not to be used as a nursing home or
sanatorium. She is rumbled when the lessors' solicitors are informed of
hospital equipment being moved in. It is then noticed that the lease is from
the same estate that owns Boodle Court, and Wren (a 'retired' solicitor)
realises that this is the very estate of which Oliver is trustee. Consequently,
when Chenda and Oliver fulminated against the wicked landlord of
Boodle Court who kept raising its tenants' rent, they were attacking
themselves. 'Oh, Jimbo! Jimbo! I see it all', exclaims Chenda. 'You mean
that *I* am the owner of this horrible place, that it is *I* who live at ease
because these poor creatures live in misery. Oh, where can I hide myself?'
She tears up the lease and announces that she wants to go back to him.

The development of the plot is well paced in the first two acts, but in
the third the expostulations of the various East Enders (particularly Dinah
Kippin) do approximate to an 'interlude' of their own, however
entertaining. Similarly, Wren's epigrammatic rants in the first act might be
show-stopping. But it seems wrong to assume that these features are
'faults of construction'. They present, rather, a plenitude within the
otherwise strictly controlled framework of the plot. We know from
Calderon's own practice that he had no aversion to rewrites for
performance. It would be perfectly acceptable, then, to cut *The Fountain*
wherever desired to make it play effectively in the modern theatre.

The plot is Labichean in that it is implicitly a search for something that
is found only in the last five minutes of the play – the identity of the
'rackrenting landlord' of Boodle Court. The fact that the audience may
guess her identity long before does not matter, since the play, the *comedy*,
is about the heroine's slowness to guess it herself. Nevertheless, on
George's own admission *The Fountain* is a 'thesis play'. This does not
mean that it simply 'demonstrates' a thesis. The aim of a thesis play is to
tease out, to play with a thesis, presenting a fan of living perspectives on it.

In this respect the play is Shavian, but in another it is not. When George changed its title to *The Fountain* he shifted the play from naturalism to allegory. The image of the fountain that in Wren's words pumps up money 'out of Oliver's parishioners' pockets all the time' and then sprays it back into their begging bowl, overarches our whole perception of the play. It becomes an allegory in a way that Shaw's plays generally are not, and allegory is a key instrument of satire as Wren implies in Act 3. Yet the irresistible humanity of Chenda always saves it from *bitter* satire. At the end of the play, in its Stage Society version, even after Chenda has been made to look a complete fool, the East Enders cheer her and sing 'He's a jolly good fellow' to her offstage. In his 1911 Preface George quoted a line from Victor Hugo's *L'Année terrible*: '*Personne n'est méchant, et que de mal on fait!*' His desire to portray everyone in *The Fountain* as 'good' may seem merely Edwardian, but it is not. The allegory is analytical, final, closed – and George's thesis seems dogmatic – but the play's people are just the opposite, and this perhaps is the source of its durable fascination.

The Fountain was definitely a success in the Stage Society's two-day showing, but where could it go from there? Max Beerbohm wrote in the *Saturday Review* of 3 April 1909:

Mr Calderon's play [...] made me regret once more the cessation of Vedrenne-Barker. Here is a comedy which could not, probably, have a long run, yet a comedy of which two performances do not nearly exhaust the number of people who would delight in it.

The reviewer of the *Morning Post* also believed it should 'certainly be heard of again, though whether it would prosper in an evening bill', i.e. in the West End, was 'another question'. Kittie made strenuous efforts to get actor-managers to see the performances, but none would risk a production.

Meanwhile, as we have seen, in the spring of 1909 Calderon was active in the anti-suffrage cause. Probably he was also collecting and digesting further material for his 'Opus 2', as he described it to his mother, which was the play about Thomas Cromwell that he had conceived in 1907. In May 1909 he, Kittie, and 'Mr Jones' stayed with the Pyms, who had moved to Banstead Manor near Newmarket. Their visit coincided with the first birthday of Violet and Evey's first child, Jack, and a visit by the golf-writer Bernard Darwin and his wife Elinor, *née* Monsell and a cousin of George's one-time flame Geraldine. Later in the summer, probably, Kittie went with Jones to stay with Nina Corbet at Acton Reynald and it was whilst Nina was absent that the venerable terrier expired. Nina wrote from London: 'I do <u>indeed</u> feel for you. I know so well too how he was part of the past – in a way how he was part of Archie and your mother.' She was sure that 'Reggie' (Reginald Astley, the manager of the estate) would 'see to anything you may want specially done', and Jones was buried at Acton Reynald. The next dog the Calderons acquired was less thoroughbred: an 'odd tangle-haired scapegrace', as Percy Lubbock described him, called Tommy.

George's luck with the alternative theatre held. 'Vedrenne-Barker' was exported to the provinces in the form of two repertory companies. Annie Horniman founded the first at Manchester in 1907 and Glasgow Repertory Theatre opened with Shaw's *You Never Can Tell* on 5 April 1909. The force behind the Glasgow experiment was Alfred Wareing, one of the most innovative minds in twentieth-century British theatre. At some point in the summer of 1909 he approached Calderon about reviving *The Fountain* in Glasgow. Stunningly, he proposed that after that he would present George's translation of *The Seagull* and George should direct it. This would be the first time a play by Chekhov had been performed in Britain, and probably the first time anywhere in English.

The Calderons travelled to Glasgow in early September, arriving on the day of the inauguration of the autumn season. This was, as Kittie put it, 'a great function held on the stage with municipal Glasgow largely represented', because the Repertory Theatre (officially the Scottish Playgoers' Company) was a Citizens' Theatre funded by local shareholders. She was helped on and off the stage by 'a genial dignitary called the Deacon Convenor', who was chairman of the Board of Directors.

In fact Wareing had not been able to maintain the theatre as a true 'repertoire company' performing three or four different plays a week; he had had to settle for short runs of plays using a resident company. *The Fountain* ran between 20 and 30 October and was even better than the

Stage Society production. Not only did Mary Jerrold play Chenda again, it was once more directed by Norman Page on loan from the Haymarket Theatre in London. Calderon wrote to his mother that Page himself would be playing Wren ('in a hat of my own') and this and other re-castings would be an improvement on London.

He also thought the play was 'better for my alterations'. Above all he had rewritten the ending. Whereas in London Chenda had torn up the lease for the Settlement and flounced out with Wren, leaving a solicitor to explain that the lease was still valid and Tom Oliver to have the last word, in Glasgow Wren persuaded Chenda to stick 'at it' and with him, to see 'if we can't give your tenants better value for their money' –

And if we can spare any time from mending our own ways, we'll spend it harassing employers, landlords, insanitary people, brewers, publicans, everyone who battens on the poor.
CHENDA: All the other Chendas, in fact.
WREN: Yes, all the other Chendas. What fun it'll be!

George now gave his audience what most of them wanted from an ending: he reconciled wife and husband in 'A long kiss'. But this in itself is not the end of the play. The 'South Sea Islander' now wakes up on his sofa and mutters: 'Wish I was back in Raparoa wid de ole wife and little chillun.' 'And so you shall be, by Gad,' cries Wren, 'as fast as ship can carry you, and curses on the infernal rascal that [...] brought you over here to see the squalid barbarism in which your pretended betters pass their days.' On he rants, and 'The Curtain descends and leaves him talking'. This was reminiscent of the closing lines of *Man and Superman*, but it was a very fine ending and was retained in all published forms of the play.

Obviously, the schedules of repertory companies were tight. Calderon would have been rehearsing *The Seagull* during the run of *The Fountain*, with several of the same actors. We shall look at the production and his whole engagement with Chekhov in the next chapter.

About the middle of November he and Kittie moved to St Andrews. Kittie, George wrote his mother, had 'resuscitated a lot of old friends up here – ranging up to ninety and over', and 'while she has been drinking their tea I have been studying golf', which he could play there 'for nothing'. However, the reason he had not written to Clara for a month was that he had been working 'very hard [...] trying to finish a play against time'. This was *Cromwell: Mall o' Monks*, an 'Historical Play in Five Acts'.

It may seem extraordinary that Calderon had decided to write it in verse, but probably he was responding to what he saw as a gap in the market. A memorandum in his 1907 diary could be taken to mean that he had been asked by the Poet Laureate Alfred Austin, whom he may have met through the *Westminster Gazette*, to find him an 'historical setting' for a verse play, but took over the subject himself. The vogue for 'poetic drama', as it was called, had been started by a spectacularly successful production of Stephen Phillips's *Paolo and Francesca* at St James's Theatre in 1902. Beerbohm Tree had staged many verse plays by Phillips and others, and in 1907 Laurence Binyon had a hit with his *Attila* at His Majesty's with Oscar Asche in the title role and music by Stanford. George had regularly met Binyon in 1907, he attended *Attila* shortly after it opened, and there was talk of their collaborating on a play. However, all of the poetic dramas just mentioned were exotic and involved extravagant sets. No-one, it seems, had taken a subject for a verse play from English history, possibly because the Shakespearian precedent was too daunting.

Whatever made George settle on Thomas Cromwell, it was a subtle choice. I remember seeing the film *A Man for All Seasons* in 1973 in the company of an English historian and his remarking as we walked home: 'Thomas Cromwell is a far more interesting character...' Even as I write, we await the RSC's dramatisation of Hilary Mantel's award-winning novels based on Cromwell's life, which must be regarded as a compliment to Calderon's discrimination. What form will the RSC's dramatisation take? How 'Shakespearian' will it be?

George avoided this problem by telling his story 'in the ancient fashion', as his Prologue puts it – i.e. in a form pre-dating Shakespeare. There are elements of the morality play. The title, meaning 'Hammer of the Monks', has an archetypal ring to it, and songs are used from *Gammer Gurton's Needle* (1550s?), *Ralph Roister Doister* (1553), and supposedly by Henry VIII himself. Cromwell is presented almost as an exemplar of 'hem that stode in heigh degree, | And fellen so that there was no remedie | To bring hem out of hir adversitee', in the words of Chaucer's Monk. The scenes are intended to be fast-moving and contrasting, the prevailing impression to be of 'epic' theatre. To help achieve this, the sets are directed to be 'simple and quickly shifted'.

But we are also encouraged by George's Prologue (a town crier) to 'seek a moral for today' in *Cromwell*. This possibly refers to the career of Lloyd George. Henry needs money, in particular because 'the envious Almain [Germany] buildeth ships'. When Calderon was writing his play, Lloyd George's 'People's Budget' was still being obstructed by the House of Lords. The suggestion is that Cromwell's raising money for the King's fleet by stripping the monasteries is like Lloyd George hammering the British aristocracy with a land tax to pay for Dreadnoughts. Doubtless Calderon suspected Lloyd George of a similar hubris and was inviting his audience to ask themselves where it would all end for the country and the Liberal Party.

These admonitory, allegorical aspects of the play appear at variance, however, with its main thesis. For Thomas Cromwell tells us that his secret motivation is to create 'Freedom' in England: freedom of thought, belief, and speech. He will use even the lessons he has learnt from Machiavelli to that end, manipulating the King to destroy vested interests, achieve independence from Rome, and form an alliance with Lutheran Germany. The Cromwellian Reformation, then, is presented as a great explosion of civil freedoms, national sovereignty, and secularisation – all 'modern' values in which Calderon himself believed. But whilst pursuing these values, Cromwell is shown to betray his own humanity and himself be betrayed by the King. Thomas More is portrayed as a dour and bloody reactionary.

The play's thesis is bold and still of interest today. The trouble is that it is easy to lose sight of it amongst the plethora of 'interludes' in the action. Reviewing the published text in 1922, the *Manchester Guardian* described it as a 'swift, actable, debonair tragedy' marred by many 'fine inconsequences'. But these would present no difficulty to a dramaturg today, because the play's framework, like that of *The Fountain*, is so firm. The dialogue, although occasionally degenerating into 'tushery', is a remarkable achievement – the marriage of an encyclopaedic vocabulary with a natural linguistic vitality.

On 22 December 1909 George wrote from St Andrews to his mother that the play was 'finished [...] and sent away on its rounds', meaning presumably in typescript to the various West End managements that had presented verse drama so far. Alas, he had mistimed it. The vogue for 'Poetic Drama' was already over and as far as can be ascertained *Cromwell: Mall o' Monks* has never been staged.

The next day he and Kittie left for Christmas at Acton Reynald.

They returned to Heathland Lodge on New Year's Day and the painter Margaret Bernadine Hall is recorded as having died there on 2 January 1910, a fact for which I am indebted to her biographer John Hussey. Hall's best-known work is the haunting 'Fantine', inspired by the character of that name in *Les Misérables*, which hangs in the Walker Gallery in Liverpool. She was a distinctive painter, who had trained in Paris and lived there many years. Given that her father was a famous philanthropic mayor of Liverpool, it is possible that the Calderons knew her through the Dowdalls. But no-one knows why she was at Heathland Lodge that day. The natural assumption is that she was merely attending a social occasion there. However, although she was only forty-six, her death certificate names the causes as 'Cardiac failure. Debility and wasting disease of long standing' and present at her death was one Constance Ross. Perhaps the latter was a companion-carer and Margaret Hall had been staying at Heathland Lodge for some time. Possibly Kittie had informally let a few of the spare rooms to her.

After nearly four months absence, George was 'quite curious', he told his mother, 'to see London again'. Between 11 and 31 January 1910 he and Kittie revisited the Pyms at Banstead Manor. He was probably already working on his next play, *Revolt*. This stands in a definite relationship to Galsworthy's play *Strife*, which had had great success under Barker's direction at the Haymarket Theatre the previous spring. Perhaps, then, George had been mulling over his new play since 1909.

He seems to have felt that he should launch it in the same way as *The Fountain*, through a production by the Stage Society. But there was a problem. Few would have contested that the inner circles of the Society had what Max Beerbohm called 'a socialistic bias'. *The Fountain* had been subtextually anti-socialist, but at least it was an irresistible comedy. *Revolt* was ostensibly anti-union and manifestly serious. It would not possibly be selected by the Council for a Stage Society production. Characteristically, George therefore set about trying to change the composition of the Council.

His ally in this was the poet Thomas Sturge Moore, to whom Calderon's letters about the matter have survived. 'What we need is people of intelligence', George wrote to him on 25 June 1910. 'It is the stupidity of the Stage Society Council that annoys me; the ease with which they are deceived by bad stuff and faded progressiveness.' He proposed that at the AGM later that summer they put up seven of their own candidates against the third of the Council that had to retire each year but would be eligible for re-election. He asked Sturge Moore and Alice Rothenstein to suggest some names, and he came up with two (both women) himself. The list included W.B. Yeats, the theatre designer Charles Ricketts, and Laurence Binyon. If Whelen was one of the retiring members, George was for re-electing him, because he was 'clever, keen and well-intentioned; Bernard Shaw I would gladly reject, because he sees little outside himself and his circle of ideas, though he moves rapidly and exhilaratingly about inside that circle'. The interesting thing is that Sturge Moore put himself on the candidate-list, but Calderon did not. George referred to them and their nominees as 'conspirators' and his language waxed Tudoresque: one Council member he would 'gladly reject and kill him with a hatchet', another 'I would banish, but unwillingly, because he has such a handsome daughter'. But it was all play-acting. Yeats was dropped because George was not sure about his 'theatrical ideals', Binyon because 'he would not want to spend either the time or the money', and Ricketts had not even joined the Society. In the end their list contained only three certain candidates, and the putsch probably fizzled out.

On the face of it, this did not matter. When George returned from Belgium in mid-September 1910 he found a letter waiting for him from the Director of the Haymarket Theatre, Herbert Trench, proposing to stage *Revolt* there subject to 'the approval of my financial authorities'. Trench was referring to the fact that the play would be 'very expensive to produce, because of the large cast and the necessity for employing the very finest actors in order to interpret your ideas'. One of his conditions for the production was 'a slight modification of the extreme end of the play which I think as it stands considerably weakens the force of the main thesis'. George was not one to object to that, so plans for the production went ahead.

Freed from the necessity of subjecting *Revolt* to the Stage Society, Calderon submitted another play, entitled *White Raven*. It was a one-acter and was accepted for production in a triple bill at the Aldwych in January 1911. However, the work performed then was called *The Little Stone House*, which prompted Sturge Moore to ask on a postcard from France whether it was the same play. We do not have George's answer, but probably it was *White Raven* renamed. Obviously, given Kittie's sobriquet the latter title raises certain expectations. But these were probably just a joke on George's part and he was actually thinking of the Russian expression that means 'a rare person/occurrence' and is applied in *The Little Stone House* to its principal character. George probably abandoned the original title because it conveyed nothing in English and was in any case not strictly accurate, as the Russian expression is 'white crow'.

Meanwhile, on 20 December 1910 Sir Walter Corbet died at Ludlow from a perforated duodenal ulcer. He was fifty-four. Kittie arrived at Acton Reynald the same day and stayed with Nina until 2 January. The Visitors Book does not indicate that she was joined by George, who cannot therefore have attended Walter's funeral on 23 December. Christmas at Acton Reynald must have presented a terrible contrast to the year before. Jim Corbet, aged eighteen, now succeeded to the title, and at forty-three Nina faced the prospect of becoming the Lady Dowager.

The curtain went up on *The Little Stone House* at an evening performance on Sunday 29 January 1911. It was preceded by Ashley Dukes's *Pride of Life* and followed by the German star-vehicle *The Passing of Talma*, translated by Stage Society member H.A. Hertz.

As mentioned earlier, George's play is an adaptation of his 1898 story 'Lipa Sidorovna' set in St Petersburg. The masterly way in which he in effect *translated* this narrative work into dramatic form will be examined in chapter 13. Suffice it to say that for a forty-minute play *The Little Stone House* is extremely strongly built, but in theatrical parlance its 'tone' is very 'uncertain'. It sets out to evoke an 'alien world' as one reviewer put it, and the naturalistic description of the lodging-house keeper's sitting-room, down to 'eikons on a shelf in the corner with a wick in a red glass bowl burning before them, paper flowers and Easter eggs on strings', seems to emphasise this. But the next set of stage directions suggests the intention is less to evoke Russian life than to parody it:

There is an atmosphere of silence, solitude and Russian monotony. The clock ticks. A man is seen passing in the street; his feet make no sound on the snowy ground. There is the sound of a concertina and a man who laughs in the distance out of doors. Then silence again.

The principal male character, Astéryi, is a stock Russian figure 'in slippers and dirty dressing-gown', who for a third of the play lays out a game of patience, 'pausing' and 'meditating', then 'murmuring, "Oh, Hóspodi!" ["Lord!"] as if in surprise at being so terribly bored'. Another key character, the stone-mason Spiridón, is 'a man with a cringing, crafty manner, in a sheepskin coat with snow on it'. The play seems to ask to be seen as a take-off of the stereotypes of Russian literature. However, that effect too is uncertain. All of the dialogue is written in slow, plonking, complete-form English that can only be described as 'translationese'. It is as though George felt that he could make his audience believe they were watching a slice of Russian life only if he gave them dialogue that sounded like bad contemporary translations of Russian literature. Is the whole play a parody, then, of the Edwardian 'discovery' of Russia? It could certainly be presented that way on the stage today, with uproarious effect.

Yet the play clearly has a serious intent as well. Whereas George's story had dealt with Lipa Sidorovna's 'dream' of her dead son, here the focus is a much colder, philosophical one on 'ideas' and their ontology. Lipa, renamed here Praskóvya, has an 'idea' of her son that the lodger Fomá calls 'a fantastic image', an *idée fixe* that in his eyes makes her 'mad'. Astéryi disagrees:

We call everyone mad who is faithful to their ideas. If people think only of food and money and clothing we call them sane, but if they have ideas beyond those things we call them mad. I envy Praskóvya. Praskóvya has preserved in her old age what I myself have lost. I, too, had ideas once, but I have been unfaithful to them; they have evaporated and vanished.

These, he tells us, were 'political' ideas: 'Liberty' and revolutionary 'regeneration'. 'But I have lived my ideals down [sic] in the dull routine of my foolish aimless life as an office hack, a clerk in the District Council, making copies that no-one will ever see of documents that no-one ever wants to read…' This too, of course, is a prime cliché of Russian literature, but there is no sense that Calderon is presenting it as such. At first Astéryi proposes 'worshipping' Praskóvya 'as something holy, for her fidelity to an idea in this wretched little town where ideas are as rare as white ravens'. After Praskóvya has rejected her flesh and blood son, however, and handed him over to the police, Astéryi is given the last line of the play: 'What's a man compared to an idea?' This 'thesis' is followed by the final stage direction 'PRASKÓVYA rolls over, dead'.

The second half of *The Little Stone House* is mounting melodrama. To modern eyes this makes the play fundamentally unstable – and few things are more difficult to bring off in today's theatre than a combination of parody and melodrama.

But the Edwardian audience did not see it that way. Not one of the twenty reviews that followed the matinee performance on 30 January referred to anything comic about it and hardly any described it as melodrama. It was 'tragedy' (*Sheffield Telegraph*), a 'harrowing study' (*The Times*), a terrifying play 'calculated to send many home with an uncomfortable feeling of fear as to whether they too may not be sacrificing the real to the illusion' (*Justice*). It was precisely the ending that was 'fine' (*Morning London*); the 'final tableau' was 'extraordinarily effective' (*Morning Post*). Its story was 'a very good one' (*Star*), rendered plausible by 'really great skill' (*Westminster Gazette*), and in the view of the *Daily Telegraph*:

Mr Calderon has put into it rare qualities of thought and imagination. It rings true and poignant, with the sad music of the ultimate mystery. […] Its theme is not foreign or local. It is concerned with universal humanity. Sad though it is, it has dignity. It may bring upon the stage some of the darkest of the tragic issues of life, but its characters have nobility, and even the meanest of them is something greater than the ugly fate which he has earned for himself. This power to dignify and ennoble his theme and his characters gives to Mr Calderon's play a rare distinction. It belongs to only great work.

Several reviewers agreed with the *Planet* that George's one-acter was 'far and away the best of the three'. It was 'very heartily applauded' (*Westminster Gazette*) and subsequently became the most-performed of his plays.

Through the winter of 1911 Trench gave no indication of when *Revolt* would be put on. Calderon therefore interested Will Rothenstein's younger brother, Albert, in producing sketches of a set design, with the aim of 'alluring' Trench, as he put it in a letter of 29 March. But nothing more is known of the Haymarket production after that date.

Four days later the census of 1911 was held. George entered himself as 'writer (author)'. In addition to himself and Kittie, there were two people domiciled at Heathland Lodge: Ruth Hopkins, 'general servant' aged thirty-one from Dublin, and Kittie's niece Mary ('May') Hamilton, 'teacher (governess)' aged twenty-three. May had probably moved the year before from Godolphin School, Salisbury, to work in London. She was an intelligent young woman who had virtually been adopted by the Calderons after she was ejected from the family home by her father, John Pakenham Hamilton, in scenes reminiscent of H.G. Wells's *Ann Veronica*. Around 1911 Nina Corbet began to rent a house from Clara Butt in Hampstead, 'so as to be near to Aunt Kittie', as Nina's daughter told me in 1986. On the day of the census, however, she is recorded as being at 44 Rutland Gate, S.W., with Jim, Lesbia, 'Mrs Stewart of Torquay', and seven servants.

Although Calderon had no more new plays performed in 1911, he was still very active in the theatre world. *The Fountain* was published and a series of public 'Dramatic Debates' held throughout the year, to which he contributed. In the summer he worked with Ballets Russes during their momentous season in London, becoming particularly friendly with Fokine. On 9 October *The Little Stone House* opened simultaneously at the Royalty Theatre, Glasgow, and the Gaiety Theatre, Manchester. For the whole of December Lydia Yavorskaya's production of Gorky's *Lower*

Depths ran at the Kingsway Theatre and on 15th George gave a lecture there on Gorky 'to a large audience' (*The Times*). George's contact with Yavorskaya and Fokine will be discussed in chapters 11 and 13 respectively.

It was most probably in the festive season of 1911/12 that George's 'Ibsen pantomime' *Cinderella* was first performed at Emmetts by him, the Lubbock brothers, children and guests. In Kittie's word, it was an 'impromptu', therefore probably worked up by George and others in a single day like the Christmas 'charades' at Heathland Lodge. But it was so successful that the company adopted the name 'Rosmersholm', with George as their 'President', and the pantomime was performed elsewhere. It is impossible now to say what the first version was like, although Percy Lubbock felt that that production 'perhaps [...] was never equalled'. The text published by Kittie in 1922 is clearly a longer, more literary one that George worked on after the performance; yet it still contains plenty of improvisatory brio.

The bare essentials of the traditional plot of *Cinderella* are retained, and there is a Demon and a Fairy, but the other characters are spoofs of Ibsen heroes. 'Cinderella' is called Hilda. When she is bullied by her stepsister Hedda, she resembles Mrs Elvsted in *Hedda Gabler*, but once she has become 'a real rickety rackety Ibsen girl' she behaves like Hilda Wangel from *The Master Builder*. The pantomime dame, Mrs Inquest (played by George), is a blend of several depressed Ibsen heroines, but turns out to be Nora Helmer, who soon returned to the Doll's House, gave birth to Hedda, and drowned Torvald 'in the mill-race'. In her words, they live in

a gloomy place, situated on a bleak and cheerless heath overlooking the fjord. We have no friends; no neighbours. There is no human habitation within miles and miles, except the gas-works. And here we all live side by side, cheek by jowl, but miles apart in soul, Hilda and Hedda and I, and we all detest each other heartily. Hedda is mad; Hilda is mad; we are all more or less mad.

The gas-works has been built by Stockfish, whose tall buildings tumbled down with such regularity that he became known as 'the plaster-builder' and resolved to build only gas-works, in places 'far from all human habitation, [...] where they can nev-ver, nev-ver be of any use to anybody at all'. Knitting, clockwork mice and White Horses are all, of course, 'symbolical', and there is even a song 'It's a Symbol'. Stockfish, who keeps a guinea pig rather than a wild duck, is in fact the father of Tesman, who is always having to dodge Hedda's pistol-shots and bores her with his rhapsodising about the pair of old 'goloshes' given them by his aunt Jemima as a wedding present (cf. his slippers in *Hedda Gabler*).

The 'goloshes' play a vital part in the dénouement of the pantomime. 'Inscrutably afraid' of his father, Tesman exits so precipitately that he leaves the 'goloshes' behind before Stockfish arrives to announce the bride-seeking party he is throwing. In the absence of glass slippers, the disguised Hilda wears Tesman's 'goloshes' and Stockfish falls in love with her. She leaves a 'golosh' behind her at the party and when the Stockfish Prince Charming tracks her down she demands that, as an act of 'Scandinavian love', he climb the gas-works and blow himself up. He does this, to a running commentary from the women characters, then Tesman rushes in 'weeping':

TESMAN: Blown up! Gone to glory! I shall nev-ver, nev-ver see them again.
MRS INQUEST: Them? What's them?
TESMAN: It's the little things that hurt one most, the things that some people would look on as almost nothing.
MRS INQUEST: Come, Tesman, what things do you mean?
TESMAN: He went up in my goloshes!
HEDDA: Your goloshes?
TESMAN: My beautiful big goloshes that Aunt Jemima gave me.
HILDA (Waving a handkerchief and dancing): My plaster-builder!
TESMAN: My goloshes!
HILDA: My plaster-builder!
TESMAN: My goloshes!

CURTAIN

In fact this ending is a 'double chord', since it parodies the last line of *The Master Builder* and Trofimov's obsession with his galoshes in the last act of *The Cherry Orchard*, which George had by then translated.

The published text of *Cinderella: An Ibsen Pantomime in Three Acts* is so full of inconsequences, incongruities, fantasy and surrealism as to resemble the 'Mabbot Street dialogues' in Joyce's *Ulysses*, or *Ubu Roi*. It is hardly performable as it stands, but once again Calderon has provided an abundance of action, language and effects from which another playwright could make his/her own choices. The performance would have to have flawless pace. Perhaps this and the special effects could best be achieved in cartoon. Radio would also be adequate to the task. At the time of writing, Librivox audiobooks have a project to produce an online recording.

Although the 'Ibsen Pantomime' contains traditional English effects such as puns, topical political references, double acts and men in drag, most of its energy is directed to sending up Ibsen's plays, which George clearly knew extremely well. The original excuse for the pantomime given by the Prologue was, according to Lubbock, that 'the old must have their pantomime', whilst the young in the audience 'still cling to their Ibsen with their severer realism'. Presumably, then, George could rely on the latter to pick up the references in his brilliant travesties of Ibsen's plots, psychology, symbols and dialogue. There was no satire here, but one could not overlook some serious themes. When Hilda 'finds herself as a woman' and becomes destructive, she is compared to a suffragette, whilst Mrs Inquest lectures Demon and Fairy on the fact that 'Right and Wrong have quite gone out; they have been abolished. [...] In place of them, we have nowadays the Expression of our Personality'. Altogether, one could hardly escape the impression that George was not an Ibsen fan.

The new year, 1912, was the high point of his practical involvement in the theatre. His epoch-making *Two Plays by Tchekhof* appeared on 29 January and had repercussions over the next twelve months. On 14 February 1912 Basil Dean's production of *The Fountain* opened at the Liverpool Repertory Theatre, which had been established the previous November. The following week another production of the play opened, at the Gaiety Theatre in Manchester. Miss Horniman's 'permanent' company was on tour in Canada (where *The Little Stone House* was on their bill) and one of her leading collaborators, 'Miss Darragh' (Letitia Marion Dallas), had taken the Gaiety for her own season. In the local press Miss Darragh accused Basil Dean of putting on *The Fountain* a week earlier in order to 'steal a march' on her. 'I can only regard it as an ungracious act on Mr Dean's part,' she said, 'especially as it is to me that he owes his present position within the Liverpool company.' This drew a lengthy counterblast from Dean and both productions surely benefited from the publicity.

Dean's was probably the better. In the early years of the repertory companies local journalists divided their reviews between explaining the plot of a new play and expressing amazement at the high quality of its acting. The Liverpool *Fountain* reflected 'the greatest possible credit on the producer, Basil Dean', wrote the *Courier*, and Dean himself 'scored a distinct success' acting Wren 'with typical abandon and freshness' (*Birkenhead Advertiser*). The Chendas of the two productions were 'charming', superbly 'feminine', 'radiant' and 'tremendously gay'. Indeed, the *Manchester Guardian* reviewer could have 'done without some 90 per cent of the exuberance that abounded last night' at the Gaiety Theatre, although he conceded that 'these character parts came along tremendously, they imposed themselves on us furiously, and altogether it was a triumph of vigour'. This was proof again of the 'actor-friendliness' of George's play – the fact that the performers enjoyed it more and more – but it proved a liability when Dean's production went on tour.

In the week beginning 4 March 1912 the company appeared for three days at the New Theatre, Oxford, with *The Fountain*, C.B. Fernald's curtain-raiser *The Cat and the Cherub*, and Ibsen's *Pillars of Society*. The *Oxford Magazine* found that 'from the largest down to the least important parts' the acting 'left room for nothing but praise'. Of Estelle Winwood as Chenda the *Oxford Chronicle* wrote that 'everybody must have had the impression that she has real acting talent of a high order after seeing her charming piece of unstressed, if artificial comedy'. 'Artificial' was an adjective applied to the Manchester Chenda, Muriel Pope, as well, and it seems that both actresses played to their audiences to 'get them on their side'.

One of the most perceptive and balanced analyses of *The Fountain* as a play appeared in the *Isis* of 9 March. For the reviewer it was 'an example of the New Drama, on that point there is no doubt: there is a certain amount of novelty and a conspicuous absence of drama'. 'Like so many plays in the new movement', it lacked 'concentration and therefore interest'. However, a great deal of the 'workmanship' was 'masterly' and the dialogue 'for the most part, really brilliant'. 'Was "Jim Crow", hailing apparently from *Uncle Tom's Cabin*, really necessary to the development of the thesis?' asked the reviewer, but concluded: 'With all its faults of self-consciousness and inconclusiveness *The Fountain* is well worth seeing.' Furthermore, 'on the fall of the curtain' on 4 March 'Mr Calderon introduced to his audience a side of his character with which they gained closer acquaintance next morning on the cab-rank outside Trinity'.

It has often been said that the Edwardians theatricalised their politics and made their theatre political; but George's action in Oxford must count as the perfect fusion of both. Britain was in the grip of the first National Coal Strike, which was beginning to have alarming effects. Called onto the stage to take his bow as author, George did so, then burst into a rousing appeal to the undergraduates present to form a body to go and work in the mines. 'I was simply cold with terror', wrote Kittie later: 'I had no notion this had been in his head.' He invited volunteers to meet him outside Trinity College next morning, in the evening he led a mass debate in the college hall about what action to take, and by the end of the day an Oxford University Strike Emergency Committee with 300 members had been formed under George's chairmanship. Next day, 6 March 1912, he and Kittie left for London to coordinate with activists there, and on the day after that George travelled alone to Cambridge for the opening night of *The Fountain* at that city's New Theatre.

By now the 'gaiety' of Basil Dean's company was getting out of hand. In the Edwardian theatre it was considered good manners vis-à-vis the audience and supportive of the actors if the author was in the house on the first night, as Calderon had been at Liverpool, Manchester and Oxford. The audience on 7 March in Cambridge was small and the actors 'livened things up' with some adlibbing. In particular, Estelle Winwood changed her line in Act 2 inquiring whether rents at Boodle Court had been raised because of the (1911) Insurance Act, to: 'Do you think, perhaps, it has anything to do with the Coal Strike?' This 'corpsed' the other actors and both they and the audience 'joined in a hearty laugh', as the *Cambridge Daily News* reviewer put it; and he took a dim view of the actors being in this 'elated state'. According to a later report in the same paper, there were 'calls for the author' afterwards and George was 'prepared to take a call', but was prevented 'possibly because Mr Basil Dean thought the time and the place were hardly suitable for propaganda'.

This did not prevent George from addressing a meeting of over two thousand undergraduates that had already been organised for the day after in the new (now Large) Examination Hall. The debate was reported at length in the *Cambridge Daily News*. We shall look at what Calderon said, the political context, his views and plan of action, in chapter 12. Suffice it to say that the Cambridge students also decided to set up a Strike Emergency Committee, but George declined to lead it. Whether he stayed for the last night of *The Fountain* in Cambridge (9 March) is not known. Immediately afterwards, at least, he was travelling all over England attempting to whip up support, and instructing Kittie by telegram as his assistant.

On 31 March George was almost certainly in London for the performance of his translation of *The Seagull* at the Little Theatre. The Coal Strike ended on 6 April. A month after that, Miss Horniman's company opened a seven-week season at the Coronet Theatre, London, with *The Little Stone House* in its repertoire. Through May, June and July George took part in recruiting 'free labour' to help break the London Dock Strike and he worked in the docks himself. On 13 June newspapers published the names of signatories to a petition to the Home Office calling for implementation of the recommendations of the 1909 Joint Committee of Lords and Commons on Censorship. Over sixty dramatists had signed, including Calderon, but paradoxically not Shaw. At the same time, George was adapting a story by Rabindranath Tagore into *The Maharani of Arakan: A Romantic Comedy in One Act*, which was performed at the Royal Albert Hall on 30 July. Whether he collaborated with Tagore on this, and what his opinion of Tagore's work and philosophy was, we do not know. Most probably he had got involved through Will Rothenstein, who was an admirer of Tagore and one of the organisers of the reception accorded him on his current visit. By now George had also completed Hankin's last, unfinished play *Thompson* at the request of his widow. But these works were hybrids – interactions with some other dramatic voice – and will be considered with similar forms of George's creativity in chapter

13. There had still been no productions of his latest original full-length play, *Revolt*.

Most unusually, the dog days of 1912 found the Calderons still at Heathland Lodge. Probably George was recovering from his physical exertions in the London Dock Strike. Kittie was suffering from an unspecified medical problem, possibly menopause. Undoubtedly George was immersed in a range of literary projects. He may have been working on his ballet scripts for Fokine (who was, however, out of the country) and on a number of one-act plays intended to form a collection. But the main reason the Calderons stayed at home through August and September was that they had put Heathland Lodge on the market and were awaiting developments.

They had been extremely happy at Heathland Lodge for over ten years. It was also perfect for their soirées and for inviting swarms of Russian conference delegates to experience a typical English garden party with croquet and pot-cricket. There were now numerous reasons for downsizing. By today's reckoning the house contained seventeen rooms, yet as far as we know their only live-in guests were May Hamilton and a domestic servant/cook. Moreover, they were short of funds. As Kittie wrote later, George's engagement with the strikes involved financial sacrifice: 'Not only of course did he cease to <u>produce</u>, but he also had to spend a considerable amount – going about the country, holding meetings etc, all cost money.' She dispensed with their last servant, and 'a treasure of a woman I had known for a long time used to come in before her regular day's work'. Unbeknown to her husband, Kittie did the rest of the housework herself, including cooking for the first time in her life. When the Dock Strike collapsed at the end of July and George came back into permanent residence, he insisted she employ a servant again (they also had a part-time gardener, of course), but manifestly they were left with a cash flow problem. It did not prevent him attending the Fourth International Congress for the History of Religions at Leiden between 9 and 13 September, where he read a paper about Slavonic elements in Greek religion. Thus on top of everything else, in 1912 he had been revisiting his research for *Demon Feasts*.

A buyer for Heathland Lodge was found, who let it to the actress-manager Olga Nethersole for thirty years afterwards, and on the last day of September the Calderons left for a holiday at Foxwold. 'Evey' Pym's stepmother had died there on 22 May 1912 and Violet and Evey moved into 'Foxwold Chase', as it was then called, on 17 July. The visitors book records that the Calderons were the young family's fifth and sixth houseguests and were joined on 5 October by Percy Lubbock. Kittie left on 7 October. It is possible, then, that the fine Autochrome photograph (Fig. 15) featuring George, Percy and the Pyms was taken at this time. The late Victorian custom of guests donating a limerick on a visit was still observed, it seems, for on one of Evey's scrupulously recycled pieces of scrap paper at Foxwold George wrote:

> There was a young lady of Brasted
> Whose efforts at wedlock were wasted:
> It wasn't the lack
> Of cash at her back
> That prevented the match: but her face did.

Above he drew a spike-nosed 'party' in a large hat with a roguish look on her face, and the outline of a church on the horizon. On another sheet of recycled paper he produced a watercolour of Maria Piltz *en pointe* as Chiarina in Ballets Russes's 1912 London production of *Carnaval*. He and Percy left Foxwold on 8 October.

He now learned that Annie Horniman proposed putting on *Revolt* during the Manchester Repertory Theatre's 1912-13 season and inviting her star director, Lewis Casson, to stage it.

Evidently George had not looked at *Revolt* for some time. 'Suddenly', he told his mother, 'I found that I had to alter the play; rereading it, I found it out of date and false in many ways.' He revised it at top speed in London, dictating to a typist, but when he met Casson in Manchester they reopened the subject. 'Casson lunched with me today', he wrote Kittie on 22 October 1912, 'and approved the alterations proposed. I killed off Renie too by lunch.' The latter sounds very drastic, as she was the love-interest of the play, but the part must have been swiftly restored as it was played to great acclaim by Casson's wife, Sybil Thorndike. Calderon's contribution

Fig. 15 Tea at Emmetts, October 1912. For key, see p.ix

to the production did not stop there. He attended rehearsals every day from 10.30 a.m. to 3.00 p.m. and on 5 November wrote to Clara: 'We alter bits here and there. It promises to be a fine finished performance.' The following day Kittie arrived from Acton Reynald, attended one rehearsal and the dress rehearsal, and both of them stayed for the week the play was performed, 11-16 November.

Miss Horniman was a superb publicist. The play preceding George's at the Gaiety was *Hindle Wakes*, a then notorious drama about extramarital sex written by northerner Stanley Houghton. Thorndike starred, Casson directed, and the production came from a steady run in the West End that summer. Much to Horniman's glee, the Vice Chancellor of Oxford University had banned it on tour because 'the general tendency of it was immoral'. It ran in Manchester for a fortnight. Possibly Horniman planned to perpetuate the good box office with a play that 'obviously' echoed Galsworthy's hit *Strife*, was by a known 'anti-unionist', and came on the heels of a strike by Merseyside dockers. Perhaps she hoped for workers' riots in the theatre.

If so, she was disappointed. There is a strike at the end of *Revolt*, followed by Luddite destruction of the beginnings of nuclear power, but the play is concerned with a variety of manifestations of 'revolt'. The Hodder family, all male, have revolt in their genes. The father had himself dabbled in 'atoms and the constitution of matter', as he puts it, and when the play opens is selling all his property to finance his son Vernon's private atomic research (clearly inspired by the Curies and Einstein). The other sons are a poet, a painter, and an engineer, who all reject established career paths. The heroine, Renie Dalrymple, is of 'noble ancestry' but rebels against her class's conventions of marriage. Another character is a Wykehamist turned socialist working in a bicycle shop. Even the strikers break the mould, since they claim that they are not syndicalists or socialists, and merely stand for 'profit-sharing'.

Nevertheless, the strike and the blowing up of the workshop that contains the 'formulae' for nuclear energy are the climax of the play's action and ideas. Casson was quite wrong to declare later that the play's 'chief interest' lay in 'the foretaste of the atomic age', remarkable though this may appear on George's part. The actions of the workmen in *Revolt* show that they are innately opposed to new ideas and technology. The real subject of the play is *intellectual* revolt. 'Thought must be free', declares Dr Hodder; his son Jeff believes that scientific discoveries are made 'out of pure curiosity'; and all the time that investors could see 'no hope of gain' in his brother Vernon's research they were content to let him literally starve to death in a garret. Jeff concludes: 'First it's the Capitalists; now it's the workmen. God seems to have given Englishmen brains only for devising ways of hindering thought.' The play, then, enacts a political message far removed from the essentially psychological focus of *Strife* and the judicial impartiality on which Galsworthy prided himself.

In that context, it is worth noting that Calderon, or possibly Casson, had told a local reporter that Jeff Hodder's revolt was 'against the prevailing view (so much insisted on by the passing generation of "intellectuals") that the material contests, of employers and working men, are chiefly significant for the present phase of our history'. A 'third factor, thought, aspiration, idealism, now drowned in the battle cries of class warfare' was 'really the only one that matters', and 'the protest of the play is directed as much against our dramatic intellectuals, the Galsworthys and the Bernard Shaws, as it is against the masses of the public' (*Manchester Guardian*, 9 November 1912). *Revolt*, then, is a post-Marxist play.

As was to be expected, it was finely directed and acted. George wrote to his mother that he was 'astonished at the care and industry that they spend in getting every detail of word and action right'. Sybil Thorndike, 'looking very Elizabethan in pure white', gave genuine romantic 'life' to the part of Renie (*Manchester Courier*, 12 November 1912). Casson almost stole the show in his single scene as the dying Vernon Hodder. Even the smallest parts reaped praise. The only substantive criticism was that the scenes with large numbers of characters talking were more vivacious than audible. This is interesting, as these were the only scenes in which the actors were asked to improvise: at the start of the lunch scene in Act 3, for instance, Calderon has the direction 'the actors are to say and do whatever is natural to be said and done by them under the circumstances, but so as not to interfere with the things set down for them to say'. This was startlingly innovative, and probably asking a lot from Edwardian actors.

The play itself was evaluated in long reviews by two of the country's top theatre critics. In the City Edition of the *Manchester Guardian* on 12 November 1912 Charles Edward Montague wrote:

[It] has two threads of subject running through it – a love story in which one does not feel sure that the author's heart is wholly engaged, and a story of genius tragically baulked, in which one feels that the author's heart is engaged passionately.

The love story 'hardly moved us at all', continued Montague, but 'the drama of the inventive spirit's vicissitudes and final defeat is deeply moving and [by] far the best thing of the kind that we have seen on the stage'. A.B. Walkley, in *The Times* of 13 November, agreed:

Nothing could be finer than the way in which Mr Calderon makes the presence of the idea, the possibility of new knowledge for the world, dominate the play, or the way in which the excitement of its struggle for existence works up to the distant little thud of the explosion which puts an end to it.

Both clearly identified the originality, within the 'Capital versus Labour' genre, of George's 'third way'. Neither was happy about the large ensemble scenes. Fresh from reading Calderon's Introduction to his Chekhov translations, Montague jumped to the conclusion that these 'passages of purely atmosphere-spreading dialogue' were conceived under Chekhov's influence. As we shall see in the next chapter, there was possibly some truth in this. But such ensemble scenes as Act 1 of *Three Sisters* or Act 3 of *The Cherry Orchard* are very carefully scripted by Chekhov and do not actually call for improvisation.

Montague's and Walkley's analyses of the strengths and weaknesses of *Revolt* were finely balanced and have stood the test of time. The former even suggested that 'Mr Calderon may have intended some significances more delicate than were, or could be, conveyed in the acting'. This would seem true, for example, of Renie, as there are clear indications that George saw her as more sado-masochistic than 'romantic'. But as Montague concluded his review, 'The audience applauded the play without any sign of such reservations as these, and Mr Calderon had to answer a warmly repeated call.' 'It all went very well', George wrote Clara on 12 November. 'The success of the evening was a supper which we gave afterwards to the whole company on the stage.'

Yet the production did not go into repertoire and was never revived. George's 'thesis' about capitalists and workers was not sensational enough to give *Revolt* the notoriety that *Strife* and *Hindle Wakes* had commanded. Another factor was that the Gaiety production used a cast of thirty-four, of whom some were local skilled amateurs. This made it very difficult to tour.

Even more surprising, Calderon seems never to have attempted another full-length play. The reason for this may emerge from some 'Notes for plays' that he wrote down in his cipher at Heathland Lodge on 10 August 1912. Some of them relate more to characters:

Play. Joseph Smith the Mormon; showing the success of patent humbug. Cf. *Peer Gynt*.
Anti-motor play. An anti-motorist converted into a bad motorist. Act I. He is musical; he composes an anti-motor symphony, with a motor horn at intervals breaking up various scenes of happiness; sylvan beauty, farmyard, sheep etc. Funeral march where he kills a man and goes on just the same. He plays it on the piano and imitates the horn with his mouth. This is a comical part for a play in which he is only a character.
Char[acter]. An intellectual workingman who attends meetings in the hope of escaping the boredom which consumes him; a lonely, elderly man.

Others are 'ideas' for plays:

Play. Write a play to prove the thesis that the true morality is to increase the sum total of happiness, not the happiness of most. [...]
Play. To show that pleasure is to be had only by refraining from it. It is a thing of the imagination. It is too confused in reality. The mirage goes.
Play. An apparently strong will[ed] original mother. Her ideas are really formed for her by anyone with any influence, by the last outside man that she has met. Her son has sunk his personality in hers; he has lost his own will and given in to hers, because of her strong face and Roman nose. Therefore it is seen on the stage that his actions are the result of her chance meetings with people outside.

Evidently there were also ideas for plays that Calderon was carrying in his head but did not detail in these notes: 'the play about the goldmine under a man's house', 'the Evil Eye play', 'the "Jealousy" play'. What nearly all the play ideas have in common, however, is the motive of 'proving' or 'demonstrating'. They would have been essentially 'thesis plays'. Perhaps, then, George grew bored with this form, or formula, of play, as he had with the neat, 'finished' form of his short stories a decade earlier? Certainly, as we shall see in chapter 13, by 1912 he had begun to experiment in much more varied, and mixed, dramatic genres. Perhaps the *Ibsen Pantomime* was a forerunner of this.

An in-depth critique of George's full-length plays and his classic *The Little Stone House* is overdue. This is not the place in which to undertake it, but some salient conclusions could be drawn from the present treatment.

Henry Newbolt wrote to his mother that George's plays were 'Bernard Shawish, but chaotic'. The adjective 'chaotic' was also applied to them by reviewers. Yet it misinterprets the openhandedness and playfulness – the *freedom* – of George's full-length plays. The 'theses' of these plays give them an irreducible structure, but this always contains interstices in which actors and audience can enjoy themselves to the full, not to mention the extraordinary innovation of inviting the actors to improvise. These features are what filled *The Fountain* and parts of *Revolt* with the 'gaiety' and life-affirming qualities universally remarked on. Tempting though it might be, then, to feel that George was too absorbed by *ideas* to become a full-blooded dramatist, his concentration on character, laughter, and above all language, makes him arguably more full-blooded than Shaw. George's dialogue is usually so energetic, nuanced, and rooted in 'heart' that it is still recognisably English as it is spoken today. Shaw's, by comparison, is overwhelmingly 'frontal', 'head' speech.

The 'Theatre of Ideas' and the Shavian revolution made Calderon's whole career as a dramatist possible, but he took the Edwardian play beyond Shaw and offers rich opportunities to today's theatrical adapters.

11

'CHEKHOV IS SUCH A GREAT MAN…'

In parallel with his own theatrical career, and everything else he was doing between 1907 and 1912, Calderon pursued an interest in contemporary Russian drama that was eventually to make him Britain's expert on the subject.

Whilst George was preparing to leave for Tahiti in March 1906, the Moscow Art Theatre (MKhT) was setting Europe ablaze with its first foreign tour, the repertoire of which included *Uncle Vanya* and *Three Sisters*. George probably paid little attention, as he had more pressing concerns. Constance Garnett, however, was quick to react. At this very time she wrote to her husband Edward that she had heard rumours MKhT was coming to London that summer, so she had started translating *The Cherry Orchard* 'on spec'. Despite having written to Chekhov in 1896 asking for his blessing on 'trying my luck' with *The Seagull*, there is no evidence that she tackled that play. Meanwhile, as translations of Chekhov's stories appeared in magazines and a small collection, literary England certainly noticed them. Knowing Laurence Irving's interest in Russian literature, Bernard Shaw wrote to him on 25 October 1905: 'I hear that there are several dramas extant by Whatsisname (Tchekoff, or something like that) – the late Russian novelist who wrote 'The Black Monk' &c. Have you any of them translated for the Stage Society?' Garnett showed her translation of *The Cherry Orchard* to Galsworthy and had it typed up whilst George was on the high seas. But MKhT did not come to Britain that summer.

According to Dr Tebb, Calderon bought Chekhov's plays and read them at the same time as he was studying Labiche and 'beginning to write' his own. We know from George's recently discovered diary that this was in 1907. The diary also reveals that he met Constance Garnett for the first time at the social historian Lawrence Hammond's on 26 January 1907. One imagines that some of their conversation, at least, concerned Russian literature. Did Garnett reveal to Calderon her interest in Chekhov's plays and that she had translated *The Cherry Orchard*? If so, she may inadvertently have given George the idea of investigating Chekhov's plays himself, as there is no evidence that he had read them before. However, he also joined the Stage Society that year, so he could have heard at one of its meetings that Constance had translated *The Cherry Orchard* and the Society was going to put it on. This turned out to be 'a false alarm, perhaps even a baseless rumour', as her grandson and biographer Richard Garnett has described it. She therefore offered her translation to Laurence Irving, but he did nothing with it either.

It was this situation, perhaps, that impelled George to get on with translating *The Seagull*. He wrote later that *The Cherry Orchard* was 'difficult, *rébarbatif* and very Russian', whereas *The Seagull* was 'easy, *entraînant*, not much unlike a Western play'. He might, therefore, have a better chance of getting his translation performed than Garnett had with hers. Being George, he read everything he could get hold of about Chekhov before he put pen to paper. In the bibliography of nine very substantial works that he appended to his translations in 1911, six were published before 1908. We happen to know that the very important one published in Russia in 1908 itself – Meyerhold's 'Naturalistic Theatre and the Theatre of Moods' – was not read by him before 1909, as his copy is inscribed by him with that year and annotated by him. The thickest compendium of Russian critical views, with a provocative article about *The Seagull*, was published in 1907 and George's copy of it, with his annotations, has also survived. It seems likely, then, that he translated *The Seagull* in 1908, especially as there is no mention of it in his diary for 1907. Thus when, in his 'last conversation' with Arnold Bennett, St John Hankin told him that he had read Chekhov's plays 'in manuscript', he was probably referring to both Garnett's version of *The Cherry Orchard* and Calderon's of *The Seagull*. Hankin could have read the first in his capacity as a member of the Stage Society's scripts committee, and the second as a close friend of George's. Hankin died on 15 June 1909.

Fig. 16 George Calderon, 1909

Having decided to present *The Fountain* at Glasgow Repertory
Theatre, Alfred Wareing probably did not need much persuading to risk
putting on George's translation of *The Seagull* the week after. Wareing
was passionate about introducing European drama to British audiences
and must have realised very quickly that George was a serious student of
Chekhov's plays. Retaining its star, Mary Jerrold, *The Fountain* was bound
to be a success in Glasgow. George came across as a popular and
personable man of the theatre (see Fig. 16) and his direct input into the

production 'on the back of' *The Fountain* could maximise *The Seagull*'s chances of success with actors, audiences, and critics alike. George would approximate to the modern director of the play, Wareing himself to its producer, and there was a further 'Stage Director' responsible for all practical matters, H. Ralph Kimpton. Moreover, although George was new to directing, the very experienced actor-director Norman Page (playing Wren in *The Fountain*) would 'fill me with good advice before he goes', as George wrote his mother on 10 October 1909.

Wareing knew that there were other circumstances, too, that could safeguard the British première of *The Seagull* against the disaster of its Russian première. Since the Scottish Playgoers Ltd had opened in April, Glasgow audiences had, in his biographer's words, 'proved the best Alfred Wareing had ever known: intelligent, sensitive, responsive, friendly, though rightly critical'. They cultivated a rivalry with the London theatre, as well they might because they were more cosmopolitan. The biggest international trade exhibition Britain had ever seen was put on in Glasgow in 1901. As Catherine Cooke has written, 'Scotland had old established trading links with Russia in her own right'. The Russian pavilions at the exhibition were the most stunning and had been designed by Chekhov's lifelong friend Fedor Shekhtel', who in the following year was responsible for the 'Moderne' style of MKhT's new theatre. Shekhtel' himself had lived in Glasgow for four months and on his return to Russia was instrumental in making Rennie Mackintosh the most popular foreign designer of Art Nouveau in Russia. Glasgow audiences, then, would hardly be deterred by the artistic modernity or 'Russianness' of Chekhov's play.

Meanwhile, since 1907 Calderon had informed himself about the best practices of modern theatre direction and those of MKhT in particular. He undoubtedly saw a production as an exercise in total artistic design. He 'choreographed' the play in advance by making a model of the stage and spending 'hours moving the tiny cardboard puppets about', as Kittie recorded in her memoirs. He wrote to Clara that 'of course we see the company daily all the time we've been here', and he strove to create a sense of ensemble among them. Before rehearsals began, Kittie tells us, 'the whole cast came one afternoon to us and George read and expounded the play and Anton Tchekhof to them'. The production was of 'intensest interest to him' and 'the actors and actresses were very responsive to his efforts'.

They were experienced professionals. At thirty-two, Mary Jerrold was ten years too old for the part of Chenda in *The Fountain* and a dozen years too young for Arkadina in *The Seagull*; but she was a versatile actress. Shamraev was played by her husband, Hubert Harben. Milton Rosmer, playing Arkadina's son Treplev, was only four years younger than Jerrold, but with his volatility as an actor he was probably well cast (he went on to fame at the Manchester Repertory Theatre). Campbell Gullan, playing Trigorin, was also only twenty-eight, and Laurence Hanray as the sixty-year-old Sorin was actually thirty-five. It was a young company, then, with plenty of energy.

As a final insurance against failure, Wareing decided to expose Glasgow playgoers and critics to George's charm and skills as a public speaker. On the afternoon of Friday 29 October Calderon gave a lecture on Chekhov's method as a dramatist, which was apparently well attended. It is generally assumed that the substance of the lecture was as in the introduction to his 1912 edition of *The Seagull* and *The Cherry Orchard*, but it must have been much shorter and this introduction contains many references to events after Glasgow, especially George's engagement with *The Cherry Orchard*. The lecture, it seems, was a success.

The first known performance of a Chekhov play in English went up at 7.45 on the evening of Tuesday 2 November 1909 in Glasgow's Royalty Theatre, at the intersection of Sauchiehall Street and Renfield Street, to an audience that all the critics agreed was 'large'.

What was the production really like?

As far as one can tell (for it was demolished in the 1950s), the Royalty Theatre was a conventional Victorian playhouse with a proscenium stage. It had a seating capacity of 1314 – greater than any other repertory theatre at that time. For performances of *The Seagull* the orchestra pit was presumably uncovered, as music by Tchaikovsky, Glazunov, Liadov and others was played before the play and during its three intervals. The Company's musical director was Calderon's friend Albert Cazabon, who also played Wieniawski's solo violin piece, 'Airs Russes'. Although today we might regard so much interval music as a distraction, or even a trivialisation of the play, it was probably a shrewd decision. It helped 'perspectivise' the drama as a *Russian* theatrical experience. Even the presence of the orchestra pit may have accentuated this distancing effect, whereas today we would want maximum immediacy of communication between Chekhov's characters and the auditorium.

The set was also cleverly handled. Each act of *The Seagull* happens in a different place, although the first two are outdoors and the last two indoors. Evidently, painted backcloths were still the norm at the Royalty, but they were expensive. A single new backcloth was used for the first half, clearly featuring the all-important lake, and a single new one for the second half, described in the programme as 'Dining Room in Sorin's House'. However, by introducing ten-minute intervals between Acts 1 and 2 and Acts 3 and 4, scenery could be completely changed, whilst in the 'real' interval, lasting fifteen minutes between Acts 2 and 3, the whole set and backcloth could be replaced. 'We are to have lovely scenery for it,' George told Clara, 'and they are going to buy a "property tree", rounded towards the audience, with a seat round it; moonlight twinkling on the waves during the first act, and the sound of the wind in the last.' The sets were by T.F. Dunn and reviewers found them excellent.

Almost certainly changes were made to George's script in rehearsal to suit actors and circumstances, but these were not usually perpetuated in the published text. The changes, cuts and even adlibbing permitted might have struck us as outrageous today. For instance, the name of the estate-manager, Shamraev, was changed to Petroff because it was easier to pronounce, and Medvedenko changed to Stoll for presumably the same reason; but Stoll is an *English* name. (Possibly it was chosen because its overtones of 'stolid' echo the 'bearishness' of the Russian name, possibly it was a company joke on Oswald Stoll the impresario.) Similarly, we know from a note of George's in the published text that Treplev's lines in Act 1 beginning 'Ay, but to live | In the rank sweat' were felt to be too explicit in English and the actor Laurence Hanray suggested an 'excellent substitute' from earlier in *Hamlet*.

Since none of the reviewers complained of longueurs or lugubriousness, the pace must have been quite brisk. The play was conspicuously billed as 'A Comedy', the principal actors were experienced at comic timing, and George himself believed that all Chekhov's plays had 'the texture of comedy'. But there was one feature that would certainly have struck us as odd today.

In the months before the production, George had read Meyerhold's essay 'Naturalistic Theatre and the Theatre of Moods' (or 'Atmospheres') and found it a 'masterly analysis'. Unfortunately, he concluded from it that 'in Tchekhof's plays many things are said and done which have no bearing on the action, but are directed *only to creating the atmosphere* [my italics]'. Therefore, in his view, the players have to 'show, by difference of tone and gesture, when they are speaking to the action, which concerns them as individuals, and when they are speaking to the atmosphere, which concerns them as members of a group'. In *Two Plays by Tchekhof* he gave examples of how this affected his direction of *The Seagull* at Glasgow:

In the second act, where a squall of nerves is brewing, the conversation and behaviour of the personages have nothing to do with the action of the piece, but are directed to convey the atmosphere of tedium and heat in which such squalls are possible. Here we had yawns and fannings and moppings of the brow. With the entrance of the boorish land agent the passive group-emotion becomes suddenly active. Everyone abandons his listless attitude, alert with the sense of impending perturbation. 'There are no horses to be had.' A gust of anger goes through all the company; each breaks out in turn.

This must have produced very contrasting blocks of 'action' and 'atmosphere' – almost an 'alienation' effect. In fact it disrupted what today we would understand as the 'through-line of the action' and begs the question of what Calderon understood to be action in a Chekhov play. The reviewers did not criticise it, however, because they had been warned about it in George's lecture.

Both the *Glasgow Herald* and the London *Stage* found the ensemble superb. Mary Jerrold, the *Evening Times* (Glasgow) wrote, played Arkadina 'with exquisite delicacy, [she] portrayed the flippant selfish woman of the world admirably'. This reviewer appreciated that Trigorin was a 'difficult part', exciting 'a peculiar combination of dislike and pity', and praised Gullan for bringing it off. However, although Irene Clarke as

Nina was 'excellent' in the first three acts, the same reviewer found her 'hardly intense enough in the long, drawn out interview of the last act'. In fact, Kittie tells us in her memoirs, George had 'reduced Miss Irene Clarke to tears' in rehearsal trying to achieve 'the concentrated passion needed at the end of the play'. ('He was much upset' by this, 'but I think he comforted her.')

The audience on 2 November 1909 gave the production an 'enthusiastic reception' (*Glasgow News*) and the play evidently made a deep impression on reviewers. It was 'a drama of realism which ought to be seen by everyone who is a serious student of the stage' and Chekhov's power was 'remarkable' (*Evening Times*). The play was felt to be 'full of more than Ibsenite symbolism' (*Glasgow University Magazine*). It was certainly apprehended as Russian, but 'the whole is illumined by comedy, and the humanity of the play is so warm and appealing that it somehow touches and interests more than it depresses – a rare virtue in Russian fiction', wrote the *Glasgow Herald*.

Manya Ross had made one of her cultural forays out of Newcastle, and was with George and Kittie on the opening night. It would have been very interesting to hear her reaction as a Russian. Kittie's verdict was: 'It really was a remarkably successful performance considering the shortness of time for rehearsal in a Repertory Theatre.' The production was even a financial success. It grossed the equivalent of £14,000 today over five evening performances and one matinee, although at two performances the theatre was less than half full. Kittie described the kindness of Wareing and his company as 'immense', leaving 'a most warm glow in our hearts'. The usual last-night dinner was held, and it was probably then that George was presented with a silver cigarette-case engraved: 'In recognition of the very sporting manner in which he has conducted the rehearsals.'

As we know, in 1910 George was writing *Revolt*, trying to find a producer for it, and turning his story 'Lipa Sidorovna' into *The Little Stone House*. It is a reasonable assumption that this is also when he translated *The Cherry Orchard*. His annotations in *"Theatre": A Collection of Articles about the New Theatre*, published by 'Shipovnik', and Pokrovskii's *Anton Chekhov's Life and Works*, show that he was fascinated by the play and its characters. It must have rapidly become clear to him, however, that his version of *The Cherry Orchard* would not be presented by the Stage Society. Firstly, in late 1910 they had accepted *The Little Stone House* for production, secondly they had a commitment to Constance Garnett's translation of 1906. It was therefore Garnett's version that was used for the British première of *The Cherry Orchard* at the Aldwych Theatre on Sunday 28 and Monday 29 May 1911.

This production was the disaster that Wareing had avoided. Although the cast contained three actors from the Glasgow *Seagull*, it had had no experience of working as an ensemble and it is safe to assume that each 'played for himself'. Katherine Pole was far too young and inexperienced for the part of Ranevskaia. 'It was unutterably sad to witness this charade', wrote a Russian correspondent: the costumes were a grotesque travesty, Nigel Playfair shamelessly hammed the part of Pishchik, and the audience 'hooted in amazement'. *The Cherry Orchard*, wrote Clifford Bax much later, was 'too baffling even for the Stage Society audience. During the first act it became restive; during the second [...] it walked out'. In a letter to George Moore, Shaw complained of the Stage Society audiences' backwardness: 'An exquisite play by Tchekoff was actually hissed.'

The 'frightful *débâcle*', as Walkley called it, had bad repercussions for Constance Garnett. Drama critics did not blame her translation, but the Stage Society Committee were perhaps looking for a scapegoat. Some of its members questioned whether the translation was 'correct'. Since it had been checked word for word by her usual Russian consultant, Natalie Duddington, the latter vouched that it was. Unfortunately, another Stage Society member told Garnett that George had been overheard telling Whelen, the Chairman of the Council of Management, that the translation was 'wretched' and 'now no-one would be willing to take up a Tchehov play anywhere as this poor translation would set the public against it' (letter to Edward Garnett, 6 June 1911). Whether this reproduces George's words or not, the incident certainly shows how internecine the Stage Society was. Garnett's feisty response was to try to publish her *Cherry Orchard* 'at once' and 'not for a moment consider Calderon's feelings'.

But she was too late. By then George had assembled his translations with an introduction and submitted them as a book to Smith, Elder. He was already engaged on another Russian project.

As he had read the 'Shipovnik' book about New Theatre, he had jotted down at the back in Russian the names of all the contemporary playwrights (18) and drama critics (7) mentioned in it. He now had the idea of writing a long article about the Russian theatre. He got hold of plays by as many of the Russian dramatists as he could, but he also wanted to hear a Russian view of the subject from someone qualified. Who better than Vsevolod Meyerhold, whose article, the longest in the book, George so admired?

Meyerhold had played Treplev in the triumphant 1898 MKhT production of *The Seagull* and was now an avant-garde director on the Imperial Theatres staff in St Petersburg. George wrote to him on 25 June 1911 enclosing a list of Russian plays he possessed and asking Meyerhold to cross out the ones that he thought insignificant and write in those he thought should be added. This really fired Meyerhold up. Less than three weeks later, he replied to George in Russian enclosing 'a) an account of the development of modern Russian drama, b) a chart showing this development, and c) a list of plays that I recommend you read'. The first two were published the following year in Meyerhold's book *About Theatre*. Meyerhold also asked George if he would reciprocate with 'a short account of the development of recent English dramatic art' – which George did in October.

Meanwhile, Calderon heard that Smith, Elder were not going to publish his translations of *The Seagull* and *The Cherry Orchard* 'because they think that the public would not take enough copies of the plays to remunerate them', as he wrote to Grant Richards on 30 July 1911. Kittie, of course, had had excellent relations with Richards since the 1890s. Richards now invited George to submit the book to him. Calderon was able to do this on 4 August 1911, explaining 'this text of the translation is not for the printer; I am going through it and making it more exact', and adding the familiar bait: 'The Moscow Artistic Theatre is going to act a Tchekhof play in London next year.' A month later George wrote to Richards for a decision; he had 'the text (very much altered) ready for printing now; it only remains to add a few notes'. On 17 September he was able to write:

I am delighted to hear that you will publish the Tchekhof book. There are several reasons why you should not expect to lose over it. Tchekhof is such a great man that he will be more and more famous here. Next summer the Moscow Artistic Theatre will act one of his plays (in Russian) in London. I suppose that they will go on to America. Gertrude Kingston wants to put *The Cherry Orchard* (with Ellen Terry) on the stage. I should be glad if you could have it printed in the States and preserve the copyright and acting right over there. [...] Certainly, pay me by results.

Five weeks later he had read the proofs. He praised the 'beautiful and attractive' layout of the book. In next to no time he was sending Richards a proposal for a book on 'the present state of British Drama', presumably inspired by his work for Meyerhold.

Two Plays by Tchekhof was coming out at a time when the British interest in Russian culture was tipping into a craze. Anna Pavlova had opened music hall eyes to ballet in 1910, in June 1911 the Ballets Russes had danced before the newly crowned monarchs and caused a public sensation, and Diaghilev was returning in 1912. Even *The Cherry Orchard* had sparked media controversy about Chekhov's plays; 'a row', as Arnold Bennett put it, that was 'a very fine thing'. Ever-responsive to theatrical fashion, Lydia Yavorskaya ('Princess Bariatinsky') put on Gorky's *Lower Depths* at the Kingsway Theatre throughout December 1911 with herself in the female lead.

George had probably met the Bariatinskys through the Stage Society. Recognising his expertise, they invited him to give a lecture on Gorky at the Kingsway on the afternoon of 15 December 1911. 'It was a large audience', *The Times* reported, and the 'Prince' presided. George began by giving an impressively detailed account of Gorky's life to date, then examined some of his plays. Yavorskaya may have been alarmed when he described *Lower Depths* as not a realistic play since 'the people were not actual', but relieved to hear him define it as 'a dynamic discussion-play – not a mere discussion, when nothing happened and nobody changed their minds – and the discussion was of ideals'. Unfortunately, George continued, for Gorky 'the test of a truth was not its power of being proved but its power of being useful to man', in particular to 'his favourite strong man', who with the 'strong woman' was prepared to 'commit any crimes

for the sake of strength for future generations'. Although George denied
that Gorky was either a Socialist or a 'follower of Nietzsche', this was an
insightful judgement in view of Gorky's later entanglement with
Bolshevism. George concluded by saying that Gorky was 'moved more by
hatred than by love' and 'failed of the highest art because he caricatured
the detested gentry, instead of [...], like Tchekoff, looking with pity on
both sides'.

In the week of 21 January 1912 Richards announced in the press that
Two Plays by Tchekhof would be published on 29 January (Chekhov's
birthday). He enthused in the *TLS*: 'Many readers will like the
introduction as much as the plays. Mr Calderon is combative, lively – and
he knows his Russia and his theatre. In fact he's written the deuce of a
preface!'

It was true. In twelve short sections George covered a huge range of
fundamental issues to do with Chekhov's plays, and he discussed these
issues with his usual analytical clarity and wit. He began with an
hypothesis that 'the interest of [the plays] is, so to speak, "centrifugal"
instead of self-centred' and compared them to modern theories of the
atom. Naturally he dwelt on 'Group Emotions', Meyerhold's 'Contrasts of
Moods', 'Realism' and 'Symbolism', but he also addressed head-on the
problem of English actors performing Chekhov. The 'English method of
acting' was 'ill-suited to Tchekhof's work' because 'centrifugal' drama
'requires above all things "centripetal" acting, acting designed to restore
the unity of impression'. In the 'general struggle for conspicuity' on the
English stage,

a sportsmanlike code has been established to give everyone a fair chance. As each
actor opens his mouth to speak, the rest fall petrified into an uncanny stillness,
like the courtiers about the Sleeping Beauty, or those pathetic clusters that one
sees about a golf-tee, while one of the players is flourishing at his ball in
preparation for a blow. But it is the very opposite of this cataleptic method that is
required for the acting of Tchekhof. His disjunctive manner is defeated of its
purpose unless the whole company keep continuously alive.

Probably Barker, Hankin, and even Shaw would have agreed with George
about the misplaced 'individualism' of English acting, but George's was

one of the sharpest formulations of the problem in Edwardian theatre-writing.

His sections on 'Good and Evil' and 'Villains and Heroes' – the irrelevancy of such concepts to Chekhov's plays – may today strike us as quaint, but they were very necessary in a world of lingering Victorian moralism, and they echo what Chekhov himself said in letters. These sections are also, in my view, influenced by George's reading of Taoist texts. According to him, Chekhov 'endeavoured to establish Man's relationship to his environment because it is only by reference to his environment that Man's nature, his doings and his sufferings, can rightly be interpreted':

To sever the individual, to abstract him in thought and try to determine the forces that sway him without reference to the rest of humanity, is as if a philosopher living at the sea's edge, by a gully in the rocks, should watch the water rise and fall in his gully, should observe the fishes and floating weeds and bits of wreckage that pass through it, and endeavour to explain their appearance and disappearance without taking into account the wide sea beyond, with its ebb and flow and changing incidents. He would not be merely limited in the scope of his conclusions; he would be positively wrong. And so, since ever we began to think in Europe, we have been wrong about Man.

The last sentence and the extended simile involving water suggest that the 'profound philosophy' George believes Chekhov has 'embraced' in his plays is that of the *Tao*. Whilst many critics have written of Chekhov's 'pantheism' and this could be described as 'Taoistic', as far as I am aware Chekhov never flirted with philosophical Taoism itself. Similarly, George goes on to apply to Chekhov's plays the Taoist view that evil is not the result of human will but of an imbalance in the forces 'flowing *through* men's souls'; yet it is difficult to think that the author of *Sakhalin Island* or 'Ward No 6', with his intense belief in ethical self-responsibility, could have accepted this.

For George's contemporaries, probably the most arresting section of his introduction was 'Tragedy and Comedy'. 'Life is never pure comedy or pure tragedy', it began.

Tchekhof had that fine comedic spirit which relishes the incongruity between the actual disorder of the world and the underlying order. Seeking as he did to throw our eyes outwards from the individual destiny, to discover its relation to surrounding Life, he habitually mingled tragedy (which is Life seen close at hand) with comedy (which is life seen from a distance). His plays are tragedies with the texture of comedy.

George believed that Chekhov endowed some characters, e.g. 'Old Sorin' in *The Seagull*, with 'his own insight'. In *The Cherry Orchard*, however, characters such as 'Yásha, Dunyásha, Epikhódof, perhaps Charlotte and Gáyef too' would not be 'out of place in a knockabout farce', although 'these folk are not random laughing-stocks; they are all sub-varieties of the species "nedotëpa" or "job-lot", and are expressly designed to carry out the central motive of the play'. Although possibly influenced by an article by Aikhenval'd, in his section 'The Illusion of the Ego' George most likely originated the English view that Chekhov's plays are about 'non-communication'.

Obviously Calderon felt that Chekhov was a profound, superbly innovating modern playwright, in fact 'one of the best models' for 'our new Drama'. Nowhere in his introduction, however, does he elaborate on why he thought Chekhov was 'such a great man'. Indeed he was so determined to avoid biography that he reduced it to the last two lines: 'P.S. – I ought to have mentioned that Tchekhof was born in 1860, studied medicine at Moscow, and died in 1904.' Nevertheless, his numerous footnotes throughout the volume convey a detailed knowledge of Chekhov's life and suggest he was intrigued, even charmed, by Chekhov as a man. He intuitively questioned the oppositionism and millenarianism attributed to Chekhov in his Yalta period by writers such as Gorky and Kuprin (their memoirs are now widely discredited). 'If Tchekhof, who saw so clearly that in real life all tales end badly, had to console himself by supposing that some day they would all begin to end well,' wrote George, 'it is enough to strike panic into one.' Yet there was consolation in 'the assurance that whatever becomes of this husk of a planet, the inner meaning of it, hope itself, God, man's ideal, continually progresses and develops'. If that was not what Chekhov meant, it seemed 'at any rate the best interpretation of what he wrote'.

Agreement and disagreement with George's introduction rippled through the writings of literary and theatrical critics for the rest of 1912. The essay became a departure-point and benchmark for discourse about Chekhov's plays. Ten years later, in a letter to the *TLS*, the American Slavist William Lyon Phelps called it 'the most subtle and penetrating essay on the Russian dramatist that I have seen anywhere'. It ought to be a set text on any university course about Chekhov's theatre, since it invites discussion in terms of what in it is purely of its time and what can be said to be still true today.

Understandably, hardly anyone commented on the quality of the translations. Meyerhold thought they were 'brilliant'. The conventional wisdom in the British theatre for the past fifty years has been that they are 'quirky' and 'dated'. But this is to forget not only how much the English language has changed since 1912, but how different today's *theatrical* language is, too. The language of George's translations of *The Seagull* and *The Cherry Orchard* is theatrical in the sense of being both an Edwardian theatrical language and recognisably George's own stage language. When he chooses a distinctive ('quirky') word there is usually good reason for it. His translator's notes are far more useful than in any modern English edition. Constance Garnett's translations are more literal and their language is hardly theatrical at all; it has 'speakable' energy only about half of the time. Because George's translations of Chekhov's plays were recognisably his, they were dropped once Edwardian theatre slipped into the past, whereas Garnett's (first published in 1923) could be treated as plain, literal versions which directors could adapt to their own theatrical language. But today dramaturgs increasingly recognise the advantages of translations whose language is contemporary with the original text, and they can subtly re-energise them. In 2009 this was very successfully done with George's translation of *The Seagull* by playwright Stuart Paterson for a centenary production by the Royal Scottish Academy of Music and Drama in Glasgow and subsequently on Radio 3.

Neither Calderon nor Garnett translated the Russian stage directions (as seen from the auditorium) into their English equivalents (as seen from the stage), which suggests that they did not know the difference. Both had some dubious renderings and at least one howler. On the whole, however,

Garnett had fewer, which is probably a tribute to Natalie Duddington's collaboration and confirms the emphasis on literalism in Garnett's translation. For Trigorin's line at the end of Act 3 of *The Seagull*, 'I've forgotten my walking-stick. I think it's on the verandah', George had 'I've left my stick behind. I think she's out there on the verandah', meaning Nina, who promptly enters. There is no doubt that George has mistaken the nominative feminine pronoun representing an inanimate feminine noun (stick), for the feminine third-person singular (she) here – his scenic imagination ran away with him. Conversely, Garnett translated Trigorin's '*vdovii tsvet*' as 'widow's flower', a bad mistake as *tsvet* can only mean 'colour' here. But George had difficulty with it too: in *Two Plays by Tchekhof* he rendered it as 'mourning shade', but in the margin of his mother's copy he wrote 'widows' colour'. Actually this crux demonstrates the difficulty of translating languages that have different structures and are at different stages of development. The Russian *vdovii* is a possessive adjective of a kind that hardly exists in English. Calderon and Garnett had no alternative but to use an apostrophe. Today, however, the attributive use of a plural noun would be possible: 'widows colour', and a case might even be made out for 'vidual hue'.

On 22 January 1912 it had been announced in *The Times* that the actor Maurice Elvey's theatre company, the Adelphi Play Society, was going to put on a single performance of *The Seagull* in George's translation on Sunday 25 February. Whether Yavorskaya, whose stage name in Britain was 'Yavorska', had already been cast as Nina is not known. The performance was soon postponed to Sunday 31 March, however, and on 6 March George asked Grant Richards to send her a copy of his book, which was done. She was then in Brighton and visited her long-standing friend Kropotkin. She must have shown him *Two Plays by Tchekhof*, as George credited Kropotkin in the second edition for a footnote 'and some corrections made since the first edition'. At some point Yavorskaya, who was after all a 'star', agreed to play opposite another 'star', Gertrude Kingston, for one performance in the Little Theatre, the smallest West End venue (seating capacity 250).

There was a bitter irony in Yavorskaya playing Nina. She discreetly put it about London's theatrical world that Chekhov had written *The Seagull* for her and that she had been his original Nina. This made its impression. In fact she had never played Nina and Chekhov's friends recognised her as, in Aleksei Bartoshevich's words, 'the prototype of the *cabotine* Arkadina'. Apparently her reputation for mendacity had not preceded her to Britain. Yet in a sense she *was* now acting in 'the play Chekhov had written for her': she had asked him for a one-acter to be entitled *Fantasies* and for its last line to be 'It's a dream!', and she would be uttering these very words as the last line of Act 2 of *The Seagull* in the character of a girl who does live in a fantasy-world. 'You either adore her or you can't stand her,' Prince Bariatinsky said of his wife. George, one strongly suspects, had got the measure of her, since he remarks in a footnote: 'Arcádina would have insisted on playing Nina'!

Gertrude Kingston was very different. She had acted in Shaw opposite Barker and specialised in classical Greek roles. She was a suffragist campaigner and played the title role in *Lysistrata*, with which she opened her management of the Little Theatre in 1910. She had fitted out this theatre with the latest technology, including dimmer-boards. It was by no means just a 'fringe theatre'.

Unfortunately, brilliant though Maurice Elvey's career would become, in 1912 he was only twenty-five. He was the presenter of the production, nominally its director and set-designer, and he was playing Trigorin. Writing a fortnight later in the *Saturday Review*, John Palmer felt that the production had not been directed 'at all'. As 'a young man', Palmer wrote, Elvey was 'entirely unable to compel Miss Gertrude Kingston or the Princess Bariatinsky to behave as she should', and their primadonnery had torn the ensemble apart.

In the 1950s Robert Tracy interviewed Elvey and was told by him that he had been 'delighted to find the translator eager to advise him, and willing to lecture to the audience on Chekhov's art as he had done in Glasgow'. The lecture was advertised for before the performance, but George did not give it. Palmer speculated whether Calderon had 'merely missed the train'. The *Era*'s reviewer thought the lecture had been abandoned because 'there were very few persons present at the advertised time for the performance to begin'. Given that the Coal Strike was not yet over, George could indeed have been hurrying to London from as far away as Scotland. Palmer actually thought, however, that Calderon had decided to bow out of the lecture because he was aware of the 'impossible situation' of the production.

Nevertheless, there is no evidence that George missed the performance itself on 31 March 1912. He made a point of having the cast-list printed in subsequent editions of *Two Plays by Tchekhof*, along with the Glasgow cast-list and that of the 1911 *Cherry Orchard*. It is possible that he even enjoyed some of it. Walkley found Kingston's performance with Elvey in Act 3, Elvey's own in Act 2, and Mary Mackenzie's as Masha, 'first-rate', although 'the scenery was not well managed'. Most interesting of all, according to the *Era*, the forty-something Yavorskaya rose to the occasion as Nina in Act 4. None of the other reviewers remarked upon a poor house. Palmer believed that since the *Cherry Orchard* fiasco 'players, audience and critics had [...] been instructed how to pretend a wisdom if they had it not [...] by Mr George Calderon's preface to an admirable translation', and 'things were a little better in the auditorium' this time. He even conceded that Kingston and Yavorskaya were 'not seriously wrong for more than half the time' and they 'heavily impressed the audience'. Even such an unstable production, then, probably furthered the causes of Chekhov on the British stage and George's income from the book.

He was proactive in writing advertisements, circulating leaflets, despatching review copies, and identifying major bookshops that did not have it in stock. Richards found an American publisher for it. He obtained a certificate registering the rights in Washington, but the certificate stated that he, Richards, owned the copyright. George therefore stressed to him in a letter of 14 June 1912 that 'as regards the book-rights, the difference is perhaps only formal; but it must not be allowed to complicate the playing rights. The copyright is actually, by our agreement, vested in me'. In October Richards produced a revised second edition. Unfortunately, by then George had failed to meet his deadline with him for the book on 'the present state of British drama'.

In July, whilst he was embroiled in the London Dock Strike, George's article 'The Russian Stage' came out in the *Fortnightly Review*.

Ostensibly it is a review of play texts by eight Russian dramatists, but at the end of the bibliographical data about them George has added: 'And other works.' Although he did not dig back as far into Russian theatrical history as Meyerhold had, he did cast his net very widely. His opening claim was ambitious:

If we want to learn the inner secrets of Russian thought during the national crisis of the last few years, the heart-searchings, the aspirations, there is hardly a better, more intimate way of doing it than by the discriminating study of their drama.

This did not include the 'necessary and delightful by-products' of 'the popular playwrights, the entertainers, who bulk biggest in the daily programme', as they 'reveal nothing; they have no place in the history of intellectual forces'. Nor did it apply to 'that intermediate sort of purveyor, who flourishes everywhere nowadays', the playwright who strives to 'represent new phases of thought, and yet to please the many; to be true if he can, but always to be effective'; the writer who has 'an air' of probing intellectual questions 'without giving offence by penetrating further than his public has gone before him'.

The perfect type in Russia of this intermediate sort is Leonid Andreyef, a gifted and versatile craftsman, famous already in England, while the work of better playwrights is till unknown. He can turn his hand to anything; he is ready to do you the realistic, the mystic, the modern, the antique, the biblical, the medieval – whatever you please. Tragedy or comedy, it is all one to him; he will give you hope if you want it, or despair if you prefer it. If he has a talent more peculiarly his own, it is the big symbolical 'bow-wow'.

In Andreyev's famous plays *The Life of Man* and *Anathema* 'everything is on the large symbolical scale', with 'mysterious "Hims" and "Its" that stand silent, with their hats pulled over their eyes'. 'Like Bilibin's painting', Andreyev's writing was 'rich, astonishing, ingenious, hollow, and insincere'.

  The quality which 'won Russian literature the position it holds in European esteem' was, however, its 'restless, probing sincerity', and George now turned to a clutch of dramatists he termed 'realists', since 'it is in the guise of realism that we are accustomed to Russian sincerity'. They included Iushkevich, Naidenov, Lev Tolstoi as a playwright, Chirikov, Dymov, and above all Gorky. Meyerhold had classed all of these except

CHEKHOV   313

Tolstoi and Gorky as 'epigones' of Chekhov. Calderon does not use the word 'epigone', but he identifies both the subject and techniques of Gorky's plays as 'openly Tchekhovian', and even Tolstoi's *Living Corpse* as influenced by Chekhov. In this discussion, George's devastating sense of the ridiculous comes out of its burrow. The 'younger generation' of Russian realists has not 'escaped the danger that lies in wait for realists – the painting of things in too sombre colours':

The type is too well fixed to be avoided; it is a sort of *tragédie de moeurs*; a poor but intellectual middle-class family, living in a small provincial town (how realists everywhere delight in small provincial towns!), inspired by hearty dislike for their nearest relatives, and practising the marriage customs of the early Stone Age.

'Do mothers really sell their daughters in Russia?' he asked of Iushkevich's *Dina Glank*. 'One is not wholly convinced.' In any case, these 'realists' were equally concerned with showing what was going to 'overcome' reality – the 'future', even 'the Millenium'. Gorky's 'new world' was 'vague': 'it would be covered with engine-sheds, and peopled by strong men with black oil on their hands'; the 'people who can lead the rest to the Golden Age' were 'rough, blunt, good-natured folk, as a rule, like great St Bernard dogs'.

This millenarianism, George continued, was an illusion. By contrast, the 'constant theme' of all Chekhov's plays was 'disillusion'. 'Tchekhof has painted disillusion with a melancholy grace that makes it seem more beautiful than achievement.' Few, probably, would accept today that disillusion is the super-theme of Chekhov's plays, but Calderon believed that at least it ensured 'his plays will never go out of date'. Here he was fundamentally at variance with his mentor: Meyerhold had said in his article that after 1905 'Chekhov's Theatre' was as good as dead.

From here George turned to plays by Chulkov and Briusov that actually depict Golden Ages. They might be 'fantastic and unreal', but he believed all of the dramatists he had discussed so far were stirred by the 'yearning and the discontent' of 'the rest of their generation'. However,

Through all the plays of the last generation in Russia runs the same cry for liberty, for emancipation; not for political emancipation – the lack of a share in the sovereign power weighs very little on the individual – but for emancipation from every sort of restraint, for an ideal and impossible freedom. The impulse is fundamentally aimless and unconstructive. [...]

While our Western playwrights, confined within the boundaries of the attainable, wage a heavy-handed polemic with social institutions and conventions, the Russians are at grips with the deepest cravings of their inward nature. While our Hervieus and Brieux are railing at unjust marriage-laws, the Russians are crying out against the bonds of love itself.

These Russians were the Decadent and Symbolist dramatists, whom George considered in the remaining half of his article.

The best of them in his opinion were Sologub and Blok. Sologub 'has humour, dignity and charm; he is a perfect master of dramatic form; and the full rich music of poetry runs through all his work'. George was particularly taken with the 'unearthly beauty' evoked in Sologub's *Night Dances*, based on a Grimms fairytale. His 'groups of women coming and going are always delicious – the twelve Princesses, scornfully rebellious, threading to their places', and in *The Gifts of the Wise Bees* 'the imagination is arrested by recurrent felicities of phrase and vision'. Blok's plays were 'the last word in modernity; he is the creator of the Subjective Drama'. His plays were 'lyrics', representing 'experiences of the soul, not external events', and George aptly juxtaposed Blok's verse cycle 'Verses about the Beautiful Lady' with his play *The Stranger* (*Neznakomka*).

Although George faithfully paraphrased the plays of other decadents, he was clearly exasperated by them. Bal'mont's *Three Blossomings* was 'poor, stilted stuff', and of its lines 'The Red, the Yellow, the Blue, | Three blossomings... | Before the victory of White | Dreams breathe...' he exclaimed: 'Heaven only knows what it means!' The men in Zinov'eva-Annibal's plays have 'distended nostrils and smell all manner of smells; they love with the fury of buffaloes – it is her own comparison'. All the characters in her play *Rings* 'suffer from acute neurasthenia, and, in this country, would be consigned to Parkhurst or Bedlam'. Kuzmin, on the other hand, was 'a decadent only in the sense of one who departs from tradition. He has a delicate irony and the light hand of a Frenchman – a rare gift among the Russians'.

'To sum up,' George wrote, 'the chief characteristic of the decadents is solitude of spirit', or egocentrism: 'They have elevated the identification of the Ego and the Cosmos to the dignity of a philosophy, under the name of Solipsism.' Thus the decadent plays were not dramatic: 'The world stands still during a solipsist play; there is no ebb and flow of life about it; men and women have no visible occupations but love and suffering.' Most perceptively, he analysed the phenomenon of 'everything is symbolic' that he had lampooned in his *Ibsen Pantomime*: symbolism was 'a disease which attacks all thought too exclusively concentrated on its object', i.e. it was a form of paranoia, the Russian disease *par excellence*. 'How refreshing after this is the live, warm, pantheistic world of Shakespeare or of Tchekhof! They loved everything that God created for its own sake.' In sentence after sentence he accurately distinguished the 'pseudo-chromaesthesia', 'tremulousness' (*zybkost'*), 'recurrent pseudoanamnesia', and *Doppelgänger*-mania of these dramatists. For them love is 'inseparable from anguish' and from this it was 'not far to Sadic excitements and an unholy delight in pain, tumult, fear and death'. This was 'a very real thing [...] in Russia nowadays, and not confined to writers, as witness Vadim the Vampire and the St Petersburg Suicide Club. Solipsism is a widespread social malady'. Since, as George had stressed, it was not accompanied by any desire for democracy or political self-responsibility, it sounds eerily like post-Communist Russia.

It is a tribute to George's objectivity, however, that he added: 'But this is only the pathological side of a movement which cannot be neglected in an estimate of intellectual forces. For it is the ultimate consequence of a passionate sincerity of thought of which we have very little in England.' If he had 'laid stress on the aberrations of the movement, on the runaways and their adventures in the ditches', it was because 'the contemplation of them enables us to characterise more clearly the general direction of the rest'.

What have we over here that we can safely put in competition with the recent dramatic literature of Russia? Our favourite playwrights, the Sutros, the Maughams, the Pineros, are too healthy, too well-balanced to come creditably out of the comparison. They are men of action who have taken entertainment for their sphere to the kindly end of refreshing other men of action when the day's work is done. One turns rather to less popular names – Hankin, Lady Gregory, Bennett, Barker, Davidson, Yeats, Martyn, Synge and Shaw (another unmistakable solipsist, by the by).

If the parenthesis seems gratuitous, it was indisputably accurate. Maintaining his focus, George questioned whether any recent British dramatist had 'travelled so far away from the common track', or 'revealed such vistas or explored such penetralia as the Russians'. In the last lines of his essay he unequivocally asserted that none of his British contemporary dramatists had 'attained such mastery of their medium as Tchekhof or Sologub'. It was praise indeed of the Russians.

This article, for which George carried out three years research and consulted with one of the twentieth century's greatest theatre directors, is on a par with his introductory essay about Chekhov's plays. Like that, it would richly repay synchronic and diachronic discussion at university level. As Laurence Senelick has written (1997), it is 'the best informed article on the subject in any western language'.

The year 1912 was the height of Calderon's involvement with Chekhov and the Russian theatre. In England his 1909 Glasgow *Seagull* had hardly been recognised as an event. But *The Little Stone House, Two Plays by Tchekhof,* and 'The Russian Stage' rode the rising wave of 'Russian mania' centred on London and made George's reputation as an authority on Russian drama. Along with Maurice Baring, he was the natural person to consult about such matters. Grant Richards, for example, was desperate to have his assessment of the 'publishability' of a translation of Leonid Andreyev's play *The Life of Man*. In his long response of 27 February 1912, George does his utmost not to commit himself. He is 'no judge' of the play's 'publishability'; 'I can only tell you what I think about it as a work of art.' It was 'very arresting, like all Andreyef's work', it had had 'immense success on the stage in Russia', and Baring had said some 'enthusiastic' things about it. Yet George cannot conceal his fundamental antipathy. The play had 'the air of being very symbolical and very wise about Life in general. But to my mind it is, at bottom, false and unreal; aiming at effect, not at Truth'. Its 'idea' was 'finely conceived', but 'warped by the endeavour to work up an excitement; and to please those who regard the attribution of a gloomy purposelessness to Life as the mark of high philosophic genius'. Its 'great success was as a play', it was 'better adapted for the illusions that stun the judgement on the stage', yet 'I think it is quite likely that it might have some success as a book', and so on and so on... 'In fact, in three words, I don't know.'

In fact, Andreyev had become something of a *bête noire* for Calderon. When Miss Darragh wrote to him about an avant-garde theatre company she was planning and asked him about the modern Russian and Spanish repertoires, he immediately recommended plays by Blok and Sologub, but added that she should at all costs avoid Andreyev, whom everyone would recommend, because he was essentially false and insincere – although his *Life of Man* might have success. He mentioned two Spanish dramatists whose work he knew, then closed by saying that Russian 'successful' plays were no better than English 'successful' plays, unless she meant successful with a select public, which, he believed, should take her straight to Chekhov.

There is no finer judgement of George's work with Chekhov than Jan McDonald's in her article 'Naturalism and the Drama of Dissent'. She writes that 'Calderon understood better than his contemporaries the true form of a Chekhov play' and concludes that in Edwardian Britain 'with the exception of Calderon, there was no director sufficiently at ease with the material to recreate the dramatist's vision on stage'. It is curious, therefore, that there is no documentary evidence of George's response to the next Chekhov production in Britain, the Stage Society's *Uncle Vanya* at the Aldwych Theatre on 10 and 11 May 1914 in R.S. Townsend's translation and with Guy Rathbone as Vanya. There is no evidence, indeed, that he saw it. It was relatively successful and Shaw is reported to have said afterwards: 'When I hear a play of Chekhov's I want to tear my own up.'

Similarly, it is intriguing that Calderon hardly ever referred to Chekhov's most visceral, and some would say greatest play, *Three Sisters*, and that there is no extant record of any further involvement by him with Russian drama after his letter to Miss Darragh of 6 January 1913.

The truth is, what he most wanted to see was a successful production of *The Cherry Orchard* in his own translation. His attention to that play in his introduction and in a short piece he wrote for the *Manchester Playgoer* entitled 'The Four Walls' in December 1912, strongly suggests this. But after the 1911 disaster London was unlikely to risk another production of *The Cherry Orchard* (it did not happen until 1920). Doubtless Wareing would have been happy for George to direct another Chekhov success for him, especially as *The Cherry Orchard* was increasingly recognised by literati, but Wareing's position at the Glasgow Repertory Theatre was becoming more precarious. So George never saw his translation of the great play performed in his lifetime. As we shall see, however, its day did come, and with far-reaching consequences.

12

THE TROUBLE WITH TRADE UNIONISM

> In Hyde Park I heard a Socialist orator holding
> forth on the iniquity of the feeding system in
> Salvation Army shelters. 'What I say is this,' he
> kept repeating, 'bring the food to our homes.'

> Herbert Beerbohm Tree, *Note-books*

To us it may seem that the Edwardians had a mania for creating 'leagues', 'committees', 'councils' and 'associations'. In so far as the interests of these bodies are today represented by the state, political parties, or charities, we may dismiss the phenomenon as a manifestation of the Edwardians' infamous 'amateurism', or indeed dilettantism. It is also possible, however, to see it as part of the explosion of middle-class democracy and pluralism that occurred in Edwardian Britain.

Thus there is nothing eccentric about George Calderon's involvement in a whole series of public causes both before and after his anti-suffrage activism. As someone who regularly used the amenity of Hampstead Heath, he supported the Hampstead Heath Extension Council formed by Henrietta Barnett in 1903, wrote letters about the project to the press, and helped raise public contributions to buy land that was part of Eton College's Wyldes Farm. This was successful: in 1907 eighty acres were acquired and they came to be known as the Heath Extension. Around 1908 George either joined the recently founded Anti-Motorist League, or started a pressure group of his own called the Road Defence Committee. It seems that he objected to both the terrorization of the 'plain man' on the roads by rich automobile-owners and the pollution of the countryside by cars; conceivably, he would later have joined the Council for the Preservation of Rural England along with Henry Newbolt.

When Bernard Pares initiated a School of Russian Studies at Liverpool University in 1909, George was brought onto its committee, whose meetings were chaired by the Lord Mayor of Liverpool, Howard Dowdall. In 1911 he was active on the Committee for Organizing a National British Festival of Arts.

But these causes were of a completely different order from his engagement with the Coal Strike and London Dock Strike of 1912. Here he gave his political philosophy its fullest practical and intellectual expression.

The period 1910-1914 saw an unprecedented level of strikes in Britain and has been called 'The Great Unrest'. A contemporary, J.B. Priestley, felt there was 'really a secret war between the syndicalist idea and "diehard" capitalism (with the Liberal Government running around in neutral territory)'. In 1910, when violence erupted at Tonypandy after a lock-out and strike throughout the South Wales coalfield, troops were sent to assist the police. The following year 145,000 workers took part in a week-long railway strike and there were stoppages among dockers, seamen and carters all over the country. The situation was particularly serious in Liverpool, where two strikers were shot dead by soldiers. Obviously these strikes threatened fuel and food supplies and materially disrupted the life of the community as a whole. Nor were they popular with some other unions, whose members were laid off and had to be compensated from union funds. On 1 March 1912 the first national miners' strike began, in support of a minimum wage. It is estimated that 850,000 men came out and another 1.3 million were made idle in ancillary industries. Some called it 'the greatest industrial strike in modern history'. *The Times* described it as 'the greatest catastrophe that has threatened the country since the Spanish Armada'. Many felt revolution was imminent.

Although Calderon's calls to Oxford students on 4 and 5 March 1912 to volunteer for work in the mining industry caught Kittie unawares, he had undoubtedly been thinking about the relationship of militant trade unionism to the community for some time. Rothenstein believed he was influenced by William James's ideas earlier in the century about 'social conscription'. It is possible that Harold Dowdall's memory of George arriving at his house unexpectedly one Sunday morning and asking him for 'an introduction to Lord Derby, who was then Lord Mayor, to summon a meeting to call for volunteer strike breakers', relates to the Liverpool Dock Strike of 1911. Dowdall, having recently been Lord Mayor himself, explained 'what was possible at the Town Hall' and presumably declined.

As we saw in chapter 10, George's campaigning in Oxford was successful. He left the city on 6 March 1912 with a Strike Emergency Committee in place and over 300 undergraduates signed up to provide volunteer labour at mines to be specified. However, by the time he arrived in Cambridge the picture had changed. The Duke of Abercorn had set up a volunteer organisation called the Civilian Force, which was now featuring prominently in the press. In a letter published in *The Times* on 4 March Abercorn had announced that a 'quick response' from the public had led to 'an enormous addition to our numbers' and he was appealing for 'further assistance from patriotic citizens in both men and funds'. 'In this time of national emergency', he wrote, the mission of his organisation was to make 'the necessary arrangements to anticipate any trouble or disorder which may arise, and to secure the continuance of the public services'. He too spoke of organising on behalf of 'the community at large'.

When Calderon arrived at the mass meeting called in Cambridge on the evening of 8 March he found he was sharing the platform with two representatives of the Civilian Force. As reported by the *Cambridge Daily News*, the chairman, a college Fellow, explained the purpose of the occasion thus:

They met to consider what was to be done in one of the gravest situations that had ever arisen in this country within the memory of man. He asked them in various capacities, first as members of the University, therefore as men who should study questions affecting their country and the welfare of their fellow creatures; secondly, as citizens of this great nation they should try to do their best to help to deal with this crisis and to avert those miseries which were bound to arise from it. It was their duty to do this, it was their duty to set an example in it. (Cheers.)

He then put the resolution 'That in the opinion of this meeting it is desirable to form an organisation of members of the University to be ready to help avert the disaster with which the nation is threatened by the coal strike'. Calderon spoke next, for the motion. The newspaper report is the only near-verbatim account we have of a long speech by George, and on its evidence he was a charismatic and entertaining speaker.

He began by telling his undergraduate listeners that there was no need for him to 'talk about the gravity of the situation', because 'the very fact that they were there in such large numbers showed that they realised it'. He then promptly ignored the chairman's *caveat* that it must not be a 'party meeting'. First he cast aspersions on 'the Liberal papers' and implied that the Liberal government was paralysed, then he attacked the Socialists:

A Socialist leader said 'See what comes of the party system'. We [at this meeting] were not concerned so much with cause as with possible results. Bernard Shaw, one of the idols of this generation – (uproar) – well, one of the idols of a past generation, remarked at a lunch that they were fiddling while Rome was burning, and that he was rather glad to be so occupied. He [Calderon] thought this crisis would bring him [Shaw] and other idols of their generation out of their exalted position in the public favour.

If the government could do nothing, this was a time for 'the whole community' to come to the rescue. They had to organise themselves, but he was against them joining the Civilian Force. George was right in implying that at that moment no-one was sure what the Civilian Force was going to do, but that its 'chief aim' seemed to be 'to keep order'. He continued:

What was wanted at a time like this was not the mere keeping of order. They must go to the root of the disease, and in this case want of coal was the disease they had got to remedy. (Cheers.) Let them be ready to do anything for which they were called, even to the extent of getting coal. (Cheers.) If they expressed their readiness to go down and get the coal that would include their readiness to do everything else. They did not want conciliation. Unless people were willing to go the whole hog they did not want them to enrol. (Cheers.)

He then considered objections to his scheme, including that 'it was unfair for them to interfere in a dispute between two classes'. The organisation he was advocating 'sided with neither side, but they would side with the side that sided with the community'. In his peroration he accused the miners of 'enjoying this wild dream of limitless power' and claimed, to applause, that 'if the community did not wake them from this dream, they would have nobody left to sell any coal to'. He moved the motion and a Mr Fenwick from Trinity seconded it.

At this point, the representatives of the Civilian Force addressed the meeting. This might suggest that they were opposing the motion, but they were not. The first, a Mr Gordon, spoke of the need 'whatever they did to keep inside the law' and of how 'the police force of this country was not sufficient to deal with any widespread disturbance'. The second, a Mr Mitford, stressed that 'the object of the Civilian Force was that men should come forth voluntarily without remuneration to keep public services going in cases where they were dislocated by labour disturbances'; this might include going down mines, but they would still have to provide their own 'protection'.

In the words of the *Cambridge Daily News* reporter, 'This so annoyed Mr Calderon, that he continually interrupted them and told Mr Gordon that his speech was entirely irrelevant to the motion before the meeting. The audience roared with delight at the spectacle of a platform disagreement.' When someone asked from the floor whether 'permission' had been 'obtained from the Government' for George's 'scheme', he quipped that he 'did not think permission was necessary to avert a national danger or to work in the mines'.

George's performances certainly enlivened the meetings in both Oxford and Cambridge. His analyses appeared rigorous, bold, even irrefutable, and his language was forceful and succinct. Yet from impeccably rational beginnings he could tease out his ideas rather artistically until they resembled comic fantasies. In Oxford, according to the *Isis* of 9 March, he 'suggested the excellent moral effect that would be created throughout the country, were three hundred public-spirited undergraduates to be blown up in the service of society'. In Cambridge he touched on famine, chaos, civil war, and the spread of the miners' megalomania to Europe and America, concluding that if the strike was not quickly stopped by some method 'a disaster would happen to this great civilisation which had been built up since the fall of the Roman Empire to which the invasion of the Goths and Huns was a mere trifle'. Indeed, at one point in Cambridge the dialogue descended into farce:

'What part will you take? Will you be the leader?'
'That has not been discussed by the Committee,' Mr Calderon replied. 'Personally, I regard that question as an insult.'
'What Committee do you refer to?' asked the Questioner.
'I mentioned no Committee,' said Mr Calderon.
There was an uproar and shouts of 'You did'. After further argument, Mr Calderon said, 'I do not understand your question', and the undergraduate who had asked it replied, 'I am endeavouring not to quibble, sir.' (Laughter.)
Mr Calderon eventually said, 'I made an inadvertent reply. There is no committee at present. I referred to the organisation you have agreed to form.'

Obviously, these features could undermine the credibility of George's arguments, however crystalline. According to the *Isis*, it was widely thought in Oxford that 'the talented author of *The Fountain* has planned the whole affair as a practical joke'. A correspondent to the *Cambridge Magazine* dismissed him as 'that indefatigable humorist'.

Nevertheless, the motion at the Cambridge meeting was over-whelmingly carried. It was this that led the *Cambridge Daily News* to begin its report by announcing that 'Cambridge undergraduates decided to follow the example of Oxford in forming a Strike Emergency Committee'. But after the vote the meeting turned again to the role of the Civilian Force. Calderon and Gordon were invited to speak for five minutes each. George said that 'Mr Gordon and Mr Mitford simply kept putting difficulties in the way and talking about protecting people. That was simply marking time. At this moment of crisis what was wanted was that they should do something rash. (Cheers.)'. Gordon declared that 'the policy of the Civilian Force was very simple. It was to enable John Bull to be master in his own house inside the law, and not outside the law. (Cheers.)'. A proposal for the Cambridge Strike Emergency Committee to join the Civilian Force was carried by 313 votes to 172. Obviously George could not have been happy about this. However, he had said earlier in the meeting that he was 'going into Manchester to organise a similar meeting the following day, and he would like to have the weight of their opinion behind him', and to a large extent he did have it.

We may assume Calderon went to Manchester on 9 March, and we know that he was in Edinburgh on 29 March, but where he was active inbetween might only be ascertained by trawling provincial newspapers. Even Kittie 'never quite knew' where he was. Presumably with others active in the London volunteer movement, he organised and addressed recruitment meetings up and down the country. There is no indication that these were heckled or disrupted by miners, unionists, or others who supported the strike. We know from a number of sources that George consulted mine-owners about the suitability of undergraduates and other unpaid volunteers to work in the mines. According to a letter from him published in the *Cambridge Magazine*, 'the prevailing opinion among coal owners seems to be that, properly diluted with experienced men – the most likely case – they would be able to give a very good account of themselves'. But there is no evidence that they were actually used by the owners, who in addition to 'blacklegs' could call on their own sources of 'free labour' as strike breakers.

Meanwhile, George's achievements at the two universities were unravelling. Abercorn announced in *The Times* of 11 March that 'the undergraduates at both Oxford and Cambridge have organised "University Special Service Divisions" of the Civilian Force, and considerable progress is reported from both centres'. On 12 March questions were asked in the House of Commons about the remit of the Civilian Force and the answer came back that 'members of the proposed force are only to be employed on public duty after being sworn in as special constables and under the orders of the responsible police authorities'. The Liberal Government, then, was not going to allow Abercorn a private army either on the streets or down the mines. Still the men of Oxford and Cambridge Universities – even presidents of colleges – continued to appeal to students past and present to join their branches of the Civilian Force. Yet according to the *Isis*, everyone was confused about its purpose: one day the 'main object of the movement was to provide "aristocratic blacklegs"', the next day 'the volunteers were only to be glorified "special constables"', on a third day 'we understand that the Committee has fallen back again on the coal-hewing idea'.

At this stage, Calderon's message was, in Kittie's words, that 'however much the Community might sympathise with the Miners in the end they desired to attain, the way to get their end was not [by] making war on the Community, which was in no way their enemy'. Calderon seems to have approved of the miners' wage claim and he certainly supported improving their working conditions. He believed in their right to strike against mine-owners. But he did not believe that they had a right to attack and intimidate the rest of society. In his view it was also naïve and irresponsible of the Government to suppose that its role should be to 'keep the ring', to be impartial and ensure that the fight between labour and capital 'should be at least a fair one', as Campbell-Bannerman had put it, when the rest of the country was affected by the fight, too. Thus, again in Kittie's words, George believed that 'the *only* practical way for the Community to put an end to such methods was to show that it could do without them – and let Oxford lead the way'.

The Government, however, was not paralysed. It had been holding almost daily discussions with both sides since before the strike. By 15 March these efforts had got nowhere, so on 19 March it introduced a bill proposing a statutory minimum wage for the miners, to be determined locally by new boards. This was comfortably passed. A majority of miners then voted against resuming work, but on 6 April the leaders of the Miners Federation ordered a return on the grounds that constitutionally a two-thirds majority against resumption was required. After that it was generally felt that the Act worked well.

As George failed, presumably, to coordinate his volunteers with mine-owners who could use them, and as the Civilian Force acquired a higher profile, so enthusiasm for his solution leached away. Towards the end of March Kittie received telegrams from him asking her to 'go down to Oxford and finish up the disappointing results there and so on'. 'Well, of course,' she wrote later, 'the disappointment was great after all this effort.' He was also 'in some direction hurt'.

But he certainly did not show it. The day after the Coal Strike ended he was writing to Grant Richards that the reason he had missed his deadline for the 'book on the English Theatre' was that he had been 'very busy lately, trying to form an organisation to prevent the recurrence of disasters like the Coal Strike'. His train of thought and the nature of the organisation he had in mind can be seen in an article commissioned from him by the *Cambridge Magazine* and published on 20 April. 'The nation', he wrote, was 'still staggering from the blow dealt it by the combination of the miners to withhold one of the necessaries of life':

However much we may all sympathise with the ultimate intention of these attacks, the enrichment of the poor (an object which all decent citizens must applaud), there is no doubt that this is the most extravagant of all methods for achieving it, and can only lead to chaos and destruction. When the community sees its very existence threatened, one thing is certain, that it will rise and defend itself; and we have to consider how that can be most effectively done, with the least permanent injury to our national life (or, more hopefully, with the greatest possible benefit to it) and how we can at the same time remove the causes of the discontent which inspires those attacks. A New Era looms, both threatening and inspiring, before us.

In the first instance, the 'threatened strikes' would have to be broken by 'the readiness of the community to do for itself what it can of the work that the strikers refuse to do'. But the miners had proved that 'the movement of our national life lies almost wholly outside the orbit of Parliament and legislation'. Therefore 'good citizens' who break the future strikes must come together in 'an alliance of all patriotic and progressive citizens, to save the existence of the nation', in a 'great national organisation for ushering in the New Era'. The progressiveness of this organisation would be seen in its determination to 'abolish poverty and underpayment', remove 'the outward distinctions of classes', and 'restore to the worker that interest in his work and comradeship with his master which the nineteenth century has been so busy destroying'. Interestingly, he believed 'apprenticeship and artisan training' were needed, to 'turn unskilled labour into skilled. Every man who works must become a partner in the capital and management of what he works at. That will soon equalise fortunes'.

The nub of George's article was that 'extra-governmental forces must be met by extra-governmental forces'; so he made no mention of a new political party. On 21 April, however, he was writing to Newbolt enclosing the draft manifesto of precisely such an organisation. It was to be called 'the Centre Party' because it would 'stand between the forces of Revolution and Reaction, and reconcile them'. Its aim was to 'rally to one centre all those who realise the gravity of our situation and are determined to remedy it'. The policy of the new party, drafted by several people, appears to have been lost, but George described it to Newbolt as 'anti-revolutionary and at the same time progressive'. He had been 'about from city to city, finding little groups of people who are of like mind', and wanted to visit Newbolt to 'persuade you that it is your own view of English affairs'. Nothing further is known of this proposal, but in the 1930s Newbolt described it as 'a farsighted view of what was coming'.

Calderon's article in the *Cambridge Magazine* provoked a lively correspondence over the next four issues. One writer believed George's 'methods' would 'certainly introduce a New Era – of humour – into England', because they were so 'unpractical and fantastic'. Another felt he had been 'fooled' by George's oratory in Cambridge. Two more, however, asked 'what is the objection to Mr Calderon's scheme?', since Cambridge undergraduates reading engineering would be 'competent to work the hauling machinery'. A fifth detected a 'germ of truth' in the article, namely that trade unionism could sideline Parliament. '*What can Parliament do?* That is the question by which we are really faced, the question which Mr Calderon has very aptly raised.' George himself summed up on 18 May by claiming that mine-owners did think undergraduates could work at the coal face, and added: 'How wonderfully monosyllabic and expressive language is becoming! The words "mush", "tosh", "bilge", etcetera, which your correspondents apply to my ideas, were hardly known as terms of controversy in my undergraduate days.'

Five days later the National Transport Workers Federation (NTWF) called a countrywide strike over the Port of London Authority's right to employ non-union workmen. This played out completely differently from the Coal Strike. The call was widely ignored in the provinces, the Government's repeated attempts at a solution failed, and the chairman of the PLA, Lord Devonport, was determined to face the unionists down.

This time, instead of going it alone, George appears to have joined the Emergency Service League run by a Mr Loring. Nothing more is known about this body, but George's public profile and his rhetorical skills must have been an asset to it. On 30 May 1912 he appeared in a carefully crafted media-event at Speakers Corner. The *Daily Express* reported:

A sensation was caused among the Socialist orators near the Marble Arch yesterday morning by the appearance of a well-dressed speaker, wearing a quiet tie, who addressed a meeting in their very midst with the object of collecting volunteers from among his audience to march boldly to the docks and help in the work of unloading food from ships till such time as the transport workers return to work.

The speaker was Mr George Calderon, author and playwright, of Heathland Lodge, Hampstead Heath, who had advertised his intention of holding the meeting.

'We are not concerned with the struggle between masters and men, and do not take sides,' he said, 'but we consider the attempt to deprive London of its food supply as an insult to the community.'

He invited all those who were willing to go to the docks to enrol themselves at the Fusiliers' Drill Hall, Tufton Street, Westminster, which would be open for the purpose after three o'clock this afternoon.

When he called for those who were ready to join him to hold up their hands about fifty men responded.

The men, he added, would be kept on board ship while they were at the docks. The accommodation would not be luxurious, and the food might not come up to that at the Ritz, perhaps. They would be afforded board and lodging and 30s. a week.

According to Kittie's memoirs, this was not the only occasion on which George 'made speeches in the Park', and she regarded it as 'a very great risk'. Speakers Corner had been dominated by orators of the Socialist Party of Great Britain since 1904. More than likely George had some protection from the Emergency Service League, but in any case, as Dowdall put it, he was 'always fearless'. At the London docks themselves, there were pitched battles between strikers and 'scabs', and police on foot and horseback guarded the entrances through which 'free labour' and volunteers had to pass to enrol for work. The seventy-five men taken on from 300 who assembled at Tufton Street on 30 May were, the *Daily Express* added, conveyed to the docks at midnight with 'considerable secrecy'. The conflict became so bitter that at one point Ben Tillett, the NTWF's leader, called on God at an open air meeting to 'strike Lord Devonport dead'.

Kittie felt George was risking his life 'in going unlading [sic] meat at the Docks'. But she 'knew' there would have been 'no smallest use' in asking him whether it was fair to her. 'It would not have made one pennyworth of difference – even if I had been left starving afterwards – it was his job – he saw it – he had to do it.' When Rothenstein wanted to visit George at Victoria Dock, where he was helping unload the *S.S. Mimiro* from Australia, George sent him a postcard with instructions on how to negotiate the police guard, 'if they are difficult', and penetrate to the 'Tufton Street gang' of volunteers to which he belonged.

It seems Calderon was mainly employed in the docks at night. Sometimes he had to sleep there, sometimes he returned to Heathland Lodge at two in the morning. Doubtless it was hard work. There were other men of his class with him, for instance H.M. Isaacs, brother of the Attorney General, who was pictured by the *Express* in a collar and tie 'assisting in the unloading of 1300 cases of lemons'. But as the strike continued through June, George felt the 'sacrifice' more keenly – 'primarily', wrote Kittie, 'of the work that he truly loved, his literary and scholarly work'. She had to write to Grant Richards herself to excuse George for not delivering his manuscript:

No reason except this one of fighting for the Community could be adequate. [He says] that unless the Community rouse itself to do as he is doing neither you nor he nor anyone else will have any work left to do...but essentially not to think he does not see your point.

I'm sure this last fact is true...by doing what he is doing he is really saving your business from engulfment. Do try and believe this and forgive him – and encourage the cause and egg others on to be alive and to refuse to have their chests sat on by a gang of Tilletts.

Kittie wrote in her memoirs that she was 'with him heart and soul' in this matter.

The employers' creation of a strong force of 'free labour', volunteers and blacklegs, became a decisive factor in the London Dock Strike. The Shipping Federation was soon informing journalists that it had 'more labour than we know what to do with'. Therefore when the Liberal Government attempted to resume negotiations in the middle of June, the

PLA was able to refuse. On 16 June George himself wrote to Grant Richards that the strike would soon be over and he would be able to resume work on his book. But it was not over in June. George had attempted in his letter to turn the tables on Richards: 'I am serving you very materially with what I am doing; it is a more tangible profit than anything you will get out of my book; I expected your letter would contain a large cheque for the Patrol' (volunteers' security). Another attempt at mediation between the NTWF and employers failed, so George carried on stevedoring. No more is heard of his book on the contemporary theatre and he appears never to have had personal dealings with Richards again.

The strike finally collapsed on 27 July. In Henry Pelling's words, 'Lord Devonport had stemmed the tide of successful strikes; and although 1913 was a year of continued unrest, no great national conflicts took place'.

One might conclude, then, that George's activism had been vindicated. The 'Community' had fought back to protect its imported food supply, and volunteers had helped to break the strike. The use of volunteers to ensure essential services and sap a strike began to become part of government strategy. In the 1919 Railway Strike, as George had dreamt, students did stand in for workers, and even more so in the General Strike of 1926. Some of George's friends therefore felt that, far from being cranky, his ideas had been before their time.

By contrast, his thinking about an extra-governmental 'alliance of all patriotic and progressive citizens' to counter the 'extra-governmental force' of the trade unions, was confused. At times of social and economic unrest people often conclude, as George wrote in the *Cambridge Magazine*, that 'Parliament no longer stands for the community, but only for aggregations of sectional interests'. Essentially, this had been his criticism of British politics in *Dwala*. If by 'the mischievous effects of the measures taken by successive Governments to pacify unrest', as the 1912 'draft manifesto' put it, he was referring to the Trade Disputes Act of 1906, which many felt gave the unions excessive freedom of action, then that too would be understandable. But the most concrete form George could offer for the extra-governmental alliance he had in mind was 'an eager, resolute body, sworn to do nothing for their class and everything for the community at large', which acerbic critics suggested George himself was ambitious to lead. Not surprisingly, in the 1930s Newbolt felt that 'today the writer of such a manifesto would probably be accused of leaning towards "Fascism"'. Indeed, George's image of this 'eager, resolute body' was somewhat paramilitary: he referred to it as 'Samurai' acting in accordance with a 'Bushido tradition' that the community would have 'consciously constructed' – an idea taken perhaps from H.G. Wells's *A Modern Utopia* (1905). As Newbolt immediately added, however: 'There was no sense of infallibility in George – he arrogated to himself no kind of superiority.' Again as in *Dwala*, the fact that George eventually proposed a 'Centre Party' tells us that his thinking returned to democratic, parliamentary channels.

If it comes as a surprise that in his *Cambridge Magazine* article George called for the removal of 'fine gentility', 'extravagant living', and 'the outward distinctions of classes', it should be remembered that the Great Unrest was caused not only by accumulated economic grievances but also by conspicuous consumption. 'Luxury', he wrote, 'divides the classes and it squanders the potential capital of the community.' We all had to be 'plain, industrious citizens together' and earnings had to be more equalised. Perhaps he was influenced here by the 'Distributist' ideas of Belloc, Chesterton and others, although he makes no mention of *ownership*. An entry in cipher on his 'Notes for Plays' sheets dated 10 August 1912 reads: 'The fault of our age, the cause of the great struggle, is that we all live too richly. The richer we have got the higher we have put our standard of luxury. The return to simplicity would save the community.'

Perhaps the most original part of George's political thinking is his holistic approach to British society (although 'society' was evidently not a word that he liked). 'I want to see the only thing in this country which is unorganised organised,' he wrote to C.K. Ogden, editor of the *Cambridge Magazine*, on 29 March 1912, 'namely, the Community; to resist the blows dealt it from every side – by classes, and by parties.' Trade unions represented only a section of the community and, like Dickens in *Hard Times*, George saw in them the seeds of selfishness, conformism and autocracy. He feared that the Liberal government had encouraged them to see themselves as above the law and parliament. Not that he ever spelt out what the effective alternatives to union action for working-people were. But for him 'Capital' too was only a 'section', and just as bloody-minded. It was absurd of a government to insist on staying on the sidelines of a conflict between labour and capital, when the community which it represented was more affected than anyone and the government's own democratic authority was at stake. The community had to restore the wholeness of British society by voluntary action, by empowering itself. As Kittie wrote later, the reason George voluntarily gave months of his life to fighting the great strikes was precisely that he 'cared desperately for the people and he felt they were going wrong'.

As in *Revolt*, then, Calderon's thinking about trade unionism moved beyond the labour-capital polarity, beyond socialism, Marxism and Toryism alike. There are obvious affinities between his thinking and the 'Big Society' of recent Conservatism. But it seems true to say that in Britain over the past forty years both governments and trade unions have had to listen more and more to holistic, 'centre party' politics. In many respects George Calderon's communitarianism has been proven right.

13

Wilder Shores of Translation

The Calderons appear to have completed their move from Heathland Lodge in December 1912. On the twenty-third they left for Christmas at Foxwold.

The new home was 42 Well Walk, NW3. In many ways it was the complete opposite of Heathland Lodge. As Kittie put it, it was 'in a street' – between Hampstead Village and the Heath, described by estate agents today as 'this most historic quarter of Hampstead'. Number 40 was of brown brick, had been built in the early 1800s, and was once John Constable's main home. It was now occupied by Sturge Moore and his family. Masefield lived opposite. Numbers 42 and 44 were of red brick, built in the mid-nineteenth century, and much taller. Including the basement and servant's room in the roof, 42 Well Walk (Fig. 17) had five storeys. Thus, whereas life at Heathland Lodge had been secluded, quasi-rural, and generously horizontal, here it was public, urban, and vigorously vertical. Even so, 42 Well Walk had almost as many rooms, they were quite spacious, and the décor was stylish. A drawback for both George and Kittie, however, was the relative smallness of the back garden. It meant that he could not indulge his taste for outdoor games, and she had less scope for applying William Robinson's principles of English gardening. But George joined Hampstead Golf Club and a lawn tennis club, and Kittie redesigned the garden with help from Frederic Lubbock. As at Heathland Lodge, she employed a gardener for maintenance, and a general maid.

Over Christmas 1912 Percy Lubbock and his brothers Alan and Roy also stayed at Foxwold, so it is a fair assumption that they put on a pantomime improvised by the president of 'Rosmersholm'. But after returning to Well Walk on 4 January 1913, George approached the novelist and angling-writer William Caine about collaborating on a pantomime for commercial performance. The idea had, apparently, been

Fig. 17 42 Well Walk, Hampstead, c. 1922

suggested to George by the composer Martin Shaw more as a 'children's fairy play' to which he could 'put music' (Shaw had had some success with similar productions in 1911 and 1912). George chose the Grimms fairytale 'The Valiant Little Tailor'. Caine agreed to write 'a pantomime' with him on this theme, as it meant he would be 'engaged upon a bit of fun with Calderon. Together we were to concoct absurdities. There would be laughter'. George had known Caine since at least 1900, when he played bridge with him. He had first met Martin Shaw, who was seven years younger than him, when they served on the committee to organise a dinner honouring Gordon Craig at the Café Royal in 1911. As Martin Shaw described in his memoirs, George and Kittie's friendship had also helped 'carry' him through 'one of the worst periods of my life'. George, Caine and Shaw duly signed a contract for collaboration.

In fact Calderon had started on a 'fairy play' with Laurence Binyon back in 1911. Perhaps he was now resuming work on it with Caine and for financial reasons it was being reinvented as a pantomime. There is evidence that he was particularly fond of the story of the inventive little man whose adventures begin with him killing seven flies in one swipe. The story had been included by Kittie's relation Andrew Lang in his best-selling *Blue Fairy Book* (1889) and George knew of its folklore variants in other cultures. Perhaps it was the very open, 'chaotic' quality of its narrative that appealed to him, as well as its high fantasy. According to Shaw and Caine, George set to work with 'characteristic energy', concentrating on the scenes with giants and dwarfs.

But he was soon affected by his old problem of nervous exhaustion. This is hardly surprising, as 1912 had been the busiest year of his life. The publication of *Two Plays by Tchekhof*, his involvement in two productions of *The Fountain*, one of them touring, his completion of 'The Russian Stage', a month touring the country addressing meetings about the Coal Strike, followed by two months working at the London docks, then the premiere of *The Maharani of Arakan* at the Albert Hall, the premiere of *Revolt* in Manchester, and much more, would have strained the nervous health of any man. Evidently a busy family Christmas at Foxwold and Emmetts had not been relaxing enough.

The reason we know that George was ill is that he was unable to accompany Kittie to Nina Corbet's wedding to Reginald Astley at Moreton Corbet on 27 January 1913. Nina refers to the fact in a letter that she wrote to Kittie four days later from Gibraltar on her 'wedding journey', as Kittie annotated the envelope. It was the third calendar year after Sir Walter Corbet's death. Astley was his respected agent and now a trustee of the estate. It may seem surprising that the wedding took place in the Corbet family church of St Bartholomew's, where both Sir Walter and Vincent lay buried near the entrance to the churchyard, and on Lesbia Corbet's eighth birthday, but *noblesse oblige*: it was important to display dynastic continuity until Nina's surviving son, Jim, came of age, even though Lady Corbet now became plain Mrs Astley. In fact Jim gave his mother away and his cousin, Dick Sutton, was Reginald Astley's best man. Nina ended her letter to Kittie: 'I am feeling A.1. and ever so happy – R. is *perfect* as a husband [...]. I only hope we won't get broke in our travels. Bless you darling always yr T['] O[ther].'

At some point George's condition improved and he continued with his literary projects. One of these was a series of libretti for Michel Fokine.

The culture-changing visit to London by Ballets Russes in the long summer of 1911 was engineered by Diaghilev, of course, but also by certain social, theatrical, musical and commercial networks at the highest levels of British life. Since he was an active member of some of these networks, it is not surprising that Calderon became involved. He attended rehearsals before the company opened at the Royal Opera House on 21 June 1911 with *Le Pavillon d'Armide*, *Carnaval*, and *The Polovtsian Dances*, all choreographed by Fokine. George's Russian presumably enabled him to act as an interpreter and fixer for the company; indeed, according to Kittie he was 'able to be of real help to [the Fokines] in a trying affair', although we do not know what this was. On 24 June 1911 *The Times* published a 'long and serious article' (Richard Buckle) entitled 'The Russian Ballet', which is probably the most-quoted piece of contemporary writing about the 1911 visit (it is reprinted in full in Cyril Beaumont's classic *The Diaghilev Ballet in London*). Recently it has been identified as being by George Calderon, rather than by the regular *Times* Music Critic, J.A. Fuller-Maitland. In it George wrote that the difference between Russian Ballet and 'that which we have hitherto known in England' lay not in the Russians' 'exquisite technique', but in 'the variety and imaginative quality of those ideas which the dancing succeeds in expressing'. These were 'artistic ideas, ideas, that is, conceived at a high pitch of emotional intelligence' – surely one of the earliest instances of the expression. Was it surprising, George asked, that 'we fall to so greedily', when the 'inventive genius of a Benois and a Fokin' and the 'interpretative genius of a Nijinsky, a Karsavina' introduced British audiences to 'a whole range of ideas such as we have never met before'? George was particularly entranced by *Carnaval*, in which Vera Fokine danced Chiarina, Nijinsky Harlequin, and Karsavina Columbine. This was 'a quite new and brilliant notion of Schumann's work, purged of all possible suspicion of any Germanic seriousness of purpose [...] immensely serious as Art, but never for a moment serious as Life'.

Fokine and Calderon became friends. Not only, as Kittie put it, did Fokine find 'an understanding artistic sympathy in George', the two men were quite similar: polymathic, 'quick', humorous, intensely musical. Whenever George took Kittie to one of the Russian ballets for the first time, he would play the score through to her on the piano 'note by note', with a running commentary, 'so that I should not miss one thing in the exquisiteness of the ballet'. The Fokines visited Heathland Lodge in the summer of 1911, and to the Calderons they became in Kittie's words 'like birds of the air. None of the ordinary things of life seemed to touch them – they adored each other and their little boy Vitalie, this and their wonderful art were literally all that counted to them'. They also had a mutual friend in the sculptor Emanuele Ordoño de Rosales, who made many figures for Fokine and in August 1911 married Kittie's American art student friend Louise Bagg at Moreton Corbet.

Whether George had seen much ballet before 1911, we do not know, but he had certainly fallen in love with the 'new ballet' of which Fokine was the leading exponent. For his part, wherever he went in the world Fokine sought new inspiration and creative artists who might produce ideas for new ballets. Obviously he knew of George's dramatic accomplishments, and given the influence of MKhT's reforms on his own theatrical revolution he probably saw eye-to-eye with him about Chekhov. At some point in 1911, they must have agreed that George would draft some one-act libretti for Fokine and they probably discussed the kind of subject that Fokine would relish and that might go down well with Diaghilev.

Before moving from Heathland Lodge, George produced his longest ballet script, *The Red Cloth: A Comedy without Words*. This may have been inspired by a story in *One Thousand and One Nights*, but it is set in 'the Harem of the SHEIKH's house in Cairo; early 19th Century' and reads more like a comic version of *Schéhérazade*, which had first been seen in London on 20 July 1911, choreographed by Fokine.

Abetted by her Odalisques, the Sheikh's young wife arranges an assignation with her lover, but unlike the Golden Slave in *Schéhérazade* this lover is a nincompoop. The Sheikh, 'pompous, bearded', discovers his wife's infidelity, but all the women escape the fate of their counterparts in *Schéhérazade* thanks to an almost pantomime donkey. Like some of Fokine's own libretti, *The Red Cloth* was illustrated by George in its margins. There are references to accompanying music throughout and the illustrations focus on balletic gestures and groupings. Clearly the humour of the piece, and its parody of *Schéhérazade*, would have appealed to Fokine, but less to Diaghilev. In June 1912, however, Fokine resigned from Ballets Russes and did not come to London with the company. According to a note by Kittie, *The Red Cloth* was accepted for production by MKhT – presumably one of Stanislavsky's 'studios' that was experimenting with wordless drama.

Returning to the winter of 1913, the first libretto that George drafted was possibly *Pandora: A Ballet in III Scenes*. A really amusing rendering of the Prometheus myth, this was sure to please the creator of *Daphnis et Chloé*. The next short script, *Passover Time: A Wordless Play in I Act*, would have been more problematical. It is set in Aleppo, in the house of 'HADASSI, a rich and noble Jew'. A young Arab attempts to seduce Hadassi's wife in this house, but is repulsed. In revenge, the Arab kills Hadassi's young Arab servant and tries to frame Hadassi for murder; 'a Jewish ritual murder' at Passover. As in *The Red Cloth*, Islamic justice triumphs in the figure of the Pasha. But *Passover Time*'s balletic potential seems low: there is no reference to musical accompaniment and the abiding effect is almost as sombre as *The Little Stone House*.

Short though these libretti are, they required sustained concentration to create. An appropriate story had to be found, from a wide range of sources, or invented; it had to be reduced to the kind of ballet-length that Fokine favoured; every move in it had to be visualized; and an ideally spare description of the action had to be produced on the page. It is possible that in the winter of 1913 Calderon got as far as his fourth libretto, as well as writing new one-act plays. But by the beginning of March his nervous health was so precarious that he had to resort to his tested remedy: a cruise.

On 20 March he was seen onto the *S.S. Aguila* in Liverpool by Mary Dowdall and her fourteen-year-old daughter Ursula. The ship was bound for Lisbon, Madeira, and the Canaries. It was 'very decent and comfortable; about twice the size of the steamer I went up the Pacific on', he wrote to Kittie ten minutes before its departure, and he had a cabin to himself.

Poor dear all alone in our big rambling house; I'm sorry; but tho' I'm all alone myself, I can't say I feel <u>lonely</u>, as I'm not in an accustomed place. Dearest love; I shall feel lonely in my bunk because that'll be in the dark and nothing but a wooden wall to kick.

During his absence, Kittie had Lesbia Corbet to stay, visited relations in Devon, and spent some time at Acton Reynald. George wrote to her regularly and these letters give a very clear picture of his attitude to the 'cruise experience'.

Writing from Portugal on 25 March 1913, he gave a sociological breakdown of all the passengers:

22 men and 7 women; ten Lancashire men, cottonspinners, burly, accented, with wives who put on smart frocks at night; 5 Irishmen; 2 Scotchmen; a parson, a musical critic, a coroner, and a boy in a sailor suit. One pretty girl, who brought 16 evening frocks aboard and finds it is not so smart as she expected; she and her Aunt or whatever she is look like musical comedy actresses.

Three days later he fleshed out all their biographies and characters for Kittie over ten closely written pages. The middle-class and even, as he pointed out, working-class origins of the company perhaps enabled him to let his hair down more than he could amongst the 'smarter' Corbets and Lubbocks. He was in great demand as a pianist and had to 'accompany all the songs'. 'We had a concert last night and tonight. I haven't read ten pages of my books. We've a Sports Committee (I'm on it) and plan whist drives, deckgame tournaments, a mock trial, all sorts of things.' Later the master of the *Aguila* wrote George that he did not expect to see 'so lively a crowd' for a long time afterwards, and missed 'your own face in particular'.

At Lisbon, Calderon spent 'a terrible hard day on expeditions' to palaces, acting as Portuguese interpreter, and sitting through a 'satirical, political' revue that had 'more characters than people in the audience'. After that, the 'Gang' (George and male friends) tended to opt out of excursions in favour of less strenuous forms of tourism such as shops, cafés and wine bars. From Las Palmas ('in the first Spanish country I have ever visited') he wrote to Kittie on 2 April that the 'Gang's' only plan each day was 'not to go on the official journey for the day'.

The only remaining feature of our plan is to take Miss Strachey in our care. This is a very highly educated intelligent Suffragette, about 32, but sadly tinged with old maid, limp, appealing, grateful. Prostrated with work for the Cause, she was prostrated with the voyage next but perked up by Madeira.

She was Philippa Strachey, the sister of Lytton, actually aged forty, and 'secretary of the London Society for Women's Suffrage (Mrs Fawcett's brand)', as George put it. In other words, she was not a suffragette but a suffragist. George and the other men clearly felt solicitous, chivalrous, or paternal about her, and perhaps George was especially sympathetic as she had come on the cruise for the same reason as himself. One wonders, however, whether their relationship cooled when Miss Strachey 'suddenly realised that I am the Anti-suffrage monster, and discovered that we have held official correspondence about debates and things'. George would surely have been astonished to learn from today's *Oxford Dictionary of National Biography* that she went on to organise the Women's Service in two world wars, lived to be ninety-six, and was visited by friends at her nursing home to cheer *themselves* up!

On 6 April the *Aguila* docked at Santa Cruz de Tenerife and George sent his last postcard. Six days later he picked up his last mail at Las Palmas. He arrived back at Liverpool on 15 April 1913.

Whilst he was away, a new run of *The Little Stone House* had opened at the Gaiety in Manchester and Kittie kept him informed of other theatrical developments. These included the forthcoming premiere of *Thompson* at the Royalty Theatre, London, under Vedrenne and Eadie's management. 'I'm glad Vedrenne doesn't mean to strangle Thompson', George wrote to Kittie from Lisbon on 28 March, presumably referring to the possibility of Hankin's and his text being reworked whilst he was away. The play was due to open on 22 April, so one can be confident that Calderon appeared at rehearsals soon after his return to Hampstead. As it happens, we can see what changes were made in rehearsal by comparing the text published in early May 1913, which had been set up earlier under a contract signed in 1912, with the immaculately kept prompt copy donated to the V&A by Dennis Eadie, who played Thompson. The changes, which must have been made at George's suggestion, or at least with his consent, are generally surficial, but in one case significant.

Why had Vedrenne and Eadie not premiered *Thompson* a year earlier? A notice in *The Times* of 20 March 1912 announced that they had 'obtained the rights of *Thompson*, the last play written by the late Mr St John Hankin, which after his death was completed by Mr George Calderon' and it would be presented in a new series of matinées opening on 9 April 1912 with Brighouse's *The Odd Man Out*. Perhaps the news that a collected edition of Hankin's works would come out over the next year persuaded them to wait until what they considered the most favourable moment. If so, their sense of timing was impeccable. On 31 March 1913 Olga Nethersole was to present J. Forbes Robertson in the London premiere of *The Light that Failed*, a stage version of Kipling's novel that came from Broadway and was expected to have a lengthy West End run. Vedrenne and Eadie had bagged the rights to premiere Kipling's first-ever play, *The Harbour Watch*, and proposed opening with it on 22 April in a double bill with *Thompson*. Advertisements for Secker's edition of Hankin's and George's play would start to appear during the run of matinées, which was due to end on 9 May.

In his preface, George writes that Hankin's widow had sent him the manuscript 'soon after' Hankin's death, i.e. presumably in 1909. She sent him 'the MS. of the play as he had left it, and asked me to finish it', which George must have done well before March 1912. 'Manuscript', however, seems a misnomer. George describes the first act as 'written out with a certain air of finality' and the rest as 'a pretty full sketch, covering some twenty pages', but later he calls these 'notes' and 'directions'. He allowed himself 'full liberty in dealing with [Hankin's] notes', carried out 'some of his directions', and 'modified others that did not fit in with the central notion as I saw it'. He does not tell us what he took the central notion to be, nor what he means by 'comedy-scheme' when he says that the 'pretty full sketch' presented 'the sort of comedy-scheme that I should have liked to invent myself'. It is highly debatable, then, how much of *Thompson* is by Hankin, and how much by Calderon. Let us consider this question after looking at the play and its 1913 reception, but note in advance that although George says that *Thompson* is 'not the result of a collaboration', he hopes that it has 'something of the effect that St John Hankin and I would have got if we had worked on it together'. In other words, he was not attempting to complete the play in Hankin's 'style' or produce an imitation of him, let alone a pastiche.

There are two narratives to *Thompson*, one 'official' and one 'unofficial'.

When the play opens, twenty-two-year-old Helen Vaughan is still mourning the death of her fiancé, James Thompson, who was eaten by a shark two years earlier whilst rescuing some women from a trans-Atlantic shipwreck. Thompson had been her father's secretary but was considered an unsuitable match for Helen, sacked, and advised by Mr Vaughan to seek his fortune in America. Without realising whose house he is in, Thompson now turns up during a business trip to Britain, and it transpires that the heroic Thompson was his namesake: he, the real James Thompson, chose to go on a liner that did better food. Helen Vaughan had even kept an album of newspaper cuttings describing 'Thompson's' heroism, which she morbidly mooned over. Helen's mother now declares that she and her husband will not oppose the marriage. But Helen discovers that not only is the real Thompson unheroic, he wholly disparages the Edwardian cult of heroes. At this point Gerald, a young army captain recently awarded the D.S.O. for his exploits in Afghanistan, shoots a lion that has escaped from the local circus. Coincidentally he has just inherited £1500 a year from an uncle. His aunt disabuses Helen of her romantic infatuation with Thompson, who confesses to her mother that he is already engaged to someone in Kentucky, and Mrs Vaughan engineers a new engagement – to Gerald. Thompson, the self-confessed philosopher of 'drift' rather than heroism, promptly departs for America.

The 'unofficial' plot is rather different. Mrs Vaughan, although referred to as 'Mamma', is actually Helen's step-mother and aged thirty-five. Thompson is thirty. Mrs Vaughan ('Matilda') is 'pretty', 'charmingly dressed', 'amiable', and more intelligent than any of the other characters. She had already engineered the dismissal of Thompson's predecessor as secretary because the latter was a 'most deplorably good-looking' woman. Thompson's engagement to Helen is a fiction of Matilda's, who came upon him kissing Helen's hand and insisted to her much older 'curmudgeon' husband that the 'engagement' be broken off. Moreover, when reports of the other Thompson's heroics appeared in all the newspapers, it was Matilda's idea to 'finally dispose of' James Thompson by not checking whether it was the *same* Thompson and telling Helen that it was... In two separate comments she inadvertently implies that she found/finds the real Thompson attractive. When he suddenly reappears, she has a near-hysterical fit. In the final scene, which is between the two of them and the longest duet in the play, Thompson declares: 'Under pretence of being a little airy, flibberty-gibberty coquette, you are the most designing, meddling, managing busybody that ever went poking their pretty finger into other people's pies' – and makes a veiled pass at her. 'Mrs Vaughan' declares that now that she knows he is leaving, she has experienced 'quite a revulsion [i.e. reversal] of feeling' and 'positively likes him'. However, she funks taking any initiative and he confines himself to kissing her hand, a gesture which throughout the play has been presented as the height of impropriety.

It will be seen that the play, although ostensibly a drawing-room farce, has a thick, almost Pinterian sub-texture. There is no doubt that Thompson and 'Mrs Vaughan' have some things in common. 'Mrs Vaughan' is actually the vibrant young woman Matilda, who transmutes her frustration into supreme manipulativeness, wit, and a passion for clothes. When Thompson finally leaves, it is possible to imagine that in a modern production Mrs Vaughan/Matilda would collapse in tears.

A comparison of the published ending with the prompt book shows that George accentuated this sense of the ending for performance. In the published script, Thompson says goodbye, checks that no-one is coming in, kisses her hand, then exits by the French windows 'waving his hand, and smiling'. He says 'Good-bye!', she repeats the word, and the curtain comes down. The prompt book, however, has:

Good-bye! [They shake hands; he goes R. to window, then stops and turns to her] Is nobody going to come in? [Mrs V. turns L. and looks towards door; he comes back to her, takes her hand and kisses it; then returns to window, where he turns and waves his hand to her; she stands looking after him]

CURTAIN

Taking the last scripted line away from the leading lady clearly creates an open ending in which she could act, or be directed, in a more interesting range of ways. Truly, as Herder put it, 'wordless emotion is the most powerful'.

Although only a matinée, the double bill was a major theatrical event in London that week and reviewed in all the national newspapers. Essentially, *Thompson* was treated as a star-vehicle. Lottie Venne, playing Mrs Vaughan, was a famous comedienne who specialised in the knowing smile. Thus as well as bringing out Mrs Vaughan's vivacity, she doubtless conveyed some of her moral ambivalence. The critics raved about Venne's performance, but nearly all of them referred to her as Helen's 'mother'. This was not surprising, as Venne was over sixty! The whole dimension of Matilda's emotional turmoil must have been invisible, therefore, and most of the sexual chemistry missing with Thompson, as Dennis Eadie was himself forty-four (whereas Athene Seyler, playing Helen, was the right age). In a word, although Venne excelled as 'Mrs Vaughan, a silly, loquacious little lady' (*Era*), 'the most feather-brained of mothers' (*Illustrated London News*), 'an old lady who changed from one gorgeous frock into another' (*Westminster Gazette*), she did not address the depths of 'Matilda'. In the *Saturday Review* John Palmer devoted a whole essay to his thesis that 'the audacity of Hankin's heroes is in their not being heroes at all', without suspecting that *Thompson* might have something important to say about Edwardian hero-worship; and no reviewer seemed to suspect that Mrs Vaughan was really Matilda trying to break out of her Doll's House.

Nevertheless, the majority of reviewers lauded the play. Although it was 'thin in texture as all the Hankin plays are', wrote the *Manchester Guardian*, it had 'real comedy quality throughout'. It was 'full of fine wit, not effervescent, not precisely sparkling, but of a most agreeable bouquet' (*Daily Telegraph*). The *Westminster Gazette* even felt that 'in the nimbleness of its wit it recalls nothing so much as *The Importance of Being Earnest* [...] it was all so calm and cool and natural and fantastically absurd'. Possibly the most interesting aspect of the critical reception was the hint of uncertainty over whether it was really a comedy. For the *Sunday Times*, 'as badinage the play had pleasant moments, but for a comedy there was not enough substance in it'. The *Pall Mall Gazette* believed that actually it was *farce*, but the company 'played it as Comedy, with results that may be described as slightly anaemic'; if it had not been for Lottie Venne, *Thompson* 'would, we fear, have been rather a solemnising business'. The *Daily Mail*, indeed, felt its humour was 'forced', and the *Manchester Guardian* that Venne's 'full-blooded farcical method was a little out of the picture in Hankin's play'.

Calderon was congratulated on completing the play 'deftly'. 'Though it may be possible to trace some differences of craftsmanship, the work has been so well done that there is no awkwardness and no discord', judged the *Daily Telegraph*. Yet 'perhaps one or two theatrical moments – especially in the last act – are too consciously effective for Mr Hankin, and may betray Mr Calderon trying hard to avoid the Tchekov manner', felt the *Manchester Guardian*, as though Hankin's reading of Calderon's and Garnett's translations was known to have influenced him more than George's own engagement with Chekhov's plays had influenced George. The main dramaturgical criticism was indeed of Act 3, the last act, which the *Sunday Times* characterised as 'verbose and overcrowded with incidents' and the *Illustrated London News* as 'curiously devoid of the special Hankin irony'. *The Times*, however, reckoned that 'a great deal of the dialogue is unmistakably Mr Hankin's'.

A computer analysis of *Thompson*'s language could be revealing, but it would not tell us anything about how Calderon changed the *plot* sketched out by Hankin. George says in his Preface to the published script that Hankin had written out the whole of Act 1 – and many people feel its language is predominantly Hankin's – but the mere fact that George says he introduced the 'plainly artificial business' about an uncle's legacy means that some of Act 1's dialogue is his. As he continues in his Preface:

A playwright can never tell how his idea is going to "pan out" till he has finished with it. The middle and end are bound to have a retroactive effect on the beginning and Hankin himself would probably have altered many things which had an air of being settled.

This surely implies that George had more input into Acts 2 and 3.

In a personal communication, the Hankin scholar Alan Andrews has written that he detects 'Hankin's fingerprints all over the dialogue at the end of Act 2', and I agree. However, we know from George's Preface that he was responsible for changing Hankin's intention of having Gerald save a man from drowning to having him shoot the lion that has chased its tamer (who can swim) into the river. Calderon most likely rejected the rescue from drowning, and Hankin's original setting of the play in a riverside hotel, because they were too reminiscent of Hankin's suicide and his last published story, in which a suicide begs to be allowed to drown. The fact that George introduced the lion and its tamer means, of course, that a substantial part of Act 2 is by him, and one indeed senses a more juicy and robust language at work. This in its turn, as Andrews has put it, creates 'a shift in tone from Hankin's humorous irony to farce'.

But if the business with Gerald's legacy is George's, what of Hankin's does it replace? The legacy is crucial in persuading Gerald's aunt and Matilda to plot his engagement to Helen Vaughan. If the legacy replaces nothing of Hankin's, then that suggests that Hankin was not going to 'resolve' the play with Gerald's engagement at all. Could this explain Hankin's original sub-title, 'A Rather Heartless Comedy', which George cut? In other words, might Helen have netted neither Thompson nor Gerald and been left at the mercy of her stepmother? Perhaps Hankin was planning an even more radical ending, like that of his previous full-length play, *The Last of the De Mullins*? It is clear from a letter of Hankin's to George in 1909 or 1908 that George 'hated the morals' of this play.

Conceivably, then, George found the ending sketched out for *Thompson* too 'cynical' as well. On the whole, the arrival in the first act of the business with Gerald's uncle suggests that George largely wrote, or rewrote, the last act. This is borne out by the difference in the dialogue's register, its comparative wordiness, odd legalistic touches typical of George, and a far more excitable portrayal of the female psyche (reminiscent of *The Fountain*). Vitally, George went for an 'open' ending, where Hankin's endings seem more 'sealed'.

To sum up, at least half of the words on the page in *Thompson* may be George's, and he may have fundamentally changed Hankin's sketched out dénouement, but that is no reason for accepting William H. Phillips's verdict that it 'should be considered a Calderon creation lacking Hankin's sureness of style and deft humour'. The latter qualities are still present, but combined with *George's* more outrageous, emotive and liberating style. The last scene, between Matilda and James, is still very funny, but moves into deeper water and could be regarded as the best part of the play. It seems likely that it was George who turned 'Mrs Vaughan' into a full-blown, even schizophrenic character. The play, then, is not by Hankin, nor is it a 'Calderon creation' alone, it is by Hankin-Calderon, a third term altogether. Although Hankin was physically dead, his words still spoke to George; George listened to them, and responded. As he wrote in his Preface, *Thompson* had 'something of the effect that St John Hankin and I would have got if we had worked on it together'. In short, it *is* a collaboration.

Thompson is one of Calderon's finest pieces of work for the theatre and cries out for a production that would recognise its Pinterian depths and realise the full scope of Mrs Vaughan/Matilda's character. One reason that it has rarely been seen since 1913 is, of course, that it is not a full-length play. But it could be very appropriately teamed with Hankin's last one-act play, *The Constant Lover*.

Thompson appears to have been performed at the Royalty only six times over three weeks, but its double bill with Kipling was a superb offering, there was a large matinee-going London audience, and according to reviewers the play was well received. One should also remember that a successful matinée presented by Vedrenne could be the springboard to a commercial production.

Meanwhile, in May 1913 George's paper at the 1912 Leiden congress, 'Slavonic Elements in Greek Religion', appeared in *The Classical Review* (it will be looked at in the next chapter); *Thompson: A Comedy in Three Acts* was published; *The Little Stone House* played at the Royal Court in its Manchester production for two weeks as curtain-raiser to St John Ervine's *Jane Clegg*; then it came out in Sidgwick and Jackson's series of one-act plays. Some of George's past work was therefore enjoying high-profile exposure, but as well as the pantomime collaboration he himself was probably most absorbed in writing new one-act plays.

Assuming that he produced his adaptation *The Little Stone House* in 1910, George's first extant original one-acter must be *Peace*, probably written in 1911. It was a collaboration with the actor Walter Herbage, who later told Kittie that 'the idea was originally his'. This could mean several things. Perhaps Herbage suggested writing a farce about a pacifist who ditches his beliefs as soon as his own safety is threatened, or had the idea of a loquacious imperialist burglar, or was responsible for the crashing pun with which the farce ends and which renders it unactable today. But the strongest part of the playlet is its guying of smug pacifism and appeasement, and George must have had a hand in this as there are features that resemble the Universal Races Conference which he attended in London 26-29 July 1911.

George and other anthropologists had been dismayed to discover that there were no 'sections' at this conference and the sessions were dominated by grandstanding delegates from what the chairman, Liberal peer Lord Weardale, described as 'the great peace movement which was now taking possession of the world. (Cheers.)'. To quote the *Manchester Guardian* of 31 July 1911, at the closing session George said:

They had all been obliged to be in one hall and listen to all the speeches at the same time. The result was that the scientific side was one they had been blind to. They had instead had to listen to sloppy expressions of good intentions for two or three days. (Hear, hear.) Many of them had thought that they were to consider the scientific aspect of the question; nothing was said, at the commencement, about peace. The papers presented had not been properly discussed, and in fact many of them had not been read by the delegates. (Hear, hear.)

The farce *Peace*, then, was highly topical and there is some evidence that it was written for a private audience, which is occasionally addressed directly and may well have been anti-appeasement. For example, when the Burglar asks 'And how is England to be ready to repel violence with violence?' he himself answers: 'By having a strong army and a strong navy. Loud applause.' Moreover, the pacifist M.P. is named Sir Blennerhassett Postlethwaite, which was too obvious a reference to the late Germano-phile Sir Rowland Blennerhassett to survive into public performance (which *Peace* appears never to have had).

On 29 February 1912 Calderon wrote to Grant Richards offering him 'a volume of four short plays'. As well as *The Little Stone House*, this would contain 'two realistic modern plays and one, very adventurous, a "subjective" play'. The likeliest candidates for the 'realistic' plays are *Derelicts* ('A Play in One Act') and *Parkin Bros.* ('A Comedy in One Act'). The one-acter *Longing* is actually subtitled 'A Subjective Drama in Two Scenes'. So these three short plays were probably written in 1911/early 1912, especially as they appear influenced by George's reading for his article 'The Russian Stage'.

Derelicts exemplifies George's understanding of Chekhov's 'system of contrasts', as he described it in his Introduction to *Two Plays by Tchekhof*. It is set in a hotel garden on a summer's night. Upstage a family gathering is in full swing, with Chinese lanterns, dance music, laughter, and a preponderance of 'pairs of young people'. Downstage, on a garden seat, older characters pour out their pain and regrets. The 'derelicts' are a man of fifty-two and a woman of forty-seven, who are both unmarried, have known each other since they were children, but never been close. In a manner also characteristic of Chekhov, they use a 'technical' patois (their hobbies are early Norman churches and Palaeolithic flints respectively) to conceal emotion. But the contrast between the aridity of the woman's spinsterhood and a love declaration upstage between two young people sets her weeping almost hysterically:

Oh, Robert, Robert! Everything about [around] us seems so full of love and poetry; and you and I sit here babbling about brass rubbings and flint implements... (Sound of laughter) Oh dear, oh dear! What have I done with my life? my little life, the only life I had to live, the life that was meant to live and love in. (Laughter) Oh, you'd better go; I'm only fit to be alone. No, don't go.

As Rex Walford and Colin Dolley have put it, the 'middle-aged pair teeter towards marriage and away from it, in the midst of a quite profound discussion about the merits and disadvantages of the institution'. The man (Robert) uses a powerful image to express their need for each other:

To know that the darkest hour of all will come and find one all alone... (A pause) In moments of general terror people cling together in search of comfort. In cities suddenly overwhelmed by earthquake the bodies of children are found hand in hand in long lines. But we... Agatha! is it too late? We who both know the same fear, cannot we take hands like the children?

But Agatha retreats to 'common sense', believing that they have 'passed through a sentimental crisis together, that is all. It is pity that moves us, but only pity for ourselves, wrought up by the surroundings of this summer night, the scent of the flowers, the moonlight, the music, the lovers'. The ending, in which Robert is left lighting his pipe and sitting silently 'pondering', seems very Chekhovian.

In *Parkin Bros.*, which also uses an atmospherically split stage, the contrast is between the self-pity and fantasy of the old man and the realism of the young. Parkin, a 'small grocer', has just gone bust. 'Disgraced and ruined! Bankrupt!' he declaims. After the death of his wife, 'there was no-one to send the bills out regular', his customers defaulted, and his own credit evaporated. Lacking capacity to sort the mess out, he now has to rely on his son (a draper's assistant) and his son-in-law (clerk to a chartered accountant) to wind the business up. They are highly competent, but have no time for his memories and failed ambitions. His *apologia pro vita sua* is delivered to the counterpoint of their dry book-keeping language, his frustration aggravated by their 'understanding' and 'kindness'. His heart is breaking, but they pay him to go away, with the words 'there's half-a-crown, and fourpence for the bus. Go and hear Harry Lauder or one of these funny chaps sing. Have a good laugh, that's what you want'...

Calderon's 1912 article 'The Russian Stage' had associated 'Subjective Drama' only with Aleksandr Blok. Certainly one can see resemblances between the latter's Beautiful, or Unknown, Lady and the wordless figure Margaret in George's *Longing*, but his generic characters ('Man', 'Death', 'Vanity' etc) and use of incoherent exclamations seem more reminiscent of Leonid Andreyev. On the other hand, the epigraph to *Longing* is George's ancestor's play-title *La vida es sueña* (*Life Is a Dream*) and *Longing* contains some conventional cosmological elements.

In the first scene Man is packing to leave for Canada, as he can no longer stand his yearning for Margaret, or at least his fixation with her image. Once he has left,

Some other man will have her, some great wonderful man, when I've half forgotten her. She'll be conquered, be made like other women, have babies and get tired. That's a revenge! Yes, I want revenge for all that longing. (*Taking a pistol-case*) How ripping the smell of new leather is! So fresh and innocent, and yet so vigorous too. Let's have a look at the pistol again. (*Taking it out*) I love mechanical things.

'PHANTOMS, muffled in grey hoods' close in on him, he begins to lose his reason, he describes the parts of the pistol in terms of Margaret's body, puts the barrel in his mouth, and shoots himself. The second scene, entitled 'From Beyond', appears to be set in Limbo, or a kind of Purgatory, since Man is told by Voice that it is 'only by longing, by unsatisfied longing' that he can 'get higher'. In view of George's writings for the *TLS* about spiritualism, it is interesting that Man is shown being able to look into the world that he has left, but no-one in that world can see out or communicate with him. A particular torment is The Colonel, who taunts Man with not having taken the initiative with Margaret (Voice says, 'A touch would have done it; a little boldness; if you had taken her hand even'). The Colonel's anarchism and his intoning of nonsense words such as 'Boomboll' and 'Boomanóonoo' suggest Chebutykin at the end of *Three Sisters*. George's play deliberately ends in verbal and numerical incoherence, and creates an even stronger sense of void than *The Adventures of Downy V. Green*.

The two one-act plays that one surmises George wrote in the summer of 1913 were *Geminae* and *The Two Talismans*. Although very different in genre and locale, they curiously mirror each other.

The action of *Geminae*, which is subtitled 'A Farce' and set in an Edinburgh hotel, is propelled with break-neck pace by one pair of terms after another. Alexander, 'a noble and romantic Scotchman', and Charles, 'his friend, a plain Lancashireman', both want to marry, but the first wants a wife with no money who will therefore 'owe everything in the world to me', the second wants a wife with plenty of money. Alexander, although he has a castle and is head of a clan, has no money, but Charles already has 'brass'. Alexander is guardian to two penniless young cousins, the identical twins Rose and Violet, who are about to visit him on 'some business'. They are both so beautiful and have such lovely natures that he loves them both equally. Charles suggests that the way to choose is to propose to both and see which one blushes and which one leaves the room. When Rose and Violet arrive, they are in fact announced by the hotel waiter as one person:

WAITER: If you please, sir, there's a lady to see you.
ALEXANDER: A lady? Are you sure it isn't *two* ladies?
WAITER: Mebbe you're right, Sir; but they're so varra much alike that I ascribed it to a deeficulty of vision to which I am sometimes subject.

Unfortunately, Rose and Violet themselves love Alexander with 'equal devotion' (Rose) and 'equal ardour' (Violet), and call upon him, 'as the man', to choose between them. They will go out whilst he decides. Before they go, he gives Rose a rose and Violet a spray of violets; when he is not looking, they exchange these because they are sick of being given their 'name-flowers'. Whilst they are out of the room, Charles opens an envelope that they have brought Alexander, and the friends discover it contains the twins' uncle's will, leaving £20,000 a year to Rose and nothing to Violet. So Alexander will marry Violet and Charles marry Rose. The twins come back and the two men propose to them in a form supposedly binding under Scottish law. But the men have relied on the flowers to tell them which was which, so they have married the wrong twin!

The necessary fiction behind *Geminae* is that identical twins *are* identical. This suggests the paradox that they are two people but one person, which in turn gives the play its frisson: if twins are 'identical', why can't a man marry them both? (It is already accepted in the play that Alexander may marry a cousin, and a much younger one to whom he is guardian, at that.) Indeed, why can't a man love any two women equally? ('We men, with few exceptions, are all Mormons at heart', Calderon had written in 1908.) Whilst *Geminae* juggles bewilderingly with duality and mistaken identity, in the best farce tradition it also hints at forbidden fruit.

In *The Two Talismans*, which is set 'outside an Arabian city' in an indeterminate past, two sages make a bet about human nature. Hafiz wagers that 'in the end, for all his blessings, you shall find the grumbler discontented still; and the contented man triumphant over his afflictions, though they be countless as the seeds of the pomegranate', whilst Hariri is convinced 'on the contrary, that prosperity will so sweeten the one and adversity so sour the other, that in the end their characters will be totally changed'. Hariri proposes testing this with two talismans that he owns. The amethyst confers on a man 'perpetual good luck in all his dealings', the ruby 'nothing but misfortune'. Two young carpet merchants promptly come along and it rapidly becomes clear that Saoud conforms to Hafiz's grumbler type and Abulfeda to his contented man. The amethyst is given to Saoud and the ruby to Abulfeda. Immediately, one blessing after another comes to meet Saoud and disasters rain on Abulfeda, until the first has acquired a fortune, been proposed to by Zaïda (the most beautiful woman in Arabia), and is about to be made King, whilst the second has lost everything and is condemned to death. But all through this Saoud has found fault and Abulfeda remained content with his lot. Saoud has coveted the ruby and persuades Abulfeda, before he goes to his death, to exchange talismans (paralleling the flowers in *Geminae*). Immediately, Zaïda (which means 'fortunate') comes to her senses, denounces Saoud's character, chooses the long-suffering Abulfeda as a worthy husband, and the latter is elected King. Hafiz has won his wager, confirming, as Hankin believed following Heraclitus, but Bernard Shaw did not, that 'character is fate'. The play ends with music, singing, and dancing, on a stage whose acting areas have been very finely apportioned by the dramatist.

Obviously, in the full perspective of the play Abulfeda's possession of the ruby led – because of his 'character' – to good fortune, and Saoud's possession of the amethyst led – because of *his* character – to misfortune. Paradoxically, then, as agents of 'fate' the talismans seem both to prove and disprove that it exists. One is reminded of the ambiguity about *Kismet* at the end of 'The Lieutenant's Heroine', or the unreliability of Richard K. Whittington's cat. There is no doubt that the plots of George's two one-acters written in 1913 are ingenious, and the Edwardians relished and valued ingenuity. To us this ingenuity may appear too cerebral to be a theatrical virtue. Possibly George's focus on 'self-referential' paradoxes in *Geminae* and *The Two Talismans* derives from him following coverage of Russell's Paradox in the press, or even reading Russell's 1903 book *The Principles of Mathematics*, in which he discusses this type of contradiction in set-theory.

Each of the short ballet libretti created 1912-13, and each of the one-act plays written 1910-13, deserves detailed attention. However, given the limitations of space it seems more important to address the fundamental question about them all: what is going on here? Why, with the exception of his collaborations with Hankin and Caine, had Calderon turned exclusively to small dramatic genres? Why were these genres so varied – from farce to Chekhovian 'mood' studies, from Oriental parable to 'subjective drama'? And why did they all derive from outside English culture? Could George be guilty of precisely what he had charged Leonid Andreyev with – 'turning his hand to anything' and producing writing that was 'rich, astonishing, ingenious' but also 'hollow and insincere'?

There is little doubt that the brevity and diversity of these works may suggest to readers today the dreaded word 'dilettante'. The works risk appearing 'slight' and the product of 'flitting' from one culture to another. But this is a modernist (or post-modernist) reading. Each work is not slight; it repays meticulous analysis because in it George always creates a discrete world. We need to look at these works in the context of *ante*-modernism and Calderon's creative biography as a whole.

It has long been accepted that, in Samuel Hynes's words, 'the discovery of Europe is an important aspect of English cultural history in the last years of the Edwardian era' and 'Russia in particular was discovered and extravagantly admired during those years'. But British creative artists were also feeling out to cultures beyond these. W.B. Yeats, Will Rothenstein, Sturge Moore and others were eager to acquaint themselves with Rabindranath Tagore's philosophy, poetry and Indian music. George dramatised Tagore's story 'Dallia' for a Tagore Evening at the Albert Hall in 1912. Indian philosophy was attracting Western minds, for example the young T.S. Eliot's. There was a surge of informed interest in the Islamic world, reflected in Flecker's verse, the impact of *Schéhérazade*, George's own ballet *The Red Cloth*, and Gertrude Bell's archaeological research. Others were 'discovering' the culture of China and Japan. In 1912 Ezra Pound was studying Japanese art in the British Museum under the direction of Laurence Binyon and experimenting with haiku. Yet others, including George, were attracted by translations of Chinese philosophical texts, for which British publishers had discovered a market.

The irresistible conclusion is that these creative minds could no longer find inspiration in the art and philosophy of the great Victorian era. In particular, the almost Brunel-scale genres of the Victorian novel and multi-act play had lived themselves out. Nothing new and alive, it seemed, could now be said in them. George's generation and younger were searching both for new things to say and new ways of saying them. This did not mean imitation. It meant 'extending oneself' to foreign cultures, going out to their ethos, their content and their forms, in order to come back with a self. The subsequent post-War development of British modernism would probably have been impossible without this pre-War stage of invigoration from foreign cultures. The turn to exotic styles and genres in George's 1911-13 theatre writing should be seen in that context. It is deeply relevant that Joyce, Pound and Eliot, say, were, like George, polyglots.

Ought we to conclude, then, that on the eve of World War I George Calderon was a proto-modernist, or at least 'moving towards' modernism?

Ever since Virginia Woolf suggested that 'on or about December 1910 human character changed', a touchstone of contemporaries' attitudes to modernism has been their response to the first exhibition of Post-Impressionist paintings that opened at the Grafton Gallery on 8 November 1910. It has to be admitted that George Calderon passes this test only up to a point.

As well as nine paintings by Manet, the exhibition included twenty-one by Cézanne, thirty-five by Gauguin, twenty-two by Van Gogh, three by Matisse, two by Picasso, six by Rouault, and many other modernist works. It met with an explosion of public dudgeon and derision. George promptly visited the show and wrote an article about it in *The New Age* of 24 November 1910. This in itself is astonishing, as the magazine was then a socialist organ associated with G.B. Shaw. George began with a call for calm:

All through the galleries I am pursued by the ceaseless hee-haw of a stage duke in an eye glass. It is not a matter of artistic taste; all that is wanted is a little politeness, a little reflection that the brain that pondered between the palette and the canvas was probably as huge a one as that in your small silk hat. It is almost too obvious to need saying, that we must go to a work of art for what is good in it, not for what is bad; that we must seek the artist's meaning, and not be set laughing, like a set of factory girls, at the least unexpectedness.

He found many of the paintings 'often badly, stupidly grotesque, conveying no emotion of a thing seen or imagined to my mind'. He passed these by 'without cackling', to the 'hundred and more that save the city'. He concentrated on Gauguin, comparing the 'great patch of red hair' of his 'Christ in the Garden' to Sharlotta suddenly producing a cucumber and eating it in the second act of *The Cherry Orchard*: 'The reality of their inconsequences raises the value of their adjacent pathos.' Only Gauguin had rendered the 'grim savage dignity' of Tahitian life. George urged *New Age* readers to 'fly to the Grafton', and when they came out to 'note how flat, stale and unprofitable have become all those engravings, pictures and statues in the art dealers' windows, that represent the bare photographic semblance of reality'. The next issue of *The New Age* printed two letters about George's piece, one tearing into him for 'praising the most brainless and degrading of all the downward movements', the other approving of his 'intelligent treatment'.

However, in its issue of 23 November 1911 *The New Age* published an airy article by Huntley Carter, 'The Plato-Picasso Idea', together with a monochrome reproduction of Picasso's Cubist painting 'Mandoline, wine glass and table'. Without colour it was very difficult to gain an idea of the

painting and there was even some doubt whether it was shown the right
way up. George wrote to the editor (in impeccable French):

> Hotel Langworthy
> Gower Street
> Wednesday 28 [*sic*] November
>
> Sir,
>   Through a most vexatious oversight your well-intentioned contributor Mr
> Huntley Carter has, in communicating to you the study that you do me the
> honour of reproducing in the issue of your esteemed magazine of 23 November,
> confused its subject with that of another one by me, also hanging in the Galérie
> Kahnweiler. The study illustrated in your magazine does not represent a
> mandoline, wine glass and table as you say, but a Cherkess mother suckling her
> child beneath a wild banana tree.
>
> Picasso

Presumably A.R. Orage realised this was a spoof, but he probably had no
idea who it was from. The next issue contained six vituperative and
hilarious letters about the painting, and correspondence warred on until
February 1912. In his general sympathy with modernism, we can assume
that George drew the line at Cubism. Similarly, it may be significant that
there is no recorded comment of his about Nijinsky's *Le Sacre du
printemps*, that 'key work in the development of early modernist
choreography' (Ramsay Burt), which was first seen in London in July 1913.
Yet in his *Times* article of 1911 George seems to have appreciated the
modernist implication of Fokine's *Carnaval*: 'This is pure choreography
[...] abstracted from all drama or mimesis.'

Rather than regarding George's short theatrical works of 1910-13 as
'hybrids' of foreign sources and English authorship, we should see them as
examples of an expanded form of something that he had done all his life,
namely translation. Although probably only one of these works (*The Red
Cloth*) pre-existed in a foreign language as such, each had to be *translated*
from one artistic language into another.

An early example of this is the one-acter *The Little Stone House*.
George's original 1898 story 'Lipa Sidorovna' was, of course, written in
English. However, it contained no direct speech. To produce dramatic
dialogue, George had to imagine his Russian characters speaking. It is

probable that he imagined them speaking in Russian, since their dialogue contains many recognisably Russian turns of phrase. But at the same time, he had to translate it in his head into English, and this may account for the 'translationese' that they speak, with no colloquial English short forms of verbs. He translated their Russian into 'theatre-translation English'.

Moreover, to produce a powerful play from the story 'Lipa Sidorovna' he had not so much to 'tinker' with it as translate a first-person narrative written in the past tense into a narrator-less theatrical experience in real time. There are actually two narrators in the original story: an 'I' and a third-person narrator, Baron Schatz, who operates within the I-narrative. For the play, the third-person narrator became a major character, renamed Asteryi Ivanovich, and he had to have as his interlocutor an entirely new character, Foma. Similarly, the difficulty for Lipa in the story of twice raising money to put a roof over her 'son's' tomb, is *dramatised* by creating the character and viewpoint of the man to do the work, who is not even mentioned in the story. Two lines in the story telling us that Schatz plays a game of patience every evening translate into a stage game that lasts for a third of the play and superbly winds up the tension. The focus of the story is Lipa Sidorovna, who transmutes into 'the white raven' for the original title of the play – when it was still centred on a personality – but George transmuted this in turn into *The Little Stone House*, which puts the emphasis on an insensible object. In fact this shift may have occurred only when he saw the theatrical need to translate the 'square wooden house with glass doors' and roof repairs into a single, more dramatic symbol. Finally, in the original story Sasha, the murderer-son returned, visits his mother several times and stays around for a page and a half. This had to be concentrated for the play into a single scene culminating in Sasha's arrest. But this in turn transmogrified a Lipa who was 'struggling between the demands of the innocent long-cherished Sasha, who needed a roof to his tomb, and the sordid unacknowledged reality, who wanted the means to live', into a Praskovya who chooses a totem over a flesh and blood person, her own son. *The Little Stone House* is a masterly translation not from one national language to another, but of one literary genre into another.

Interestingly, in a letter of 15 August 1912 to Ajit Kumar, Tagore himself spoke of Calderon having 'translated' his story 'Dallia' into 'the form of a drama', although this operation did not involve translating from Bengali, only from a narrative English text into a dramatic English text ('A Romantic Comedy in One Act'). *Peace* and *Geminae* could be said to be translations by George of his own theatrical ideas into farce forms derived from the French farce and possibly his reading of Chekhov's vaudevilles. In *Longing* very English situations and characters are translated into Symbolist forms. In *The Two Talismans* not only has Old Araby been translated to the English stage, but the characters speak an ornate English that gives the impression, again, of translationese. Calderon's 'Comedy without Words' *The Red Cloth*, his ballet *Pandora*, and the 'Wordless Play' *Passover Time*, are translations from speech into pure body language and music.

It is also noticeable that after 1910 Calderon's literary activity became more collaborative, whether with the dead Hankin, Herbage on *Peace*, William Caine and Martin Shaw on *The Brave Little Tailor*, or Fokine on ballet. He had always, of course, been prolific with ideas that he gave away to others. Newbolt, for instance, fulsomely acknowledged George for having inspired him in 1905 to write his novel *The Old Country*. Now Calderon occasionally wrote out of the blue to young writers whose work he had just read, encouraging them with his praise and offering assistance.

In *Lithuania* Rupert Brooke had written a one-act play resembling *The Little Stone House*, except that the latter's melodrama became in Brooke's hands Grand Guignol. It was about to be premiered by Wareing when, in the spring of 1913, Wareing finally had to give up in Glasgow and retire to his house in the Vale of Health, where George undoubtedly visited him. George then wrote to Brooke telling him that he liked his work and suggesting an American producer for his play. On 18 July 1913 Brooke replied from Toronto. He valued George's compliment 'very highly: for I know your judgement', although from what he had seen of American theatre he was 'doubtful if America would care for' *Lithuania*. In fact it was premiered in Chicago on 12 October 1915 and published in Cincinnati the same year.

One answer, then, to our fundamental question about Calderon's literary activity after 1910 might be that he became increasingly engaged with duality and dialogue. The duo *Geminae* and *The Two Talismans*, probably written together in 1913, is the starkest example of the former. But in all of his one-act and wordless plays, as well as his personal creative partnerships, he is now engaged in dialogue with some manifest other, whereas it seems fair to say that *Downy V. Green* and *Dwala*, for example, are more one-voiced ('monological'). By 1913 Calderon was at the cutting edge of Edwardian literary experimentation. Certainly we can say that he had become part of the Modernist 'movement'.

Although George seems not to have written anything about *Le Sacre du printemps* (in *The Times*, at least), he could still have seen it. The London premiere was on 11 July 1913 and he and Kittie left the day after for Oxfordshire, where they were guests of the critic Basil de Sélincourt (1877-1966) and his wife, the popular American novelist Anne Douglas Sedgwick (1873-1935). De Sélincourt had built a large house called Far End on the edge of the village of Kingham in 1907 and it had become a literary hub prefiguring Garsington. The Calderons had first been invited there in December 1912, most likely thanks to the stir created by George's volume of Chekhov's plays, as the de Sélincourts were great admirers of Russian literature. Basil and George shared an intellectual incisiveness, and played difficult piano duets in Far End's music studio. Kittie and the elegant, vivacious Anne Sedgwick also got on well. Nevertheless, when the Calderons left Far End on 14 July, George wrote '(The barbarian)' in Greek beneath his signature in the Guest Book. 'Barbarous' and 'barbarian', applied to men, were favourite adjectives of Anne Sedgwick's in her 1911 best seller *Tante*. Both she and her husband were progressives, so perhaps George had been challenged about his views on suffragism.

The last of the three performances of *Le Sacre du printemps* was on 24 July 1913 and the following day he and Kittie left for Foxwold. A month later they were at Acton Reynald for the coming of age of Sir Roland James Corbet (Jim). About a thousand people attended the festivities. Complete with Punch and Judy, a merry-go-round, the Shropshire Yeomanry Band, Chinese lanterns and a firework display, it was a happy occasion because the Corbets were genuinely popular with their tenantry. Proposing Jim's health, a tenant farmer said he believed that 'every man on the estate would be prepared to follow the lead of the Corbet family, confident in the belief that they had a sound leader'. Jim himself apologised for the fact that his career in the Coldstream Guards and the 'extraordinary and heavy death duties which the Government had thought fit to impose' had so far prevented him from living on his estate. He had a very strong sense of duty to his country, his family, and Shropshire, but there was also a softer side to him. When he visited a young London actress whom he admired, he took his sister Lesbia with him. He was also a serious ornithologist. Among the long list of presents he was given were two books by the naturalist W.H. Hudson from 'Mr and Mrs George Calderon'.

Jim's and Lesbia's mother, Nina Astley, herself now left Acton Reynald, with her husband Reggie, to live mainly in London and Berkshire.

Some time in September, probably, George and Kittie returned to 42 Well Walk. Evidently a full-scale theatre production of *The Maharani of Arakan* was being planned, as Albert Cazabon wrote to George on 29 October 1913 about providing authentic Indian lute music for it; but nothing came of the production immediately. At the Royal Court Miss Horniman revived her May offering of *Jane Clegg* preceded by *The Little Stone House*, and they ran from 3 to 15 November 1913. *Geminae* was premiered on 3 November as a curtain raiser to G.K. Chesterton's comedy *Magic* at Devonshire Park, Eastbourne, where both were being previewed. The double bill transferred to Gertrude Kingston's Little Theatre on 7 November and *Geminae* ran there until 20th, whilst *Magic* went on until 28 March 1914. *The Times* described *Geminae* merely as 'a new one-act farce by Mr George Calderon' and the *Era* as 'a mildly amusing effort', but its performers were praised and the whole bill was 'artistically produced' by Kenelm Foss of 1911 *Cherry Orchard* fame.

As winter set in, George's mind turned to Tahiti.

14

'A New and Unknown Adventure'

By January, Calderon was well into writing *Tahiti*, but he was also working on *The Brave Little Tailor* with Caine and Shaw, and it was probably in this month that he started translating Il'ia Tolstoi's *Reminiscences of Tolstoi*, recently published in Berlin. Until August, the year 1914 was entirely devoted to large literary projects.

Tahiti was an extraordinary example of creative hysteresis (effect lagging behind cause). According to Kittie, George approached the writing 'almost with dread, lest he should not be able to recapture his old sense of the wonderful island':

I remember the joy with which he told me that he was completely reliving those Tahitian days, that their atmosphere was all round him as he worked; while his own experience fell into line with the knowledge that he had since acquired.

By the latter, Kittie meant his research into 'the history of the European influences to which the island had been exposed', the Tahitian language, and 'the more remote history of the island, its manners and customs'. But since 1906 Calderon had also had at least one exchange of letters with his friends on Tahiti. In 1907 Maná and Tahiri wrote to him, using his Tahitian name, in their inimitable French:

Cher Tihoti vous vous rappelez toujours de notre cher Tahiti et vous m'écrivez que c'était dous [sic] *d'être a* [sic] *Tahiti.*
    Reviens cher Tihoti pour voir encore le beau pays que vous aimiez tant.
    Reviens le voir encore une fois.
    Oh quand [comme] sera heureus [sic] *de vous voir encore auprès de nous cher Tihoti. Si vous voyiez ou bien si vous écriviez à Aritana vous lui direz que je ne l'ai pas oublié.*

Simply to re-read this letter was to be enveloped again in the spirit of the island's free and sophisticated women, which had beguiled him so much.

Since it was the pantomime season, Calderon probably went to see several new examples of the genre, and certainly *The Cockyolly Bird*, which ran for fifteen matinée performances at the Court. This was a children's play by the hugely talented writer, performer and children's illustrator Mabel Dearmer, with music by Martin Shaw. *The Times* described it as 'a play full of adventure and gaiety and fun' and predicted that it would be revived. We can be sure that Calderon and Caine noted its innovativeness and success.

It is also likely that George and Kittie took Lesbia Corbet to see it. On 27 January they gave a birthday party for her, at which George was master of ceremonies. John Masefield, whose ten-year-old daughter Judith attended the party, remembered George's performance for the rest of his life; he felt that this kind of entertainment was Calderon's forte. Judith herself recalled: 'He said, "Let's play Queen Elizabeth and Sir Walter Raleigh and the cloak, and I'll be the mud".'

To be chosen to translate Il'ia Tolstoi's memoirs of his father was a coup for George and probably lucrative. The world was expecting revelations and the book would be published simultaneously in London and New York. At 80,000 Russian words, it was not long, but obviously the translation had to be faultless. George was also commissioned to supply plentiful notes. The British publisher, Chapman and Hall, owned the popular *Fortnightly Review* and proposed first printing extracts there from June to September.

Meanwhile, following Nijinsky's dismissal, in February 1914 Fokine was reinstated as choreographer of Ballets Russes. The Calderons soon heard that Michel, Vera and the company would be coming over from Paris in the summer. This may well have impelled George to complete his remaining extant libretti, *The Khan and His Son* ('A Mimodrama') and *Mademoiselle de Maupin* ('A Ballet'). Both seem well tailored to Fokine's and Diaghilev's tastes. The first is 'adapted from Gorky' and set 'in the Crimea, 15th century'. The Khan's son is jealous of his elderly father's young Cossack wife, Bogumila, who loves the Khan. Rather than honour an oath to give his son 'whatever in the world he may choose', the Khan throws Bogumila over a parapet into the sea, choosing the same death for himself moments later. The intense love drama and orientalism of the subject seemed sure to appeal to the choreographer of *Schéhérazade*. The second, longer libretto derives from Théophile Gautier's historical romance of the same name. Gautier was a favourite author of Diaghilev's and his works lay behind two of Ballet Russes's major successes – *Giselle* and *Le Spectre de la Rose*. 'Mademoiselle de Maupin' was the flamboyant seventeenth-century fencer and opera singer Julie d'Aubigny. George gave full play to her cross-dressing and bisexuality, producing a very fast-moving, liberated text.

In March a second edition of *The Fountain* appeared. At some point that month George and Caine finished *The Brave Little Tailor*, although Shaw had written only half of the pantomime's music. Caine then departed for six months in America, 'leaving Calderon to find us a manager' as he wrote later. Before he went, however, Caine had given a lunch party at Oddenino's restaurant in Regent Street, where George met the controversial publisher John Lane, who promised to introduce him to William Lestocq, the London manager of American theatrical producer Charles Frohman. Calderon and Caine could not have set their sights higher, as it was Frohman who had produced *Peter Pan* in London at Christmas 1904! But subsequently Lane merely asked George for a copy of the typescript to 'show to a manager'.

On 11 April 1914 *Brer Rabbit and Mr Fox* by Mabel Dearmer, again with music by Martin Shaw, opened for sixteen matinée performances at the Little. The cast was a mixture of adult actors and children. 'The piece was enthusiastically received', wrote *The Times*, 'by an audience largely composed of children, and it deserves its success.' George was certainly taken by it: he wrote to Alice Rothenstein on 22 April that he had seen it three times 'and delighted in it'. Unfortunately, on the last occasion he had 'expatiated' on its faults 'just by the ledge of the authoress' box'... This could not have appealed to Mabel Dearmer, who was a feminist, socialist and pacifist, and probably well aware of who Calderon was. She was also a long-standing friend of John Lane.

Shortly after this, George received a letter from the publishers James Nisbet drawing his attention to two recent *TLS* reviews by Stephen

Graham of modern Russian fiction, in which there was 'a very straight tip
in particular about Kouprin, and Remizov sounds attractive'. Nisbet
invited George to translate 'a volume of either'. Graham had in fact
written on 9 April 1914: 'Someone of sympathetic genius should translate
the new fairy tales of Remizov. These are the most delicate and fresh
creations of to-day.' With his profound knowledge of Russian folklore and
his delight in strange words, George would have been the ideal translator
for Remizov's prose. He might have successfully introduced this highly
original writer to Britain, who is only now being appreciated here. But he
was still busy with *Reminiscences of Tolstoy*, most or all of which he
delivered to Chapman and Hall in May. Even so, he noted on the back of
the letter in Russian some writers for possible translation: 'Chekhov.
Dymov (and others). Kuprin *Single Combat*. Plays of Sologub, Blok.'

On 7 June George wrote to John Lane: 'You kindly took a copy of the
pantomime "The Brave Little Tailor" [...] to show to a manager. If the
copy is available again, I should be glad to have it back, as we are rather
short of copies.' Nothing is known of the pantomime after that. One
cannot help thinking it was hubristic of Calderon and Caine to aim for a
West End theatre rather than premiering it on the Fringe as Martin Shaw's
previous musicals had been.

By now, however, George was swept up in the visit by Ballets Russes.
Fokine was not only the company's choreographer, but its principal
dancer. This was in fact the only season in which Fokine ever danced in
London. His and Ravel's masterpiece *Daphnis et Chloé* opened at the
Theatre Royal, Drury Lane, on 9 June 1914, and its beauty was rapturously
received. The London premieres of *Papillons, Le Coq d'Or, Midas,* and *La
Légende de Joseph,* all choreographed by Fokine, occurred one after
another through June. George attended many performances both with and
without Kittie, was available to Fokine as an interpreter-fixer, and quite
possibly discussed his libretti with Fokine, as there were already plans for
the latter to create seven new ballets for Diaghilev. This London season
was one of the pinnacles of Fokine's career, and Calderon is the most
likely candidate for having translated Fokine's famous letter to *The Times*
of 6 July 1914, in which he set out his Five Principles of modern ballet.

However, the English seems slightly too stiff and to contain too few semi-colons to be George's work.

The weather was often as glorious as during the ballet company's first visit in 1911. The weekend of 27-28 June was particularly hot. On the Sunday, Archduke Franz Ferdinand of Austria-Hungary was assassinated in Sarajevo. In Max Hastings's words, 'most of Europe received the news with equanimity, because acts of terrorism were so familiar'. Given that the assassin was part of a wider Serbian conspiracy, everything depended on how Austria would now react. For weeks it appeared to do nothing. To George with his knowledge of Russian and Balkan politics, the perils must have been clear: if Austria tried to annex Serbia as it had Bosnia-Herzegovina in 1908, Russia could intervene and Germany ally itself with Austria-Hungary. Indeed it may have been at this point that Calderon told his friends that if it came to war he would 'genially and resolutely insist on' a commission, as Percy Lubbock recalled after 1918.

In his spare time from assisting Fokine, Calderon carried on writing *Tahiti* and may have drafted his last play, the one-acter *The Lamp*.

On 23 July Austria-Hungary delivered an ultimatum to Serbia. The London season of Ballets Russes closed on 25th. That afternoon, Serbia rejected the key demand in the Austrian ultimatum, and on Wednesday 29 July the Austrians started shelling Belgrade.

It was probably on that day that George said goodbye to the Fokines, who were returning to Paris where Ballets Russes were based. There is no evidence that George had taken a break since Easter. On 30 July, therefore, he set out to join the Pyms in a holiday on the Isle of Wight, with Kittie to follow later. That evening he wrote to her from Seaview, north of Bembridge:

Trains full of sailors all recalled by early telegrams this morning. Soldiers moving everywhere. Men at all the guns along the shore on the mainland and in Isle of Wight. Groups of soldiers in marching order posted on watch at improvised telephone stations on the beach. It looked as if the Germans were expected at any moment. Strict regulations about all unofficial craft; no-one to move on sea after sunset, or to approach men of war at any time.

He soon heard that 'the first fleet went out 2 days ago no-one knows where'. Actually it had been sent to its war station at Scapa Flow. But the European tension did not prevent George from enjoying the Pyms' company. Despite recent whooping cough, their two young children Jack and Roly were 'good and hearty; they came running over to greet me at my room in the villa opposite'. In the evening he went crab-dipping with them, played billiards at the 'new constitutional club', and 'we wandered out to an outdoor concert'. Violet Pym was seven months pregnant and Evey, as a captain in the Suffolk Yeomanry, must have been wondering when he would be recalled to barracks.

On Friday 31ˢᵗ the holiday party probably heard that Russia had mobilised, but they carried on sailing, swimming, and playing with the children. The following day, however, news was received that Germany had sent ultimatums to Russia and France, and that the German and French armies were mobilising. Evey decided to take his family back to Foxwold the next morning, and George left with them.

When he arrived in London, instead of going to Well Walk he made for the headquarters of the Inns of Court Officer Training Corps (ICOTC). Although 2 August was a Sunday, he guessed correctly that somebody would be there. His intention was to enlist with them by appealing to his experience in the Artists Volunteers and Inns of Court Volunteers twenty years earlier. Unfortunately, there was no-one present who could tell him whether it would be possible to 'rejoin' the Regiment at the age of forty-five years and eight months. But he did learn that they were leaving for camp next day.

When he arrived home, he explained what he wanted to do. In Kittie's words:

We spent the rest of that day rummaging and collecting the most suitable sorts of garments for Camp – and most of the night stitching hard – as most of them were very ancient – and he and his ruk-sak were on the platform of the station where the Regiment was to entrain at I think it was 6 a.m. next morning.

She had taken her own steps to contribute to the war effort, if necessary. A long reference for her from Dr Tebb, dated 1 August 1914, indicates that Kittie intended to become a Red Cross 'VAD' (Voluntary Aid

Detachment). Tebb described her as possessing 'all the best of the mental qualities which go towards, and are absolutely necessary for, the making of an efficient nurse', together with adequate experience from nursing her mother.

The ICOTC could trace its origins to at least the sixteenth century. The regiment had been nicknamed 'The Devil's Own' by George III because it was comprised of lawyers! Given its popularity in the Inns of Court, it is quite possible that on 3 August 1914 Calderon was not the only ex-barrister in his mid-forties attempting to rejoin on the station platform. If so, like him they were all turned down by the Adjutant.

Wearing his improvised field dress, he returned to Hampstead, where the annual Cockney Carnival was in progress, since it was 'St Lubbock's Day' (August Bank Holiday). The weather was fine, but according to the local paper the Carnival was 'a dismal affair [...] the true holiday spirit as only was to be expected was absent'. Mobilisation orders were now being sent out. That afternoon, Sir Edward Grey addressed the House of Commons on what he saw as the country's moral duty. Bank Holiday crowds gathered in Whitehall and outside Buckingham Palace. Far from disheartened, George plotted to get round the ICOTC's initial rejection.

German troops crossed the Belgian border next morning. Somehow (perhaps by telephone) George arranged to see the Colonel of the Inns of Court Regiment, who was previously unknown to him. At first the Colonel rejected him on the same grounds as his Adjutant had, but in Kittie's words 'as he talked I suppose [the Colonel] grasped that here was a man who would be an asset, 45 though he might be'. The Colonel may also have had an inkling of how short of officers the British Army would soon become. By the end of the afternoon Calderon had passed a medical examination at Lincoln's Inn, taken the oath of allegiance, and been accepted for four years service in the Territorial Army. His 'Attestation' was dated 4 August, the day Britain declared war.

After that, Kittie wrote, 'we lived in an atmosphere of drill – I don't only mean the drills etc and general training that he was going through, but at home: books on drill, books on everything, Morse codes, other codes, German military handbooks of all sorts'. Calderon was training hard. On 15 August he wrote to his mother:

Get up about 5.30, read military books; breakfast at 8; go off early, usually with a bit of shopping to do, a knife or a compass or something to buy. Drill all the morning in the beautiful garden of Lincoln's Inn, among the Chancery lawyers; the rest of the battalion in the Temple Garden and Gray's Inn.

In the afternoon, more drill, and lectures on the grass under the trees. Tea, and then signalling, and back home for dinner; a little bit of reading and then bed. [...]

Last Sunday we had a capital day prancing like goats among the bracken in Richmond Park, attacking a hill.

Already, he told Clara, the Colonel had recommended him for a commission. 'In a few days I hope to know the result.' The commission would be in a regular regiment (between 1914 and 1918 the ICOTC trained 11,000 such officers). It failed, however, to materialise.

This put George in a quandary; Kittie too. When he signed his Attestation, it committed him in wartime to the Army Reserve. He was most likely, then, to be based for a long time in the United Kingdom, if he saw action abroad at all. Kittie assumed this, which is why in her mind's eye she saw 'two little figures which were George and Reggie Astley standing by two immense guns somewhere up near John o'Groats House waiting for the German invasion'. Calderon, however, wanted to fight at the Front. When he went to ask the advice of Lieutenant-Colonel Coote Hedley, who lived not far away and whose acquaintance he had probably made at Hampstead golf club, Hedley exclaimed: 'My dear fellow, unless it comes to a case of the nation in arms you'll never be accepted as a combatant.' This must have been reassuring to Kittie, but she wrote later that 'well before August was over' she was 'up against' a 'finality' in George that reminded her of his singlemindedness in the strikes of 1912.

On 23 August, at Mons, the British Expeditionary Force (BEF) clashed with the German Army for the first time. By the evening it had suffered heavy losses and was retreating southwards. The bad news hit the British public two days later. However, it was accompanied by a call for 'every man who is able and willing, to do his duty by his country in this crisis of England's fate' (*The Times*), by joining Kitchener's 'New Army'. Intriguingly, no age limit was specified. Patriotic enthusiasm seized the nation and recruitment soared.

It was probably at this point that Calderon went to see Hedley again. He may well not have known how high up in the war machine Hedley really was (he was in charge of the General Staff's foreign maps section, which was to become part of Military Intelligence). Kittie had described George's ICOTC garb as 'a reach-me-down out of the general pile', but Hedley confided to Mrs Hedley that 'even in that awful old Inns of Court private's uniform [...] he managed to look such a soldier'. This time, Hedley made a highly informed suggestion: the 'most feasible way' of getting to the Front 'appeared to be to go as an interpreter, for he was an accomplished linguist'. When George asked him if there was anything else he could do to 'get out', Hedley said that an interpreter should be able to ride – which George could not do very well. Hedley then lent him some riding breeches and George was at the Royal Horse Guards (the 'Blues') riding school by 7.30 next morning.

In actual fact, the BEF was not short of interpreters, as the French had provided it with a large contingent on landing. Nor were interpreters usually combatant. In any case, how could George's Colonel in the ICOTC find him a place as an interpreter with a company leaving for France, when he was already committed to finding him a place in a reserve regiment? But Calderon's strategy was deeper. As Kittie put it, the non-combatant commission as an interpreter was 'only regarded as a stepping stone to a combatant one. He felt sure if he could only get out there the combatant one would soon come along and no fuss about age'. It was therefore necessary simultaneously to complete his officer training and prepare for work as a military interpreter. He arranged for Dryhurst, Assistant Secretary at the British Museum, to give him a reference mentioning the 'high marks' he had achieved in 1900 in the Civil Service Commissioners' French examination. He started learning military word-lists in French, Walloon, Flemish and German. He carried on with his daily exertions at the Blues' riding school. The problem remained, though, *who* was going to take him on as a military interpreter?

It solved itself in a very Calderonian way. George made himself so personable as a senior 'private', and approached the challenges of horsemanship with such enthusiasm, that the Corporal Major of the riding school recommended him to the Blues commanding officer, Colonel

Gordon Wilson, who was himself forty-nine. Calderon and Wilson hit it off. Following the long retreat from Mons, during which the BEF had lost 15,000 men, a Second Cavalry Division had had to be formed and sent out fast. Now a Third was proposed, which would include the Blues. Around 9 September George was invited to go with them as Wilson's interpreter, and promptly accepted.

He was due to report to the Windmill Hill Camp on Salisbury Plain on 16 September. The day before, however, he was thrown against a wall by his horse and his back badly bruised. To continue in Kittie's words:

He arrived home in great pain which got worse and worse. The doctor said of course he could not possibly go the next day. As he said it, I wondered in my own mind if the doctor quite knew his man. I said as much when alone with him, he smiled and said the pain and stiffness would be such he could not possibly go. In reply to my further question 'if he insisted, would it make him worse?', he said, no. Moving would do no harm but he would not be able to go. When I returned to George's room from seeing the doctor off, he said, 'Of course you know I am going.'

With Kittie's help he got up and dressed at 6.00 a.m., his luggage was put on a car outside 42 Well Walk, and just after eight o'clock he and Kittie emerged. At this point he was handed a telegram from Colonel Wilson saying that he need not be in Camp until the day after.

Since he was packed, he and Kittie decided to go to Waterloo Station anyway, leave the luggage there, cross London to say goodbye to his brother Frank, and travel down to Hampshire to spend the night with his mother at Ringwood in the New Forest. Clara had a cottage there, at which she also regularly holidayed with George's sisters. Next day, 17 September, he and Kittie travelled to Southampton, where they said goodbye for the time being, and George took himself and his luggage by train to Ludgershall. That evening he was alone in a tent at Windmill Hill Camp, but preparing to dress for dinner in the Blues' mess.

A number of major themes run through the letters that George wrote to Kittie every day. First, the Blues' officers were extremely hospitable. Many of them were titled and practically financing themselves as professional soldiers. They were 'all very big and robust'. On 19

September George wrote that he felt 'rather out of it not being the Marquis of anything or having three chargers and a motor car'. Second, the Colonel personally directed his training and instructed him in his duties as an interpreter, which would particularly involve taking messages on horseback and negotiating billets. George accompanied Wilson on exercises and Wilson explained modern cavalry tactics to him, for example the role of machine guns as 'the pivot of an attack'. Third, there was a never-ending list of items of equipment that he had to ask Kittie to buy and send on to him.

Another leitmotif was whether George was to have a servant or not. On 17 September a hussar called Paterson had reported to him and announced 'with what sounded uncommonly like a break in the voice, that he had no duties henceforth but to look after me; but I couldn't think of anything to tell him to do'. Paterson's main duty, in fact, was to groom George's horse, which was hard work. Unfortunately, four days later Colonel Wilson 'broke it to me gently' that he had discovered War Office regulations were that 'Interpreters have no servants, and have to groom their own horses'.

Kittie followed this up herself. On 8 September Jim Corbet had been wounded in the Battle of the Marne. On 22 September, with Nina and Reginald Astley, Kittie visited Jim in a London hospital. During lunch with the Astleys at the Automobile Club, she met a mutual acquaintance, Gerard Thorpe, who had been a soldier. In the only letter from Kittie to George that has survived, she wrote that day:

[Thorpe] says you had much better just pay one of the men to come and 'do' for you – the only point is that that [way] you have not a servant entered as yours – you might find out about that – he says that is certainly what he'd do.

As to grooming your horse I'd do that at any rate for a bit not to seem as if you minded. I'll tell you why. Can you believe it some men who went out as interpreters with the first lot were such creatures that they made objections to having to groom their horses on active service – can you believe it (they were members of 'White's' and were sent back!!). But anything not to be mixed up with such scum – for of course you would never mind what you did – only, there on Salisbury Plain when someone else might easily do it and you might be doing something else of more important training, as G.T. said, it is waste of time. As a matter of fact you'd want to do it for a bit to get to do it well. Post goes Hugs K

The following day, Calderon came home for twenty-four hours leave. In the afternoon of 22 September, incidentally, Nina had written to Kittie from Mayfair 'only this line to tell you what I could not do with my voice – that I love you more than I can express – and that your magnificent courage is just as wonderful as George's and that is saying everything'. She was referring, of course, not to Kittie's commitment as a VAD, but to her endurance of George's obsessive desire to get to the Front.

Much as Calderon made light of it in his letters, he was lonely and missing her badly. The Blues were unfailingly 'affable', as he put it, but he was always odd man out. This was uncomfortably brought home to him when George V, Queen Mary, and the Prime Minister reviewed the 3rd Cavalry Division at Windmill Hill on 28 September (Kittie was by then staying at Foxwold). It was 'rather a dull day', George remarked wryly. 'I let the Division ride past the King without me (as I am not a *member* of it) and trotted about with a Transport officer in something of the same position, on the outskirts.' He 'chatted a bit' with Constance Sutton, whose son Dick was in the 1st Life Guards, then turned his attention to an intruder – 'a wretched little crazy fellow, or else a spy, dressed up in what he said was an Indian uniform'. This man had wandered into the Blues' mess, where he was affably treated and promised a job 'if anything turned up'. During the Review, he was 'everywhere in the crowd, chatting with everybody, ladies, soldiers, chauffeurs and policemen', then he 'went off across the Plain on foot'. A Military Policeman, 'having his attention directed to him, said Oh, he was all right; they knew all about him; he was the Interpreter'... The next day, George wrote to Kittie pointedly:

As I rode home alone I practised sword exercise all alone in a field under the hill on a row of dummies on poles, made of sacking and straw, as directed by the Colonel. However the horse was very shy of them, and horribly alarmed when the sword went into them, and shied and galloped about; and it was rather lonely, poking dummies all alone in a big field, even when a battalion of Kitchener's men began to drill in a distant corner.

To make matters worse, as he admitted to Kittie, 'my position as *the* Interpreter to the Blues has suffered a severe shock, for I hear that the Colonel has *eleven* more coming'. He was also still suffering from his fall on 15 September and had to be 'heaved' into the saddle. Nevertheless, he was now officially 'Second Lieutenant Calderon'.

The most positive thing one can say of his experience, perhaps, is that his position as an outsider gave him a writerly sense of 'distance' that might one day bear fruit. He was not so much an 'intruder' or 'impostor soldier', as a war correspondent in disguise.

After a combined exercise on 1 October, it was clear that the 3rd Cavalry Division would soon embark for the Front. George advised Kittie not to come to Windmill Hill Camp to see him off. Suddenly, however, he was given leave for the weekend 3-4 October. When he arrived at 42 Well Walk, their gardener, who had worked for them for seven years, told George that he wished he were 'young enough to go as your servant, sir'. Similarly, as he left the house next morning their housekeeper, Elizabeth Ellis, burst into tears. 'It was always a surprise and touched him to find people cared for him', Kittie wrote later.

Fig. 18 George Calderon, 6 October 1914

Most of the next day, 5 October 1914, the Blues stood ready to leave for Southampton. Calderon had enough time to write letters to Kittie and his mother (he told Clara, 'The Germans are nearly beaten now'), and one to the press headed 'Philosophy and the War'. The gist of this was that Nietzsche had had less influence on the Germans' 'outlook on their historic purpose' than Hegel. Both the Kaiser and the Tsar were professed Hegelians who believed in 'the imposition of the newest and highest [national civilisation] on the world at large'. In the Russians' case this 'civilisation' was a blend of Slavophilism, Orthodoxy, and Russian nationalism. 'It would be a poor office for the Belgians, French and British', George wrote, 'if we were fighting merely to set up a Slav world-domination instead of a Teutonic.' The argument echoes his 1900 lecture 'Russian Ideals of Peace' and seems more prescient of the next World War than 1914-18. It is, moreover, paradoxical, since Calderon concludes by claiming that the Tsar's Hague peace initiatives prove that the 'ideal at which Russia aims' is a 'civilisation in which every national type is preserved and allowed its fullest expression'. The letter does not appear to have been published.

Delayed at first by suspected U-boat activity in the Channel, the 3rd Cavalry Division arrived at Zeebrugge early in the morning of 8 October with a crack regular infantry force, the 7th Division. Dick Sutton, now twenty-three, was present with the 1st Life Guards, which was part of the 7th Cavalry Brigade that included the Blues. The 7th Division's orders were to proceed to Antwerp, but that was now an inferno and the Allies were abandoning it. The 3rd Cavalry Division marched through Blankenberge on the Bruges road, but after less than a mile

[we] plunged aside into the sand dunes (just like St Andrews) and bivouacked there for the night. Very cold and very beautiful. Sea plashing, moonlight, long grass and red smoke of camp fires. Many awake all night for the cold. The sand too soft for picket pegs. I lay half the night holding two horses that awoke me, plunging after tufts of feather grass whenever I nodded off.

His own mount was 'a genuine old black Blues' charger' worth thousands of pounds.

On the morning of 9 October they set off for Bruges, ten miles away, passed through it, and that night were billeted at a village 'in the great iron buildings of a horticulturist (the great business here)', as he wrote Kittie. He was active now as Gordon Wilson's interpreter, liaising with the mayor and spending 'two hours or more telephoning the Colonel, to establish communication with our Brigade Headquarters'. He got to bed 'after everybody and slept on the bricks among the horses'. All through the night cars, taxicabs and London omnibuses streamed past, full of Belgian and Royal Naval Division troops from Antwerp heading for Ostend, as well as refugees. At 3.30 next morning he went on reconnaissance with an NCO towards Torhout, 'to see that the country was clear of Germans for the Regiment to move'. In fact German cavalry had been active for five days further south, but were now withdrawing. That evening the Blues did not reach Torhout, but were billeted in a château near the village of Ruddervoorde.

At this point, George developed a cold. On the night of 11 October, therefore, at a country bivouac, he was allowed to sleep on straw in a kitchen. We know from Dick Sutton's diary that next day the Life Guards set off early towards Izegem, twelve miles further south, 'confident we should meet patrols of the enemy', but they did not. Sutton's squadron took up a defensive position at Lendelede, about three miles beyond Izegem, and it seems the Blues also bivouacked there that night.

Reveille for the Blues on 13 October was at four, and two hours later George's B Squadron of the 7th Cavalry Brigade was moving south again, towards Gullegem, where it could turn westwards to approach Ypres. A German reconnaissance plane flew slowly over the column and the whole regiment fired at it. That morning George went out on a mounted patrol. There was no sign of the enemy, so the Blues advanced. In the afternoon, he wrote Kittie, there was

great excitement on the road. Colonels, adjutants, orderlies galloping madly up and down, and across the fields to the right flank. German cavalry in sight. [Lord] Anglesey was sent with a patrol to gallop round in a big circle. As he rode forward parallel to our own line a half mile away, we could see Uhlans (2 or 3) galloping away before him between the pollard willows. He never saw them, there were trees between. A force of 500 was reported to be coming down the road towards us.

An ambush was set for this force, which meant George 'borrowed a gun', but the force did not materialise. He made the disturbing discovery that he was passing blood in his urine. The weather had been fine, but now it started raining heavily.

The report of the advancing German force may have been connected with developments at Menin, about ten miles away. The Life Guards were first off on 13 October and learned from their advance guard when they reached Geluwe that Germans were arriving at Menin thick and fast. They prepared to attack them, but were recalled to Izegem to protect 3rd Cavalry Division HQ. Next morning the whole Division was ordered to march immediately to Ypres and, in Dick Sutton's words, 'if possible, effect a junction with the British Main Army', which effectively meant Thompson Capper's 7th Division since Haig's I Corps and others were still on their way to Ypres from the Aisne. If the 3rd Cavalry Division had not done this, it could have been surrounded.

Calderon's cold had got worse, he was run down, and riding was very uncomfortable. He therefore 'decided (with permission) to ride to battle on the baggage wagon' – but could not find one. With the help of an unspecified drug that he bought at a chemist's, he 'kept up pretty gaily all day, now with one troop of our squadron, now with another', and rode into the centre of Ypres at noon. 'It seemed like history.'

That night the Blues were billeted on the road to Kemmel. George's friend, Captain Fitzgerald of B Squadron, broke his toe in an accident in the dark. Next morning Fitzgerald went 'on the sick list', and George decided to join him for 'a few days rest'. It was now 15 October. It took six days to evacuate them to a hospital set up in the casino at Dunkirk and George became so critical of the British Army's medical system that he asked Kittie to 'get Bruce Richmond [editor of the *TLS*] and Theodore Cook [editor of The *Field*] to collect all the evidence and destroy the man at the War Office' responsible for it. 'Let him be wounded and jolted in a motor lorry and hanged on a high gallows in Whitehall.' Marooned at Dunkirk, George was now missing the 1st Battle of Ypres, which the

Germans had unleashed on 19 October. Worse, he seems to have fallen prey to the kind of depression that afflicted him at Taravao in 1906. He signed his letter to Kittie of 23 October from Dunkirk 'Pore Peeky Peety'.

At Ypres, a doctor had diagnosed his haematuria (blood in the urine) as 'gravel from gout'. The doctor prescribed 'Contrexéville and some drugs'. However, there is no mention of a second opinion at Dunkirk, or of any other treatment. George recovered there from his cold and fatigue, but it seems likely that the haematuria persisted.

Meanwhile, the Brigade Major and Brigade Interpreter of the 7th Cavalry arrived at the hospital in Dunkirk. Colonel Wilson now had the bilingual twenty-seven-year old Baron Alexis de Gunzberg as his Interpreter, so George was appointed the new Brigade Interpreter and returned to Ypres on 24 October.

Next day, he reported to Brigadier-General Kavanagh about three miles behind the southern half of the Front. He wrote to Kittie on the afternoon of 26 October:

It is not certain that General K. can keep me, as movement by motor car is not always feasible, but, if the worst comes to the worst, I must blue my pay over a cart and a driver rather than get left behind.

The implication is that he found it too painful to ride a horse. Yet there is still no mention of a plausible diagnosis.

Calderon was now politely marginalised as an interpreter. He spent the morning of 26th 'in the sun by the roadside on a chair, studying Flemish', he heard that Dick Sutton had been wounded at Zandvoorde the day before, and he was asked by the Blues to liaise for them with the locals. This consisted of preventing peasants from coming too close to trenches, or 'spying'. When he tried to move forward with the Blues, he was 'turned away' by the new captain of B Squadron. He wrote to Kittie on 28 October that he had to 'fill up the day by inventing jobs for myself'.

That day, however, he was suddenly able to implement his strategy for becoming combatant. In the morning he reported to Brigade HQ, then wandered over to a field dressing station run by Surgeon Major Basil Pares, the brother of Bernard Pares with whom George had worked on the committee setting up the School of Russian Studies at Liverpool

University. He asked Pares for a second opinion of his medical condition. Pares examined him and declared that he was 'not gouty at all', but had 'an enlarged prostatic gland (and varicose at that) from riding. There's nothing at all the matter with me but the riding'. This, George felt, freed him to apply to an infantry regiment forthwith – the 2nd Battalion Royal Warwickshires, who were part of 7th Division and 'very good, but sadly reduced'. He had already taken part in two searches with them for a sniper who was pestering them, and in the course of trying to smoke him out of a farmhouse George had come under shrapnel fire from the Germans, who were only 700 yards away.

Next morning, 29 October 1914, he brought the Royal Warwickshires a note from the 7th Cavalry Brigade to say that he could join them as Interpreter. However,

we altered the function. [...] The regiment has been blown to bits by Black Marias [German howitzer shells]; about three hundred men remain and about eight officers. A captain commands the battalion. When I brought my note he asked me if I really wanted to interpret. I said No, what I wanted was a fighting job. 'Then you're just the man for us; sit down; we're just reorganising the regiment.' So they were: re-distributing the officers, appointing new sergeants and so on. So I was attached as Junior Subaltern to A Company. [...] I went over the road to my billet and burnt my interpreter's brassard. [This and subsequent quotations concerning Calderon's activity on 29 October 1914 are taken from a long letter written to Kittie on 30 October and in part published by Percy Lubbock; the original is lost.]

He was given a Royal Warwickshire Regiment badge, a rifle, equipment, and a greatcoat tied up with string. 'Then we started for the battle.'

On 29 October the Germans were attempting to push in the salient between the Menin Road and Zandvoorde, in preparation for a massive attack next day during which Army Group Fabeck was due to punch through the Messines Ridge to Hollebeke, completely breaking the British line (see Fig. 19). The 2nd Battalion Royal Warwickshires had spent the night near Klein Zillebeke, so this is presumably where George joined them. By mid-morning they were moving towards Zandvoorde, reoccupying British trenches abandoned on 27th. When they had passed the last of them, George and another 'trotted on to see what was there and thought we saw Germans on the left, half a mile away, moving in column'. As A Company advanced, they came under fire from a wood that was 'thick with Germans, who had no right to be there, quite on our side of the battlefield'.

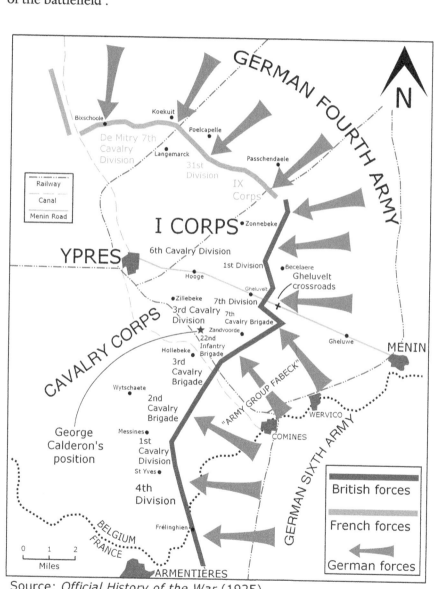

Source: *Official History of the War* (1925)

Fig. 19 First Battle of Ypres, approximate positions, nightfall 29 October 1914

They took cover in some empty trenches. George volunteered to fetch help from the regiments behind, to clear the wood. He 'hopped out and ran like a hare'. However, the troops he encountered would do nothing, because they were 'tired out and their nerves shattered by perpetual shell-fire, Black Marias, shrapnel and machine guns'. George therefore sprinted off again, almost completing a two-mile circle, when he came across a general and his staff 'leaning over a five-barred gate'. He gave the general an 'exact account' of the front line he had come from, 'with numbers, points of compass, names of regiments'.

The general told me that he was sure the wood had already been evacuated by the Germans, for a large body of men had gone forward while I was hunting around. So I slung my gun over my shoulder and went forward again over the fields [...] towards the spot where I had left my C.O. and the thirty men. There were no shots flying over it; it was perfectly empty; there was not a human being in sight anywhere. When I was half-way across, pip, something whacked my left ankle and knocked me over. I simply, without any pause, rolled as fast as I could, like a rolling-pin and quite as blindly, and I hadn't rolled over three times before I went pop into a nice newly-dug roadside trench, dug to carry the water off, 18 inches deep and wide.

More shots hit the road where he had first fallen. He 'rammed' his head back into the mud as far as possible and achieved complete cover. The time was about 3.30 p.m.

The battle in front of Zandvoorde hotted up whilst Calderon lay there. 'I was slap in the middle of the battlefield, snugly ensconced, but a little anxious. Shrapnel, rifle shots and machine gun fire fizzed and pipped over my head.' By 5.30 it was dark and he was found by 'some delightfully tender-hearted English soldiers', who carried him until he was met by stretcher-bearers. The rain was now pouring down. At 7.30 they reached a 'Field Ambulance', and at 10.30 he was collected by the general's 'own car', probably because he (Brigadier-General S.B.T. Lawford) felt guilty for having assured George the wood was clear of Germans. At midnight George arrived at a casualty clearing station seven miles away.

It was from here that he wrote Kittie a letter of at least 1700 words on 30 October. He was being well cared for and was unmistakably on a high:

I really haven't had a moment's depression since I joined the regiment [i.e. twenty-four hours ago], though I was pretty low-spirited before, with nothing to do. As I was carried out of the field ambulance last night, and said good-bye to the less lucky, a wounded officer wanted to know whether it was 'that cheery cove'. I really enjoyed my day yesterday; I believe we cleared a bit of country, though I never saw a German [...] and never fired a single shot. At any rate we are reported to have retaken lost ground in the course of the day.

This was true, but it was on 30 October that the Fabeck task force went into action. The Germans took Zandvoorde and the Royal Warwickshires were forced to entrench 1200 yards behind it. By the following morning many of these trenches had been completely destroyed, the occupants buried in them. This, then, might have been George's fate if he had not been wounded on 29th.

Had his 'military career' to date contributed anything, or had he been a liability? He admitted to Kittie in his next breath, 'If I didn't see any Germans all day, I suppose on consideration that I didn't drive any back; the others must have done it while I was lying in my ditch.' On the other hand, we should not underestimate the courage of a man who had no previous experience of war but was 'combatant' alongside career officers and regular troops. He had certainly put himself in the firing-line.

He was now suffering from acute stress. He reached Sussex Lodge Hospital, off Regent's Park, on 1 November, and Kittie visited him that day with his younger brother Fred, who had signed up in Canada and was on his way to Salisbury Plain for training. Kittie wrote that this was 'an immense pleasure, he was devoted to Fred and they had not met for years. But it all rather over-excited him and he was allowed to see no-one but me for a few days after'. When Coote Hedley visited him, George wanted to tell him all about 'his battle', but in Kittie's words 'the doctor said he must not be encouraged to talk about the battle – it was too exciting'. Then Calderon learned that Colonel Wilson had been killed on 6 November about a mile from where he himself had been wounded. 'When he heard [the news] he downright cried – he saw I was upset by his crying[,] it was so unlike him, and he said quite angrily, "Why on earth shouldn't I cry?".' She felt his experience had changed him: 'I noticed that his heart went out to others in a way it had not done before the War – I think he really *loved* those men he was most with for that short time in Flanders.' Wilson's Interpreter, incidentally, had been killed beside him at the same time.

As therapy, Kittie taught George to knit. He began a muffler, which became 'a network of intricate patterns that he invented as he went along'. In the middle of it he knitted a small cauldron. Perhaps in his mind he was beginning to connect his soldiering with his ancestors' campaigning in the Crusades. On 23 October, apropos of having been accommodated at a seminary dedicated to St Francis of Assisi, he had described the saint in a letter as 'the family friend', referring to St Francis staying at his ancestors' house. For the time being, however, there was no evidence that George was *mythologising* his military commitment in that direction.

Word was getting about that he was back from the Front, wounded, but when Alice Rothenstein tried to visit him in early November he was 'not easy enough in limb', as he wrote Will, to do more than send a message thanking her for her flowers. On 5 November his translation of *Reminiscences of Tolstoy* was boldly advertised in the *TLS*, and Kittie must have brought him a copy of the new novel by Anne Douglas Sedgwick, as Sedgwick wrote to him on 14 November thanking him for his letter of appreciation and expressing the hope that 'the leg is too badly injured to allow you to go back again!'. The danger of sepsis passed, the cartilage was mending, and he became psychologically more stable. On 22 November he wrote to Sturge Moore's children, signing himself 'Field Marshal Calderon' and expecting to be out of hospital 'in a day or two'.

When he returned to 42 Well Walk, George met the three young Belgian refugees Kittie had taken in. One was living in his study, another in his dressing-room. He enjoyed talking with them, and spent a lot of time sitting in a long low chair in the drawing-room knitting a patterned quilt for his god-daughter Elizabeth Pym, who had been born at Foxwold on 8 October. It was about now that Michel, Vera and Vitalii Fokine visited him. After war broke out they had left France for Spain, expecting to return to Russia by the Black Sea and to winter as usual in St Petersburg. On 29 October, Turkey entered the war on Germany's side, so they were now en route to Norway. The Fokines were, in Kittie's words, 'terribly concerned to find him wounded', and Vera 'very distracted': 'She knew what would happen. The Germans would capture the steamer –

Michel would be seized being of military age – and she and Vitalii would eventually be sent on to Russia – never to see Michel again.' In the Calderons' eyes these fabulous dancers were 'creatures of the sun'. 'How could they ever exist in the world as the world had become? That is what we wondered.'

On 29 November George was fit enough to present his knitted quilt in person at the christening of Elizabeth Pym in Brasted. Military duties prevented the child's father, Evey Pym, from attending, so the event was managed by Violet and her parents, Frederic and Catherine Lubbock from nearby Emmetts.

The question on everyone's minds, of course, was whether George was intending to return to the Front. Kittie's friends felt strongly that he should not; he had caused her enough stress already. As an 'interpreter', he would have had no difficulty in retiring now from active service, especially as he passed his forty-sixth birthday on 2 December 1914. In fact the War Office did not accept he had ever been more than an interpreter. But as Kittie put it, once he was home he 'began working hard on his military books' and 'the moment George was fit for anything he meant to get back to soldiering'. He therefore wrote to the Adjutant General on 17 December explaining the circumstances in which he had been appointed a 'combatant officer' by the 'commander' of the 2nd Battalion of the Royal Warwickshire Regiment on 29 October in Flanders.

Kittie and George returned to Brasted on 23 December for Christmas at Foxwold. They took with them their Belgian refugees Raymond Dereume and Jean Ryckaert (the third had found a job), and this Christmas was remembered for many years after. According to Percy Lubbock, Calderon was 'at his kindest and sunniest; he made that strange holiday seem even natural'. Lubbock recalled his 'whimsical, interested face as he [described] the delight of searching a ruinous farmhouse in the dark, where a German sniper is known to be concealed'. Dereume and Ryckaert entered into the spirit of the occasion and George taught them to play billiards, build a toy theatre, and perform polyglot charades. Percy, Roy, Alan and Cecil Lubbock were present, with at least five Lubbock and Pym children. As Kittie recalled, together they produced 'one of those glorified charades that George was so splendid at evolving', for the troops stationed in the village. It was 'extraordinarily funny and clever', but she saw only the rehearsals before she fell ill. She and George returned to Hampstead on New Year's Eve.

The following day, Calderon wrote to William Rothenstein thanking him for his and Alice's invitation to stay with them at Far Oakridge in Gloucestershire; but 'I do not see it as practicable just now'. He had 'fallen into a routine of slight occupations, which seems never to leave me free for the decencies of life. Massage, exercises, military reading, repose, visitors, what not'. Kittie set an 'exaggerated value' on his company, but he could 'still less leave [her], because she has been far from well for a long time, and has been through an anxious and wearing time, exerting her beyond her powers'. The latter appears to refer to having Belgian refugees 'in the house since the middle of October'. They were 'hearty young men, who ought to be in the army, but I can't tell them so'! He himself had applied to the War Office for a 'commission as a combatant officer' and 'must soon go before a Medical Board for examination'. He was still in the Corps of Interpreters, he told Will, so he was sure that he would go back to the Front 'in one quality or the other'.

Published statements by Kittie and Percy Lubbock suggest that Calderon took steps to leave a number of manuscripts in a state that would enable other people to complete them if he did not come back from the war. Perhaps he started on this work now. He made a synopsis of *Tahiti*, for example, which in Kittie's words 'showed how he meant to construct it'. Some parts of the book were 'practically finished', others 'existed in many forms', but it was possible from this to complete it for publication in 1921.

Similarly, it seems that he 'wrote up' parts of the comparative study of early western religions that he had been working on since 1896. The extract published in 1913 posits an historical link between 'Slavonic folk rites and early Greek ceremonies for rain-getting and fertility', mediated through Thrace. The present Professor of Slavonic Studies at Cambridge, Dr Simon Franklin, has very kindly given me his opinion of George's argument. He points out that although George refers to 'the evidence of *Nestor's Chronicle*' as supporting his hypothesis, 'Nestor' never actually mentions Thrace. George's approach is to describe several ancient

Slavonic rites and Dionysian/Delphic rituals and discover homologies or analogies between them. George also maintains that 'the hypothesis of historical connection can be supported by philological evidence'. However, the latter seems at times strained and implausible. Altogether, Franklin believes that Calderon's exposition would not be rigorous enough by today's academic standards. Nevertheless, he felt the article was 'very cleverly and impressively written' and certainly offered 'a way into the history of mankind'; which seems praise indeed. So in writing up sections of *Demon Feasts* in 1915, perhaps George sought to present his arguments with the rhetorical cogency that he displayed in this article.

He probably took his medical in the first week of January. According to Kittie, his wound had 'not yet absolutely closed'; but he was pronounced fit. On 9 January a major wrote on George's Application for Appointment to a Temporary Commission in the Regular Army for the Period of the War: 'Temporary Commission as Lieutenant in 9 Battln Oxford Bucks Light Infantry and order to join.' This was very good news indeed for George. Not only was he going straight into the Regular Army as a lieutenant, not second lieutenant, but the 'Ox and Bucks' was a famous regiment that had been on the Western Front since August 1914 and distinguished itself at Ypres. As Kittie put it, George had 'felt sure his former Commission in the Field, his wound and Sir Coote Hedley between them would this time get him over all difficulties', and perhaps he was right.

He joined the regiment at Portsmouth on 15 January 1915, and two days later wrote to the Sturge Moore family apologising for not saying goodbye to them:

I began to take a touching farewell of a young lady, saying, with sigh, I am off tomorrow. She announced, without even turning pale, 'Oh, you'll always be turning up again.' From that moment I resolved to make no farewells; because it is quite true, I shall turn up again. Not so often as I expected; for we are a garrison. In fact, tomorrow we move into a fortress: those who have inspected it say, it is just like being in prison; I don't know how he [*sic*] knew.

Not long afterwards, Calderon received a letter from Nina Astley. Although chatty, at the centre of it was a serious concern: 'I saw Kittie on

Friday. She was I was glad to see a little better – not very stalwart yet! But even a slight improvement is a comfort. She makes one very anxious at times.'

The fortress George referred to was Fort Brockhurst on the north side of Gosport. It was built in the mid-nineteenth century to protect Portsmouth, is moated, and indeed resembles a prison. Unfortunately, soon after he arrived there it was hit by flu and tonsilitis. Like much of Kitchener's New Army at this time, George's battalion (which was part of K4) was ill-equipped. 'Not only [were there] absolutely no "comforts", but no ordinary necessities of life, and no proper medicines', wrote Kittie. As soon as Calderon could travel, he was sent home on sick leave. He was still very ill, so his leave must have been quite extended.

At home, he lambasted the 'mismanagement' that had led to this 'unnecessary' epidemic. He also described, or impersonated, the ineptitude 'from the moment in the morning when a belated orderly would come round with their gargle in a pitcher on to the end of the whole awful day' in such a way that Kittie and others 'rocked with laughter'. However, as at Ypres when Calderon had experienced the army's ambulance service, 'tears and rage were not far off'. Lieutenant Calderon did not suffer military fools gladly.

He had now got his study back. According to Kittie, he worked there 'at military lore', but it seems probable that he also used his free time to continue to put his literary projects in order. As well as *Tahiti* and the *magnum opus*, this must have included his last play, *The Lamp*, since in her preface of 1921 to all George's one-acters Kittie says that parts of it 'existed only in the form of rough draft', yet she was able to present it in a credibly finished state.

The Lamp has the makings of a curtain-raiser to rival *The Little Stone House* in popularity. There is an obvious resemblance: *The Lamp's* protagonist, Theophanes, is as obsessed with keeping his 'holy lamp' burning, to the exclusion of fundamental human values, as Praskóvya was to build her 'tomb-house'. However, there is no revenant figure as there was in *The Little Stone House* (and its imitation, Brooke's *Lithuania*), nor any sense of parody to unsettle the tone as there was in the 'Russian' play. The scene is set in Syria around AD 50, but is deliberately eclectic: a stage direction requires 'Soft "Arabian night" evening sky' and it is easy to see how *The Lamp* could have been cast as a ballet for Fokine. Its language is stylised, formal, verging on 'translationese', yet remarkably elegant and consistent. The general effect is more classical than any other of Calderon's one-acters. Yet true to his form, it is full of paradoxes and peripeteia's.

Theophanes has been converted by St Paul and is revered as a hermit (perhaps his name alludes to a Russian saint, Feofan the Recluse). But he is really an idolater, a totemist, because he is fixated on a lamp that he has 'vowed to keep [...] always burning to the glory of God'. He is described as an 'ascetic of about forty-two or -three', yet he is married to a 'beautiful woman of about twenty-eight or thirty' and they have a son, Yanoula, 'a fair, handsome boy of nine or ten'. The wife is called Myrrhina, which may derive from Oscar Wilde's unfinished play *La Sainte Courtisane*, as George's heroine is also a noblewoman who has been converted by a Christian hermit, and George knew the Wilde canon.

When the play opens, the 'holy lamp' on an altar in their hut is about to go out for lack of money to buy oil. Myrrhina loves her husband for converting her, but her beliefs enable her to see the lamp in perspective:

If it go out, has not its flame lighted a flame in a thousand bosoms that will never die? [...] If God needed your vow, he would send you the means to fulfil your vow. No, though your vow fail, yet shall we still continue in the joy of his blessing, we three together, you and I and our son.

At this point, a 'sleek and prosperous' merchant, Kolónimos, appears with a bag of gold. He is a slave-trader and 'the greatest sinner in Antioch', but he too has made a vow: he will 'make restitution to God' by endowing money to buy oil for the lamp in perpetuity, and he throws the gold on the altar. At first Theophanes welcomes this as a miracle, but since Kolónimos will not renounce his calling, the hermit rejects the 'unclean' money. As obsessional as Theophanes, the merchant says he cannot break his vow, either. He tries to make Theophanes accept the money as payment for 'some charm or philtre to restore the waning lustiness of youth', but Theophanes objects: 'I have naught to sell.' Then the slave-trader sees Yanoula and twists the story of Abraham and Isaac to persuade

Theophanes that it will be 'the will of God' to sell his son into (paedophile) slavery. For the sake of the lamp and in the name of sacrificing 'earthly joy' – his own son – Theophanes agrees and the deal is struck. But Kolónimos leaves Yanoula with his parents until morning. When Myrrhina returns and hears what her husband has done, she tries to reason with him, but he is blinded by the belief that he must sacrifice *others* to attain what he sees as his *own* glory in heaven. She continues to counter his arguments, implores Theophanes to leave the lamp and their unhappy home, but he will not. She takes Yanoula and as they depart she 'strikes down the dying lamp'. The play ends with the direction: 'The man stays with the money about him, and the lamp broken, weeping.'

A summary cannot do justice to the sheer dialectics compressed into eighteen pages of play. There is a similar binary deadlock in *The Lamp* to those in George's one-acters that we examined in the previous chapter: Theophanes has made a vow, Kolónimos has made a vow, neither will break his vow, but the two vows are made mutually exclusive by their sub-conditions. Kolónimos 'solves' the paradox, however, by intuiting Theophanes's vanity – although there is a hint of this solution even before Kolónimos's arrival, when the 'ascetic' says to his son: 'If one so loves the things of this earth that one cannot sacrifice them for things above, then one loves them too much.' Kolónimos's dialectical triumph opens Myrrhina's eyes: 'Trapped out in rags, your humbleness was nothing but pride disguised', she tells her husband. The dialogue is subtly differentiated: Theophanes speaks overwhelmingly in single blocks, Kolónimos's speech tends to be in two strophes, Myrrhina's tends to an elegant, diminishing triple structure.

By the end of the play her voice is by far the most persuasive:

[Exchange] the sun of my sky, the moon of my night, for a smoky flame? My child, my life, God's special voice to me? No. [...] The voice of life speaks in me, drowning the murmurs of your sullen creed.

This world was made for happiness. The sunshine and the trees, the singing birds and water running joyfully, these are the true symbols of God on earth, not lamps that smoke in the dark corners of hermit caves and huts. [...]

God's lamps are lighted not in bowls of earthenware, but in the hearts of men.

This was George's last word on established religion. It is in complete contrast to his other anti-totem play, *The Little Stone House*, in that the ending is positive. In *The Lamp*, the religious totem is smashed, Theophanes does not die, and the mother and her child escape into the world of humane values, the 'true and simple happiness of life' that Myrrhina believes is Godly. She seems to speak with a particular Calderonian conviction.

★   ★   ★   ★

It seems unlikely that George returned to Fort Brockhurst before the beginning of March 1915. His training then began in earnest. He grew a moustache and altogether looked more like a professional soldier (Fig. 20). He began a course in machine-gunnery on nearby Hayling Island which seems to have enabled him to come home from Friday to Monday.

Thus he was probably with Kittie when on Saturday 17 April she received a telegram from Nina at Brinsop Court to say that 'the worst has happened': Jim Corbet had been killed by a sniper at Givenchy two days before. On the back of the telegram George drew numerous configurations of trenches and a detailed section of one that demonstrated how little headroom it had. Jim's commanding officer, however, explained to Nina that he had not been in a trench, but walking down a 'breastwork' in thick fog, and 'perhaps he may have thought that he could not be seen and have over-exposed himself'. The concept of 'over-exposed' is challenging, and unfortunately the very photograph of Jim taken at about this time and given to Kittie shows him leaning against such a structure in a vulnerable position.

In a letter three days later, Nina assured Kittie that she felt 'your dear spirit just wraps me round and holds me *close*', and mentioned that she had had 'such a darling letter from George'. This has not survived, but Nina's own letter to George of 2 May has. She hardly ever had cause to write to him, so this, her last letter, is all the more special. 'My dear George,' she began,

From my heart I thank you for your dear letter. Yes it is splendid and I thank God every minute – it was instantaneous, so that he could not regret – even for a moment all he was leaving behind him.

For him – one can have no regrets. He is merely gone to a fuller life.

But for the poor girl [Elizabeth Hayes] who was to have married him – it's terrible. At that age it's so hard to keep one's faith in anything – when your whole world has crumbled to ashes in one moment. She is so plucky – so worthy of Jim – but every day her little face gets whiter and smaller.

Dear George, always you have had a very warm corner in my heart. But more than ever now I feel I may say:

Your friend

Nina

It must have seemed to Calderon that the death of friends, especially of young friends, was closing in on him. He had lost several young comrades amongst the Blues and Life Guards at Ypres, he received letters informing him of the death of his friends' sons, he had known Jim Corbet since Jim was seven, and now the twenty-two-year-old Francis Newbolt, who had written to George enthusiastically from the Ox and Bucks on 6 December, was brought home from the 2nd Battle of Ypres severely shellshocked.

Meanwhile, there had been two military developments that affected Calderon profoundly.

First, on 10 April 1915 the 9th Battalion of the Ox and Bucks was converted from a Service Battalion to a Reserve Battalion. Whereas the former was intended to provide combat support to a brigade and fight in a defensive role, the latter trained recruits and officers for the Front. As George explained to his mother, who was back at Ringwood thirty miles away:

four platoons of the best men have been chosen as the first line of reserve, the first to be called on for the front. [...]

Well, the 55 best men of our company, some of the best men in the regiment, are under my command, specially preparing; so I'm pleased and proud of my warriors. [...]

We go about when we can and do attacks and defences on open ground and play the Boy Scout generally. Then there's bayonet fighting, bayonet fixing and a heap of other things; besides lectures which we mug up and deliver to the men now and again.

Fig. 20 Officers of the 9th Battalion Ox and Bucks, winter 1915. Second row, seated, extreme right: George Calderon

The implication is that George (with another subaltern) was commanding the best platoon of the company of four which was the first reserve. He was full of 'splendid enthusiasm', Captain Maxwell Labouchere told Kittie, and 'he took everyone's heart by storm'. His lectures to the ranks, as well as to the officers he was increasingly involved in training, were brilliant, and he showed 'unending invention and energy in getting up sham fights etc'. The eighteen-year-old lieutenant Michael Davidson described George at Fort Brockhurst as 'a gay, whimsical, slightly ironical person, bubbling with wit and good humour and ever ready with kindness and the sensible solution of some tiresome military problem'. His piano-playing also made him popular.

As a married officer, George was entitled to live outside Fort Brockhurst in digs. Kittie explained why this did not happen:

And why did I not go down and make him some comparatively comfortable sort of home somehow? Because he was firmly convinced that if he lived in rooms with me he would not learn one quarter as much of soldiering as by living in barracks – and time at best was short.

I had not the faintest doubt that he was right, we had mutually accepted that only one thing was to be thought of, one end to be worked for, and my going to live down there would not only not help but would hinder the best achievement of that end. So that was that.

Nevertheless, George often visited the home of a young brother officer and his wife, the Peels, whose 'little, young household', as he described it later, provided 'such a rest from barrack life'. Another officer's wife, he told Kittie, thought that he was in love with the twenty-five-year-old Helen Peel. He denied this, but Kittie heavily 'appled' out the suggestion in his letter.

It would be very interesting to know more about the 'only thing to be thought of', the 'one end to be worked for' that George and Kittie had 'mutually accepted'. In fact, she still occasionally questioned what he was doing: 'Could he not really serve the Cause equally well at home as on some Front? Were not men such as he just what were wanted to train the New Army?' This was also Coote Hedley's attitude. He knew that the Corps of Interpreters had now become part of the Intelligence Service.

George with his linguistic, cryptographic and analytical skills could have done valuable work 'away from the firing line', as Hedley put it. But, Kittie wrote, 'I knew exactly what such suggestions were worth when I made them. They were worth Nothing.' No letters between George and Kittie have survived from the entire period that he was at Fort Brockhurst, conceivably because this subject continued to exercise them.

The other military development that impacted on George was the allied expeditionary force landings at Gallipoli on 25 April 1915, which were reported in the British press on 27th.

The Gallipoli campaign was not going well. During the First Battle of Krithia, on 28 April 1915, Sir Ian Hamilton's army at Helles had advanced about a third of the way towards its first-day objective, the 718-foot-high Achi Baba six miles inland. After the Second Battle of Krithia, 6-8 May 1915, Hamilton had lost 6500 men – about a third of his Helles force – and total allied casualties were by then over 20,000. Hamilton had no reserves left and was begging Kitchener for reinforcements.

Given that the Ox and Bucks did not fight at Gallipoli, it is not transparent how Calderon came to be sent there. However, throughout the British Army there was a shortage of junior infantry officers, as their combat life was about six weeks. It seems, therefore, that the 9th Battalion Ox and Bucks, now a Reserve Battalion, received a call for officers to volunteer for active service 'in the East', which might mean Egypt or Mesopotamia (Iraq). They would go out as 'unattached' officers and join a regiment 'in the field'. As at Ypres, George saw a sudden opportunity and took it. Labouchere and another officer seem to have tried to dissuade him. Later they felt the regiment should not have let him go. 'But they could not have kept him,' Kittie wrote, 'he would have found another way.'

At tea-time on Friday 7 May she received a telegram from George to say that he would be home that evening but had to return to Fort Brockhurst next day to 'await immediate orders to go on active service'. She had been expecting him for Friday, Saturday and Sunday nights, as had become the pattern, and had therefore invited his mother, sister Marge, a brother, and some friends to dinner on the Saturday night. Telephoning

around, she managed to bring this forward to Friday. George arrived
when the meal was almost over:

I heard his knock and went out to let him in. I think even then in that first minute
I felt there was something different about him.
    He was extraordinarily himself except that he looked years and years younger.
His smile was radiant but something, some part of him had gone...

Kittie was not alone in feeling this. To others present, according to Percy
Lubbock, it seemed that he had become 'years younger, in the immediate
prospect of arriving where he wished to be'; although Lubbock does not
say where that was.

    The war, of course, was discussed at the dinner party, so now would
seem an appropriate point at which to attempt an explanation of
Calderon's determination to go and fight.

    He does not, as far as I know, anywhere use the phrase 'For King and
Country'. Yet given his views on liberty, pluralism, social responsibility
and the rule of law as we have seen them in the course of this biography, it
seems obvious that he must have been fighting for 'the British way of life'.
Indeed, as his father had said, the Calderon family felt themselves utterly
'English', so it is quite possible to imagine George picking up a handful of
earth and saying, with Edward Thomas, that he was fighting 'literally, for
this'.

    Yet at a dinner party before the war, Laurence Binyon writes, George
had 'somewhat startled the company by maintaining that England never
fought a war except for an idea'. So, assuming Calderon still believed this,
what was the 'idea'? Although he did not hate Germans, there is plenty of
evidence in his letters that he hated the brutality of Prussian militarism and
the amorality of the Hohenzollern political system. Was he fighting, then,
for 'decency', constitutional monarchy and liberal democracy?
Undoubtedly. And his awakened interest in his Spanish ancestors, during
late 1914, even suggests that he saw himself as a Crusader for civilised
values – although nowhere near as much as his friends saw him that way
after the War.

    More likely, in my view, is that he believed he was fighting for an idea
of the future. Not long after the party of 7 May, George wrote a letter to

Leonora Bagg, the mother of Kittie's lifelong friend Louise, both of whom were there. The letter is lost, but Bagg gave her own account of it:

The impression which I received [...] was of one who felt and fully understood the vast impact of the world conflict in which he was giving his all, of one who had penetrated far below and beyond the material horror of the battles and felt the present phase of the conflict was a preface to a greater revolutionary cataclysm to come which would transform the world. [...] [He felt] that the vast majority had, comparatively speaking, the understanding of children of the conflict which was shaking the world to its foundations.

This sounds plausible, if we recall the millenarianism of George's views expressed in 1912 in the *Cambridge Magazine* and elsewhere. Surprisingly, perhaps, for a conservative thinker, George had looked forward then to a more classless society, more equal incomes, and an end to Edwardian 'luxury'. Quite possibly he saw the present cataclysm as leading to a 'New Age' of that kind.

But one cannot deny, and Kittie certainly did not, that Calderon was seeking 'Adventure' in the War. Difficult though this concept is to accept today, we must remember that 'Adventure' was the Edwardian male's drug. For the first year of the war, at least, most young ex-public-school officers joined up for that very reason. 'Adventure' went with a bravery that sometimes seems brainless. Certainly Calderon was fearless, but at Ypres he also behaved foolhardily, indeed irresponsibly. His determination to go where the fighting was fiercest is reminiscent of Peter Pan's belief that 'dying will be an awfully big adventure'. Conceivably, by now Calderon believed self-sacrifice to be the highest wartime ideal. Or had he even, perhaps, been diagnosed with a terminal complaint, for example prostate cancer, kept this from everybody, and was planning death in battle as 'assisted suicide'? Given what we know of his physical condition to date and beyond, it is a thinkable hypothesis, at least.

Evidently there are multiple reasons why George was determined to fight, including his desire to have the experience and write about it afterwards (as is clear from his directions to Kittie about his long letters). If there are many plausible or imaginable answers to this question, it is probably insoluble.

Unlike October 1914, Kittie went with George to see him off. They travelled down to Fort Brockhurst on 8 May. En route they quite possibly read a letter in *The Times* from Michael Furse, now Bishop of Pretoria. Furse had been visiting South African troops and their chaplains in Flanders. He was outraged by the effects of the Germans' use of poison gas at the Second Battle of Ypres, which he had witnessed, and disgusted by the shortage of munitions among the British Army. He called for the economy to be galvanized into weapon production and the whole population to be 'mobilised' in a form of National Service. The letter caused a sensation. Furse had charisma. Soon he had inspired Lloyd George personally to tackle the Shell Crisis. Whatever Calderon may have thought of Michael's 'muscular Christianity' and possible pass at the widowed Kittie in 1899, he must have approved of his proactivity now.

George and Kittie had two days together at Brockhurst, during which he was, in her words, 'full of zest, playing tennis, making final preparations'. But

I was anxious about him physically in spite of his energy, in spite of that extraordinary look of youth. If for a moment at rest in our lodgings he would fall asleep in his chair, when night came he would literally fall into bed and sleep what looked like a sleep of sheer exhaustion – this was difficult to combine with his unflagging and evidently <u>spontaneous</u> energy in all directions. It frightened me, but there was no use saying anything [,] he had passed the medical test for active service.

It sounds as though Calderon had pushed himself to his limits; that he was 'willing' himself on. Kittie was convinced that 'his strength of purpose was such that he simply hypnotised the Medical Officer into believing him fit'. But if so, what was his true, underlying condition?

Early on Monday 10 May they set out on the long journey to Devonport, where George was to embark. 'He was full of thoughtful lovingness', Kittie remembered.

Yet a strange feeling hung over everything; not of foreboding, but as though there were millions of miles of distance – distance that was <u>bridged</u>, but yet <u>there</u>.

But it was not bridged in ordinary ways – somehow the warm clasp of his hand as he sat by me in the train speeding down to Devonport didn't seem to have anything to do with being <u>near</u> him.

I think we can trust Kittie's memory here. The George Calderon she had known – wit, linguist, scholar, writer, dramatist, activist, entertainer – was again becoming 'someone different', a person living 'on another plane'. She felt 'his whole being had become one pure flame of Idealism and Clear Seeing'.

With other wives, Kittie probably said goodbye to George at his barracks in Devonport late in the afternoon of 10 May. A naval officer whispered in her ear the name of the ship George was to sail in – the enormous *R.M.S. Orsova*. That evening, after 11.00, he wrote to her from on board:

Poor dear old Keety – don't trouble over me; I'm off on a new and unknown adventure, but it either ends ill or very well, and no thought can alter it – so rejoice in the colour and vigour of the thing – and drink deep with jolly friends while it's doing – with Catta [Catherine Lubbock] and Violet [Pym] and other Rabelaisians. Your wishes for good, will work all the better when two or three of you are gathered together.

This was the only serious note in the letter. The rest described the troops' 'comical' embarkation, the ship, his cabin-companion Lieutenant Reeves (who had also been wounded at Ypres, not far from where 'Peety fell'), news and views. As always on a voyage, he was exhilarated. By the close of the letter, the *Orsova* was moving to an anchorage. He finished: 'Goodnight and goodbye, dear Keety; your loving old spouse P.'

Kittie stayed in a hotel at Devonport and watched the ship at its buoy for the next two days. At midnight on 12 May it left with a destroyer escort. She returned to her lodgings at Brockhurst, thence to Well Walk, and by 18 May was with Violet Pym and her children at Foxwold, where she stayed three days.

The *Orsova*'s escort left it at Ushant and when George wrote next, on 16 May, the ship was due to reach Gibraltar that evening. Again his letter was packed with news and descriptions. There were fifty nurses on board,

who were 'mostly suited with officers now, and there isn't a corner on the
boat deck of a night that it's kind to peep round'. He sketched some of
these nurses, as he had sketched women on Tahiti, and cultivated the
company of three who were always together. An Ox and Bucks comrade,
Captain Hogan, 'has a cabin with silly old Inman […] and is nearly driven
mad by foolish questions, such as how you charge with a bayonet and
flourish a revolver at the same time'. George was playing 'deck games,
bridge, chess, piano' and 'reading a little of Tolstoy's Sebastopol in Russian
to brush up the lingo'. He half seriously thought that the language might
be put to use if they were sent to the Dardanelles and met the Russians in
Constantinople. His other Slavonic languages might then be exercised if
they fought 'on thro Bulgaria and Servia or whatever comes next'...

On 18 May, however, expecting to reach Malta next day, Calderon
wrote that 'nobody knows where he's going'. The day before, he had
boxed with Hogan, a prize fighter, who had given him a nosebleed and
then taken his name off the competition list 'as I was too old to run the
risk of a knockout'. 'Had a concert last night; I played Sibelius' Valse Triste
and the accompaniments.' This letter reached London on 1 June and was
promptly redirected to Emmetts.

Another reason Calderon was reading Tolstoy's Sebastopol sketches
may well have been that he was thinking of the kind of prose in which he
would eventually cast his own experience of war. On 22 May he wrote
Kittie from Alexandria in a sentence very suggestive of Tolstoy:

Here we are in the great big harbour of Alexandria, out in the midst, among
shoals of ships, with coal barges, launches, sailing boats alongside, full of brown
fellahs and big black Africans, all shouting and blowing steam whistles with all
their might to make as jolly a row as they can and a windlass hanking away and
nurses and officers and tommies all peering over the sides and chatting idly in a
tropical air.

As always, George closely observed the 'parsons', of whom there were
many on board as padres. He gave an amusing word-portrait of one and
gossiped about other passengers. There is talk in the body of the letter of
possibly sailing from Egypt to the Dardanelles, but when he had already
signed off as 'Your very tender P.' he scribbled on the back page: 'Doctors,

nurses and chaplains are for the shore (a sister will post this). We are bound in this ship for Lemnos, 50 miles from the Dardanelles.'

They reached the Allied base of Lemnos on the night of 24 May, but in his letter next day he could not name the island, or Gallipoli, as 'the veil of secrecy has descended suddenly, with a thump; I may name nothing, describe nothing, criticise nothing'. Nevertheless, he described the *Orsova*'s passage through 'countless islands of famous names', and Mudros harbour, in some fine lyrical sentences. Twelve hours earlier than expected, a lugger had arrived to take them on to the Dardanelles, and at 9.00 a.m. they were about to set off. The six officers from the 9th Ox and Bucks were 'undivided'. They still did not know to which regiments they would be attached, but 'not to our own, in any case'. So, George wrote, 'Little P. enfolds Mrs P. and departs for the seat of war.'

Calderon arrived at Helles on 26 May, when the whole Gallipoli campaign was in disarray. The navy's attempt to force the Straits had been abandoned after heavy losses; a month after the infantry landings the first day's objectives had still not been reached; Admiral Fisher had resigned over Gallipoli, and the Liberal Government had fallen as a result of that and the Shell Crisis. The Second Battle of Krithia had advanced the line by only 600 yards. Churchill had been sacked from the Admiralty and a Coalition Government was announced on 26 May, from which Sir Ian Hamilton was desperately waiting for a decision about reinforcements. The day before George's arrival, the *Triumph* had been sunk off Anzac Cove by a U-boat and the day after, the *Majestic* was sunk at Helles in his sight.

Understandably, he did not refer to these events in his letter to Kittie of 27th. After landing, the unattached officers were marched to 'a square place of sand, pegged out with barbed wire', where 'the men were drawn up, the draft, in their companies'. A shell exploded 100 yards away. They loaded a supply column of mule carts and the officers were told that they were all going to be attached to the 1st Battalion King's Own Scottish Borderers (KOSB). This was 'a first-rate regular battalion' and George wished 'vanitously' that he could 'get hold of a glengarry, with the red and white dice border – and have myself photographed in colours'.

That night, 26 May, 'in the young moonlight', Calderon accompanied the mule carts up to 'the lines'. In his letter he was still, perhaps, experimenting with a Tolstoyan style:

The firing had fallen still. Up the hill and onto a rolling plain, with broom and heath and a minty low shrub with a mauve flower. Two miles away a mound on a hill [Achi Baba], the molehill top of a low mountain – that's Him [often italicized by Tolstoy for 'the enemy']. And all the rolling plain lies open before him; he shells about, but does little harm. After breakfast the shrapnel flew over our heads to the beach camp or the sea; our men laboured digging without concern. Officers sat in a group, maps, telescopes, rangefinder, cigarettes – till a shell fell short and another long and we went our ways to different places.

He was aware of the danger, but indulged his paradoxical humour. He found an unexploded shell with its time fuse marked in Turkish characters. An officer buried it,

Then a sergeant said it ought to be 'handed in'; so I dug it up again and carried it across the camp. Six soldiers pronounced it dangerous and recommended reburial. I left them digging its grave. One said, 'the fuse is set to time'. I said: 'I expect the time's expired now.' They were silent awhile then one laughed and they all laughed.

Above all, he was affected by the landscape. He slept in 'a big lonely ditch at the left of the line, with the stars above, the moon aslant and a nightjar rattling softly'. As with George's beliefs about the War ending in 1914 and the Allies taking Constantinople, one is shocked by his lack of realism about the Gallipoli campaign:

It is strange, this careless, rather amused life […] in full view of Him on the big moleheap. Surely it must discourage him to see the tip-end of a big civilisation leisurely going about the routine of life while it closes up to swallow him.

The possibility arises that George and his fellow Ox and Bucks officers really had not known any more about the campaign than that its object was to capture Constantinople, and they thought they were going to do this. George presumably had not heard of the massed Turkish attack and slaughter at the Anzac bridgehead a week earlier.

In his next letter, however, written on Sunday 30 May, he could not conceal that things were hotting up. About eighty shells had fallen in or around their camp that day. At the Church Parade, from which George seemed to take some consolation, the padre had just begun to preach 'on the symbolism of Moses' rod' when

shells began to fall so mightily close by that we threw ourselves on the ground. But not at once. We had to remain sitting, looking as unconcerned as possible, while the men dispersed gently, a platoon at a time. There were about 20 of us trying to take cover behind one slim tree. The men went to the trenches [...] The shelling has gone on, off and on, for a couple of hours. There are two men wounded, I think. [Actually one was killed and one wounded]

Modelling himself, perhaps, on the survivor Vlang in Tolstoy's third Sebastopol sketch, George kept 'diving into trenches' and 'bobbing up and down like a moorhen'. He had not smoked, he told Kittie, since Lemnos. The previous night he was 'rather wakeful and heard a great noise of fighting, rifle and cannon'. Nonetheless, it was 'one of the most beautiful nights I ever saw; a full moon shining on the waters to right and to left of me; a clear starry sky; a landscape of hills and woods and distances like an early Victorian steel engraving'. Even the 'big spiders' and 'horrible centipedes as fat as my fountain-pen and six to eight inches long' could not spoil his aesthetic pleasure.

He had been given a platoon, number 8, of about fifty men. They were 'all lovely Scots'. The platoon was one of four comprising B Company, which was commanded by Captain Grogan (Hogan commanded D). There were four such companies in the 1st Battalion KOSB, which itself formed a quarter of 87th Brigade. George's daily programme involved getting up just before six, putting his men through physical exercises, spending much time 'fiddling with machine guns', inspecting rifles, and talking about 'the need of leaving no rubbish about for flies'. He was not sure, he wrote Kittie on 1 June, how far the men recognised the new officers attached to them. The previous night, when he had been instructing some of them in 'bomb throwing', 'one of my men, being asked, in my presence, whose platoon it was, said "Sergeant Smith's"'.

The reason for this was that they were professional soldiers who had been fighting on the Peninsula ever since landing at Y Beach on 25 April, where they had been fiercely opposed. The 1st Battalion KOSB were part of the very backbone of Hamilton's main force, the 29th Division under Major-General Aylmer Hunter-Weston. It was indeed a 'great honour', as George wrote, to be attached to them.

But ever since leaving England he had been assuring Kittie he would be with 'the territorials' or 'in reserve'. Even on 27 May he told her that the 1st KOSB were in reserve, 'neither on the beach nor in the firing line'. 'Nothing in my letters need make you anxious', he wrote on 1 June, 'for you'd know if I was a casualty thro the W.O., before any letter had time to alarm you.' Even though the battalion had heard that the Turks might attack that night, '[we] expect nothing much for ourselves; there are two or three lines between us and them'. 'We [87th Brigade] pride ourselves that we are held in reserve to deliver the smashing and decisive blow.'

The truth was devastatingly different.

After the Second Battle of Krithia, Hunter-Weston ordered the 29th Division to reduce the gap between the opposing trenches from half a mile in the middle of the line to an 'assaulting distance' of 200-250 yards. This was to be done by sapping and night advances. By the third week of May he was satisfied that enough progress had been made to launch a general attack along a line from the Aegean coast to the Straits. The new commander of the French right flank, General Gourand, agreed with him. Hamilton would have preferred to wait for the reinforcements that Kitchener had now promised him (52nd Division), but he was desperate to push forward. On 24 May, therefore, Hunter-Weston was promoted to Lieutenant-General and the 29th Division, 42nd Division, and Royal Naval Division were put under his command as 'VIII Corps'. Given the arrival of the 'replacement drafts' on 26 May, including Lieutenant Calderon, on 31 May Hamilton decided to fight a Third Battle of Krithia. Its aim would not be to reach Achi Baba in one day, but to advance the whole Allied line by 800 yards.

The battle plans presented by Hunter-Weston and Gourand on that day were exceptionally carefully thought out. 'Every detail was provided for,' wrote one company commander, 'and the plan seemed invincible.'

Orders were issued by GHQ on 2 June for the attack to take place two days later.

Thus when George wrote to Kittie on 3 June, he knew what the general role of the 1ˢᵗ Battalion KOSB was to be. It was transferred to the 88ᵗʰ Brigade and together with the Hampshires, Royal Fusiliers and Worcesters was to take the Turkish trenches along Fir Tree Spur, in front of Krithia itself. On 3 June VIII Corps issued its orders, 'for the first time accompanied by a trench diagram showing the various objectives to be reached' (*Official History*). As all writers agree, the battle was the first at Gallipoli to be fought as though it were trench warfare on the Western Front. There were to be two waves of attack, and the first was to be launched at noon on 4 June.

'My dearest Mrs P., When there's a brickfield we're the Jims', Calderon began his letter of 3 June. He was referring to the particularly bloody 'Battle of the Brickstacks' at La Bassée in January 1915, which Jim Corbet took part in with the Coldstream Guards. George is implying, then, that if there is a showdown he will be in danger.

The previous night, 2 June, he had gone up Gully Ravine (on the extreme left of the front) with a hundred men of B Company, to the firing line:

Sandstone cliffs shelved with green, white sand bottom with a stream along the edge, Sikhs [from the 29ᵗʰ Indian Brigade], and all manner of folk; muleteers, camps, with innumerable little fires in every chink of the cliffs; patient pickets of horses. Bullets plocked and hummed overhead, from the battle. [...] They were most of them forty feet above us I suppose; though a few fell in the nullah. [...] Sometimes a rattling fusillade, silenced by a bang-whizz-bang of a round or two from the big guns, firing over our hollow. Beautiful flashlights, a curved rocket with golden sparks ending in a bright silver star that hangs and illuminates.

At 11.30 guides took them up 'precipitous cliff paths, across a hilly heath into a great winding corridor of sand, endless and monochrome, with caves here and there in it, plocks and zims over the edge, and tired men lying sleeping in the pathway'. From there, 'through a side door', they emerged 'on an open heath again – where the plocks and zims had a personal air'. This was presumably the section of the front between the

Indian Brigade and 42nd Division (see Fig. 21), from which they would attack on 4th. They took over from troops creating a new trench and 'by 3 a.m. we had done a decent job of cover for those who are to succeed and deepen the work in the daylight'. Here, George wrote, 'the bullets seemed to be fired with some personal animosity'. He had told Kittie on 1 June that he was 'sleepy all the time', and at 4.30 a.m. on 3 June he 'staggered home at the head of my company like a drunken man'.

Judging from other accounts, the 1st KOSB went up to their section of the front at about the same time on the night of 3 June. They had exchanged their glengarries for pith helmets. They may have reinforced 'trenches' again (in extant photographs these look more like 'sangars' built up with sandbags), but they did not return to their base camp.

Earlier that day he had finished his letter to Kittie:

Well, nobody knows what may be happening to him in this land of adventure. But we all hope for the best, and nothing is safer than success, at which we all aim, and for which we are not ill provided. I only hope that the Turks will recognise the regiment; then they'll fly for Byzance yelling, Allah, it's them Scots again! and nobody will find out that I'm a timid little penman from London.

Anyway I'm always a fortnight behind the newspapers, and always your loving little P., who wishes he were safely back in the bosom of Tommy [the dog] Shady [the cat] Elizabeth [Ellis] & Co., but is nevertheless very well pleased to be where he is. P.P.P. [Pore Peeky Peety]

Now he got about three hours sleep in the KOSB's support trenches.

Friday 4 June dawned a beautiful summer's day, with a stiff north-easterly breeze. As planned, at 8.00 the British howitzers started registering and bombarded the enemy's strong-points until 10.30. At 11.00 the artillery pounded the Turkish front line. B Company of the 1st KOSB were in rear trenches extending from about 200 yards left of Twelve Tree Copse to the 400-yard mark. As arranged, at 11.20 the British guns fell silent, the KOSB cheered, and showed their fixed bayonets above the trenches. This was to tempt the Turks back to their parapets. 'There was no doubt about them being there,' wrote the battalion's Adjutant, 'as I have never heard such heavy rifle and machine-gun fire.' At 11.30 the British barrage resumed more intensely. It was perhaps at this point that

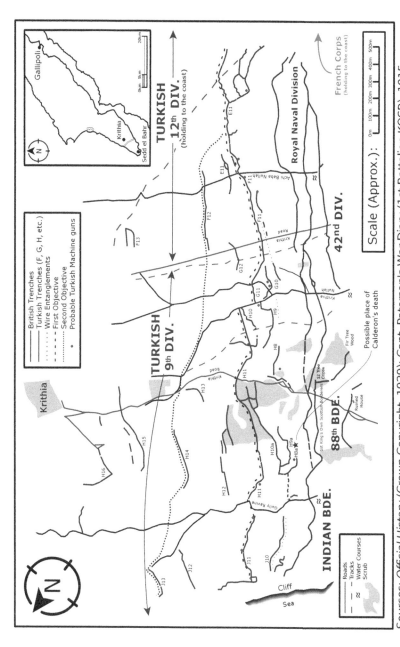

Fig. 21 Trench diagram of the Third Battle of Krithia, 4 June 1915

Sources: *Official History* (Crown Copyright, 1929); Capt. Paterson's *War Diary* (1st Battalion KOSB), 1915

George is recorded as giving men of his platoon a drink of brandy, picking a leaf from a shrub, and telling them to do the same and chew it, as the Turks believed it gave them strength. All the men near to him did this.

At 11.55 companies A and B moved up to the front trench. Despite the 'feint' and barrage, the Turkish gunfire was still heavy. The British batteries lengthened their range beyond the first line of enemy trenches. The plan was for A Company, as half of the first wave, to go over the top at noon. They mounted the ladders and the whistle blew. Precisely at this moment Turkish machine guns opened fire along the top of the KOSB's parapet. In the words of a sergeant-major in C Company, 'instead of going forward, A Company either fell back again wounded or killed. The majority in fact hardly got their heads over the parapet'. To their left, B Company were already on their ladders. The stretcher-bearers rushed to the aid of A Company, there was a lull in the Turkish fire, then the whistle blew again.

With a convincing shout, George led his platoon forward into a cloud of wind-driven smoke and dust.

15

AFTERMATH AND MASTERPIECE

Weep, you may weep, for you may touch them not.
Wilfred Owen

On 4 June 1915 Kittie was at Foxwold. She helped Violet Pym with her three children and probably worked in the garden that she had designed before 1910. Temperatures were in the seventies. The last letter she had received from George was that of 18 May, in which he said the *Orsova* was nearing Malta. So she still did not know that his destination was Gallipoli. On 10 June she returned to Well Walk, having received George's next four letters out of sequence. She now knew that he had arrived at Gallipoli, been attached to the KOSB, and was cheerful. Kittie was probably reassured to read that the KOSB were 'in reserve', and tittered over George's humorous descriptions.

The following day, Friday 11 June, she received a telegram from the War Office: '2nd Lieut. Calderon Oxford Light Infantry attached K.O.S. Borderers was wounded June 4th. Further news will be telegraphed when received.'

It is unlikely that she panicked, as George had been wounded before. On the other hand, in Flanders he had telegraphed her himself. By Sunday evening, no further telegram had come from the War Office, so she went to see Coote Hedley. There had been confusion at the War Office over George's name before, and this time they had got his rank wrong – there was no doubt that he was a full lieutenant. This could be significant on hospital lists etc. Hedley therefore sent an internal memo to Casualties next day, drawing attention to the error. Kittie also wrote to Gertrude Bell, who was running the Enquiry Department for Wounded and Missing at the Red Cross in London. Bell replied immediately that she had sought further information about George by telegraph on 13 June 'at the request of the War Office'.

The thirty-six-year-old Percy Lubbock was unfit for military service because of his very poor sight and had therefore enrolled with the Red Cross. It seems that he had just returned from working with a Field Ambulance on the Western Front. When no further news about George had been received by 15 June, Kittie and Gertrude Bell appear to have decided that Percy should be sent to Alexandria on a general Red Cross mission but with the special purpose of searching the hospitals there for George. He probably left for Egypt on 17 June.

By then Kittie was staying with Nina at the Cottage at the Crossways, Hoe Benham, in Berkshire. Nina had withdrawn there to grieve after Jim Corbet's death in April. The cottage was secluded in beautiful countryside. Kittie had acted very fast in the six days since receiving the War Office's telegram, but there was nothing more she could do in London. The two women were the best possible support to each other. They may have been joined by Constance Sutton, as Dick Sutton's mansion Benham Valence was only three miles away and Constance had written to Kittie sympathising with 'the awful state of anxiety in which you must be living' even before she knew that George was 'wounded'.

On 20 June Kittie received George's letters of 1 and 3 June, forwarded by Elizabeth Ellis. In Nina's presence the opening words of the letter of 3 June – 'When there's a brickyard we're the Jims' – could not have been more disturbing. She stayed on, it seems, for another ten days, but no more letters from George arrived.

Back in London, Kittie again sprang into action. She kept in touch with Hedley, Labouchere at the 9th Ox and Bucks HQ in Dorset, and Gertrude Bell. Percy had arrived in Alexandria on about 25 June but Bell had had no news from him. Kittie wrote to Sir Ronald Ross, the discoverer of the malarial parasite, who was about to leave for Alexandria to investigate the epidemic of dysenteric diarrhoea at Gallipolli; he assured her he would do 'everything in my power to endeavour to trace your missing husband'. Labouchere had heard that Captain Hogan had been wounded on 4 June, but not George. Hogan seems now to have written to Kittie suggesting that George was missing. However, he could not himself have seen

George in the battle, as he, Hogan, went over the top with D Company forty minutes later.

On 10 July Nina telegrammed: 'Still a fighting chance shall I come to you if no answer shall understand prefer be alone your welcome here always ready Dina.' But two days later the War Office wired that 'in reply to special enquiry it is stated that Lt. G. Calderon Ox and Bucks LI previously reported wounded is now reported missing'. A letter from Percy told Kittie that this was also the official position in Alexandria, but 'enquiries will at once be started in all the hospitals in Egypt'.

Kittie was now desperate. If George was missing, she needed every scrap of information from soldiers who might have seen him and since been invalided home. She therefore wrote to *The Times*, who published a 'Missing' notice on 15 July, and this was followed by appeals for information in all the national newspapers well into August. As the news spread, she was deluged with letters from well-wishers, who knew that 'missing' could mean 'taken prisoner', but more often meant something worse. 'My dear Mrs Calderon, it never entered my head that George was anything but lightly wounded', wrote William Rothenstein. 'The thought of him lying untended and alone I cannot easily bear [...] Our dear, brave, witty and lovable George without you by him, or any of those who love him in that strange hostile place.'

Meanwhile, in Alexandria a VAD had taken a statement from 'Sergeant-Major Allan', who had been with B Company on 4 June, and this reached Gertrude Bell on about 21 July. It is not clear whether Bell communicated its contents to Kittie, but there is a copy in George's War Office file. The witness's opinion was that 'it is probable that [Lieutenant Calderon] was killed outright, and the body left on the open ground'. Two days later Bell wrote to Kittie that 'Sergeant Smith, KOSB, returning on the hospital ship *Delta* can give some information'. This seems to have been the very Sergeant Smith who had led 8 Platoon before George took over. Again, there is no copy of a statement by him amongst Kittie's papers, or evidence that she met him on his return to Britain. But Percy Lubbock obviously knew Smith's account, as in a letter to Kittie from Alexandria on 6 August he called it 'much the clearest I have heard'. He also knew the contents of Allan's statement, so must have discussed both with Kittie on his return to London. Smith was the most likely source for Percy's later published assertion that George was 'seen to fall, severely wounded, in the open'.

The source of Percy Lubbock's further assertion, 'when he was reported missing there was a chance that he might prove to be a prisoner', was Sir Ian Hamilton himself. On 11 July Wolfram Onslow Ford, a fellow-officer of George's in the 9th Ox and Bucks who knew Sir Ian, wrote to him asking for 'news' of George. On 8 August, in the thick of the Suvla landings fiasco, Hamilton dictated a reply. He had contacted the Adjutant General, 'Base', and 'the Medical people', but could get 'nothing but negative information'. Nevertheless:

Owing to regiments pushing on further in attacks than they are able eventually to make good, there have been a good many cases of missing officers. Occasionally, when we have [...] retaken trenches, we have found these wounded men with first dressings put on them by Turks who, on the whole, seem to have behaved quite decently in these respects. I feel then that one might fairly suggest that there is quite a glimmer of hope still in such a case as this.

Onslow Ford presumably received this assessment around 20 August and passed it to Kittie. On 8 August Ian Hamilton also dictated a letter to 'The Officer Commanding, 1st Bn. K.O.S.Bs.' to say that he would be 'much obliged if any officer who saw Lieutenant Calderon on the day of his disappearance, or could say anything to comfort his widow, would write a line or two to Mr Ford and give him some message for Mrs Calderon from her husband's comrades'. The revealing word here, of course, is 'widow'.

On 26 July Kittie wrote to the War Office formally asking for George's name to be added to 'your list of "Missing" – probably prisoner of War in Turkey'. Efforts were made at the highest possible level to verify the latter. At Gertrude Bell's bidding, the last British ambassador to Turkey, Sir Louis Mallet, wrote to the Red Crescent. The War Office inquired of the 'Ottoman Foreign Office' through the American Embassy in Constantinople, but the Americans' reply dated 26 August was that George had 'not been made a prisoner of war by the Imperial forces'. At about the same time, Kittie received a statement taken by a solicitor in Bristol from Captain Frank J. Martin of the Worcestershire Regiment, who claimed to have been the 'Senior Subaltern' in B Company of the 1ˢᵗ KOSB on 4 June and the only officer in that company not to have been killed. His 'private opinion' was that 'Lieutenant Calderon was killed outright' and 'probably his body was buried, together with many others by a shell, or by the enemy, or even by British troops'. At the beginning of September, Kittie heard from Sir Ronald Ross in Alexandria. Frustrated by the lack of information there, he had written to the KOSB's commanding officer at Gallipoli. This was Major G.B. Stoney, who was in charge on 4 June. 'I regret much to have to inform you', Ross told Kittie, 'that he thinks there is very little hope of your husband being alive.'

We know from George's War Office file that behind the scenes they had come to the same conclusion. On 9 September 1915 they telegrammed Kittie: 'Deeply REGRET TO INFORM YOU THAT Lieut. G. Calderon Oxford & Bucks L.I. previously reported wounded and missing 4ᵗʰ June now unofficially believed killed in action 4ᵗʰ June and Lord Kitchener expresses his sympathy.'

*   *   *   *

Comparison of official histories of the Third Battle of Krithia, KOSB war diaries preserved in the Imperial War Museum, two eyewitness accounts amongst Kittie's papers, and other documentary material, persuades me that George got to within a hundred yards from the enemy trench in front of him (H9a) before he was mown down. Most of the Turkish soldiers in it had been killed during the intensive bombardment between 11.30 and noon. The brunt of the fire directed at the KOSB therefore came from its flanks – the machine gun redoubts at H8 and H8a (see Fig. 21). But after these had slaughtered A Company on its parapet, they had to attend to their own flanks, where the Sikhs and Worcesters were attacking on the KOSB's left and the Royal Fusiliers and Hampshires on its right. This short lull, combined with George's sprinting ability, enabled him and others in B Company to cover about fifty yards without being hit. But then the machine guns turned back on them and most were caught in their fire. According to the KOSB's Adjutant, each was hit six or seven times. George must have died instantly, or very quickly, at about 12.05.

Some of the survivors charged on and the commander of B Company, Captain Grogan, was seen firing his revolver on the Turkish parapet before he was blown to pieces by a shell or grenade. Others took shelter in a shallow nullah, waiting for a lull in the machine gun fire or for C and D Companies to reach them. But Major Stoney considered it too risky to send them in at 12.15 as planned. At 12.25 the Turkish fire slackened, the Sikhs captured the redoubt at H8a and the Fusiliers seemed to be making good progress on the right, so eventually Stoney ordered C and D to advance in 'platoon rushes'. This worked. With relatively few casualties, the KOSB captured all the First Objective trenches (H9a-H11) and pressed on. By 1.00 p.m. the 88th Brigade as a whole had taken hundreds of prisoners and even reached its Second Objective, half a mile from Krithia.

After the KOSB had advanced beyond the First Objective, consolidating forces swiftly moved in to strengthen H9a-11 and in particular to construct a trench from them back to the old front line. However, the lack of progress on the Dardanelles and Aegean flanks meant that the Allies' centre was being exposed to devastating enfilade fire. They were forced to retreat and 'conform'. Shortly after 5.15 p.m. the Turks counterattacked. To protect themselves, the excavators piled up the corpses from B Company's attack on either side of the new communciation trench. George's body was presumably among them.

Over the next three days, the Turks pushed in the Allied salient until it stabilised along trench H11 – the original First Objective. At this point, the 1/5th Battalion (Territorials) of the KOSB, who had arrived at Helles on 6 June, were given the terrible task of burying the KOSB dead of 4 June. The probability is that George's body was removed by them and buried in a cemetery behind Fir Tree Wood. The fact that between June and September Kittie received conflicting War Office telegrams about George's fate suggests that his identity disc was not removed. 'I find it difficult to believe an *officer* should have been buried unidentified', Percy wrote to her on 28 August 1915, but the body may not have been distinguishable as a lieutenant's if the KOSB's officers had removed their insignia to avoid being specially targeted; or the corpses may have been too decomposed to remove the discs safely. After 1918, the graves from Fir Tree Wood Cemetery and elsewhere were transferred to a new one at the site of the original Twelve Tree Copse. It is reasonable, then, to assume that George Calderon's remains rest today with those of 2225 other unidentified servicemen at Twelve Tree Copse Cemetery near Alçitepe (Krithia).

Kittie probably never heard the whole truth about George's death. The Staff at Gallipoli certainly knew that the KOSB dead of 4 June had been piled into a 'ghastly avenue', as the *Official History* (1929) puts it. Major Stoney knew, Allan and Smith possibly knew, and Coote Hedley probably found out, but they rightly felt it was too horrific to tell her. This could only foster the myth that George's body had not been found; that he was therefore 'missing'.

The 'Kitchener Telegram' that Kittie received on 9 September must have shaken her, but she came out fighting. Sergeant-Major Allan and Captain Martin thought George had been 'killed outright', but Captain Hogan and Sergeant Smith did not. The same day, Kittie wrote a frantic letter to the War Office, culminating in:

Mrs George Calderon is most anxious that this [unofficial death] should not yet be reported in the Casualty Lists – for an American went out to Turkey several weeks ago to do nothing except search for Lieut. George Calderon and it is just possible he might be able to find out more than any official service would be able to.

She described at length the 'many cases' in Germany 'where names of [British] officers are not allowed to come through', and the cases 'in Flanders' of 'badly wounded men being dumped in houses and left there and never being put on the regular register of prisoners till long after'... She finished by pleading that 'the American specially searching might possibly get onto some such clue – so it seems reasonable to wait for his report which Mrs Calderon will at once communicate to the War Office'.

Until further notice, the military agreed to keep George's name on their 'wounded and missing' list. A few weeks later, the American sent by Kittie's friends reported that he had not even been allowed into 'Asia Minor'.

Kittie now collapsed both nervously and physically. She wept incessantly and succumbed to one illness after another. It is impossible to say what she was doing between October 1915 and March 1916, even whether she spent Christmas at Foxwold. Some of her friends, such as Labouchere, continued to tell her that 'Turkish lists must be incomplete'. In the middle of October she received a letter from Fokine in Petrograd desperately asking for news of George. On Christmas Eve Rothenstein wrote to her: 'It is long since we heard news from you [...] We have [our son] John back with us [...] He is an ardent admirer of George, and I tell him he, of all my friends, is the most gallant and golden. But these are evil times.' In a *TLS* review (16 March 1916) of *The Maharani of Arakan*, which K.N. Das Gupta had published to precede a star production at the Coliseum, Harold Hannyngton Child wrote of George as dead. On 3 April 1916 George's brother Fred was killed at Ypres.

But Kittie had always lived by *faith*. It is doubtful whether in 1916 this was what Constance Sutton in a letter to her called 'the real faith to feel that "all is well" with your beloved one – whether this side the veil, or the "other"' (Constance had become more articulate about the 'other side' since marrying the retired priest Hubert Astley). Rather, Kittie brought all her believing powers to bear on George's survival. She would live 'as if' he were coming back. She also stayed in touch with the 1st KOSB in France, sending them letters, mittens and sweets.

She began a project to erect a memorial tablet to her father by the causeway at her birthplace, St Ernan's in Donegal. Being a lifelong supporter of the Arts and Crafts movement, she chose Eric Gill to carve the inscription and in the summer of 1916 visited him at Ditchling Common. Here she met Gill's twenty-four-year-old apprentice Joseph Cribb, who was conscripted and sent to France. Kittie corresponded with him for the rest of the War, sending him cakes, sweets and 'lemonade tabloids'.

In November 1916 Sheffield's first probation officer, the thriller-writer Robert Holmes, persuaded Kittie to correspond with a soldier called Clement Quinn, who was stationed in Lucknow. Quinn was an ex-miner, only twenty-one, and distinctly intelligent. His letters were long and although Kittie's have not survived, one may assume that she replied in kind. They seem never to have met, but the correspondence was therapeutic for them both.

On 11 July 1917 Quinn asked Kittie to send him a photograph of herself, 'if it is your wish for me to have one, as I shall always remember you, for how good you have been to me whilst I have been out here'. (She had also sent him food, tobacco, books, and a fountain pen.) With his letter of 28 July 1917 he enclosed a pressed rose. In January 1918 Kittie sent him one of the studio portraits of her that she had had taken after the death of Archie (see Fig. 4). Cribb responded: 'You say under your hat there is Grey Hair, but you look quite young yet, but [*sic*] Mr Jones does look a nice dog.' He hung the picture above his bed. When the end of the War was in sight, Quinn wrote 'I hope and trust you have the Honour of seeing your hubby now the Turks are mastered', but suddenly added: 'Do you know what I'm thinking of now is when you were skating last winter and the Zepps came over.'

Although Kittie *believed* George was alive, she was alert to any opportunity to confirm it. In 1916 the highly respected physicist Oliver Lodge published *Raymond, or Life and Death*, which described the communication he believed he had had with his dead soldier-son at seances. Kittie wrote to Lodge. The only surviving fragment of a letter from him to her ends: 'I am constantly more and more impressed with the fact that the spiritual world is a great reality.' However, when Violet Pym arranged for Kittie to meet a medium called Mrs Thomas, who told her that George was alive, Kittie was more interested in developing her own telepathic powers to communicate with him than using Mrs Thomas. Telepathic communication was, it will be remembered, something George and she had always tried to do. Judging from her own remarks to Percy Lubbock, Kittie was as sceptical about 'spiritualism' as George had expressed himself in his *TLS* reviews.

The first two anniversaries of George's departure for Gallipoli were particularly harrowing. When Violet invited her to visit Foxwold in early May 1917, Kittie explained why she had been slow to reply:

I was feeling almost as if I could not write to anyone I cared for – or who was as dear and loving to me as you are – even now I'm breaking down and crying imbecilely – and it's only because I'm talking and it churns me up – and my control slips – I don't think really as a whole I'm less controlled – but these days – he sailed last night two years – – and there ended sight – – but letters will go on till the June 4th [*sic*] and one just lives every minute of them...and I think I am better here alone till that date is past and the third year of silence begins.

However, that summer Kittie started 'visiting' again. She stayed for long stretches at Foxwold and Emmetts, at Hove with the Skipwiths, at Benham with Nina, and probably elsewhere.

Thus she strove to pull herself through.

When the War ended on 11 November 1918, Kittie wrote to Constance Sutton celebrating the fact and that both Dick Sutton and her son by her second marriage, Philip Astley, had survived. 'It was just like you to throw yourself into my joy,' Constance replied on 18 November. 'My heart is overflowing with thankfulness.' But during the night of 29 November Dick Sutton died in a hospital at Wimereux from Spanish Flu. A memorial service was held for him at Benham Valence on 10 December, and another later in the month at St James's, Piccadilly. Kittie did not attend the first, but forced herself to go to the second. It was taking place, of course, at the church in which she and George had been married.

On 1 January 1919 Constance Sutton wrote her a long letter from Brinsop Court:

I have left you till all outside [letters] had been got through. And now what can I say – just that I love you and thank you, and feel all the time that your hand is in mine, and that it helps me. I only have to go back in thought to that time, so many years ago, to realise what I owe you – for you with your faith, your intense belief in the love of God and the nearness of the Unseen – lifted me out of a slough of despair – and the lesson you taught me then has never been forgotten, and is now, 27 years later, bearing fruit, and enabling me not to be an utter coward under this knock-down blow. And so when I say thank you it is from my heart, and not a mere conventional phrase. And I thank you too darling Kitty for coming to that Service at St James'. It was brave indeed of you, and I can realise what the strain must have been – but I am glad to think you were there, near me in the body as well as in the Spirit.

Constance was referring to the death of her first husband in 1891. In August 1915 she had written that she looked upon George as 'one of the heroes which made me proud of Englishmen'. It was fitting that she should now pay tribute to Kittie's bravery too.

*   *   *   *

In April 1919 the last lists of British prisoners in Turkey were published. George Calderon's name was not on them. At this point Kittie must have decided to accept that George had been killed and his body never found, because Nina wrote to her:

Perhaps now it is easier in a way – for as you say what <u>was</u> a true attitude – was becoming a mask – and that implies effort in wearing it. I said 'easier', but nothing is easy is it?

Oh! Dina – <u>How</u> I love you, or would shield you from this pain if I could – but I can't.

Dear George – I shall never think of him as dead – He was far too vital for that – He lives in his friends' hearts and still inspires them – of that I'm sure. Of course I'll come to you Dina on night of 2nd [May] when I've seen Legs [Lesbia] off to school. […]

I clasp you close Dina – your very insufficient T.O. [T'Other]

On 28 April 1919 Kittie instructed the War Office to publish George's name 'as soon as possible […] in the Official List of those Killed in Action'. On 5 May a very fine obituary by Percy Lubbock appeared in *The Times*. This was the clearest signal to Kittie's friends that she accepted George was dead, and they wrote to her from all over the country. The *Manchester Guardian* published a long letter from William Caine on 12 May that claimed George had 'died before his work had won the recognition it deserves. Had he lived he must soon have been among the first of our playwrights'.

But the War Office could not do what Kittie had requested. On 2 May they wrote to her with certain questions and enclosing a form for the 'winding up of accounts' with them. The whole acceptance process had clearly been debilitating for her, as she did not reply for a month and her letter was very confused. She pleaded that it was 'known' there were 'over six thousand British Prisoners of War from the Gallipoli Campaign in Turkey' and 'the names of only some six hundred are known', so 'would it not seem more reasonable to wait till the names of the thousands in Turkey are known?'.

On 18 June Kittie left for a week at Foxwold. By then the last surviving British prisoners had returned from Turkey. It was left to Coote Hedley to confirm to the War Office that Kittie did desire 'the official insertion of her husband's death'. Yet in a letter dated 8 July 1919 the Casualties department informed her that the Army Council had decided 'no further official announcement shall be made in the official casualty list in the case of officers whose deaths have been officially accepted solely on account of the lapse of time since they became Missing'. George's death was never officially published, therefore, but it was officially accepted and probate juddered forward.

However, on one level Kittie never did accept it. She told her teenage god-daughter Lesbia that she always expected George to 'turn up' as he had after Tahiti or one of his 'walking tours'. Clearly, maintaining this fiction helped her.

A single idea now gripped Kittie: to bring out a book-length 'memoir' to George and a multi-volume edition of his works previously published and unpublished. Percy Lubbock wrote to her enthusiastically from Italy on 10 May 1919 accepting her commission to help with both. She began to go through George's unfinished manuscripts, she selected dozens of his letters to show Percy, and she most probably started writing her own memoir of life with George. This vibrant document she intended to be the basis for Lubbock's personal input into the memorial volume.

On his return to England, Percy and Kittie discussed George's manuscripts and Kittie handed over her selection of his letters. Percy wrote to her on 22 September 1919: 'I am reading to and fro among the letters with such a sense of the life and strength and wit and truth that flows in them. Something can come of this – I feel nearly sure.' But Lubbock had been working on his own two-volume edition of Henry James's letters (1920) and had acquired a hard nose for publishing. He wrote to Kittie from Emmetts on 28 September that, after all, the letters he had been shown were 'too light' and he recommended that she concentrate on assembling George's 'South Sea letters and diaries (with so much of the Tahiti book as was written)'. She took Percy's advice, setting aside the unpublished short plays plus *Revolt* and *Cromwell* for the time being.

She also wrote to George's friends from all through his life, inviting them to contribute their memories of him to a volume edited by Percy. The concept of the volume was Kittie's, but she would not appear in it personally. Her love-tribute to George would, as it were, be the whole book. At this time it was to be a composition of letters of George's, friends' testimonies, and a biographical essay by Percy that would contain his own tribute. 'I like your idea,' wrote Laurence Binyon to Kittie in early December, 'it has simplicity and grandeur.' On 23 January he told her that as well as his memoir he wanted to write a poem about George. He referred to the volume as 'Percy Lubbock's book'.

Fig. 22 Percy Lubbock, 1923

Through the winter of 1920 Kittie received tributes from people as varied as the Bradby brothers, Harold Dowdall, A.B. Lowry, Coote Hedley, Sturge Moore, Masefield, Lawrence Hammond, and Ordoño de Rosales. The longest and best was Binyon's. The biographical content of these memoirs has frequently been used and acknowledged in the present biography, whilst the more nuanced observations in Binyon's and others' tributes will be discussed in my 'Afterword'.

None of these personal memoirs appeared in Percy Lubbock's *George Calderon: A Sketch from Memory*, and none has been published in its entirety since. Kittie had them typed up and sent to Percy, but in January 1920 he wrote to her: 'I <u>couldn't</u> read any one else's account while I am in the middle of my own. [...] you will understand how one <u>can</u> only do the thing in one's own way, and how one may be hampered by the sight of some one else's way.' The book was rapidly turning from an exercise in the familiar 'memorial volume' genre of post-1918 Britain to being an 'account' of George Calderon by Percy Lubbock. Nevertheless, the memoirs were used (unattributively, by agreement) at numerous points in the *Sketch*, as of course was Kittie's memoir. Strictly speaking, therefore, the 'Memory' of the book's sub-title cannot be Percy's alone.

Whilst living in the Master's Lodge of Magdalene College, Cambridge, where he was caring for the ailing A.C. Benson, Percy worked hard on what he now called 'the portrait'. He argued with Kittie that George's war letters should not stand alone and complete the volume, but be enclosed in his, Percy's, narrative. He won. By the beginning of July 1920 he considered the book finished enough to submit with Kittie's creation *Tahiti* to her old friend the publisher Grant Richards. Both projects had had Kittie's intense attention and undermined her health, as can be seen from the fact that on 9 July 1920 her solicitor, William Ripley, had to apologise to the War Office for Kittie failing for two months to swear to the administration papers for George's probate. 'I believe she has pernicious anaemia', wrote Ripley, and he would be 'writing her peremptorily today'.

Grant Richards instantly recognised the commercial potential of bringing out Percy's book first, to prepare the market for a new work by George Calderon followed by further volumes. Agreement was reached and both Kittie and Percy went straight into revising their respective books. An extract from Letters of Administration made by William Ripley on 20 July 1920 reveals that George died intestate, his estate naturally went to Kittie, and it had a gross value of two hundred and four pounds, ten shillings and seven pence – which would have an economic power value today of £54,220. Meanwhile, Kittie was embroiled in correspondence with the War Office to obtain George's correct medals.

On 26 August 1920 Binyon wrote to Kittie enclosing the first draft of his poem 'In Memory of George Calderon'. It was not generally elevated in tone or metre. Binyon explained:

I fear [the verses] may read rather cramped and bald in style: but somehow I could not write of George in the traditional elegiac strain. I wanted to be as exact as I could, and the thought of him cannot be anything but tonic, and an astringent to sentiment.

He also alluded anxiously to Kittie's health. His package was actually redirected to the Lubbocks' at Petersfield, then to Constance Sutton at Brinsop Court, where Kittie had been convalescing.

Binyon's poem contained proto-Modernist elements typical of him, which Percy Lubbock, aesthetically conservative, criticised in a letter to Kittie of 7 September. He hoped that in subsequent drafts Binyon would 'improve' the metre and 'raise and vivify the diction'. He took particular exception to the final lines of the poem for being 'prosaic' and 'rather conventional', namely: 'He went to the very end; | He counted not the cost: | What he believed, he did.' Binyon revised his text at least three times, but these lines, reminiscent in sentiment of the last line of 'For the Fallen', he never changed. Kittie told him that she particularly loved the last stanza. The poem was first published at Christmas, 1920, in Binyon's collection *The Secret*, then at the front of Percy's *Sketch*.

The galley proofs of the book arrived in November. Meanwhile, Kittie had personally designed the covers and taken on the Arts and Crafts binder Sybil Pye (a friend of Sturge Moore's) to create the prototype for Grant Richards. It was in plain cloth of a distinctive cobalt blue, with a gold-tooled emblem on the front:

Fig. 23

Given that Kittie's name at birth was 'Catherine', as well as standing for 'George Calderon' the outlying dots could symbolise George and Kittie's 'selves', as in the emoticon they used at the end of letters. The two rings, surely, signify their marriage; perhaps even the marriage of their 'souls'. We know from a letter of Percy's that the ear of corn across the intersection of the rings is a 'barley stalk'. This would suggest that it does not refer to Christ's words 'except a corn of wheat fall into the ground and die, it abideth alone; but if it die, it bringeth forth much fruit', even though Kittie admired *The Karamazov Brothers*, of which this is the epigraph. More likely, given Kittie's membership of the Irish Literary Society, it derives from Robert Dwyer Joyce's ballad 'The Wind that Shakes the Barley', in which barley symbolises the immortality of men who left their loved ones behind when they went off to fight (I am indebted to Katy

George for this interpretation). Another Arts and Crafts component of the *Sketch* was its fine photographs, which had been finished by Emery Walker, a confrère of Eric Gill's.

But Kittie's 'staunchest' contribution to the book was to ensure that George was presented as a 'Crusader', a 'paladin', a 'knight-errant'. This view of him was shared by people as varied as William Caine, Constance Sutton, William Rothenstein, Leonora Bagg, and G.F. Bradby. Of course, it was a commonplace of the time for fallen officers. It is doubtful, however, whether Percy would have focussed on it quite so much without Kittie's influence. Moreover, she gave it a specifically Christian turn by prefacing the whole book with the Calderon motto, '*Por la fé moriré*' – 'I will die for the Faith'. Admittedly George seems to have become more interested in his forebears during the War, but there is no evidence that he saw *himself* as a Crusader, and he probably died an agnostic. However, the whole point of the Crusader topos was to 'settle' the public's image of the fallen and assist 'closure'.

In a letter of 1923, Kittie described Percy's *Sketch* as 'quite beautiful' and George's 'Life'. It is certainly not the latter in the sense of 'a biography'. There were also elements in it that she disliked. The book was a compromise between her and Percy as authors, but mainly it was a solipsistic version of the past prefiguring *Earlham*. Percy recognised Kittie's dissatisfaction when he wrote to her on 21 July 1920: 'All I can think of is the way in which I find it impossible to help you as I could wish.' He was delighted, however, when Kittie read the book to George's mother in December 1920 and she approved. Clara died two months later, on 16 February 1921, aged eighty-four.

George Calderon: A Sketch from Memory was published on 10 May 1921. Masefield wrote to Kittie six days later that 'the book has made its mark already as a fine piece of biography'. In the *TLS* of 12 May Harold Child regretted that Percy had not written more about George's place 'in drama and its place in George Calderon', but appreciated that 'to Mr Lubbock his friend was not, as to the outer world, a dramatist named Calderon, but George Calderon who happened to write some plays. His book sensitively and simply sets before us a man'. This was the response of George's friends and most reviewers. 'What a noble and entrancing portrait of a most remarkable and lovable and fascinating character', Mary Cholmondeley wrote Kittie on 15 May. Four days later, Newbolt told Kittie: 'Your book has stirred me as few books could – it makes me realise with pain and thankfulness how deeply I loved George.' William Caine, in a letter to Kittie of 22 May, summed up for his contemporaries: 'What we wanted was not a detailed account of George's doings and an elaborate analysis of his various works, but what we have here – this brief and brilliant impression. [...] the man himself is there.' It was a 'portrait', then, not a 'Life'.

The success of Percy's *Sketch* was intended by Richards to pave the way for the publication of *Tahiti* at the end of July. First, however, Kittie met and corresponded with her old friend Ray Lankester about publishing George's anthropological *magnum opus*. It was to be edited and annotated by a 'Professor Rose of Leipzig', who has not been identified but was presumably one of George's colleagues from the international congresses on the history of religions. As Controller of Oxford University Press, Lankester thought they would be the best publisher, but he also gave Kittie excellent advice about approaching a commercial one. In a letter dated 2 August 1921 Mary Cholmondeley rejoiced that 'George's great book *will* be written after all'.

But *Tahiti* had hardly come out before Kittie was hit by the worst disaster since George's disappearance at Gallipoli. On 5 August 1921 Nina Corbet died of peritonitis in a hotel at Lugano.

The month before, Kittie had told her friends she would be going with the Red Cross to Copenhagen to fight a cholera (?) epidemic. The preparations prevented her from seeing Nina, Lesbia and Reggie Astley off at Victoria for their villa on Lake Como. 'If you had come', Astley wrote her on 2 August, 'you would perhaps have realised how bad Nina was, and given us good advice.' Nina thought she was suffering from indigestion, but the pain worsened and at Lugano she was hustled off the train into the Hotel Metropole, where acute appendicitis was diagnosed. Astley telegrammed Kittie at Foxwold not later than 4 August and Kittie immediately left for Torquay to be at Nina's mother's side when the dreaded news arrived.

The reviews of *Tahiti* were immediately positive. Like Gauguin, wrote the *Observer* on 1 August 1921, George had found the 'savage and unconscious life' on Tahiti – 'found it by modesty and patience, and a resolute scepticism about the substitutes'. 'The scrupulous sincerity of vision here is remarkable', agreed *The Times* on 2 August. The same day, the *Morning Post* called *Tahiti* 'the best study of all of the manners and customs of a community which still keeps the freshness of its allurement despite the corroding influences of civilisation so-called'. It was 'undoubtedly the book of the week' (*Glasgow Evening News*); an 'arresting work, marked by a vision and a felicity of phrase rarely to be met with in a book of travel' (*Scotsman*). Several reviewers expressed the view that if George had written nothing else, 'it alone would show how fine a writer was lost when he died' (*Evening Standard*). The word 'genius' began to be applied.

There can be little doubt that *Tahiti*, as assembled and edited by Kittie, is George Calderon's masterpiece. Almost every page demonstrates with what sensitivity, economy, and attention to cadence he wrote it. Other contemporary books about Tahiti are journalism by comparison.

The poetic power of George's book owes much to its allusiveness. The spirits of *Le Mariage de Loti* and *Paul et Virginie* hover over it. Unattributed Latin quotations from Horace and Virgil, together with references to the Homeric world, invoke the classical Golden Age. The fact that George was writing 'from memory' is probably another source of its nostalgia. Not that the book is romantic: it looks unflinchingly at the darkest sides of Tahiti's history, and the image of barbed wire regularly brings the reader back to the reality of twentieth-century 'civilisation'. But, characteristically, this image is not a given either. First, barbed wire blights what is thought to be the paradisial 'Bain de Loti'; then George injures his foot on some, affecting his walking for days; finally he sees 'a piece of coral reef still growing with a piece of English barbed wire embedded in it' and this images for him his 'faith' that 'the Tahitians have resolved to cut their losses, to yield what must inevitably go, and save the rest; save their existence, at any rate'.

For all its sense of being a limpid record of George's stay on the island, *Tahiti* is a profoundly fictive world. It was accepted practice in such travel writing to change the names of real people, or places, or ships, as George does, but in a manuscript note quoted by Kittie in her Preface George disconcertingly explains that he has 'disguised the personality' of individuals too, 'so that no-one should recognise them'. Are Tahiri-i-te-rai's and Tupuna's characters imagined, then? It is possible that the sketch entitled 'Manu' was not drawn on Tahiti but is a later pastiche of a figure in Gauguin's *Tahitian Women with Mango Blossoms*; whilst the unsourced story of the white doe that concludes 'Songs of the South Seas' could well be by George himself. Similarly, Kittie's personal ordering of the book into forty-eight chapter-fragments, some very short, and her decision to retain here and there the present tense of George's notebooks, produce extremely potent effects of 'parataxis'. It may be that George himself meant the narrative to be less disjunctive, more horizontal than this, but the gains in meditative 'verticality' are undeniable. In this sense, *Tahiti* is the culmination of George and Kittie's lifelong creative synergy.

But the breadth of theme addressed in *Tahiti* is also a vital part of its appeal. There is plenty for everyone, from the lover of travel, landscape, women, human character, wit, to the anthropologist, folklorist, musicologist, historian and anti-colonialist. Central, though, is the question debated by 'Dumford', by Europeans 'gone native', missionaries, and George himself as he reclined in his *pareu* and garland with Lantérès 'looking through the tops of coco-trees on to the blue sea': how could twentieth-century man 'regain his liberty' and 'return to Nature'? It was a question that many post-War readers were asking themselves.

By the second week of August 1921 *Tahiti* was the number one bestseller in central London (it was reprinted in October). On 13 August Binyon wrote Kittie a superb appreciation of the book, which he felt produced a 'not less vivid picture of George' than of the island. Enthusiastic reviews continued to pour out and by the end of the year Kittie had been sent over thirty of them by the two press cutting agencies she employed.

We have no idea how she reacted, or even where she was. She probably stayed with Mrs Stewart for weeks – she *was* a second daughter to her – and then wandered from one friend to another. We do not even know where she spent Christmas. Constance Sutton was well aware of

AFTERMATH AND MASTERPIECE

Kittie's state of mind. In a letter dated 28 November 1921 she tried to reset Kittie's emotions on George and on her own achievement in the last two years. 'It has been I know a real labour of love to you,' she wrote of *Tahiti*, 'and with this and Percy Lubbock's tribute you can feel that George's personality and genius are safe to be recognised for all time.'

Immediately after Christmas, Richards published George's *Eight One-Act Plays*. This could easily have been a miscalculation, as readers were expecting something substantial after *Tahiti* and Richards himself had rejected George's proposal for such a volume in 1912. But the extreme polarisation of the book's reception proved good publicity. For some the playlets were 'very trifling dramatic sketches' (*Bookman*) and not all of them were 'actable' (*Glasgow Herald*). For *The Times*, however, they were 'miniature experiments' that breathed a 'keen, sometimes biting, vitality' and had a 'specifically dramatic quality'. For the *Liverpool Post* they were even 'commercial experiments in comedy and farce, in romantic, realistic and subjective drama' and only *Longing* 'presents any real difficulty to the producer'.

In the spring Kittie visited Foxwold and Emmetts for a long time, returning on Easter Monday (17 April). Five days later she was with the de Sélincourts at Far End. The only known event in her life in the next three months is the publication of *Three Plays and a Pantomime* on 13 July 1922. By the time reviews were appearing, she was at Mrs Stewart's side in Torquay for the anniversary of Nina's death. She stayed several weeks.

The new volume contained, in order, *Revolt, The Fountain, Cromwell: Mall o' Monks*, and *Cinderella: An Ibsen Pantomime*. It invited definitive assessment of George as a dramatist. 'Fresh from reading these plays,' wrote Harold Child in *The Times* of 27 July, 'one is inclined to say that Calderon's loss was the heaviest blow which struck the English drama during the war.' Several reviewers echoed him. But, as in George's lifetime, the consensus was that *The Fountain* was superior to *Revolt*, and hardly anything was added by reviewers to the themes aired when *The Fountain* and *Revolt* were first performed. On the other hand, everyone was astonished to discover that George had written a five-act historical drama in verse, and the critical responses to it were surprisingly up-beat. The *Manchester Guardian* described *Cromwell* as 'swift, actable, debonair' and *Eve*'s favourable comparison of it with competitors was typical: 'It is so vigorous and so rich in life, in humour, and in tragic matter that it has no room for the feebleness and dullness of much modern historical drama.' Similarly, although most reviewers had cavils about *Cinderella*, they appreciated it as 'a typical Calderon extravaganza [...] first-rate fun' (*Liverpool Post*).

The most interesting thing, however, about the twenty reviews of *Three Plays and a Pantomime* sent to Kittie by her cutting agencies was that they comprised a dialogue about 'who' George was as both a writer and man. They will therefore be discussed in my 'Afterword'. Important themes in this dialogue were, for example, whether George was 'just' an amateur (post-War youth viewed this subject differently from the Edwardians), whether 'pure intellect' predominated in him over 'the creative spirit' and 'humaneness', why he was felt to be 'a man of genius, who yet left behind him only a collection of incomplete and not particularly impressive works' (*Glasgow News*), and what really was his 'character'. When, in the *TLS* of 3 August 1922, Harold Child suggested that 'outside Mr Lubbock's book, Calderon's plays and *Tahiti* are all that is left of a fine spirit and a fine brain', he was contradicted by a letter published on 14 September 1922 from William Lyon Phelps, one of the brightest stars in the American academic firmament and a specialist in Russian literature. Phelps wrote that he regarded George's Introduction to *Two Plays by Tchekhof* as 'the most subtle and penetrating essay on the Russian dramatist that I have seen anywhere' – a view which many would still accept.

Kittie was probably gratified by Phelps's intervention, since she regarded much that was said about George in reviews as 'rot'.

But by now she had other things on her mind. She had bought a three-bedroom Victorian cottage just outside the village of Sheet, a mile from Petersfield in Hampshire, and finally moved there with her housekeeper Elizabeth Ellis in December 1922. George's and her last home, 42 Well Walk, was sold. 'My beloved London I had left forever', she wrote later, but 'for two whole years I had loathed living there.'

16

WHITE RAVEN

Kittie chose the Petersfield area for several reasons. Her godson Alan Lubbock was married to Helen Bonham-Carter and they lived in the latter's family home at nearby Adhurst St Mary, which Kittie had visited. In 1919 Kittie's neighbours at Well Walk, the Sturge Moores, moved to the village of Steep, which was within walking distance of Kittie's cottage. Before that, the painter Flora Twort, whom Kittie probably knew, had also left Hampstead for Petersfield, where there was a thriving Arts and Crafts community. From Sheet, Kittie could go walking on the South Downs, which she loved doing.

She had every intention of making this her permanent home. She had brought with her a new dog, Bunty the Cairn terrier, and at least one of her and George's cats Shadrach, Meshach and Abednego. She began 1923 by planning an extensive garden, with Frederic Lubbock's advice, and ordering plants. As if to emphasise her residency, she changed the name of her house from Hurst Cottage to Kay's Crib.

But somehow she could not settle. She spent the summer visiting friends in various parts of the country, returned to Sheet in the autumn, then left again on 8 December and returned only three times in the next two years.

Part of the reason was doubtless that Mrs Stewart of Torquay had now entered a long illness and Kittie wanted to be with her. Equally, Kittie wanted to continue publicising George's legacy, but for this purpose London and other urban intellectual centres beckoned. She was, in fact, poorly prepared for rural life. The break with her past had been too abrupt. Eight years after George's death, 'closure' was still elusive.

In the winter of 1923 William Rothenstein corresponded with Kittie about a talk he was going to give on George, probably in Oxford, but Kittie could not get there and had to rely for an account on a letter from

Gladys Raikes, who was a friend of the Pyms. She also corresponded with William Caine about his narrative version of the pantomime that he and George had completed, *The Brave Little Tailor*. This was published by Grant Richards in September as a lavishly illustrated children's book, on whose cover George was billed as first author. Kittie was probably also instrumental in the publication of *Thompson* by Samuel French in 1924, and certainly edited *Two Plays by Anton Tchekhof and One by Alfred de Musset*, which Richards brought out in the familiar cobalt covers in June of the same year.

This literary event may have spurred the Irish theatre-man J.B. Fagan to risk staging *The Cherry Orchard* in George's version at the Oxford Playhouse in January 1925. Like George, Fagan was an alumnus of Trinity College, Oxford (he matriculated the year after George graduated). He must have known of the stir that George's *Cherry Orchard* had created in Dublin six years earlier. In his *Verdict at Midnight* Harold Hobson wrote that the Oxford Players' production, which he saw as an undergraduate, was 'not one of Fagan's best'. Even so, Nigel Playfair transferred it to the Lyric Theatre, Hammersmith, where it opened on 25 May 1925. Despite violently opposed reviews, it became a famous success, moved to the Royalty Theatre in Soho, and eventually crossed the Atlantic. Truly, Hobson emphasised when I met him in 1977, it was 'an Oxford man' who introduced Chekhov to the British stage...

Kittie went to London to see the production. Perhaps it was on the back of its success that *The Fountain* was republished in 1925. But the year rapidly deteriorated for her. In May Constance Sutton's husband died, in July Kittie's friend Mary Cholmondeley, in September William Caine. By this time she was in residence at The Croft, Torquay, where she nursed Mrs Stewart as she had her own mother. Nina's mother died at the age of eighty-four on 24 November. There is no evidence that Kittie attended a performance of *The Fountain* staged by the Harben family under the auspices of the International Labour Party at the Strand Theatre, Aldwych, on Sunday 13 December. Completely drained, she retired to Foxwold for Christmas.

Alan and Helen Lubbock brought her back to Sheet by car on New Year's Day, 1926. There is a suspicion that like George she kept a diary only when she was trying to give structure to her life; and 1926 is one of three years for which a diary has survived. On 11 February Kittie started work on the garden by 'planting seedlings from The Croft all day', but noted: 'Weeds in garden even worse than I feared. Sent S.O.S. to Gertrude Corbet [Constance Sutton's sister] asking her to come and help me clear it.' Gertrude arrived on 19th, gardened solidly with Kittie for the next fortnight, then Kittie continued almost daily for three weeks. Lesbia Corbet, now aged twenty-one, was Kittie's last remaining blood-link with Nina. She visited Kittie monthly, they grew closer than ever, and Kittie approved of Lesbia's choice of fiancé, Victor Mylius. A stream of other visitors are recorded in the 1926 diary. The Sturge Moores, Percy Lubbock, and the Hedley family came to tea, Calderon and Ripley relations dropped in, and old friends of Kittie's came to stay. She had not been able to see the premiere of *The Lamp* at St Paul's, Covent Garden, on 28 February 1926, because 'the trains altered', but she got to London in October to attend to business and see J.B. Fagan's hit *And So to Bed*. On her return, she began teaching in Sheet's Anglican Sunday school.

Her diary suggests that in 1926 she threw herself into the village's social life. She collected for the church's Clothing Club and helped manage its Fabric Fund. She visited the infirm and attended village events. By the end of the year she was regularly calling on or taking tea with a third of the village's Private Residents named in *Kelly's Directory*. This brought its complications. Within five months of resuming residence at Sheet, she was losing sleep over a letter she felt she must pen to a retired army captain that would 'prevent [the] idiot kink in village socialities'. She had come in at the very top of Sheet society, and this created waves.

Meanwhile, Kittie was determined to use her good relations with Richards to continue publishing George's *Works*. The question was: which works? Interestingly, the idea of republishing *The Adventures of Downy V. Green* seems never to have been raised, although a Richards edition of *Dwala* was. Percy Lubbock was not enthusiastic about this, and Smith, Elder would surely not have parted cheaply with the rights. In 1920 Percy had been in favour of collecting 'the stories etc in the magazines' for a Richards volume, but there would not have been enough and the longest, 'Lipa Sidorovna', had been superseded by *The Little Stone House*.

Now, therefore, Kittie turned to George's unpublished ballets and 'mimodramas'. She prepared them for Fokine to see at the publisher's, and Fokine offered to write a preface to them. As with the stories, they would have covered barely forty pages of print. Nothing more is heard of the project after 1927. This means that the Chekhov/de Musset volume of 1924 is the last in Grant Richards's edition of George's works. The idea of 'Professor Rose of Leipzig' editing George's anthropological *magnum opus* for publication was dropped in 1925 after Rose found the task impossible and returned the 'Index' to Kittie. In 1927, however, Percy brought off the coup of transferring George's 1912 Chekhov volume to his own publisher, Cape, who issued it in their popular series 'The Travellers' Library'. This edition was reprinted through the twenties and thirties and remained the most readily available text. In 1928 *The Two Talismans* was published as a single volume, which appears to be the last new publication (as opposed to reprint) of a Calderon work ever.

But the performance life of George's plays had never been so active. Kittie managed this through the theatre agents Joseph Williams. *Perdican and Camilla* was premiered at the Blackfriars Theatre, London, in December 1926. *Peace, The Two Talismans, Derelicts* and *Thompson* all received their radio premieres between 1925 and 1929. *The Little Stone House* was broadcast six times in the same period, as well as being revived by theatre companies.

The success of Fagan's production of *The Cherry Orchard* in George's translation gave the manager Philip Ridgeway the idea of a Chekhov season at the Little Theatre and Barnes Theatre between October 1925 and November 1926. All four of Chekhov's greatest plays were included, three directed by Theodore Komisarjevsky. The versions used were by Constance Garnett – probably because Komisarjevsky wanted to treat them as literals and adapt them to his personal purposes, which Kittie would not allow. Nevertheless, it was certainly George's and Fagan's work that gave impetus to this important further step in establishing Chekhov on the British stage. In September 1926 Kittie granted exclusive rights to Her Majesty's Theatre, Sydney, to premiere *The Cherry Orchard* in Australia in George's version.

After the supreme effort Kittie had made in 1926 to settle into the community at Sheet, early in 1927 her residency there began to fall apart again. On 21 January Violet Pym died at Foxwold from cancer, aged forty-five. Her husband Evey needed every support he could get, especially with his youngest children, Jeremy (seven) and Elizabeth (twelve). Kittie stayed for three weeks after the funeral. When she returned to Sheet, she gave a homily to her Sunday school class on St John 14 that flowed from her conversations with Jeremy:

Do not let us be afraid of death. It brings us who remain in the world sorrow when someone we love dies. Their having gone away must make us sorry, but we would be full of sorrow if they went right away from us into another country – sorrow does not mean fear. [...] Jesus promised his disciples – his friends – that he would pray God to give them the Comforter – and that comforter he said was the spirit of truth – that he might be with them for ever. 'I will not leave you comfortless,' he said, and it is that Spirit of Truth that is comforting that little boy and giving him strength. He, the Comforter, has made him understand that all is well with his Mother – and that there is nothing in Death itself to fear.

Undoubtedly this was her own belief. In April she helped at Foxwold for five weeks. She had Jeremy Pym and his nurse to stay with her 'and Bunty' at Kay's Crib, and was always available to Evey for advice about Elizabeth, his only daughter. In June Violet's father Frederic Lubbock died and Kittie rushed to Emmetts to comfort his wife and children. She made at least two other long visits to Foxwold and Emmetts in the year. In December 1927, it seems, she gave her last Sunday school class at Sheet.

Really, then, Kittie had found her 'family' with the now motherless Pyms in Kent. Simultaneously, she felt a desire to travel. In December 1926 Percy Lubbock had married Lady Sybil Cuffe, the owner of Villa Medici near Florence, and the couple invited Kittie and Victoria Cholmondeley to stay in October 1927. This fell through because Kittie was needed at Foxwold. Her next plan was to visit Villa Medici in May 1928 'from Constantinople', as Percy recorded. By April 1928, however, this had changed to visiting Villa Medici on her way to Gallipoli for the anniversary of George's death. This too fell through, because she had urgently to attend Elizabeth Pym at Foxwold. In 1929 and 1930 four projected visits to Percy and Sybil were cancelled at short notice either because Kittie was ill, or for family reasons.

The most important of these was Kittie's role in persuading Evey not to oppose the engagement of his eldest son Jack to Diana Gough, when in 1929 both were still at university. Diana's mother, the widow of Brigadier-General Sir J.E. Gough, V.C., was equally apprehensive about the marriage of her only child. Evey, who was not at ease in such matters, relied greatly on Kittie to sound the feelings of all parties. Fortunately, as a war widow herself she got on extremely well with Lady Gough. Both were reassured by what they saw of the couple, and Kittie conducted an intensely empathetic correspondence with Jack Pym at Cambridge. She was possibly the pivotal figure in negotiating the obstacles to what became a long and successful marriage. She postponed yet another projected visit to Percy and Sybil until the wedding was fixed for December 1930, and finally got to Villa Medici in November. As far as is known, she never visited Gallipoli.

Percy Lubbock came to rely on Kittie more and more. They corresponded almost weekly. The vividness of her accounts of life at Foxwold and nearby Quakers, where his mother lived after vacating Emmetts, delighted and sustained him. Kittie was also expert in finding nurses to care for Sybil, who was famously neurotic and often bedridden. In October 1929 Percy wrote to Kittie: 'I do need and shall often need this winter – what I told you before, the kind of support that your presence would give me – just your presence (I don't mean that I should cast my cares *on* you).' Later, they made what he called 'a pact' that if he could not cope, he would telegram her and she would leave for Italy immediately.

Here, then, were two considerably younger men to whom Kittie was a full-time counsellor. Her experience and emotional intelligence were welcomed by many. She also provided monthly financial assistance to her half-great-niece Rose Foster in Dublin and her widowed niece Mary Dakin in Australia. She was intimately involved in her god-daughter Lesbia's recovery from a miscarriage in 1931 and was at Catherine Lubbock's side in her final illness (she died in 1934).

Such activities took Kittie away from Sheet. She retained great affection for the Lubbocks at Adhurst St Mary and she became best friends with

Sophie Malcolm, the wife of a retired surgeon who in 1929 moved into Sheet House in the village itself. 'With a house of that size', writes local historian Vaughan Clarke, 'they would have been the wealthiest residents of Sheet.' But there is no evidence that Kittie was still involved in the community as a whole. By now she may have regarded it as artificial and conflicted. The village's Early English church had been built in 1868 and exogenous residents preponderated over villagers. There were especially many navy and army officers of a kind that Kittie did not like. Although she was a Hamilton and the widow of a war hero, her house was modest. In a later memoir, she even described Hampshire as 'my prison'.

Rather as in 1915 after George's 'disappearance', Kittie now left Elizabeth Ellis to mind Kay's Crib whilst she herself wandered. Between April and August 1933 she stayed at Foxwold and Quakers at least four times. Judging by a letter from Percy Lubbock of 19 October 1933, she had now broken with Sheet altogether and was living with, or near, George's sister Margie at Cuckfield in Sussex. On 19 December 1933 Lesbia wrote to her from the marital home on Lake Como: 'I do love you so much [...] and I'm most worried about you as I don't know how you are or where you are or anything. Have you got a house and where will you be for Christmas?' According to the Visitors Book, she was not at Foxwold. Between January and September 1934, however, she stayed there two months, and after that went to live with the widowed Kathleen Skipwith (née LLoyd) in Hove.

Sometime in 1933, it seems, Kittie had devised a brilliant plan. Her brother John Pakenham Hamilton and his wife Sarah had moved to Ashford in Kent to be close to their eldest son, Edward, who managed a local estate. It was probably Edward who drew Kittie's attention to Kennington, a mile or so from the centre of Ashford and only forty from Foxwold. Kennington was an authentic village (with a twelfth-century church). Kittie found a building plot here 'in a cornfield', as she put it, but within walking distance of the village, and she asked Jack Pym, now a qualified architect, to build a house for her on it, to be called 'White Raven'. She moved into it from Hove in November 1934, when George's *Perdican and Camilla* was revived at the Fortune Theatre, London.

The three-bedroomed white house looked simple and modern, with its black outside doors and black metal window-frames, blockhouse garage at the west end and loggia behind, but the deep enveloping roof in pinkish tiles was an unmistakable Arts and Crafts touch. The name 'White Raven' referred, of course, to the sobriquet Nina had given Kittie – although few knew that. It was perhaps a statement of being comfortable now with who she was. Friends liked the house's name and Roland Pym's painting of the Corvid above the front door.

In spring 1935 Kittie set about planting a very spacious garden on the south side of the house. Helen Lubbock supplied her with roses, Percy and Sybil with a ceanothus, and friends with much else. Through Edward Hamilton, Kittie met the families of two partners in the important Ashford firm of estate agents and auctioneers, Burrows Clements and Winch. The Burrowses attended the same church as Kittie, St Mary's Kennington, the Clements family lived round the corner from her, and they and her nearest neighbours were very supportive. She seems to have hosted at least one meeting of the Women's Institute at White Raven, and may have given talks about George. In 1930, incidentally, she had commissioned a silverpoint 'portrait' of him from the young artist Arnold Pienne and presented it to Trinity College. It was a portrait of George as a post-Edwardian. Pienne had softened the assertiveness of Hollyer's original photograph, and the combination of silverpoint with a creamy paper gave it an ethereal quality (Fig. 24). Kittie described it to Trinity's President Blakiston as 'delightful' and kept a facsimile of it by her.

At Kennington she was regularly visited by her brother and his wife, godchildren, friends and relatives. Altogether, one has the impression that she became part of a genuine community here. Truth to tell, it was probably her first experience of living amongst middle-class people. They valued and respected her. The name 'White Raven' had proved auspicious.

Kittie continued, as a friend put it, to 'do good by stealth'. She not only carried on sending Mary Dakin five pounds a month in Australia, in her Will of October 1935 she made Mary (without telling her) her sole residuary legatee. She got her solicitor to draw up a further provision for Rose Foster in Eire. In 1937 an Australian first cousin once removed,

Nancy Lang, came to England for medical treatment and lived with Kittie for two months. Kittie supported innumerable charitable causes. Sometimes she was taken advantage of. In December 1935, for instance, she lent a fishmonger's roundsman seventy-five pounds (four thousand five hundred at today's prices!) and never saw it again. If a friend was ill or in trouble, Kittie's instinct was to rush to their side. When, in March 1937, she received a note from Sophie Malcolm to say that her husband had died that morning, Kittie 'suddenly', as she expressed it in her diary, left to be with her, arriving in Sheet at 10.30 p.m. More than ever, Kittie's was a life of giving herself to others.

Fig. 24 Portrait of George Calderon by Arnold Pienne, 1930

She promoted George's works whenever she could. Isabel Fry suggested that the young Slavist Fritz Epstein, a refugee from Nazi Germany who had settled in the United States, might be interested in seeing George's research for the *magnum opus*. Epstein wrote to Kittie on 29 May 1938: 'I should be very glad indeed if I can be of any assistance to you in fructifying these materials for the benefit of Slavonic philology and folklore.' It seems possible that the papers were got to him in Cambridge, Massachusetts. However, despite the fact that Epstein himself became a distinguished Curator of Slavic Collections at Stanford and Indiana Universities, no trace of them can be found today. In the theatre, whilst there were doubtless many amateur productions of George's one-acters, professional interest focussed on his Chekhov translations.

Kittie also had her worries. Now in her early seventies, she suffered from serious eye-problems and was prone to falling asleep without warning. This was diagnosed as chronic exhaustion. But in November 1938 she had an unspecified accident that left her concussed. After spending New Year at Foxwold, she wrote in her diary of how during her stay she would fall asleep for three or four hours whilst undressing, wake up, finally get to bed 'at perhaps 5 or 6', then sleep till mid-day. She prayed 'nightly for return of "grip" after Prayer for Peace'. She followed national and international politics closely and after Hitler's invasion of Czechoslovakia in March 1939 she remarked in her diary 'Atrocious' and actually wrote out her prayer. She was also depressed by the drop in her income from the Ripley Trust following the economic slump. However, she could sell jewels, had a large amount of silver deposited in her bank, and received legacies.

To take Kittie's mind off all this, in July 1939 Louise Rosales organised a motoring holiday in Ireland. It culminated in a visit to Kittie's birthplace, St Ernan's Island in Donegal. On arriving at the causeway, they alighted to contemplate the memorial tablet to John Hamilton that Kittie had commissioned from Eric Gill in 1916. They spent the night as guests of the owners of the house that Kittie's father built on the island in 1826:

O so wonderful [...] The sound of the lapping sea – and the sea birds crying – my earliest memories. Louise slept in old <u>night</u> nursery, I in the old <u>Nursery</u> – door open between. This nice plan made me feel <u>in</u> both rooms. Impossible to describe sensation – beyond all words. How I do thank Louise for bringing me home and God for allowing it to actually happen.

Seven weeks later, the war that Kittie's generation dreaded so much broke out. Her god-daughter Lesbia barely made it across Europe by train to Paris with her four-year-old son, and thence to the Stewart estate of St Fort in Fife.

Fig. 25 Kittie Calderon and Bunty at White Raven, 1936/1937

The war was the most dangerous and debilitating time of Kittie's life. Realising very quickly that Ashford would be in the front line, Lesbia invited her to St Fort to help manage refugee children, whilst Raymond Dereume, one of the Calderons' Belgian refugees in 1914 and now an American businessman, invited Kittie to live with him and his family in Pittsburgh. She gracefully declined both, so Dereume sent her food parcels. It seems that both Kittie and Elizabeth Ellis were determined to stay at White Raven as an act of defiance.

When war was declared, Kittie's German neighbours on one side were interned and their house was occupied by the military. In June 1940 the Battle of Britain began, followed by the Blitz, which targeted Ashford as a railway hub. The racket above White Raven from dogfights and bombers was so great that, as Kittie wrote Percy, she and Elizabeth would 'sit in the kitchen laughing together' as they were 'bounced into the air by the shocks overhead'. Percy and Sybil escaped from Villa Medici to Montreux just days before Mussolini declared war on 10 June 1940. In August Alfred Burrows launched an appeal in Kennington to raise £1000 for the YMCA, who ran a Services Club at Ashford station and a mobile canteen covering a wide area. Kittie's response, it seems, was to offer the rights for an amateur production of George's *Cherry Orchard*, with all proceeds to the appeal. In September Kittie was badly affected by the death of Constance Sutton. The bright spot of 1940, however, was that she was able to attend Lesbia's marriage in London on 2 November to her second husband, Captain (later Admiral of the Fleet) Charles Lambe, whom Kittie adored.

Personal travel involving petrol had now become difficult, and in March 1940 Kittie paid her last recorded visit to Foxwold. However, after a Heinkel 111 bomber crash-landed at Kennington in a nearby field on 11 May 1941, it seems Kittie was able to take a 'holiday' in a guest-house at Hythe, twelve miles away. But this was technically on the front line and the owners vacated it not long afterwards to avoid shelling from across the Channel!

If Kittie's sleep pattern had been erratic before the war, the air raids destroyed it completely. There was such a shortage of coal that in any case Kittie and Elizabeth took to their beds in the daytime to keep warm. Kittie spent the evening and much of the night wrapped in a travelling rug going through all her and George's papers, sometimes accompanied by her nephew Edward. She segregated manuscripts and letters that were to be burned after her death, labelled over 500 photographs, and even annotated some of the letters that were to survive. She also wrote incessantly. The number of her correspondents was already large, but when she was writing to people like Percy and Lesbia her pen ran away with her. Her failing eyesight sometimes turned these letters into what she called 'tangled skeins'. Parts of her letters to Lesbia detailed – with unimpaired accuracy – aspects of their shared family history, or events in Archie's and George's lives. They were tantamount to memoirs and have been invaluable to the present writer. Particularly interesting is her denunciation of the Victorian era. Watching the 'Little Old Lady' and her 'Procession of Princes' at the Jubilee of 1887, Kittie had been suddenly overcome by a 'sense of Portent' that 'such might and splendour could not last':

What then was the matter? <u>Money</u>. It <u>is</u> the root of all evil once it becomes respected for itself. It was the stumbling block of the Victorian Age – both <u>of the Rich and of the Poor alike</u>. And why? Because <u>on it selfishness thrives</u>, sowing false standards which are accepted and easily attracting younger people to the cheaper type of thought.

Increasingly housebound, she needed to *converse*, if only on paper. Her wartime correspondence, her memoir-fragments, her annotations on photographs and letters, were her dialogue with a lifetime's friends, loved ones, even perhaps a biographer. Her G.P. told Louise Rosales: 'If <u>only</u> Mrs Calderon would sleep at night and <u>get up</u> and do her writing by day' her whole health would benefit, including the chronic gastric problem that Kittie nicknamed 'the Curse'.

She had thought long ago about who might look after her in old age. This is probably what lay behind leaving White Raven to Mary Dakin in her Will. In 1936 she invited Mary to live with her, but her niece, then forty-eight, would not leave Australia and her daughter. Kittie therefore changed her Will, leaving White Raven to Lesbia, and in 1941 pursued a different idea. Elizabeth Ellis was seventy-two and herself beset with health problems. Kittie proposed that Elizabeth retire, and her half-great-niece Rose Foster come to live with her and 'do'. Evey Pym and others firmly advised against this: Rose had psychological problems and owing to a genealogical quirk was seventy herself. Rose was desperate to be provided for by Kittie in this way, but wartime restrictions would not permit her to leave Eire. Kittie's 'valued old servant', as she described Elizabeth Ellis in a codicil, therefore stayed on at White Raven.

In June 1944 the flying bomb attacks started. Up to a hundred a day roared overhead and Ashford became the worst-hit area after London. On

25 October John Pakenham Hamilton's wife died. After the funeral, his sons invited him to live with them, but he would not move from Ashford. The most he would agree to was for Kittie and Elizabeth to go and stay with him for a few days. They duly left White Raven on 1 November. Shortly afterwards, a flying bomb came down in the back garden. It blew half the tiles off White Raven and the ceilings collapsed onto Kittie's and Elizabeth's beds. There is little doubt that they would have been killed if they had been there. In the New Year Kittie's brother sold up and went to live with his son Edward in Nottinghamshire, which Edward himself had moved to in 1942.

As Kittie went into 1945, then, all her plans for care in her old age had come to nothing. Lesbia and her husband again invited her to live with them in Fife, but Kittie's doctor opposed it.

Through no fault of her own, she was also having cash-flow problems. The manager of her bank in Ashford suffered a breakdown, during which he switched the monthly payment of her pension into government war loans, so that at one point she was the equivalent of £25,000 overdrawn. Louise Rosales became extremely concerned at the bank manager's apparent attempt to take over the running of Kittie's financial affairs completely and advised her to ask her trusted solicitor, Mackarness of Petersfield, to step in. At the same time, Kittie's gastric complaint prevented her, as she put it to Lesbia, from going 'further than the front gate', and Elizabeth Ellis was also often housebound. When cheques arrived totalling today's equivalent of £2227 for royalties on a production of *The Seagull* that opened at Birmingham Repertory Theatre on 15 May 1945, Kittie's agent Joseph Williams complained about her not paying them in.

Nevertheless, as the news spread that Kittie had been 'blitzed', friends from all over the country rallied round. Louise Rosales, who lived at the Connaught Hotel in London, regularly visited her, as did Nancy Knox (*née* Lang), who was working in Britain. Throughout 1945 there was a steady flow of letters to and from White Raven. Kittie continued to wrestle with Rose Foster's problems, and was now making monthly payments to her sister Mary in Belfast as well. The war in Europe ended in May. Mrs Clements took Kittie in her car to vote in the General Election.

Percy Lubbock could now return to Italy, but without Sybil, who had died in December 1943. Kittie had wanted to fly to Switzerland to stand by Percy as agreed, but it was militarily impossible. Still in Montreux, Percy closed his letter to her of 10 October 1945: 'I was thinking lately how much your letters have done for me and given me first and last, in my life abroad.'

Then suddenly Kittie's dialogue breaks off. Nothing written by her or to her is known after 2 January 1946. Sometime that year her health must have deteriorated drastically. Perhaps she had a stroke, but there is no independent evidence of that. Elizabeth Ellis still lived with her and helped out. As Kittie's attorney, Louise Rosales arranged home care with the help of Kittie's doctor, the church, and neighbours. However, in December 1947 both Kittie and Elizabeth moved to Brighton for sustained professional care. Most of White Raven's furniture was put in store; the house was cleared; papers for burning were sent to Mackarness; the rest were sent to Lesbia; the house was let.

It is possible that at first Kittie and Elizabeth lived with Kathleen Skipwith at 'Milldean', Dyke Road Avenue, Hove, then moved to 72 Pembroke Crescent. But on 3 September 1948 Elizabeth died at Lee House, a nursing home at 12 Dyke Road, and by January 1950 Kittie had also moved there. Lesbia and Charles Lambe visited her in the middle of that month. Lesbia reported to Edward Hamilton that Kittie was 'very frail of course and rather wandering, but was so pleased to see us and she still had that wonderful sparkling laugh'. Kittie died peacefully at Lee House on 30 January 1950, in her eighty-third year.

As we might expect, she had made her own funeral arrangements long before. Announcements in *The Times* of 31 January and 1 February described her as 'daughter of the late John Hamilton, of St Ernan's, Co. Donegal, widow of Archie Ripley and of George Calderon'. The cremation was to be 'private', with 'Please, no flowers'. Although Lesbia came down to London immediately, she could not attend because of an attack of bronchitis, nor could Edward Hamilton. The service took place in Hove, with Louise Rosales, Kathleen Skipwith and Nancy Knox present, and probably members of the Hamilton and Pym families.

At Kittie's request, her ashes were scattered. Where, nobody knows.

Who George Calderon Was

> Temper your sharpness, disentangle your
> ideas, moderate your brilliancy, live in
> harmony with your age. This is being in
> conformity with the principle of Tao. Such a
> man is impervious alike to favour and
> disgrace, to benefits and injuries, to honour
> and contempt.
>
> Laozi

Kittie's was a 'good' death in more senses than one. In April 1939, after listening to a radio production by Val Gielgud that attempted to give a balanced account of the Gallipoli campaign, she had written in her diary: 'At long last.' What would she have made, then, of the rubbishing of the First World War in the early 1960s by Alan Clark, Joan Littlewood, and even an establishment historian, A.J.P. Taylor, who in David Reynolds's words implied that 'there was nothing to choose between the two sides and [...] the only fault of the Germans was to have lost'? Furthermore, the new 'kitchen sink' drama specifically targeted Edwardian values, the Edwardian military, and the whole 'romantic picture', as Jimmy Porter called it in *Look Back in Anger*, of 'the Edwardian brigade's brief little world of high summer'. The theatrical revolution also rubbished Edwardian plays – with the exception of Shaw's. When George's version of *The Seagull* was produced at the Lyric, Hammersmith, in 1949 with Paul Scofield as Treplev and Mai Zetterling as Nina, it was attacked for its brisk pace, which reviewers identified with Edwardian drawing-room drama; what they wanted was the slow, 'poetic' playing of Chekhov that afflicted British productions in the 1950s and 60s. George's translations went out of fashion therefore in the theatre, but his version of *The Seagull* maintained its place on radio from 1942 to 1966 precisely because it practised an Edwardian economy with stage time. On the other hand, not one of George's own plays was performed in London between 1940 and 1960. The general passing of deference for the Edwardian period was symbolised by the removal of Captain Scott from Madame Tussaud's to make way for the Beatles.

But the critical evaluation of George Calderon's personality and achievement had begun long before. To venture an opinion in the twenty-first century on who George 'was', it is vital to follow this process of evaluation by journalists, critics, and George's friends alike.

Even the brief notices of George's disappearance that newspapers published through the summer of 1915 were surprisingly uncertain in focus and tone. Nearly all identified him as 'the Slavonic scholar' and a dramatist. *London Opinion* noted that he was 'the first British playwright to appear in the casualty list' and the *Daily Sketch* believed 'the literary world could ill spare him'. Mention of his 'versatility', however, was the cue for some to remark on the 'eccentricity' of its political manifestations:

He was always breaking out in some fresh and generally rather original direction, as, for example, when he tried to start a Consumer's League to combat the rise in prices, and during the last great coal strike stumped the university towns to advocate the amusing scheme of working the mines with voluntary armies of undergraduates. He was, besides, secretary of the Men's League for Opposing Women's Suffrage. In fact, you might call George Calderon a cheery reactionary whose irresponsibilities were balanced by an occasional flash of insight.

In the circumstances, this comment from the *Manchester Guardian* of 16 July 1915 seems extraordinarily flippant, but no more so than the *Daily Sketch*'s 'he is a quiet, genial man, a good conversationalist, and – looks like Alfred Lester' (a music hall comedian), or the *TLS*'s description of George as a 'playboy'.

When George's death was confirmed in 1919, the tone of the published and private tributes was deeply respectful, but their content was understandably influenced by their context. 'That which the theatre has suffered cannot, of course, be estimated, but that it is a heavy one is certain', wrote William Caine in a letter to the *Manchester Guardian*. Had George lived, he 'must soon have been among the first of our playwrights.

He died at the very moment when his powers were ripe for the fulfilment of their promise'. Whether Caine had seen George's latest, unpublished short plays, or his libretti for Fokine, we do not know, but he offers no evidence for his assertions. The real emphasis of Caine's letter was, of course, on George's altruism: 'This war, for him, was a crusade; in this cause no sacrifice – not the last – could be other than a joy. It is to this spirit in Calderon – and in how many others! – that England owes her life. He is content – and they.' Percy Lubbock's obituary of George ended on the same note. The most interesting variation, however, was the suggestion that his willed death was the true fulfilment of his activism in the rest of his life. In his (unpublished) tribute Laurence Binyon did not baulk at stating that there was 'no little of the Don Quixote' in George's blood, but that he 'seemed born for a life of action' and 'heroic action claimed him in the end', whilst in his (partly published) tribute G.F. Bradby wrote that the various causes George had fought for denied him 'the opportunity for heroic and decisive action' but 'when he vanished into the smoke of battle, we know that his heart was satisfied for he had at last found the Great Cause for which a Paladin can fight and die'.

When Kittie began to receive the memoirs from George's friends that she had invited for the compilation of Percy's book, she must have been struck by the conflicting diversity of their impressions. They did not even agree on George's complexion: for Newbolt it was 'brown', for H.C. Bradby his 'colouring' was 'striking', for Masefield George's face was 'rather pale', for Sturge Moore it was 'swarthy'. Arthur Lowry, George's old college friend and flatmate in London, wrote of him as someone inexhaustibly patient with every fool and bounder: 'He had the faculty of seeing and drawing out what was good in a man to such an extent that the bad was altogether obscured. In fact he was full of charity.' For the social historian Lawrence Hammond, George's wit was 'fundamentally good tempered, without any suspicion of malice or sourness'. Herbert Blakiston, in 1907 elected President of Trinity College, Oxford, would hardly have agreed with either memoirist after George's caricature of him as the Junior Fellow in *Downy V. Green*, and as we have seen, in suffragist and political circles George had a reputation for nastiness. Even Percy Lubbock referred to his 'rich gift of anger'. Several memoirists hinted at the existence of what George himself had called his 'blue devil days', yet Harold Dowdall was 'certain that Calderon kept his cheerfulness for his friends, and his times of depression for himself'; his mind was 'quick and alert and ready for any adventure or enterprise, and incurably optimistic'. Masefield felt that 'to be charming and nice to others, with a ready and pleasant mind [...] used more of him than any of his other interests', but Kittie commented to Percy: 'This of course is quite wrong.' For Sturge Moore and his children George had always seemed 'at leisure' and Coote Hedley was 'under the impression that he took life rather easily' (a 'playboy'?); but Moore came to realise 'what a profound and hard-working scholar he was' and 'on the outbreak of war' Hedley 'discovered my mistake'.

The memoir that most frankly expressed George's contradictions, yet balanced them finely in a whole that could not cause offence, was Laurence Binyon's. Closely written, much corrected, and covering three large manuscript pages, it presented memories and generalisations in a chronological narrative, which had the advantage that none of Binyon's judgements seemed final, only relative. Thus he could write of George as an undergraduate:

There seemed to be a freakish vein in his mind. Paradox attracted him. [...] All were agreed about his gifts, but no one was confident of the direction in which they would carry him. I confess that at that time I underrated the quality of his mind. He disconcerted me at times by a love of rather perverse ingenuities of argument. I doubted whether he would ever concentrate his powers productively. His dialectical skill seemed rather sterile. But this did not prevent him from being entirely attractive and lovable.

Obviously, although strictly 'time-referenced', this disquisition on George's mind (much longer than I have quoted) invites the question: but was it true later in life as well? There is a feeling that Binyon meant us to speculate on that.

In the 1890s, Binyon discovered 'an inexhaustible kindness of heart' in George and that George was 'nothing if not adventurous' (a point stressed by several memoirists). But Binyon soon returns to his undergraduate theme of George's 'easy brilliance, his versatility'. After 1900, 'one never

knew what fresh subject he might not be engrossed in. Not only subjects
engrossed him, but causes; and in some of these he developed a sort of
fanaticism that seemed incongruous with his charming humour'. When
George began his career as a dramatist, Binyon felt that he had 'found the
true medium for his genius'. 'Often one wished he would concentrate on
that. But how well he did other things! His intellectual curiosity was
unbounded.' Binyon concluded, in fact, that George's versatility was *not*
'shallow'. Stepping out of narrative time, in a long final paragraph he tried
to sum up George's character and qualities, prefacing it with 'George
Calderon was a man whom it took long to know truly, sociable and
accessible though he was':

I seemed always to be discovering something new in him. He had his moods; but
in the mood of radiant and inventive gaiety, finding interest and fun in the
simplest things of life, he seemed most himself. He was perfect at a children's
party. Yet how he revelled in the world of ideas! He was English in many things,
but had a Latin quickness and lucidity of comprehension, a Latin pursuit of logic
to its end in action. Adventurous and fearless, [...] impulsive, wayward, he often
seemed; but one thing was always constant in him, an innate chivalry of mind.
There was nothing soft about him, but nothing cold, either. [...] He was vivid; he
quickened life for all whom he was with. Not till we had lost him did I know to
the full how much I honoured and loved him.

'Did one human body ever hold quite so simple yet quite so complex a
soul?' Kittie asked in her own memoirs, written only for Percy's eyes, and
she must have felt that Binyon had conveyed some of that complexity.

Understandably, when Binyon came to write his ode to George's
memory he focussed on George's positive qualities. One of these Kittie felt
bound to query. In its first draft, the opening lines read 'Wisdom and
Valour, Faith, | Justice and Temperance – names | Of virtue's quest and
prize'. On 31 August 1920, the day after receiving Binyon's manuscript at
Brinsop Court, Kittie wrote to him:

Was George 'temperate'? It's very difficult for he certainly was not what one
means by 'intemperate' – but but [sic] there was a swift white heat about him that
with all his gentleness and tenderness burnt things up without hesitation – I
wonder if you know what I mean in him – I cannot find any words that exactly

express it – – neither did it always burn up – it was sometimes a driving force – – – whatever he did he did with a sort of passion – – oh – I can't get at it – that sounds exaggerated – but I think you may know what I'm trying for – – it never <u>blinded</u> his justice or integrity – which is so often the effect of this quality I think – yet it <u>did</u> burn up.

Binyon changed the lines in his next draft to: 'Wisdom and Valour, Faith', | Justice – the lofty names | Of virtue's quest and prize.'

In her own memoirs, very diplomatically, Kittie describes behaviour that does strike one as intemperate. She and George 'occasionally had fearful heated battles' over things in the newspaper:

They weren't just battles of words. I always felt and still feel he <u>sometimes</u> prevented people [from] seeing the truth of what he was upholding by being too violent. He did not mind it when I said it in that sort of way in quiet talk. But when suddenly it took tangible form over some question in the paper – we clashed and banged – and he would for the moment hate me and not care one scrap how much he hurt by refusing to see the grains of sense there might be among my mushiness – and I would become furious and despairing.

'Hate me' is strong, and Kittie explains at some length that George apologised – was 'almost child-likely "sorry"' – but only when he had convinced himself that he had reached the wrong 'verdict' about the subject in the first place. Yet in his letters of 1898-99 to Kittie George himself admitted he could be 'brutal', 'a monster', 'peevish', 'blunt', 'not an admirable character; very weak; ready to take, having nothing to give'.

With the benefit of long hindsight, we can see that many of the apparently conflicting features of George Calderon's character and life are quintessentially typical of the Edwardian male. The arrogant nastiness that the latter was prone to was surely the product of an elite education and the confidence of Empire ('never complain, never explain' was the mantra). In Peter Brent's words, 'for the pre-1914 British, chauvinism was the cement which held the social fabric together'; and their social cantankerousness probably derived from that. It could, of course, be accompanied by charm and perfect manners. As Kittie wrote, if George's human surroundings were 'congenial' he would 'expand and blossom'. Similarly, George's lifelong passion for games and sport was natural in a

Rugbeian and Oxfordian of his generation, and his belief in sporting amateurism wholly to be expected of an Edwardian 'gentleman'. His love of 'Adventure' and his need for heroic action are very characteristic of the times; some might say that his actions in 1915 show that he suffered from a 'Scott Complex'. His polymathery and tendency to work himself into 'nervous prostration' were typical of the age, too. Perhaps they were not unconnected with a life of private income, servants, and massive wage inequality. Even George's self-financed activism in political and social causes was not as unusual as it may strike us today, for as Paul Thompson has written: 'Innumerable unknown Edwardians gave their life's enthusiasm to the creation of a better society; a higher proportion, I suspect, than at any other time in Britain.'

However, by the time that *Tahiti*, Lubbock's *Sketch*, and the volumes of George's plays had come out in the early 1920s, the Edwardian age was past. Many reviewers no longer remembered the full syndrome, as it were, of the Edwardian personality. Others were downright mystified by it. Lubbock, wrote the *Glasgow News*, had shown 'a strange, brilliant creature who [...] did a number of brilliant things vividly'. 'Before his death', the *Queen* wrote curiously, George had 'led a dispersed and rather disappointing career', and his 'political adventures' were 'fantastic'. A common thread was that he was 'greatly gifted', 'many-sided', 'a splendid influence', 'remarkably versatile', but it was 'too much, indeed, to allow him to achieve greatness in any single branch of activity' (*Glasgow Evening News*). What could one make of it all? 'Were they all romantics at heart, those figures of the Dramatic Renascence that came before the war and withered at its blast?' asked the *Manchester Guardian*. In 1921 a reviewer of the younger generation, Edgell Rickword, could understand George only as 'that valuable anomaly, a romantic with a passion to see clearly' (*New Statesman*).

But by far the commonest contention was that George Calderon was 'an amateur'. Harold Child in *The Times* may have described his death as 'the heaviest blow which struck the English drama during the war', but a week later in the *TLS* he conceded that 'it is possible to look upon Calderon as a brilliant amateur'. For the reviewer of *Eve* George's loss was 'incalculable to the British drama'; for the *London Mercury* his short plays were 'the work of an amateur'; for the *Observer* there was 'a certain quality of the amateur' in his dramatic work; for Rickword again, George was 'the amateur of modern drama'.

This takes us, I believe, to the heart of the question of who Calderon 'was'. His post-contemporaries definitely tended to use the word 'amateur' pejoratively, yet how could they call someone a genius and an amateur at the same time? No reviewer I have read seemed to notice this contradiction and attempt to resolve it. Indeed, hardly anyone defined what they meant by 'amateur', presumably because they did not feel they needed to. The *Saturday Review* ennumerated George's many activities – translating Chekhov and Tolstoi, being a Russian scholar and dramatist, holding 'unfashionable views on socialism' – and suggested that 'all this pointed to a wandering talent and a fugitive individualism', but no-one explicitly linked his versatility, i.e. polymathery, with his being an 'amateur', for if they had they would presumably have reached for the word 'dilettante', which none of them did. True, the young Rickword (who seemed almost obsessed with the 'enigma' of Calderon and wrote some of the longest and most penetrating reviews of him) came to the conclusion that 'Calderon wrote as he lived, as though it were not his trade, but his hobby', yet Rickword's imputation of 'amateurism' was the exception, presumably because it was generally recognised that George's *versatility* had not prevented him from attaining *excellence*, for example in *Tahiti*, his long plays, and his Chekhov translations. As Binyon stressed, 'his was no shallow versatility'. However, some reviewers voiced their criticisms of George's works in terms that did suggest why they regarded him as an 'amateur'. For the *London Mercury* George wrote 'always to amuse himself and never with the final seriousness of the artist'; he 'never penetrated deep enough into his subjects to be excited about them: he was excited only by what he was doing with them'. In other words, he practised the *superficiality* of the supposed amateur.

The most sustained attempt to grapple with George's writing was published in the *Glasgow News* of 27 July 1922 and entitled 'Water and Wine: Art and the Intellectuals'. Its unnamed author was profoundly unsettled by his perception that modern art (Bernard Shaw, Jacob Epstein and Wyndham Lewis are mentioned) exemplified the 'predominance of pure intellect over emotion, feeling, sentiment, colour, call it what you like'. This 'thesis', he explains,

occurs to me now purely in relation to the case of George Calderon, a man of genius, who yet left behind him only a collection of incomplete and not particularly impressive works. What seems worth while establishing is the theory – as exemplified in Calderon – that pure intelligence can kill what we call the creative spirit in a man and that the works of the sharply intelligent man are apt to be *jeux d'esprit* rather than the products of cosmic conviction. That, in other words, there is a tremendous gulf between pure genius and pure intelligence.

For this writer, George's plays were 'not great plays. But they suggest, somehow, that their writer was a great man, whose talents were dissipated by the strength of his critical faculties'. Thus *The Fountain* was 'a tract, almost a polemic. It touches the fuzzy realities of life only here and there'. Technically, 'Calderon was a first-rate dramatist; but he was not a humane artist. He could feel – we know on direct evidence [*Tahiti*] – as warmly as anybody; when he took his pen in hand, the hard, critical intelligence prevailed.' *Revolt* was 'a thesis with an eminently human moral, but it is still a thesis, a coldish brittle thing'. George's was 'not a metallic intelligence like Shaw's; it was more gently humorous and whimsical; but it was always concerned more with theories than actualities'.

If we think of *Dwala*, or *The Fountain*, these aspersions may ring true – although plays such as *Derelicts, Parkin Bros.* or *The Lamp* are surely the works of a humane writer. But what really strikes one in this and other reviews of the early 1920s is the shift in feeling and values since the war. The rationalism, cleverness, paradox and 'fun' of the Edwardians were no longer enough, in fact they were wrong: what post-war Britons wanted was a 'life and death' engagement with reality, with 'emotion, feeling, sentiment, colour', with 'actualities' rather than ideas. It is not difficult to see what experience had brought the 'new' values into being. Edgell Rickword's description of George could have been of the archetypal Edwardian officer: 'He had a strong, wilful character, but a narrow and rather small mind.' As Asquith thought Sir Ian Hamilton had 'too much feather in his brain', so Rickword, who was soon to join the Communist Party, thought George was 'overweighted with moral and intellectual bagage'. Behind the new 1920s emphasis on professionalism and specialism lay the perceptions of Edwardian crass 'amateurism' at Gallipoli and the Somme.

Nevertheless, the post-war critical dialogue about who George Calderon was did not produce a consensus. The reason hardly any post-war reviewer defined what they meant by 'amateur' was that in fact they had largely carried its meaning over from the Edwardian age and strangely respected it. An Edwardian 'amateur' could embody the highest standards in an activity, for example cricket and exploration; it was still not an unambiguously pejorative word. Thus in 1922 *The Times* could remark rather subtly that it might be possible to regard George as an amateur, but 'a man's work is not necessarily the worse because it is a parergon', i.e. subsidiary to his main employment, and *The Observer* even acknowledged that 'for his generation at any rate' George's 'quality of the amateur' in his dramatic work 'does not enfeeble it, but adds a curious individual spontaneity'. It was the perceived superficiality and inefficiency of the Edwardians' programmatic *versatility*, their 'we British can do everything' attitude, that had become denigrated by the 1920s. Yet even this did not work when applied to Calderon: if you thought his plays second-rate, you still had his non-fiction *Tahiti* which wasn't; if Harold Child thought these works were 'all that is left of a fine spirit and a fine brain', William Lyon Phelps could object that George's Introduction to his Chekhov translations was 'the most subtle and penetrating essay on the Russian dramatist that I have seen anywhere'. Finally, George might have left 'only a collection of incomplete and not particularly impressive works' displaying a brittle 'pure intelligence', as the *Glasgow News* reviewer put it, but even for the latter he remained 'a man of genius'. How, one is bound to ask, could this be?

A century after the passing of the Edwardian period we can, I think, dissociate its faults from the Great War, understand its ethos more clearly, and appreciate its values more positively.

The all-pervading impulse of the period was diversity. As Samuel Hynes has written, Queen Victoria's long tenure resulted in 'an ossification of authority that encased and cramped the new: the *forms* of values had become the values; institutions had become more important than the ideas they embodied'. The result under Edward VII was an *explosion* of ideas. There has never been a period in the life of Britain when democratic discourse was as vibrant, exciting and individualistic as 1901-1914; under the Liberals, it very nearly blew the country apart. The Edwardians' discovery of pluralism, versatility, polymathery, Adventure, heroism, style and mass entertainment, was part and parcel of that discourse, and in this context even their belief in the 'amateur' was a force for good. George Calderon saw the amateur as subverting the imitative, received and established in art. Of the 'amateur' women writers Ross and Somerville, for instance, he wrote (not knowing their gender) that he rejoiced 'at the coming of an amateur with all his [her] artistic innocence and the smack of real life, from which he [she] emerges'. With *Dwala* he could be said to have subverted the novel of the Aesthete establishment, with *The Fountain* the play of the Fabian establishment. His determination to remain a (technically professional) 'amateur' placed him outside all literary establishments, or as Percy Lubbock called them, 'schools', and may account for George's exclusion from the establishment narrative of Edwardian literature ever since. Moreover, although the introduction of Ibsen's plays to the British theatre was a part of the left-wing establishment's cultural narrative, the introduction of Chekhov's plays was not. George was always to some extent an amateur 'outsider' and this was probably reinforced by perceptions that he was not actually English. In complete contrast, the young Percy Lubbock passionately desired to be part of the Jamesian establishment and regarded even Mary Cholmondeley as a 'devoted amateur' incapable of bringing to a novel 'the straight cool understanding of a craftsman'. As a littérateur George sought innovation, not craft guild production. He therefore comes across in Percy's book about him as an amateur whose oeuvre, in the words of Percy's 1927 *Dictionary of National Biography* entry, was 'always to some extent hampered by his great versatility'. The war poets themselves were regarded by this particular cultural establishment as amateurs.

However, it would be a serious misapprehension to assume that George Calderon effortlessly sailed into a fulfilled life of versatility and professional amateurship. In Russia he had decided to embark on a single, academic career, concentrating on Russian literature, folklore and anthropology. Back in Britain he pursued this by applying for the Cambridge lectureship. But he frankly admitted to Kittie in the same year that he felt 'too practical to be academic, too academic to be practical'. He was torn in these two directions, then, but by 1899 he was also a published creative writer and torn in that direction. The first conflict seemed to be resolved by giving up for good the idea of an academic career. He took a practical job at the British Museum, but still did scholarly research, and he wrote fiction. This three-way strain also proved too great. After his nervous breakdown and convalescence on Tahiti, he stopped writing scholarly articles, took up reviewing for the *TLS*, and felt his way to satisfying his practical talents in theatre, politics, and eventually war. Thus his 'versatility', which now looks so typically Edwardian, was actually an arduous personal journey that had taken in several blind alleys such as his etymological anthropology, his 'universal language', and Biblical exegesis. His 'career' was hard won. Moreover, it contained two paths that were practically unbroken: writing for the stage, and contributing to the daily and periodical press

If George's belief in the amateur, his love of sport, travel, Adventure, 'visiting' and 'café life', and even his cantankerousness and depression, were thoroughly Edwardian, so was his passion for exploring other cultures and philosophies. Here too were pluralism, new knowledge, fresh inspiration. When George decided to involve himself in democracy on the streets, he was similarly original and innovative: he saw beyond Capital, Labour and class warfare, beyond the ineffectual Liberal consensus of his day, *beyond* suffragism and anti-suffragism, to a modern Communitarian centrism. He was open to the newness, the un-Englishness, of Chekhov, modern ballet, and Post-Impressionist painting. He accomplished a remarkable journey from the extreme maleness of his Victorian education to a new empathy that flowered in his war experience (let us recall that he actually used the expressions 'to feel your feelings' and 'emotional intelligence', and Kittie wrote of him 'never did I come across anyone so sensitive to his human surroundings').

The only known manuscript of a Calderon play was discovered in the final stages of writing this book. It is of George's collaboration with William Caine, the 'Musical Play' *The Brave Little Tailor* from 1914. It is

207 pages long and the final typescript 134 pages long! It reads as the epitome of Edwardian humour, of what they understood by 'fun': interminable facetiousness, campery, paradox, slapstick, word play and lively rhymes. It certainly strikes one today as irremedially 'amateur' in the sense of done for the authors' own enjoyment (as Caine put it, it was 'a bit of fun with Calderon' and 'there would be laughter' – for them). But is that merely a po-faced modern response? The humour of this script reminds one of Baden-Powell's injunction to 'smile and whistle under all circumstances'; indeed, it might be a very good Scout pantomime. Perhaps Edwardian 'fun' was a form of defence mechanism or therapy? Perhaps innocuous 'entertainment' that releases endorphins and serotonin was more beneficial, more civilised, than aggressive humour that merely generates testosterone? Perhaps with Edwardian humour it is a case of 'never such innocence again' (Philip Larkin, 'MCMXIV')?

We know today that the self-referential ('Barber') species of paradox that George Calderon favoured was in its set theory form debunked by Bertrand Russell as 'just noise without meaning', and by Ludwig Wittgenstein as 'nonsense'. Yet the *literary* use to which George put his 'pure delight of paradoxes' was far from sterile. As with Oscar Wilde, Bernard Shaw, Bertolt Brecht, or Tom Stoppard, George's paradoxes 'make strange' reality. They question Edwardian assumptions, they operate as 'alienation effects' that make us think – all the while generating laughter's release. Perhaps his typically Edwardian love of paradox was not superficial, but as sane and beneficial as 'fun'. Perhaps in our 'serious' age we can learn from both?

George Calderon, then, was 'in harmony with his age', in fact at the very growing point of his age. But does that make him a 'genius', as he was posthumously agreed to be? Were his powers too dispersed to be a genius? Does polymathery *preclude* genius?

Whilst we may think that the essence of genius is a constant (supreme creative innovative power), the form it takes is not. A genius is always at the sentient core of his/her time; the form of their genius is historical. Hildegard of Bingen and Dante are medieval geniuses, Rabelais and Shakespeare Renaissance geniuses, Darwin and Charlotte Brontë Victorian geniuses. I would contend that *Dwala*, George's essay on Tolstoi, *The*

Fountain, his essay on Chekhov, and *Tahiti*, are touched by genius. But the very essence of the Edwardian age was diversity, versatility, polymathery, and George seems to me the personification of these combined with quality of performance. No-one, not James, say, Shaw, Wells, Masefield or Galsworthy achieved such diversity of such quality. George was the quintessential *Edwardian* genius.

This, I believe, is who George Calderon was. Who he 'is', only the future can tell.

ACKNOWLEDGEMENTS

Many people have contributed to making this book since I first became interested in George Calderon over thirty years ago; they too are its authors. I apologise to any whom I may have omitted from this 'chapter', and would ask them to contact me as soon as possible so that I can make amends, for example on **calderonia.org**, the blog of the project.

Private archives
During the 1970s, Russianists became seriously interested in British citizens who had lived in Russia before the Revolution, including George Calderon. When in the early 1980s I began to research Chekhov's plays on the British stage, several Russianists informed me that there were no Calderon papers in institutional archives and they themselves had been unable to trace any. After drawing a blank with every Calderon in the London telephone directory and the last known addresses of George's siblings, I felt that all I could do was appeal for information on the pages of the *Times Literary Supplement* and *Spectator*.

My appeal in the *Spectator* brought an immediate response from Mr Roland Pym, Kittie Calderon's great-nephew by her first marriage. Roland (Roly) Pym and his brother John (Jack) had known George Calderon as children, and their sister Elizabeth, born in 1914, was his god-daughter. I met all three at the family home of Foxwold in Kent, which George and Kittie had often visited, and they showed me their Calderoniana and shared with me their memories of Kittie. Roly was sure that the Calderons' papers would be in the possession of Lady Petra Lambe, *née* Lesbia Rachel Corbet, who as Kittie's god-daughter and the daughter of her closest friend, Nina Corbet, was Kittie's heir. I am uniquely beholden to Roly and Jack Pym, and their sister Elizabeth Cobb, and I treasure their memory. I shall acknowledge the full extent of my debt to the Pym family below.

In October 1984 I contacted Lady Lambe at Knockhill House on her estate of St Fort in Fife. She enthusiastically welcomed my interest in the

Calderons and invited me to visit her the following year. It can be said without exaggeration that the attic of Knockhill House contained the 'Calderon Papers': nearly a thousand letters from and to George and Kittie, hundreds of documents including Kittie's own memoir of George, water colours by both, and 700 photographs. After Kittie's instructions to burn certain papers had been carried out by her executors, Petra had been adamant that nothing further should be destroyed. The Papers were preserved in her attic exactly as they had been received after 1947, where she occasionally read them. With unfailing kindness, Petra invited me back to sort and catalogue them, and lent me George's letters to his parents from Russia for publication. However, she did even more than that: she told me everything she remembered and felt about George and Kittie in two recorded interviews and continued to correspond with me about fresh memories and archival discoveries.

It is a plain fact that this book would never – *could* never – have been written without Lady Lambe's careful preservation of the Calderon Papers for forty years and her unstinting encouragement. It is fitting, therefore, that the book should be dedicated to her memory.

But my gratitude extends to the next generation of descendants of Nina Corbet as well. Petra died in 1990. When her daughter, Louisa Scherchen, took up residence in Knockhill House, she regularly invited me to view new material that she had discovered, to identify George and Kittie's surviving books in the library at Knockhill House, and to catalogue them (247 volumes). Louisa too has been unfailing in her enthusiasm and support of the project, for which I thank her from the bottom of my heart – as well as for bringing me restorative glasses of whisky and serving Arbroath Smokies for breakfast! I should also mention that she transcribed Nina Corbet's diary of 1890-91, Nina's 'Thoughts and Musings' of 1893-94, her 'Log of the Two Girls and the Boy with the Sailor Hat' (1894), 'The Coming of Age of Sir Roland James Corbet' (1913), and the latter's war diary of 1914, all of which have been invaluable to me in interpreting Kittie's link with the Corbet family. Finally, Louisa allowed me to remove the whole Calderon archive and library to Cambridge for the duration of my writing the biography, which greatly lightened my task, and she has given me complete freedom to quote from the Calderon Papers. Louisa has been the perfect owner of a private archive and I shall never be able to thank her adequately.

I must also thank Louisa's brother, James Lambe, for his readiness to be consulted on family history, for his encouragement, and particularly for unearthing the Visitors Book of Acton Reynald and making its contents available to me. To Lady Lambe's son Andrew Mylius I am obliged for his warm welcome to St Fort, consultation, and drawing my attention to stray items from the Calderons' library. I am deeply indebted to all the grandchildren of Walter and Nina Corbet for permission to quote from their grandparents' papers. I also tender my thanks to David Scherchen for his expert remastering of the tapes of my interviews with Lady Lambe, for his contribution to transcribing Corbet documents, and his always stimulating conversation.

There are no direct descendants of George's parents resident in Britain today. The last was Mrs Joan Tower, the daughter of George's brother Frank. Thanks again to Roland Pym, I was able to contact Mrs Tower in 1984, two years before her death. She was most generous with her memories of her uncle and details of his siblings' histories, all of which have enhanced this book.

In 2011 my indefatigable genealogical researcher Michael Welch traced certain descendants of Kittie's father, 'John Hamilton the Great', on both sides of the Irish Sea. It has been very good to make contact with them and enjoy their company. I am particularly grateful to Mrs Tibs Evans for showing me a document relating to Mary Hamilton, Kittie's mother.

At the same time I also decided to get in touch again with the Pym family. I was serendipitously assisted in this by Professor Laurence Senelick of Tufts University, whose scholarly contribution is recognised in my Bibliography. The way in which Jack Pym's son, John (Johnnie) Pym, dedicated himself to the biography of his grandparents' friends, has been tantamount to having a second research assistant. He dug out letters from George and Kittie to members of his family and painstakingly digitised them for my use. He transcribed all relevant entries from Foxwold's Visitors Book – a key aid to piecing together Kittie's life after May 1915. He and his wife Hope showed me every photograph and book from Foxwold that might interest me. Johnnie has educated me about the gardens of Foxwold and Emmetts, to whose creation Kittie contributed, and never baulked at answering whatever question I fired at him concerning the Pym and Lubbock families. Thus the last two chapters of the book owe more to Johnnie Pym than to anybody else, especially as he is deeply informed about his great-uncle Percy Lubbock. Above all, Johnnie has permitted me to reproduce photographs and quote documents from his family archive, to publish excerpts from Percy Lubbock's writings, to print George's Brasted limerick from the autograph in his possession, and to make copies of the only extant typescripts of George's ballet libretti, which were given to his uncle Roland by Kittie herself. The true expression of my thanks to Johnnie and Hope Pym is our abiding friendship.

Last but by no means least, I thank Katy George, who in 2015 found a significant letter from Kittie inside a book at a charity shop and offered it to the archive.

Archival institutions and libraries

My 1984 appeal in the *Times Literary Supplement* was answered by Paul Sorrell, Reed Rare Books Librarian at City of Dunedin Public Library, New Zealand, who enclosed copies of George's letters of 1898 to the editor of the *Nineteenth Century*. His initiative proved extremely fruitful.

Since then, I have consulted the following archival institutions and libraries and am indebted to them and the persons named for their professional assistance: Bibliothèque Nationale de France; Bodleian Library, University of Oxford (Simon Bailey, Rachael Gardner, Gillian Humphreys); British Library (Peter Hellyer, Helen Melody, Andra Patterson, Katya Rogatchevskaia, Christopher Scobie, Zoe Stansell); Burberry Heritage Archive (Suzanne Doolin); Cambridge University Library (Frank Bowles, Jacqueline Cox, Emily Dourish, Suzanne Paul, Ray Scrivens); Harry Ransom Center, University of Texas at Austin (Anna Chen, Richard Watson); Houghton Library, Harvard University (James Capobianco, Heather Cole, Susan Halpert, Emilie Hardman); Imperial War Museum (Angela Wootton); John Rylands Library, University of Manchester (Fran Baker, Suzanne Fagan, Elizabeth Gow, James

Robinson); Kent History and Library Centre (Patricia Kelly); Leeds Russian Archive (Richard Davies); Liddell Hart Military Archives, King's College, London (Adam Cox); Mary Lago Collection, University of Missouri (Karen Paulik Witt); Merton College, Oxford (Julia Walworth); Mitchell Library, Glasgow (Bernadette Gallacher); National Archives, Kew; National Library of Ireland (James Harte, Caroline Montgomery); Oriel College, Oxford (Robert Petre); Philip Robinson Library, Newcastle University (Lucy Keating, Sam Petty); Princeton University Library Manuscripts Division (Charles E. Greene, AnnaLee Pauls); Royal Academy of Arts (Sidney C. Hutchinson); Royal Commission on Historical Manuscripts (Sonia Anderson, Isabel Kenrick); Royal Regiment of Fusiliers (Royal Warwickshire) Museum (Harry Morton); Rugby School (Rusty MacLean, Tracey Ahmet); Rush Rhees Library, University of Rochester (Phyllis Andrews, Richard Peek, Rosemary Switzer, Melinda Wallington); Senate House Library, University of London (Tansy Barton); Slade School of Fine Art, Archive (Lou Adkin); Stony Brook University Special Collections and Archives (Kristen J. Nyitray); Tate Gallery Library and Archive (Andrew Gent, Leah McGowan); Theatre Collection, University of Bristol (Bex Carrington); Trinity College, Oxford (Clare Hopkins); UCL Art Collections (Andrea Fredericksen); UCL Records Office (Robert Winckworth); UCL School of Slavonic and East European Studies Library (Gillian Long); University of Glasgow Library (Ruth Jones, Claire McKendrick); University of Manchester Library (Suzanne Fagan, Elizabeth Gow); Victoria and Albert Theatre and Performance Collections; Women's Library, London Metropolitan University (Sonia Gomes, Gillian Murphy).

I owe a special debt of gratitude to Clare Hopkins, Archivist of Trinity College, Oxford, for giving me the full benefit of her knowledge as the college's historian. For what one might call an 'inside' view of George's student life at Trinity, I warmly recommend reading Clare's guest post of 9 December 2016 on **calderonia.org**, entitled 'One Man and His College'. Throughout the project Clare's suggestions, comments and ideas have shaken up my thinking in innumerable productive ways.

Permissions

I am extremely grateful to the following institutions and trustees for their kind permission to publish quotations from the items and collections specified:

Harry Ransom Center, University of Texas at Austin, Box 8, Folder 3 (John Lane)

Houghton Library, Harvard University, MS Eng 1148 (218, 219) (William Rothenstein)

Leeds Russian Archive, Leeds University Library, MS.1073 (Ross)

Manuscripts Division, Department of Rare Books and Special Collections, Princeton University Library, C0125 (Grant Richards)

Reed Collection of Rare Books and Manuscripts, City of Dunedin Public Library, Editorial Papers (*Nineteenth Century*)

Senate House Library, University of London, MS978/1/2/11 (Thomas Sturge Moore)

The Imperial War Museum, Documents.15403 (Third Battle of Krithia)

The President and Fellows of Trinity College, Oxford, Ref. OF20/22 (Herbert Blakiston)

The Syndics of Cambridge University Library, UA CUR 113.V, UA VCCon. IX.5, Cam Papers EE113 (University Archives); Elizabeth Hill Papers, Boxes 19-23 (Russian Dramatists on the British Stage)

The Trustees of the Liddell Hart Centre for Military Archives, Hamilton 7/1/27 (Sir Ian Hamilton)

The Women's Library at LSE, 2WNA/E/01 (Women's National Anti-Suffrage League)

Most documents quoted in this book are drawn from the Calderon Papers, and most of these are copyright of the Calderon Estate. Letters to George and Kittie contained in the Calderon Papers are, however, copyright of the descendants of their authors, or of bodies identified as their copyright holders today. I am thankful indeed to the following for their permission to quote from such letters: Richard Astley; Thomas Cholmondeley; Gertrude Bell Archive; Edmund Gray; James Lambe; George E.C.

Lankester; London School of Hygiene and Tropical Medicine Library and Archives Service; Mary Lowe; Andrew Mylius; Marcia Newbolt; Julian H. Pardoe; Johnnie Pym; Louisa Scherchen; The Society of Authors as the Literary Representative of the Estate of John Masefield; Stanford Collection, Newcastle University Library; Trustees of the Joseph Conrad Estate.

Local history consultants

A biography that ranges from Soho, Eastcote and Hampstead to St Petersburg, Tahiti and Petersfield needs experts on each of these places to acquaint its author intimately and authoritatively with their pasts. This consultancy has been generously provided by the following, often in person and *in situ*: Helen Axworthy; Sheila Ayres; Julian and Helena Bates; Mary Boase; Sylvia Bovington; Robin Britcher; Cyril Brown; Jean-François Cauvin; Vaughan Clarke; Sue Cowan; Mrs F.A. Curry; Richard Davies; Melodie Foreman; Frith Street Gallery, Golden Square; Janis Hardiman; Hayling Island Tourist Office; Jo Hobbs; Clare Hopkins; Paul Lush; Members of the Ruislip, Northwood and Eastcote Local History Society research group; Geoff Munge; Mr and Mrs N. Osborne; Marion Pont; Port Authority of Papeete; David Powell; Johnnie Pym; Jane Ramsay; John Richardson; Service du Patrimoine Archivistique et Audiovisuel, Tahiti; Karen Spink; David Sullivan; Shirley Temple; Rebecca Tomaszewski; Olivia Tottle; Nick Truss; John Tucker and colleagues, Torquay Library; Simon Walker; Richard Wheeler; Wimereux Tourist Office; Melanie Winterbotham.

I am particularly indebted to Karen Spink, who showed me Eastcote on three highly enjoyable visits, facilitated my entry to several properties associated with the Calderons in Eastcote and elsewhere, and has shared with me her deep knowledge of London history generally; and to Vaughan Clarke, Chairman of Petersfield Museum, for his part in establishing the history of Kittie's cottage at Sheet and for sharing with me his encyclopaedic knowledge of the area.

Biographical consultants

I take the 'historical' opportunity here of thanking Percy Lubbock for writing *George Calderon: A Sketch from Memory*. Before the Calderon Papers were located, this book was the principal source of biographical information about George; and it was approved by Kittie herself. Percy took his own memories and the materials Kittie decided to show him, and made of them a work of art.

At the same time, I gratefully acknowledge the readiness of descendants of those who feature in the biography, experts on them and their contexts, or people who knew them personally, to help me answer the often highly specific questions I had about them: Richard Baldwin; Véronique de Beaulieu; Stephen Bennett; Susan Chitty; John Fleming; Isabelle Fokine; Elizabeth Gow; Peter Hellyer; Jill Hoare (née Pym); Hugh Honour; Henry Hurst; Sidney C. Hutchinson; Alan Lubbock; Joe Lubbock; Roy Lubbock; Derwent May; Nick Mays (Archivist, News UK); Edward Morgan; Marcia Newbolt; Johnnie Pym; Katya Rogatchevskaia; Valeria Ordoño de Rosales; Rear Admiral G.C. Ross; Graeme Smith; Clothilde Trouvé; Robert Winkworth.

'Specialist' contributors

Cutting across every area of this biography has been the work of my research assistant, Michael Welch. Mike has investigated for me censuses, genealogies, electoral rolls, local directories, passenger lists, timetables, births, marriages and deaths, and George's War Office file (National Archives, WO 339/13518). The extent of my indebtedness to him may be judged by the fact that his efficiency, knowledge and lateral thinking probably shortened the writing of this biography by a year. Without his forensic and internet skills I would have lost my way.

In the area of Russian studies, I thank the following for their expert and always enthusiastic assistance in resolving a range of issues: Rosamund Bartlett; Anthony G. Cross; Richard Davies; Simon Franklin; Michael Holman; Roger J. Keys; James Muckle; Harvey Pitcher; Donald Rayfield.

Finally, I have been helped by a veritable host of people whose special interests range from military history to graphology, and I am deeply obliged to them: Alan Andrews; Georgia Atienza; Lyulph Avebury; John and Sheila Baddeley; Ian Beckett; Laurence Brockliss; Greville Corbett; Jill Court; Madeleine Descargues; Richard Easterbrook; Howard Erson; Dorothy Galton; Peter Gibson; Damian Grant; John B. Hall; Peter Hart; John Hussey; Caroline and Paul Johnson; Annina Lubbock; Jan McDonald; William Miles; Bryan Missenden; Juliet Nicolson; Charles Nisbet; Stella Panayotova; Christopher Pountain; Christopher Prior; David Reynolds; Nicholas Robinson; Laurence Senelick; Nigel Steel; Crispian Strachan; James Strachan; Andrew Tatham; Barbara Weaver; Graeme Wright.

Readers

I have been saved from folly numerous times by Peter Gibson, Clare Hopkins, James Lambe, Derwent May, Alison Miles, James Muckle, Andrew Mylius, Harvey Pitcher, Johnnie Pym, Louisa Scherchen and Karen Spink, who meticulously read for me drafts of chapters in their particular field. I thank them deeply.

Personal

My wife Alison and my son James proposed to me the idea of 'Calderonia', a blog about the Calderons, and I am profoundly grateful to them for its creation of a Calderon 'web presence' and the enjoyment it has given me to write. James designed and launched **calderonia.org** and has managed the blog site for me since 2014. I also thank him for drawing the maps of the First Battle of Ypres and Third Battle of Krithia, his skilful preparation of the illustrations generally, and typesetting the entire book.

Alison has not only had to live with me writing this biography for six years, she has had George and Kittie living with us too. Her interest, involvement and advice, her truly Edwardian staunchness and stamina, have been a constant support to me.

BIBLIOGRAPHY

1. The published works of George Calderon

In the interests of biography, publications are presented chronologically. Only first editions are included. Most newspaper publications were unsigned, but those listed here are attributed to George Calderon beyond reasonable doubt, for example from letters or by the TLS Historical Archive.

1895

'A Russian Tavern', *Pall Mall Gazette*, 10 December 1895, p. 2

'I Seek Lodgings in St. Petersburg', *Pall Mall Gazette*, 19 December 1895, p. 3

'I Engage Lodgings in St. Petersburg', *Pall Mall Gazette*, 21 December 1895, p. 3

1896

'On and Off in Petersburg', *Pall Mall Gazette*, 7 January 1896, p. 4

'Some Diversions of Petersburg', *Pall Mall Gazette*, 20 February 1896, p. 3

'A Russian Bath', *Pall Mall Gazette*, 7 April 1896, p. 3

1897

'Scene in a Russian Cemetery. Grave and Gay', *Pall Mall Gazette*, 11 May 1897, p. 8

'Laughing Aspen', *Cornhill Magazine*, n.s. 3 (December 1897), pp. 759-68

1898

'Lipa Sidorovna', *Temple Bar*, 113 (February 1898), pp. 269-74

'Tarakanof's Idyll', *Cornhill Magazine*, n.s. 4 (March 1898), pp. 358-66

'Richard K. Whittington', *Cornhill Magazine*, n.s. 5 (October 1898), pp. 543-48

1899

'Russian Tragic Drama', *Literature*, 21 January 1899, pp. 58-59

'No Room to Live' [Letter to Editor], *Daily News*, 13 February 1899, p. 5

'The Academy of Humour', *Cornhill Magazine*, n.s. 6 (April 1899), pp.459-71

1900

'Russian Literature', *Literature*, 31 March 1900, pp. 257-58

'The Lieutenant's Heroine', *Cornhill Magazine*, n.s. 9 (November 1900), pp. 600-08

1901

'Russian Ideals of Peace', *Proceedings of the Anglo-Russian Literary Society*, 29 (1901), pp. 66-87

'The Wrong Tolstoi', *Monthly Review*, 3 (May 1901), pp. 129-41

'Tolstoy's Novels', *Literature*, 31 August 1901, pp. 197-202

'Korolenko', *Monthly Review*, 4 (September 1901), pp. 115-28

'Dobrynia: A Russian Bŭilina', *Monthly Review*, 5 (December 1901), pp. 148-61

1902

The Adventures of Downy V. Green, Rhodes Scholar at Oxford (London: Smith, Elder, 1902)

1903

'The Obstinacy of the Romanoffs', *Monthly Review*, 11 (April 1903), pp. 85-91

'Hampstead Heath Extension' [Letter to Editor], *Daily Chronicle*, 15 July 1903, p. 3

'Hampstead Heath "Extension"' [Letter to Editor], *Daily Chronicle*, 18 July 1903, p. 3

1904

Dwala: A Romance (London: Smith, Elder, 1904)

1905

'Bulgarian Folklore', *The Times Literary Supplement*, 17 February 1905,
p. 56

'Beauties of Russian Literature', *Proceedings of the Anglo-Russian
Literature Society*, 43 (1905), pp. 5-23

1907

'Europe and the Turks', *The Times Literary Supplement*, 14 June 1907,
p. 187

'A Word Collector's Cabinet', *The Times Literary Supplement*, 5 July
1907, p. 214

'Life as an Indian', *The Times Literary Supplement*, 12 July 1907, p. 222

'Maori Legends', *The Times Literary Supplement*, 19 July 1907, p. 227

'Israel in Europe', *The Times Literary Supplement*, 6 September 1907,
p. 270

1908

'Folk Lore', *The Times Literary Supplement*, 6 February 1908, p. 44

'The Man Who Was Thursday', *The Times Literary Supplement*, 5 March
1908, p. 78

'The Virgin Widow', *The Times Literary Supplement*, 12 March 1908,
p. 86

'Prince Urussov's Memoirs', *The Times Literary Supplement*, 16 April
1908, p. 122

'Folklore and Tradition', *The Times Literary Supplement*, 7 May 1908,
p. 146

'Duke and Tramp', *The Times Literary Supplement*, 14 May 1908, p. 156

'Servia', *The Times Literary Supplement*, 14 May 1908, p. 157

'The Spanish Jade', *The Times Literary Supplement*, 14 May 1908, p. 157

'Tangled Wedlock', *The Times Literary Supplement*, 14 May 1908, p. 157

'Folklore as an Historical Science', *The Times Literary Supplement*, 21
May 1908, p. 166

'Restitution', *The Times Literary Supplement*, 28 May 1908, p. 173

'The Court of Russia', *The Times Literary Supplement*, 11 June 1908,
p. 188

'Gospels of Anarchy', *The Times Literary Supplement*, 25 June 1908, p. 203

'The Phenomena of Spiritualism', *The Times Literary Supplement*, 9 July 1908, p. 219

'The Singular Republic', *The Times Literary Supplement*, 23 July 1908, p. 235

Woman in Relation to the State: A Consideration of the Arguments Advanced for the Extension of the Parliamentary Suffrage to Women (London: The Priory Press, 1908)

'The Maori Spirit', *The Times Literary Supplement*, 6 August 1908, p. 253

'A Laughing Matter', *The Times Literary Supplement*, 6 August 1908, p. 255

'Occultism and Common Sense', *The Times Literary Supplement*, 27 August 1908, p. 275

'Further Experiences of an Irish RM', *The Times Literary Supplement*, 10 September 1908, p. 293

'Mr Chesterton's Orthodoxy', *The Times Literary Supplement*, 1 October 1908, p. 319

'Salvator', *The Times Literary Supplement*, 1 October 1908, p. 324

'Salthaven', *The Times Literary Supplement*, 8 October 1908, p. 336

'Reminiscences of a Stonemason', *The Times Literary Supplement*, 15 October 1908, p. 343

'Discourse at Large', *The Times Literary Supplement*, 15 October 1908, p. 344

'M. Anatole France', *The Times Literary Supplement*, 22 October 1908, p. 353

'Junia', *The Times Literary Supplement*, 22 October 1908, p. 363

'David Bran', *The Times Literary Supplement*, 29 October 1908, p. 376

'A Summer Tour in Finland', *The Times Literary Supplement*, 5 November 1908, p. 389

'The War in the Air', *The Times Literary Supplement*, 5 November 1908, p. 390

'John Silence', *The Times Literary Supplement*, 19 November 1908, p. 418

'The Conquest of the Caucasus', *The Times Literary Supplement*, 31 December 1908, p. 493

1909

'The World of Helen Keller', *The Times Literary Supplement*, 4 February 1909, p. 39

'Tolstoy', *The Times Literary Supplement*, 11 March 1909, pp. 92-93

[With others] 'Mr G. Howard's Bill' [Letter to Editor], *The Times*, 19 March 1909, p. 6

'Woman Suffrage and Women's Wages' [Letter to Editor], *The Times*, 13 April 1909, p. 8

'Casual Realism', *The Times Literary Supplement*, 22 April 1909, p. 152

'The Grateful Dead', *The Times Literary Supplement*, 15 July 1909, p. 261

'The Mongols in Russia', *The Times Literary Supplement*, 19 August 1909, p. 303

'The Polar Eskimo', *The Times Literary Supplement*, 16 September 1909, p. 335

'John Dee', *The Times Literary Supplement*, 23 September 1909, p. 346

'The Literature of Russia', *The Times Literary Supplement*, 11 November 1909, p. 426

1910

[Review of A.A. Grace, *Folktales of the Maori*], *Folk-lore*, 21 (1910), no. 1, p. 128

'Landmarks in Russian Literature', *The Times Literary Supplement*, 24 March 1910, p. 106

'The South Seas', *The Times Literary Supplement*, 14 April 1910, p. 131

'A Bath-Chairman's Autobiography', *The Times Literary Supplement*, 2 June 1910, p. 200

'Mr Chesterton on the World', *The Times Literary Supplement,* 30 June 1910, p. 231

'Peace Alley', *The Times Literary Supplement*, 25 August 1910, p. 303

'The New Spiritualism', *The Times Literary Supplement*, 8 September 1910, p. 317

'Mr Maude's Life of Tolstoy', *The Times Literary Supplement*, 6 October 1910, p. 355

'The Post-Impressionists', *New Age*, 24 November 1910, pp. 89-90

'Woman Suffrage Canvasses' [Letter to Editor], *The Times*, 31 December
 1910, p. 12

1911

The Organisation of Buying: A Policy for Women (London: The Priory
 Press, [1911])
The Fountain: A Comedy in Three Acts (London: Gowans & Gray, 1911)
'The Russian Ballet', *The Times*, 24 June 1911, p. 13
'The Russian People', *The Times Literary Supplement*, 2 November 1911,
 p. 421
[Unsigned reply to letter of M. Baring], *The Times Literary Supplement*,
 23 November 1911, p. 481

1912

'Father Sergius', *The Times Literary Supplement*, 11 January 1912, p. 14
Two Plays by Tchekhof: 'The Seagull', 'The Cherry Orchard', Translated,
 with an introduction and notes, by George Calderon (London:
 Richards, 1912)
'Cambridge and the Coal Strike', *Cambridge Magazine*, 20 April 1912,
 pp. 229-30
'Mr Calderon Sums Up', *Cambridge Magazine*, 18 May 1912, p. 351
'The Russian Stage', *Quarterly Review*, 217 (July 1912), no. 432, pp. 21-42
'The Four Walls', *Manchester Playgoer*, n.s. 1 (December 1912), no. 2,
 p. 45-48

1913

[With St John Hankin], *Thompson: A Comedy in Three Acts* (London:
 Secker, 1913)
The Little Stone House: A Play in One Act (London: Sidgwick & Jackson,
 1913)
'What Women Want' [Letter to Editor], *The Times*, 23 May 1913, p. 10
'Slavonic Elements in Greek Religion', *Classical Review*, 27 (May 1913),
 no. 3, pp. 79-81

1914

Reminiscences of Tolstoy by his son Count Ilya Tolstoy, Translated by
    George Calderon (London: Chapman & Hall, 1914)

1915

*The Maharani of Arakan: A Romantic Comedy in One Act founded on the
    story by Sir Rabindranath Tagore* (London: Francis Griffiths, 1915)

1921

Tahiti (London: Richards, 1921)

1922

Eight One-Act Plays (London: Richards, 1922)
Three Plays and a Pantomime (London: Richards, 1922)

1923

[With William Caine], *The Brave Little Tailor, or Seven at a Blow*
    (London: Richards, 1923)

1924

*Two Plays by Anton Tchekhof: 'The Seagull', 'The Cherry Orchard' and
    One by Alfred de Musset: 'Perdican and Camilla' ('On ne badine pas
    avec l'amour')*, Translated, with an Introduction and Notes by George
    Calderon (London: Richards, 1924)

1928

The Two Talismans: A Comedy in One Act (London: Sidgwick & Jackson,
    1928)

2. Secondary literature

This comprises publications consulted or specifically referred to by author in the biography.

Angenot, Marc, and Nadia Khouri, 'An International Bibliography of Prehistoric Fiction', *Science-Fiction Studies*, 8 (1981), no. 23, pp. 38-53

Aspinall-Oglander, C.F., *Military Operations: Gallipoli*, History of the Great War Based on Official Documents by Direction of the Historical Section of the Committee of Imperial Defence, 4 vols (London: Heinemann, 1929)

Astley, Constance, and Mildred Isemonger, *Richard Vincent Sutton: A Record of his Life Together with Extracts from his Private Papers* (London: George W. Jones, 1922)

Aston, Sir George, *Secret Service* (London: Faber & Faber, 1930)

Bain, R. Nisbet, *Tales from Tolstoi* (London: Jarrold, 1901)

_____ *Tales from Gorky* (London: Jarrold, 1902)

Bakhtin, M.M., *Literaturno-kriticheskie stat'i (Essays in Literary Criticism)* (Moscow: Khudozhestvennaia literatura, 1986)

Bank, Jonathan, ed., *St John Hankin Reclaimed* (New York: Granville Press, 2007)

Baring, Maurice, *Landmarks in Russian Literature* (London: Methuen, 1910)

_____ *The Russian People* (London: Methuen, 1911)

_____ *What I Saw in Russia* (London: Thomas Nelson, 1913)

Barker, Harley Granville, *Three Plays: The Marrying of Ann Leete, The Voysey Inheritance, The Madras House* (London: Sidgwick & Jackson, 1909)

Bartlett, Rosamund, *Tolstoy: A Russian Life* (London: Profile Books, 2010)

Bartoshevich, Aleksey, 'The "Inevitability" of Chekhov: Anglo-Russian Theatrical Contacts in the 1910s', in *Chekhov on the British Stage*, ed. by Patrick Miles (Cambridge: Cambridge University Press, 1993), pp. 20-28

Beaumont, Cyril W., *Michel Fokine & his Ballets* (London: the author, 1935; repr. London: Dance Books, 1996)

_____ *The Diaghilev Ballet in London*, 3rd edn (London: A. and C. Black, 1951)

Beckett, Ian F.W., *Johnnie Gough, V.C.: A Biography of Brigadier-General Sir John Edmond Gough, V.C., K.C.B.* (London: Tom Donovan, 1989)

_____ *Ypres: The First Battle, 1914* (London: Routledge, 2013)

Beckett, Lorna C., *The Second I Saw You: The True Love Story of Rupert Brooke and Phyllis Gardner* (London: The British Library, 2015)

Bede, Cuthbert [Edward Bradley], *The Adventures of Mr Cuthbert Bede, an Oxford Freshman* (London: Nathaniel Cooke, 1853)

Beecroft, Arthur, *Gallipoli: A Soldier's Story* (London: Hale, 2015)

Beerbohm, Max, *The Poet's Corner* (London: Heinemann, 1904)

_____ *Herbert Beerbohm Tree: Some Memories of Him and of his Art* (London: Hutchinson, 1920)

Bell, Yvonne, *The Edwardian Home* (Oxford: Shire Publications, 2012)

Bennett, Arnold, *Books and Persons: Being Comments on a Past Epoch, 1908-1911* (London: Chatto & Windus, 1917)

Bentwich, Helen C., *The Vale of Health on Hampstead Heath 1777-1977* (London: Camden History Society, 1977)

Binks, Doreen, Jean Gard, and Mary Ray, *The Story of Petersfield* (Petersfield: Petersfield Museum, 2009)

Binyon, Laurence, *The Secret: Sixty Poems* (London: Elkin Mathews, 1920)

Booth, Michael R., and Joel H. Kaplan, eds, *The Edwardian Theatre: Essays on Performance and the Stage* (Cambridge: Cambridge University Press, 1996)

Bostridge, Mark, *The Fateful Year: England 1914* (London: Viking, 2014)

_____ 'Portrait of 1914: Behind Trenches and Treaties', *The Ship*, University of Oxford, St Anne's College Record (2014-2015), no. 104, pp. 57-61

Bradby, G.F., *The Great Days of Versailles: Studies from Court Life in the Later Years of Louis XIV* (New York: Scribner; London: Smith, Elder, 1906)

Bradby, H.C., *Rugby* (London: George Bell, 1900)

Brendon, Piers, *Eminent Edwardians: Four Figures Who Defined their Age: Northcliffe, Balfour, Pankhurst, Baden-Powell* (London: Pimlico, 2003)

Brent, Peter, *The Edwardians* (London: BBC, 1972)

Bright, Michael, 'Remembering Sir Henry Newbolt: An Essay and Bibliography', *English Literature in Transition, 1880-1920*, 33 (1990), no. 2, pp. 155-78

Britcher, Robin, *Kennington at War 1939-1945* (Ashford: the author, 2016)

Brockliss, L.W.B., *The University of Oxford: A History* (Oxford: Oxford University Press, 2016)

Buck, Martin, '"What Has Happened to Poor Tebb?": A Biographical Sketch of Conrad's Physician', *The Conradian*, 23 (1998), no. 1, pp. 1-18

Buckle, Richard, *Nijinsky*, 3rd edn (London: Phoenix Giant, 1998)

Bullock, Philip Ross, 'Tsar's Hall: Russian Music in London, 1895-1926', in *Russia in Britain, 1880-1940: From Melodrama to Modernism*, ed. by Rebecca Beasley and Philip Ross Bullock (Oxford: Oxford University Press, 2013), pp. 113-28

Burt, Ramsay, '*Le Sacre du printemps* in London: The Politics of Embodied Freedom in Early Modernist Dance and Suffragette Protest', in *Russia in Britain, 1880-1940: From Melodrama to Modernism*, ed. by Rebecca Beasley and Philip Ross Bullock (Oxford: Oxford University Press, 2013), pp. 129-45

Bush, Julia, *Women against the Vote: Female Anti-Suffragism in Britain* (Oxford: Oxford University Press, 2007)

Caine, William, *An Angler at Large* (London: Kegan Paul, Trench, Trubner, 1911)

_____ *Fish, Fishing & Fishermen* (London: Philip Allan, 1927)

Camden, London Borough of, *Hampstead Conservation Area Statement* (Camden: Conservation & Urban Design Team, 2001)

Carpenter, Humphrey, *OUDS: A Centenary History of the Oxford University Dramatic Society 1885-1985* (Oxford: Oxford University Press, 1985)

Carrick, Edward, *Gordon Craig: The Story of his Life* (London: Gollancz, 1968)

Chapman, Don, *Oxford Playhouse: High and Low Drama in a University City* (Hatfield: University of Hertfordshire Press, 2008)

Chekhov, A.P., *Polnoe sobranie sochinenii i pisem v tridtsati tomakh (Complete Collected Works in 30 Volumes)* (Moscow: Nauka, 1975-83)

Chitty, Susan, *Playing the Game: A Biography of Sir Henry Newbolt* (London: Quartet Books, 1997)

Cholmondeley, Mary, *Red Pottage* (London: Edward Arnold, 1899)

_____ *Moth and Rust* (London: Murray, 1902)

Cohen, Susan, *Medical Services in the First World War* (Oxford: Shire Publications, 2014)

Cole, G.D.H., and Raymond Postgate, *The Common People, 1746-1946*, 2nd edn (London: Methuen, 1961)

Conrad, Joseph, *The Collected Letters of Joseph Conrad*, ed. by Frederick R. Karl and Laurence Davies, 9 vols (Cambridge: Cambridge University Press, 1983-2007)

Cooke, Catherine, 'Fedor Osipovich Shekhtel: An Architect and his Clients in Turn-of-the-Century Moscow', *Annals of the Architectural Association School of Architecture*, 5 (1984), pp. 3-31

Cornwallis-West, G., *Edwardians Go Fishing: Or Many Days on Many Waters* (London: Putnam, 1932)

Cross, Anthony, *Cambridge – Some Russian Connections: An Inaugural Lecture Delivered before the University of Cambridge on 26 February 1987* (Cambridge: Cambridge University Press, 1987)

_____ *St Petersburg and the British: The City through the Eyes of British Visitors and Residents* (London: Frances Lincoln, 2008)

_____ ed., *A People Passing Rude: British Responses to Russian Culture* (Cambridge: Open Book Publishers, 2012)

Das, Santanu, *Touch and Intimacy in First World War Literature* (Cambridge: Cambridge University Press, 2005)

Davidson, Michael, *The World, the Flesh and Myself* (London: David Bruce and Watson, 1973)

Dobbs, Brian, *Edwardians at Play: Sport 1890-1914* (London: Pelham Books, 1973)

Donohue, Joseph, 'What Is the Edwardian Theatre?', in *The Edwardian Theatre: Essays on Performance and the Stage*, ed. by Michael R. Booth and Joel H. Kaplan (Cambridge: Cambridge University Press, 1996), pp. 10-35

Doyle, Peter, *The British Soldier of the First World War* (Oxford: Shire Publications, 2008)

Easterbrook, Richard, *In Search of Harold and Elsie Neville: A Family Memoir* ([Sidcup]: the author, 2016)

Edmonds, Sir James Edward, *Military Operations: France and Belgium*, History of the Great War Based on Official Documents by Direction of the Historical Section of the Committee of Imperial Defence, 17 vols (London: Macmillan, 1922-47)

Ellman, Richard, ed., *Edwardians and Late Victorians: English Institute Essays, 1959* (New York: Columbia University Press, 1960)

Emeljanow, Victor, ed., *Anton Chekhov: The Critical Heritage* (London: Routledge, 1981)

_____ 'Towards an Ideal Spectator: Theatregoing and the Edwardian Critics', in *The Edwardian Theatre: Essays on Performance and the Stage*, ed. by Michael R. Booth and Joel H. Kaplan (Cambridge: Cambridge University Press, 1996), pp. 148-65

Ensor, R.C.K., *England, 1870-1914* (Oxford: Clarendon, 1968)

Eyffinger, Arthur, *The 1899 Hague Peace Conference: 'The Parliament of Man, the Federation of the World'* (London: Kluwer Law International, 1999)

Fairs, P.J., 'Russian Publications in the British Museum in the Nineteenth Century', *Solanus*, no. 5 (1970), pp. 13-16

Faust, Drew Gilpin, *This Republic of Suffering: Death and the American Civil War* (New York: Knopf, 2008)

Feeney, William J., *Drama in Hardwicke Street: A History of the Irish Theatre Company* (Rutherford, NJ: Fairleigh Dickinson University Press; London: Associated University Presses, 1984)

Feuchtwanger, E.J., *Democracy and Empire: Britain 1865-1914*, The New History of England, 9 (London: Edward Arnold, 1985)

Fevral'skii, A.V., and B.I. Rostotskii, eds, *V.E. Meierkhol'd: Stat'i, pis'ma, rechi, besedy (V.E. Meierkhol'd: Articles, Letters, Speeches, Talks)* (Moscow: Iskusstvo, 1968)

Fokine, Michel, *Fokine: Memoirs of a Ballet Master*, trans. by Vitale
Fokine, ed. by Anatole Chujoy (London: Constable, 1961)

_____ *Protiv techeniia. Vospominaniia baletmeistera. Stsenarii i zamysly
baletov, stat'i, interv'iu i pis'ma (Against the Current: Memoirs of a
Choreographer (Libretti and Ideas for Ballets, Articles, Interviews and
Letters))*, ed. by Iu.I. Slonimskii and G.N. Dobrovol'skaia, 2nd edn
(Leningrad: Iskusstvo, 1981)

Forster, E.M., *A Room with a View* (London: Edward Arnold, 1908)

Foster, Joseph, *Oxford Men 1880-1892, with a Record of their Schools,
Honours and Degrees* (Oxford: James Parker, 1893)

Frazer, James George, *The Golden Bough: A Study in Comparative
Religion*, 2 vols (London: Macmillan, 1890)

Frye, Northrop, *Anatomy of Criticism: Four Essays* (Princeton: Princeton
University Press, 1957)

Furse, Michael, *Stand Therefore!: A Bishop's Testimony of Faith in the
Church of England* (London: S.P.C.K., 1953)

Galsworthy, John, *Strife: A Drama in Three Acts* (London: Duckworth,
1977)

Galton, D., 'The Anglo-Russian Literary Society', *Slavonic and East
European Review*, 48 (1970), no. 111, pp. 272-82

Garnett, Richard, *Constance Garnett: A Heroic Life* (London: Sinclair-
Stevenson, 1991)

Gerard, Jessica, 'Lady Bountiful: Women of the Landed Classes and Rural
Philanthropy', *Victorian Studies*, 30 (1987), no. 2, pp. 183-210

Gillon, Stair Agnew, *The K.O.S.B. in the Great War* (London: Nelson,
1930)

Gitovich, N.I., I.V. Fedorov and A.K. Kotov, *Chekhov v vospominaniiakh
sovremennikov (Chekhov as his Contemporaries Remembered Him)*,
2nd edn (Moscow: GIKhL, 1954)

Goldie, Grace Wyndham, *The Liverpool Repertory Theatre 1911-1934*
(London: The University Press of Liverpool; Hodder & Stoughton,
1935)

Goodman, Susan, *Gertrude Bell* (Leamington Spa: Berg, 1985)

Gough, Hubert, Sir, *Soldiering on* (London, Arthur Baker, 1954)

Graham, Stephen, *Undiscovered Russia* (London: John Lane, 1912)

_____ *Part of the Wonderful Scene: An Autobiography* (London: Collins, 1964)

Graves, Robert, *Poems Selected by Himself* (Harmondsworth: Penguin Books, 1972)

Gregory, Adrian, *The Last Great War: British Society and the First World War* (Cambridge: Cambridge University Press, 2008)

Hamilton, George, *A History of the House of Hamilton* (Edinburgh: J. Skinner, 1933)

Hammond, Bryn, 'The Third Battle of Krithia, 4th June 1915', The Joint Imperial War Museum / Australian War Memorial Battlefield Study Tour to Gallipoli, September 2000 (London: IWM, 2001)

Hankin, St John, *The Last of the De Mullins: A Play without a Preface* (London: A.C. Fifield, 1909)

_____ *The Dramatic Works*, 3 vols (London: Secker, 1912)

Hare, Augustus J.C., *The Gurneys of Earlham*, 2 vols (London: George Allen, 1895)

Harris, P.R., *A History of the British Museum Library 1753-1973* (London: The British Library, 1998)

Harrison, Brian, *Separate Spheres: The Opposition to Women's Suffrage in Britain* (London: Croom Helm, 1978)

Hart, Peter, *Gallipoli* (London: Profile Books, 2011)

Haslam, Jonathan, *Russia's Cold War* (New Haven: Yale University Press, 2011)

Hastings, Max, *Catastrophe: Europe Goes to War 1914* (London: William Collins, 2014)

Hatcher, John, *Laurence Binyon: Poet, Scholar of East and West* (Oxford: Clarendon Press, 1995)

Hattersley, Roy, *The Edwardians* (London: Abacus, 2006)

Hearnshaw, F.J.C., ed., *Edwardian England, A.D. 1901-1910: A Series of Lectures Delivered at King's College, University of London, During the Session 1932-3* (London: E. Benn, 1933)

Heffer, Simon, *The Age of Decadence: Britain 1880 to 1914* (London: Random House, 2017)

Heimburger, Franziska, 'Fighting Together: Language Issues in the Military Coordination of First World War Allied Coalition Warfare', in

Languages and the Military: Alliances, Occupation and Peace Building, ed. by Hilary Footitt and Michael Kelly (Basingstoke: Palgrave Macmillan, 2012), pp. 47-57

Herbert, A.P., *Half-Hours at Helles* (Oxford: Blackwell, 1916)

Hobson, Harold, *Verdict at Midnight: Sixty Years of Dramatic Criticism* (London: Longmans, Green, 1952)

Holroyd, Michael, *Augustus John: The New Biography* (London: Chatto & Windus, 1996)

Hope Simpson, J.B., *Rugby Since Arnold: A History of Rugby School from 1842* (London: Macmillan, 1967)

Hopkins, Clare, *Trinity: 450 Years of an Oxford College Community* (Oxford: Oxford University Press, 2005)

Hudson, Cyril E., 'Michael Furse', *Church Quarterly Review*, 159 (1958), no. 1, pp. 89-105

Hunter, Jefferson, *Edwardian Fiction* (Cambridge, MA: Harvard University Press, 1982)

Hussey, John, *Finding Margaret: The Elusive Margaret Bernadine Bell* (Birkenhead: Countyvise, 2011)

Hynes, Samuel, *The Edwardian Turn of Mind* (Princeton: Princeton University Press; London: Oxford University Press, 1968)

Isaac, Winifred F.E.C., *Alfred Wareing: A Biography* (London: Green Bank, 1951)

_____ [Letter to Editor], *The Prompter*, May 1953, no. 75, p. 4

James, Dermot, *John Hamilton of Donegal 1800-1884: This Recklessly Generous Landlord* (Dublin: The Woodfield Press, 1998)

Johnson, Barry C., ed., *Tea and Anarchy!: The Bloomsbury Diary of Olive Garnett 1890-1893* (London: Bartletts Press, 1989)

Joubert, Carl, *Russia as It Really Is* (London: Nash, 1904)

Keable, Robert, *Tahiti: Isle of Dreams* (London: Hutchinson, c. 1925)

Kemp, Sarah, Charlotte Mitchell, and David Trotter, *The Oxford Companion to Edwardian Fiction* (Oxford: Oxford University Press, 2002)

Kemp, W.A.G., *The Story of Northwood and Northwood Hills, Middlesex* ([Northwood, Eng.]: the author, 1957)

_____ *The History of Eastcote, Middlesex* ([Northwood, Eng.]: the author, 1963)

Kennedy, Dennis, *Granville Barker and the Dream of Theatre* (Cambridge: Cambridge University Press, 1985)

_____ 'The New Drama and the New Audience', in *The Edwardian Theatre: Essays on Performance and the Stage*, ed. by Michael R. Booth and Joel H. Kaplan (Cambridge: Cambridge University Press, 1996), pp. 130-47

Kernan, Alvin B., *The Plot of Satire* (New Haven: Yale University Press, 1965)

Keynes, Geoffrey, ed., *The Letters of Rupert Brooke* (London: Faber & Faber, 1968)

Korshunova, V.P., and Sitkovetskaia, M.M., eds, *V.E. Meierkhol'd. Perepiska. 1896-1939 (Vsevolod Meierkhol'd: Correspondence 1896-1939)* (Moscow: Iskusstvo, 1976)

Kulikov, Sergei V., 'Emperor Nicholas II and the State Duma: Unknown Plans and Missed Opportunities', *Russian Studies in History*, 50 (2012), no. 4, pp. 44-78

Lachinov, Serge, 'Kal'deron, Dzhorzh' ('George Calderon'), <https://ru.wikipedia.org/wiki/Kal'deron,_Dzhorzh> [accessed 19 March 2010]

Lansdall-Welfare, Thomas, and others, 'Content Analysis of 150 years of British Periodicals', *Proceedings of the National Academy of Sciences*, 114 (2017), no. 4, E457-465

Lao Tsŭ, *The Sayings of Lao Tsŭ*, trans. by Lionel Giles (London: Murray, 1905)

Larkin, Philip, *Collected Poems*, ed. by Anthony Thwaite (London: The Marvell Press and Faber & Faber, 1988)

Laurence, Dan H., ed., *Bernard Shaw: Collected Letters*, 4 vols (London: Reinhardt, 1965-88)

Leslie, Anita, *Edwardians in Love* (London: Hutchinson, 1972)

Lester, John A., Jr., *Journey through Despair, 1880-1914: Transformations in British Literary Culture* (Princeton, NJ: Princeton University Press, 1968)

Lewis-Stempel, John, *Where Poppies Blow: The British Soldier, Nature, the Great War* (London: Weidenfeld & Nicolson, 2016)

Leyburn, Ellen Douglass, *Satiric Allegory: Mirror of Man* (New Haven: Yale University Press, 1956)

Lubbock, Percy, 'Obituary: George Calderon', *The Times*, 5 May 1919, p. 19

_____ *George Calderon: A Sketch from Memory* (London: Richards, 1921)

_____ *The Craft of Fiction* (London: Jonathan Cape, 1921)

_____ *Earlham* (London: Jonathan Cape, 1922)

_____ 'Calderon, George (1868-1915)', in *Dictionary of National Biography 1912-1921*, ed. by H.W.C. Davies and J.R.H. Weaver (London: Oxford University Press, 1927), p. 85

_____ *Mary Cholmondeley: A Sketch from Memory* (London: Jonathan Cape, 1928)

Luckhurst, Mary, and Jane Moody, eds, *Theatre and Celebrity in Britain, 1660-2000* (Basingstoke: Palgrave Macmillan, 2005)

Lunacharskii, A., and others, *"Teatr". Kniga o novom teatre. Sbornik statei ("Theatre": A Collection of Articles about the New Theatre)* (St Petersburg: Shipovnik, 1908)

Martin, Christopher, *The Edwardians* (London: Wayland Publishers, 1974)

Masefield, John, *Gallipoli* (London: Heinemann, 1916)

_____ *The Tragedy of Nan* (London: Heinemann, 1926)

Matthew, H.C.G., *The Liberal Imperialists* (London: Oxford University Press, 1973)

May, Derwent, *Critical Times: The History of The Times Literary Supplement* (London: HarperCollins, 2001)

_____ 'The Rediscovery of George Calderon', *London Magazine*, August/September 2010, pp. 73-75

McBean, Jim, 'Captain and Mrs Bennett Edwards of Haydon Hall', *Journal of Ruislip, Northwood and Eastcote Local History Society*, 1991, pp. 14-16

McDonald, Jan, *The 'New Drama' 1900-1914: Harley Granville-Barker, John Galsworthy, St John Hankin* (London: Macmillan Education, 1986)

_____ 'Chekhov, Naturalism and the Drama of Dissent: Productions of
Chekhov's Plays in Britain before 1914', in *Chekhov on the British
Stage*, ed. by Patrick Miles (Cambridge: Cambridge University Press,
1993), pp. 29-42

McEvansoneya, Philip, '"A Libel in Paint": Religious and Artistic
Controversy Around P.H. Calderon's "The Renunciation of St
Elizabeth of Hungary"', *Journal of Victorian Culture*, 1 (1996), no. 2,
pp. 254-79

McKean, Erin, 'The Lure of Invented Languages', *International Herald
Tribune*, 14 May 2012, p. 9

Meister, Charles W., *Chekhov Bibliography: Works in English by and
about Anton Chekhov: American, British and Canadian Performances*
(Jefferson, NC: McFarland, 1985)

Michelin, *Ypres and the Battles of Ypres: An Illustrated History and Guide*
(Clermont-Ferrand: Michelin, 1919)

Miles, Patrick, *Chekhov on the British Stage 1909-1987* (Cambridge:
Sam&Sam, 1987)

_____ ed., *Chekhov on the British Stage* (Cambridge: Cambridge
University Press, 1993)

_____ 'Letters from George Calderon to his parents in England, 1895',
Slavonica, 2 (1995/1996), no. 1, pp. 7-25

_____ 'Chekhov at 150: The "Hampstead Connection"', *London
Magazine*, June/July 2010, pp. 98-102

_____ 'Cromwell Pedigree' [Letter to Editor], *The Times*, 22 January
2015, p. 35

Moody, Oliver, 'Age of Celebrity Born as Victoria Died', *The Times*, 10
January 2017, p. 3

Moore, Lucy, *Nijinsky: A Life* (London: Profile Books, 2013)

Moorehead, Alan, *Gallipoli* (London: Hamish Hamilton, 1956)

Morgan, Edward, 'Lydia Yavorska', *Theatrephile*, 3 (1990), no. 9, pp. 3-7

Morton, Vanessa, 'Earlham Hall Unwrapped', *Ziggurat*, University of East
Anglia, 2014/15, p. 23-26

Mottram, R.H., *Portrait of an Unknown Victorian* (London: Hale, 1936)

Muckle, James, *The Russian Language in Britain: A Historical Survey of
Learners and Teachers* (Ilkeston: Bramcote Press, 2008)

_____ 'Ivan Nestor-Schnurmann (1852-1917): a Pioneer of the Teaching of Russian in Great Britain', *Australian Slavonic and East European Studies*, 24 (2010), no.'s 1-2, pp. 103-116.

Munro-Faure, Alice, *Flora Twort: A Petersfield Artist*, Hampshire Papers 7 (Portsmouth: Hampshire County Council, 1995)

Murland, Jerry, *Aristocrats Go to War: Uncovering the Zillebeke Churchyard Cemetery* (Barnsley: Pen & Sword Military, 2010)

Naaké, John T., *Slavonic Fairy Tales* (London: Henry S. King, 1874)

Najder, Zdzisław, *Joseph Conrad: A Life*, trans. by Halina Najder (Rochester, NY: Camden House, 2007)

Newbolt, Henry, *My World As in My Time: Memoirs of Sir Henry Newbolt, 1862-1932* (London: Faber & Faber, 1932)

_____ *The Later Life and Letters of Sir Henry Newbolt*, ed. by Margaret Newbolt (London: Faber & Faber, 1942)

Nicolson, Juliet, *The Perfect Summer: Dancing into Shadow: England in 1911* (London: Murray, 2006)

Obraztsova, Anna, 'Bernard Shaw's Dialogue with Chekhov', in *Chekhov on the British Stage*, ed. by Patrick Miles (Cambridge: Cambridge University Press, 1993), pp. 43-53

O'Brien, Frederick, *Mystic Isles of the South Seas* (London: Hodder & Stoughton, 1921)

Okey, Thomas, *A Basketful of Memories: An Autobiographical Sketch* (London: Dent, 1930)

Orwell, George, *Coming Up for Air* (London: Gollancz, 1939)

Owen, Roger, *Lord Cromer: Victorian Imperialist, Edwardian Proconsul* (Oxford: Oxford University Press, 2004)

Pache, Mary, 'Thrills and Swoon in Eastcote', *Journal of Ruislip, Northwood and Eastcote Local History Society*, 2002, pp. 41-44

Paget, H.L., Right Rev., *In the Day of Battle* (London: Longmans, Green, 1915)

Papernyi, Z., E.A. Polotskaia and L.M. Rozenblium, *Chekhov i mirovaia kul'tura (Chekhov and World Culture)*, Literaturnoe Nasledstvo, 3 vols (Moscow: Nauka and IMLI RAN, 1997-2005)

Paterson, John, *Edwardians: London Life and Letters, 1901-1914* (Chicago: Dee, 1996)

Payne, Pamela, *Voices of Petersfield and District* (Stroud: Tempus
    Publishing, 2003)

Pegler, Martin, *Soldiers' Songs and Slang of the Great War* (Oxford:
    Osprey Publishing, 2014)

Pelling, Henry, *A History of British Trade Unionism* (Basingstoke:
    Macmillan, 1992)

Phillips, William H., *St John Hankin: Edwardian Mephistopheles*
    (Rutherford: Fairleigh Dickinson University Press; London: Associated
    University Presses, 1979)

Piketty, Thomas, *Capital in the Twenty-First Century*, trans. by Arthur
    Goldhammer (Cambridge, MA: The Belknap Press of Harvard
    University Press, 2014)

Pitcher, Harvey, *When Miss Emmie Was in Russia: English Governesses
    before, during and after the October Revolution* (London: Murray,
    1977)

_____ *The Smiths of Moscow: A Story of Britons Abroad* (Cromer:
    Swallow House Books, 1984)

Pobyedonostseff, K.P., *Reflections of a Russian Statesman*, trans. by
    Robert Crozier Long (London: Richards, 1898)

Poems of the Great War, 1914-1918 (London: Penguin Books, 1998)

Pogson, Rex, *Miss Horniman and the Gaiety Theatre, Manchester*
    (London: Rockliff, 1952)

Pokrovskii, V., ed., *Anton Pavlovich Chekhov. Ego zhizn' i sochineniia.
    Sbornik istoriko-literaturnykh statei (Anton Chekhov's Life and Works:
    A Collection of Literary-Historical Articles)* (Moscow: Spiridonov and
    Mikhailov, 1907)

Pollock, John, *Time's Chariot* (London: Murray, 1950)

Priestley, J.B., *The Edwardians* (London: Heinemann, 1970)

Pritchard, Jane, ed., *Diaghilev and the Golden Age of the Ballets Russes,
    1909-1929* (London: V&A, 2010)

Pugh, Martin, *The March of the Women: A Revisionist Analysis of the
    Campaign for Women's Suffrage, 1866-1914* (Oxford: Oxford
    University Press, 2000)

Pym, Caroline Fox, *A Rhine Sketch Book* (London: Racquet Court Press,
    1900)

Pym, John, 'Emmetts Garden in 3-D', *Kent Gardens Trust Newsletter*, 36 (Autumn 2010), pp. 2-3

Quinn, Tom, *Mrs Keppel: Mistress to the King* (London: Biteback, 2016)

Reynolds, David, *The Long Shadow: The Great War and the Twentieth Century* (London: Simon & Schuster, 2013)

Richardson, Gavin, *For King and Country and the Scottish Borderers: The Story of the 1/4th (Border) Battalion The King's Own Scottish Borderers on the Gallipoli Peninsula, 1915* (Hawick: Gavin Richardson, 1987)

Ripley, H.W., and N.Y. Harlem, *Genealogy of a Part of the Ripley Family* (Newark, NJ: A. Stephen Holbrook, 1867)

Rogachevskaia, E., 'Istoriia formirovaniia slavianskikh kollektsii v Britanskoi biblioteke (po arkhivnym materialam: 1837-1900 gg.)' ('The History of the Slavonic Collections in the British Museum from Archival Sources 1837-1900'), *Bibliografiia*, 2008, no. 6, pp. 122-34

Rose, Jonathan, *The Edwardian Temperament, 1895-1919* (Athens, OH: Ohio University Press, 1986)

Roskina, N.A., and others, eds, *Dnevnik Alekseia Sergeevicha Suvorina (A.S. Suvorin's Diary)* (London: The Garnett Press, 1999)

Rothenstein, William, *Men and Memories: Recollections of William Rothenstein*, 2 vols (London: Faber & Faber, 1931-32)

Rouse, W.H.D., *Rugby* (London: Duckworth, 1898)

Rowell, George, and Anthony Jackson, *The Repertory Movement: A History of Regional Theatre in Britain* (Cambridge: Cambridge University Press, 1984)

Ruby, Jennifer, *The Edwardians and the First World War* (London: Batsford, 1988)

Ruislip, Northwood and Eastcote Local History Society, *Eastcote: A Pictorial History* (Pinner: The Society, 1984)

Russell, Dave, 'Varieties of Life: The Making of the Edwardian Music Hall', in *The Edwardian Theatre: Essays on Performance and the Stage*, ed. by Michael R. Booth and Joel H. Kaplan (Cambridge: Cambridge University Press, 1996), pp. 61-85

Sage, Adam, 'What's the Wardwesân for...?', *The Times 2*, 2 February 2011, pp. 4-5

Salmond, Anne, *Aphrodite's Island: The European Discovery of Tahiti* (Berkeley, CA: University of California Press, 2010)

Scurr, Ruth, 'Lives, Some Briefer Than Others', *Guardian Review*, 28 February 2015, pp. 18-19

_____ *John Aubrey: My Own Life* (London: Chatto & Windus, 2015)

Seidel, Michael, *Satiric Inheritance: Rabelais to Sterne* (Princeton: Princeton University Press, 1979)

Senelick, Laurence, *Russian Dramatic Theory from Pushkin to the Symbolists: An Anthology* (Austin: University of Texas Press, 1981)

_____ *The Chekhov Theatre: A Century of the Plays in Performance* (Cambridge: Cambridge University Press, 1997)

_____ '"For God, for Czar, for Fatherland": Russians on the British Stage from Napoleon to the Great War', in *Russia in Britain, 1880-1940: From Melodrama to Modernism*, ed. by Rebecca Beasley and Philip Ross Bullock (Oxford: Oxford University Press, 2013), pp. 19- 34

Shaw, Bernard, *Plays Pleasant and Unpleasant*, 2 vols (London: Constable, 1898)

_____ *The Complete Plays of Bernard Shaw* (London: Constable, 1931)

Shaw, Martin, *Up to Now* (London: Oxford University Press, H. Milford, 1929)

Silkin, John, ed., *The Penguin Book of First World War Poetry*, 2nd edn (London: Penguin Books, 1981)

Sires, Ronald V., 'Labor Unrest in England, 1910-1914', *Journal of Economic History*, 15 (1955), no. 3, pp. 246-66

Smith, Graeme, *The Theatre Royal: Entertaining a Nation* (Glasgow: Glasgow Publications, 2008)

Smith, Marilyn Schwinn, 'Aleksei Remizov's English-Language Translators: New Material', in *A People Passing Rude: British Responses to Russian Culture*, ed. by Anthony Cross (Cambridge: Open Book Publishers, 2012), pp. 189-200

Spink, Karen, 'The Missing Link: A Writer at South Hill Farm', *Journal of Ruislip, Northwood and Eastcote Local History Society*, 1999, pp. 7-12

_____ 'In Memoriam', *Journal of Ruislip, Northwood and Eastcote Local History Society*, 2015, p. 1

Stead, W.T., *Truth about Russia* (London: Cassell, 1888)

Stokes, John, '"A Woman of Genius": Rebecca West at the Theatre', in
    The Edwardian Theatre: Essays on Performance and the Stage, ed. by
    Michael R. Booth and Joel H. Kaplan (Cambridge: Cambridge
    University Press, 1996), pp. 185-200

Stone, Norman, *World War One: A Short History* (London: Penguin
    Books, 2007)

Storey, George Adolphus, *Sketches from Memory* (London: Chatto &
    Windus, 1899)

Stray, Christopher, ed., *An American in Victorian Cambridge: Charles
    Astor Bristed's 'Five Years in an English University'* (Exeter: University
    of Exeter Press, 2008)

Sullivan, David, '"Old Wyldes" and "Wyldes": A Short History of Two
    Houses', *Camden History Review*, 37 (2013), pp. 15-19

Taylor, A.J.P., *The First World War: An Illustrated History* (London: H.
    Hamilton, 1963)

Thompson, Paul, *The Edwardians: The Remaking of British Society*, 3rd
    edn (London: Routledge, 1992)

Thompson, Paul, and Gina Harkell, compilers, *The Edwardians in
    Photographs* (London: Batsford, 1979)

Tidcombe, Marianne, *Women Bookbinders, 1880-1920* (New Castle, DE:
    Oak Knoll Press; London: British Library, 1996)

Tolstoï, Serge, *Les Enfants de Tolstoï* (Paris: Perrin, 1989)

Tolstoy, Leo, *The Kingdom of God and Peace Essays*, trans. by Aylmer
    Maude (London: Oxford University Press, 1936)

Tomlinson, Richard, *Amazing Grace: The Man Who Was WG* (London:
    Little, Brown, 2015)

Tracy, Robert, 'The Flight of a Seagull: Chekhov on the English Stage'
    (unpublished doctoral thesis, Harvard University, 1959)

_____ 'A Čexov Anniversary', *Slavic and East European Journal*, 4 (1960),
    no. 1, pp. 25-34

Trewin, J.C., *The Edwardian Theatre* (Oxford: Blackwell, 1976)

Walford, Rex, and Colin Dolley, *The One-Act Play Companion: A Guide
    to Plays, Playwrights and Performance* (London: A&C Black, 2006)

Wallace, Donald Mackenzie, *Russia*, 2nd edn, 2 vols (London: Cassell
    Petter & Galpin, 1877)

Warner, Oliver, *Admiral of the Fleet: The Life of Sir Charles Lambe* (London: Sidgwick & Jackson, 1969)

Wearing, J.P., *The London Stage, 1890-1899: A Calendar of Plays and Players*, 2 vols (Metuchen, NJ: The Scarecrow Press, 1976)

_____ *The London Stage, 1900-1909: A Calendar of Productions, Performers, and Personnel*, 2nd edn, (Lanham: Rowman & Littlefield, 2014)

_____ *The London Stage, 1910-1919: A Calendar of Plays and Players*, 2 vols (Metuchen, NJ; London: The Scarecrow Press, 1982)

_____ *The London Stage, 1920-1929: A Calendar of Productions, Performers, and Personnel*, 2nd edn (Lanham: Rowman & Littlefield, 2014)

_____ *The London Stage, 1930-1939: A Calendar of Productions, Performers, and Personnel*, 2nd edn, (Lanham: Rowman & Littlefield, 2014)

_____ *The London Stage, 1940-1949: A Calendar of Plays and Players*, 2 vols (Metuchen, NJ: The Scarecrow Press, 1991)

_____ *The London Stage, 1950-1959: A Calendar of Productions, Performers, and Personnel*, 2nd edn (Lanham: Rowman & Littlefield, 2014)

_____ *The London Stage, 1890-1959: Accumulated Indexes*, 2 vols (Lanham: Rowman & Littlefield, 2014)

Wells, H.G., *A Modern Utopia* (London: Chapman & Hall, 1905)

_____ *The War in the Air* (London: George Bell, 1908)

_____ *Ann Veronica: A Modern Love Story* (London: Fisher Unwin, 1909)

_____ *Tono-Bungay* (London: Macmillan, 1909)

Wheeler, Richard, 'Frederic Lubbock and Emmetts: Stereoscopic Views of an Edwardian Plant Collector', *National Trust Historic Houses & Collections Annual 2010*, pp. 26-33

Whishaw, James, *A History of the Whishaw Family*, ed. by M.S. Leigh (London: Methuen, [1935])

Wilson, A.E., *Edwardian Theatre* (London: Barker, 1951)

Wilson, A.N., *After the Victorians* (London: Hutchinson, 2005)

Wood, Sydney, *The Edwardians* (Edinburgh: Oliver & Boyd, 1981)

Young, Stuart, '"Formless", "Pretentious", "Hideous and Revolting": Non-Chekhov Russian and Soviet Drama on the British Stage', in *Russia in Britain, 1880-1940: From Melodrama to Modernism*, ed. by Rebecca Beasley and Philip Ross Bullock (Oxford: Oxford University Press, 2013), pp. 87-112

Zetland, Lawrence John Lumley Dundas, Marquis of, *Lord Cromer: Being the Authorized Life of Evelyn Baring, First Earl of Cromer* (London: Hodder and Stoughton, 1932)

3. Websites

http://1914ancien.free.fr/bef_1914.htm

https://www.artrenewal.org

http://avalon.law.yale.edu

http://www.british-history.ac.uk

http://www.cwgc.org

http://genome.ch.bbc.co.uk

http://www.historyanswers.co.uk/2015/3/10/gallipoli-dissected-what-did-britain-get-wrong

http://www.iccy.org.uk

http://www.iwm.org.uk/history/gallipoli

http://www.longlongtrail.co.uk

https://measuringworth.com

http://www.michelfokine.com

http://www.oxforddnb.com

http://www.thepeerage.com

http://www.thesuffragettes.org

http://www.violetbooks.com/lostrace.html

http://www.william1.co.uk/w176.htm

INDEX

'A' and 'The' are retained in their initial position in the titles of literary works. George Calderon's published and unpublished writings are indexed under 'Works' in the sub-index for the entry 'Calderon, George'.

Sam&Sam is an Anglo-Russian publisher founded in 1974.
It has published over thirty literary, theological, philosophical and historical titles in both Russian and English, sometimes in collaboration with other Russian publishers.
The following RUSSIAN-LANGUAGE works are currently in print.
Some are available on Amazon, but all may be purchased at reduced price plus postage and packing by emailing **bychkovserser@gmail.com**.

Religious and historical

- *Sobranie sochinenii G.P. Fedotova (Collected Works of Georgii Fedotov)*, Moscow, 1996-2014, 12 vols., 400 Rb. per vol., individual vols available.
- *Sviatye zemli russkoi (The Saints of Russia)*, Moscow, 'Belyi bereg', 2002, 2nd edition, 3000 Rb.
- *Pravoslavnaia rossiiskaia Tserkov' i imperatorskaia vlast' (The Russian Orthodox Church and Tsarist Power)*, Moscow, 2015, 300 Rb.
- *Bol'sheviki protiv Russkoi Tserkvi 1917-1941 (The Bolshevik Persecution of the Russian Church 1917-1941)*, Moscow, 2006, 400 Rb.
- Father Sergii Zheludkov, *Liturgicheskie zametki (Notes on the Liturgy)*, Moscow, 2004, 200 Rb.
- *Stradnyi put' arkhimandrita Tavriona (Archimandrite Tavrion's Calvary)*, Moscow, 2007, 2nd edition, 400 Rb.
- *Osvobozdenie ot illiuzii: Zhizn' i podvig arkhiepiskopa-ispovednika Ermogena [Golubev] (Freeing Oneself from Illusions: The Life and Achievement of Archbishop-Confessor Hermogenes [Golubev])*, Moscow, 2010, 400 Rb.

Literary

- Sergei Bychkov, *Tikhie ogni: Izbrannye poeticheskie perevody, vospominaniia, interv'iu (Still Lights: A Collection of Poems, Verse Translations, Memoirs and Interviews)*, Moscow, 2011, 2nd edition, 400 Rb.
- Iurii Dombrovskii, with illustrations by Boris Sveshnikov, *Izbrannoe (Selected Poems)*, Moscow, 2017, 1000 Rb.
- Sigizmund Krzhizhanovskii, *Mysli raznykh let (Thoughts over the Years)*, Moscow, 2017, 500 Rb.
- Georgii Shengeli, *77 sonetov (77 Sonnets)*, Moscow, 2011, 400 Rb.
- Georgii Shengeli, *Izbrannoe (Selected Works)*, Moscow, 2013, 1000 Rb.
- Mark Tarlovskii, *Izbrannoe (Selected Works)*, Moscow, 2011, 400 Rb.